# Injury and Causation in Trade Remedy Law

James J. Nedumpara

# Injury and Causation in Trade Remedy Law

## A Study of WTO Law and Country Practices

Springer

James J. Nedumpara
Jindal Global Law School
O.P Jindal Global University
Sonepat, Haryana
India

ISBN 978-981-10-2196-1 ISBN 978-981-10-2197-8 (eBook)
DOI 10.1007/978-981-10-2197-8

Library of Congress Control Number: 2016947504



Printed on acid-free paper

This Springer imprint is published by Springer Nature
The registered company is Springer Science+Business Media Singapore Pte Ltd.

*In memory of*
*my father*
*Mr. Joseph Nedumpara*

# Foreword

Trade remedy instruments have gained a unique significance in international trade. In the last few years, several emerging economies such as Brazil, China, and India have made increasing use of trade remedies. While such remedies are actively pursued by traditional and new users alike, there has been rich body of literature as to how such remedies could impede international trade.

It is widely accepted that trade remedies have a public choice function. Equally accepted is the fact that the extent of injury needed to trigger the application of these instruments is not necessarily a matter of mathematical precision. However, the use and conduct of these measures are regulated by various agreements under the WTO. For example, the WTO agreements on antidumping, subsidies and countervailing measures as well as safeguards provide fairly strong disciplines on the circumstances in which these measures can be applied. The extent and nature of injury required in the importers' domestic market may vary depending on the circumstances, and there are practical limitations that need to be taken into account. Another perennial source of controversy is the nature of causal link required to establish connection between imports and the injury to the domestic industry. For example, the causation standard itself has undergone major treaty changes, especially in the context of antidumping from the Kennedy Code to the present Uruguay Round Antidumping Agreement. The Rules Negotiations under the Doha Round too witnessed a rich menu of proposals on injury and causation.

Trade remedy measures have been frequently challenged before the WTO. A number of such measures have been brought to the WTO panels and the Appellate Body. In fact, more than 50 % of the adjudicative work before the panels and Appellate Body consumes trade remedy disputes. The jurisprudence under the various trade remedy agreements is dense and complex. It is important that certain scholarly work is done in the area of injury and causation to understand this jurisprudence and examine its implications on the existing agreements.

In that context, this study by James Nedumpara on injury and causation in trade remedy law with a focus on the WTO law and certain members' practices is a significant contribution to the existing body of literature in this field. This book has traced the origins of the injury and causation provisions in all the three trade remedy agreements and has provided a rich and thorough examination of the existing WTO trade remedy jurisprudence. In addition, it has also provided some useful comparative perspectives by examining the practice of various WTO members and, in particular, India. Some of the findings and conclusions of this study will be of immense help to the users of trade remedy instruments and for negotiators looking for future revisions or improvements to the existing trade remedy agreements.

Geneva
May 2016

Gabrielle Marceau
Counsellor, World Trade Organization
Associate professor, Law Faculty, University of Geneva
President, Society of International Economic Law (SIEL)

# Preface and Acknowledgements

Trade remedy laws are firmly rooted either in the complex world of economics or in the intricacies of accounting. This is not typically a lawyer's discipline. For whatever reason, I developed a liking for this subject without fully appreciating the multi-disciplinary character of this field. This was not entirely surprising considering that trade remedy practice is one of the most prominent areas of international trade law practice and provides a lifeline for lawyers committed to remain in this specialization of practice. In particular, this area of practice flourished in India in the early 2000s and like any other trade lawyer, I wanted to plunge deep into this field.

Any introductory text book on trade remedies will straightaway mention that there are only three focal points in a trade remedy case: imports, injury, and causation. In other words, the requirement to establish causation between imports and injury to the domestic industry is a vital element. It is central to determining the liability for the exporters involved in trade remedy cases and for the domestic industry to get import relief. However, it was not difficult for me to realize that the international treaty provisions on establishing injury and causation were significantly deficient when compared to other disciplines of trade remedy law such as the determination of dumping or subsidization.

Several scholars have pointed out the logical fallacies in making imports a cause of injury. Much of the criticism came from the economists. The disconnect could not have been more apparent, as most of the legal practitioners and policy makers assumed that imports themselves are a cause of injury. Despite the logical contradictions and structural infirmities, trade remedy actions deserve a special place in international trade law practice. It is easy to condemn this branch of international trade law or policy, but for lawyers, businesses, and policy makers, the need for trade remedies cannot be overemphasized. Rather than condemning the application of trade remedy measures, I was convinced that the focus should be on making in the injury and causation findings coherent within the context of the present international legal framework. This study is a modest attempt in achieving a semblance of coherence or at least in highlighting the need for more structured enquiries in this field.

A substantial body of this publication stems from my doctoral research on the issues of injury and causation in trade remedy law both within the context of the WTO and member practices. The work heavily rests on the existing literature, journal articles, and various interviews, most of which are referenced in this book. During my research, I had a chance to meet with and speak to some of the leading exponents of trade remedy practice in various jurisdictions. The discussions were enriching and inspiring, but most of the practitioners and experts agreed that the present practices in demonstrating injury and causation required some deeper study and course correction. Some of the respondents addressed the need for a counterfactual "but-for" enquiry in injury and causation analysis. I found the discussion on the counterfactual analysis especially illuminating. I have devoted an entire chapter on the utility of Common Law analytical tools in the injury and causation analysis.

My own findings and observations emphasize the need for recasting the injury and causation standards in WTO trade remedy law based on the general theories of causation in law. In other words, the suggestions for incorporating terms such as "principal cause," "substantial cause," and "a cause in and of itself" are by no means new and are somewhat unnecessary, in my view. Some of these suggestions have been discussed at length and explicitly discarded in previous trade negotiations. Trade remedy instruments have a particular public choice function. The negotiating history of the various trade remedy agreements should not be lost sight of in this debate.

The use of quantitative tools is another interesting issue. Quantitative tools are almost impenetrable to most lawyers and there is a general aversion to using such tools, at least in trade remedy practice. It is surprising that the lack of faith in economic tools is deep even within some of the advanced jurisdictions. On the whole, most of the trade remedy users increasingly use qualitative tools—a method which is generally descriptive and fairly easy to use.

I am grateful to a number of people who helped me navigate the process of completing this work. I am indebted to Prof. O.V. Nandimath who has been a great source of support for me by offering valuable guidance and suggestions in improving the research design and fine-tuning the arguments at various stages of this research. I am grateful to him for devoting time for guiding me in this research work despite his multitudinous responsibilities. For several valuable discussions and suggestions, I am grateful to Prof. A. Jayagovind, Prof. T. Ramakrishna, Prof. Abhijit Das, and Prof. Thomas Prusa. I have been significantly benefitted by the discussions with Ms. Nithya Nagarajan, Prof. Raj Bhala, Mr. Sharad Bhansali, Mr. A.K. Gupta, Mr. Sanjay Notani, Mr. Ashish Chandra, Prof. Mukesh Bhatnagar, Mr. Terence Stewart, Mr. Jorge Miranda, Ms. Jennifer Hillman, Prof. Mark Wu, and Dr. Chad P. Bown. Their inputs have helped me explore the field of trade remedies with greater ease.

The National Law School of India University (NLSIU), Bengaluru, where I completed my doctoral research, and my employer O.P. Jindal Global University, Sonipat, provided me exceptional institutional support in the process of completing this work. I am grateful to Prof. R. Venkata Rao, Prof. Jasphet, and Ms. Padmavathi at NLSIU for their invaluable support. This is also an opportunity to thank

Prof. C. Raj Kumar and Prof. Y.S.R. Murthy at O.P. Jindal Global University who gave me unstinted support for pursing this research. I also gratefully acknowledge the research and editorial help provided by Vandana Gyanchandani and Rishabh Raturi.

I would also like to express my gratitude to Ms. Sagarika Ghosh and Ms. Nupoor Singh of Springer for their inordinate patience and the most helpful cooperation at all stages of the production of this book.

Last but not least—as always—I owe a great debt to my family, my mother Tresa, my wife Sharmila, and son Joseph for their constant encouragement and love. I am also hugely indebted to my parents-in-law and my siblings for their unwavering support. Finally, this book is dedicated to my father Joseph Nedumpara who took the pains, even in his advanced age, to read the final draft and suggest corrections, but could not live long enough to see I complete this work. I dedicate this book in his memory.

New Delhi
June 2016

James J. Nedumpara

# Endorsements

While much attention has been focused on the WTO dispute settlement system's jurisprudence regarding dumping margins and subsidies, Professor James Nedumpara's book shines a bright and illuminating light on one of the other major components of trade remedy law—the requirement to demonstrate that dumped or subsidized or increased imports have caused injury to a domestic industry. His remarkable book thoroughly covers the entire terrain of causation and injury, from its evolution in the GATT and the WTO, to its practice in India and jurisdictions around the world, to the methodologies—both quantitative and qualitative—used in many jurisdictions to demonstrate a causal link between imports and injury. His book includes a wealth of data tucked into clear and concise tables that elucidate the precise differences in the approaches taken by countries around the world to demonstrating causation, along with an excellent discussion of various theories of causation from other areas of the law. This book is equally useful to trade law practitioners and scholars.

**Jennifer A. Hillman**
*Visiting Professor, Georgetown University Law Center,*
*Former member of the WTO Appellate Body*

"James Nedumpara's extensive analysis of injury and causation in trade remedy investigations is a significant scholarly contribution in the field of international trade law. Trade remedies are increasingly critical to the developed and developing countries in the WTO and it is important to examine how the use of such remedies could be made more coherent. This book is a must-read for anyone handling trade remedy investigations at the domestic level or in WTO dispute settlement."

**Rajeev Kher**
*Member, Competition Appellate Tribunal*
*& Former Commerce Secretary, Government of India*

"James Nedumpara's book on injury and causation in the context of WTO trade remedy rules will become the one-stop shop for those litigating in this field. James examines in great detail and depth the origins of such rules, how they have been interpreted in WTO dispute settlement, and how they have been applied in several national jurisdictions. This is an outstanding contribution to the analytics of world trade law."

**Jorge Miranda**
*Consultant, King & Spalding, Washington, D.C.*

*Injury and Causation in Trade Remedy Law* provides an insightful and illuminating analysis of one of the underexplored areas of trade remedy practice. This path-breaking study has a contemporary resonance as it analyses in incisive detail how the WTO Members are currently complying with this requirement. The book's important claim is that injury and causation standards should derive its strength from the public choice theory considerations of these agreements, and not necessarily from causal maximalist positions supported by rigorous economic approaches. The book is a marvelous read and its contents are comparative and wide-ranging. It is an excellent and enriching contribution in the area of legal analysis of trade remedies.

**Abhijit Das**
*Professor and Head, Centre for WTO Studies, New Delhi*

# Contents

# About the Author

**James J. Nedumpara** is an associate professor of law and the executive director of Centre for International Trade and Economic Laws (CITEL) at Jindal Global Law School. He has several years of experience in the field of international trade and has worked with leading law firms, corporate firms, and also UNCTAD before joining academia. His specialization is in trade remedy law and international trade regulation. James received his Ph.D. in law from the National Law School of India University, Bangalore, and holds master of laws (LL.M) degrees from the University of Cambridge, UK, the New York University School of Law, USA, as well as the National University of Singapore, and a bachelor degree in law from the Mahatma Gandhi University, Kerala, India. He was also a part of the Indian delegation that appeared before the WTO Appellate Body in *India—Import Restrictions on Agricultural Products* (Avian Influenza) dispute.

# Abbreviations

| | |
|---|---|
| AD | Antidumping |
| ADA | Antidumping Agreement |
| ASCM | Agreement on Subsidies and Countervailing Measures |
| ASEAN | Association of Southeast Asian Nations |
| BoP | Balance of payments |
| CCFRS | Certain carbon flat-rolled steel |
| CEGAT | Customs, Excise and Gold (control) Appellate Tribunal |
| CESTAT | Customs, Excise and Service Tax Appellate Tribunal |
| CITT | Canadian International Trade Tribunal |
| CNCE | National Foreign Trade Commission (Argentina) |
| CNV | Constructed normal value |
| COGS | Cost of goods sold |
| COMPAS | Commercial Policy Analysis System |
| CVD | Countervailing duties |
| DBM | Dead burnt magnesite |
| DECOM | Department of Trade Defense (Departamento de Defesa Comercial) Brazil |
| DG Safeguards | Directorate General of Safeguards |
| DGAD | Directorate General of Anti-Dumping and Allied Duties |
| DSU | Dispute settlement understanding |
| EC | European Commission/European Communities |
| ECJ | European Court of Justice |
| ECOSOC | United Nations Economic and Social Council |
| EEC | European Economic Community |
| ELT | Excise Law Times |
| FAN | Friends of Antidumping |
| FFTJ | Fittings, Flanges and Tool Joint |
| GATT | General Agreement on Tariffs and Trade |
| GDP | Gross domestic product |
| GOES | Grain oriented flat-rolled electrical steel |

| | |
|---|---|
| INUS | Insufficient but necessary part of an unnecessary but sufficient set |
| ITAC | International Trade Administration Commission |
| ITO | International Trade Organization |
| Kennedy Code | Kennedy Antidumping Code signed on 30 June 1967 |
| LAB | Linear alkyl benzene |
| LTFV | Less than fair value |
| MOFCOM | Ministry of Commerce (China) |
| NAFTA | North American Free Trade Agreement |
| NESS | Necessary element of a sufficient set |
| NGR | Negotiating Group on Rules |
| NIP | Non-injurious price |
| NME | Non-market economy |
| NSR | Net sales realization |
| PCN | Product control number |
| POI | Period of investigation |
| PPA | Protocol of Provisional Application |
| PSF | Polyester staple fiber |
| PTA | Purified terephthalic acid |
| PVC | Polyvinyl chloride |
| QR | Quantitative restrictions |
| ROCE | Return on capital employed |
| RTA | Regional trade agreement |
| SECOFI | Secretariat of the Economy (Secretaría de Economía) |
| SIL | Special import licenses |
| SIMA | Special Import Measures Act 1984 |
| The 1921 Act | The US Antidumping Act, 1921 |
| Tokyo AD Code | Tokyo Anti-Dumping Code under GATT (1979) |
| Tokyo Subsidies Code | Tokyo Subsidies Code under GATT(1979) |
| UNCTAD | United Nations Conference on Trade and Development |
| UPCI | Unidad de Practicas Comerciales Internacionales |
| USAFC | US Court of Appeals for Federal Circuit |
| USDOC | US Department of Commerce |
| USITC | US International Trade Commission |
| WTO | World Trade Organization |

# List of Figures

# List of Tables

# List of Cases

## WTO Dispute Settlement Reports

### Appellate Body Reports

*Argentina—Safeguard Measures on Imports of Footwear,* WT/DS121/AB/R (December 14, 1999)

*Brazil—Measures Affecting Desiccated Coconut*, WT/DS22/AB/R (February 21, 1997)

*China—Countervailing and Anti-Dumping Duties on Grain Oriented Flat-Rolled Electrical Steel from the United States,* WT/DS414/AB/R (November 16, 2012)

*China—Measures Imposing Anti-Dumping Duties on High-Performance Stainless Steel Seamless Tubes ("HP-SSST") from Japan* (October 14, 2015)

Appellate Body Report, *European Communities—Anti-Dumping Duties on Malleable Cast Iron Tube of Pipe Fittings from Brazil*, WT/DS219/AB/R (July 22, 2003)

Appellate Body Report, *European Communities—Anti-Dumping Duties on Imports of Cotton-type Bed Linen from India*, WT/DS141/AB/R (March 1, 2001)

Appellate Body Report, *European Communities—Countervailing Measures on Dynamic Random Access Memory Chips from Korea*, WT/DS299/AB/R (April 21, 2006)

*Japan—Countervailing Duties on Dynamic Random Access Memories from Korea*, WT/DS336/AB/R (March 5, 2010)

*Korea—Definitive Safeguard Measure on Imports of Certain Dairy Products*, WT/DS98/AB/R (December 14, 1999)

*Mexico—Definitive Anti-Dumping Measures on Beef and Rice*, WT/DS295/AB/R (November 29, 2005)

*Thailand—Anti-Dumping Duties on Angles, Shapes and Sections of Iron or Non-Alloy Steel and H Beams from Poland*, WT/DS122/AB/R (March 12, 2001)

*United States—Anti-Dumping Act of 1916*, WT//DS162/AB/R (August 28, 2000)

*United States—Anti-Dumping Measures on Certain Hot-Rolled Steel Products from Japan*, WT/DS184/AB/R (August 23, 2001)

*United States—Continued Dumping and Subsidy Offset Act of 2000*, WT/DS217/ARB/BRA (August 31, 2004)
*United States—Definitive Safeguard Measures on Imports of Circular Welded Carbon Quality Line Pipe from Korea*, WT/DS202/AB/R (March 8, 2002)
*United States—Definitive Safeguard Measures on Imports of Certain Steel Products*, WT/DS252/AB/R (November 19, 2003)
*United States—Definitive Safeguard Measures on Imports of Wheat Gluten from the European Communities*, WT/DS166/AB/R (December 22, 2000)
*United States—Final Countervailing Duty Determination with respect to certain Softwood Lumber from Canada*, WT/DS257/AB/RW (December 5, 2005)
*United States—Subsidies on Upland Cotton*, WT/DS267/AB/R (March 3, 2005)
*United States—Sunset Review of Anti-Dumping Duties on Corrosion-Resistant Carbon Steel Flat Products from Japan*, WT/DS244/AB/R (December 15, 2003)
*United States—Customs Bond Directive for Merchandise Subject to Anti-Dumping/Countervailing Duties*, WT/DS345/AB/R (July 16, 2008)
*United States—Safeguard Measures on Imports of Fresh, Chilled or Frozen Lamb Meat from New Zealand and Australia*, WT/DS177/AB/R, WT/DS178/AB/R (May 16, 2001)
*United States—Countervailing measures on certain hot-rolled carbon steel flat products from India, WT/DS436/AB/R* (December 8, 2014)

**Panel Reports**

*Argentina—Definitive Safeguard Measure on Imports of Preserved Peaches,* WT/DS238/R (April 15, 2003)
*Argentina—Definitive Anti-Dumping Duties on Poultry from Brazil,* WT/DS241/R (April 23, 2003)
*Argentina—Definitive Anti-Dumping Measures on Carbon-Board from Germany and Definitive Anti-Dumping Measures on Imports of Ceramic Tiles from Italy,* WT/DS189/R (September 28, 2001)
*Argentina—Safeguard Measures on Imports of Footwear*, WT/DS121/R (June 25, 1999)
*China—Anti-Dumping and Countervailing Duty Measures on Broiler Products from the United States,* WT/DS427/R and Add. 1 (September 25, 2013)
*China—Definitive Anti-Dumping Duties on X-Ray Security Inspection Equipment from the European Union*, WT/DS425/R and Add.1 (April 24, 2013)
*Dominican Republic—Safeguard Measures on Imports of Polypropylene Bags and Tubular Fabric*, WT/DS417/R (January 31, 2012)
*Egypt—Definitive Anti-Dumping Measures on Steel Rebar from Turkey,* WT/DS211/R (October 1, 2002)
*European Communities—Anti-Dumping Duties on Malleable Cast Iron Tube or Pipe Fittings from Brazil,* WT/DS219/R (March 7, 2003)
*European Communities—Anti-Dumping Measure on Farmed Salmon from Norway,* WT/DS337/R (November 16, 2007)

*European Communities—Countervailing Measures on DRAM Chips*, WT/DS299/R (June 17, 2005)
*European Communities—Definitive Anti-Dumping Measures on Certain Iron or Steel Fasteners from China,* WT/DS397/R (December 3, 2010)
*Guatemala—Definitive Anti-Dumping Measure on Grey Portland Cement from Mexico,* WT/DS156/R (October 24, 2000)
*Korea—Definitive Safeguard Measures on Imports of Certain Dairy Products*, WT/DS98/R and Corr.1 (January 12, 2000)
*Korea—Measures Affecting Trade in Commercial Vessels,* WT/DS273/R (March 7, 2005)
*Mexico—Anti-Dumping Investigation of High Fructose Corn Syrup (HFCS) from the United States,* WT/DS132/R (February 24, 2000)
*Mexico—Definitive Countervailing Measures on Olive Oil from the European Communities*, WT/DS341/R (October 21, 2008)
*Thailand—Anti-Dumping Duties on Angles, Shapes and Sections of Iron or Non-Alloy Steel and H Beams from Poland,* WT/DS122/R (September 28, 2000)
*United States—Anti-Dumping Act of 1916, Complaint by Japan,* WT/DS162/R and Add.1 (September 26, 2000)
*United States—Anti-Dumping Measures on Certain Hot-Rolled Steel Products from Japan*, WT/DS184/R (February 28, 2001)
*United States—Sunset Review of Anti-Dumping Duties on Corrosion-Resistant Carbon Steel Flat Products from Japan,* WT/DS244/R (August 14, 2003)
*United States—Countervailing Duty Investigation on Dynamic Random Access Memory Semiconductors (DRAMS) from Korea,* WT/DS296/R (February 21, 2005)
*United States—Customs Bond Directive for Merchandise Subject to Anti-Dumping/Countervailing Duties*, WT/DS345/R (August 1, 2008)
*United States—Definitive Safeguard Measures on Imports of Carbon Steel Products*, WT/DS252/R (July 11, 2003)
*United States—Definitive Safeguard Measures on Imports of Circular Welded Carbon Quality Line Pipe from Korea*, WT/DS202/R (October 29, 2001)
*United States—Measures Affecting Imports on Certain Passenger Vehicle and Light Truck Tyres from China*, WT/DS399/R (October 5, 2011)
*United States—Safeguard Measures on Import of Fresh, Chilled or Frozen Lamb Meat from New Zealand and Australia*, WT/DS177/178/R (December 21, 2001)
*United States—Subsidies on Upland Cotton,* WT/DS267/R (September 8, 2004)

**GATT Panel Reports**

*Canadian Countervailing Duties on Grain Corn from the United States*, SCM/140and Corr.1—39S/411 (February 21, 1992)
*European Union—Imposition of Anti-Dumping Duties on Imports of Cotton Yarn from Brazil*, ADP/137 (April 4, 1995)
*United States—Imposition of Anti-Dumping Duties on Imports of Fresh and Chilled Atlantic Salmon from* Norway, ADP/87 (November 30, 1992)

**National cases**

*Supreme Court of India*

Reliance Industries v. Designated Authority, 2006 (10) SCC 368 (Supreme Court of India)

*State High Courts in India*

Nirma Limited v. Saint Gobain Glass India Limited, 2012 (281) E.L.T. 321 (High Court of Madras)

Rajasthan Textile Mills Association v. Directorate General of Anti-Dumping and Allied Duties, 2002 (144) E.L.T. 45 (High Court of Rajasthan)

**Custom Tribunals in India: CESTAT/CEGAT**

Agfa Gevaert A.G. v. Designated Authority, 2001 (130) E.L.T. 741 (Custom Excise & Service Tax Appellate Tribunal, Delhi)

Indian Spinners Association v. Designated Authority, 2004 (170) E.L.T. 144 (Custom Excise & Service Tax Appellate Tribunal, Delhi)

Kothari Sugars and Chemicals Ltd. v. Designated Authority, 2005 (187) E.L.T. 185 (Custom Excise & Service Tax Appellate Tribunal, Delhi)

M/s. Sasol Solvents v. Union of India through Ministry of Finance, Department of Revenue and the Designated Authority, MANU/CUST/0057/2008-Customs, March 11, 2008 (Custom Excise & Service Tax Appellate Tribunal, Delhi)

Refractory Makers Association v. Designated Authority, 2000 (119) E.L.T. 319 (Custom Excise & Service Tax Appellate Tribunal, Delhi)

Urals Heavy Machine Building Plant v. Designated Authority, 2005 (197) E.L.T. 194 (Custom Excise & Service Tax Appellate Tribunal, Delhi)

Videocon Narmada Glass v. Designated Authority, 2003 (151) E.L.T. 80 (Custom Excise & Service Tax Appellate Tribunal, Delhi)

*United States*

Bratsk Aluminum Smelter v. United States, 444 F. 3d. 1369, 2006 (Court of Appeals, Federal Circuit, Washington D.C., United States)

Gerald Metals Inc. v. United States 132 F. 3d716 (U.S. Federal Circuit, 1997)

*European Union*

Miwon v. Council of European Union, T-51/96, March 30, 2000 (Judgment of the Court of First Instance, Third Chamber, Extended Composition)

Sinochem Heilongjiang v. Council of Europe, T-161/94, July 11, 1996 (Judgment of the Court of First Instance (First Chamber, Extended Composition)

**National antidumping/countervailing/safeguards investigation reports**

**Indian Antidumping Investigation Reports**

*Imports of Acetone originating in or exported from European Union, Chinese Taipei, Singapore, South Africa and the United States of America, No. 14/4/2006 (Ministry of Commerce, January 4, 2008) (Final Findings)*

Imports of Acrylic Fiber from Turkey, Hungary and the European Union, No. 34/1/1998 (Ministry of Commerce, March 24, 2000) (Final Findings)
Imports of Acyclic Alcohols originating in or exported from Singapore, Brazil, Romania, Malaysia and South Africa, No. 63/1/2001 (Ministry of Commerce, July 29, 2003) (Final Findings)
Imports of Bias Tyres originating in China PR and Thailand, No. 14/9/2005 (Ministry of Commerce, June 29, 2007) (Final Findings)
Imports of Bisphenol-A originating in or exported from the European Union and Taiwan, No. 47/1199 (Ministry of Commerce, December 6, 2000) (Final Findings)
Imports of Bisphenol-A originating in or exported from USA, No. 15/5/95/ADD (Ministry of Commerce, March 18, 1997) (Final Findings)
Imports of Butter oil from New Zealand, No. 14/49/2002 (Ministry of Commerce, September 17, 2003) (Notice of Termination)
Imports of Carbon Black used in rubber applications originating in or exported from Australia, China PR, Iran, Malaysia, Russia and Thailand, No. 14/21/2008 (Ministry of Commerce, December 24, 2009) (Final Findings)
Imports of Certain 'Compressors' originating in or imported from China PR and Malaysia, No. 14/7/2004 (Ministry of Commerce, July 13, 2005) (Notice of Termination)
Imports of Certain Phosphorous based chemical compounds originating in or exported from China PR and European Union, No. 14/3/2009 (Ministry of Commerce, April 7, 2010) (Final Findings)
Imports of Certain Polyester Staple Fibres (PSF) originating in or exported from Korea, Thailand, Taiwan and Indonesia, No. 29/1/1998 (Ministry of Commerce, January 21, 2000) (Final Findings)
Imports of Circular Weaving Machines having six or more shuttles for weaving PP/HDPE Fabrics originating in or exported from People's Republic of China, No. 16/25/2008 (Ministry of Commerce, November 16, 2010) (Final Findings)
Imports of Citric Acid from the People's Republic of China, No. 29/1/1997 (Ministry of Commerce, March 15, 1999) (Final Findings)
Imports of Coated Paper and Paper Board from China, Singapore, Japan, Hong Kong, Korea and Finland, No. D-22011/25/2009 (Ministry of Commerce, November 13, 2009) (Final Findings)
Imports of Coated paper of 80 GSM exported from European Union and Indonesia, No. 14/7/2003 (Ministry of Commerce, December 15, 2004) (Final Findings)
Imports of D (-) Para Hydroxy Phenyl Glycine Base (PHPG Base) originating in or exported from the European Union, No. 14/6/2002 (Ministry of Commerce, March 1, 2003) (Final Findings)
Imports of D (-) Para Hydroxy Phenyl Glycine Methyl potassium Dane Salt (PHPG Dane Salt originating in or exported from China and Singapore, No. 14/23/2002 (Ministry of Commerce, June 24, 2003) (Final Findings)
Imports of Digital offset printing plates originating in or exported from People's Republic of China and Japan, No. 14/7/2011 (Ministry of Commerce, October 3, 2012) (Final Findings)

Imports of Dry Batteries originating in or exported from People's Republic of China, No. 53/1/2000 (Ministry of Commerce, July 13, 2001) (Final Findings)
Imports of Electrical insulators from People's Republic of China, No. 14/6/2011 (Ministry of Commerce, March 20, 2013) (Notice of Termination)
Imports of Gypsum Plaster Board from Indonesia and Thailand, No. 14/10/2003 (Ministry of Commerce, September 2, 2003) (Notice of Termination)
Imports of Hot Rolled Coils/Sheets/Plates/Strips from Russia, Kazakhstan and Ukraine, No. 14/1/1997 (Ministry of Commerce, November 18, 1998) (Final Findings)
Imports of Lead Acid Batteries originating in or exported from Japan, Korea, China and Bangladesh, No. 67/1/200 (Ministry of Commerce, December 1, 2001) (Final Findings)
Imports of Linear Alkyl Benzene from Iran, Saudi Arabia, Qatar and Switzerland, No. D-22011/23/2008 (Ministry of Commerce, November 18, 2009) (Final Findings)
Imports of Magnesium from People's Republic of China, No. 7/1/97/ADD (Ministry of Commerce, July 24, 1998) (Final Findings)
Imports of Melamine originating in or exported from European Union, Iran, Indonesia and Japan, No. 14/35/2010 (Ministry of Commerce, June 1, 2012) (Final Findings)
Imports of Metallurgical Coke originating in or imported from Japan, No. 14/41/2002 (Ministry of Commerce, May 14, 2004) (Final Findings)
Imports of Optical Fibre from Korea, No. 24/1/99 (Ministry of Commerce, November 5, 1999) (Final Findings)
Imports of Para Hydroxy Phenyl Glycine Base originating in or exported from China and Singapore, No. 51/12001 (Ministry of Commerce, October 1, 2001) (Notice of Initiation)
Imports of Penicillin-G originating in or exported from the China, No. 14/10/2008 (Ministry of Commerce, May 22, 2009) (Final Findings)
Imports of Phtalic Anhydrite from Korea, Pakistan, Taiwan, Indonesia and Iran, No. D-22011/32/2008 (Ministry of Commerce, May 28, 2009) (Final Findings)
Imports of Polyester Staple Fibre (PSF) from Korea, Thailand, Taiwan and Indonesia, No. 29/1/98 (Ministry of Commerce, January 21, 2000) (Final Findings)
Imports of Potassium Carbonate from Russia, Thailand and United States of America, No. 14/6/2007 (Ministry of Commerce, January 23, 2009) (Notice of Termination)
Imports of Power steering gear system originating in or exported from China, No. 14/13/2007 (Ministry of Commerce, June 5, 2009) (Notice of Termination)
Imports of Pre-sensitized Positive Offset Aluminum Plates (PS Plates) from Bulgaria, China, Malaysia, Singapore and South Korea, No. 14/6/2006 (Ministry of Commerce, August 23, 2007) (Final Findings)
Imports of Pure Terephthalic Acid from Japan, Malaysia, Spain and Taiwan, No. 27/1/98 (Ministry of Commerce, April 20, 2000) (Final Findings)
Imports of Soda Ash from Russia and Turkey, No. 14/3/2011 (Ministry of Commerce, February 9, 2013) (Final Findings)

Imports of Sports Shoes (both branded and un-branded) originated in or exported from China, No. 56/1/2000 (Ministry of Commerce, November 20, 2000) (Notice of Initiation)
Imports of Styrene Butadiene Rubber from Japan, Korea, Turkey, Taiwan, United States, Germany and France, No. 30/1/97 (Ministry of Commerce, June 2, 1999) (Notice of Termination)
Imports of Vinyl Acetate Monomer from Singapore and Iran into India, No. 58/1/2001 (Ministry of Commerce, February 15, 2002) (Notice of Termination)
Imports of Viscose Staple Fibre excluding Bamboo Fibre originating in or exported from China and Indonesia, No. 14/6/2009 (Ministry of Commerce, May 17, 2010) (Final Findings)
Imports of Vitamin B12 originating in or exported from China, Hong Kong and Japan, No. 14/12/2006 (Ministry of Commerce, October 29, 2007) (Notice of Termination)

**Indian safeguard investigation reports**
Imports of Bisphenol-A from China, Germany, United States, Singapore, Taiwan, Korea and Japan, No. SG/INV/1/2003 (Ministry of Finance, October 27, 2003) (Final Findings)
Imports of Coated Paper and Paper Board into India, D-22011/25/2009 (Ministry of Finance, November 13, 2009) (Final Findings)
Imports of Dimethoate technical from China, Notice of Initiation, No. D-22011/07/2009 (Ministry of Finance, May 14, 2009) (Final Findings)
Imports of Epichlororhydrin from Japan, United States, Belgium and Korea, No. SG/INV/1/2002 (Ministry of Finance, June 25, 2002) (Final Findings)
Imports of Flexible Slabstock Polyol of molecular weight 3000-4000 used in the manufacture of Slabstock foams and polyurethane foams mattresses from Singapore and Japan, No. SG/V/4/97 (Ministry of Finance, September 17, 1998) (Final Findings)
Imports of Hard Board (High Density Fibre Board) from Thailand, South Africa, Malaysia, Italy and Pakistan, No. SG-REP/4/98 (Ministry of Finance, November 12, 1998) (Final Findings)
Imports of Linear Alkyl Benzene from Iran, Saudi Arabia, Qatar and Switzerland, No. D-22011/23/2008 (Ministry of Finance, November 18, 2009) (Final Findings)
Imports of Methylene Chloride from Taiwan and Hungary, No. SG/INV/2/2000 (Ministry of Finance, December 15, 2000) (Final Findings)
Imports of Phenol from Germany, Italy, United States, Tokyo, Korea, Taiwan, South Africa and Switzerland, No. SG/INV/2/98 (Ministry of Finance, May 12, 1999) (Final Findings)
Imports of Phtalic Anhydrite from Korea, Pakistan, Taiwan, Indonesia and Iran, No. D-22011/32/2008 (Ministry of Finance, May 28,1999) (Final Findings)
Imports of Starch; Manioc (Cassava, Tapioca) based sago and modified starches from Thailand, Netherlands, China, United States and Korea, Final Findings, No. SG/INV/1/2004 (Ministry of Finance, February 16, 2005) (Final Findings)

Imports of Uncoated Paper and Copy Paper from Indonesia, Thailand, Finland, China, Hong Kong, Japan, Singapore and the United States, No. D-22011/27/2009 (Ministry of Finance, November 5, 2009) (Final Findings)

**Antidumping investigation reports of South Africa**

Imports of Feed Supplements containing by mass 40 % or more Lysine, whether or not containing added anti-biotics or added melengestrol acetate, commonly known as L-Lysine Sulphate and its By-Products from fermentation (biolys) originating in or imported from the United States of America, Investigation Report No. 193 (Ministry of Trade and Industry, September 11, 2006) (Final Findings)

Imports of Polyethylene terephthalate originating in or imported from China, Thailand and Indonesia, Report No. 157 (Ministry of Trade and Industry, June 15, 2006) (Final Findings)

Imports of Stainless steel tubes and pipes originating in or imported from China, India and Malaysia, Final Findings, Report No. 160 (Ministry of Trade and Industry, July 18, 2006) (Final Findings)

Imports of steel wheel originating in or imported from Brazil, China, Chinese Taipei and Turkey, Report No. 125 (Ministry of Trade and Industry, July 4, 2005) (Final Findings)

Imports of toughened glass for incorporation in vehicles originating in or imported from China, Report No. 184 (Ministry of Trade and Industry, September 6, 2006) (Final Findings)

Investigation into the alleged dumping of polyethylene terephthalate (PET) originating in or imported from the People's Republic of China, India, Indonesia, South Korea, Chinese Taipei and Thailand, Report no. 154 (Ministry of Trade and Industry, February 9, 2006) (Final Findings)

**Trade remedy investigations by the United States**

Circular Welded Non-Alloy Steel Pipe from China, Investigation Report, No. TA-421-6, 3807 (International Trade Commission, 2005) (Final Findings)

Imports of Bicycles from Czech Republic, 25 Federal Register 9782 (International Trade Commission, 1960) (Final Findings)

Imports of Carbon Steel Bars and Shapes from Canada, 29 Federal Register 12599 (International Trade Commission, 1964) (Final Findings)

Imports of Cold-Rolled Steel Products from Argentina, Inv. No. 731-TA-829-40 (International Trade Commission, 2000) (Final Findings)

Imports of Ferrite Cores from Japan, 36 Federal Register 1934 (International Trade Commission, 1971) (Final Findings)

**Trade remedy investigation by Canada/against Canada under NAFTA**

Hot Rolled Steel Sheet Originating in or Exported from Canada (Dumping) MEX-96-1904-03 (Binational Panel Review Pursuant to the North American Free Trade Agreement, June 16, 1997) (Final Findings)

Imports of Refined sugar originating in or exported from the United States of America, Denmark, the Federal Republic of Germany, the Netherlands, the United Kingdom and the Republic of Korea, Final Findings, Inquiry No. NQ-95-002, (Ministry of Trade and Commerce, November 6, 1995) (Final Findings)
Refined Sugar from the United States, Denmark, Germany, the Netherlands and the United Kingdom, Inquiry No. NQ-95-002 (Ministry of Trade and Commerce, November 6 and 21, 1995) (Final Findings)

# Legal Instruments/Documents

**International legal treaties**

Agreement on Implementation of Article VI of the General Agreement on Tariffs and Trade 1994 (Anti-Dumping Agreement), Annex 1A, THE LEGAL TEXTS: THE RESULTS OF THE URUGUAY ROUND OF MULTILATERAL TRADE NEGOTIATIONS 1868 U.N. T.S. 201

Marrakesh Agreement Establishing the World Trade Organization (the WTO Agreement), Annex 1A, THE LEGAL TEXTS: THE RESULTS OF THE URUGUAY ROUND OF MULTILATERAL TRADE NEGOTIATIONS,1867 U.N.T.S. 154

Agreement on Safeguards, Annex 1A, THE LEGAL TEXTS: THE RESULTS OF THE URUGUAY ROUND OF MULTILATERAL TRADE NEGOTIATIONS, 1869 U.N.T.S. 154

Agreement on Subsidies and Countervailing Measures, Apr. 15, 1994, Marrakesh Agreement Establishing the World Trade Organization, Annex 1A, THE LEGAL TEXTS: THE RESULTS OF THE URUGUAY ROUND OF MULTILATERAL TRADE NEGOTIATIONS 231, 1869 U.N.T.S. 14

General Agreement on Tariffs and Trade 1994, Apr. 15, 1994, Marrakesh Agreement Establishing the World Trade Organization, Annex 1A, THE LEGAL TEXTS: THE RESULTS OF THE URUGUAY ROUND OF MULTILATERAL TRADE NEGOTIATIONS 17 (1999), 1867 U.N.T.S. 187, 33 I.L.M. 1153 (1994) [April 14, 1994]

**GATT/WTO-related and other international documents**

Communication from Japan, *Negotiating Group on MTN Agreements and Arrangements*, MTN/GNG/NG8/W/11 (September 28, 1987)

Communication from the Delegation of Hong Kong, *Negotiating Group on MTN Agreements and Arrangements*, MTN/GNG/NG8/W/51/Add/1 (December 22, 1989)

Communication from the Republic of Korea, *Negotiating Group on MTN Agreements and Arrangements*, MTN/GNG/NG8/W/3 (May 20, 1987)

Negotiating Group on Rules Communication from the United States, *Causation (ADA Article 3.5; ASCM Article 15.5)*, TN/RL/GEN/59 (July 13, 2005)

Negotiating Group on Rules Communication from the United States, *Identification of Additional Issues Under the Anti-Dumping and Subsidies Agreements,* TN/RL/W/98 (May 6, 2003)

ECOSOC, *Verbatim Report of the Seventh Meeting of Committee of the International Conference on Trade and Employment, II,* E/PC/T/C/II/PV/7, held in the Hoare Memorial Hall, Church House, Westminster, S. W. (November 1, 1946)

Group "Non-Tariff Measures" Sub-Group "Technical Barriers to Trade", *Agreement on Interpretation and Application of Articles VI, XVI, and XXIII of the General Agreement on Tariffs and Trade*, MTN/NTM/W/226 (April 5, 1979)

Negotiating Group on Rules, *Submission by Australia*, TN/RL/W/86 (April 30, 2003)

Negotiating Group on Rules, *Communication from Egypt*, TN/RL/ W/56 (February 10, 2003)

Negotiating Group on Rules, *Communication from the Chairman*, *Agreement on the Implementation of Article VI of the General Agreement on Tariffs and Trade*, TN/RL/W/254 (April 11, 2011)

Negotiating Group on Rules, *Communication from the United States*, TN/RL/W/130 (June 20, 2003)

Negotiating Group on Rules, Communication of Australia, *Paper by Australia: Comments on Document*, TN/RL/W/6, TN/RL/W/22 (October 15, 2002)

Negotiating Group on Rules, Paper from South Africa, *Proposals on Issues Relating to the Antidumping Agreement,* TN/RL/GEN/136 (May 29, 2006)

Negotiating Group on Rules, *Draft Consolidated Chair Texts of the AD and SCM Agreements*, TN/RL/W/213 (November 30, 2007)

Negotiating Group on Rules, Hong Kong, China; Japan; Korea, Rep. of; Norway; Switzerland; and the Separate Customs Territory of Taiwan, Penghu, Kinmen and Matsu, TN/RL/W/233 (March 12, 2008)

Negotiating Group on Rules, *New Draft Consolidated Chair Texts for AD and SCM Agreements*, TN/RL/W/236 (December 19, 2008)

Negotiating Group on Rules, *Paper by Friends of Antidumping, Antidumping: Illustrative Major Issues*, TN/RL/W/6 (April 26, 2002)

Negotiating Group on Rules, Paper from Friends of Antidumping, *Second Submission of Proposals on the Determination of Injury,* TN/RL/W/38 (March 23, 2005)

Negotiating Group on Rules, *Paper from South Africa: Proposals on Issues relating to the Antidumping Agreement*, TN/RL/GEN/136 (May 29, 2006)

Negotiating Group on Rules, *Proposal of the People's Republic of China on the Negotiation on Antidumping, WTO Negotiating Group on Rules*, TN/RL/W/66 (March 6, 2003)

Negotiating Group on Rules, *Second Submission of India: Antidumping Agreement*, TN/RL/W/26 (October 17, 2002)

Negotiating Group on Rules, *Submission from the People's Republic of China, Replies to the Questions and Comments of the WTO Members Concerning the Proposal of China*, TN/RL/W/94 (May 5, 2003)

Negotiating Group on Rules, *Working Document from the Chairman*, TN/RL/W/232 (May 28, 2008)

Negotiating Group on Safeguards, *Communication from Australia, Hong Kong, Korea, New Zealand and Singapore*, MTN/GNG/NG9/W/8 (October 5, 1987)

Negotiating Group on Safeguards, *Communication from Brazil, Elements for a Comprehensive Understanding of Safeguards*, MTN/GNG/NG9/W/3 (May 25, 1987)

Negotiating Group on Rules, Paper from Friends of Antidumping, *Second Submission of Proposals on the Determination of Injury*, TN/RL/W/38 (March 23, 2005)

*Report of the Inter-sessional Working Party on the Complaint of Czechoslovakia Concerning the Withdrawal by the United States of a Tariff Concession under Article XIX of the GATT,* GATT/CP/106 (October 22, 1951)

Sub-Committee on Non-Tariff Barriers Group on Anti-Dumping Policies, *Draft Report on the Group on Anti-Dumping Policies*, TN/64/NTB/W/19 (April 24, 1967)

Submission from the Nordic Countries, *Negotiating Group on MTN Agreements and Arrangements,* MTN/GNG/NG8/W/15 (November 16, 1987)

World Trade Organization, *ADP Committee, Recommendations for Data Collection for Antidumping Investigations*, G/ADP/6 (May 16, 2000)

WTO Negotiating Group on Rules, *Communication of Australia, Paper by Australia: Comments on Document*, TN/RL/W/6, TN/RL/W/22 (October 15, 2002)

WTO Negotiating Group on Rules, *Proposal of the People's Republic of China on the Negotiation on Antidumping,* TN/RL/W/66 (March 6, 2003)

WTO Negotiating Group on Rules, *Second Submission of India: Antidumping Agreement*, TN/RL/W/26 (October 17, 2002)

WTO Negotiating Group on Rules, *Submission from the People's Republic of China, Replies to the Questions and Comments of the WTO Members Concerning the Proposal of China*, TN/RL/W/94 (May 5, 2003)

WTO, *Ministerial Declaration of 14 November 2001*, WT/MIN (01)/DEC/1, 41 I.L. M. 746 (2002)

Archive of European Integration, *The First Commission Report on Anti-Dumping and Anti-Subsidy Activities*, Information Memo P-87/83 (September 1983)

Committee on Trade and Development, Communication from the European Communities, *WTO Work Program on Special and Differential Treatment—Some EU Ideas for the Way ahead*, TN/CTD/W/20 (November 18, 2002)

**Statutes and Regulations**

*India*

Customs Tariff Act (Amended), 1975

Foreign Trade (Development & Regulation) Amendment Act of India, 2010

Antidumping Rules [Customs Tariff (Identification, Assessment and Collection of Anti-Dumping Duty on Dumped Articles for Determination of Injury) Rules, 1995

Collection of Anti-Dumping Duty on Dumped Articles and for Determination of Injury, Amendment Rules, 2011
Customs Tariff (Anti-Dumping) Rules of India, 1995

*United States of America*
Anti-Dumping Act of 1916, 15 U.S.C. 72 (1994)
Clayton Antitrust Act (1914), 15 U.S.C. §§ 12–27, 29 U.S.C. §§ 52–53
Customs Tariff Act, 1897
The Revenue Act, 1962, Pub.L. 87–834
Sherman Antitrust Act, 1890, 15 U.S.C. §§ 1–7
Tariff Act, 1890 (a.k.a. "Mckinley Tariff")
The Tariff Act, 1930, Pub.L. 71–361
Tariff Commission Act, 1970
The Antidumping Act, 1921 19 U.S.C. 160
The Trade Act, 1974, 19 U.S.C. 12
The Trade Agreements Act, 19 U.S.C. §§ 2501–2581

*South Africa*
International Trade Administration Act of South Africa, 2002

South Africa Customs Tariff Act, 1914

*Canada*
Antidumping Act of Canada, 1970
Customs Tariff Act of Canada, 1897
Special Import Measures Act of Canada, 1984

*UK*
British Safeguarding of Industries Act, 1921

*China*
Anti-Dumping Regulations of the People's Republic of China, 2004

*European Union*
Council Regulation (EC), 1372/ 2005 (August 19, 2005)

*Australia*
Customs Act of Australia, 1904

# General Introduction

This book is a comprehensive treatment of injury and causation in the context of trade remedy law—an arcane area of international trade law. But the book touches upon, rather eloquently, a larger issue of demonstrating causal link or determining legal responsibility within the context of economic legislations. Even within the domain of Common Law, the philosophical and practical nuances of establishing a link between the cause and effect have puzzled a large section of legal community for centuries. Having analyzed James Nedumpara's work, I am convinced that this problem is more acute in the context of international trade law. One of the vexing issues is that, in the strict sense, imports need not be a cause-in-fact or a cause in the economic sense, but is deemed as a cause by virtue of the trade remedy legislation. But leaving aside that issue, the nature and extent of causal connection itself is contentious.

This book has several purposes. It has provided a rounded analysis of the WTO case law and the areas where coherence is needed. In addition, the book has analyzed the puzzling areas of injury and causation in trade remedy law in the context of various WTO members including India. The book has provided a facile introduction to the evolution of injury and causation in trade remedy law and has examined the legislative history in the USA and several other GATT/WTO members. The legislative history is key to understanding the role and purport of these agreements.

The issue of injury and causation in trade remedy will continue to receive good attention. It is not easy to solve the conundrum, but it will be important to shape the causality determination in light of a clearer and better appreciation of the changing role of these instruments. This is where this book could be of immense help and guidance to the trade law community. While the world is embracing sophisticated versions of preferential and regional trade agreements, the temptation for import protection has not diminished in any sense. The WTO statistics indicate that trade remedy cases have increased in the last decade when compared to the previous periods in history.

I have no hesitation in saying that this is a unique contribution and I am glad to have advised Nedumpara as a research guide in shaping the contours of this research. The readers can gain a broad perspective of how trade remedy instruments are implemented among various jurisdictions. The book also provides a compelling analysis of the challenges posed by the WTO panels and the Appellate Body in the area of injury and causation. The twin assessment of the WTO law and the member practices is bound to create significant interest for any reader who is keen to know more about the conduct of trade remedy investigations.

Bengaluru
June 2016

O.V. Nandimath
Professor and Registrar
National Law School of India University

# Chapter 1
# Injury and Causation in Trade Remedy Law: An Introduction to the Enquiry

**Abstract** Trade remedy laws predicate their foundation on the very existence of "injury" to the domestic industry. While the nature and degree of causal relationship is unspecified in the WTO trade remedy agreements, the WTO panels and the Appellate Body have crafted certain treaty specific standards on injury and causation in all three categories of trade remedies. This introductory chapter examines the currently available literature on the application of appropriate injury and causation standards in WTO trade remedy law. This chapter sets out the key focus of enquiry of this book and the desirability of achieving coherence in evaluating injury and the causal link.

## A Introduction

The World Trade Organization (WTO) treaty seeks to liberalize international trade and remove barriers to movement of goods and services. However, the WTO treaty also permits a member country, in certain circumstances, to impose import restrictions in the form of higher tariffs or quotas for addressing the harm caused to its domestic country industry from imports. The unilateral actions permitted under the WTO include antidumping (AD) actions, countervailing duty (CVD) actions, and safeguards. An AD action is taken when a foreign exporter sells a product in the foreign market at a price lower than its home market price, and consequently injures the domestic industry. A CVD action may be filed against foreign exporters or producers who benefit from a government subsidy in their home market and, as a result, injures the industry in the importing country. In both instances, the effect of the subsidy or dumping must be to cause or threaten to cause certain harm or damage, known in trade parlance as "material injury", to a domestic industry or to "materially retard the establishment of a domestic industry". The third category, namely, safeguard actions are taken when increased imports cause "serious injury" to the domestic industry. A triumvirate of these actions is popularly known as 'trade remedies'.

Trade remedy investigations have significant political appeal and have been used by various domestic constituents to seek import relief. Such measures raise tariffs or adopt similar measures to specific goods, and effectively neutralize, in a significant measure,



J.J. Nedumpara, *Injury and Causation in Trade Remedy Law*,
DOI 10.1007/978-981-10-2197-8_1

the tariff concessions made in previous trade negotiations. Especially after the establishment of the WTO, there has been a significant increase in such actions. Multilateralizing trade remedies through the WTO resulted in a number of countries, which had hitherto no experience or domestic legislative framework for such instruments adopting and enforcing them with rigour. As trade liberalization resulted in lowering of tariffs or other protection across countries, recourse to trade remedy instruments became widely common. More than 4900 antidumping investigations have been initiated by WTO members in the last 20 years. The other two trade remedy measures, viz., countervailing duty actions (CVD) and safeguard actions are also not infrequent.[1]

Trade remedy laws predicate their foundation on the very existence of "injury" to the domestic industry. The WTO Treaty and, in particular, the relevant covered agreements ensure that the afore-mentioned trade remedies can be resorted to only when there is a causal relationship between dumping/subsidization or increased imports and the injury to the domestic industry. The domestic industry may suffer injury on account of a number of factors, which could be a few or many depending on the facts and circumstances. However, trade remedy measures can only be used to offset the injury attributable to unfair/increased imports and not for serving protectionist purposes. Stated differently, injury and causation provisions act as filters or anti-abuse provisions to the application of trade remedy measures.

Trade remedy measures predated the WTO and even the GATT 1947. However, the causation (or causality; throughout this book both the terms 'causality' and 'causation' are interchangeably used) language in the GATT/WTO was often contentious and called for negotiating compromises. The causation language in international trade remedy treaties has undergone myriad changes since the establishment of the GATT in 1947. Some of the changes were canvassed by countries that were keen to ensure harmony between their domestic legislation and international treaties.

The following sections outline the complexities of the problem, the questions that remain unresolved as a consequence of the interpretation of the WTO dispute settlement panels and the Appellate Body and the research design of this study. A review of the relevant literature is also attempted in the introduction to the research problem. The following discussions also deal with the structure of enquiry and the methodology adopted in this study.

## B Injury and Causation in Trade Remedies: Persisting Issues

Trade remedy actions occupy an important role in international trade, although they are widely considered as antithetical to the concept of free trade. Trade remedy measures enable governments to pursue trade liberalization as they act as a buffer

---

[1]Chad P. Bown (2014), *Global Antidumping Database*, http://go.worldbank.org/KR19BT5EQ0 (updated as of December, 2014); see also World Trade Organization, Documents online, http://docs.wto.org (last visited May 26, 2015).

against unforeseen situations where imports are perceived to be causing injury to the domestic industry. The very concept of injury varies depending on the laws governing the investigations.[2] While antidumping and countervailing duties deal with 'material injury', safeguards investigations deal with 'serious injury'. Both these terms are not properly defined in the WTO treaty, but refer to a general decline in the economic parameters of the domestic industry.

There are built-in restraints in various trade agreements against the indiscriminate use of such measures. The WTO covered agreements, however, require that the above trade remedies can be resorted to only when there is a causal relationship between dumping/subsidization or increased imports and the injury to the domestic industry. However, the WTO agreements that deal with trade remedies provide only limited guidance on the meaning, degree or nature of the causal relationship. As outlined earlier, the absence of a definition on what could constitute "material injury" or "serious injury" can be problematic; however, the greater challenge for the investigating authorities is in performing the "non-attribution" test. The non-attribution test is about isolating and explaining away the role of factors other than imports to ensure that the injury caused by other factors is not attributed to dumped, subsidized or increased imports.[3]

As originally conceived, the non-attribution analysis entailed certain weighing and comparison of causes. The negotiating history of injury and causation provisions under the Kennedy and Tokyo Rounds or even the WTO treaty established under the Uruguay Round can provide certain explanatory force to this effect. It is more or less clear from the negotiating history that the drafters wanted the investigating authorities to take into account the influence of "other factors" in examining whether they break the chain of causation or not, rather than examining the individual impact of each known factor. However, the WTO panels and the Appellate Body have been extremely critical of the conduct of the non-attribution analysis of the various national trade remedy investigating agencies.[4] The WTO Appellate Body in a number of cases involving trade remedy measures had ruled that the investigating agencies have an obligation to segregate and distinguish the "other known factors" from dumped/subsidized or increased imports and make sure that the injury caused by such factors is not attributed to such imports.[5]

---

[2]J.J. Fetzer, *Inference for economic modeling in antidumping, countervailing duty and safeguard investigations*, 8(4) World Trade Review 545, 545-556 (2009).

[3]Jorge Miranda, *Causal Link and Non-Attribution as Interpreted in WTO Trade Remedy Disputes*, 44(4) Journal of World Trade 729 (2010) (explaining how non-attribution is conducted in the context of WTO cases).

[4]Alan o. Sykes, The Wto Agreement On Safeguards: a Commentary 174 (2006). *See infra*, Chap. 2 of this book for a detailed discussion on this topic.

[5]Appellate Body Report, *United States – Anti-Dumping Measures on Certain Hot-Rolled Steel Products from Japan*, WT/DS184/AB/R, (August 23, 2001)[hereinafter "Appellate Body, US-Hot-rolled Steel); Appellate Body Report, *United States – Safeguard Measures on Imports of Fresh, Chilled or Frozen Lamb Meat from New Zealand and Australia*, WT/DS177/AB/R, WT/DS178/AB/R (May 16, 2001).

This requirement is broadly known as the "non-attribution" requirement. The United States, for instance, lost most if not all safeguard cases in the WTO where its conduct of non-attribution analysis was challenged. As Appendix of Chap. 3 of this book demonstrates, several disputes in the WTO have examined the matter of non-attribution in injury and causation.[6]

The WTO cases after the *US—Hot-rolled Steel* have elevated the "non-attribution" test to the status of an inviolable requirement necessitating the need to identify and, where possible, separate the role of each factor. Such an approach is evident from a few selected statements of the Appellate Body in cases such as *US—Line Pipe,*[7] *US—Hot rolled steel*[8] and *US—Wheat Gluten.*[9] For example, in the *US—Line Pipe*, the Appellate Body ruled that one of the objectives of the non-attribution is to make sure that only an appropriate share of overall injury is attributed to increased imports.[10] However, neither the panels nor the Appellate Body has provided any clarity as to how this could be done.

There is a strong body of literature that suggests that the injury and causation standards in the trade remedy field have become incoherent and confusing.[11] Jorge Miranda comments that some of the methodological tools used for the non-attribution have limitations and could prove misleading or inconclusive.[12] Alan Sykes argues that the causal connection between increased imports and injury is fundamentally incoherent. As Sykes argues, from the standpoint of economic logic, import quantities are not a causal or exogenous variable—they are endogenous and result from other forces.[13] Assuming that the imports and domestic products are perfect substitutes, according to Sykes, the quantity of imports will just equal the difference between domestic demand and domestic supply at the equilibrium price. Within this framework, the exogenous factors are the determinants of domestic supply, domestic demand, and the import supply curve. Factors such as consumer tastes and incomes

[6]*See infra*, Chap. 3, Appendix.

[7]Appellate Body Report, *United States – Definitive Safeguard Measures on Imports of Circular Welded Carbon Quality Line Pipe from Korea*, ¶ 252, WT/DS202/AB/R (March 8, 2002) [hereinafter Appellate Body Report, *US- Line Pipe*].

[8]Appellate Body Report, *United States – Anti–Dumping Measures on Certain Hot–Rolled Steel Products from Japan*, WT/DS184/AB/R (August 23, 2001).

[9]Appellate Body Report, *United States – Definitive Safeguard Measures on Imports of Wheat Gluten from the European Communities* ("US- Wheat Gluten"), WT/DS166/AB/R ¶ 69 (January 19, 2001) (emphasizing the need to "distinguish" the injury caused by imports from the injury caused by other factors).

[10]Appellate Body Report, *US- Line Pipe*, ¶ 252.

[11]Alan Sykes, *The Safeguard Mess: A critique of WTO jurisprudence*, 2(3) World Trade Review 261 (2003); Chad P. Bown, Why are Safeguards Under the WTO so Unpopular, 1 World Trade Review 47 (2002); Douglas Irwin, '*Causing Problems': The WTO Review of Causation and Injury Attribution in US Section 201 Cases*, 2(3) World Trade Review 297 (2003).

[12]Jorge Miranda, *Causal Link and Non-Attribution as Interpreted in WTO Trade Remedy Disputes*, 44(4) Journal of World Trade 729, 760(2010).

[13]Alan o. Sykes, *The Safeguard Mess: A critique of WTO jurisprudence*, 2(3) World Trade Review 261 (2003).

can affect domestic demand; other factors such as costs of inputs in production and the state of available production technology can determine domestic supply; other factors affecting supply and demand in other countries can also determine import supply. Based on this reasoning, the quantity of import is determined by the interaction of these forces.

In addition to Sykes, a number of authors have investigated whether affirmative results of injury and causal link in trade remedy investigations can be explained by "injury from imports". These studies include the research published by Kelly,[14] Pindyck and Rotemberg,[15] Grossman and Mavroidis,[16] etc. Some of the studies, especially in the field of economics, have found that non-import related factors—as proxied by general macroeconomic conditions such as movements of GDP, employment or other conditions could be determined as the dominant reasons for injury depending on the facts of each individual case.[17] According to this view, the prices and quantities of imported and domestic goods in commonly used supply and demand models of markets in international trade are endogenously determined. The major shortcoming, in the opinion of certain economists, is that imports per se cannot be the cause of injury and that it is incorrect to assume that import volumes or quantities 'causes' decline in price or output in the domestic industry.[18] However, based on a public choice analysis of the trade remedy laws, Sykes and others argue that instead of ascribing economic logic to such laws, one has to view them as part of a grand and political compact among major trading nations.[19] Other commentators have also argued that the economic rationale of trade remedy laws rests on murky theoretical foundation and is not empirically sustainable.[20]

A detailed literature review on injury and causation in trade remedy law is provided in Chaps. 2 and 3 of this book.

---

[14]K. Kelly, *An Analysis of Causality in Escape Clause Cases*, 37(2) Journal of Industrial Economics, 187-207 (1998).

[15]R.S. Pindyck & J.J. Rotemberg, *Are Imports to Blame? Attribution of Injury under the 1974 Trade Act*, 30 Journal of Law and Economics 101 (1987).

[16]Henrik Horn & Petros C. Mavroidis, *United States- Safeguard Measures on Imports of Fresh, Chilled or Frozen Lamb Meat from New Zealand and Australia: What Should be Required of a Safeguard Investigation?*' in The Wto Case Law of 2001 (H. Horn and P.C. Mavroidis eds., 2003).

[17]*See for example*, J. Michael Finger, *Flexibilities, Rules, and Trade Remedies in* The Gatt/wto System in the Oxford Handbook on World Trade Organization 428 (Amrita Narlikar et al. eds, 2012).

[18]H. Horn and P.C. Mavroidis, *United States- Safeguard Measures on Imports of Fresh, Chilled or Frozen Lamb Meat from New Zealand and Australia: What Should be Required of a Safeguard Investigation?*' in The Wto Case Law of 2001 (H. Horn and P.C. Mavroidis eds., 2003). See also Alan O. Sykes, The Economics of Injury in Antidumping and Countervailing Duty Investigations, 16 International Review of Law and Economics 5, 10 (1996).

[19]A.O. Sykes, *The Economics of Injury in Antidumping and Countervailing Duty Cases*, 16 International Review of Law and Economics 5 (1996).

[20]Michael J. Trebilcock & Robert Howse, The Regulation of International Trade 259 (3rd edn., 2010).

This analytical work would like to steer clear of this debate and assumes that imports, fair or unfair, are causal under antidumping, CVD and safeguards investigations. Such an assumption lies at the heart of trade remedy legislations. In that context, this study enquires whether it is essential to insist on econometric approaches to establishing injury and causation as hinted by some of the WTO Panel and the Appellate Body decisions.[21] It is important to ask whether most of the WTO members are capable of doing such a rigorous analysis involving econometrics and sophisticated statistical tools.[22] While an econometric approach to establishing injury and causation has certain intuitive appeal,[23] does the evidence from various countries suggest that the WTO members have the capability to routinely conduct and establish such analysis? In the light of the above, it is examined in this study whether the non-attribution test is a process requirement rather than an economic concept aimed at precise identification of injury and causation. In order to address this issue, it is important to examine the practices of the key users of trade remedies to get an understanding of how they conduct injury and causation. The trade remedy agreements provide a significant amount of leeway to the member countries in establishing causation and the scope of interference by WTO panels is narrow in the light of the standard of review suggested for the dispute settlement panels. Therefore, rather than examining whether such investigations do conform to the requirements of the WTO treaty text and dispute settlement jurisprudence, it is more pertinent to ask how the key users conduct their injury and causation analysis so as to ensure their treaty obligations. It is pertinent to add here that the question as to how the role of various causal factors can be measured or separated is an economic or statistical enquiry whereas the focus of this study is to examine what treaty obligations the WTO members have assumed in respect of injury and causation analysis and how the members could potentially meet their treaty obligations. Towards this end, it is necessary to examine the WTO member practices as evidenced by the WTO dispute settlement proceedings examining trade remedy investigations and domestic investigations by some of the key players. Although the purpose of the non-attribution language is to ensure that injurious dumped/subsidized/increased imports should have, without the help of other factors, caused the injury, it should not result in foisting a requirement on WTO members which is not easy to meet with.

It is also seen that the non-attribution analysis is tied to the nature and degree of causal relationship between imports and the alleged injury to the domestic industry. Prior to the conclusion of the Uruguay Round (1986–1994), various GATT rounds had addressed the issue whether imports should be the “principal cause” of injury,

---

[21]Appellate Body Report, *US –Line Pipe*, ¶ 252.

[22]J.P. Durling & M. P. McCullough, *Teaching Old Laws New Tricks: The Legal Obligation of Non-Attribution and the Need for Economic Rigor in Injury Analyses Under US Trade Law*, in Handbook of International Trade (E. Kwan Choi & James Hartigan eds., 2004).

[23]K. Kelly, *An Analysis of Causality in Escape Clause Cases*, 37(2) Journal of Industrial Economics 187-207 (1998); G.M. Grossman, *Imports as a Cause of Injury: The Case of the US Steel Industry*, 20 (3 &4) Journal of International Economics 201, 223 (1986).

or "substantial cause" of injury, or the "predominant cause of injury" or a just a "a cause". These issues invoked significant epistemological difficulties from a causation point of view.[24] This analytical work proceeds on the proposition that causation in trade remedy law is a policy dependent matter and that a scientific or econometric approach is neither necessary nor strictly enforced in practice. To elaborate, a strict non-attribution may be required if the authorities have to establish a "genuine and substantial relationship of cause and effect" between imports and the alleged injury; however, the degree of cause will be less rigorous if imports have to be just a "cause". In order to examine this proposition, this research seeks to examine the evolution and the traditional role of each of the trade remedies dating back to the early twentieth century.

Furthermore, a review of WTO case law[25] and the discussions in the Rules Negotiations[26] under the Doha Round clearly indicate that the current state of play in injury and causation is controversial and is lacking in coherence. For instance, Terence, Dwyer and Hein argue that the Appellate Body has "overreached" its mandate in these cases.[27] While negotiations are taking place in Geneva on reforming the Antidumping Agreement and the Subsidies and Countervailing Measures Agreement, it is perceived that the injury and causation issue cannot be addressed without introducing conceptual clarity on the meaning of causation itself. However, current negotiations do not indicate that such an effort has been made. This research study is an attempt in understanding the meaning of injury and causation in the context of trade remedy law by grounding its basis in the general theories of causation in law. It is further examined whether the Necessary Element of a Sufficient Set (NESS) test elaborated upon by Richard Wright could provide a conceptual grounding to the theory of causation in trade remedy law.

## C Purpose of the Enquiry on Injury and Causation

Establishing injury and causality or even conducting non-attribution is not necessarily legal, but may require multidisciplinary approaches. There could be umpteen economic or non-economic factors which could explain the poor state of the domestic industry and, therefore, it will be difficult to establish whether a factor

[24]Raj Bhala, Modern Gatt Law 804 (2005).

[25]Douglas A. Irwin, '*Causing Problems': The WTO Review of Causation and Injury Attribution in US Section 201 Cases*, 2(3) World Trade Review 297 (2003); Jorge Miranda, *Causal Link and Non-Attribution as Interpreted in WTO Trade Remedy Disputes*, 44(4) Journal of World Trade 729 (2010); Alan Sykes, *The Safeguard Mess: A critique of WTO jurisprudence*, 2(3) World Trade Review 261 (2003).

[26]*See Infra* Chap. 6.

[27]Terence P. Stewart, Amy S Dwyer & Elizabeth M. Hein, *Trends in the Last Decade of Trade Remedy Decisions: Problems and Opportunities for the WTO Dispute Settlement System*, 24 (1) Arizona Journal of International and Comparative Law 251, 277 (2007).

alone or in combination with other factors is substantially causing injury to the domestic industry in the importing country. One of the key objectives of this research is to understand the scope and meaning of non-attribution, which is an important element in the injury and causation determination. The emphasis on separating and isolating the impact of each causal factor is fraught with imperfections and inaccuracies. This study seeks to provide a thorough and comprehensive analysis of the WTO jurisprudence on injury and causality with special reference to the non-attribution test. While doing so, this study also seeks to bridge the information gap regarding the WTO member practices in the field of injury and non-attribution analysis in trade remedy investigations.

Several developed and developing nations have become prominent users of the trade remedy instruments. While the United States, Canada and the European Union have been the traditional users, new users such as India, China, Brazil, and Argentina have also been aggressive in pursuing trade remedy actions. This book has examined the injury and causation analysis of both the traditional and new users. In particular, an effort has been made to understand the key determinants which are given weightage or consideration in the injury and causation analysis. Every effort was made to understand how the traditional and new users conduct the non-attribution test in the injury and causation analysis. Another consideration was whether the major users are receptive to using rigorous economic analysis and quantitative tools.

In addition, this study proceeds on the basis that the key to resolving the causation muddle in trade remedy law is to find out an appropriate conceptual standard in the general theories of law. For example, this book has devoted several pages for examining the utility of the "but-for" test. Central to this enquiry is the nature of causal connection itself, i.e., whether the imports should be the necessary cause, sufficient cause or a mere cause, including the degrees of necessity and sufficiency required in this connection. Based on this premise, this research seeks to ground the injury and causality debate in trade remedy in the general principles of law. This enquiry is based on the assumption that the current approaches to establishing injury and causation, especially the approaches suggested by the WTO Appellate Body are, to an extent, incoherent and impose an onerous procedural requirement on trade remedy authorities.

Issues relating to injury and causality in antidumping and subsidies are central to the ongoing Rules negotiations of the Doha Round in the WTO. This study is aimed at informing the debate of the ongoing negotiations and filling the existing gaps in knowledge in this field. Towards this objective, there is a fairly detailed analysis of the proposals in the Rules negotiations under the Doha Round. A major hypothesis of study was that injury and causation determination in trade remedy investigations is a policy dependent exercise and is not amenable for a strict and rigorous standard of causation.

## D Methodology

The study involves an understanding of the evolution of injury and causality instruments in various domestic legal systems and under various international trade agreements. A large part of the analysis undertaken in this work is descriptive and analytical.

The primary source for evaluation of injury and causation are international treaties on trade remedies and various national legislations and executive orders enforcing the trade remedy law. In fact, an evaluation of the legislations in the United States starting from the U.S. Antidumping Act, 1916 are found to be extremely useful in understanding the historical background and context for developing trade remedy statutes. Likewise, the Basic Regulations and the successive treaties that led to the formation of the European Union (EU) can provide useful insights into the implementation of trade remedies in the EU. Furthermore, several countries including Canada and South Africa had implemented trade remedy measures, especially antidumping measures even before the establishment of the GATT 1947. This study has traced the origin of trade remedies in various domestic jurisdictions and how the current language on injury and causation in the GATT/WTO was shaped and influenced by domestic legislations of some of the major users.

More than one-third of the cases brought for WTO dispute settlement are trade remedy cases.[28] The vast body of WTO jurisprudence available in the field of trade remedies is instructive in understanding the injury and causation provisions under the GATT/WTO. A bulk of this study is based on the interpretative approach of the WTO panels and the Appellate Body in reviewing trade remedy cases and, to this extent, is doctrinal. The discussion of the WTO case law is to provide a systematic, analytical and evaluative exposition of the WTO jurisprudence in injury and causality. In this regard, a detailed analysis of the injury and causality arguments involved in the WTO disputes during the last 20 years (1995–2014) and a few GATT disputes (1947–1994) is attempted. In addition to the analysis of the reported WTO cases, this analysis has also examined the various written submissions made by WTO members in the WTO dispute settlement, to the extent that they are available in the public domain.[29] The study has also examined the negotiating proposals of various WTO members submitted as part of the Rules Negotiations of the Doha Round. All the negotiations proposals and submissions are available from the *Documents online* portal of the WTO.[30]

---

[28]WTO's Dispute Settlement Gateway at http://www.wto.org/english/tratop_e/dispu_e/dispu_e.htm.

[29]Only a limited number of WTO members such the European Union and the United States provide public access to their submissions to the dispute settlement body.

[30]World Trade Organization, *Documents online*, *available at* https://docs.wto.org.

In addition to doctrinal approach, this research study has also conducted a qualitative assessment of injury and causation determination based on detailed case studies of antidumping and safeguards investigations held in India. Case studies are often seen as prime examples of qualitative research which adopts an interpretive approach to data or practices.[31] The purpose is to examine the process and type of analysis adopted in conducting injury and causation in trade remedy cases. Nineteen (19) cases were chosen in the field of antidumping and twelve (12) cases were chosen in the field of safeguards. These cases have been selected from different time periods in order to obtain a broadly representative understanding as well as to gather a better appreciation of the shifts in the analytical approaches of the investigating agencies over time. Since India has limited experience in conducting full-fledged countervailing duty (CVD) or anti-subsidy investigation, such a case study was not possible in the field of CVD actions. Furthermore, in order to understand the practice of other key users, a review of the secondary literature, including scholarly works and other articles published in professional journals was made.

The qualitative examination is based on a critical evaluation and observation of the final findings of the Indian antidumping agency, namely the Directorate General of Antidumping and Allied Duties (DGAD). India is one of the leading users of antidumping actions and has completed more than 550 antidumping cases. Therefore, in the case of antidumping investigations, the case studies are taken from a pool of cases in which the findings of injury and causal link was a matter of central enquiry in the investigation. In order to select the cases for detailed observation analysis, a review of all antidumping cases between 1995 and 2013 was initially undertaken to examine in how many of such cases injury and causality was relevant.[32] Since it is impossible to provide a qualitative analysis of the process, methodologies and the nature of analysis on injury and causation involved in each of these cases and also with a view to achieving precision, a list of nineteen antidumping cases was drawn up based on the following criteria: (a) whether the final findings contain a reasonable discussion on injury and causation, or (b) whether any respondent/exporter had challenged the maintenance of investigation for any alleged lack of injury/causation before the investigating authority or before any appellate forums. This approach was chosen to ensure that the selection of cases does not omit or disregard the significant or pertinent cases on injury and causation. This approach was also necessitated by the fact that a number of parties, especially foreign exporters or traders do not participate in the investigation and that relevant arguments on injury and causation would not have been raised. The findings in such cases are typically made on the basis of *facts available*.[33]

[31]Jerry Wellington and Marcin Szcerbinski, Research Methods for Social Sciences 91-92 (2008).

[32]The injury and causation findings in all original findings have been compiled and documented (on file with author).

[33]See Article 6.8 and Annex II of the Antidumping Agreement. When interested parties do not submit information within a reasonable period of time, the investigating authority is free to use the best information available, which is also known as *facts available*.

Furthermore, in order to ensure that the case studies have included the relevant cases, the details were further cross-checked with the Global Antidumping Database maintained by Chad Bown of the World Bank.[34] The Global Antidumping Database maintains a detailed profile of antidumping cases conducted by India and other WTO members. It also provides quantitative data on all aspects of the investigation including dumping and injury. However, this database does not provide details of how the decision was taken or why injury and causal link were found to be existent or non-existent. However, during the analysis it was reconfirmed that the nature or approaches to injury and causality analysis do not drastically change from case to case although one could conclusively argue that there is a trend towards a more thoroughgoing analysis of cases conducted after 2003. Accordingly, the investigations were classified into two phases. Phase-I deals with cases conducted between 1994 and 2003 and Phase-II dealing with cases examined between 2004 and 2014. The cases were adopted on a broad longitudinal timeframe, i.e., over a 20 year period in order to accurately capture the change in antidumping practices and the nature of examination over time.

Furthermore, the case studies are chosen from diverse sectors of manufacture to fully appreciate the approach and pattern in antidumping cases across products and sectors. This methodology is expected to provide a better and comprehensive understanding of the processes, methodology, reasoning and approach in antidumping cases involving India. In addition, in order to understand the injury and causation determination practices of other countries, a comparative analysis based on a review of secondary literature such as published articles and case reports was carried out. These countries account for more than 80 % of the world-wide antidumping orders and can provide rich insights into the antidumping practices.

In the case of safeguards, choice of case studies for closer examination was much easier. India had concluded only 30 odd safeguard cases. Out of these, 12 cases were chosen for careful study. In choosing the cases for detailed examination, effort was made to choose cases spread across representative time frame, products and sectors.

The case studies in antidumping and safeguards chosen for India systemically examine whether the DGAD examined each of the material injury factors during the injury investigation period. It also examines whether the DGAD conducted a non-attribution analysis and how such an analysis was carried out. The pertinent question was whether the authorities conducted a detailed examination of factors other than imports in the causality determination. The case studies also enquire whether the "other causes" were limited to the standard causes which are enlisted in the Antidumping or the SCM Agreements or whether they were they based on a case specific enquiry. Furthermore, in Appendix of Chap. 3, a detailed examination of all the "other causes" identified by the WTO panels in all trade remedy

[34]Chad P. Bown, *Global Antidumping Database*, The World Bank (2014), *available at* http://econ.worldbank.org/ttbd/gad/.

investigations brought to the WTO Dispute Settlement Body (DSB) between the period 1995–2015 is provided.

The study has also used scholarly articles in exploring alternative conceptual framework for causation in trade remedies. There is a rich body of literature explicating the causation issues in the context of tort and contract law. These general theories of law are not often referred to while suggesting reforms to injury and causality in trade remedy law, although there have been a few recent attempts.[35] The literature on causation in the general theory of causation is considered instructive in the field of trade remedy law as well.

In addition to examining the primary documents, the study has been benefitted by one to one exchanges with several practitioners, academicians and policy makers in the field of trade remedy in India, EU and the United States.[36] These interactions helped the process of understanding the nature of injury and causation determination in several jurisdictions.

## E Structure and Organization of the Book

The organization of this book is as follows: In order to understand the injury and causation with respect to various trade remedy instruments, emphasis was laid on identifying the role and function of each trade defense instrument under the GATT/WTO. An important question was the following: how did the international treaties on trade remedies adopt the current language? What was the rationale for adopting a particular language for a specific trade remedy agreement? The political economy considerations might have had a major influence in shaping a particular causation language as opposed to various other alternatives. A review of GATT/WTO treaty and their negotiating history is key to understanding the objectives of the specific trade defense instruments and their role within the treaty context. Chap. 2 of this book entitled *Historical Evolution of Injury and Causation in Trade Remedies under GATT/WTO* is an attempt to discern the normative justifications as well as the political economy considerations that led the GATT Contracting Parties to elect for a particular language in various trade remedy agreements.

The decisions of dispute settlement bodies and other tribunals can throw immense light on the application of causation provisions in the underlying domestic

---

[35]Dukgeun Ahn & William J. Moon, *Alternative Approach to Causation Analysis in Trade Remedy Investigations" : ' Cost of Production' Test*, 44 (5) Journal of World Trade 1023, 1047-1051 (2010).

[36]Interactions were conducted with Jennifer Hillman, Terence P. Stewart, Abhijit Das, Sharad Bhansali, Sanjay Notani, Mukesh Bhatnagar, Mark Wu, Thomas Prusa, Nithya Nagarajan, Rajnish Jaiswal, Peter Koenig, Jitendra Singh, Ashish Chandra, Jorge Miranda, Han Yong and several other experts working in this field to understand the conduct of causality in several jurisdictions. The concerned details of the interviews are mentioned at the relevant section.

proceedings in various jurisdictions and how the reviewing courts would interpret and evaluate the causation determination in such cases. Therefore as a logical second step, this book undertakes a review of most of the GATT/WTO disputes (1947–2015) which had some discussion on injury and causation in the fields of antidumping, subsidies and countervailing measures, and safeguards. The disputes which are of particular importance in this area include the decisions of the Appellate Body, in *US—Hot Rolled Steel* (antidumping),[37] *EC—Pipe Fittings* (antidumping),[38] *Mexico—Rice* (antidumping),[39] *Argentina—Footwear* (safeguards),[40] *US—Line Pipe* (safeguards),[41] *US—Lamb* (safeguards),[42] *US—Wheat Gluten* (safeguards),[43] *US—Steel* (safeguards),[44] etc. In addition to these landmark cases, this book will examine the role of other panel decisions which have a jurisprudential significance. In the above light, Chap. 3 of the book, which is entitled *Injury and Causation in Trade Remedy Law: An Analysis of the WTO Jurisprudence* provides a critical analysis of the WTO jurisprudence on injury and causation issues in trade remedy investigations.

As outlined above, one of the key research questions is whether the WTO members are capable of performing the non-attribution requirement along the lines of various panel and Appellate Body rulings. In the above context, it is necessary to evaluate the substantive and procedural components of the non-attribution test. Accordingly, this study undertakes an examination of the injury and causation analysis in India by focusing on a select list of cases in the field of antidumping as well as safeguards investigations. Chapters 4 and 5 of this book examine India's experience of conducting injury and causation in antidumping and safeguards investigations respectively. In addition, Chaps. 4 and 5 include a secondary literature review of injury and causality determinations of other active users of antidumping and safeguards instruments.

The ongoing Rules negotiations under the Doha Round is an appropriate occasion to understand the views and reflections of the WTO members on injury and causation. The views of the WTO members will be influenced by their

---

[37]Appellate Body Report, *United States – Anti-Dumping Measures on Certain Hot-Rolled Steel Products from Japan*, WT/DS184/AB/R, adopted 23 August 2001.

[38]Appellate Body Report, *European Communities – Anti–Dumping Duties on Malleable Cast Iron Tube or Pipe Fittings from Brazil*, WT/DS219/AB/R (August 18, 2003).

[39]*Mexico – Definitive Anti-Dumping Measures on Beef and Rice*, WT/DS295/AB/R (November 29, 2005).

[40]Appellate Body Report, *Argentina–Safeguard Measures on Imports of Footwear*, WT/DS121/AB/R (Jan.12, 2000).

[41]Appellate Body Report, *United States – Line Pipe.*

[42]Appellate Body Report, *United States – Safeguard Measures on Imports of Fresh, Chilled or Frozen Lamb Meat from New Zealand and Australia*, WT/DS177/AB/R, WT/DS178/AB/R, (May 16, 2001).

[43]Appellate Body Report, *United States – Wheat Gluten.*

[44]Appellate Body Report, *United States – Definitive Safeguard Measures on Imports of Certain Steel Products*, WT/DS248/AB/R, WT/DS249/AB/R, WT/DS251/AB/R, WT/DS252/AB/R, WT/DS253/AB/R, WT/DS254/AB/R, WT/DS258/AB/R, WT/DS259/AB/R (December 10, 2003).

understanding of the domestic application of these remedies and the interpretations accorded to these provisions by the WTO dispute settlement panels and the Appellate Body. In the light of the developments made under the Rules negotiations, this study explores whether the substantive proposals made by various members are capable of addressing the injury and causation issues. Accordingly, Chap. 6 examines the various negotiating proposals under Rules negotiations under the Doha Round to examine some of the key proposals and the suggestions made in the Chairman's texts.

One of the points of enquiry in this study is the applicability of causation standards in Common Law to trade remedy investigations. In order to provide a conceptual framework for trade remedies, this book examines some of the dominant writings on causation in Chap. 7. In particular, this book examines the work of H. L. A. Hart and Tony Honoré,[45] as well as Richard Wright.[46] This study further examines the suitability of the "Necessary Element of a Sufficient Set", popularly known as the NESS Test in providing a robust conceptual basis for the causal relationship between the imports and the injury. According to the NESS test a particular condition will be treated as a cause to a specific result only and only if it was a necessary element of a set of actual conditions that was sufficient for the occurrence a result. The NESS test has strong philosophic roots and can satisfactorily address a causal enquiry where multiple factors are involved. The book seeks to examine the utility of the NESS test when compared to the "but-for" test or other quantitative approaches involving economic or statistical tools.

Finally, this book examines if there is a need for the WTO Membership to seriously consider the need to make clarifications or amendments to the treaty text itself in order to reflect the current day practices, realities and exigencies that underlie the use of various trade defense instruments. Chapter 8 summarizes some of the key findings and observations.

## F Limitations of the Study

This book addresses the issue of injury and causation from a legal perspective. As Hart and Honoré said, causation need not be a legal issue, but law will have to systematize the causal relationship.[47] In relation to causation, there have been several suggestions to use economic tools to evaluate the causal relationship in the context of trade remedy proceedings.[48] This research does not address arguments either in favour of or against the use of economic tools. The focus of this research is

---

[45]H L A Hart & Tony Honoré, The Causation in Law (1959).

[46]Richard Wright, *Causation in Tort Law*, 73 California Law Review 1735 (1985).

[47]Hart & Honoré, *supra* note 45.

[48]*See* for example A. Keck *et al, A 'Proababilistic Approach to Use of Econometric Modeling in Sunset Reviews*, 6(3) World Trade Review 371 (2007).

on understanding the historical background and current application of injury and causality provisions under the WTO trade remedy agreements and to suggest a conceptual framework which could adequately answer the causation enquiry. The practice of some of the key users such as India is also examined, but it is neither logically desirable nor practically feasible to examine the practices of all major users of trade remedies. The scope of the examination was to find out the methodology applied by various jurisdictions including India in determining injury and causation and to analyze how the key users are conducting the enquiry, what analytical or economic tools are being used and how they comply with the requirements imposed by the panels and the Appellate Body of the WTO. Having said this, the clarification of causal concepts and the making of causal judgements in trade remedy cases will be an unending journey; we can only seek to make the journey a bit more stable, but not to predetermine the path itself.

# Chapter 2
# Historical Evolution of Injury and Causation in Trade Remedies Under GATT/WTO

**Abstract** This chapter traces the history of trade remedy legislations and the evolution of various international instruments that were developed to discipline the misuse and proliferation of trade remedy measures. In particular this chapter lists out the key developments in the United States which emerged as a major user of trade remedies. This chapter also examines the key developments that led to specific trade remedy provisions under the various negotiating rounds of the GATT.

## A Introduction

Trade remedy laws typically refer to national laws that impose import restrictions against certain specific contingencies such as increased imports, or unfair imports. Such remedies are often used by industries to seek protection from such fair or unfair import competition. Establishing causal link in trade remedy investigations between such unfair or fair imports and injury is an essential, but often problematic part of all trade remedy investigations. The Antidumping Agreement as well as its related trade contingency instruments, viz., safeguards and countervailing duty investigations, provide a significant amount of discretion to the investigating agencies as to how a causal link between injury and increased imports (or, dumped imports in the case of the latter) has to be established.

At present, trade remedy investigations are governed at the multilateral level by the World Trade Organization (WTO). A number of regional trade agreements and economic partnership agreements also regulate trade remedy actions. However, trade remedy actions are not anything new. Such actions have been maintained and implemented by a number of countries, mainly industrialized countries, for well over a century. However, most developing countries and emerging economies started using it after mid-1990s.



J.J. Nedumpara, *Injury and Causation in Trade Remedy Law*,
DOI 10.1007/978-981-10-2197-8_2

At the multilateral level, trade remedy actions are subject to the WTO Agreements which include, the Marrakesh Treaty Establishing the World Trade Organization[1] and other covered agreements under the WTO. These agreements include the General Agreement on Tariffs and Trade (GATT) 1994, the Agreement on the Implementation of Article VI of the GATT (the Antidumping Agreement, or AD Agreement), the Agreement on Subsidies and Countervailing Measures Agreement (SCM Agreement), and the Agreement on Safeguards (Safeguards Agreement). The specific trade remedy agreements referred to above elaborate and explain the treaty provisions of the GATT 1994.

Of the various trade policy instruments, antidumping is the oldest and perhaps, the most commonly used trade remedy instrument.[2] Antidumping measures are invoked to counteract the injurious effects of dumping. In international trade law parlance, dumping is often defined as international price discrimination.[3] It occurs when an exporter sells merchandise in the importing country at a price significantly below that at which it sells like merchandise in its home country.[4] Specific actions against such price discriminations were taken unilaterally by the importing countries.

Unilateral enforcement of trade remedy measures created significant friction among trading nations and several countries wanted to discipline the use of such remedies. Antidumping or, for that matter, countervailing duties and safeguard actions are no longer unregulated especially after the establishment of the WTO.

The original GATT 1947 had certain skeletal mechanism for regulating the use of trade remedies. The Antidumping Agreement (ADA)[5] and the Subsidies and Countervailing Measures Agreement (SCMA),[6] which have originated from the Uruguay Round trade negotiations (1986–1994), unequivocally state that specific action against dumping or subsidization can only be conducted within the framework of these agreements. Efforts by WTO members to implement legislation that are at variance with the AD Agreement and the SCM Agreement have been rejected by the WTO panels and the Appellate Body in recent times.[7]

---

[1]Final Act Embodying the Results of the Uruguay Round of Multilateral Trade Negotiations, Apr. 15, 1994, The Legal Texts: The Results Of The Uruguay Round Of Multilateral Trade Negotiations 2 (1999), 1867 U.N.T.S. 14, 33 I.L.M. 1143 (1994) [hereinafter *Final Act*].

[2]Igne Nora Neufeld, *Anti-Dumping and Countervailing Procedures – Use or Abuse? Implications for Developing Countries*, Policy Issues in International Trade and Commodities Study Series No. 9, UNCTAD (2001), also available at: http://unctad.org/en/docs/itcdtab10_en.pdf.

[3]Giancario Gandolfo, International Economics I: The Pure Theory of International Trade 131 (2d ed. 1994).

[4]Richard D. Boltuck, *An Economic Analysis of Dumping*, 21(5) Journal of World Trade 45 (1987).

[5]Agreement on Implementation of Article VI of the General Agreement on Tariffs and Trade 1994, April. 15, 1994, LT/UR/A-1A/3.

[6]Agreement on Subsidies and Countervailing Measures, Apr. 15, 1994, Marrakesh Agreement Establishing the World Trade Organization, Annex 1A, The Legal Texts: The Results Of The Uruguay Round Of Multilateral Trade Negotiations 231 (1999), 1869 U.N.T.S. 14.

[7]Panel Report, *United States – Anti–Dumping Act of 1916, Complaint by Japan*, WT/DS162/R and Add.1 (September 26, 2000), upheld by Appellate Body Report WT/DS136/AB/R, WT/DS162/AB/R,

Trade remedy investigations differ from typical state actions. In principle, such actions are regulated and governed by multilateral agreements, but each country retains its own systems and procedures for conducting such actions. Although they are adopted by importing countries, the actions are initiated at the level of private actors. First, the domestic industry in the importing country must file a case with the government petitioning for increased tariffs against a trading partner. A government may also proactively begin investigating a case *ex officio*. Then, the case is adjudicated through domestic administrative proceedings. Provided certain conditions are met, a country may impose unilateral tariffs against goods from a trading partner.

Trade remedy instruments are generally considered as protectionist instruments. Although the perceived purpose is to preserve a "level playing field" on which domestic and foreign producers can compete on the basis of who makes the best product at the lowest cost, such actions, to an extent, have come into the hands of protectionist lobbies. Michael Finger, a World Bank Economist, referred to antidumping as an "ordinary protection with a grand public relations program".[8] Generally, the trade-remedy measures administered through duties, tariffs, priced based mechanisms such as price undertaking, or in certain cases, through quotas have often a narrow goal. They seek to help provide the domestic industry a higher market share, increase in production and better sales realization. In other words, most trade remedy investigations seek to help the domestic industry claw back profits and recover to pre-import situation. Many firms or petitioners of trade remedy actions complain that without such protection, the industry would be forced to close down or scale back production and employment. In essence, the antidumping measures play a strategic role by creating an additional cost to the new foreign entrant and have strong interfaces with strategic industrial policy.[9] In other words, antidumping actions can be an important component of certain multifaceted strategic contests between rival firm to acquire greater shares of global markets.[10]

The purpose of this chapter is to provide an analysis of the historical evolution of injury and causation provisions in trade remedies. A vast majority of the discussion will focus on the developments in the United States and the European Union (including its previous institutions). A bulk of the discussion examines how a particular causation language was inserted in the first place in some of the domestic legislation, and how such standards were grafted in international treaties. This

(Footnote 7 continued)

DSR 2000:X; *see also* Panel Report, *United States – Customs Bond Directive for Merchandise Subject to Anti–Dumping/Countervailing Duties, WT/DS345/R* (August 1, 2008) as modified by Appellate Body Report *WT/DS343/AB/R/WT/DS345/AB/R, DSR 2008:VIII.*

[8]J.Michel Finger, Nellie T. Artis, *The Origins and Evolution of Antidumping Regulation, in* ANTIDUMPING: HOW IT WORKS AND WHO GETS HURT 34 (J.M. Finger ed., 1991).

[9]Michael O. Moore and Mark Wu, *Antidumping and Strategic Industrial Policy: Tot-for-Tat Trade Remedies and the China—X-Ray Equipment Dispute* (Robert Schuman Centre for Advanced Studies Global Governance Programme, 2014).

[10]*Ibid*, at 33.

chapter will also discuss the negotiating history of trade remedy sections in various international treaties concluding with the Uruguay Round of trade negotiations.

An analysis of the historical evolution of injury and causation in trade remedy cases could provide a perspective on the domestic compulsions, negotiating compromises, and the balance struck by some of the key users and proponents of the trade remedy instruments. Traversing the history and evolution of injury and causation provisions will help gain a better understanding of why a particular causation provision or terminology was chosen in the first place. A perusal of the various iterations of the negotiating texts in the past negotiating rounds can also be instructive in understanding the evolution of the injury and causation language.

This chapter is organized as follows. Sections B, C and D provide an evolution of antidumping laws and examine how various particularities in the U.S. antidumping statute, including the language on injury and causation provisions made their way into the GATT/WTO; Section E examines the origin and evolution of injury and causation provisions under the Tokyo Subsidies Code and the SCM Agreement; Section F deals with the genesis and evolution of injury and causation provisions under the Safeguards Agreement. Section G provides a summary of developments on injury and causation at the end of the Uruguay Round trade negotiations. Section H concludes.

## B Genesis of Antidumping Law

Trade remedy legislations have a history of over 100 years. Within the discipline of trade remedy measures, antidumping measures have a history longer than any other trade remedy measures. Among the industrialized countries, Canada enacted the first antidumping law in 1904.[11] According to Jacob Viner, a neoclassical Canadian economist, the 1904 legislation was a response to the U.S. Steel Corporation's practice of selling its exports at prices significantly lower than its domestic prices.[12] It was, however, the U.S. that began implementing the antidumping measures with a definite purpose and regularity.[13]

---

[11]An Act to Amend the Customs Tariff Act, 1897, 4 Edw. 7, ch 11 & 19. *See* J. Viner, *infra note* 10. The 1904 Canadian Act, as amended in 1907, provided that any imported product, of a class or kind manufactured in Canada, would be assessed as additional duty (subject to a cap), whenever the price charged for the product in Canada, less the cost of the shipment, was less than the price in the exporter's home market.

[12]J.A. Viner, DUMPING: A PROBLEM IN INTERNATIONAL TRADE 86 (1923).

[13]Douglas A. Irwin, *The Rise of U.S. Antidumping Activity in Historical Perspective,* 28(5) THE WORLD ECONOMY, 651–668 (2005) (noting that the number of antidumping activities conducted in the 1930 and 1950 s have been surprisingly large).

The genesis of the U.S. antidumping regulation derives from anti-trust concerns rather than from the protection of the domestic industries from foreign imports.[14] Influenced by the antitrust sentiments in the late 19th century, which led to the enactment of the Sherman Act of 1890,[15] the first U.S. antidumping statute namely, the Antidumping Act of 1916,[16] required the existence of "predatory intent" to punish foreign dumping, and also imposed criminal liability for violation.

The 1916 Act made it illegal to sell imported products at prices substantially lower than the market value in the exporting country "with the intent of destroying or injuring an industry in the United States, or of restraining or monopolizing any part of trade and commerce in such articles in the United States".[17] The 1916 Act was an antitrust law that extended to foreign commerce the anti-price discrimination of the 1914 Clayton Act.[18] In other words, before the passing of the Antidumping Act of 1916, there was no remedy against a foreign company that practiced international price discrimination or predatory pricing, whereas a domestic company that practiced similar pricing policies was subject to the domestic antitrust statutes.

The U.S. Antidumping Act, 1921[19] (the 1921 Act) superseded the 1916 Antidumping Act.[20] However, the 1916 Act remained on the statute book without demonstrating any effective use until recently.[21] The 1921 Act only required that there be "injuries" to the domestic industry allegedly caused by foreign dumping without a separate requirement of predatory intent. In economic terms, the effect of dumping is to cause an outward shift in foreign supplies (imports), which implies that consumers would shift towards the imports as against the domestic products. This shift in demand is demonstrated as injury to the domestic industry. The 1921 Act, unlike the 1916 legislation, introduced the concept of "special dumping duty" in the place of monetary fines or jail sentences to combat unfair dumping. The 1921 Act also introduced the notion of "fair value", which was a departure from the idea that antidumping measures were meant strictly to protect markets and consumers

---

[14]§§ 12-26, §§ 12-27 Clayton Antitrust Act, 29 U.S.C. (1914).

[15]§§ 1-7 Sherman Antitrust Act, 15 U.S.C. (2006).

[16]Title VIII of the Revenue Act of 1916, 39 Stat. 756 (1916); 15 U.S.C. § 72.

[17]*See* Finger, *supra* note 8.

[18]The Clayton Act of 1914 made price discrimination an illegal practice if it reduced competition or tended to create monopoly.

[19]§ 1305(a) 19 U.S.C. § 1305(a).

[20]19 U.S.C 1673.

[21]The Antidumping Act of 1916 was held to be in violation of the WTO Antidumping Agreement by a WTO panel, and later by the Appellate Body. The violation was established on the condition that GATT Article VI (2) limits the remedy of dumping to antidumping duties or price undertakings as prescribed by the Antidumping Agreement. Criminal penalties and treble damages which were stipulated by the 1916 Act were found as impermissible remedies. The European Union filed a dispute against the United States in 1998 since the U.S. Antidumping Act of 1916 existed in parallel with the Tariff Act of 1930 and Court actions were pending against European parties as on the date of seeking consultation. In 2000, the WTO Appellate Body affirmed the panel finding against the United States in this matter.

from the effects of anticompetitive practices.[22] The 1921 Act also authorized the Tariff Commission, the U.S. domestic investigating agency, to determine whether a domestic industry was being injured by reason of sales at less than fair value.[23] The use of "by reason of" language introduced the requirement of causal connection between dumping and injury.

In many ways, the 1921 Act ushered in flexibility which enabled the government to manage trade policies in the interests of domestic industries, and in tune with the protectionist climate.[24] As mentioned earlier, the only remedy available under the 1921 Act was the imposition of duties equivalent to the magnitude of dumping. In other words, the antidumping measure was in the nature of a higher import duty.

At the same time, the 1921 Act introduced the basic confusion between antitrust and protectionist purposes into the U.S. law—a confusion that sustains until date. The objective of the 1921 Act was to prevent "domestic industries from being destroyed in a price war, after which the foreign producer, then unopposed, would increase his prices and recoup losses".[25] The 1921 Act was consistently justified as combatting an unfair practice, namely predatory dumping. Furthermore, the 1921 Act contained all the elements of what we now recognize as antidumping: that duties may be imposed if the exporter's sales price is less than the foreign market value; that foreign costs of production may be calculated if the foreign market value is not ascertainable; that the dumping must be related to injury suffered by the domestic industry, and; that higher import duties are the appropriate remedy, etc.[26] Put simply, the 1921 Act was the prototype of future antidumping legislations.

The operative language of the 1921 Act assailed any dumping that injured the domestic producers, not just predatory dumping. More importantly, any mention of antitrust criteria—conspiracy, combination, or restraint of competition—was eliminated.[27] Although the legislative history of the 1921 Act, including the Congressional reports and floor debates made reference to predatory dumping, it is more than evident that the 1921 Act had broader objectives.[28] There were also many who spoke for and understood that some of the key features of the 1921 Act—namely, converting criminal penalty to a duty remedy, eliminating the need of any proof of predatory intent, and incorporating a mere 'injury to industry' test—lent

---

[22]Gregory Mankiw and Philip L. Swagel, *Antidumping: The Third Rail of Trade Policy*, Foreign Affairs 107, 111 (2005).

[23]Committee on Finance, United States Senate, *The Antidumping Act 1921 and the International Dumping Code* (July 5, 1968) *available at:* http://www.finance.senate.gov/library/prints/.

[24]*See* Finger, *supra* note 8, at 12, 13.

[25]H. R. Rep. No. 1, 67th Cong., 1st Sess. 23-24 (1921).

[26]Under the 1921 Antidumping Act, the Treasury Department was responsible for determining whether the sales were made at less than fair value and the Tariff Commission was tasked with the determination of injury.

[27]*See* Finger, *supra* note 8, at 22.

[28]*See* H. R. Rep. No. 1, 67th Cong. 1st Session, 23 (1921) ("the legislation will protect and our industries and labor against a now common species of commercial warfare of dumping goods on our markets at less than cost or home value if necessary until our industries are destroyed").

**Table 1** U.S. statutes on unfair trade and injury to industry

| Name of legislation | Disciplines on injury |
|---|---|
| Sherman Act, 1890 | Antirust statute; Injury not required |
| Wilson Tariff Act, 1894 | Antitrust statute; injury not required; focus on intent to restrain trade |
| Antidumping Act, 1916 | Offense to sell imports below actual market value of imports; requires intent to restrain competition |
| Antidumping Act, 1921 | Importing below market value; injury to the U.S. domestic industry required |
| Fordney—McCumber Tariff Act, 1911 | Effect or tendency to destroy or substantially injure |
| Smoot Hawley Tariff Act, 1930 | Title VII inserted in 1979. Section 731 requires USITC to determine whether a U.S. industry is materially injured or threatened with material injury. |
| Tariff Act, 1974 | Expanded the definition of dumping to include home market sales below the average cost of production |
| Trade Agreement Act of 1979 | Amended the 1930 Tariff Act to insert Title VII to the Tariff Act of 1930 |
| Trade and Tariff Act of 1984 | U.S. International Trade Commission to cumulate the imports of all countries subject to an antidumping investigation when making an injury determination |

this pioneering legislation significant protectionist potential. In other words, the purpose of the 1921 Act was to lessen the rigours of the 1916 Act and to mollify the domestic manufactures who could not receive tariff protection (Table 1).

In addition to the U.S., four other countries had enacted antidumping legislations by 1921. These countries included the United Kingdom, South Africa, Australia and New Zealand. Of these countries, the United Kingdom and Australia made some form of injury a prerequisite for imposition of duties as well. The British Safeguarding of Industries Act 1921[29] provided that employment in a United Kingdom industry had to be or likely to be seriously affected by foreign articles sold below cost of production. The Australian Industries Preservation Act[30] included the requirement that detriment might result to an Australian industry by reason of dumped imports.[31] The New Zealand antidumping law did not require an injury standard.[32] The South African antidumping legislation,[33] which dates back to 1914, imposed the first antidumping duty in 1921.

[29]British Safeguarding of Industries Act, 1921 (11 & 12 Geo. V c. 47).

[30]Australian Act of 1916, Act No. 9 (1906).

[31]*Id.* at §§ 18(1).

[32]A. Pangratis & E. Vermulst, *Injury in Anti-Dumping Proceedings: The Need to Look Beyond the Uruguay Round Results*, 28(5) Journal of World Trade 61, 63 (1994).

[33]Customs Tariff Act 1914, Statutes of the Union of South Africa (1914).

## 1 *Economic Rationale of Antidumping Laws*

### (a) Viner on Dumping

A vast majority of economic literature in the field of antidumping builds on the work of Jacob Viner who attempted to provide an economic rationale for antidumping laws.[34] Viner placed great emphasis on the length of time one could expect dumping prices to endure. Accordingly, he classified dumping as:

- "sporadic"; dumping,
- "short-run" dumping, and
- "permanent" dumping.

In the case of sporadic dumping, one or two shipments of dumped imports may take place within a short span of time; in the case of intermittent or short run dumping, dumping may last for several months or perhaps even a year; in the case of permanent or long-run dumping, the dumping takes place for an indefinite period of time.

Viner was concerned about dumping by foreign companies based on his assumption that dumping was transitory. In other words, Viner considered only short run dumping as objectionable and required some remedial action. This conclusion was based on two premises: (a) the low price will be temporary, and; (b) a temporary low price will be injurious to domestic producers.[35] According to him, short lived consumer benefits in the form of lower prices could not offset serious injury to domestic producers in the form of reduced output/sales.

Viner's arguments against dumping, although not restricted to predatory situations, was at least predicated on the existence of substantial injury to the domestic manufacturers. The "substantiality" requirement presumably aimed to offset the loss of consumer benefits, and also discounted the possibility that unobjectionable long-run dumping be involved in any given dumping case.[36]

Viner accepted that trade remedy laws can coexist with free trade. Free trade theories have certain demonstrable welfare gains. However, departure from free trade principles may be required in situations where the domestic industry in the importing countries face import competition. Tariff barriers provided adequate relief to various economies, at least until the 1970s. The establishment of the GATT and the various preferential trade agreements, however, constrained the freedom which countries had generally enjoyed in maintaining high tariffs.

In that context, the general thrust of trade remedy laws is to allow withdrawal of negotiated tariff concessions where a trade agreement results in such an influx of imports as to cause serious injury to domestic industry producing the same or

---

[34]*See* Viner, *supra* note 12, at 1-30.

[35]*See* Viner, *supra* note 12, at 139-140; *see* also for a discussion on Viner's theory, Alan O. Sykes, *Countervailing Duty Law: An Economic Perspective*, 89(2) Columbia Law Review 199 (1989).

[36]John J. Barceló III, *Antidumping Laws as Barriers to Trade - The United States and the International Antidumping Code*, 57(4) Cornell Law Review 491, 515 (1972).

competitive product. Anecdotal evidence suggests that the ability to impose antidumping duties has served as a *quid pro quo* for trade liberalization in negotiations for some of the most ambitious trade agreements the world has seen so far.[37]

According to Viner, the 1921 Act was a "model of draftsmanship" and was indeed superior to the Canadian law. Viner observed:

> The limitation of antidumping duties to a product which injures or is likely to injure an American industry leaves it open to a wise customs administration to refrain from interference with all dumping whose benefit to the American consumer is not clearly offset in part at least by an injury, actual or prospective, to American industry.[38]

As noted by Horlick and Shea, several developed countries started using antidumping as a tool of "back-door" industrial policy as well as "escape-valve" for protectionist pressures.[39] Especially in the late 1970s, there was an effort to justify the antidumping measures as a short term exception to the free trade principles that allowed certain sectors of a national economy to face the challenges and vigour of import competition.[40]

The protectionist features of antidumping laws were also highlighted by Michael Finger. Finger explains how the 1921 Act became a harbinger of contingent protection:

> [U]nder the softer standards of interpretation and proof, administration of the law could follow changing political pressures for protection much more quickly than a more rigorous, rule-of-law standard would allow. Thus, it prepared the way for eventual emergence of anti-dumping as the main vehicle for import-competing interest to press for protection- and for governments to respond to those pressures.[41]

Although domestic producers were able to use trade laws to obtain protection from foreign competition, antidumping duties were rarely imposed between the 1930 and the 1960s.[42] Despite the relatively steady number of antidumping cases filed in the 1950s and 1960s, actual determinations of injuries were occasional during this period. The reasons for this trend could be partly attributed to the presence of tariff barriers which provided effective protection against import competition.

Growth in antidumping actions occurred remarkably in the 1980s.[43] Between 1980 and 1995, the US, Canada, Australia, and the EC were responsible for 95 % of

---

[37]Wentong Sheng, *Reforming Trade Remedies*, 34 Michigan Journal of International Law 151, 166(2012).

[38]Viner, *supra* note 12, at 262.

[39]Gary Horlick & E.C. Shea, *The World Trade Organization Anti-Dumping Agreement,* 29 Journal of World Trade 5, 6-7 (1995).

[40]Douglas Irwin, *The Rise of U.S. Antidumping Activity in Historical Perspective*, 28 The World Economy 651, 654 (2005).

[41]*See* Finger, supra note 8, at 35.

[42]The Fordney-McCumber Tariff pushed the U.S. tariffs rates back or up to the rates that had been force at the end of the 19th Century.

[43]Douglas A Irwin, Sam Laird, Julio Nogues, *Trade Policy and Debt Crisis* 18 (World Bank WPS No. 99, Sept. 1988) (noting that the number of antidumping actions after the 1980s have been alarming). *See* also Horlick and Shea, *supra* note 39, at 6.

all dumping cases worldwide.[44] During the decade of the 1980s, more than 1,000 antidumping actions were taken collectively by these jurisdictions.[45] In addition to the traditional users, other developed countries such as Japan, Switzerland, Norway, Sweden and Finland incorporated antidumping laws on their statute books.[46] In short, antidumping became a key policy instrument for industry seeking protection from import competition.

## 2 *Movement from Predatory Intent to Injury Standards*

As is common knowledge now, the purpose of the trade remedy laws was to help the domestic industry get back to profitable levels by addressing the injurious effects of unfair trade or increased imports. In this context, the 1916 Act did not adequately address injury to the domestic industry. The 1921 Act[47] on the other hand, required that the injury to the domestic industry be caused "by reason of" dumped merchandise. As stated by Raj Bhala, the 1930 Tariff Act did not require the domestic industry or the investigating agency to show that the class or kind of merchandise subject to investigation is the direct, immediate, proximate or even the substantial cause of injury.[48]

The developments until the 1960s also indicated that antidumping agencies started to make injury determination on objective factors and with limited focus on predatory intent. The U.S., in 1954, decided to divide the administration of U.S. antidumping law between the Treasury Department, which continued to determine whether less than fair value sales occurred, and the Tariff Commission (now called the International Trade Commission or USITC).

Despite the administrative change, predatory intent, an important relic of the U.S. antitrust statutes remained a key component of the U.S. antidumping investigations. Until the 1960s, the Tariff Commission (USITC's predecessor) often based its injury finding on the existence of predatory intent. During this period (i.e., 1920–1960), the Tariff Commission often arrived at a negative finding on injury in the absence of predatory intent.[49] As predatory intent requirement has taken back seat over the years, leading users of antidumping substituted the predatory intent requirement with the

---

[44]Raj Bhala, *Rethinking Antidumping Law,* 29(1) George Washington Journal of International Law & Economy 4 (1995); *See also*, Archive of European Integration (AEI), *The First Commission Report on Antidumping and Anti-subsidy Activities, Information Memo P-87/83* (1983), *available at* http://aei.pitt.edu/31453/1/P_87_83.pdf.

[45]Christian Conrad, *Dumping and Antidumping Measures from a Competition and Allocation Perspective*, 36(3) Journal of World Trade 563(2002).

[46]Edwin Vermulst, *Adopting and Implementing Antidumping Laws: Some Suggestions for Developing Countries*, 31(2) Journal of World Trade 5 (1997).

[47]This statute initially was enacted as part of the *Tariff Act of 1930* and is sometimes called the *Smoot- Hawley Tariff Act.* Tariff Act of 1930, Pub L. No. 71-361, 46 Stat. 590 (1930).

[48]Raj Bhala, *Rethinking Antidumping Law*, supra note 44, at 51.

[49]*See e.g.*, Bicycles from Czech, 25 Fed. Reg. 9782 (1960); Carbon Steel Bars & Shapes from Canada, 29 Fed. Reg. 12599 (1964).

"injury" test.[50] As a consequence, an antidumping petition would fail if certain imports, no matter how fair or unfair they may be, do not cause injury to the domestic industry.

An important shift also occurred with the passage of the Trade Agreement Act 1979.[51] The most significant change introduced by this Act was the adoption of the "material injury" test which provided a means to measure the harm suffered by the domestic industry.[52] The Senate Finance Committee Report[53] to the 1979 Trade Agreements Act also clearly stated that the new legislation did not limit the reach of the antidumping laws to predatory pricing situations. The Report, in fact, did not define dumping as "unfair" price discrimination, but rather as selling in another country's market at prices less than fair price. The Senate Finance Committee stated:

> [T]he Act is primarily concerned with the situation in which the margin of dumping contributes to underselling the U.S. product in the domestic market, resulting in injury or likelihood of injury to a domestic industry…When clear indication of injury, or likelihood of injury exists, there would be reason for making affirmative determination.[54]

The "rule of reason" analysis, when applied to the antidumping duty, has a per se element. The purpose of antidumping laws is to remedy the injury caused or threatened to be caused by dumped imports to a domestic industry. Price discrimination which causes material injury or threat thereof is per se "unfair" and therefore must be proscribed.[55] But if dumped imports do not result in injury, such price discrimination should be permitted. Based on this logic, only a few dumping practices were challenged.

In other words, the evolution of antidumping laws can be best explained by the public choice theory. It helps the administrative branch to remain answerable to the concerns of the domestic producers. Especially when things go wrong, or when the domestic market finds a surge of imports during phases of economic instability, there is a great tendency or even insistent demand from both labour and business to claim import relief. In that context, trade remedies allow governments to address future developments or critical circumstances that are highly unpredictable.[56]

---

[50]There are strong theoretical reasons and empirical evidence suggesting that predatory pricing and, in particular, international predation, will be a very improbable occurrence. *See* Michael J. Trebilcock & Thomas M. Boddez, *The Case for Liberalizing North American Trade Remedy Laws*, 4(1) Minnessota Journal of Global Trade 1, (1995).

[51]S.Rep.No.1298, 93rd Congress, 2nd Session (1974) reprinted in 1974 U.S.C.C.A.N. 7186, 7316.

[52]Diana Jean Carloni, *An Analysis of Material Injury under the 1979 Trade Agreements Act,* 4 Loyala Los Angeles International and Comparative Law 181 (1981).

[53]Report on the Trade Agreement Act of 1979, Senate Finance Committee Report, S. Rep No. 249, 96th Session. 1.st Sess. 75 (1979).

[54]*Id.*

[55]William DeGrandis, *Proving Causation in Antidumping Cases,* 20 International Lawyer 563 (1986).

[56]*See* Dani Rodrik, One Economics, Many Recipes: Globalization, Institutions and Economic Growth 213–36 (2008). ("Countries may legitimately wish to restrict trade or suspend existing WTO obligations… for reasons going beyond competitive threats to their industries ….

Despite this reality, antidumping proceedings and legal proceedings will have limited legitimacy without a sound and rational legal framework.

The following discussion will track the development of injury and causation requirements in multilateral bodies such as the GATT especially in the context of country practices in some of the key jurisdictions.

## C Injury and Causation in Antidumping Under GATT 1947

In 1946, the United Nations Economic and Social Council (ECOSOC) established preparatory committee to prepare an agenda for a United Nations Conference on Trade and Employment. During the first session of the Committee in London, the U. S. submitted a suggested Charter for International Trade Organization (ITO) of the United Nations. Article 11 of the Charter dealt with antidumping duties.

It is observed that exceptions for trade remedies were included in the GATT in 1947 because some countries including the U.S. would not have agreed for trade liberalization without such a recourse. According to Professor John H. Jackson, Article VI of the GATT 1947 recognizes the legitimacy of certain policy objectives, but at the same time has established conditions that may be imposed to secure the attainment of those objectives.[57]

The 1947 GATT provisions on trade remedies were significantly influenced by the United States. In many ways, several substantive and procedural aspects of the current antidumping law have been adopted from the 1921 Act and its successor legislations.[58] Article VI of the GATT which contains the general principles relating to the application of antidumping as well as countervailing duties read as hereunder:

*GATT 1947: Article VI (1)*

> The contracting parties recognize that dumping, by which products of one country are introduced into the commerce of another country at less than the normal value of the products, is to be condemned if it causes or threatens material injury to an established industry in the territory of a contracting party or materially retards the establishment of a domestic industry….In order to offset or prevent dumping, a contracting party may levy on any dumped product an antidumping duty not greater in amount than the margin of dumping.

According to Article VI (2) of the GATT 1947, the remedy for dumping lies exclusively with the importing country in the nature of imposition of antidumping

(Footnote 56 continued)

Developmental priorities are among such reasons, as are distributional concerns or conflicts with domestic norms or social arrangements in the industrial countries".)

[57]John Jackson, The World Trading System: The Law and Policy of International Economic Relations 236–242 (1997).

[58]Douglas A. Irwin, *supra* note 13 (noting that the 1921 Act formed the textual basis for Article VI of the GATT).

duties. Article VI of the GATT 1947 lays down the key requirements for imposition of antidumping duties, which has remained fairly unchanged until this date. The essential requirement under the GATT 1947 is that there should be dumping; it should cause material injury or threat thereof; and that there should be causation between the two. In other words, the injury caused by dumped imports should be affecting those domestic industries that produce "like products" of the dumped imports.

In many ways, Article VI of the GATT 1947 closely followed the requirements under the 1921 Act.[59] The 1921 Act used the phrase "by reasons of importation of such merchandise into the U.S." However, Article VI of the GATT 1947 had certain glaring omissions which included the absence of a definition of key terms such as "material injury" and "domestic industry".[60] These ambiguities persisted for several decades, until the Trade Agreement of 1979 (amending the 1930 Tariff Act) defined "material injury" to mean "harm which is not inconsequential, immaterial, or unimportant".[61] Strangely, there is still no definition of the term "material injury" under the GATT/WTO.

Interestingly, this tautological definition which was supplemented by a list of statutory factors appears more vague and unclear.[62] Within the U.S., the USITC has held in certain cases that "material injury" as per Section 421 represented a lesser degree of injury than "serious injury" under Section 202 of the U.S. Trade Act of 1974 (1974 Act).[63] Further, the GATT 1947 had not even provided a list of illustrative factors that could be used to determine injury. More importantly, the nature of causal link required to be established between dumping and material injury remained unclear and vague under the GATT.

On the positive side, GATT 1947 was the first international trade agreement to set forth among other concepts, an injury standard for antidumping.

## 1 *Antidumping Under Kennedy Round*

As stated earlier, the antidumping provisions in GATT 1947 had borrowed heavily from the 1921 Act to develop core disciplines. During this period, the function of the

---

[59] *Id.*

[60] M. Matsushita et al., The World Trade Organization: Law, Practice and Policy, 418 (2nd edn, 2006).

[61] Pub. L. No. 96-39, Section 101 (codified at 19 U.S.C Section 1677 (7) (A)].

[62] *See* Wentong Sheng, *Reforming Trade Remedies*, 34 Michigan Journal of International Law, 151, 175 (2012) (noting that under S. 1677 (7) (B) of the Tariff Act, the factors that should be considered in making material injury determination include the volume of imports of the subject merchandise, the effects of imports of that merchandise on prices in the United States for domestic like products, … the impact of imports of such merchandise on domestic producers of domestic like products … [and] such other economic factors as are relevant to the determination regarding whether there is material injury by reason of imports.).

[63] *See, e.g.,Circular Welded Non-Alloy Steel Pipe from China*, Investigation No. TA-421–6, 3807 (United States International Trade Commission, October 2005).

antidumping laws, especially in the context of the U.S., was to preserve the openness of the domestic market rather than restrict foreign imports. According to some statistics, from 1921 till 1967, the U.S. government had conducted more than 700 antidumping cases. Out of this, all but 75 actions resulted in a negative injury determination.[64]

In making a causal link between dumping and injury, the U.S. Tariff Commission and later the USITC insisted that the successful penetration of imports was directly attributed to the less than fair imports (dumped imports), and not merely the availability of goods.[65] Further, more countries, including a number of European countries, had started implementing antidumping legislations.[66] The U.S. was keen on ensuring that such laws were not used in an overly protectionist manner given the export interests of U.S. industries.[67] Concerns were also raised about the possible abuse of antidumping laws. But the abuse was thought of in ways similar to abuse of a safeguard law—too frequent resort to duties in the absence of real price discrimination or import related material injury. Thus, negotiators focused their attention on defining price discrimination and limiting the antidumping duty to the margin of dumping. During this round, the U.S. officials also wanted to ensure that exports accused of dumping had access to all non-confidential information on their case, and had opportunity to present evidence and provide rebuttal.

At the end of the Kennedy Round of GATT negotiations from 1963–1967, the Kennedy Anti-dumping Code (the Kennedy Antidumping Code) was signed on 30 June 1967 by eighteen Contracting Parties (see Appendix 1 of this chapter).[68] The Kennedy Code was created as a separate document from the GATT, and the Contracting Parties remained free to sign the Code or refrain from doing so. The negotiators were concerned with three general problems: (1) the lack of an injury test in third country antidumping laws (especially the Canadian law)[69]; (2) the possibility of a revised antidumping mechanism through weak tests on substantive aspects such as definition of material injury, industry and causation, and (3) the elimination of procedural delays, uncertainties and arbitrariness.[70] The problem relating to Canadian

[64]Michael Finger & Tracy Murray, *Antidumping Duty Enforcement in the United States*, *in* ANTIDUMPING: HOW IT WORKS AND WHO GETS HURT 34 (J.Michael Finger ed.,1991).

[65]Unites States International Trade Commission Publication, Washington, D.C. (1981).

[66]Michael Finger, *The Origins and Evolution of Antidumping Regulation*, 26 (World Bank Working Papers, 783, October 1991).

[67]Robert E. Baldwin, *Imposing Multilateral Discipline on Administered Protection*, in THE WTO AS AN INTERNATIONAL ORGANIZATION 303 (Anne O. Krueger ed., 1998).

[68]Sub-Committee on Non-Tariff Barriers Group on Anti-Dumping Policies, *Draft Report on the Group on Anti-Dumping Policies*, TN.64/NTB/W/19 (April 24, 1967) *available at* http://www.wto.org/gatt_docs/English/SULPDF/91890175.pdf (last visited May 26, 2015).

[69]Canada did not have a material injury provision in their antidumping law.

[70]John J. Barcelo III, *A History of GATT Unfair Trade Law—A Confusion of Purposes*, 14(3) THE WORLD ECONOMY 311, 324 (1991)[hereafter BarceloIII, *A History of GATT Unfair Trade Law*].

law was resolved in the Kennedy Round through Canada's adherence to the Antidumping Code and the amendments of its domestic law by adding an injury test.[71]

One of the important changes introduced by the Kennedy Code was the new "causation" standard in antidumping. The Code stated that in order to impose antidumping duties, the authorities must determine that the dumped imports are the "principal cause" of injury to the domestic industry. The concerned provision is reproduced below:

> *Article 3: Determination of Injury*
>
> A determination of injury shall be made only when the authorities concerned are satisfied that the dumped imports are **demonstrably the principal cause of material injury or of threat of material injury** to a domestic industry or the principal cause of material retardation of the establishment of such an industry. In reaching their decision the authorities shall weigh, on one hand, the effect of the dumping and, on the other hand, all other factors taken together which may be adversely affecting the industry. The determination shall in all cases be based on positive findings and not on mere allegations or hypothetical possibilities. In the case of retarding the establishment of a new industry in the country of importation, convincing evidence of the forthcoming establishment of an industry must be shown, for example that the plans for a new industry have reached a fairly advanced stage, a factory is being constructed or machinery has been ordered. *(emphasis added).*
>
> ---
>
> *Footnote 1*: When in this Code the term "injury" is used, it shall, unless otherwise specified, be interpreted as covering cause of material injury to a domestic industry, threat of material injury to a domestic industry or material retardation of the establishment of such an industry.

The purpose of this language was to ensure that if dumping had a minimal effect upon the industry as opposed to other economic factors, then no finding of causal link between dumping and injury could be made.[72] According to Robert Hudec, the "principal injury" was a very close normative statement—that domestic industry is not deserving of relief from import competition if most of its troubles are on account of factors other than dumped imports.[73]

The Kennedy Code, by itself, did not define material injury, but required an examination of all factors relevant to determining the state of the domestic industry in question. The Kennedy Code provided for the "evaluation of effects of dumped imports on the industry". Article 3(b) of the Kennedy Code listed out factors that should be considered by an investigating agency in the evaluation of the state of the domestic industry.

---

[71]The amended Canadian Antidumping Act directs the Tribunal to determine whether "the dumping of the goods... has caused, is causing or is likely to cause material injury..."Antidumping Act, CANADA REVISED STATUTES, A-15, amended by Ch.1, 10 (2nd Supp. 1970-71).

[72]Diana Jean Carloni, *An Analysis of Material Injury under the 1979 Trade Agreements Act*, LOYALA LOS ANGELES INTERNATIONAL & COMPARATIVE LAW REVIEW 87, 91 (1981).

[73]Robert Hudec, *Antidumping and Countervailing Duties,* in ANTI-DUMPING LAW AND PRACTICE: A COMPARATIVE STUDY (John Jackson & Edwin Vermulst eds. 1989).

The factors included the following:

- Development and prospects with regard to turn over
- Market share
- Profits
- Prices
- Export performance
- Employment
- Volume of dumped import and other imports
- Utilization of capacity of domestic industry
- Productivity
- Restrictive trade practices

The Kennedy Code also introduced the concept of non-attribution, albeit indirectly. An additional requirement of weighing and comparing the role of other factors "individually or in combination" was for the first time introduced in the Kennedy Code. Article 3 (c) of the Kennedy Code which deals with weighing the role of other causal factors reads as follows:

*Kennedy Code: Article 3(c)*

In order to establish whether dumped imports have caused injury, all other factors which, individually or in combination, may be adversely affecting the industry shall be examined, for example: the volume and prices of undumped imports of the product in question, competition between the domestic producers themselves, contraction in demand due to substitution of other products or to changes in consumer tastes.

On the injury and causation standard, the Kennedy Code was at variance with the U.S. domestic law. As stated earlier, the U.S. statute merely stated that the USITC must find that the U.S. domestic industry has been "injured by reason of" dumped imports (see Table 2).

The Kennedy Code was fully implemented, at least in a formal sense, only in Europe. The new European Economic Community (EEC) Antidumping Regulation of 1968 (1968 law) conformed faithfully to the language of the Kennedy Code.[74] There was stiff resistance to the injury language of the Kennedy Code (Article 3) within the United States. Although the objective of the Kennedy Code was to limit the use restrictive antidumping measures among the signatories to the GATT, the

[74]Angelika Eymann & Ludger Schuknecht, *Antidumping Enforcement in the European Community*, *in* ANTIDUMPING: HOW IT WORKS AND WHO GETS HURT 221-238 (J.M. Fingers ed., 1991). The Common Trade Policy was set out in Articles 110 to 116 of the EEC Treaty (Treaty establishing the European Economic Community) which entered into force on January 1, 1958. The transitional period of 12 years ended 31 December 1969 (Article 8 of the EEC Treaty). The initial EEC Anti-Dumping Regulation 459/68 entitled *Protection against Dumping or the Granting of Bounties or Subsidies by the Countries which are not Members of the European Economic Community* was adopted on April 5, 1968 (Reg. 459/68, [1968] O.J. L93/80).

**Table 2** Key differences between the US antidumping legislation and the Kennedy code

| The 1921 U.S. antidumping act | The Kennedy antidumping code |
|---|---|
| *Major differences* | |
| The Act requires that the Commission shall determine whether an industry in the United States is being, or is likely to be, injured *** by reason of the importation of such merchandise | The Code states that before dumping duties can be imposed it must be found that the dumped merchandise is demonstrably the principal cause of material injury or threat of material injury to a domestic industry (Art. 3 (a)) and that the authorities shall weigh, on the one hand, the effect of the dumping and, on the other hand, all other factors taken together which may be adversely affecting the industry |

U.S. did not ratify the Code because it thought that it would undermine the protection available to manufacturers, producers, wholesalers and retailers.[75]

Urged on by the opponents of the Kennedy Code, the U.S. Congress enacted a law in 1968 instructing the U.S. Tariff Commission not to be constrained by the elements of the Kennedy Code while implementing the Antidumping Act of 1921.[76] The 1968 law did not, in principle, prevent the U.S. Tariff Commission from interpreting the implementing legislation to conform to the apparently higher injury thresholds of the Kennedy Code, but in practice the Tariff Commission applied a less rigorous injury and causation standard and frequently found injury in several cases.[77]

In fact, during the Senate Finance Committee hearing in this matter, the lawyers for the administration took the position that the term "demonstrably the principal cause of material injury" was designed to result in the same interpretation—a determination of injury when dumped imports caused injury to the domestic industry in any degree higher than *de minimis*—which the Tariff Commission had given in the past. For example, the majority of the Tariff Commission reasoned in *Whole Dried Eggs from Holland*[78] that as opposed to the material injury test of the 1967 Kennedy Code, a showing of anything more than a trivial and consequential effect on the domestic industry was sufficient to trigger antidumping duties.

Similarly, in *Ferrite Cores from Japan*, the Tariff Commission also rejected the principal cause language of the Kennedy Code and accepted a very weak test based on the injury being 'attributable in part' to the alleged dumping.[79] Following this

---

[75]Eugenia S. Pintos & Patricia J. Murphy, *Congress Dumps the International Antidumping Code*, 18 Catholic University Law Review 180, 190-191 (1969).

[76]*Id.* at 188.

[77]Barcelo III, A History of GATT Unfair Trade Law, *supra* note 70, at 318.

[78]35 Fed. Reg. 12500, 12501 (1970).

[79]United States Tariff Commission, 36 Fed. Reg. 1934 (1971) (The Tariff Commission noted, "[w]e agree that if injury is attributable solely to factors other than LTFV, an affirmative finding should not be made. However, if injury is attributable in part to the LTFV sales… and such injury is more than *de minimis*, we must make an affirmative determination." A negative determination on causation between dumping and injury was recorded by Commissioners Leonard and Young).

trend, the majority of the Commissioners noted in *Pig Iron from Canada, Finland and West Germany* that it was not necessary to show that imports were the sole cause or even the major cause of injury as long as the facts show that less than fair value (LTFV) imports were more than a *de minimis* factor in causing injury. The overall approach of the ITC was supported by the views of the Senate Committee on Finance which noted as follows:

> "In short, the Committee does not view injury caused by unfair competition, such as dumping, to require as strong a causation link to imports."

The Kennedy Code also introduced other operational difficulties in conducting the injury analysis. The Kennedy Code acknowledged that injury could be caused on account of several factors. Article 3(c) of the Kennedy Code provided that "in order to establish whether dumped imports have caused injury, all other factors which, individually or in combination, may be adversely affecting the industry shall be examined". Similarly, Article 3(a) of the Kennedy Code provided that "the authorities shall weigh, on one hand, the effect of the dumping and, on the other hand, all other factors taken together which may be adversely affecting the industry". The manner of interpretation by leading users of antidumping such as the U.S. posed certain questions. For example, the Senate Finance Committee in its Report 1974 noted that injury due to other causes was immaterial to the injury test under the U.S. law.

The key issue was whether the injury attributable to dumping should be more than 'inconsequential' or 'immaterial'. According to this view, the test mandated under the U.S. law required isolation of the economic harm caused by dumping and finding out whether injury caused by the harm was more than immaterial. This can be better explained with the help of a hypothetical. Assume that five factors A, B, C, D and E are the known causes of injury to the domestic industry seeking antidumping relief. According to the economic isolation test, the economic harm caused by dumping will have to be assessed. If the extent of harm can be identified and the nature of the harm is considered as more than immaterial, then causality is determined. Following this logic, even a relatively low injury contribution (assuming that factor E represents dumping) could be classified as not immaterial and as causally sufficient.

According to another view, which had significant supporters, the USITC should assess the overall injury, measure the causative influence of dumping on that overall injury, and determine whether dumping has enough significance to be called a 'cause' of this larger condition.[80] According to this view, the share of dumping in causing injury will have to be determined. In the hypothetical provided in Fig. 1, only Factor A, which contributes to 60 % of the material injury could be considered as a principal cause. It is a cause which is greater than all other causes combined (i.e., A > (B + C + D + E)); further A is a cause which is greater than any other

[80]United States International Trade Commission, Portland Hydraulic Cement from Mexico, AA1921–161, 795 (1976).

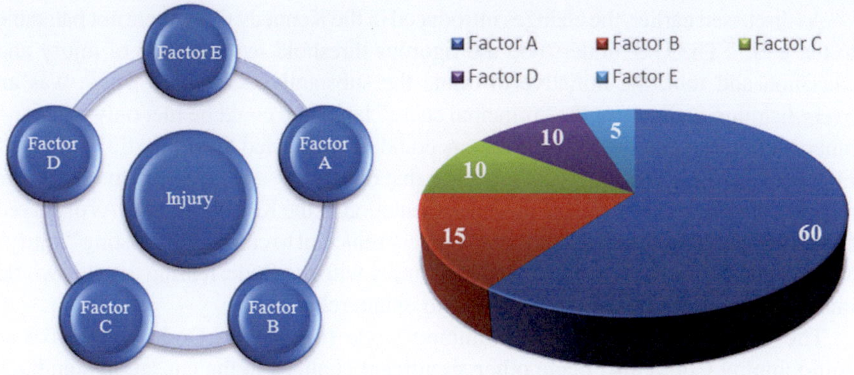


**Fig. 1** Antidumping enquiry and multiple causal factors

cause (i.e. A > B, or A > C, or A > D, or A > E). Based on this reasoning, if factor A were dumping, it could easily meet the injury and causation requirement. However, the concept of weighing and comparing the effects of dumping and other causes was considered to be an exceptionally onerous procedural burden.

The Kennedy Code also introduced provisions for the simultaneous investigation of both dumping and injury. Article 5 (b) and (c) of the Code clearly established that evidence of both dumping and injury should be considered simultaneously in the decision regarding initiation of the investigation, and thereafter, during the course of the investigation.

## 2 *Antidumping Under the Tokyo Round Code*

The Tokyo Round trade negotiations took place between 1974 and 1979. By the mid-1970s, a number of industrialized countries had started the use of antidumping actions. The leading users of antidumping, in addition to the U.S., included Australia and Canada. The U.S. had been facing competition from Japan and other industrialized countries, and considered the trade remedy provisions as a means to guard against fair and unfair imports.

There was an increased awareness of the uses of the antidumping instruments and several GATT Contracting Parties considered that antidumping laws would confer some inherent rights—rights that should be "improved" by making relief more readily available. For example, the U.S. pressed for the elimination of below cost sales in normal value calculation in international antidumping law. Accordingly, the Contracting Parties agreed to a new antidumping code that reproduced most of the Kennedy Code's provisions with some important amendments.

As discussed earlier, the changes introduced in the Kennedy Code were not palatable to the U.S.[81] The U.S. understood the rigorous threshold requirements of injury and causation and took the initiative to dilute the substantive standards. There was an overwhelming feeling that the "principal cause" language could be met only where no other economic, social or political factors could have affected the domestic industry.[82] Furthermore, there was empirical evidence that only a few antidumping investigations reached affirmative stage during the implementation of the Kennedy Code. As observed by John H. Jackson, the U.S. Congress was very reluctant to change the existing "injury" test under U.S. law to "material injury" to comply with the Code, fearing that this would make it more difficult for U.S. industries to obtain relief.[83]

The 1979 Tokyo Round Antidumping Code (the Tokyo Code or the Tokyo Antidumping Code) also made other significant changes in the causation standards in the Kennedy Code. The "principal cause" standard was expressly weakened in the Tokyo Code. The deletion of the principal cause standard was to make antidumping remedies more flexible and available for use when dumping is no longer the main cause of injury. The explicit requirement to weigh the role of dumped imports compared to a combination of all other factors in the Kennedy Code was also deleted in the Tokyo Code. Further, the language on causation requiring all other factors to be assessed individually or in combination was deleted in the Tokyo Code. More importantly, the list of "other factors", which was originally stipulated in the main text of the Kennedy Code was relegated to the footnotes. Professor Barcelo considered the reformed Tokyo Antidumping Code as an alternate safeguard law, which could be triggered by per se price discrimination, based on weakened injury standards, and applied on a selective basis.[84]

*Article 3.4: Tokyo Antidumping Code*

"It must be demonstrated that the dumped imports are through the effects[4] of dumping, causing injury within the meaning of this Code. <u>There may be</u> other factors[5] which at the same time are injuring the industry, and the injury caused by other factors must not be attributed to the dumped imports". (emphasis added).

---

*Footnote 4*: As set forth in paragraphs 2 and 3 of this Article.

*Footnote 5*: Such factors include, *inter alia*, the volume and prices of imports not sold at dumping prices, contraction in demand or changes in the patterns of consumption, trade restrictive practices of and competition between the foreign and domestic producers, developments in technology and the export performance and productivity of the domestic industry.

---

[81]Eugenia S. Pintos & Patricia J. Murphy, *Congress Dumps the International Antidumping Code*, 18 Catholic University Law Review 180, 190-191 (1969).

[82]Diana Jean Carloni, *An Analysis of Material Injury under the 1979 Trade Agreements Act,* 4 Loyola Los Angles International & Comparative Law Review 87, 91 (1981).

[83]John Jackson, *supra* note 57.

[84]Barcelo III, *A History of GATT Unfair Trade Law*, *supra* note 70, at 313.

Non-attribution language was a significant contribution of the Tokyo Antidumping Code although it was not considered as a bright line test for causation determination at the time of its introduction.[85] One of the objectives of this non-attribution requirement was the need to avoid attributing causation of injury to dumped imports, when in reality, some other factors were assumed to be responsible.[86] Beseler and Williams analyzed the causation standard contained in the revised Agreement on Implementation of Article VI of the General Agreement (1979) as follows:

> The new Code provides more realistic criteria in that the initial requirements that the dumped imports should be 'demonstrably the principal cause' of the injury suffered by the domestic industry, outweighing all other factors combined, is now replaced by a requirement to segregate the injury caused by dumping from the injuries caused by other factors and then to make an assessment of injury caused by dumping alone.[87]

In the years since the adoption of the Tokyo Code, the principal users of the antidumping remedy were the U.S., Canada, the EEC, and Australia. Japan had not had an active antidumping policy. Beseler and Williams have noted that despite the tough injury standards, EEC's resort to antidumping remedies rose dramatically after the 1977–78 recession.[88] Within the U.S., there was a move for the zealous enforcement of AD/CVD laws post conclusion of the Tokyo Round fueling a criticism that such laws have been used for protectionist purposes.[89]

## 3 *Injury and Causation in Antidumping Under Uruguay Round*

The Uruguay Round Agreements were formally completed on 15 August 1994 with the signing of the Marrakesh Declaration, and entered into force with effect from 1 January 1995. In a way, the Uruguay Round brought about the most significant reform of the world's trading system since GATT was created. It covered more issues and involved more countries than any previous trade round. All areas of trade remedies including Antidumping was one of the covered agreements under the WTO Treaty.

The Uruguay Round negotiations under the GATT achieved across the board reductions in industrial tariffs. The average tariff in the developed countries plummeted from roughly 40 % in 1947 to approximately 3.9 % at the end of the

---

[85] Jorge Miranda, *Causal Link as interpreted in WTO Trade Remedy Disputes*, 44 (4) Journal of World Trade 730 (2010).

[86] Raj Bhala, Modern GATT Law 796 (2005).

[87] Beseler and Williams, Antidumping and Anti-Subsidy Law: The European Communities 167 (1986).

[88] *Id.*

[89] Douglas A. Irwin, *The Rise of U.S. Antidumping Activity in Historical Perspective*, *supra* note 13.

implementation period of the Uruguay Round.[90] The reduction in tariff levels had compelled some scholars to argue that "[t]ariffs no longer matter in international trade law".[91]

Most developed countries that had brought down their tariffs, increasingly resorted to antidumping measures in the early 1990s. This was especially true for the U.S. which, by that time, was at a high point in using antidumping as a tool for "back door" industrial policy as well as an "escape valve" for protectionist pressures.[92] Apart from the U.S., other industrialized countries too were not very keen for specific changes in the field of antidumping. It is also observed that a limited number of GATT contracting parties—approximately only 22 signatories to the Antidumping Code of the GATT had antidumping laws in force as of October 1990.[93] It is therefore not surprising that the GATT Ministerial decision which launched the Uruguay Round did not mention anything about antidumping.[94]

There was a well-ingrained belief at this time that antidumping investigations were private matters concerning private companies.[95] On the other hand, subsidies were considered as a more pernicious protection being handed out by governments. However, during the Uruguay Round of negotiations, countries including Korea, Japan, Nordic countries and India submitted various proposals which sought to address the way antidumping investigations were conducted. Most of the proposals centered around issues such as dumping margin calculation, anti-circumvention, transparency, etc.[96] Although there was resistance on the part of the U.S. and the European Community (EC) to introduce key changes to the fundamental issues, a special Informal Group was established under Charles Carlisle, the Deputy Director General of the GATT.[97] The Informal Group was instrumental in fleshing out the details of the reforms in this field. The Informal Group considered various proposals, including certain proposals on injury and causation.

## 4 *Antidumping, Injury and the Overarching Obligations*

Article 3 of the AD Agreement became the cornerstone of injury and causation determination in antidumping investigations. Article 3 elaborated a number of

---

[90]*See* Raj Bhala, *supra* note 86, at 3.

[91]*Id.*

[92]*See* Gary Horlick & E.C. Shea, *supra* note 39, at 6.

[93]Terence Stewart et al., The Gatt Uruguay Round: A Negotiating History (1986-1992).

[94]*See* Gary Horlick & E.C. Shea, *supra* note 39.

[95]*See* Roger P. Alford, *Why A Private Right of Action against Dumping Would Violate GATT?*, 66 New York University Law Review 696 (1996).

[96]Chin Lim & Margaret Liang, Economic Diplomacy, Essays And Reflections by Singapore's Negotiators (World Scientific 2011).

[97]Margaret Liang, *Antidumping negotiations in the Uruguay Round*, *in* Economic Diplomacy, Essays and Reflections by Singapore's Negotiators (Chin L. Lim & Magaret Liang eds., 2010).

concepts included in the Tokyo Code. The key provisions in Article 3 which deal with injury and causation determination are Articles 3.1, 3.2, 3.3, 3.4, 3.5 and 3.7.

Article 3.1 is an overarching provision that establishes a WTO Member's fundamental, substantive obligation in injury and causation determination.

*Anti-dumping Agreement: Article 3.1*

A determination of injury for purposes of Article VI of GATT 1994 shall be based on positive evidence and involve an objective examination of both *(a)* the volume of the dumped imports and the effect of the dumped imports on prices in the domestic market for like products, and *(b)* the consequent impact of these imports on domestic producers of such products.

The rest of this provision explains in detail what precisely needs to be done in order to establish injury and causation. Article 3.1 incorporates the core requirements of "positive evidence" and "objective examination". In other words, an objective examination is hinged on positive evidence. Generally speaking, positive evidence is concerned with the quality of the evidence that authorities may rely upon in making a determination.

The incorporation of the term "positive evidence" has significance for injury and causation determination, as authorities cannot enter such findings based on "allegation, conjecture or remote possibility". The Appellate Body in *Mexico—Rice* noted, "... we would expect an investigating authority to substantiate the reasonableness and credibility of particular assumption".[98] Especially since the conditions to impose an antidumping duty are to be assessed with respect to a current situation, the determination of whether injury exists should be based on data that provide indications of the situation prevailing when the investigation takes place. In short, the requirement of positive evidence requires an unbiased and objective assessment.[99]

The volume of dumped imports and their price effects play a crucial role in injury and causation analysis. One of the critical issues is whether an increase in imports (relative or absolute) is an additional requirement—an independent analytical tool in the assessment of causation? There is a view that an investigating agency can still impose duties even if there is no absolute or relative increase in dumped imports.[100] Article 3.2 of the ADA, which deals with volume and price effects reads as follows:

*Anti-Dumping Agreement: Article 3.2*

With regard to the volume of the dumped imports, the investigating authorities shall consider whether there has been a significant increase in dumped imports, either in absolute terms or relative to production or consumption in the importing Member. With regard to the

[98]Appellate Body Report, *Mexico- Definitive Anti-Dumping Measures on Beef and Rice*, fn. 228, WT/DS295/AB/R (November 29, 2005) [hereinafter Appellate Body Report, *Mexico- Rice*].

[99]Appellate Body Report, *Mexico—Rice*, ¶ 7.86.

[100]Petros C. Mavroidis et al., The Law and Economics of Contingent Protection in the WTO 100 (2010).

effect of the dumped imports on prices, the investigating authorities shall consider whether there has been a significant price undercutting by the dumped imports as compared with the price of a like product of the importing Member, or whether the effect of such imports is otherwise to depress prices to a significant degree or prevent price increases, which otherwise would have occurred, to a significant degree. No one or several of these factors can necessarily give decisive guidance.

Article 3.2 of the Antidumping Agreement does not require an investigating authority to analyze the price and volume effect of dumped imports on a country-by-country basis. However, the Antidumping Agreement has introduced the concept of cumulation. Cumulation implies that if "like" imports from two or more countries are subject to the antidumping investigation, and if such imports compete with one another and the "like" domestic product, then the investigating agency must cumulate the volume and effect of such imports to determine material injury. This was a novel concept, as prior practices of leading investigating agencies indicated that small or insignificant share of imports was generally considered as inadequate to establish a finding of injury.[101] The provision on cumulation provides as under:

*Anti-Dumping Agreement: Article 3.3*

Where imports of a product from more than one country are simultaneously subject to anti-dumping investigations, the investigating authorities may cumulatively assess the effects of such imports only if they determine that (a) the margin of dumping established in relation to the imports from each country is more than *de minimis* as defined in paragraph 8 of Article 5 and the volume of imports from each country is not negligible and (b) a cumulative assessment of the effects of the imports is appropriate in light of the conditions of competition between the imported products and conditions of competition between the imported product and the like domestic product.

The cumulative analysis is logically premised on the ground that the domestic industry may face the impact of dumped imports as a whole. As the WTO Appellate Body mentioned in *EC—Tube and Fittings*, "…the negotiators appear to have recognized that a domestic industry confronted with dumped imports originating from several countries may be injured by the cumulative effect of those imports, and that those effects may not be adequately taken into account in a country specific analysis of the injurious effects of dumped imports".[102] The cumulation requirement introduced during the Uruguay Round specifically addressed this particular problem.

In sum, Articles 3.2 and 3.3 spell out the essential conditions for treating imports as cause of injury.

---

[101]Gary Horlick, *History of the One/Three Formula for Antidumping*, 8(1) Global Trade And Customs Journal 25-26 (2013) (noting that the US Tariff Commission and the International Trade Commission had hardly found injury from import sources with less than 3 percent import before the introduction of the cumulation language in the domestic legislation).

[102]Appellate Body Report, *European Communities – Anti-Dumping Duties on Malleable Cast Iron Tube or Pipe Fittings from Brazil*, WT/DS219/AB/R, ¶116 (July 22, 2003).

## D Material Injury and Non-attribution in Antidumping Investigations

One of the crucial aspects of an antidumping investigation is whether injury has been caused to the domestic industry on account of imports. Article 4 of the Antidumping Agreement defines "domestic industry" as a major proportion of the domestic producers of the "like products". Articles 2.1 and 2.6 clarify that "like product" refers to products that are either identical or closely resembling the product that is alleged to have been dumped. When examining the existence and extent of injury to the domestic industry, authorities may initially determine which of the following categories is relevant: "material injury to domestic industry"; "threat of material injury to domestic industry"; or, "material retardation to the establishment of domestic industry"[103] Among these categories of injury, the most commonly invoked category is the material injury to the domestic industry.

Article 3.4 of the AD Agreement provides a non exhaustive list of items used to gauge the impact of dumped imports on the domestic industry.

*Anti-Dumping Agreement: Article 3.4*

> The examination of the impact of the dumped imports on the domestic industry concerned shall include an evaluation of all relevant economic factors and indices having a bearing on the state of the industry, including actual and potential decline in sales, profits, output, market share, productivity, return on investments, or utilization of capacity; factors affecting domestic prices; the magnitude of the margin of dumping; actual and potential negative effects on cash flow, inventories, employment, wages, growth, ability to raise capital or investments. This list is not exhaustive, nor can one or several of these factors necessarily give decisive guidance.

### 1 *Causation and Non-Attribution: Insights from Uruguay Round Negotiating Texts*

Injuries caused by dumping are an essential element of all antidumping investigations.[104] While Article 3.4 explains how material injury to the domestic industry can be established, Article 3.5 provides the all-important language on causation. Although the core idea behind non-attribution was included even in the Tokyo Code, the softer language "there may be" was replaced with a stricter "shall… examine" formulation during the Uruguay Round.[105] According to Beseler and Williams, this language imposed an obligation to isolate the injuries caused by each

---

[103]Prakash Narayan, *Injury Investigations in "Material Retardation" Antidumping Cases*, 25(1) North Western Journal of International Law and Business 37, 41 (2004).

[104]Sungjoon Cho, *Anticompetitive Trade Remedies: How Antidumping Measures Obstruct Market Competition,* 87(2) North Carolina Law Review 357, 377(2009).

[105]Terence Stewart et al., *supra* note 93.

of the other factors including dumping and to treat each as a separate injury.[106] The objective of this language was to require that the effect of the dumped imports was such as to cause injury.

Injury can be caused by a number of factors, most of which may not be familiar even to the parties or the investigators. Some of the common examples of injury include the evolution of market conditions such as demand for diversification, competitive advantage of the foreign companies in price, quality, organization and such other factors which can be considered as part of acceptable competition. Injury can also be self-inflicted through, for example, wrong commercial strategies, bad management policies, rise or escalation in production costs, poor investment decisions, production inefficiencies, etc. Last not but the least, injury can also be caused by dumping.

The proposals on incorporating a non-attribution language were particularly contentious during the Uruguay Round as it was during the Tokyo Round. The following discussion traces the negotiating history of non-attribution under the Uruguay Round Antidumping Agreement.

Carlisle, the acting Chairman of the informal group submitted on his responsibility a draft text to reform the antidumping code. The draft contained no brackets and was considered only as a starting point for discussion. The Carlisle I[107] Draft on Injury and Causation reads as follows:

*Carlisle I Draft: Article 3.5*

It must be demonstrated that the dumped imports are, through the effects[3] of dumping, causing injury within the meaning of this Code. The demonstration of the existence of causal relationship between the dumped imports and the injury to the domestic industry shall be based on positive evidence and not on mere assumption. ~~There may be~~ The authorities shall consider whether there are other factors[4] which at the same time are causing injuring the industry, and the injuries caused by other factors must not be attributed to the dumped imports. Determinations of injury shall contain explanations of how such factors have been considered.

---

*Footnote 3*: As set forth on paragraphs 2 and 4 of this Article

*Footnote 4*: Such factors include, inter alia, the volume and prices of imports not sold at dumped prices regardless of their origin, including from an exporting country subject to investigation, contraction in demand or changes in the pattern of consumption, trade restrictive practices, the nature and extent of ~~and~~ competition in the domestic market among domestic producers in the country as a whole and between the foreign and domestic producers, changes or development in technology and the export performance and productivity of the domestic industry.

---

[106]Beseler and Williams, *supra* note 87.

[107]General Agreement on Tariffs and Trade, Communication from the Delegation of Hong Kong, MTN.GNG/NG8/W/51/Add. 1, at 3 (December 22, 1989).

Carlisle I draft was opposed by most of the negotiating countries on the ground that the text was unbalanced. Carlisle prepared a second draft which included alternate (bracketed) proposals. The Carlisle II[108] draft was released on August 14, 1990.

*Carlisle II Draft: Article 3.5*

[It must be demonstrated that the dumped imports are, through the effects of dumping, causing injury within the meaning of this Code.] [The demonstration of the existence of a causal relationship between dumped imports and injury to the domestic industry ~~shall~~ should be based on positive evidence and not on mere assumption.] [The authorities shall consider whether there are] [There may be] other factors[6] which at the same time are injuring the industry, and the injuries caused by other factors must not be attributed to dumped imports. ~~Determinations of injury shall contain explanations of how such factors have been considered.~~

---

*Footnote 5:* As set forth in paragraphs 2 and 4 of this Article

*Footnote 6:* Such factors include, inter alia, the volume and prices of imports not sold at dumping prices [regardless of their origin, including from an exporting country subject to investigation], contraction in demand or changes in the patterns of consumption, [the nature and extent of competition in the domestic market among domestic producers in the market as a whole] [the price behavior of domestic producers] and competition between the foreign and domestic producers, changes or developments in technology and the export performance and productivity of the domestic industry.

As explained earlier in the discussion on Tokyo Code, if together with dumped imports, other low-priced non-dumped imports had entered the market, one would ask whether it was possible to distinguish between the effects of dumped imports and other non-dumped imports. According to the non-attribution language, the causation of the material injury from factors other than dumping had to be evident and direct if the investigators were to conclude that those factors had caused the material injury, and thus declare dumping non-injurious. The U.S. delegation "roundly criticized" the Carlisle II draft stating that it was not an improvement over Carlisle I draft since the use of a number of bracketed texts left too many issues unresolved.[109]

These differences left the causation language under the ADA not substantively different from the language under the Tokyo Antidumping Code. Article 3.5 of the ADA reiterates the requirement under the Tokyo Code that there must exist a causal relationship between dumped imports and injury to the domestic industry.

*Anti-Dumping Agreement: Article 3.5*

It must be demonstrated that the dumped imports are, through the effects of dumping as set forth in paragraphs 2 and 4 of this Agreement, causing injury within the meaning of this Agreement. The demonstration of a causal relationship between the dumped imports and

---

[108]Terence Stewart et al., *supra* note 93, at 1518. *See also* J. Croome, Reshaping The World Trading System: A History Of The Uruguay Round 180-181 (1999).

[109]Lijuan Xing, *Behind the Multilateral Trading System: Legal Indigenization and the WTO in Comparative Perspective*, fn 619 (SJD Dissertation, 2012) (unpublished).

> the injury to the domestic industry shall be based on an examination of all relevant evidence before the authorities. The authorities shall also examine any known factors other than dumped imports which at the same time are injuring the domestic industry, and the injuries caused by these other factors must not be attributed to the dumped imports. Factors which may be relevant in this respect include, inter alia, the volume and prices of imports not sold at dumped prices, contraction in demand or changes in the patterns of consumption, trade restrictive practices of and competition between the foreign and domestic producers, development in the technology and the export performance and productivity of the domestic industry.

As noted by Miranda, a conceptually and intellectually challenging aspect of the causation requirement under the AD Agreement is the reference to the term "through the effects of dumping" mentioned in the first sentence of Article 3.5 of AD Agreement.[110] This provision closely resembles the U.S. antidumping law. The first critical factor examined by the USITC in an injury examination is whether the volume of imports was "significant" or not. The USITC determines 'significance' as an absolute amount and in terms of market share percentage. The USITC also examines the timing of the increase in volumes of less than fair value (LTFV) imports in relation to domestic production, sales and consumption. The second criterion is whether the dumped imports depressed prices of "like" domestic products or prevented price increases that would have occurred but for the dumped imports.

In order to gather information for its investigation, antidumping agencies send questionnaires to the respondents to elicit data and detailed information on the cost of production, sales, profit, net revenues, wholesale and retail prices, and other data related to the article in question. The agencies also seek information to determine whether factors unrelated to dumping influence the purchaser's decision. If such other factors causing injury exist, then the task of an agency is difficult. As the USITC 1979 Report observed, the USITC does not have to determine that the dumped imports are a principal, substantial and significant cause of injury.[111] It was sufficient under the U.S. law that "imports are *a cause* of material injury".[112] The position was adopted even in the EC at the time of the conclusion of the Uruguay Round. In sum, it is more than evident that the U.S. and EC antidumping practices have substantially influenced the language of injury and causation even under the WTO Antidumping Agreement. This language reiterated that dumping need not be a substantial cause of injury, but a cause; further, there was no categorical requirement to separately examine and weigh the role of each possible causal factor. The negotiating history of the AD Agreement only reconfirms that dumping was treated as just a cause and not as a significant or substantial cause for the purpose of antidumping actions. A detailed examination of the non-attribution language with respect to GATT/WTO disputes is provided in Chap. 3.

---

[110] Jorge Miranda, *supra* note 85, at 732-735.

[111] United States International Trade Commission, ANNUAL REPORT (1979), *available at* http://www.usitc.gov/publications/annualreport/pub982.pdf.

[112] William D. DeGrandis, *Proving Causation in Anti-dumping Cases*, 20(2) THE INTERNATIONAL LAWYER 563, 568-569 (1986).

## 2 *Causation in Sunset and Interim Reviews*

Article VI of the GATT did not envisage sunset reviews. Under the previous Tokyo Code, an antidumping measure could remain in force only as long as, and to the extent necessary, to counteract dumping which is causing injury. There was a provision under the Tokyo Code to review the continued imposition of antidumping duties, which could be initiated *suo motu* by the investigating authority or at the request of an interested party. However, there was no guidance under the Tokyo Code to set a limit on the maximum duration of an antidumping measure.[113] The sunset provision was included in the AD Agreement based on the proposals of Korea,[114] Japan,[115] and other Nordic countries.[116] Article 11.2 of the ADA deals with interim reviews and Article 11.3 deals with sunset or expiry reviews of antidumping measures.

*Anti-Dumping Agreement: Article 11.2*

The authorities shall review the need for the continued imposition of the duty, where warranted, on their own initiative or, provided that a reasonable period of time has elapsed since the imposition of the definitive anti-dumping duty, upon request by any interested party which submits positive information substantiating the need for a review. Interested parties shall have the right to request the authorities to examine whether the continued imposition of the duty is necessary to offset dumping, whether the injury would be likely to continue or recur if the duty were removed or varied, or both. If, as a result of the review under this paragraph, the authorities determine that the anti-dumping duty is no longer warranted, it shall be terminated immediately.

*Anti-Dumping Agreement: Article 11.3*

Notwithstanding the provisions of paragraphs 1 and 2, any definitive anti-dumping duty shall be terminated on a date not later than five years from its imposition (or from the date of the most recent review under paragraph 2 if that review has covered both dumping and injury, or under this paragraph), unless the authorities determine, in a review initiated before that date on their own initiative or upon a duly substantiated request made by or on behalf of the domestic industry within a reasonable period of time prior to that date, that the expiry of the duty would be likely to lead to continuation or recurrence of dumping and injury. The duty may remain in force pending the outcome of such a review.

According to Article 11.3 of the AD Agreement, initiation of sunset reviews can be done in two ways: either on an application by the domestic industry or by the concerned authority itself. However, there is an obligation on the authorities to determine whether the expiry of the duty would be likely to lead to continuation or

---

[113] Abhijit Das & Meghna Sharafudeen, *Sunset Reviews: Important Provisions Made Irrelevant*? 5 (1) Jindal Global Law Review 79, 82 (2014).

[114] Communication from the Republic of Korea, *Negotiating Group on MTN Agreements and Arrangements*, at 5 MTN.GNG/NG8/W/3 (May 20, 1987).

[115] Communication from Japan, *Negotiating Group on MTN Agreements and Arrangements*, at 3-4, MTN.GNG/NG8/W/11 (September 28, 1987).

[116] Submission of Nordic Countries, Negotiating Group on MTN Agreements and Arrangements, at MTN.GNG/NG 8/W/15 (November 16, 1987), at 4.

recurrence of dumping and injury. The non-existence of dumping or injury during the period of investigation is not dispositive of the probability of dumping or injury recurring in the future. Sunset reviews take place subsequent to the application of the antidumping measures, which one would expect to have neutralized the injury caused by the investigated imports.[117] A sunset review may, therefore, justify the continuation of the measure even after the dumping and injury have ceased. This is especially the case in situations where the exporters assume price undertaking, leading to increase in the import prices. This would not constitute current injury.

Another key issue is the applicability of the key disciplines of the Antidumping Agreement, such as Articles 2 (provision on dumping) and 3 (provision on injury and causation) of the ADA to the interim and sunset review proceedings. There is no explicit reference in Articles 11 of the Antidumping Agreement to Article 2 and 3. A WTO panel in *United States—Corrosion Resistant Steel Sunset Review* examined the issue whether the determination of likelihood of continuation or recurrence of dumping in a sunset review must be based on the determination of a dumping margin calculated in conformity with Article 2.4.[118]

The Panel noted that the substantive disciplines of Articles 2 and 3 did not apply in determining the likelihood of continuation or recurrence of dumping under Article 11. The Appellate Body, on the other hand, held that if the likelihood of injury determination is based upon the likelihood of dumping determination, then the dumping determination must be WTO-consistent. This implies that the substantive principles of Articles 2 and 3 could still apply in a sunset proceeding. The Appellate Body clarified the position as follows:

> Our conclusion that the establishment of a causal link between likely dumping and likely injury is not required in a sunset review determination does not imply that the causal link between dumping and injury envisaged by Article VI of the GATT 1994 and the Antidumping Agreement is severed in a sunset review. It only means that re-establishing such a link is not required, as a matter of legal obligation, in a sunset review.[119]

The above finding of the Appellate Body reaffirms that in a sunset review what is more important is the establishment of nexus between the "expiry of the duty" and the likelihood of "continuation or recurrence of dumping and injury". Reestablishing causal link in a sunset review is unnecessary according to the current thinking on this matter.

The foregoing paragraphs examined the evolution of injury and causation provision and examined the history and evolution of causal link in antidumping proceeding. The discussion also revealed how the protectionist concerns in antidumping laws influenced the injury and causation standards.

---

[117]Jorge Miranda, *supra* note 85, at 735.

[118]Panel Report, *United States – Sunset Review of Anti–Dumping Duties on Corrosion–Resistant Carbon Steel Flat Products from Japan*, WT/DS244/R (August 14, 2003).

[119]Appellate Body Report, *US –Corrosion-Resistant Steel Sunset Review*, WT/DS244/AB/R, ¶124 (December 15, 2003) [hereinafter Appellate Body Report, *US- Corrosion Resistant Steel* (*Sunset Review)*].

Section E of this book shall examine the injury and causation language in respect of subsidies and countervailing measures.

## E Injury and Causation in Subsidies and Countervailing Investigations

Subsidies and countervailing measures, which form the second pillar of trade remedy law remain one of the complex trade remedy instruments. Like antidumping, countervailing duties are trade remedy measures adopted to rectify what is seen as an unfair trade practice.

A subsidy is generally the bestowal of goods or services by a government upon the manufacture, production, or exportation of a product on terms that are preferential or inconsistent with commercial considerations. Subsidies have been addressed right from the days of GATT 1947, and several countries have adopted country specific legislations. Subsidies are offset through countervailing duty proceedings and are administered through tariffs pursuant to lengthy investigation proceedings.

The GATT 1947 did not mention any distinction between export and domestic subsidies. It only referred to a "bounty or subsidy bestowed, directly or indirectly, upon the manufacture, production or export of any merchandise".[120] However, the Tokyo Subsidies Code which was introduced in 1979 contained an outright prohibition on export subsidies to manufactured and mineral items. The Tokyo Code also contained an illustrative list of prohibited subsidies, all of which condition the subsidy in some manner on export or export performance.[121]

The first countervailing duty laws were enacted by the United States in 1890 and Belgium in 1892.[122] These laws were aimed at offsetting bounties paid by Continental European countries primarily on the export of sugar products, but also on other products such as flour and alcoholic beverages.[123] Viner suggested that these bounties on exports were not originally intended to promote export, but resulted from complex, clumsy tariff and excise tax laws—that is, rebates and drawbacks greater than the taxes or duties actually paid. Despite the fairly long

[120]General Agreement on Tariffs and Trade, art.VI:3, Oct. 30, 1947, 61 State. A-11, 55 U.N.T.S. 1994 [hereinafter GATT]. (this definition seems to be derived from the U.S. Tariff Act of 1930 which provides for the imposition of countervailing duties to offset any "bounty or grant" paid or bestowed upon the imports under investigation, although nowhere is the phrase "bounty or grant" defined.)

[121]Group "Non-Tariff Measures" Sub-Group "Technical Barriers to Trade", *Agreement on Interpretation and Application of Articles VI, XVI, and XXIII of the General Agreement on Tariffs and Trade*, MTN/NTM/W/226 [hereinafter referred to as the *Tokyo Subsidies Code*].

[122]Tariff Act of 1890, Chapter 1244, Sect. 237, 26 Stat. 584, as cited in G Bryan, Taxing Unfair International Trade Practices 250 (1980).

[123]Jacob Viner, *supra* note 12, at 90-91.

history of countervailing duty laws, such duties were not used to a significant extent by nations other than the United States.

Subsidies were disciplined for the first time at the multilateral level under GATT 1947.[124] As compared to the antidumping, GATT 1947 had fairly lenient provisions with respect to subsidies. Contracting Parties whose industry was injured by subsidized imports were allowed to impose countervailing duties up to the amount of subsidies. This was permitted by GATT Article VI (3). However, a GATT Contracting Party was required to establish that the domestic industry in the importing country had suffered material injury or threatened with material injury or was such as to materially retard the establishment of the domestic industry.

The GATT Article VI provisions on countervailing duties closely mirror the provisions on antidumping. Apparently, the drafting countries readily agreed to include countervailing duties along with antidumping duties under the rubric of Article VI despite the obvious differences between the two regimes. It appears that the controversy was limited to the need for an injury test in the application of countervailing duties. The U.S. did not have the injury requirement for countervailing duties in its domestic law. Nonetheless, the use of Protocol of Provisional Application (PPA)[125] to bring Part II of GATT 1947 had the effect of allowing the U.S. to continue to enforce its countervailing duty without the application of the injury test.[126] Although the conduct of CVD actions without an injury test was a clear departure from the GATT requirements in view of the limited CVD actions during 1948–1980, countervailing duties did not receive serious attention during this period.[127] However, as a consequence of the Tokyo Round, the U.S. accepted the "material injury" clause in its CVD law by inserting a new Title VII to the Tariff Act of 1930.[128] One of the most important changes made by the 1979 Act was the requirement of an injury test in all CVD cases involving imports from "countries under the Agreement".[129] However, the 1979 Act defined material injury as "harm which is not inconsequential, immaterial, or unimportant", which was undoubtedly soft injury standard.[130]

---

[124]*See e.g.*, Ronald Steenblik, *Previous Multilateral Efforts to Discipline Subsidies to Natural Resource Based Industries*, *available at* 2 (1999), http://www.oecd.org/greengrowth/fisheries/1918086.pdf.

[125]The Protocol of Provisional Application of the General Agreement on Tariffs and Trade, October 30, 1947, 61 Stat. A2051 (1947), 55 UNTS 308 (1950).

[126]*Id.*

[127]John J. Barcelo III, *A History of GATT Unfair Trade Law*, *supra* note 70.

[128]Trade Agreement Act of 1979, Sect. 101, 19 U.S.C.A §§ 1671–1671 f (West 1980) (adding new §§ 701–707 to the Tariff Act of 1930. In the 1979 Trade Agreement Act of 1979, the AD/CVD laws were introduced as a new section, namely Title VII of the Tariff Act of 1930).

[129]Countries which were signatories to the Tokyo Subsidies Code or had assumed substantially similar obligations to those under the Code.

[130]John J. Barcelo III, *Subsidies, Countervailing Duties and Antidumping After the Tokyo Round,* 13(2) Cornell International Law Journal 257, 271 (1980).

Notwithstanding the importance of maintaining various types of subsidy programmes, not enough work was made in developing disciplines on this topic. The U.S. was the only major industrial power that had an active countervailing duty programme.[131] Countervailing duties were never authorized within the internal market in EEC, and only a few countries had a functional regime for the implementation of this implementation of this remedy. It is reported that in addition to the U.S. and the European Union, only a few GATT signatories such as Australia, Canada, Chile and Japan, had implemented such measures earlier.[132] The EEC Treaty, on the other hand, sought direct regulation of impermissible subsidy practices through treaty related practices and rules such as State-aid.[133]

Establishing subsidy in the context of the GATT was fairly straight-forward, although the GATT disciplines were not fully developed. The framework provided under the GATT for determination on injury was even sketchier. Article VI of GATT 1947 provided that determination of injury shall be based on positive evidence and an objective examination of (a) the volume of the subsidized imports and the effect of the subsidized imports on prices in the domestic market for like products, and (b) the consequent impact of these imports on the domestic producers of such products.

Article VI: 3 of the GATT explicitly permits the application of countervailing measures to subsidized imports.[134] Article VI, paragraph 6(a), of the GATT provides in relevant part:

*Article VI: 6(a) of GATT*

No contracting party shall levy any antidumping or countervailing duty on the importation of any product of the territory of another contracting party unless it determines that the effect of the dumping on subsidization, as the case may be, is such as to cause or threaten material injury to an established domestic industry, or is such as to retard materially the establishment of a domestic industry.

In the following section, I shall discuss the key changes introduced in Tokyo Subsidies Code.

## 1 Injury and Causation in Tokyo Subsidies Code

The Tokyo Round negotiations on subsidies and countervailing measures took place under the auspices of the GATT. Twenty four countries ratified the Tokyo Subsidies code formally known as *Agreement on Interpretation and Application of*

[131] *Id.*

[132] John J. Barcelo III, *supra* note 130, at 279.

[133] Art. 91(1), Treaty Establishing the European Economic Community (Treaty of Rome) 298 UNTS 11 (Adopted on March 25, 1957); *See also,* Beseler and Williams, *supra* note 78, at 32-33.

[134] Appellate Body Report, *Brazil – Measures Affecting Desiccated Coconut*, WT/DS22/AB/R Page 11 (February 21, 1997).

*Articles VI, XVI and XXIII of the General Agreement*. The Tokyo Subsidies Code entered into force on 1 January 1980.[135] Negotiations on developing disciplines for a Subsidies Code took place in tandem with the negotiations on reforming the Antidumping Code. The following is a reproduction of the injury and causality provisions under the Tokyo Subsidies Code.

*Tokyo Subsidies Code: Article 6*

1. A determination of injury[17] for purposes of Article VI of the General Agreement shall involve an objective examination of both (a) the volume of subsidized imports and their effect on prices in the domestic market for like products[18] and (b) the consequent impact of these imports on domestic producers of such products.

2. With regard to volume of subsidized imports the investigating authorities shall consider whether there has been a significant increase in subsidized imports, either in absolute terms or relative to production or consumption in the importing signatory. With regard to the effect of the subsidized imports on prices, the investigating authorities shall consider whether there has been a significant price undercutting by the subsidized imports as compared with the price of a like product of the importing signatory, or whether the effect of such imports is otherwise to depress prices to a significant degree or prevent price increases, which otherwise would have occurred, to a significant degree. No one or several of these factors can necessarily give decisive guidance.

3. The examination of the impact on the domestic industry concerned shall include an evaluation of all relevant economic factors and indices having a bearing on the state of the industry such as actual and potential decline in output, sales, market share, profits, productivity, return on investments, or utilization of capacity; factors affecting domestic prices; actual and potential negative effects on cash flow, inventories, employment, wages, growth, ability to raise capital or investment and, in the case of agriculture, whether there has been an increased burden on Government support programmes. This list is not exhaustive, nor can one or several of these factors necessarily give decisive guidance.

4. It must be demonstrated that the subsidized imports are, through the effects[19] of the subsidy, causing injury within the meaning of this Agreement. There may be other factors[20] which at the same time are injuring the domestic industry, and the injuries caused by other factors must not be attributed to the subsidized imports."

---

*Footnote 17:* Determinations of injury under the criteria set forth in this Article shall be based on positive evidence. In determining threat of injury the investigating authorities, in examining the factors listed in this Article, may take into account the evidence on the nature of the subsidy in question and the trade effects likely to arise therefrom.

*Footnote 18:* Omitted.

*Footnote 19*: As set forth in paragraphs 2 and 3 of this Article.

*Footnote 20*: Such factors can include inter alia, the volume and prices of non-subsidized imports of the product in question, contraction in demand or changes in the pattern of consumption, trade restrictive practices of and competition between the foreign and

---

[135]Agreement on Interpretation and Application of Articles VI, XVI, and XXIII of the General Agreement on Tariffs and Trade, GATT BISD 56-83 (26th Supp. 1980) [hereinafter *Subsidies Code*].

domestic producers, developments in technology and the export performance and productivity of the domestic industry.

The Tokyo Subsidies Code reiterated the material injury requirement of GATT Article VI.[136] More importantly, it did not contain a grandfather clause like the Tokyo Antidumping Code.[137] Consequently, the U.S. law was amended by the 1979 Trade Agreement Act to incorporate material injury in all antidumping investigations, and to require material injury in all countervailing duty investigations against countries that were part of the Subsidies Code.[138]

One of the contentious issues in the Tokyo Code was the interpretation of Footnote 19[139] to the SCM Agreement. The issue was whether the terms "through the effects of the subsidy" implied a meaning that was similar to the phrase "through the effects of imports"? According to David Palmeter, the Tokyo Code manifestly required the level of subsidy along with the imports to constitute the effects.[140] As will be discussed later in Chap. 3, the meaning of "through the effects" still continues to be ambiguous in the context of both AD and Countervailing Duties (CVD) investigations.

It must be noted that the Tokyo Subsidies Code, unlike the Kennedy Antidumping Code, did not contain a language on the degree of causality. However, one of the draft arrangements discussed during the Tokyo Round negotiations contained the following language: "[t]he subsidized products must be [an important contributing factor in causing or threatening] [the cause of] injury. All other relevant factors adversely affecting the industry shall be considered in reaching a determination."[141] However, this language was not incorporated in the final agreement. In other words, after the Tokyo Round, the degree of causality required in CVD investigations is almost identical to the language in AD investigations.

---

[136]Agreement on Interpretation and Application of Articles VI, XVI and XXIII of the General Agreement on Tariffs and Trade, LT/TR/A/3 (adopted on November 28, 1979).

[137]Jagdeep S. Bhandari & Alan Sykes, Economic Dimensions of International Law: Comparative and Empirical Perspectives 87(1997).

[138]John H. Jackson, *supra* note 57, at 236–242.

[139]SCM Agreement, footnote 19 read as follows: *"In the event that the request relates to a subsidy deemed to result in serious prejudice in terms of paragraph 1 of Article 6, the available evidence of serious prejudice may be limited to the available evidence as to whether the conditions of paragraph 1 of Article 6 have been met or not".*

[140]David Palmeter, *Countervailing Subsidized Imports: The International Trade Commission Goes Astray*, 2(1-2) UCLA Pacific Basin Law Journal 21(1983).

[141]General Agreement in Tariffs and Trade, *Multilateral Trade Negotiations Group "Non-Tariff Measures" Sub-Group "Subsidies and Countervailing* Duties", MTN.NTM/W/168 (July 10, 1978).

## 2 *Uruguay Round Agreement on Subsidies and Countervailing Measures*

The Uruguay Round SCM Agreement expanded and developed the procedural and substantive rules on the use of countervailing measures developed under the Tokyo Subsidies Code. Under the Tokyo Subsidies Code, the only effective remedy against foreign subsidization was application of the domestic countervailing duty law. While that law was somewhat effective in addressing the effects of subsidized merchandise in the importing country market, it was not designed to address the effects of subsidies in other markets. The Uruguay Round SCM Agreement, together with the new WTO dispute settlement procedures, provide a more substantive and detailed procedural tools for addressing distortions caused by subsidies anywhere in the world.[142]

As regards injury and causality, the SCM Agreement did not make substantive changes to the Tokyo Subsidies Code. Part V of the SCM Agreement "… permit[s] WTO Members to levy countervailing duties on imported products to offset the benefits of specific subsidies bestowed on the manufacture, production or export of those goods". However, Part V also conditions the right to apply such duties on the demonstrated existence of three substantive conditions (subsidization, injury, and a causal link between the two) and on compliance with its procedural and substantive rules, notably the requirement that the countervailing duty cannot exceed the amount of the subsidy.

The key provisions with respect to injury and causality were consolidated under Article 15 of the SCM Agreement. Article 15.5 of the SCM Agreement remains the single most important provision on injury and causation determination, but it refers to Articles 15.2 and 15.4.

Similar to Article 3.1 of the AD Agreement, Article 15.1 of the SCM Agreement introduces the requirement of positive evidence and the need to conduct an objective examination of volumetric and price effects of the subsidized imports.

*SCM Agreement: Article 15.1*

A determination of injury… shall be based on positive evidence and involve an objective examination of both (a) the volume of the subsidized imports and the effect of the subsidized imports on prices in the domestic market for like products and (b) the consequent impact of these imports on the domestic producers of such products.

*SCM Agreement: Article 15.2*

With regard to the volume of the subsidized imports, the investigating authorities shall consider whether there has been a significant increase in subsidized imports, either in absolute terms or relative to production or consumption in the importing Member.

---

[142]Article 5 of SCMA which deals with "Adverse effects" is aimed at addressing the distortions caused by certain subsidies in third country markets.

With regard to the effect of subsidized imports on the price of similar products, it is specified that:

> The investigating authorities shall consider whether there has been significant price undercutting by the subsidized imports as compared with the prices of a like product…, or whether the effects of such imports is otherwise to depress or suppress to a significant degree or to prevent price increases, which otherwise would have occurred, to a significant degree.

*SCM Agreement Article 15.4*

> The examination of the impact of the subsidized imports on the domestic industry shall include an evaluation of all relevant economic factors and indices having a bearing on the state of the domestic industry, including actual and potential decline in output, sales, market share, profits, productivity, return on investments, or utilization of capacity; factors affecting domestic prices, actual and potential negative effects on cash flow, inventories, employment, wages, growth, ability to raise capital or investments and, in the case of agriculture, whether there has been an increased burden on government support programmes. This list is nor exhaustive, nor can one or several of these factors necessarily give decisive guidance.

A combined reading of Article 15, clauses (1), (2) and (4) indicates that the assessment of injury is linked to the effects of subsidy. A combined reading captures the four key steps involved in a CVD investigation: (1) Is there a significant increase in imports?; (2) Is there a significant price undercutting by subsidized imports? (3) Whether the effects of these imports were to depress prices to a significant degree or to prevent price increases to a significant degree?, and (4) whether the imports in view of these factors have caused material injury to the domestic industry? It is instructive to examine Article 15.5 of the SCM Agreement which is very similar to the AD Agreement in relation to causation.

*SCM Agreement Article 15.5*

> It must be demonstrated that the subsidized imports are, through the effects[47] of subsidies, causing injury within the meaning of this Agreement. The demonstration of a causal relationship between the subsidized imports and the injury to the domestic industry shall be based on an examination of all relevant evidence before the authorities. The authorities shall also examine any known factors other than the subsidized imports which at the same time are injuring the domestic industry, and the injuries caused by these other factors must not be attributed to the subsidized imports. Factors which may be relevant in this respect include, inter alia, the volume and prices of non-subsidized imports of the products in question, contraction in demand or the change in the pattern of consumption, trade restrictive practices of an competition between the foreign and domestic producers, developments in technology and the export performance and productivity of the domestic industry.
>
> ---
>
> [47] as set forth in paragraphs 2 and 4.

The first paragraph of Article 15.5 of the SCM Agreement is almost a reproduction of the first paragraph of Article 6.4 of the Tokyo Code. Article 15.5 of the SCM Agreement also includes a requirement to examine "known factors other than subsidized imports" and that the injuries caused by these other factors must not be attributed to subsidized imports. Although the Tokyo Code had a reference to "known factors" in the footnote to Article 6(4), such an examination was omitted or overlooked in the CVD investigations conducted all along. None of the CVD disputes conducted during 1980–1994 in the U.S. or in the EU had a clear discussion on the role of known factors in the assessment of injury and causality.[143]

### *3 Similarities of SCM Agreement and AD Agreement*

This chapter examined the material injury and causation standards in AD and CVD investigations under the GATT/WTO. As exhaustively outlined in this chapter, a CVD case may be filed against exporters benefiting from a government subsidy, while an AD case may be filed against an exporter dumping a product into an import market. In effect, both AD and CVD duties are imposed against products of foreign companies, rather than against foreign governments. The material injury and causation standards are nearly the same for both AD and CVD investigations.[144]

The non-attribution requirement is also common to both the AD and SCM Agreements. The Panel in *EC- DRAM* noted that the non-attribution requirement in AD investigations has been addressed by the Appellate Body in several relevant cases.[145] The same logic and reasoning should apply in CVD cases. Furthermore, the WTO Ministerial Decision calls for a consistent resolution of disputes arising from antidumping and countervailing duty measures.[146] In conclusion, despite their almost separate and wholly unconnected evolution and existence, the injury and causality requirements of antidumping and CVD investigations have nearly merged and look almost indistinguishable now.

## F Injury and Causation in Safeguard Investigations

Safeguards, the third element in this *troika*, are generally in the nature of import restrictions imposed in the event of import surges. This is to prevent serious injury to the domestic industry, as well to make positive adjustments to import competition.[147] Such duties or protection are expected to help the concerned industries and workmen from business disruption, dislocation and economic extinction. In other

---

[143] Marc Benitah, The Law of Subsidies Under the GATT/WTO System 14 (2001).

[144] John J. Barcelo III, *supra* note 70, at 285.

[145] Panel Report, *EC—Countervailing Measures on DRAM Chips*, ¶ 7.404, WT/DS299 (June 17, 2005).

[146] As provided by the Ministerial Declaration on Dispute Settlement Pursuant to the Agreement on Implementation of Article VI of the GATT 1994 and Part V of the Agreement on Subsidies and Countervailing Measures.

[147] Sheng, *supra* note 62, at 153.

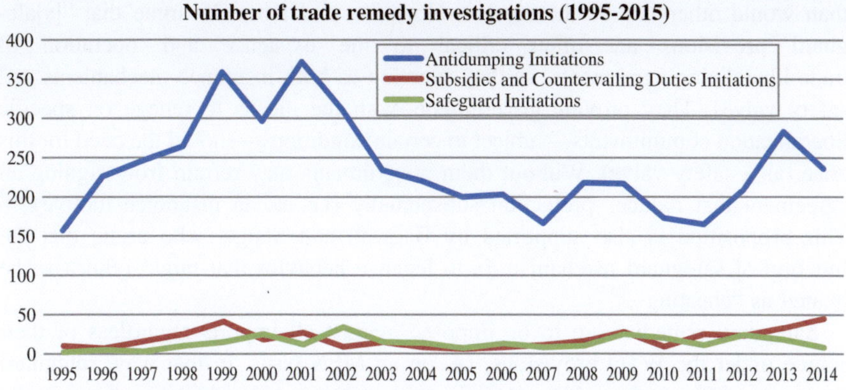


**Fig. 2** Number of trade remedy investigations (1995–2015). *Source* WTO notifications

words, safeguard duties are applied to give domestic producers some breathing space for adjustment against foreign competition[148]—competition that is perfectly fair but that nevertheless causes serious injury to domestic producers. In practice, the number of safeguard investigations conducted in a year is much less when compared to the antidumping actions. For example, while more than 4,900 antidumping actions are initiated since the establishment of the WTO, only less than 300 safeguard actions are initiated (Fig. 2).[149]

According to Cottier and Oesch safeguard measures inherently accompany the process of liberalization and of structural adjustment that go along with enhancing market access for imported products.[150] Moreover, the instrument is politically necessary in order to undertake liberalization in the first place and to find the necessary majorities to do so at home.[151] This view is significantly supported by scholarly writings. Kenneth Dam also suggests that the availability of safeguard remedies has encouraged countries to enter into a greater number of tariff bindings

[148]Negotiating Group on Safeguards, *Communication from Australia, Hong Kong, Korea, New Zealand and Singapore*, MTN/ GNG/NG9/W/8 (October 5, 1987).

[149]World Trade Organization, WTO Trade Remedies Gateway, http://www.wto.org/english/tratop_e/adp_e/adp_e.htm (last visited on July 31, 2016).

[150]According to Section 201 of the U.S. Trade Act of 1974 if an industry exhibits the conditions of injury contemplated by Article XIX, the President shall take "appropriate and feasible" action that could "facilitate efforts by the domestic industry to make positive adjustment to import competition". The Preamble to the Agreement on Safeguards also refers to the importance of "structural adjustment".

[151]Thomas Cottier and Mattias Oesch, International Trade Regulation, Law And Policy In The WTO, The European Union And Switzerland: Cases, Materials And Comments 486 (2005).

than would otherwise be the case.[152] Hoekman and Kostecki argue that "[s]afeguard provisions are often critical to the existence and operation of trade-liberalizing agreements, as they function as both insurance mechanisms and safety valves. They provide governments with the means to renege on specific liberalization commitments—subject to certain conditions—should the need for this arise (as a safety valve). Without them governments may refrain from signing an agreement that reduces protection substantially (i.e. as an insurance motive).[153] This proposition is also supported by Bagwell and Staiger who argue that the function of safeguard mechanism is to legalize behavior that might otherwise be treated as "cheating".[154]

Safeguard remedies are to be imposed against all imports regardless of their source under the WTO provisions, i.e. on an MFN basis. In that way, safeguard actions are different from AD and CVD investigations. AD and CVD actions can be taken only against those countries which are found to be engaged in unfair dumping and consequently causing injury to the domestic industry. However, safeguard actions are to be applied irrespective of the source, subject to certain flexibilities available for developing countries.

Compared to antidumping actions, safeguard actions came in several years later. The trade agreement that the U.S. signed with Mexico in 1943 was the first agreement that is known to have introduced the "escape clause".[155] When introducing the proposed safeguards mechanism, the U.S. delegate stated the purpose of the mechanism as follows:

> The purpose of this Article, generally speaking, is to give some flexibility to the commitments undertaken in Chapter IV [of US–Mexico Agreement].Some provisions of this kind seems necessary in order that countries will not find themselves in such a rigid position that they could not deal with situations of an emergency character. Therefore, the Article would provide for a modification of commitments to meet such temporary situations.[156]

Formally in 1951, the U.S. Congress empowered the Tariff Commission to conduct an "escape clause" or the safeguards investigation upon the application filed by a representative of the injured industry.[157] In other words, it had to be

[152] KENNETH W. DAM, THE GATT: LAW AND INTERNATIONAL ECONOMIC ORGANIZATION 99 (1970).

[153] BERNARD HOEKMAN & MARTIN KOSTECKI, THE POLITICAL ECONOMY OF THE WORLD TRADING SYSTEM: THE WTO AND BEYOND 413 (2nd edn., 2001).

[154] KEITH BAGWELL & ROBERT W. STAIGER, THE ECONOMICS OF THE WORLD TRADING SYSTEM (2002).

[155] Reciprocal Trade Agreement with Mexico, December 23, 1943, 57 Stat. 833 (1943).

[156] United Nations Economic and Social Council, *Preparatory Committee of the International Conference on Trade and Employment,* Verbatim Report of the Seventh Meeting of Committee of the International Conference on Trade and Employment, II, E/PC/T/C.II/PV/7 (1946), at 3.

[157] *See generally,* G. Bronz, *The Tariff Commission as a Regulatory Agency,* 61(3) COLUMBIA LAW REVIEW, 463 (1961).

demonstrated that the concession engendered imports had played a substantial part in causing injury to the petitioner. Under the 1962 Act, however, a petitioning industry must sustain the double burden of proving that the increased imports were caused "in major part" by trade agreement concessions, and that the increased imports were "the major factor" in causing the industry's serious injury. A preponderant causal connection between trade-agreement concessions and increased imports must be proved.[158] In practice, the Tariff Commission in the U.S. determined that before an affirmative finding could be made under the new Act, a petitioning industry must prove that the increased imports were caused, by trade-agreement concessions, in major parts; and that the imports were the major factor in causing serious injury to the petitioner's industry. If the petitioner failed to sustain its burden with respect to either element, the Commission said that it could not make an affirmative finding.

It will be instructive to notice that the authority to apply "escape clause" or safeguard action was tied to the Presidential authority to negotiate reciprocal tariff concessions, at least in the U.S. For example, the U.S. President had no authority to negotiate tariff concessions between 1967 and 1974 (i.e., after the conclusion of the Kennedy Round and the commencement of the Tokyo Round), and when the President was granted authority by virtue of the 1974 Trade Act, a corresponding power was granted under Title II of the Act under the category *Relief from Injury Caused by Import Competition*. Title II of the 1974 Trade Act has continued until date as the basis for safeguard investigations under the U.S. legislation.[159]

Safeguards actions were recognized in the GATT 1947[160] treaty itself although there is no evidence to indicate that any Contracting Party other than the United States had such a mechanism. Article II of the GATT 1947 provided for reciprocal reduction of tariff rates among the Contracting Parties which resulted in negotiated ceilings or tariff bindings. The drafters of GATT 1947 anticipated that tariff concessions could become unduly burdensome. In such a context, safeguard actions allowed a Contracting Party to undo a previously granted concession to protect domestic industry from import competition. In view of the concerns expressed by the negotiating parties to the GATT 1947, the drafters provided for "emergency action on imports of particular products" in Article XIX of GATT 1947.

---

[158] A "substantial cause" is one that is important and not less important than any other cause. Section 2251 (b) (4).

[159] K. Grybowski, V. Rud & G. Steppanyenko, *Towards Integrated Management of International Trade—The U.S. Trade Act of 1974*, 9 International and Comparative Law Quarterly 285 (1979).

[160] GATT, at Art. XIX.

*Article XIX (1) of GATT, 1947*

If, as a result of unforeseen developments and of the effect of obligations incurred by a contracting party under this Agreement, including tariff concessions, any product is being imported into the territory of that contracting party in such increased quantities and under such conditions as to cause or threaten serious injury to the domestic producers in that territory of like or directly competitive products, the contracting party shall be free, in respect of such product, and to the extent and for such time as may be necessary to prevent or remedy such injury, to suspend the obligations in whole or in part or to withdraw or modify the concession.

It is clear from the text of Article XIX that a Contracting Party desiring to apply safeguard measures must have experienced "increased quantities" of a "like" or "directly competitive" product manufactured by the domestic industry. Although the term "increased quantities" is not explained in Article XIX of GATT 1947, a GATT Working Party had concluded that this term would refer to an increase in import quantities either in absolute terms or relative terms.[161] The absence of any reference to a baseline for evaluating the surge in imports was considered to be major shortcoming of Article XIX of GATT 1947.[162] The lack of jurisprudence on the application and interpretation led to the persistence of ambiguity in Article XIX of the GATT 1947.[163]

Under Article XIX of the GATT 1947, a signatory cannot impose trade restrictions under the "escape clause" without compensating adversely affected members of GATT 1947 if the restrictions impair the value to them of a prior GATT concession. In particular, paragraphs 2 and 3 of Article XIX of GATT 1947 provide that a party invoking its right to suspend or modify concessions must negotiate with adversely affected parties and provide compensation in the form of alternative trade concessions. As a general rule, compensation is required from the Member applying the safeguard measures to the exporting Members.

The WTO Safeguards Agreement specifies that if no agreement on compensation is reached within 30 days of consultations required under the Safeguards Agreement, the affected exporting Members are free, within a 90 day period after the imposition of the safeguard measure, to suspend the application of "substantially equivalent concessions" (i.e., Article 8. 2 of the Agreement on Safeguards). The right of suspension is not to be exercised for the first 3 years that a safeguard measure is in effect, provided that the safeguard measure has been taken as a result

---

[161] Report of the Intersessional Working Party on the Complaint of Czechoslovakia Concerning the Withdrawal by the United States of a Tariff Concession under Article XIX of the GATT (Hatters' Fur), GATT/CP/106 (Oct. 22, 1951). [hereinafter, *Working party report, Hatter's Fur*].

[162] Alan O. Sykes, The WTO Agreement on Safeguards: A Commentary 9 (2006); see also Alan O. Sykes, *A Safeguard Mess: A Critique of WTO Jurisprudence*, 2(3) World Trade Review 261, 268-269 (2003) [hereinafter *Sykes, A Safeguard Mess*].

[163] The only written dispute report pertaining to safeguard measures during the GATT was the Hatter's Case released in 1951.

of an absolute increase in imports and that such a measure conforms to the provisions of the Safeguard Agreement.[164]

One of the key interpretative issues in the application of safeguard measures was the meaning of the terms "unforeseen developments", along with the term, "the obligations incurred by a contracting party". The first clause of Paragraph 1 of Article XIX of GATT 1947 was formulated in the context of an agreement that was expected to be short-lived and a provisional arrangement.[165] However, one of assumptions of incurring tariff obligations was that the concessions would be suspended in the event of an unforeseen development which may have an adverse impact on the domestic industry.

It appears from the provisions of GATT that it was not enough that an unforeseen import surge has resulted from a tariff concession. There is an additional requirement that the import surge has caused or is threatening to cause injury to domestic production.[166] One of the earliest cases in the GATT dealing with unforeseen development is the Hatter's Fur case.[167] The U.S. withdrew a concession that it had negotiated in 1947 with respect to women's hat bodies. The U.S. argued that an unexpected surge in imports had resulted from its 1947 concession due to an unforeseen change that benefited imports over domestic producers. Members of the Working Party in that case, in 1951, stated[168]:

> …"unforeseen developments" should be interpreted to mean developments occurring after the negotiation of the relevant tariff concession which it would not be reasonable to expect that the negotiators of the country making the concession could and should have foreseen at the time when the concession was negotiated."

It is possible that the requirement of "unforeseen developments" was conceivable and comprehensible in the early days of the GATT. When new tariff concessions were given, there arose a possibility that such concessions could result in unanticipated import surge. According to Professor Sykes, Article XIX of GATT 1947 was designed to address such unforeseen and politically inconvenient consequences of tariff liberalization under the GATT.[169] The requirement that increase in imports must be the result of "unforeseen developments" has been progressively liberalized in several jurisdictions.[170] However, in some of the earlier WTO

---

[164]Art. 8(3) Agreement on Safeguards, 15 April 1994, LT/UR/A-1A/8 [hereinafter *Safeguards Agreement.*].

[165]Sykes, *A Safeguard Mess*, *supra* note 162, at 261.

[166]*Id.* at 255.

[167]*Working Party Report, Hatter's Fur*, *supra* note 161.

[168]*Id.* at ¶ 9. This interpretation was proposed by the representative of Czechoslovakia, and was accepted by all the Members of the Working Party, with the exception of the United States.

[169]ALAN O. SYKES, THE WTO AGREEMENT ON SAFEGUARDS: A COMMENTARY 17 (2006).

[170]Alan O. Sykes, *The Persistent Puzzles of Safeguards: Lessons from the Steel Dispute,* 7(3) JOURNAL OF INTERNATIONAL ECONOMIC LAW 523 (2004); MICHAEL J. TREBILCOCK, UNDERSTANDING TRADE LAW 93-94 (2011).

decisions such as *Argentina—Footwear*[171] and *Korea—Dairy,*[172] the Appellate Body had held that Article XIX of the GATT and the Agreement on Safeguards should not be read as to exclude the requirement of establishing unforeseen developments. According to *Argentina—Footwear,* an unforeseen development is one that was not expected by trade negotiators at the time when such concessions were negotiated.[173] In view of this requirement, all safeguard investigations are required to provide a finding on "unforeseen developments". In other words, the requirement of unforeseen development is not merely an "explanatory verbiage".[174] This interpretation affirmed the continuing vitality of Article XIX of the GATT in respect of safeguards investigations.

The objective of the Safeguards Agreement was also to prohibit various grey area measures and to clarify and reinforce the disciplines of the GATT. Grey area measures referred to "voluntary restraint agreements", "voluntary export restraints" and "orderly marketing arrangements" which amounted to quantitative export limitations.[175] Article 2 of the Safeguards Agreement sets forth the conditions (i.e., serious injury and threat thereof) under which safeguard measures may be imposed. The causation requirement is set forth in Articles 2.1 and 4.2 (b).

*Safeguards Agreement: Article 2.1*

A Member (footnote omitted) may apply a safeguard measure to a product only if that Member has determined, pursuant to the provisions set out below, that such a product is being imported into its territory in such increased quantities, absolute or relative to domestic production, and under such conditions as to cause or threaten to cause serious injury to the domestic industry that produce like or directly competitive products.

Even the new Safeguards Agreement did not include other conditions for its application. For example, it was not entirely clear whether the imports of the product under examination should increase suddenly, sharply or unexpectedly. The negotiating history indicates that the Pacific- Rim countries (Australia, New Zealand, Hong Kong, Korea and Singapore) were in favour of tough disciplines.[176] The proposal of the Pacific- Rim countries suggested that the determination of serious injury or threat thereof shall depend on the establishment of a direct causal link between increased imports and an overall decline in the condition of domestic producers. Brazil also proposed that a precise definition of "serious injury" and a clear causal link between "unforeseen sudden and substantial increase in imports"

---

[171] Appellate Body Report, *Argentina- Safeguard Measures on Imports of Footwear*, WT/DS121/AB/R (December 14, 1999) [hereinafter "Appellate Body, *Argentina- Footwear*].

[172] Appellate Body report, *Korea – Definitive Safeguard Measure on Imports of Certain Dairy Products*, WT/DS 98/AB/R ¶ 97 (December 14, 1999).

[173] Appellate Body Report, *Argentina- Footwear*, ¶ 93.

[174] Appellate Body Report, Korea—Diary, ¶ 43.

[175] Jagdish Bhagwati, Protectionism (1988) (arguing that safeguard measures are known as "grey area measures", because they were neither authorized nor condemned by GATT.).

[176] Croome, *supra* note 108, at 55.

and "serious injury" would have to be established in order for a contracting party to be in a position to resort to safeguards measures.[177]

The only guidance to the meaning of the term "serious injury" and the appropriate standard of causation is provided by Article 4 of the Safeguards Agreement.

*Safeguards Agreement: Article 4.1*

"For purposes of this Agreement:

(a) "serious injury" shall be understood to mean significant overall impairment in the position of the domestic industry

It is generally considered that the concept of "serious injury" is much higher than other forms of injury. The terms "significant overall impairment" which are used to qualify serious injury themselves are ambiguous. In *Argentina—Footwear*, the Appellate Body highlighted the need to look at the "overall picture" of the industry while assessing "significant overall impairment".[178] The Appellate Body in *US-Lamb*, noted that the concept of serious injury under the Safeguards Agreement is a high standard.[179] The Appellate Body noted that the word "serious" connoted a higher standard than the word "material" which is mentioned in the AD and SCM Agreements.[180] Again, in *US—Wheat Gluten*, the Appellate Body referred to the standard of "serious injury" determination as "exacting".[181] However, how an investigating authority can differentiate between the two standards was not clearly spelt out. In many ways, it appears that distinctions in injury and causation standards that originated in the use of such instruments in some of the jurisdictions such as that of the United States were carried forward even in the interpretation of the WTO Safeguards Agreement.[182]

In regard to causation, the Safeguards Agreement provides as below:

*Safeguards Agreement: Article 4.2*

(a). *In the investigation to determine whether increased imports have caused or* are threatening to cause serious injury to a domestic industry… the competent authorities shall evaluate all relevant factors of an objective and quantifiable nature having a bearing on the situation of the domestic industry, in particular, the rate and amount of the increase of imports of the product concerned in absolute and relative terms, the share of the domestic industry taken by increased imports, changes in the level of sales, production, productivity, capacity utilization, profit and losses, and employment.

---

[177]Negotiating Group on Safeguards, *Communication from Brazil, Elements for a Comprehensive Understanding of Safeguards*, ¶. 3, MTN.GNG. NG9/W/3 (May 25, 1987).

[178]Appellate Body Report, *Argentina- Footwear*, ¶ 139.

[179]Appellate Body Report, *United States – Safeguard Measures on Imports of Fresh, Chilled or Frozen Lamb Meat from New Zealand and Australia*, WT/DS177/AB/R, WT/DS178/AB/R, ¶ 124 (May 16, 2001) [hereinafter Appellate Body Report, *US- Lamb*].

[180]Appellate Body Report, *US—Lamb,* ¶. 124.

[181]Appellate Body Report, *US—Wheat Gluten*, ¶. 149.

[182]Alan Sykes, The WTO Agreement on Safeguards (2006).

> (b). The determination [of whether increased imports cause or threaten to cause serious injury] shall be made unless this investigation demonstrates, on the basis of objective evidence, the existence of the causal link between increased imports of the product concerned and serious injury or threat thereof. When factors other than increased imports are causing injury to the domestic industry at the same time, such injury shall not be attributed to increased imports.

It is important to note that unlike the AD as well as the SCM Agreement, the Safeguards Agreement does not provide a list of other factors. Nonetheless, Article 4.2 includes a non-attribution requirement. However, the absence of an illustrative list of factors–as the discussion in Chap. 3 indicates–does not appear to have affected the performance of the non-attribution requirement.

Besides Article XIX of the GATT and the Safeguards Agreement, certain transitional product specific safeguard mechanisms are also provided in the WTO.[183] For instance, Article 16 of China's Protocol of Accession[184] authorized a WTO Member to take certain product specific safeguards if the increased imports caused or threatened to cause market disruption. Article 16(4) of the Protocol considered market disruption to take place when imports are found to be 'increasingly rapidly' so as to be a significant cause of material injury. It is noteworthy that the transitional product specific safeguard mechanism has used the material injury standard (as seen in AD and SCM Agreements) instead of the serious injury standard. Furthermore, the transitional safeguard mechanism has used the 'significant cause' requirement. In *US—Tyres (China),* China argued that the U.S. violated its commitments under the Accession Protocol since the increased imports were not a 'significant cause of injury'. However, the panel ruled that rapidly increasing imports would properly constitute a significant cause of market disruption even though their causal role is not as significant as other factors.[185] This was an important clarification that a mere choice of causal adjectives will not substantially influence the causation analysis.

Article 5.1 requires that a safeguard be imposed not only to the extent necessary to prevent or remedy serious injury, but also to facilitate the adjustment. In *US—Line Pipe,* the Appellate Body has also made the link between the Article 5.1 "extent necessary" requirement and the non-attribution requirement under Article 4.2(b), second sentence. The Appellate Body had noted that it would not be logical to require a Member to conduct the non-attribution analysis while, at the same time, permit that Member to apply a safeguard measure addressing injury caused by all factors.[186] Thus, it found that a violation of the non-attribution requirement (in that

---

[183]This study does not focus on the product specific safeguards actions provided under the Agreement on Textiles and Clothing (ATC).

[184]The China specific transitional product specific safeguard mechanism expired in 2013, i.e. after 12 years after the date of accession to the WTO.

[185]Panel Report, *United States – Measures Affecting Imports of Certain Passenger Vehicle and Light Truck Tyres from China,* ¶ 7.158, WT/DS399/R (October 5, 2011).

[186]Appellate Body Report, *US- Definitive Safeguard Measures on Import of Circular Welded Carbon Quality Line Pipe from Korea,* ¶ 252, WT/DS202/AB/R (February 15, 2002) [hereinafter Appellate Body Report, *US- Line Pipe*].

injury caused by factors other than imports has been attributed to imports) entailed a *prima facie* demonstration that the safeguard measure had not been applied "to the extent necessary" to prevent or remedy serious injury, and to facilitate the adjustment.[187] A safeguard measure that imposes a burden on imports beyond the effects that should be attributed to imports, limits competition and runs counter to the objective of the escape clause protection. As the Panel in *US—Steel* stated, there is a "need to maintain a balance between market access and safeguards rights and obligations".[188]

Safeguard investigations or the so-called "escape clause" actions do not involve a test of the fairness of import competition, but only an injury test. As can be seen from the foregoing discussion, the standards for relief under antidumping and subsidies and countervailing measures are considerably lower when compared to that of safeguards. The contingent trade protection available under Article XIX of the GATT 1947 and the Safeguard Agreement is temporary. In many jurisdictions, seeking such a relief is often discretionary. However, there are various similarities in the methodologies for conducting injury and causation, especially the non-attribution analysis.

## G Injury and Causation Provisions at the End of the Uruguay Round

The purpose of the trade remedy laws was to allow relief to domestic producers who were affected by fair and unfair imports. The existence of such laws was considered essential to encourage countries to undertake trade liberalization and, at the same time, retain policy flexibility to provide timely and appropriate protection against the disruptive effect of such imports. The Uruguay Round tried to establish an effective balance between these two policy objectives. The Uruguay Round introduced tougher and stricter standards for the conduct of trade remedy investigations. Especially with respect to injury determination, the Uruguay Round agreements put more weight than the previous codes, or even the GATT, in ensuring that imports (fair or unfair) which were causing difficulties of the domestic industry needed to be properly addressed. The Uruguay Round Agreements, by themselves, did not introduce stand-alone obligations and cannot be read in isolation from GATT 1994. Each agreement has to be read in conjunction with the corresponding GATT Articles. For example, the AD Agreement has to be read in conjunction with Article VI of the GATT; the SCM Agreement to be read in conjunction with Article VI and VII of GATT, and, the Agreement on Safeguards to be read in conjunction with Article XIX of the GATT.

---

[187]Appellate Body Report, *US- Line Pipe,* ¶ 261.

[188]Panel Report, *United States – Definitive Safeguard Measures on Imports of Certain Steel Products,* ¶ 10.13, WT/DS252/R (July 11, 2003).

It was a significant achievement for the GATT negotiating countries to develop separate agreements for the three common forms of trade contingent protection. However, the development of separate agreements did not resolve all the ambiguities. In certain areas, such as double remedies, zeroing, etc., the existing provisions did not provide significant improvements. Establishing injury and causation is yet another area where the Uruguay Round failed to introduce the desired level of clarity.

In the matter of injury and causation, the Uruguay Round trade remedy agreements have left ambiguity in certain key areas. An examination of the evolution of trade remedy agreements clearly indicates that these agreements were significantly influenced by the U.S. practice. The U.S. practice assigned a tougher injury and causality standard in escape clause or safeguard investigations.[189] Some authors prefer to call this a "first-level" injury.[190] The Safeguards Agreement has opted for the term "serious injury". The USITC implied this standard as the proxy for a first-level injury.

On the other hand, the U.S. statute defined the injury standard in the antidumping and subsidies and countervailing investigations as "material injury" which was interpreted as an injury which was not "inconsequential, unimportant or insignificant". Within the U.S., this injury standard was likened to a "second-level" injury.[191] The Uruguay Round agreements have not fully adapted the U.S. standard, although the U.S. tend to believe that their injury and causality standard in antidumping, subsidies and safeguard are by and large close to the WTO standards. Certain key provisions of the Uruguay Round agreements on trade remedies expressly retain this ambiguity. For example, terms such as "serious injury", "material injury" and "material retardation" are extremely vague. As Vermulst argues, despite the improvements made in the Uruguay Round, the injury part of AD Agreement and SCM Agreement remains far less developed that the dumping and subsidy side.[192] The concept of "non-attribution" is mentioned in all the agreements, but how this test has to be performed in these agreements is not clearly spelt out.[193] Lack of clear understanding on some of the concepts has resulted incoherent interpretations by WTO panels and the Appellate Body. Some of these issues will be examined in greater detail in Chap. 3.

---

[189] PETROS.C. MAVROIDIS, GEORGE A. BERMANN & MARK WU, THE LAW OF THE WORLD TRADE ORGANIZATION (WTO) DOCUMENTS, CASES & ANALYSIS 628, 643-645 (WEST 2010).

[190] Barcelo III, *supra* note 130, at 257, 279 (arguing that countervailing duties in the United States under the 1979 laws have triggered a weak second level injury).

[191] Barcelo III, *supra* note 130, at 279.

[192] Angelos Pangratis and Edwin Vermulst, *Injury in Anti-Dumping Proceedings—The Need to Look Beyond the Uruguay Round Results*, 28(5) JOURNAL OF WORLD TRADE 61–96 (1994).

[193] Robert S. Pindyck, and Julio J. Rotemberg, *Are Imports to Blame? Attribution of Injury under the 1974 Trade Act*, 30, JOURNAL OF LAW AND ECONOMICS, 101, 122 (1987).

## H Conclusion

Trade remedy measures are policy instruments that seek to help the domestic industry facing import competition. Each of the three trade instruments, namely antidumping, countervailing duty, and safeguard investigations have specific threshold requirements and specific objectives. The motivation for the existence of each agreement is different. Antidumping had its genesis in predatory pricing practices, whereas countervailing duty arose from a desire to a create level playing fields in sectors and products distorted by government intervention; safeguard actions sought to create a balance between trade liberalization and compensating affected sectors for certain temporary periods.

Trade remedy instruments are highly political in nature. Treating factors such as dumped/subsidized imports themselves as causal factors for injury is a policy consideration in itself. In a world without trade remedies, it is quite unlikely that factors such as imports would be treated as a real cause of injury to domestic businesses and enterprises. Therefore, a pure scientific approach to injury and causation determination is not often possible, and even if possible, not wholly desirable. Had it been possible, a uniform approach and methodology could have been prescribed. Like in the case of antidumping, injury and causation provisions of various trade agreements were influenced by domestic policy considerations in some of the jurisdictions such as the U.S., Canada and the EU. While causation is a legal requirement, it will be necessary to understand the context in which such trade remedy agreements became popular. Without an understanding of their historical origin and evolution, it will be difficult to appreciate the role of trade remedies and the reasons for their existence. While negotiators and dispute settlement panels argue that the injury and causation standards in all three agreements are of different degrees, at an objective level, the various indicators identified for injury and causation are the same. On a reading of the treaty texts, one can argue that threshold for all these actions are different, with the safeguard actions calling for the strongest relationship between injury and imports. However, at a fundamental level, no investigating authority can say that the circumstances present in a case would qualify for material injury under antidumping or subsidies, but not for serious injury under safeguards. The purpose of this chapter is to postulate that injury and causation standard in a trade agreement often serves as a justification for an otherwise breach of the agreement; safeguard actions are not expected to be used often and, therefore, has a higher injury and causation threshold. Antidumping and CVD actions have an additional requirement of identifying dumping or subsidy and, thus, possess a lower injury and causation threshold. Material injury indicators and non-attribution language further act as side constraints, but, in essence, proving causation on the basis of one or several of these factors will be difficult.

In the above light, this chapter sought to trace and map the history and circumstances that led to the choice of a particular language on injury and causality in the treaty text. This history should inform and guide how the injury and causality determination shall be made. The historical developments in jurisdictions such as the U.S. and EU are, to an extent, unavoidable and should inform the debate on injury and causation in trade remedies.

At a time when several negotiating proposals have been submitted in the Doha Round Rules Negotiations on reforming and improving the trade remedy agreements, a comprehensive understanding of the history and negotiating proposals would be helpful to appreciate how some of the leading trade remedy jurisdictions addressed the injury and causality issues. The subsequent chapters provide specific discussions in the context of WTO dispute settlement, domestic practices and the ongoing treaty negotiations in the field of injury and causation.

# Appendix 1

## *Signatories of Kennedy Round Antidumping Code*

Kennedy Round negotiations were concluded by the end of 1967. According to information by the GATT secretariat as on 14 May, 1968, the following countries began the implementation of the tariff reductions resulting from the Kennedy Round on 1 January 1968:

| Signatories as on 14 May, 1968 | The following countries began the implementation on 1 July 1968 |
|---|---|
| 1. Australia | 1. Czechoslovakia |
| 2. New Zealand | 2. Israel |
| 3. South Africa | 3. Sweden |
| 4. Austria | 4. Denmark |
| 5. Peru | 5. Japan |
| 6. Switzerland | 6. Trinidad and Tobago |
| 7. Canada | 7. European Economic Community (Belgium, France, Germany, Italy, Luxembourg, Netherlands, Korea, United Kingdom, Finland, Norway, Greece, Spain) |
| 8. Poland (import commitment) | |
| 9. Turkey | |
| 10. Ireland | |
| 11. Portugal | |
| 12. United States | |

*Source* GATT

# Appendix 2

## *Signatories of Tokyo Antidumping and Subsidies Codes*

Multilateral instruments negotiated in the Tokyo Round came into force on 1st January, 1980. 12 parties have signed and accepted the agreement on Anti-dumping and 14 parties for the agreement on Subsidies and Countervailing Measures, as on 6th October, 1980.

| Anti-dumping code | | Subsidies code | |
|---|---|---|---|
| 1 | Austria | 1 | Austria |
| 2 | Canada | 2 | Brazil |
| 3 | Czechoslovakia | 3 | Canada |
| 4 | European Economic Community<br>1. Belgium<br>2. Denmark<br>3. France<br>4. Germany<br>5. Ireland<br>6. Italy<br>7. Luxembourg<br>8. Netherlands<br>9. United Kingdom | 4 | European Economic Community<br>1. Belgium<br>2. Denmark<br>3. France<br>4. Germany<br>5. Ireland<br>6. Italy<br>7. Luxembourg<br>8. Netherlands<br>9. United Kingdom |
| 5 | Finland | 5 | Finland |
| 6 | Hungary | 6 | India |
| 7 | Japan | 7 | Japan |
| 8 | Norway | 8 | Korea |
| 9 | Romania | 9 | Norway |
| 10 | Sweden | 10 | Pakistan |
| 11 | Switzerland | 11 | Sweden |
| 12 | United States | 12 | Switzerland |
| | | 13 | United States |
| | | 14 | Uruguay |

*Source* GATT

# Chapter 3
# Injury and Causation in Trade Remedy Investigations: An Analysis of the WTO Jurisprudence

**Abstract** This chapter provides a comprehensive examination of the injury and causation standards developed by the WTO panels and the Appellate Body in trade remedy disputes. The chapter, in particular, examines the utility of the trends analysis and the non-attribution test. The chapter examines whether the investigating agencies are required to adopt quantitative tools as opposed to qualitative tools in the causation determination. This chapter also explores the role of factors other than imports in the causation enquiry and stresses the role of a meaningful identification of all known factors, as opposed to only examining the statutory list of other causes which are causing injury to the domestic industry.

## A Introduction

Chapter 2 examined the historical evolution and the political economy surrounding the concept of injury and causal link in trade remedy investigations. Chapter 2 also traced the role of policy considerations in shaping the injury and causation provisions under various trade agreements and how they underwent significant changes over time. It was instructive to know how the degree of causation in various trade remedy agreements represented the interests of domestic lobbying and negotiating strategies adopted by some of the powerful trading nations. Having understood the considerations behind certain specific language in injury and causation provisions, this chapter examines the WTO jurisprudence on injury and causation in trade remedies and how a constructive interpretation of the relevant provisions could be undertaken to ensure that trade remedy instruments do not relapse into logical incoherence and possible disuse over time. By drawing on the WTO jurisprudence, this chapter examines the analytical tools employed in trade remedies for establishing injury and causation. A major focus of this chapter is on the conduct of the so called "non-attribution" test which is an essential part of the injury and causation analysis.



J.J. Nedumpara, *Injury and Causation in Trade Remedy Law*,
DOI 10.1007/978-981-10-2197-8_3

The use of sophisticated analysis or quantitative tools is a sensitive issue in injury and causation determination. As H. L. A. Hart and Tony Honoré note, causal judgments are not specifically legal, although the law may have to systematize them.[1] The recent advances in economic theory and analytical techniques in the field of quantitative analysis have made it possible to simulate the impact of various factors including trade effects with remarkable rigor and consistency.[2] Causation enquiries increasingly make use of complex econometric modeling and simulation in other fields of law and economics. As such, nothing in the Safeguards or the Antidumping/SCM Agreement discourages the use of quantitative tools by the concerned investigating agencies. Yet, intuitive judgments and common sense approaches have their rightful place. This chapter will also touch up on the role of qualitative and quantitative tools in assessing injury and causation.

Administrative agencies have a heavy burden in establishing that fair (increased) or unfair (dumped or subsidized) imports are the cause of injury. The interested parties constituting the domestic industry in the importing country would undoubtedly allege that the foreign imports have hurt their industry. They would array facts and figures on lost volume, lost market share, declining prices, lost profits, lack of profitability, unused capacities, dwindling return on investment and many other details.[3] Further, the domestic industry applicant would, in all likelihood, assert that most of the problems suffered by the domestic industry are attributable to imports. That is a common characteristic of all trade contingency remedies. The responding parties in all cases would probably argue that imports have nothing to do with the poor condition of the domestic industry, assuming that the allegation on injury has been conceded. The attempt would then be to shift the blame from imports to possible adverse shifts in market demand or domestic supply. In this context, establishing the causal connection between the imports and injury to the industry will be a crucial issue in trade remedy cases.

As discussed in Chap. 2, antidumping laws originated from antitrust concerns involving private business, but eventually settled down to deal with international price discrimination involving firms or enterprises. Initially, the intent to injure, destroy, or prevent the establishment of an industry or restrain competition became the leitmotif of the antidumping legislation.[4] Export or domestic subsidies, on the other hand, can create market distortions and was addressed mainly through countervailing duty actions, and through direct actions at the GATT/WTO. By contrast, safeguard actions do not require any unfair trade practice. Unexpected surge in imports as a result of certain unforeseen developments is the focus of enquiry in most safeguard investigations.

---

[1]H.L.A HART & TONY HONORE, CAUSATION IN LAW lv (2ND EDN. 1985).

[2]Roberta Piermartini & Robert Teh, *The Demystifying Modeling Methods for Trade Policy* (WTO Secretariat Discussion paper No. 10, *available at* https://www.wto.org/english/res_e/booksp_e/discussion_papers10_e.pdf.

[3]For instance, factors listed under Article 3 of the Safeguards Agreement.

[4]J. Michael Finger, The Origins and Evolution of Antidumping Regulation 12- 13 (1991) *in* ANTIDUMPING: HOW IT WORKS AND WHO GETS HURT 34 (J.M. Finger eds., 1991).

This chapter is organized as follows. Section B examines the reasons for following a common approach in determining injury and causation in all trade remedy agreements; Section C examines the importance of traditional tools such as the trends analysis. Section C also examines the WTO jurisprudence on injury and causation under the above three categories of trade remedies. Section D is devoted for an examination of the non-attribution requirement. This part also provides a discussion on the use of quantitative tools in this determination and on the utility of the "but-for" test. Section E concludes the key arguments and findings of this chapter.

## B Causal Link in Trade Remedy Investigations: Issues and Challenges in Implementation

### *1 Concept of Causal Link in WTO Trade Remedy Agreements*

The common law has long depended upon the legal metaphor of a "chain of causation". Chain of causation is defined in Black Law Dictionary as: (1) a series of events each caused by previous one, and; (2) the causal connection between cause and effect.[5] The verb "cause" is defined in Merriam Webster's Dictionary as, "to make (something) happen or exist: to be the cause of (something). According to the Shorter Oxford Dictionary, word "the cause" means "that which produces an effect or consequence; an antecedent or antecedents followed by a certain phenomenon"; it "indicates a condition or circumstance or combination of conditions and circumstances that effectively and inevitably calls forth an issue, effect or result or that materially aids in that calling forth."[6] The common dictionary meaning was relied upon by the WTO panel in *US–Steel Safeguards*, noting that "if a number of factors have caused serious injury, a causal link may be demonstrated if the increased imports have, in some way, contributed to 'bringing about', 'producing' or 'inducing' the serious injury".[7]

The chain of causation is a useful metaphor in understanding causation (See Fig. 1). Distractions of "new causes", "superseding events" or other "intervening forces" need not affect the causal chain. However, if the background completely shifts, thereby introducing news events and causal themes, the chain can be said to

[5]Black Law Dictionary (6th edn).

[6]Webster's New International Dictionary, 355-356 (3rd edn, 1981).

[7]Panel Report, *United States – Definitive Safeguard Measures on Imports of Certain Steel Products*, ¶10.290–293, WT/DS248/R/WT/DS249/R/WT/DS251/R/WT/DS252/R/WT/DS253/R/WT/DS254/R/WT/DS258/R/WT/DS259/R/and Corr.1, (December 10, 2003); See also Appellate Body Report, *United States – Definitive Safeguard Measures on Imports of Wheat Gluten from the European Communities*, ¶ 70 WT/DS166/AB/R (December 22, 2000).

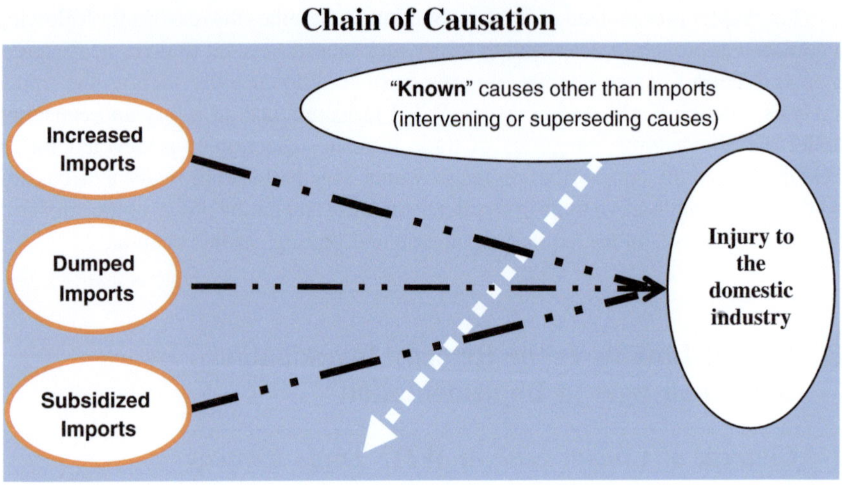


**Fig. 1** The metaphor of "chain of causation" in Trade Remedy Law

be broken.[8] As the following pictorial representation depicts, each independent event (i.e., dumped imports/subsidized imports or increased imports) could be capable of forming a causal link, unless there is a supervening event to break the chain of causation. The common law has adopted various tests such as the "proximate cause", "immediate cause", "probable cause", etc., to visualize the concept of a chain of causation. A more detailed discussion of Common Law concepts of causation is provided in Chap. 7 of this book.

## 2 *Injury and Causation: Why a Common Approach is Desirable for All Trade Remedy Actions?*

The previous chapter had examined the similarities and differences in the injury and causality provisions of the AD Agreement, SCM Agreement and the Safeguards Agreement. The previous chapter also identified several similarities between these agreements that could call for a unified approach in injury and causal link. More specifically, Article 3.5 of the AD Agreement, Article 15.5 of the SCM Agreement and Article 4.2(b) of the Safeguards Agreement have many things in common, as they provide in detail the need to establish a causal relationship between the alleged increased/dumped or subsidized imports and the injury caused to the domestic industry. The problematic issue, however, is the methodology and the manner of examination by investigating authority as to whether a causal link that was established earlier had

[8]The Panel in *EC–Fasteners* noted that the investigating agencies have a duty to examine whether causes other than the statutory causes break the causal link, *see* WT/DS 397/ R, ¶. 7.429.

snapped at any time. An unbroken chain of causation between increased imports and injury is considered as a necessary condition for the invocation of a trade remedy. While the Safeguards Agreement talks about "serious injury", the Antidumping as well the SCM Agreement requires "material injury".[9] Notably, the difference between the two terms is subtle. Serious injury is supposed to be at a level higher than the material injury.[10] While Article 4.2(b) of the Safeguards Agreement is an entirely new addition, the elements of Article 3.5 cannot be termed as something entirely new. The Tokyo Code on Antidumping had almost a similar provision. Interestingly, even the Kennedy Antidumping Code[11] contained specific provisions on injury and causality.

The treaty history of the injury and causation provisions of the AD Agreement/SCM Agreement may be a helpful reference in interpreting the causality provision in the Safeguards Agreement, considering the broad similarity in their current textual forms. As mentioned in Chap. 2, the Kennedy Code had required that dumped imports should be "demonstrably the principal cause of injury", whereas the Tokyo Code and the current AD Agreement had abandoned this test. Therefore, by analogy, one could argue that the drafters of the Safeguards Agreement had expressly avoided the "principal cause" requirement from the causation analysis. As is apparent, "principal cause" is a harsher standard than "a cause". But as this study examined in the previous chapter, there is no legislative definition of "material injury", nor is there any jurisprudential guidance on the exact scope of "serious injury".[12] The existence of a higher injury threshold under the Safeguards Agreement, in itself, does not explain why the causation analysis under both the agreements should be substantively different.[13]

Furthermore, a number previous WTO panels and the Appellate Body have made cross references to the corresponding provisions of the other trade remedy agreements and their existing jurisprudence. The panel in *US—Lamb* noted that the causation approach under the Safeguards Agreement is consistent with the reports of various GATT and WTO panels under the AD Agreement and SCM Agreement.[14] More specifically, the panel in *US—Lamb* made explicit reference to the reasoning of the reports of the Panels on *US—Atlantic Salmon* which was decided under the Tokyo Round Subsidies and Antidumping Codes.[15] As a matter

---

[9]Art. 3.4 of the Antidumping Agreement enlists the factors to be examined for assessing material.

[10]Appellate Body Report, *United States – Safeguard Measures on Imports of Fresh, Chilled or Frozen Lamb Meat from New Zealand and Australia*, ¶ 124, WT/DS177/AB/R, WT/DS178/AB/R, (May 1, 2001).

[11]Negotiated in 1967 by GATT Contracting Parties.

[12]Appellate Body Report, *Argentina – Safeguard Measures on Imports of Footwear*, ¶ 139, WT/DS121/AB/R, (December 14, 1999). [hereinafter Appellate Body, Argentina—Footwear].

[13]Petros. C. Mavroidis et al., The Law and Economics of Contingent Protection in the WTO, 479 (2008).

[14]Panel Report, *United States- Safeguard Measures on Imports of Fresh, Chilled or Frozen Lamb Meat from New Zealand and Australia*, ¶. 7.246, WT/DS 177, 178/ R, (December 21, 2000).

[15]Panel Report, *US—Lamb*, at ¶ 7.246.

of practice, most of the WTO panels have referred to the decision of the Appellate Body report in *US—Hot Rolled Steel* while explaining the meaning of the non-attribution clause in the SCM and the Safeguard Agreements.[16]

The similarities between the injury and causation provisions in the AD and CVD agreements are more evident. The provisions of Article 3.5 of the AD Agreement are almost similar to that of Article 15.5 of the SCM Agreement. Case law in WTO clearly reveals that the panels and the Appellate Body consider that interpretations given under AD Agreement could be equally valid for other trade remedy cases.[17] As the Panel in *US—DRAM* noted, there is a need for a consistent resolution of disputes on topics such as non-attribution in the injury and causation analysis.[18]

In order to provide a conceptual basis for injury and causality determination, this study provides a brief discussion of the economic rationale and the evidentiary tools used in order to establish injury and causal link in trade remedy investigations.

## 3 *Injury and Causation Under the WTO: A Comparison*

Beyond broadly incorporating the requirements of injury and causation, the current provisions of the Antidumping, Subsidies and Safeguards treaties do not explicitly clarify the methodology for carrying out such an examination. In the absence of clear guidelines, different jurisdictions interpret the injury and causation provisions differently and employ varying analytical tools. Under both the AD and the SCM Agreements, the investigating agencies are required to conduct an objective examination and provide positive evidence of dumped or subsidized imports and the consequent injury to the domestic industry. A similar requirement is present even under the Safeguards Agreement. In other words, investigating authorities are required to provide objective and verifiable information on the trend of imports and the prices at which they enter the importing country. Article 3.2 of the AD Agreement and 15.2 of the SCM Agreement require an investigating agency to consider whether there has been a significant increase in dumped or subsidized imports, either in absolute terms or relative to production and consumption in the importing country, and their price effects. A similar language is present in the Safeguards Agreement as well. Under Article 2.1 of the Safeguards Agreement, a Member may apply a safeguard measure on an article if "such product is being imported into its territory in such large quantities, absolute or relative to domestic

---

[16]*See* Panel Report, *US- Steel,* at ¶10.329; Appellate Body Report, *US—Line Pipe*, at ¶¶212-214.

[17]Panel Report, *United States – Sunset Review of Anti-Dumping Duties on Corrosion-Resistant Carbon Steel Flat Products from Japan*, ¶. 7.75, WT/DS244/R, (August 14, 2003).

[18]Panel Report, *United States – Countervailing Duty Investigation on Dynamic Random Access Memory Semiconductors (DRAMS) from Korea*, WT/DS296/R (20 July 2005). The Panel made reference to the Appellate Body's elaborate discussion on the non-attribution requirement in paragraphs 188-189 of *EC - Pipe Fittings*, an antidumping dispute.

**Table 1** Comparison of injury indicators in trade remedy agreements under the WTO

| Components of Domestic Industry Evaluation | Safeguards agreement | SCM agreement | Antidumping agreement |
|---|---|---|---|
| Sales | Sales | Sales | Sales |
| | Market share | Market share | Market share |
| Production & Operations | Production | Production | Production |
| | Productivity | Productivity | Productivity |
| | NA | Inventories | Inventories |
| | Employment | Employment | Employment |
| | NA | Wages | Wages |
| | Capacity utilization | Capacity utilization | Capacity utilization |
| Investing | NA | Return on investment | Return on investment |
| | NA | Ability to raise capital or investment | Ability to raise capital or investment |
| Financing | Profits and losses | Profits | Profits |
| General | NA | Growth | Growth |
| | NA | Cash flows | Cash flows |
| Residual factors | Rate and amount of increase in imports | Magnitude of subsidies margin | Magnitude of the dumping margin |
| | NA | Factors affecting prices | Factors affecting prices |

*Source* Own compilation. The author acknowledges Fernando Pierrola's clear exposition of this relationship between the injury factors in his book. See Fernando Pierola, THE CHALLENGE OF SAFEGUARDS IN THE WTO (2014)
*NA* means 'not available' or 'not included'

production, and under such conditions as to cause or threaten to cause serious injury to the domestic industry that produces like or directly competitive products."

Once the volume and price trends are examined, the investigating authority shall undertake to examine various economic and other factors such as actual and potential decline in output, sales, market share, profits, productivity, return on investment, capacity utilization of the industry, effects on cash flow, employment, wages, etc. Broadly, these factors can be broken down in terms of operating, investing or financing activity (see Table 1). These factors vary in the case of various trade remedy instruments. While the Antidumping and the SCM Agreements provide a more comprehensive list of injury indicators for evaluation, the Safeguards Agreement has a slightly narrower category of factors. For example, factors affecting prices is not a listed factor in Article 4 (2) of the Safeguards Agreement, although price related injury has a specific meaning under the other two agreements. A number of panels and the Appellate Body have held in several disputes that all the factors enlisted in the concerned agreements must be addressed in an investigation to provide a holistic analysis.[19]

[19]See Panel Report, *Egypt – Definitive Anti–Dumping Measures on Steel Rebar from Turkey,* ¶. 7.36, WT/DS211/R, (October 1, 2002); Panel Report, *European Communities – Anti-Dumping Duties on Imports of Cotton-type Bed Linen from India*, WT/DS141/R, ¶. 6.159; see also Panel

The factors indicated above are a priori considered to be relevant and informative of the situation of the domestic industry. This proposition was laid out by a WTO panel in *Korea–Diary*. According to the panel, a consideration of the factors listed is always relevant and unavoidable, even though the authority may later dismiss some of them as not having a bearing on the situation of that industry.[20]

Although the injury factors enlisted in the various trade remedy agreements are indicative and demonstrative of the state of the domestic industry, investigating authorities ascribe different weightage to certain injury factors even for causation determination. Oftentimes, a relative change in the market share is considered as a vital parameter, which could result from: (i) changes in total consumption, or (ii) changes in domestic sales of the product concerned. If total consumption remains the same or nearly constant, any relative changes in the share of the domestic producers could be attributed to import competition. In such a scenario, the imports are assumed to have caused market displacement. Trade remedy authorities give special emphasis to demand or market growth/loss in the context of the injury and causality determination. If the exporter gains market share at the expense of the domestic producers, it may be an indication that the exporter is gaining an advantage through price competition or through unfair means.

Profit and profitability of the domestic industry have special significance in the context of injury and causation examination. Profits and losses are the result of changes in the total sales revenue, costs and/or other expenses. At least three injury parameters enlisted in the trade remedy agreements have direct reference to profits.[21] These parameters include profitability, return on capital employed (ROCE) and cash flow. Gross profit is the amount a firm makes after deducting the cost of goods sold from its net sales; once the company deducts the selling, general and administrative expenses, it arrives at the operating profit. A company arrives at its net profit after deducting various interest and finance expenses. Profitability gives an indication of profits after depreciation and interest. ROCE is the profits after making adjustments for depreciation, but before interest. Cash flow is profits before depreciation but after interest. These financial parameters have special relevance in the context of injury and causal link.

Investigating authorities often look at the profit levels of the domestic industry and other factors such as sales, market share, return on investment, etc. in determining injury. One factor which is often examined by investigating authorities is lost sales. However, it is not a listed factor in any of these agreements although it

---

(Footnote 19 continued)

Report, *Mexico – Anti–Dumping Investigation of High Fructose Corn Syrup (HFCS) from the United States*, ¶. 7. 128, WT/DS132/R, (February 24, 2000); Panel Report, *European Communities – Anti-Dumping Duties on Malleable Cast Iron Tue or Pipe Fittings from Brazil*, ¶.7.304, WT/DS219/R, (March 7, 2003).

[20]Panel Report, *Korea – Definitive Safeguard Measure on Imports of Certain Dairy Products*, WT/DS98/R and Corr.1, ¶. 7.55 (January 12, 2000).

[21]V. Lakshmi Kumaran, The 10 Major Problems with the Antidumping Instrument in India, 39(1) JOURNAL OF WORLD TRADE 115, 122 (2005).

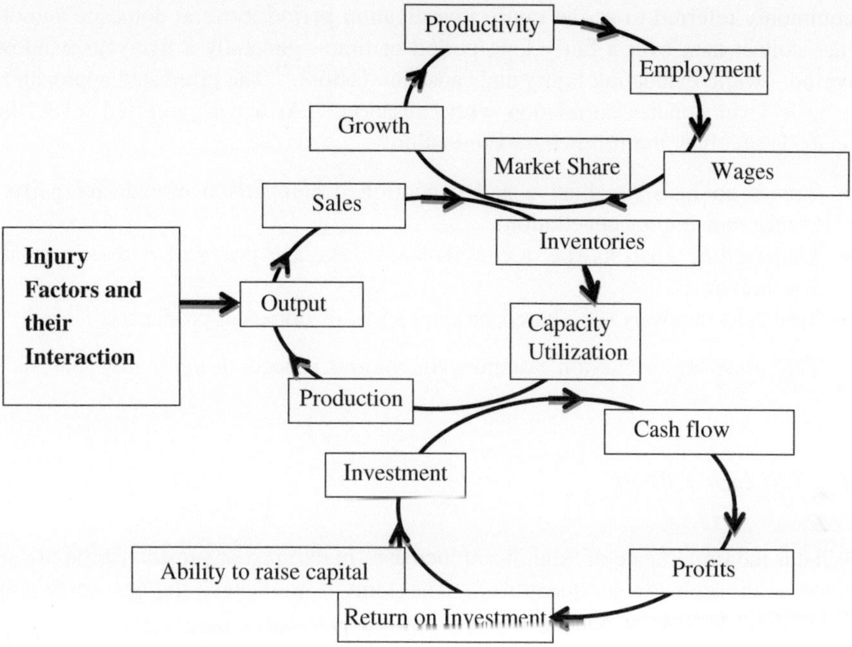


**Fig. 2** Interplay of injury factors. *Source* Own compilation

may have certain overlapping with market share. It is often seen that the various financial/non-financial factors can have cascading effects on each other as most of these injury factors are directly linked to each other (see Fig. 2).

## C Role of Trends Analysis

In the absence of clear guidelines or evidentiary tool in the conduct of injury and causation analysis, most investigating authorities depend on anecdotal evidence of domestic industry developments and simple correlation among import levels, domestic production and shipments. Certain jurisdictions, such as the U.S. have incorporated the trends analysis in their so-called "bifurcated analysis".[22] This approach first enquires whether the domestic industry has suffered the injury and second, whether the alleged imports have contributed to the injury. If the volume of fair or unfair imports increases, while the condition of the domestic industry declines in its various dimensions, causation will be typically inferred. This approach looks at the trends over a representative period of time, which is

[22]K.H. Kelly & M.E. Mokre, *One Lump or Two: Unitary Versus Bifurcated Measures of Injury at the USITC,* (Federal Trade Commission Working Paper No. 282, 2006).

commonly referred to as the injury investigation period. Several domestic authorities collect data over a fairly long period of time—generally a five-year window period—while evaluating injury and causation factors.[23] The bifurcated approach at a basic level equates correlation with causation.[24] At a disaggregated level, the analysis involves the following examination:

- Trends analysis (qualitative and uncontrolled comparison of industry performance and import penetration)
- Underselling analysis (i.e. a comparison of average prices of domestic goods and imports)
- Lost sales analysis (i.e., based on the claims of domestic producers)

The following discussion examines the various aspects of the trends analysis.

## 1 *Volume Effects*

What is the importance of "significant increase" in dumped or subsidized imports or imports in such "large quantities"? The term "significant" implies something "important, notable or consequential".[25] In *EC—DRAM*, a dispute that involved a CVD measure, the Panel noted that the term "significant" implies something more than just a nominal or marginal movement.[26] Recent trends in imports are important in the context of all trade remedy investigations and especially vital in the case of safeguard actions. As the Appellate Body noted in *Argentina—Footwear*, one of the earliest safeguards disputes at the WTO, the competent authorities are required to look at trends in imports over the period of investigation and that the "increase in imports must have been sudden enough, sharp enough, and significant enough… to cause or threaten to cause 'serious injury'"[27]

As examined in the previous chapter, the negotiating history of these agreements does not explain the importance of terms such as "significant increase" and "large quantities", in the injury and causation analysis. According to Miranda, it is at best doubtful whether this provision was meant to be part of the injury analysis.[28] Based on this reasoning, if there is a pronounced drop in the imports just before the initiation of the investigations, will an antidumping or CVD action be dropped on the ground that there is no injury? The alternative view is that the volume of

---

[23]*Sykes*, *infra* note 126 at 135; see also Appellate Body Report, *Argentina—Footwear*, ¶ 131.

[24]MICHAEL J. TREBILCOCK, UNDERSTANDING TRADE LAW 68 (2011).

[25]Panel Report, *United States—Subsidies on Upland Cotton*, ¶ 7.1326, WT/DS267/R, (March 21, 2005).

[26]Panel Report, *European Communities—Countervailing Measures on DRAM Chips*, ¶ 7.307, WT/DS299/R, (June 17, 2005) [hereinafter Panel Report *EC-DRAM*].

[27]Appellate Body Report, *Argentina—Footwear*, ¶131.

[28]Jorge Miranda, *Causal Link and Non-attribution as Interpreted in WTO Trade Remedy Disputes,* 44 (4) JOURNAL OF WORLD TRADE 729, 736 (2010).

dumped or subsidized imports could be more appropriate in the context of a causation analysis.[29] In other words, findings on volume and price effects identified under Article 3.2 of the AD Agreement and 15.2 of the SCM Agreement will have to be expressly linked to Article 3.5 and Article 15.5 of the AD Agreement and SCM Agreement respectively. This proposition was supported by the Panel decision in *EC—DRAM*.[30] The Panel noted that the causal link requirement under the AD Agreement can be met by showing a coincidence in time between the adverse price effects of the dumped imports and the decline in indicators reflecting the performance of the domestic industry.[31] In the case of the Safeguards Agreement, the coincidence-in-time or temporal analysis of imports is a distinct requirement, although it could be subsumed within the causality determination. Further, in the case of AD and SCM Agreements, the trend analysis is a key element of the causality determination, although it could be argued that it is part of a separate and distinct element.

How could a coincidence in time provide insightful information? According to Douglas Irvin, WTO Panels seem to agree that the coincidence of an increased level of imports and a lower level of domestic industry activity usually indicates that imports have caused injury.[32] To provide an example, if there is an absolute increase in the volume of imports accompanied by a declining trend in the performance of the domestic industry, the simultaneous occurrence of these factors could be a strong indicator of not only injury, but also causation. As is evident, some injury factors are linked to import-related movements. An immediate example is the rate and amount of imports and the share of consumption captured by imports. It is axiomatic that when the domestic demand remains constant, any increase in imports will result in a reduction in market share of the domestic industry. In *Argentina—Footwear*, the Panel had an opportunity to comment on the trend analysis in this type of scenarios. The Panel noted that the market share by volume and value "largely track the data on the absolute volumes and values of imports".[33] In the opinion of the Panel, "an upward trend in import volume, coinciding with a downward trend in the indicators portraying the condition of the domestic industry could be probative of causation."[34] The Panel noted:

> In practical terms, we believe therefore that this provision means that if causation is present, an increase in imports normally should coincide with a decline in the relevant injury factors. While such a coincidence by itself cannot *prove* causation (because, *inter alia*, Article 3 requires an explanation – i.e., "findings and reasoned conclusions"), its absence would

[29]Petros C. Mavroidis et al., The Law Of The World Trade Organization (WTO): Documents, Cases & Analysis 470 (2010).

[30]Panel Report, *EC—DRAM*, at ff. 277.

[31]*Id.*

[32]Douglas A. Irvin, *Causing Problems: The WTO Review of Causation and Injury Attribution in US Section 201 Cases*, 2(3) World Trade Review 297, 301 (2003).

[33]Panel Report, *Argentina –Safeguard Measures on Imports of Footwear*, ¶. 8.242, WT/DS121/R, (June 25, 1999)[hereinafter Panel Report, *Argentina—Footwear*].

[34]Panel Report, *Argentina—Footwear,* ¶ 8.229.

> create serious doubts as to the existence of a causal link, and would require a *very* compelling analysis of why causation still is present.[35]

This key observation of the Panel, which was subsequently upheld by the Appellate Body, posits that the movement in imports and the movement in injury factors should be in tandem.[36] The Appellate Body also came out with a resounding affirmation of the trends analysis in this dispute. The Appellate Body introduced the postulation that "if causation is present, an increase in imports normally should coincide with a decline in the relevant injury factors."[37] The Appellate Body agreed with the panel, which had noted:

> In making our assessment of the causation analysis and finding, we note in the first instance, that Article 4.2(a) requires the authority to consider the 'rate' (i.e., the direction and speed) and "amount" of increase in imports and the share of the market then taken by imports as well as changes in injury factors (sales, production, productivity, capacity utilization, profit and losses and employment) in reaching a conclusion as to injury and causation. As noted above, we consider that this language means that the trends—in both injury factors and imports—matter as much their absolute levels. In the particular context of causation analysis, we also believe that this provision means that it is the relationship between the movements in imports and injury factors that must be central to a causation analysis and determination.[38]

Conversely, if the trend analysis show contradictory movements, it may be possible to disprove the existence of causation. As the Panel in *Argentina–Footwear* noted, lack of coincidence would create serious doubts as to the existence of causal link.[39] In other words, a negative correlation may be an indication of lack of causation.

The coincidence analysis is in practice the first step to demonstrate a causal link between imports and injury to the domestic industry. However, further analysis may be required if there are special conditions of competition that may cast doubt on this coincidence, for example, the fact that imported and domestic goods are not price-sensitive. Furthermore, an increase in imports may not have a direct and immediate impact on injury parameters such as sales, output, production, productivity, profits and losses, capacity utilization and employment. If there is a temporal lag between the surge of imports and the manifestation of the injurious effects, can it be said that there is still a relevant coincidence? The Panel in *US—Steel* has noted that these indicators are expected "to reach shortly after an increase in imports".[40] However, the Panel admitted the possibility there might be temporal lags between increase in imports and injury.[41] In *US—Steel*, the WTO Panel reviewed product

[35]Panel Report, *Argentina Footwear,* 8.237-8.238; *See also* Panel Report, *United States – Definitive Safeguard Measures on Imports of Certain Steel Products*, WT/DS252/R, ¶. 10.320 (July 11, 2003). [hereinafter Panel Report, *US-Steel*].

[36]Appellate Body Report, *Argentina – Footwear*, ¶. 144.

[37]*Id.*

[38]Panel Report, *Argentina—Footwear,* ¶¶.8.237–8.238.

[39]Appellate Body Report, *Argentina—Footwear* ¶7.398.

[40]Panel Report, *US – Steel Safeguards*, ¶ 10.375.

[41]*Id*, ¶10.310.

specific findings of the USITC to examine whether there had been coincidence-in-time between the upward trend in import volume and in the downward trend of several economic parameters of the domestic industry. In regard to three products, namely, certain carbon flat-rolled steel (CCFRS), fittings, flanges and tool joints (FFTJ), and stainless steel bar (SSB), the Panel examined the trends in various domestic industry indicators such as (1) volume of production; (2) the volume of sales; (3) the operating margin; (4) employment; and (5) the productivity in terms of man power. The Panel noted:

> … there may be instances in which injury may be suffered by an industry at the same point in time as the influx of increased imports. However, the injury that is caused at that point in time may not become apparent until some later point in time. In other words, there may be a lag between the influx of imports and the manifestation of the injurious effects on the domestic industry of such an influx.[42]

Furthermore, the Panel in *US—Steel*, agreed with the approach followed by another WTO Panel in *Egypt—Steel Rebar,*[43] an antidumping dispute. In *Egypt–Steel Rebar*, the Panel rejected the argument made by the complainant Turkey that there must be a strict temporal connection between the increased imports and any injury being suffered by the industry.[44] The Panel in *Egypt—Rebar* acknowledged that there could be transaction costs that might impede an immediate reflection of price changes in the situation of the domestic industry. The *Egypt—Rebar* Panel noted:

> [R]este[d] on the quite artificial assumption that the market instantly absorbs, and reacts to, imports the moment they enter the territory of the importing company. Such an assumption implicitly rests on the existence of so-called "perfect information" in the market (i.e., that all actors in the market are instantly aware of all market signals.)[45]In the case of lag in imports and the manifestation of effects on injury parameters, various WTO panels have emphasised on the obligation of the investigating authority to explain this factor with objective data.[46]

The *US—Steel* Panel drew strength from the reasoning of the WTO Panel in *Egypt—Steel Rebar*. The *US—Steel* Panel noted:

> [W]hile lags may be expected in relation to some factors (for example, employment), lags in the manifestation of effects are less likely to exist in relation to other injury factors such as production, inventories and capacity utilization, which, ordinarily, would react relatively quickly to changes taking place in the market, such as an influx of imports if increased imports are causing serious injury. If the competent authority does rely upon a lag as between the increased imports and the injury factors, we consider that such a lag must be fully explained by the competent authority on the basis of objective data.[47]

---

[42]Panel Report, *US – Steel Safeguards*, ¶. 10.310.

[43]Panel Report, *Egypt – Definitive Anti–Dumping Measures on Steel Rebar from Turkey*, WT/DS211/R, (October 1, 2002)[ hereinafter, Panel Report, Egypt Steel Rebar].

[44]Panel Report, *US – Steel Safeguards*, ¶. 10.310.

[45]Panel Report, *US – Steel Safeguards*, ¶. 7. 129.

[46]Panel Report, *Egypt – Steel Rebar*, ¶.7.129.

[47]Panel Report, *US – Steel Safeguards,* ¶. 10.312.

The above discussion indicates that the question of delay or time lags is one of the most significant considerations in the coincidence analysis. The length of time lags, jointly with the homogeneity of the products as well as their likeness or direct competitiveness, sheds light on how competitive a market is. It appears that long lags jointly with rather heterogeneous or directly competitive products would call for an analysis of conditions of competition in that market. The 'conditions of competition' analysis generally looks at price related factors.

Whilst a temporal correlation has been considered as central to injury and causation analysis in the context of the Safeguard Agreement, its role in the context of AD Agreement and SCM Agreement has been somewhat uncertain. In the context of AD and SCM Agreements, some complainant members have argued that in the absence of a temporal correlation between dumping/subsidization and the decline in the performance of the domestic industry, the panel should rule that no causal link was established.[48] According to the Panel in *EC—DRAM*, an investigation authority has considerable latitude in determining whether a significant increase, either in absolute terms or relative to production or consumption, has taken place.[49] The *EC—DRAM* Panel suggested that countervailing measures may be imposed even in the absence of a significant increase in the volume of subsidized imports, provided that the price effects exist. The Panel was persuaded by a language in Article 15.2 of the SCM Agreement (last sentence of Art. 15.2 of SCM Agreement) that "[n]o one or several of these [volume and price effect] factors can necessarily give decisive guidance".[50] The *EC—DRAM* Panel preferred to concur with the observation of another WTO Panel in *US—DRAM*, which noted that there was no generalized requirement to establish a temporal correlation between increased imports and injury to the domestic industry.[51] The *US—DRAM* panel noted that the absence of a temporal correlation certainly raises a flag, but it is not an absolute barrier to finding of injury.[52]

In conclusion, the volume and direction of imports is an essential element of an injury and causation analysis although the degree of its importance could vary. Especially in the case of the Safeguards Agreement, the requirement of increased or recent surge in imports is a matter of central focus and a separate threshold; it is also an indicator in the coincidence-in-time or correlation analysis. Likewise, the AD and the SCM Agreements too lay emphasis in the movement in imports as a key step in the causation analysis.

---

[48]Panel Report, *United States – Countervailing Duty Investigation on Dynamic Random Access Memory Semiconductors (DRAMS) from Korea*, ¶ 7.318, WT/DS296/R (July 20, 2005) [hereinafter Panel Report, *US- DRAM*].

[49]Panel Report, *US- DRAM*, ¶ 7.308.

[50]Panel Report, *US- DRAM*, at fn. 277.

[51]Panel Report, *US- DRAM*, ¶. 7.320.

[52]Panel Report, *US- DRAM*, ¶. 7.320.

## 2 *Price Effects: Concept of Price Undercutting and Underselling Analysis*

The Panel in *Egypt—Steel Rebar* stated that an investigating authority must in every case include a price analysis of the type mentioned in Articles 3.1 and 3.2 of the AD Agreement.[53] The price effects also constitute a part of the trends or coincidence-in-time analysis. A failure to conduct an analysis of the price effects could be a violation of the AD Agreement or the SCM Agreement.

The scope of price analysis in the Safeguard Agreement is slightly unclear. While a price analysis is explicitly required under the AD and SCM Agreements, there is a glaring omission of this concept under the Safeguard Agreement.[54] Importantly, Article XIX of the GATT as well as Article 2 of the Safeguard Agreement refers to the phrase "and under such conditions". The Panel, in *US—Wheat Gluten*, noted that although price is not mentioned as a relevant factor that needs to be examined, it will have a role in a causation analysis as part of the *conditions of competition* between the imported and domestic product.[55] In *US—Wheat Gluten*, the Appellate Body noted that "conditions of competition" related to the "prevailing 'conditions' in the market place".[56] This approach was also supported by the WTO panel in *US–Steel*.[57] In short, the role of price effect analysis is not ruled out in safeguards investigations.

In most antidumping and CVD investigations, the investigating authority will enquire whether the dumped or subsidized imports had either depressed or suppressed prices in the import market. In particular, an investigating authority should examine whether the dumped or subsidized imports have resulted in:

(a) Price undercutting; or
(b) Price suppression; or
(c) Price depression

The investigating authorities traditionally examine the nexus between the import penetration, import selling prices and the domestic selling price. The authorities may also look at factors such as market share and lost sales. However, the traditionally

---

[53]Panel Report, *Egypt- Steel Rebar*, ¶. 7.73.

[54]Panel Report, *Korea- Definitive Safeguard Measure on Imports of Certain Dairy Products*, ¶¶ 7.51–52, WT/DS98/R (June 21, 1999) [hereinafter Panel Report, Korea—Diary].

[55]Panel Report, *United States – Definitive Safeguard Measures on Imports of Wheat Gluten from the European Communities*, ¶ 8.109, WT/DS/166/R, (July 31, 2000) [hereinafter "Panel report, *US-Wheat Gluten*"]; see also Panel Report, *Argentina-Footwear*, at ¶ 8.250-51. The European Communities argued that the phrase "under such conditions" require a price comparison, but the panel did not explain what this analysis requires. The panel, however, noted that products may compete with each other along a variety of dimensions.

[56]Appellate Body Report, *US—Wheat Gluten*, ¶ 78.

[57]Panel Report, *US— Steel Safeguards*, ¶ 10.516.

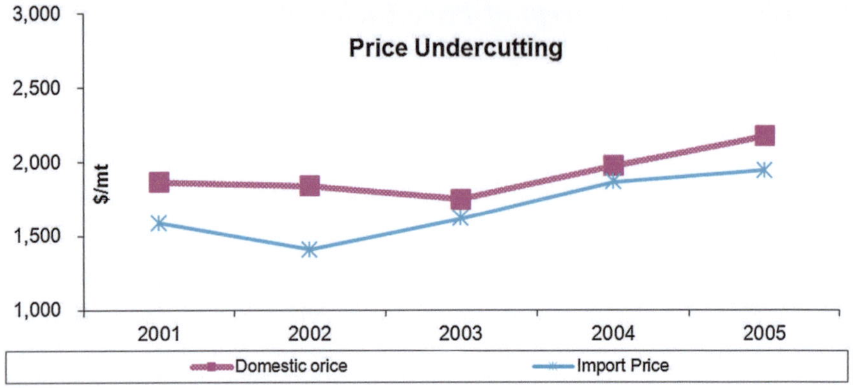


**Fig. 3** Price Undercutting illustration

used analytical tool is the "margin analysis".[58] Margin analysis corresponds to a kind of common sense understanding of dumping/subsidy and its effects. But the margin analysis is not limited to dumping/subsidy aspects only; it can also measure the impact on domestic industry prices and is widely known as "injury margin" analysis. The price/injury margin analysis is analogous to the dumping margin analysis; the only difference is that instead of taking the exporters' home market price, it takes the domestic industry net selling price or, if that price unreliable, a constructed non-injurious price, and compares it with the landed value of imports.

Injury margin or price effects analysis is done in almost all antidumping investigations and in a number of safeguard investigations in different jurisdictions.[59] Margin analyses are generally conducted through price undercutting analysis and price underselling analysis. The price undercutting margin measures (in percentage terms) the degree to which the landed price of imports is lower than the selling prices of comparable domestic like product during the injury investigation period. The price undercutting analysis assumes that under competitive conditions, imported product should be sold at higher prices than the domestic product.[60] The term price undercutting was interpreted by a Panel in *EC—Pipe Fittings* as referring to a situation where the imported products were priced below the domestic products.[61] (For an illustration, see Fig. 3). Price underselling on the other hand measures in percentage terms the degree to which the landed price of imports is lower than the target price or the non-injurious price of the comparable domestic like product.

[58]The author would like to clarify that the term margin analysis is different from the 'margin analysis' used in jurisdictions such as the United States which traditionally use dumping or subsidy margins. The author is grateful to Nithya Nagarajan for bringing explanation to his attention.

[59]Judith Czacko et al., A Handbook on Antidumping Investigations 339 (2003).

[60]A. Pangratis and E. Vermulst, *Injury in Antidumping Proceedings: The Need to Look Beyond the Uruguay Round Results*, 28(5) Journal of World Trade 61, 90 (1994).

[61]Panel Report, *EC— Pipe Fittings*, ¶. 7.268.

In other words, the margin analysis compute the extent to which the imports have led to either price depression (in the case of price undercutting) or price suppression (in the case of price underselling).

An understanding of the concept of price suppression and price depression is important in appreciating the role of price effects. In *Korea—Commercial Vessels*, the WTO panel referred to price suppression and price depression as including a certain built-in concept of causation in the sense that the extent of price suppression or depression could be reflective of the effects of the unfair imports on injury factors.[62] Neither Article 3.2 of the AD Agreement nor Article 15.2 of the SCM Agreement provides any particular methodology for conducting a price analysis. The Panel and the Appellate Body in *US—Upland Cotton* expressly referred to the meaning of these terms.[63] The Panel interpreted "price suppression" as referring to a situation where the prices are either prevented or inhibited from rising (i.e., they do not increase when they otherwise would have) or they do actually increase, but the increase is less than it otherwise would have been.[64] On the other hand, the Panel interpreted "price depression" as referring to a scenario where the prices are pressed down or reduced.[65] Although these are distinct concepts, the above interpretation would imply that both price suppression and depression could overlap in certain ways, especially in scenarios where prices are pressed down.[66] To explain, the Panel and the Appellate Body appeared to agree with the interpretation that price suppression would envisage scenarios where there is an actual decline in the domestic prices (which otherwise would not have declined and, therefore, implying price depression) as well as a less than desirable increase in prices (which would have otherwise increased to a much greater degree).[67]

Price undercutting analysis is quite helpful in establishing a presumption of causal connection. For instance, if the average domestic unit price of a product is declining, matched with declining average unit price of imports and resulting in a higher share of imports, one could conclude that there is a strong correlation between the decline in the domestic prices and imports. Pervasive undercutting is often an indication of price related injury if the import prices fall below the domestic selling price. A producer will generally reduce the selling price only if the costs of sales are correspondingly getting reduced. Otherwise, it could impact the profitability of the business. Again, a domestic industry could still sell without

---

[62]Panel Report, *Korea – Measures Affecting Trade in Commercial Vessels*, ¶ 7.534 WT/DS273/R (April 11, 2005). [hereinafter Panel Report, *Korea- Commercial Vessels*].

[63]Panel Report, *United States – Subsidies on Upland Cotton*, WT/DS267/R, Corr.1, and Add.1 to Add.3 (March 21, 2005) as modified by Appellate Body Report, WT/DS267/AB/R (March 3, 2005).

[64]*Id.*, ¶ 1388.

[65]This is interpretation is also in line with the interpretation in Panel Report in *Korea- Commercial Vessels*, ¶ 7.537.

[66]Appellate Body Report, *US—Upland Cotton*, ¶ 424.

[67]Appellate Body Report, *US—Upland Cotton*, ¶ 423; *See* also Panel Report, *US- Upland Cotton*, ¶ 7.1277.

**Table 2** Categories of HP SST

| | |
|---|---|
| Grade A | Least expensive and the lowest grade |
| Grade B | Middle grade |
| Grade C | Most expensive and the highest grade |

reducing average unit prices, but the market share and capacity utilization may get affected. Therefore, price undercutting analysis in conjunction with the performance of other financial parameters of the industry in most straightforward cases could give some inference on whether injury is attributable to imports or not.

One should add a caveat here. The relevance of a price undercutting analysis depends on obtaining accurate price levels of both the imports and the domestic industry like products. Furthermore, the results of price undercutting analysis would also differ based on the methodologies adopted and the comparison levels. For example, issues such as the level of trade, choice of comparison period, whether such comparison should be made at a transaction-to-transaction level or on a weighted average basis, etc., remain inconclusive.[68] It is important to recall the finding of the Appellate Body in *China—GOES* case wherein it was held that "when a price comparison is made for the purposes of an undercutting analysis under Article 3.2 …, it is necessary to ensure that the prices being considered are actually comparable."[69]

A similar issue arose in *China—X-Ray Equipment*[70] as well as in in *China—HP-SST (Japan)* and *China- HP-SST (EU)*.[71] Both these cases touched upon the methodology to be applied in a price undercutting finding in an injury analysis. In the *China—X-Ray Equipment* case, the MOFCOM, China's government agency, examined the price effects of the product (including both high energy and low energy scanners meant for different purposes) without ensuring model-to-model price comparison—an approach which was disapproved by the WTO panel. The Panel held that MOFCOM failed to fulfill its obligations under Article 3.2 of the AD Agreement while conducting the price effects analysis.[72] In *China—HP-SST (Japan)*, there were three categories of high-performance stainless steel in the underlying antidumping investigation. These categories were Grade-A, Grade-B, and Grade-C (Table 2).

[68]*See* Petros C. Mavroidis et al., The Law of the World Trade Organization (WTO) Documents, Cases & Analysis 470 (2010).

[69]Appellate Body Report, *China – Countervailing and Anti-Dumping Duties on Grain Oriented Flat-Rolled Electrical Steel from the United States*, WT/DS414/AB/R (Nov.16, 2012) [hereinafter Appellate Body Report, *China- GOES*].

[70]Panel Report, *China-Definitive Anti-Dumping Duties on X-Ray Security Inspection Equipment from the European Union*, WT/DS425/R, (April 24, 2013) [hereinafter Panel Report, *China – X-Ray Equipment*].

[71]Appellate Body Report, *China - Measures Imposing Anti-Dumping Duties on High-Performance Stainless Steel Seamless Tubes ("HP-SSST") from Japan*, ¶. 5.519, WT/DS454/AB/R, (Oct. 14, 2015) [hereinafter Appellate Body Report, *China - HP-SSST (Japan)*].

[72]Panel Report, *China – X-Ray Equipment*, ¶. 7.65-7.68.

The European Union argued in this case that the majority of the domestic (Chinese) production is in Grade A products and that the MOFCOM should not have made a finding of price undercutting for Grades B and C (the majority of imported product types) on a comparison to the domestic prices for the like products *as a whole* including domestic Grade A HP-SST. More specifically, while the market share held by the imported Grade A product types comprised less than 2 % of the market share, the share of imported Grade B and C product types comprised more than 90 % of the respective market segments. The MOFCOM, however, concluded that the dumped HP-SST imports had an effect on the domestic industry as a whole.

The Appellate Body observed that an objective examination of price undercutting should have taken into account the relevant market shares of the respective product types.[73] Appellate Body also noted that the price undercutting analysis should not be based on a "static" examination, but should involve a "dynamic assessment" of prices and trends.[74] This examination, according to the Appellate Body, "includes assessing whether import and domestic prices are moving in the same or contrary directions, and whether there has been a sudden and sharp increase in the domestic prices".[75]

Price undercutting comparisons are generally more difficult in the case of safeguards when compared to antidumping or CVD investigation since the product scope is much wider in the case of the former and the reported import prices may vary substantially due to product differences. Furthermore, detailed product matching based on product control numbers (PCNs) or CONNUMs are not usually done in the case of safeguard investigations as done in the case of antidumping or CVD investigations. Generally, such calculations would be based on import data which are generally quite inaccurate and unspecific. Further, there could be other factors which may affect purchasing decisions. Notwithstanding these limitations, undercutting trends could provide an overall picture of the trend of import prices and the impact it may have on domestic prices.

Price underselling analysis is also a useful indicator of injury and the existence of causal connection with imports. The premise behind the price underselling analysis is that in view of the low landed value of imports, the domestic industry is unable to pass on the higher costs such as fixed costs, variable costs and other selling expenses by way of higher product prices. Inability to pass on the higher costs to the consumers may result in operating losses and consequent injury. Existence of a "cost/price squeeze" is often an evidence of injury attributable to imports. For an illustration see Fig. 4.

In order to estimate the price suppression, the investigating agencies may have to calculate a ratio of the weighted average cost of goods sold ("COGS") to the net sales value during the investigation period. The most practical difficulty with price underselling analysis is that the investigating agency will have to compile the cost and sales data for a period of at least 3–5 years (depending the type of trade remedy

[73]Appellate Body Report, *China-HPSST (Japan)* ¶. 5.180.

[74]Ibid, ¶. 5. 181.

[75]Ibid, ¶. 5. 159.

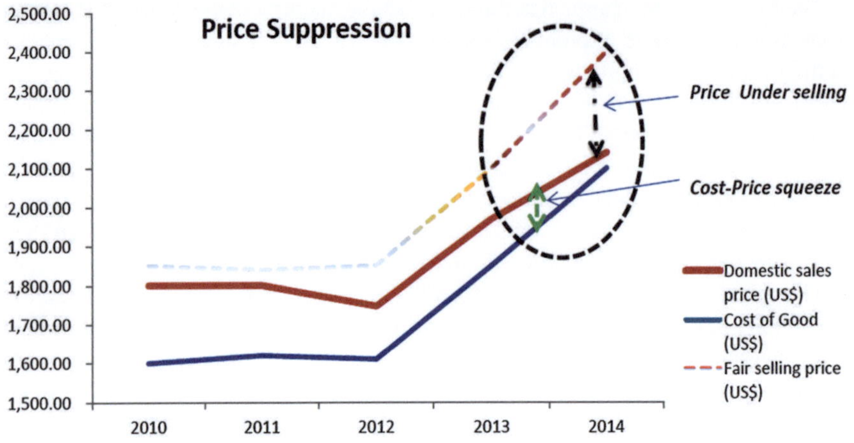


**Fig. 4** Price suppression illustration

involved) which is too cumbersome for any agency and the participating domestic producers.

It is seen in practice that price underselling analysis which is determined on the basis of target or non-injurious prices would be a more effective and scientific tool for measuring the impact of imports on domestic prices. The reasons are obvious. In certain cases, if the domestic prices are already depressed the undercutting margin would not adequately reflect the extent of injury. Again, the domestic industry might have adopted a low pricing policy to ward off domestic competition and in such a case, attributing the injury to dumped or subsidized imports may not be appropriate. Furthermore, price suppression is assessed on the basis of data pertaining to the domestic like product only and does not involve a comparison with the price of the imported product. It will not be necessary for the investigating authority to make complex adjustments for price comparison purposes.[76]

In conclusion, one could say that in practice the price effects or margin analysis has high evidentiary value in establishing injury and causation, but they are not conclusive evidence of injury and causal link. As the maxim goes, correlation is not causation. The Appellate Body ruling in *China—GOES* emphasizes that the price effects analysis can help the investigating agencies examine whether the subject imports can provide an explanatory force for the occurrence of significant depression or suppression of domestic prices.[77] As the Appellate Body notes, such an analysis can provide a "meaningful basis" in the injury and causation determination.[78]

[76]Panel Report, *China – Definitive Anti-Dumping Duties on X-Ray Security Inspection Equipment from the European Union*, ¶ 7.52–54, WT/DS425/R and Add.1 (April 24, 2013). [hereinafter Panel report, *China-X-Ray*].

[77]Appellate Body Report, *China—GOES*, ¶ ¶152,154.

[78]Appellate Body Report, *China—GOES*, ¶ 154.

A review of WTO trade remedy law and country practices suggest that the price effect or price margin analyses—even in its crude form—remain perhaps the only analytical tool applicable to a vast number of WTO Members to conduct the correlation analysis in the causation enquiry. The details of the application of margin analysis among various WTO members will be examined in the next chapter.

## 3 *Trends Analysis and Conceptualizing the Requirement of "Through the Effects"*

An examination of WTO trade remedy disputes reveals that in most jurisdictions the traditional analysis of causation has been driven by anecdotal evidence of domestic industry developments and simple correlation among import levels, domestic production and shipments. At a fundamental level, the analysis involves the trends or the correlation examination.

Under the trends analysis, if market penetration of imports has occurred when domestic industry profits, domestic prices and output have declined, it is a kind of "evidence" that imports have been causing problems. Unless there is a compelling qualitative evidence to force a disconnect in this simple analysis, import volumes and prices are considered to be the cause of injury to the domestic industry.

Article 3.5 of the AD Agreement as well as Article 15.5 of the SCM Agreement provides that dumped/subsidized imports must be shown to have caused injury to the domestic industry "through the effects of dumping" or "through the effects of subsidy" as the case may be. One of the central issues regarding this term was whether it was sufficient for the investigating agency to establishment a finding of injury purely on volume and price effects if there were other factors, perhaps more significant factors, causing injury.[79] Legal scholars such as John H. Jackson highlighted the importance of the effects of dumping or subsidy margin, which could have caused the injury to the domestic industry. In other words, it was desired that the scope of antidumping or CVD remedies would be available only when the magnitude of dumping or subsidies were to cause certain effects. According to this view, a *de minimis* level of dumping or subsidy could not have caused injury. Professor Jackson noted as follows:

> The GATT Subsidies Code explicitly states, 'It must be demonstrated that the subsidized imports are, through the effects of the subsidy, causing injury within the meaning of this Agreement'. This would seem to establish an international obligation to pursue a causal connection that would relate to the actual subsidization - i.e., the margin. A similar clause exists in the Anti-Dumping Code. Moreover, this interpretation was consistent with the object and purpose of the Agreement. The Agreement sought to prevent unjustified impediments to the flow of international trade. Consequently, the Agreement required a strong showing that the injury to be prevented was caused by the effects of dumping and thus, that the remedy (the anti-dumping measures) would, in fact offset this material injury.

---

[79]Ivo Van Bael, Jean-François Bellis, EU Anti-dumping and Other Trade Defence Instruments 700 (2011).

If the injury were to be caused by other factors, the anti-dumping measures would not offset the injury and would impede trade to no lawful purpose.[80]

In the *US—Atlantic Salmon* dispute, both Norway and the U.S. made exhaustive arguments on the meaning of these terms.[81] According to the interpretation advanced by Norway, the Agreement required an analysis in each case of whether and how the effects of the imports under Articles 3.2 and 3.3 of the Tokyo Code were the "effects of dumping". This interpretation required some focus on the "margin of dumping/subsidy". Norway argued that if Article 3.4 of Tokyo Code required only an analysis of the effects of imports (i.e., volume and price effects) under Articles 3.2 and 3.3 (of the Tokyo Code), there would be no distinction between the determination of the existence of material injury and the determination of the cause of injury. Norway argued that the principle of effective treaty interpretation ruled out an interpretation which could render the phrase "through the effects of dumping" superfluous. The United States, on the other hand, argued that in order to give effect to the phrase "through the effects of dumping", it was not necessary to analyse any factors other than the effects of the imports as mentioned in Articles 3.2 and 3.3 [Tokyo AD Code] which did not incidentally include the margin of dumping. The United States also argued that the effects of the imports under Articles 3.2 and 3.3 were by definition the "effects of dumping".[82] The GATT Panel accepted the above proposition advanced by thc United States. According to the Panel, what was needed to be demonstrated under the concerned provision was that "the dumped imports are causing injury within the meaning of this Agreement".[83] The GATT panel interpreted that the effects mentioned in Article 3. 2 and 3.3 of the Tokyo Code were not mere indicators of material injury, but provided great precision in the manner in which causal relationship was to be established.[84]

The meaning of this phrase "through the effects" has been less clear in the context of the Uruguay Round AD Agreement and SCM Agreement. There was a move to discredit the finding of the *US– Atlantic Salmon* on the ground that the finding of the GATT panel on the large issue of causation dispute was rejected by the Appellate Body in *US—Hot-rolled Steel.*[85] The terms "through the effects of dumping" and "through the effects of subsidies" are retained in Article 3.5 of the AD Agreement and Article 15.5 of the SCM Agreement respectively. However, a closer look would establish that the Appellate Body was only examining the non-attribution provision

[80]John H. Jackson, THE WORLD TRADING SYSTEM 242 (1969); *see* also *N.D. Palmeter, Dumping Margins and Material Injury: The USITC is Free to Choose*, 21(4) JOURNAL OF WORLD TRADE 173–175 (1987).

[81]Panel Report, *US—Atlantic Salmon*, ¶ 304.

[82]*Id*, ¶ 300.

[83]*Id*, ¶ *569.*

[84]*Id*, ¶ *571.*

[85]*Appellate Body Report, United States—Anti–Dumping Measures on Certain Hot–Rolled Steel Products from Japan, WT/DS184/AB/R (August 23, 2001)* [hereinafter Appellate Body Report, *US- Hot-rolled Steel*].

in the AD Agreement in *US—Hot-rolled Steel* and that the scope of the term "through the effects of dumping" was not a matter of contention in that dispute. However, the Panel and Appellate Body had an occasion to examine this phrase in greater detail in *Japan—DRAM,* a subsequent WTO dispute.[86]

A closer reading of *Japan—DRAM* would indicate that the Appellate Body has apparently blurred the distinction between "injury through the effects of dumping/subsidies" and "injury caused by dumped/subsidized imports".[87] Strictly speaking, these terms have different meanings. The Appellate Body chose to reconcile the terms "the effect of … subsidization" found in Article VI: 6(a) of the GATT and "through the effects of subsidies" incorporated in Article 15.5 of the SCM Agreement. In making this reconciliation, the Appellate Body chose to interpret the terms "through the effects of subsidies" to mean "through the effects of subsidized imports"—an approach that could take the primary focus of the causation enquiry from the margin of dumping or subsidies to the effects of dumping/subsidies on the domestic industry.[88]

In sum, the extent of subsidy or dumping margin could be a useful indicator in assessing the effects of dumped or subsidized imports on the domestic industry. A relatively small subsidy or dumping margin is expected to have far less impact as compared to a higher margin. However, the magnitude of dumping/subsidy is included as a factor in the consideration of the material injury to the domestic industry. There is a criticism that if the terms "through the effects of dumping/subsidy" required only an analysis of the effects of imports under Articles 3.2 and 3.4 of the AD Agreement or Articles 15.2 and 15.4 of the SCM Agreement, there would be no distinction between the determination of the existence of material injury and the determination of the cause of injury.[89] This view has some clear merits, but it appears that this magnitude of dumping/subsidy has been subsumed within the trends analysis, which undertakes an examination of the price and volume trends in conjunction with the injury effects on the domestic industry. In other words, the terms "through the effects of dumping/subsidies" have been used to highlight the role of trend analysis not only in material injury but also in causation analysis. The magnitude of dumping/subsidies could have been an independent factor in the causation analysis, but the reasoning adopted by the GATT panel in *US-Atlantic Salmon*, continues till date as the permissible reading of the treaty.

The trends analysis is, however, not complete in itself. The major weakness of trend analysis is that it does not often take into account the degree of causality required for import relief. The following discussion examines the utility of the trend analysis in various scenarios.

---

[86]Appellate Body Report, *Japan—Countervailing Duties on Dynamic Random Access Memories from Korea, ¶ 269, WT/DS336/AB/R (November 28, 2007)* [hereinafter Appellate Body Report, *Japan – DRAM*].

[87]Jorge Miranda, *Causal Link and Non-attribution as Interpreted in WTO Trade Remedy Disputes,* 44 (4) Journal of World Trade 729, 734 (2010).

[88]Appellate Body Report, *Japan—DRAM*, ¶ 269-270.

[89]Norway's arguments, *US—Atlantic Salmon.*

## 4 *Summary on Trends Analysis*

The trends analysis or the correlation analysis is one of the most used analytical tools in the injury and causation determination. It is fairly simple to implement and relies on descriptive explanations. The WTO panels and the Appellate Body have reiterated the importance of trends analysis. The following scenarios are presented to highlight some of its practical advantages and drawbacks of the trends analysis.

**Scenario I**: Material injury is entirely caused by factors other than dumped/subsidized imports, i.e., dumping or subsidization has not caused material injury. For instance, the injury could have been caused by fair imports, or other macroeconomic or industry specific factors. A trends analysis which examines the correlation between imports and the movement of injury parameters may not be probative of the effects of dumping or subsidization.

**Scenario II**: No factors other than dumped or subsidized imports have been identified as a cause of material injury. In this scenario a trends or correlation analysis may be helpful in establishing causation. It is possible that injury may be caused by factors which were not identifiable or hidden at the time of the investigation; however, in the absence of any contrary evidence the causal link presumed to be established between dumped/subsidized or increased imports could be assumed to remain intact.

**Scenario III**: The material injury is at least partially caused by factors other than dumped imports. In this scenario, the dumped imports could have contributed to the injury or might have triggered the injury which was aggravated by other factors. This is a highly common situation. According to a study conducted by Hansen and Prusa,[90] imports had very small or usually statistically insignificant role on prices. Hansen and Prusa also found that other factors mattered more than imports in driving down domestic prices. In such a situation, the trends analysis will not be helpful in establishing whether the injury is on account of dumped or subsidized imports.

In antidumping there is no *pro rata* scaling down of an antidumping margin to account for injury caused by factors other than LTFV imports. Instead, if the investigating authority is not satisfied that such causal link exists, it will reach a negative injury determination which will result in the termination of the antidumping proceedings.[91]

---

[90]William Hansen & Thomas Prusa, *Economics and Politics: An Empirical Analysis of ITC Decision Making*, 5 Review of International Economics 230-245(1997).

[91]Under the comparative negligence theory in tort law, damages would be apportioned between parties at fault. Such a concept does not exist in trade law.

## D Examination of the GATT/WTO Jurisprudence: The "Non-attribution" Test

As discussed earlier, there is no legal requirement under the provisions of the present trade remedy agreements that imports shall be the sole cause of injury.[92] The treaty provisions acknowledge the possibility of factors other than increased imports causing injury to the domestic industry, but no method or order as to how the demonstration of causal link between increased imports and injury to the domestic industry shall be made is spelt out. However, Article 3.5 of the AD Agreement and 15.5 of the SCM Agreement require the investigating authorities to examine any "known factors" other than dumped or increased imports which are at the same time injuring the domestic industry, and that the injuries caused by the other factors must not be attributed to increased imports. This is formally known as the "non-attribution" test. The AD and SCM Agreements have given a list of indicative factors, which include the following:

- The volume and price of non-dumped or non-subsidized imports
- Contraction in demand or changes in patterns of consumption
- Trade restrictive practices of and competition between the foreign and domestic producers
- Developments in technology
- Export performance and the productivity of the domestic industry

The requirement to segregate and analyze the injuries caused on account of other factors has often been the subject matter of a number of disputes under the GATT/WTO (see Appendix). Some of these disputes are under the AD Agreement while a vast majority of the disputes are under the Safeguards Agreement. There have been a few cases under the SCM Agreement as well. The Appellate Body observed in *US—Wheat Gluten*, one of the earlier cases under the Safeguards Agreement:

> Logically, the final determination of the injurious effects caused by increased imports must follow a prior separation of the injurious effects of the different causal factors. If the effects of the different factors are not separated and distinguished from the effects of increased imports, there can be no proper assessment of the injury caused by the single and decisive factor. As we also indicated, the final determination about 'causal link' between increased imports and serious injury can only be made after the effects of increased imports have been properly assessed, and this assessment, in turn, follows the separation of effects caused by all different causal factors.[93]

In *US—Lamb*, the Appellate Body, while interpreting Article 4.2(b) of the Safeguards Agreement, stated that a conclusion based exclusively on an assessment of only one of the factors, namely "increased imports" in the Safeguards Agreement, would rest on an uncertain foundation, because it assumed that the other causal factors were not causing injury which had been ascribed to increased

---

[92] Appellate Body Report, *US—Lamb*, ¶ 170.

[93] Appellate Body Report, *US—Wheat Gluten*, ¶ 69.

imports.[94] According to the Appellate Body, the non-attribution language in Article 4.2(b) required a satisfactory explanation of the "nature and extent" of the injurious effects of other "known factors", as distinguished from the injurious effects of the increased imports.

*US—Hot-rolled Steel,*[95] an antidumping dispute, is perhaps the most important decision in the context of "non-attribution" analysis. Japan, the complainant, had argued that the USITC failed to adequately analyze "other factors" affecting the U.S. industry, for example, the increase in capacity of mini-mills and the ensuing expansion of U.S. steel supply, the strike at General Motors, declining demand for hot-rolled steel from the pipe and tube industry and the prices of non-dumped imports. Secondly, Japan claimed that the USITC had "failed to ensure that injury caused by these other factors was not attributed to the dumped imports." This was one of the earlier cases in which the scope of non-attribution was put to test before a WTO panel. During the GATT period, only a few disputes had examined the role of non-attribution and there was no requirement to conduct this enquiry as an analytical step. For example, in *US—Atlantic Salmon,*[96] a GATT panel analyzed the role and scope of the non-attribution clause under the Tokyo AD/Subsidy Codes. Norway, the complainant in that case, argued that investigating authorities, namely the USITC should have carried out a thorough examination as opposed to a mere consideration of all possible causes of material injury to the domestic industry and should have isolated and excluded the effects of such other possible causes of injury from the effects of imports.[97] The Panel noted that, in addition to examining the effects of the imports under Articles 3.1, 3.2 and 3.3 of the Tokyo Antidumping Code, the USITC was not required to identify the extent of injury caused by these other factors. According to the panel, there was no obligation to isolate the injury caused by these factors from the injury caused by the imports from Norway.[98]

In *US—Hot-rolled Steel*, Japan also argued that the addition of the explicit requirement to "examine any known factors other than the dumped imports" under the WTO AD Agreement as opposed to the recognition of the possibility that other factors are injuring the domestic industry, constituted "a significant substantive change in the underlying treaty text [which] renders *United States—Atlantic Salmon* totally inapposite".[99] While deciding on the non-attribution language, the WTO Panel noted that responsibility of the investigating agency was to "examine and ensure that these other factors do not break the causal link that appeared to exist between dumped imports and the material injury on the basis of an examination of

---

[94]Appellate Body Report, *US—Lamb*, ¶179.

[95]Panel report, *United States–Anti-Dumping Measures on Certain Hot-Rolled Steel Products from Japan*, WT/DS184//R (August 23, 2001).

[96]Panel Report, *US—Atlantic Salmon*, ¶ 555.

[97]*Id* ¶ 545.

[98]*Id* ¶ 555.

[99]Second Submission of Japan to the Panel Proceedings in *United States—Anti-Dumping Measures on Certain Hot-Rolled Steel Products from Japan*, Annex C-1, ¶ 256.

the volume and effects of dumped imports under Articles 3.2 and 3.4 of the AD Agreement".[100] What the GATT panel implicitly said was that there was no need to quantify the injury.[101] In the appeal, the Appellate Body promptly dismissed the Panel's view and held that the requirement of separating and distinguishing the injurious effects of other known factors is essential to concluding whether the dumped imports are indeed causing injury.[102] The Appellate Body noted as follows:

> The non-attribution language in Article 3.5… applies solely in situations where the dumped imports and other known factors are causing injury *at the same time.* In order that investigating authorities are … able to ensure that the injurious effects of other known factors are "attributed" to dumped imports, they must appropriately assess the injurious effects of those factors. Logically, such an assessment must involve separating and distinguishing the injurious effects of other factors from the injurious effects of the dumped imports.[103]

According to the Appellate Body, if the injurious effects of dumped imports and other known factors remain lumped together and indistinguishable, there was simply no means of knowing whether injury ascribed to dumped imports was, in reality, caused by other factors.[104] This concern was reiterated by the Appellate Body in *US—Line Pipe* too. The Appellate Body stated in *US—Line Pipe*:

> The non-attribution language in Article 4.2(b) has two objectives. First, it seeks in situations where several factors are causing injury at the same time, to prevent investigating authorities from inferring required 'causal link' between increased imports and threat thereof on the basis of the injurious factors caused by factors other than increased imports. Second, it is a benchmark for ensuring that only an ***appropriate share*** *of overall injury is attributed to increased imports*."[105](emphasis added)

In principle, the Appellate Body ruling on 'non-attribution' has certain intuitive appeal as it seeks to locate the injury attributable to the alleged imports. However, the challenge lies in its execution. It will be instructive to examine the efficacy of this test in a real trade remedy dispute. Hot-rolled bar was one of the products involved in the *US—Steel* dispute. The respondents (exporters facing safeguard action) argued that the injury to the U.S. domestic industry was on account of rising input costs or cost of goods sold (COGS). The USITC had admitted the occurrence of rising COGS but emphasized that import competition had prevented the domestic firms from passing the cost to costumers. In a way, import competition could be a reason why the domestic firms were unable to recover their costs, but how practically feasible will it be for an investigating authority to establish that the injury on account of rising COGS is not attributed to increased imports? To take another example, exchange rate fluctuations may be a cause for injury to the domestic industry, but they could also be a reason for dumping or increased imports to take

[100]Panel Report, *US—Hot-Rolled Steel*, ¶ 7.253.

[101]*Id.* ¶ ¶ 7.260–61.

[102]Appellate Body Report, *US—Hot-Rolled Steel*, ¶ 7.217.

[103]*Id.* ¶ ¶ 222–223.

[104]*Id.* ¶ 228.

[105]Appellate Body Report, *US—Line Pipe*, ¶ 252.

place.[106] In such cases, there is an interplay of various economic factors, which cannot be properly segregated and separated for the purpose of non-attribution.

In light of the above discussion, the non-attribution analysis poses certain questions. Does it mean that all investigating agencies should quantify and eliminate the role of other known factors? Or, does it only mean that an investigating agency should provide a reasoned and adequate explanation of the injurious effects of other known factors? These two aspects are separate and distinct. There are views that an investigating authority cannot segregate the extent and nature of injurious effects except by using some mathematical computation or economic science.[107] On the other hand, if this requirement is all about providing some explanation without a through economic justification, this exercise may be a purely qualitative test–a mere procedural requirement. It appears from some of the recent cases that the Appellate Body realized the folly in imposing a standard which no one clearly understood and not many WTO Members had the capacity or ability to accomplish.[108] This study examines the persisting lack of clarity among WTO members in the use of non-attribution in the next two chapters of this book, namely, Chaps. 4 and 5 which deal with the country specific practices in the causation determination in the field of antidumping and safeguard investigations.

It is interesting that in a well-known safeguards dispute, *US—Line Pipe,* the Appellate Body while interpreting the pertinent provision of the Safeguards Agreement settled for a segregation test which was nothing more than qualitative. The Appellate Body noted:

> [T]o fulfill the requirement of Article 4.2(b), last sentence, the competent authorities must establish explicitly, through a reasoned and adequate explanation, that injury caused by factors other than increased imports is not attributed to increased imports. The explanation must be clear and unambiguous. It must not merely imply or suggest an explanation. It must be straightforward in express terms.[109]

Likewise, in cases such as *US—DRAM*[110] and *Mexico—Oilve Oil,*[111] the WTO panels have upheld the non-attribution analysis without extensively examining the methodology used for isolating and distinguishing the effects of the 'other factor'. In *Mexico—Olive Oil*, the panel stated that *Economia,* the Mexican CVD investigating authority, had "carefully examined, separated and distinguished the effects of

---

[106]GATT Panel Report, *EC—Imposition of Antidumping Duties on Imports of Cotton Yarn from Brazil*, ADP/137 (April 4, 1995). Brazil noted that temporary exchange rate fluctuations were the reasons for dumping and had to be adjusted, *see* ¶ 125.

[107]PETROS MAVROIDIS ET AL., THE LAW OF THE WORLD TRADE ORGANIZATION (WTO), fn.18, at 657 (2010).

[108]Appellate Body Report, *EC—Pipe Fittings*, ¶ 188.

[109]*Id.* ¶. 217.

[110]Panel Report, *United States—Countervailing Duty Investigation on Dynamic Random Access Memory Semiconductors (DRAMS) from Korea*, WT/DS296/R (July 20, 2005).

[111]Panel Report, *Mexico—Definitive Countervailing Measures on Olive Oil from the European Communities*, ¶ 7. 317 WT/DS341/R (October 21, 2008) [hereinafter Panel Report *Mexico-Olive Oil*].

each factor from the effects of subsidized imports, and reasonably concluded that these factors were not contributing to the injury suffered by *Fortuny* [the Mexican Olive Oil producer]".[112] In a way the panel examined whether *Economia* had examined a particular known factor and supported its finding. During the panel process, the panel requested Mexico to identify the paragraphs in the Preliminary and Final Resolutions that referred to the other injury factors.[113] Based on a perusal of the information submitted, the panel gave deference to the finding of the Mexican investigating authority and was not prepared to second-guess whether the investigating authority's analysis was quantitatively precise or not.[114] This panel finding supports the proposition that once an investigating authority has identified and listed a causal factor, and supported its non-attribution analysis with a certain reasoned explanation, the WTO panels and Appellate Body would be unwilling to disturb the finding. The panel in *US—DRAM* also followed a similar reasoning.[115]

One could argue that in terms of the "non-attribution" analysis, what the Appellate Body sought to clarify in *US—Line Pipe*[116] was still an improvement on the *status quo*. Moreover, the qualitative non-attribution analysis upheld by the WTO panel in *Mexico—Olive Oil* is an acceptance of the practical difficulty in performing this test. It is only appropriate to add that an economic analysis conducted by Chad Bown and Niall Meagher by using the facts of this case notes that the Mexican Authority had failed to properly isolate and segregate the effects of other factors of injury.[117] It was a common practice to ascribe causal link to imports in several trade remedy investigations without even acknowledging the role of other causally significant factors.[118] In such a context, an objective explanation—even a defective one at that—could eliminate the elements of arbitrariness from such investigation to an appreciable extent. As the Appellate Body noted in *US—Lamb*, if the investigating authorities fully address the nature and complexities of the data and respond adequately to the plausible interpretation of the data, the reviewing panels are unlikely to overturn the findings.[119] This observation was reconfirmed even in the *EC—DRAM* case as well where the panel said that a "satisfactory explanation" which could include even a "thorough qualitative examination" could be sufficient to meet the obligations of separating and distinguishing the injurious effect of 'other factors'.[120]

---

[112]Panel Report, *Mexico—Olive Oil*, ¶ 7. 317.

[113]*Id.* ¶ 7. 309.

[114]*Id.* ¶ 7.317.

[115]Panel Report, *US—DRAM*, ¶ 7. 369.

[116]Appellate Body Report, *US—Line Pipe*, ¶ 217.

[117]Chad Bown & Niall oMeagher, *Mexico- Olive Oil: Remedy Without a Cause*, 9(1) World Trade Review 85-116 (2010) (noting that the panel had not fully addressed causal factors such as Fortuny's loss of its distribution network, its loss of the right to use a Spanish brand name (Ybarra), and its high costs in the non-attribution analysis).

[118]See *Argentina–Footwear*; *US—Lamb*, *US—Wheat Gluten*, etc.

[119]Appellate Body Report, *US—Lamb*, ¶ 106.

[120]*Panel Report, EC—DRAM*, ¶ 7.420.

## 1 *Identifying and Separating Other "Known Factors": Who Bears the Burden?*

Under the AD and SCM Agreements, the investigating authorities are required to examine the impact of all known factors other than dumped or subsidized imports which at the same time are causing injury to the domestic industry, and to ensure that the injury caused by such factors is not attributed to dumped or subsidized imports. In accordance with Article 3.1 of the AD Agreement and 15.1 of the SCM Agreement, the investigating authority is required to base all its determinations of injury on positive evidence and objective evaluation. In order for an evaluation to be "objective", an investigating authority has the obligation to examine the potential effects of "known factors" other than dumped or subsidized imports that might be causing injury.

The Appellate Body in *EC—Pipe and Fittings,*[121] examined the role of other 'known factors' as follows:

> Critical to the effective operation of the non-attribution obligation, and indeed the entire causality analysis, is the requirement of Article 3.5 to "examine any known factors other than the dumped imports which at the same time are injuring the domestic industry", for it is the "injuries" of those known factors that must not be attributed to dumped imports. In order for this obligation to be triggered, Article 3.5 requires that the factor at issue:
>
> (a) be "known" to the investigating authority
> (b) be a factor "other than dumped imports"; and
> (c) be injuring the domestic industry at the same time as the dumped imports.

One of the pertinent issues in non-attribution analysis is the task of identifying the 'other factors' which may be causing injury to the domestic industry. The Panel in *Thailand—H Beams* stated:

> The text of Article 3.5 …. does not make clear how factors are 'known' or are become 'known' to the investigating authorities. We consider that other 'known' factors would include those factors that are clearly raised by the interested parties before the investigating authorities in the course of an AD investigation. We are of the view that there is no express requirement in Article 3.5 that investigating authorities seek out and examine in each case on their own initiative the effects of all possible factors other than imports that may be causing injury to the domestic industry under investigation.[122]

It can be implied from the findings of the Panel that the general burden on raising the known factor is on other interested parties, or preferably on the exporter. The Panel in *Thailand—H Beams* clearly spelt out this general position of law.[123] Furthermore, once an investigating agency acknowledges the presence of an injury factor, a failure to evaluate such a factor is a breach of the non-attribution

---

[121]Appellate Body Report, *EC—Pipe Fittings,* ¶ 175.

[122]Panel Report, *Thailand—Anti-Dumping Duties on Angles, Shapes and Sections of Iron or Non-Alloy Steel and H-Beams from Poland*, ¶ 7.273, WT/DSS122/R (September 28, 2000) [hereinafter Panel Report, *Thailand—H Beams*].

[123]Panel Report, *Thailand—H Beams,* ¶ 273.

requirement.[124] The ruling of the panel in *EC—Salmon* suggests that if the investigating agency has gained certain understanding of the causal factors based on prior knowledge of a product, industry or market, or common knowledge, such information and understanding "play a part" in the non-attribution analysis.[125] Certain ambiguities also persist as to the evidentiary standards applicable to qualify a causal factor as a known factor. There could be several possible causes for the alleged condition of the domestic industry. Should each such factor be acknowledged and followed up with a separate analysis? Does the investigating authority have the freedom to disregard certain factors as too irrelevant, remote or causally inconsequential? These issues beg questions. For example, in a majority of cases it is seen that the investigating authorities, or even the WTO Panels, simply accept at face value the "other factors" pointed out by the exporters or the respondent country without considering whether they are appropriate or inappropriate, relevant or irrelevant or significant to the causal enquiry.[126] The lack of clarity on these aspects is yet to be addressed through dispute settlement panels or any authoritative decisions by the WTO members.

However, on certain other aspects, the WTO Panels and the Appellate Body have filled some of the gaps in treaty language. One particular concern was whether there was any temporal limitation on raising or bringing to the notice of the authority the existence of any known factors. In *EC—Pipe Fittings*, the Appellate Body noted that there is no specific stage for raising the presence of other factors that may be causing injury to the domestic industry. The Appellate Body clarified that it is irrelevant if any interested party has raised a factor at one particular stage and not consistently throughout the investigation. The second question related to the process in which a known factor has to be dealt with. The panel in *EC-DRAM* noted that it does not suffice for an investigating authority to merely "check the box".[127] According to the Panel, an investigating authority must do more than simply list other known factors, and then dismiss their role with bare qualitative assertions. The Panel provided an illustration of qualitative comments. In certain cases, investigating authority may dismiss certain possible known factor along the following lines: "this factor did not contribute in any significant manner to the injury"; "this factor did not break the causal link between the subsidized imports and material injury", etc. According to the Panel in *EC—DRAM*, a more robust discussion of the known factor(s) is required for examining its role. As the Panel further noted, the non-attribution language in the AD Agreement/SCM Agreement requires an investigating authority to provide a satisfactory explanation of the

---

[124]Panel Report, United States—*Investigation of the International Trade Commission in Softwood Lumber from Canada*, ¶7.137, WT/DS277/R (March 22, 2004) [hereinafter Panel Report, *US—Softwood Lumber IV*].

[125]Panel Report, *European Communities, Antidumping Duties on Farmed Salmon from Norway*, ¶ 7.667, WT/DS 377/R (November 16, 2007) [hereinafter Panel Report, *EC—Salmon*].

[126]Alan Sykes, The WTO Agreement on Safeguards 188 (2006).

[127]Panel Report, *EC—DRAM*, ¶ 7.405.

nature and extent of the injurious effects of the other factors, as distinguished from the injurious effects of the subsidized imports.[128]

In Appellate Body in *US—Hot rolled Steel* recognized that there may be a number of different causal factors interacting and affecting the domestic industry at the same time and that "their effects may well be inter-related, such that they produce a *combined* effect on the domestic industry."[129] The Appellate Body went on to state that "we recognize that there may be cases where, because of the specific factual circumstances therein, the failure to undertake an examination of the collective impact of other causal factors would result in the investigating authority improperly attributing the effects of other causal factors to dumped imports."[130]

The purpose of a "known factor" is not just to fill in the requirements of non-attribution. The purpose is to locate the possible causal factors whose existence would be otherwise hidden. The causal effects of statutory causes such as dumping/subsidy or increased imports cannot be assessed unless the existence of other causes is identified or examined. That is why the Appellate Body has introduced the concept of non-attribution even when the treaty text is silent on a strict segregation of factors. In other words, this is an acceptance by the Appellate Body of the fact that any causal enquiry would entail the identification of the existence of other causal factors. For example, the WTO panels and the Appellate Body imported the concept of non-attribution while dealing with "serious prejudice" claims under Articles 5 and 6.3 of the SCM Agreement[131] and Paragraph 16.4 of China's Protocol of Accession.[132] However, there is no express language on non-attribution in these treaty provisions.

In this respect, it is often seen from the disputes raised in the WTO that each trade remedy case will have its own set of relevant factors. An analysis of the cases indicate that the list of illustrative factors mentioned in Article 3.5 of the AD Agreement and Article 15.5 of the SCM Agreement often do not have much role in the causation analysis (see Appendix of this chapter). However, an analysis of the non-attribution findings of various WTO panels in the field of trade remedies indicate that there are certain factors which may have a greater influence on the performance of the domestic industry. As could be seen from the analysis, a common reason for poor profitability of the industry is the increase in the raw materials or utility costs, referred to as rise in cost of goods sold (COGS). Second, non-tariff barriers and exchange rate fluctuations play a key role. Again, domestic industry constituents could be subject to one or another form of trade remedy action in other markets, or could be facing multiple or simultaneous trade remedy actions

---

[128]See also Appellate Body Report, *United States – Definitive Safeguard Measures on Imports of Certain Steel Products*, ¶ 304, WT/DS252/AB/R (November 10, 2003).

[129]Appellate Body Report, *US—Hot Rolled Steel*, ¶ 227-228.

[130]Appellate Body Report, *US—Hot Rolled Steel*, ¶ 228.

[131]Panel Report, *US—Cotton*, ¶ 7.1343.

[132]Panel Report, *United States—Measures Affecting Imports of Certain Passenger Vehicle and Light Truck Tyres from China*, ¶ 7.176, WT/DS399/R, (October 5, 2011), upheld by Appellate Body Report WT/DS399/AB/R.

or anticipating such actions in other jurisdictions. Domestic competition is yet another factor. The effects of any other remedial measures currently applied to the sector or the product may also have to be viewed in perspective. Third, the fall in productivity of the domestic industry could be a common cause of injury. The chilling effect of these factors will have to be adequately taken into account. Although the role of "other factors" will have to be examined and analyzed on a case-by-case basis, it will be instructive to have a more comprehensive list of illustrative factors which an authority should examine while deciding injury and causation. Some of the factors such as rise in raw material costs, domestic competition, currency exchange rate fluctuations and role of labor or management decisions merit mandatory discussion in most trade remedy cases.[133]

Having looked at the general contours of the "non-attribution" test, it would be helpful to understand the complexities of the non-attribution test in the light of the experience of the United States, which was required to defend several of its findings on injury and causality in various safeguard investigations at the WTO.

## 2 *Non-attribution: Examination of the U.S. Methodology in Trade Remedy Investigations*

The trade remedy practices in the United States have had a profound influence in shaping the application of this mechanism at the multilateral level. The obvious question was how come a country with more than nine decades of experience in injury determination lose virtually all its injury determinations in safeguards and a few antidumping cases at the WTO? For the broader WTO community, the question was how could the "non-attribution" test be carried out in a WTO compatible way? This question has evoked intense debate within and outside the U.S.[134] On a plain reading of Article 4.2(b) of the Safeguards Agreement, it is more or less clear that the competent authorities have the discretion to craft appropriate methodologies.[135] But then, it is surprising that each attempt made by the U.S. to comply with the injury and causation determination especially in the context of safeguard investigations was found lacking and falling short of the WTO standards in one respect or another.[136]

Section 201 of the US Trade Act of 1974, as amended, is the applicable legislation for safeguard investigations in the U.S.. Section 201 mandates the USITC to

---

[133]*See Infra* Appendix of this chapter.

[134]Douglas A. Irwin, *Causing Problems: The WTO Review of Causation and Injury in Section 201 Cases*, 2(3) World Trade Review 297, 298 (2003). See also Chad P. Bown, *Why Are Safeguard Measures under the WTO So Unpopular*, 1 World Trade Review 47 (2002).

[135]Appellate Body Report, *US—Lamb*, ¶ 181.

[136]Alan Sykes, *The Safeguard Mess: A Critique of WTO Jurisprudence*, 2(3) World Trade Review 261 (2003).

determine "whether an article is being imported into the U.S. in such increased quantities as to be a substantial cause of serious injury, or the threat thereof, to the domestic industry producing an article like or directly competitive with the imported article".[137] Although Section 201 refers to "increased imports", it omits the terms "under such conditions" which is mentioned in Article 2.1 of the WTO Safeguards Agreement.

The practice of USITC was to assess the injury caused to the domestic industry on account of increased imports and compare it with other factors.[138] Then the USITC took each of the other factors one at a time and examined its relative causal importance with respect to the serious injury it had previously established to exist. The USITC, under this methodology, weighed each factor individually against imports to determine whether such factor was a "more important cause of injury" and then excluded that factor as a "cause of injury" when that factor alone did not satisfy that standard.[139] The U.S statute implied that the various sources of injury should be rank ordered and that "increased imports" should be no less important factor than any other factor. In the underlying investigation on *US—Lamb*, the USITC concluded that each four of the six "other factors" was relatively less important cause than increased imports.[140] This was an implicit acknowledgement that these other factors were actually causing injury than increased imports. In *US—Lamb*, the Appellate Body ruled on the consistency of the causation test as applied by the USITC as follows:

> [B]y examining the relative causal importance of the different causal factors, the USITC clearly engaged in some kind of process to separate out, and identify the effect of different factors, including increased imports. Although an examination of the relative causal importance of the different causal factors may satisfy the requirements of the United States law, such an examination does not, for that reason, satisfy the requirements of the Agreement on Safeguards. On the record before the Panel in this case, a review of whether the United States complied with the non-attribution language in the second sentence of Article 4.2(b) can only be made in light of the explanation given by the USITC for its conclusions on the relative causal importance of the increased imports, as distinguished from the injurious effects of other causal factors.[141]

The WTO Panel in *US—Lamb*, (part of the finding which was later upheld) also noted that serious injury examination in that case was "polluted" by the injurious effects of the remaining factors.[142] The Panel noted that in this case, the U.S. assessed the injurious effects of the other factor at issue against the injurious effects of increased imports and the remaining factors. The determinations were not made

---

[137]19 U.S.C. para 2252(b)(1)(B).

[138]Panel Report, *US—Wheat Gluten*, ¶ 134.

[139]Section 202 (b) (1) (b) of the U.S Trade Act explains that the term "substantial cause" means 'a cause which is important and not less than any other cause'.

[140]Import Lamb Meat, No. TA- 201-68 (United States International trade Commission, April 1999), USITC Publication 3176.

[141]Appellate Body Report, *US-Lamb*, ¶ 184.

[142]Panel Report, *US-Line Pipe*, ¶ 7.289.

with any explicit method, but based on a loose assessment of the relative weights of each factor. Furthermore, the Panel pointed out that there was no effort to separate and distinguish the injurious effects of the increased imports from the injurious effects of other factors. This approach, according to the Panel, was not in conformity with the requirements of the Safeguards Agreement, which requires an examination as to whether there is "a genuine and substantial relationship of cause and effect" between the serious injury and the increased imports.[143]

The injury analysis in *US—Line Pipe* also highlights how an investigating agency can fail the non-attribution standard despite the existence of evidence on strong causal link between imports and the resultant injury.[144] In the investigation USITC examined six factors other than increased imports that were possibly causing injury to the domestic industry (see Appendix for details). The USITC found that the declining demand in the oil and gas industry was a factor, but held that increased imports were important than any other factor. According to the Appellate Body, the USITC recognized that the decline in oil and gas drilling and production, but did not explain the nature and extent of the injurious effects of this factor. It appears that the USITC was unable to defend its non-attribution analysis since it failed to provide a reasoned and adequate examination of the effects of this factor. In other words, a mere assertion is not enough.[145] In the view of the Appellate Body the descriptive part of the injury and causation determination should explicitly incorporate such an analysis.[146]

The postulations of the Appellate Body and the Panels may sound abstract, but the conceptual and practical difficulties with some of the existing approaches on non-attribution could be explained with the help of a simple example. Consider a hypothetical involving high fructose corn syrup (HFCS), a product which is subject matter of several trade remedy actions. The HFCS industry in country A, files an application for a safeguard investigation where the major supplying countries are W, X, Y and Z. Further, assume that six different causes of injury are existing, which include (a) inefficient management of the state-owned HFCS industry; (b) growing preference for sugar based sweeteners as against corn based sweeteners; (c) high input costs of corn in country A; (d) employees' strike in the major HFCS producing company in country A, and; (e) appreciation of the local currency in country 'A' and the consequent poor export performance of the domestic HFCS industry, and finally (f) surge in imports from countries W, X, Y and Z. These are the available known factors. Imagine a situation where the investigating agency starts to rank order items (a) through (f) with reference to the increased import, namely item (f). In some of the safeguard investigations involving the United States which were challenged before the WTO, it was found that the USITC, the injury

---

[143] Panel Report, *US-Line Pipe,* ¶ 169; *see* also Appellate Body Report, *US- Wheat Gluten*, ¶. 69.

[144] Appellate Body Report, *US- Line Pipe*, ¶ 220-222.

[145] Raj Bhala & David Ganz, *WTO Case Review of 2001*, 20 (2) ARIZONA JOURNAL OF INTERNATIONAL AND COMPARATIVE LAW 178, 194(2003).

[146] Appellate Body Report, *US- Line Pipe*, ¶ 223-262.

determination agency, sought to assign weight based on the relative importance of each of the identified factors against increased imports which it established initially. This was an exercising of decomposing, comparing and then rank ordering of various causal factors as against imports which did not satisfy the non-attribution requirement espoused by the Appellate Body.[147]

Further, what do the Panels and Appellate Body require when they insist that the national agencies should perform a "non-attribution" in trade remedy investigations? In the hypothetical just discussed, in addition to imports, there are five other factors causing injury simultaneously. Assume that the input prices of corn were unusually high in a year, but if the capacity utilization, sales realization and profitability are the highest during this time, it could be concluded that the rise in corn prices (input costs) is not affecting the causal link between increased imports and the serious injury earlier established. If higher input costs were affecting the domestic industry, it should have been reflected in any or most of the financial parameters under examination. On the other hand, if higher input prices have indeed an effect on injury, the non-attribution test requires the authority to separate and disentangle (i.e., separate and distinguish) the effects of rising input costs. Although a proper non-attribution is only possible through quantification, the recent rulings of some of the panels discussed above indicate that WTO members could comply with this requirement through an explicit and reasoned qualitative analysis provided there is identification of all factors causing injury. There should be proper identification of all factors and an examination as to how the various factors affect the domestic industry should be evident on the records. In the hypothetical above, such an analysis has to be conducted for all the five factors listed from (a) through (e) above. In other words, the non-attribution should at least be procedurally demonstrated.

The WTO jurisprudence is unambiguous on the need for non-attribution.[148] In this context, it is necessary to ask: what was the mistake that the United States committed in a long line of safeguards and certain antidumping disputes? The USITC invariably took the default position that a rise in import trends is bound to "cause" changes in domestic prices and output. A commensurate deterioration in financial and non-financial parameters such as production, market share, price, profitability and a host of similar factors with rising imports were almost assumed as conclusive of causal link. Instead of comparing the relative role of each causal factor, the USITC should have discussed and explained away how the injury alleged on account of other factors is not breaking the causal link. According to the

[147]Panel Report, *United States – Definitive Safeguard Measures on Imports of Circular Welded Carbon Quality Line Pipe from Korea*, ¶ 7.288, WT/DS202/R (October 29, 2001); see also Douglas Irwin, *Causing Problems*, supra note 134, 304.

[148]*See for example*, Appellate Body Report, *US—Gluten*, ¶ 69.

Appellate Body, the USITC's focus was on "substantial cause", and not on "non-attribution".[149]

It is important to recall that the safeguard measures adopted by the United States were found inconsistent with WTO provisions, not because they were bereft of causal sufficiency, but primarily in view of the USITC's adherence to the domestic statutory requirement. As examined in Chap. 2, the U.S. safeguard legislation has a different language from the WTO Safeguards Agreement.[150] It may look paradoxical that the United States lost the cases despite having a far stricter standard—a standard based on the "substantial cause" criterion as against the "a cause" criterion adopted by other leading users of safeguard actions. This fact underlies the conclusion that the degree of causal significance by itself is not a significant factor in WTO jurisprudence.

## *3 Non-attribution Analysis and Its Discontents: The Application of the 'but for' Test*

The foregoing discussion indicated the shortcoming of the coincidence–in-time or correlation test in establishing causation between imports and injury to the domestic industry. Nonetheless, a number of WTO panels and even the Appellate Body have emphasized the need for establishing "a genuine and substantial relationship of cause and effect".[151] The key question is how this requirement could be fleshed out in terms of a sound legal construct, and employed in real practice in conformity with the jurisprudence of the panel and the Appellate Body rulings. The "but-for" test is a regularly used legal construct for identifying/establishing the causal link in domestic proceedings. Even in trade remedy setting, the 'but for' test is suggested as a useful legal construct.[152] In the context of antidumping/safeguard investigations one could ask as follows: "but for the dumped/increased imports, would the injury have occurred?" This expression is in a counterfactual form and requires an examination of what would have been the state of the domestic industry, had the increased imports not taken place? This analysis does not ask the straightforward question of what caused the injury to the domestic industry being considered. In

---

[149] Appellate Body, *US—Line Pipe*, ¶ 219.

[150] Christy Ledet, *Causation of Injury in Safeguard Cases: Why the U.S Can't Win*, 34(3) Law and Policy in International Business, 713, 717(2003); also see Sykes: The WTO Agreement on Safeguards 174 (2006).

[151] Appellate Body Report, *United States – Final Countervailing Duty Determination with respect to certain Softwood Lumber from Canada, (Article 21.5 – Canada)*, ¶ 132, WT/DS257/R; *see also* Appellate Body Report, *United States – Wheat Gluten*, ¶ 69.

[152] Prakash Narayan, *Injury Investigation in "Material Retardation" in Antidumping Cases*, 25(1) Northwestern Journal of International Law and Business 37, 53 (2004). See also Panel Report, *Korea- Commercial Vehicles* ¶ 7.613; Panel Report, *Indonesia-* Report of the Panel, *Indonesia—certain Measures Affecting the Automobile Industry*, ¶ 5.103, WT/DS54/R (July 2, 1998).

practice, the "but-for" test is established on the basis of balance of probabilities: if it is more likely than not that an event was the cause, it is treated as if it were the cause. In the context of trade remedy investigations, the but-for test is helpful where increased imports/dumped or subsidized imports are the likeliest or the most probable cause of injury. To explain, the underlying presumption in such a case would be that the alleged increased imports, by virtue of volume, price and other trends, are the likeliest cause of injury and the purpose of this test is to reaffirm to what extent such a presumption is true or untrue.

In the context of antidumping and safeguard investigations, the but-for test is generally conducted through econometric models such as the partial equilibrium models. Normally the causal analysis is done by holding the levels of imports constant or through allocation of quotas while using actual industry values for all other variables, and then by comparing this output to the actual output. Essentially, such a comparison would attempt to approximate what the condition of the domestic industry would be in the absence of imports.[153] In jurisdictions such as the U.S., such a counterfactual test is conducted through the so-called unitary analysis. The unitary approach compares the actual performance of a domestic industry with a simulation of what its performance would have been had it had to compete with fair or unfair imports. COMPAS[154] (the currently existing model), which is generally used in the case of antidumping and subsidies, employs three key inputs and six parameters (elasticities) to determine the price and volume of effects of dumping.[155] The COMPAS model is designed to calculate the effect of dumping at specified margins on the domestic prices, the volume of domestic shipments and the overall sales revenue. The principal parameters are the following: (i) dumping margin percentage; (ii) domestic producers' market share; (iii) subject import's market share; (iv) aggregate elasticity of demand for the product under investigation; (v) domestic producer's supply elasticity; (vi) fairly traded import supply elasticity; (vii) domestic product/subject imports elasticity of substitution; (viii) domestic product/fairly traded imports elasticity of substitution; and (ix) subject imports/fairly traded imports elasticity of substitution. These elasticities are based on assumptions and are, therefore, "educated guesses" or "guestimates".[156] The WTO trade remedy agreements do not stand in the way of using such advanced

---

[153]Alexander Keck et al., *A Proababilistic Approach to Use of Econometric Modeling in Sunset Reviews*, 6(3) World Trade Review 371 (2007).

[154]COMPAS is an Armington partial equilibrium simulation model that quantifies the effects of dumping in a simple supply-demand framework.

[155]James P. Durling & Matthew P. McCullough, *Teaching Old Laws New Tricks: The Legal Obligation of Non-Attribution and the Need for Economic Rigor in Injury Analyses Under US Trade Law*, in Handbook of International Trade (E. Kwan Choi & James Hartigan eds., 2004) [hereinafter Durling & McCullough, *Teaching Old Laws New Tricks*].

[156]Thomas Prusa & David C.Sharp, *Simultaneous Equations in Antidumping Investigations*, 14(1) Journal of Forensic Economics 63–78(2001) (noting that the COMPAS results often reflect the analyst's assumptions and judgments regarding the causal relationship between the imports and the domestically produced product).

statistical/econometric modeling and even the WTO dispute settlement panels have used such techniques as a matter of routine practice, at least in arbitration proceedings.[157]

While revisiting the but-for test there has been significant literature on the utility of this test in the causation enquiry.[158] One major flaw of the but-for test is that it does not seek to search for the causes of injury at least if there are multiple causes. Let's take an example involving a struggling industry. Assume that the industry is operating with outmoded technology, lack of skilled manpower, high capital costs, lack of diversified portfolio and falling investor confidence. However, the company had trusted customers who were willing to purchase their products at competitive prices. However, when imports started coming in, the customers shifted their purchases to imports. In a trade remedy enquiry, the natural question is: but-for imports, could this domestic industry have suffered injury". The domestic industry can possibly seek antidumping protection, but the real reasons for the poor performance of the domestic industry are something else. To that extent, the but-for test does not enquire the factual reasons of an event taking place. As Fumerton and Kress argue, the but-for test seems to work well in 'garden-variety' examples of causation and not necessarily in complicated investigations that involve multiple or unknown causes and long periods of enquiry.[159] The application of but-for test in trade remedy cases varies dramatically from other personal injury or tort cases. These issues are more exhaustively dealt with in Chap. 7.

It is important to keep in mind that the but-for test is not the same as the correlation test, although both could look confusingly similar. The background assumption for the application of both tests is that dumped/subsidized or increased imports constitute the overwhelming reason for injury, but the "correlation" test assumes the default position that if two things happen at the same place, one could be the reason of the other. The but-for test does not assume such a position. Rather, it works in an "all or nothing" fashion, i.e. either something is a cause or not a cause.

It is easy to explain this problem with a simple hypothetical. Imagine a case where someone is called upon to quantify the impact of various factors on the performance of an industry. One may assume that the role of each factor is perfectly quantifiable in economic terms in this scenario. Imports from subject countries were quantified as contributing to 30 % of the overall injury and there are two additional factors causing injury. Further assume that these factors are causing injury to the

---

[157] *See* Decision by the Arbitrator, *United States – Continued Dumping and Subsidy Offset Act of 2000, Original Complaint by Brazil – Recourse to Arbitration by the United States under Article 22.6 of the DSU*, WT/DS217/ARB/BRA (August 31, 2004).

[158] John D. Rue, Returning to the Roots of the Bramble Bush: The 'But for' Regains Primacy in Causation Analysis in the American Law Institute's Proposed Restatement (Third) of Torts, 71 (6) Fordham Law Review 1744 (1985); James J. Nedumpara, Causation in Trade Remedy Law: Problems with the 'But for' Test, 10 (11&12) Global Trade and Customs Journal 402 (2015).

[159] Richard Fumerton, *Causation and the Law: Preemption, Lawful Sufficiency, and Causal Sufficiency*, 64 (4) Law and Contemporary Problems 83, 95 (2001).

extent of 35 % each. The simple enquiry is whether a trade remedy investigation can be successfully conducted by employing the but-for test?

In the above hypothetical scenario, the other two factors, which cumulatively account for 70 % of the injury, are the dominant causes of injury. One could argue that even without the imports, the domestic industry might have suffered injury. In such a case, the alleged imports cannot be treated as a cause of injury in the ordinary sense. In other words, application of the but-for test would fail to establish any link between the imports and the injury alleged. One of the major disadvantages of the but-for test is that it only accommodates a limited number of factors as causative agents. Then, one may ponder: is the 30 % contribution to injury insignificant or inconsequential? On the face of it, it is not. But can it cause injury by itself and on its own? It depends, but certainly the imports can contribute to the injury. Given this situation, how should an investigating authority proceed? One could draw a conclusion that the but-for analysis may be helpful when a limited number of factors present themselves, but when the factors are too many, it would be preferable to avoid this test. One could therefore conclude that the but-for test cannot account for the causality determination when plurality of causes is involved. But, as stated earlier, when imports are the obvious cause of injury, the but-for test could be an effective test.

The use of economic analysis is a bone of contention in injury and causation determination. The general opinion seems to be that quantification may be desirable, as far as possible. As the WTO Panel in *US—Steel* said, "[e]ven the most simplistic of quantitative analyses may yield useful insights … into the nature and extent of injury being caused by factors other than increased imports to the domestic industry"[160] Regression analysis is used to estimate the relationship between various economic variables. A particular regression technique used in similar estimations is the Granger causality analysis. But as Josling and Sapir argue, Granger causality models can be demanding in terms of data requirements. Economic models such as COMPAS, as used by the USITC, will have some utility in measuring the magnitude of impact imports on the domestic market. Again, as Durling and MacCullough suggest, these models may not be very appropriate in distinguishing the relative impact of different factors that might have simultaneously caused injury to the domestic industry.[161] Again, as Rodrik puts it, the conclusions in economic models are true only to extent their critical assumptions approximate reality.[162] It is also argued that given the narrow product lines chosen in antidumping and CVD cases, it will not be easy to gather reliable data for econometric analysis.[163] It is therefore not surprising that COMPAS results are

---

[160]Panel Report, *US – Steel Safeguards*, ¶ 10.341.

[161]Durling & McCullough, *Teaching Old Laws New Tricks*, supra note 155.

[162]Dani Rodrik, Economics Rules 18 (2015).

[163]Alan O. Sykes, *The Economics of Injury in Antidumping and Countervailing Duty Cases*, 16(5) International Review of Law and Economics, 5, 10 (1996).

generally attached to the back of staff reports that accompany the USITC decisions but need not be a basis for decision in most cases.[164]

A challenge for most trade remedy authorities could be in performing non-attribution when multiple factors are causing injury to the domestic industry. The foregoing discussion touched upon the but-for test and econometric models such as COMPAS which have been reported to useful when dumping/increased imports could be the most obvious candidates for injury.[165] However, such models can have limitations when multiple causes are involved. Considering these limitations, economists have used simultaneous equations models such as the "two-stage least squares" model to estimate supply-demand in the product being investigated.[166] For example, Professor Thomas Prusa's two-stage least square estimate was embraced by the USITC in the Investigation on Cold-Rolled Steel (2000).[167] However, these models require reliable set of time series data and are recommended only in few cases which meet the rigorous data requirements.

In sum, all approaches to causation determination and non-attribution that are in vogue, both in the U.S. and E.U. and elsewhere,[168] have significant shortcomings. A vast majority of cases examined in this chapter are based on pro-forma or checklist templates. In fact, any court or authority second guessing the determination of injury and causality could find some flaws in the approach. It is therefore no wonder that Alan Sykes remarked that no country could perhaps conduct a safeguard investigation without being challenged or the causation findings being unsettled.[169] Despite this reality, not all findings of injury and causation can be challenged successfully at the WTO, if the investigating agencies have provided a reasonable and sufficient explanation of various causal factors. According to the standard of review prevailing in trade remedy investigations, especially in antidumping, the panels and the Appellate Body are required to uphold the conclusions of an investigating authority if such findings could have been reached by an objective and unbiased investigating authority on the basis of the evidence available on record.[170] Investigating authorities while anchoring on the traditional

---

[164]Durling & McCullough, *supra* note 155, at 80-81.

[165]*Id*, at 81.

[166]David C. Sharp & Kenneth Zantow, *Attribution of Injury in the shrimp antidumping case: A simultaneous Equations Model*, 6(5) ECONOMIC BULLETIN 1 (2005).

[167]United States International Trade Commission, Investigation on Cold-Rolled Steel Products from Argentina, et al., Inv. Nos. 731-TA-829-40 (Final), Jan, 2000; see also T.J. Prusa and D.C. *Sharp, Simultaneous Equations in Antidumping Investigations*, 14(1) JOURNAL OF FORENSIC ECONOMICS 63 (2001). Prusa and Sharp's model of the cold-rolled steel industry was prepared for the US antidumping investigation of that industry during 1999 and 2000.

[168]Other major users of trade remedy instruments include India, Argentina, Mexico, Brazil, etc. A detailed discussion of the injury and causality determination of the key users of trade remedy instruments is provided in Chapters IV and V of this book.

[169]SYKES, *supra* note 126, at 252.

[170]The standard of review applicable to antidumping measures is set forth in Art. 17.6 of the Antidumping Agreement. See Panel Report, *Egypt- Steel Rebar*, ¶ 116; see also Appellate Body Report, *US – Softwood Lumber VI* (Article 21.5 – Canada), ¶ 17.

trends analysis could also seek the help of economic models in isolating and examining the role of a known factor as far as possible.

## E Conclusion

As the foregoing discussions indicate, the WTO provisions on trade remedy instruments do not clearly specify the methods and approaches by which the WTO Members may carry out the injury and causality analysis. Even the degree of causation required or the process of separating and distinguishing the injurious effects of other known factors is not uniform. However, various WTO members have been using traditional techniques such as the coincidence-in-trends or correlation analysis in determining injury and causation. Although the trends or the correlation analysis occupy a central position in injury and causation examination, various panels and the Appellate Body have also said that such analysis alone cannot prove causality.[171]

The standard set by the WTO Appellate Body does not require that increased imports or dumped imports be a 'sole', 'substantive' or 'predominant' cause of injury. The focus of various WTO Panels and the Appellate Body was to establish an unbroken chain of causation. However, it needs to be stated that the rulings made by the WTO Appellate Body to establish a chain of causation in the nature of a "genuine and substantial relationship of cause and effect" was by itself not very illuminating. The WTO Appellate Body also noted that the investigating authorities must establish explicitly, through a reasoned and adequate explanation that the injury caused by factors other than increased imports/dumped imports is not attributed to such imports–a requirement popularly known as the "non-attribution" analysis.

While the non-attribution analysis has certain appeal, the task of separating and distinguishing the impact of various injury factors is considerably more burdensome than anticipated. There is an overwhelming view that the non-attribution analysis can only be done by way of a quantitative examination. However, this view is contentious and a generally acceptable methodology for conducting non-attribution analysis is yet to be identified. The WTO case law on this aspect is still developing. In addition, the reliability of economic models will depend on the robustness of assumptions made and the accuracy of the data. This chapter discussed how certain types of simultaneous equation models such as the two-stage least square estimates were taken into consideration by the USITC in certain cases. However, the larger issue is that use of sophisticated econometric models has its own political repercussions in addition to its inherent limitations. Even assuming that econometric models are robust and useful, the regressions results can be quite difficult for non-statisticians or policy makers or judges to interpret. Therefore, such

[171]Panel Report, *Argentina- Footwear*, ¶. 142.

requirements should not be imposed on all users of trade remedy mechanisms under the WTO. In view of the uncertainty over the methodology in undertaking proper isolation or separation of the role of other causal factors, this study argues that a strict non-attribution test advocated by the Appellate Body is neither necessary nor warranted.

This study has already found that there is clear movement towards the use of qualitative methods for the conduct of the non-attribution test, although the Appellate Body is yet to give an affirmative opinion on such methodologies. Based on an examination of some of the recent rulings of the panels in cases such as *US—DRAM*, *Mexico—Oil*, *Egypt—Rebar*, and *Mexico—Pipe and Fittings* this study finds that the evolving thinking on injury and causation in WTO jurisprudence is not to opt for a strictly scientific or quantitative test, but a cogent test which should respect the underlying purpose and objectives of such trade remedy instruments. In other words, the non-attribution analysis is now being widely considered as an obligation to identify various causes of injury and demonstrate the consideration of such factors through an explicit and well-documented analysis. So long as the analysis is reasoned and logical, a reviewing panel is unlikely to overturn the injury and causation findings. In other words, if the injury and causation findings meet certain 'minimum standard of substantive rationality',[172] it should be considered as acceptable.

While acknowledging the difficulties of conducting quantitative methods, this study highlighted the emerging importance of qualitative methods. The qualitative test could subsume a two tier test, which comprises: (1) a correlation analysis, and (b) a non-attribution analysis. The correlation analysis can be conducted through the coincidence-in-time (trends analysis) and the price undercutting or underselling analysis (price effects analysis). Although correlation is not the same thing as causation, it is perhaps the best evidence of it. Therefore, all investigation agencies should routinely conduct such analysis to establish injury and causation. However, the second tier of examination, namely the non-attribution can be satisfied through a proper discovery of all causes causing injury and a proper evaluation of such causes even through descriptive means. A scrutiny of WTO disputes (listed in Appendix) clearly indicates that a strictly scientific or economic "isolation" or "separation" of the effects of other causal factors as advocated by certain panels or Appellate Body decisions is neither essential nor practically feasible for all WTO members. Barring the United States, none of the respondents in the WTO cases had availed econometric models for determining causation in some of the domestic investigations which were under challenge. In this context, it is up to the WTO members to choose a desirable approach.

This study has also examined the utility of the much talked about 'but-for' test as an alternative test in injury and causation. The but-for test which is widely used in common law jurisdictions is undeniably a good option in causal determination in

---

[172]Andrew T. Guzman, *Determining the Appropriate Standard of Review in WTO Disputes*, 42 (1) Cornell International Law Journal 45 (2009).

certain specific circumstances. However, it may have shortcomings where there are multiple causes. Furthermore, even the but-for test may require quantitative analysis if it has to be properly administered in practice. The but-for test has already been incorporated in the *Unitary analysis* in some of the established users of trade remedies such as the United States. But the overwhelming view is that the but-for test is more useful where there are only a limited causes of injury, or more accurately, where the imports are the obvious cause of injury. Furthermore, the but-for test may not be highly appropriate, especially if the imports are treated just as a "cause" and not the necessary cause of injury.

This chapter also examined the presence of other known causes of injury in the non-attribution analysis. It is important to identify all known causes in addition to the causes enlisted in Article 3.5 of the AD Agreement or Article 15.5 of the SCM Agreement. One of the ways of improving the non-attribution analysis is to require a clarification of the obligations with respect to discharging the burden of proof requirements on raising known factors/other factors in the Antidumping, Subsidies, and Safeguards Agreements. Dumping, subsidy or increased imports occupy centrality in injury and causality only because such factors are statutory causes. Yet there is a need to identify the non-apparent or non-obvious causes. WTO members can also include separate sections in their antidumping/subsidies/safeguard questionnaire to gather information on the existence of various non-listed causal factors. Calling expert witnesses is another way of seeking information on the reasons for injury to the domestic industry and their possible impacts. Identification and explanation of the various known causal factors by in itself could be a good insurance against the abusive use of trade remedy instruments. However, a long lasting solution could be found only if more relaxed standards of causation are introduced, the details of which will be further examined in the upcoming chapters.

# Appendix

| Dispute | Dispute No. | Discussion of listed and unlisted known factors in WTO disputes |
|---|---|---|
| *Antidumping agreement* | | |
| 1. Thailand—H-Beam (Panel) | 122 | ***Art. 3.5 Known factors***<br>• Increase in imports from Poland (the complainant)<br>• Actual and potential decline in productivity<br>• Obsolete technological development<br>***Other known factors*** (7.268)<br>• World-wide demand for H-Beams (including export markets);<br>• Consumption patterns (including the general economic environment and local demand);<br>• Potential trade restrictive practices of and competition b/w domestic and foreign producers;<br>• Influence of non-Polish imports;<br>• Nature of Siam Yamato Steel Co. Ltd. ("SYS") (the sole Thai producer of H-beams) entry into the H-Beam Market |
| 2. EC—Bed Linen, (Panel) | 141 | ***Art. 3.5 Known factors***<br>Imports from non-subject countries (Para. 100, First Submission of India)<br>***Other known factors*** (Paras. 102–108, First Submission of India)<br>• Increase in raw cotton prices<br>• Developments in Community Consumption and demand<br>• Competition from non-complainant producers in the Community |
| 3. EC—Bed Linen, Article 21.5 (Panel) | 141 | ***Art. 3.5 Known factors***<br>Increase in imports from third countries (6.229)<br>***Other known factors*** (6.218)<br>• Prices of Bed Linen were not able to keep pace with inflation in prices of consumer goods<br>• An increase in the cost of raw cotton. (6.223) |
| 4. U.S.—Hot-Rolled Steel from Japan (Panel) | 184 | ***Other known factors*** (7.237–7.257)<br>• An increase in the capacity of the mini-mills in the U.S. (7.240);<br>• The effects of a strike at General Motors (7.242);<br>• The decline in demand for hot-rolled steel from the pipe industry (7.245); and<br>• The effects of prices of non-dumped imports (7.247) |

(continued)

(continued)

| Dispute | Dispute No. | Discussion of listed and unlisted known factors in WTO disputes |
|---|---|---|
| 5. Egypt—Rebar (Panel) | 211 | ***Other known factors*** (7.108)<br>• The dramatic capacity expansion at the two major Egyptian rebar producers and its likely temporary effects on their cost structures;<br>• Effects of intra-industry competition;<br>• Alleged sharp contraction in demand for raw material (Falling prices for steel scrap, the primary raw material input at Al Ezz);<br>• A sharp contraction in demand in January 1999, the very month in which the prices of the rebar fell, and<br>• The effect of comparably prices, fairly traded imports |
| 6. EC—Pipe Fittings (Panel) | 219 | ***Other known factors*** (7.350)<br>• EC producers' poor export performance;<br>• Imports from the countries not subject to the investigation;<br>• Outsourcing;<br>• Rationalization efforts (restructuring efforts of the industry in 1995);<br>• Substitution of the product concerned; and<br>• The difference in the cost of production and the market perception between the two variants of the product concerned |
| 7. Mexico—Steel Pipes and Tubes AD Duties (Panel) | 331 | ***Art 3.5 known factors*** (7.215)<br>• Volume and prices of imports not sold at dumping prices;<br>• Contraction in demand or changes in the patter of consumption;<br>• Trade restrictive practices of and competition between the foreign and domestic producers;<br>• Developments in technology by the domestic industry;<br>• Export performance and productivity of domestic industry.<br>• Decline in exports<br>***Other Known factors*** (7.351)<br>• Increase in operating costs |
| 8. Japan—DRAMS | 336 | • Did not raise any factor |
| 9. EC—Salmon AD Measure (Panel) | 337 | ***Other Known factors*** (7.647)<br>• EC producers' increased cost of production<br>• Imports of Salmon from the United States and Canada |
| 10. EC—Fasteners (Panel) | 397 | ***Art 3..5 known factors*** *(7.433)*<br>• Export performance of the domestic industry<br>***Other known factors***<br>• Increased raw material prices (7.430) |

(continued)

(continued)

| Dispute | Dispute No. | Discussion of listed and unlisted known factors in WTO disputes |
|---|---|---|
| 11. EU—Footwear (China) (Panel) | 405 | ***Art 3.5 Known Factors*** (7.492)<br>• Export performance of the EU industry;<br>***Other known factors*** (7.538)<br>• Imports from other third country;<br>• Lifting of the quota;<br>• Structural inefficiencies of the EU industry and high labour costs;<br>• Outsourcing.<br>• Non-tariff barriers<br>• Exchange rate fluctuations; |
| 12. China—GOES (Panel) | 414 | ***Other known factors*** (7.263)<br>• Domestic industry's capacity and production; and<br>• Low demand and increase in inventories more than the subject imports.<br>• Value and volume of non-subject imports<br>• excess capacity |
| 13. China—X-Ray Equipment (Panel) | 425 | ***Other known factors***<br>• Global Economic Crisis 2008 (7.268);<br>• Nuctech's start-up situation (7.292);<br>• Nuctech's aggressive pricing policy (7.287);<br>• Nuctech's aggressive business expansion (7.281); and<br>• Fair competition b/w Nuctech and other producers (7.272) |
| 14. China—Autos (US) (Panel) | 440 | ***Other known factors***<br>• Decline in apparent consumption in China (7.347);<br>• Increase in average wages coupled with decline in industry productivity (7.352); and<br>• Increase in sales tax (7.358) |
| 15. China—HP-SST (Japan) (Panel) | 454 | ***Other known factors***<br>• Decline in domestic demand (7.173);<br>• Expansion of domestic production |
| 16. China—HP-SST (EU) | 460 | ***Other Known factors*** (7.169, 7.196, 7.205)<br>• Decline in apparent consumption<br>• Increase in domestic production capacity |
| *Subsidies and countervailing measures agreement* | | |
| 17. U.S.—Lumber ITC Investigation (Panel) | 277 | ***Other known factors*** (7.128)<br>• Increase in non-subject imports;<br>• Other substitutes for lumber; and<br>• Cyclical demand and housing construction cycle |
| 18. U.S.—Lumber ITC Investigation (21.5 Panel) | 277 | ***Other known factors*** (5.13)<br>• Excess supply from the domestic industry<br>• Third country or non-subject imports<br>• Integration of North American Softwood Lumber Industry<br>• Importation relative to demand<br>• Engineered wood products and other substitute products<br>• Insufficient timber supplies |

(continued)

(continued)

| Dispute | Dispute No. | Discussion of listed and unlisted known factors in WTO disputes |
|---|---|---|
| 19. U.S.—DRAMS CVD Investigation (Panel) | 296 | ***Other known factors*** (7.355)<br>• Increase in non-subject imports;<br>• Capacity increases by other suppliers; and<br>• Decline in demand and technological and production difficulties admitted by Micron |
| 20. EC—DRAMS (Panel) | 299 | ***Other known factors*** (7.436)<br>• Economic downturn in EC market;<br>• Overcapacity; and<br>• Increase in non-subsidized imports. |
| 21. Mexico—Olive Oil CVD (Panel) | 341 | ***Other known factors*** (7.307)<br>• Loss of the previous distribution network;<br>• Loss of the ability to use a leading Spanish brand name on its olive oil;<br>• Loss of the guaranty of supply that the market demanded;<br>• Lack of a guaranty of a product of the quality demanded by purchasers of olive oil;<br>• Status prior to 2002, of the relationship between Fortuny's predecessor and its distributor which was importing increasing amounts from the European Communities; and<br>• High level of Fortuny's costs |
| 22. U.S.—Carbon Steel (India) (Panel) | 436 | ***Other known factors*** (7.368)<br>• Effect of non-subsidized dumped imports;<br>• Reduced demand for line pipe as a result of reduced oil and gas drilling;<br>• Competition among domestic producers of line pipe;<br>• A decline in demand in export markets;<br>• Shift from oil country tubular goods production to line pipe production; and<br>• Decline in raw material costs |
| *Safeguards agreement* | | |
| 23. Korea—Dairy Safeguards (Panel) | 98 | ***Other known factors***<br>• Import price of basic materials for cheese (7.62);<br>• Low production of cheese affecting the production and consumption pattern of raw milk in Korea; (7.94)<br>• Domestic regulation affecting the sales of raw milk. (7.95)<br>• Increased imports (7.63);<br>• High inventory (7.64);<br>• Market share captured by third country imports (7.65);<br>• Increase in the level of dairy sales (7.66);<br>• Decrease in production of the domestic dairy products (7.67); |

(continued)

(continued)

| Dispute | Dispute No. | Discussion of listed and unlisted known factors in WTO disputes |
|---|---|---|
| 24. Argentina—Footwear Safeguards (Panel) | 121 | ***Other known factors*** (8.265)<br>• The tequila effect i.e. the domestic recession in Argentina brought on by the collapse of the Mexico peso;<br>• Imports under the Industrial Specialization regime; and<br>• Imports from Mercosur countries |
| 25. U.S.—Wheat Gluten Safeguards (Panel) | 166 | ***Other known factors*** (8.119)<br>• The effect of wheat protein premiums on the wheat protein price in the US market;<br>• Co-product markets;<br>• Increased domestic capacity;<br>• Increase in input prices; and<br>• Imports by US producers and capacity utilization |
| 26. U.S.—Line Pipe Safeguards (Panel) | 202 | ***Other known factors*** (7.283)<br>• Decline in line pipe demand resulting from reduced oil and natural gas drilling and production activities;<br>• Competition among domestic producers;<br>• A decline in export markets in 1998 and 1999;<br>• A shift from OCTG production to line pipe production; and<br>• A decline in raw material costs |
| 27. Chile- Agricultural Products | 207 | ***Other known factors*** (6.39)<br>• Chilean wheat industry was heavily affected by drought |
| 28. Argentina—Peach Safeguards (Panel) | 238 | ***Other known factors*** (7.97)<br>• Capacity utilization of the domestic industry;<br>• Productivity of the domestic industry; and<br>• Increase in employment situation in the domestic industry |
| 29. U.S.—Cotton Subsidies, Article 21.5 (Panel) | 267 | ***Other known factors*** (7.50)<br>• Substantial proportionate influence of the US on the world market for upland cotton;<br>• Mandatory and price contingent nature and revenue stabilizing effect of marketing loan;<br>• Counter-cyclical payments;<br>• The order of magnitude of the marketing loan;<br>• Counter-cyclical subsidies; and<br>• Significant gap between the total costs of production of the US upland cotton producers and their market revenue |

(continued)

(continued)

| Dispute | Dispute No. | Discussion of listed and unlisted known factors in WTO disputes |
|---|---|---|
| 30. U.S.—Lamb Safeguards (Panel) | 177, 178 | ***Other known factors*** (7.263)<br>• The termination of US- Wool Act payments;<br>• Competition from other meat products;<br>• Increased input costs;<br>• Overfeeding of lambs; and<br>• Alleged concentration in the packer segment of the industry, etc. |
| 31. U.S.—Steel Safeguards (Panel) | 248, 249, 251, 252, 253, 254, 258, 259 | ***Other known factors*** (10.561)<br>• Increases in energy costs;<br>• Declining domestic demand;<br>• Competition among domestic producers;<br>• Domestic capacity increases; |
| 32. US- Tyres (Panel) | 399 | ***Other known factors*** (7.3)<br>• Domestic industry's business strategy<br>• Voluntary plant closures by U.S. producers as part of long terms strategy<br>• Changes in demand<br>• Subject imports by U.S. producers<br>• 2008 recession |
| 33. Dominican Republic—Bag and Fabric Safeguards (Panel) | 415, 416, 417, 418 | ***Other known factors*** (7.311)<br>• Changes in the levels of sales;<br>• Productivity of the domestic industry;<br>• Increase in domestic capacity;<br>• Increase in Capacity utilization; and<br>• Favourable employment in the domestic industry |

# Chapter 4
# Injury and Causation in Antidumping Investigations: Experience of India and Other Jurisdictions

**Abstract** This chapter provides a detailed examination of the practices of the key users of antidumping instruments in conducting injury and causation by treating India as the prototype of a major developing country user. Central to this enquiry is the need for an analysis of the key practices and developments among the traditional and new users of antidumping. This chapter enquires whether the injury and causation assessment among the major users is carried out in accordance with the requirements established by the WTO rules and the observations of the panels and the Appellate Body. In addition, the following analysis has attempted to find out whether any of the key users is resorting to sophisticated economics or quantitative tools while assessing injury and causation.

## A Introduction

The previous chapters examined how trade remedy practices of industrialized nations have evolved over time. Chapter 2, in specific, evaluated the role of trade remedies as an adjunct to industrial policy and how the domestic legislations of some of the traditional users retained trade remedy as a flexible policy tool. It may be pertinent to recall that until the launch of the Uruguay Round, just four jurisdictions—the United States, European Union, Canada, and Australia—had implemented more than 90 percent of antidumping actions.[1] However, the number of trade remedy actions has increased manifold in the last few decades, especially after the establishment of the World Trade Organization (WTO) in 1995. The United States is no longer the leader in antidumping investigations, and the European Union does not figure in the list of the top three users. Emerging economies such as Brazil, China and India occupy the leading positions in using trade remedies now. Even other developing countries such as Argentina, Mexico and Turkey have catapulted themselves as some of the new top users.

---

[1]Maurizio Zanardi, *Antidumping: What are the Numbers to Discuss at Doha?* 27 (3) THE WORLD ECONOMY 403 (2003).



J.J. Nedumpara, *Injury and Causation in Trade Remedy Law*,
DOI 10.1007/978-981-10-2197-8_4

The challenges of trade remedy disputes at the WTO, however, present a different picture. The trade remedy practices of the United States and the European Union have been the subject of several WTO disputes in the last two decades. The United States was involved in more than sixty WTO disputes, whereas the European Union (formerly EC) was involved in nearly 30 disputes. The injury and causation findings by both these jurisdictions have been challenged in several disputes and the WTO panels and the Appellate Body had occasion to comment on the trade remedy practices and the methodologies applied by these jurisdictions. The details of these WTO challenges have already been exhaustively examined in Chap. 3. However, the trade remedy practices of developing countries and emerging economies are yet to be seriously tested. Among the developing countries only Argentina, Mexico and China have been involved in WTO trade remedy disputes on multiple occasions. While 7 cases were filed against Argentina, 5 cases were filed against Mexico and 11 cases against China.[2] Some of the disputes against Mexico have risen in the context of trade liberalization under NAFTA whereas the trade remedy disputes under Argentina have been initiated in the context of the MERCOSUR.[3] In other words, those disputes were bi-national disputes centered on the regional trade agreement (RTA), but brought to the WTO under the WTO Dispute Settlement Understanding (DSU). The trade remedy investigations against China have been mounted in the context of China's rising export competitiveness and its status as the world's largest merchandise exporter. Otherwise, there have been relatively few challenges to the trade remedy practices of developing and emerging economies.

India's recent use of anti-dumping mechanism has received some attraction from developed country scholars.[4] As of 2014, India is one of the largest users of antidumping actions in the world. From the inception of the WTO until December 2014, India accounted for 740 of the 4757 anti-dumping initiations adopted by Members, i.e., 15.6 % of the total.[5] Measured by the number of anti-dumping measures implemented between 1995 and 2014, India ranks first at 740 and China ranks eighth at 218—ahead of all other countries, developed or developing.[6] It is evident that India used antidumping to slow down or limit the adverse impact of globalization on Indian corporations (Table 1).

---

[2]World Trade Organization, Dispute settlement Gateway, http://www.wto.org/english/tratop_e/dispu_e/dispu_e.htm (last visited on October 12., 2014).

[3]Common Market of the Southern Hemisphere.

[4]See M. Wu, *Antidumping in Asia's Emerging Giants*, 53(1) Harvard International Law Journal 102 (2012).

[5]World Trade Organization, Anti-Dumping Initiations: By Exporting Country 01/01/1995–31/12/2013, http://www.wto.org/english/tratop_e/adp_e/AD_InitiationsByExpCty.pdf.

[6]World Trade Organization, Anti-Dumping Initiations: By Reporting Member 01/01/1995–31/12/2013, http://www.wto.org/english/tratop_e/adp_e/AD_InitiationsByRepMem.pdf.

**Table 1** Antidumping Actions by India between 1995–2014

| Year | Antidumping | Final measures |
|---|---|---|
| 1995 | 6 | 7 |
| 1996 | 21 | 2 |
| 1997 | 13 | 8 |
| 1998 | 28 | 22 |
| 1999 | 64 | 23 |
| 2000 | 41 | 55 |
| 2001 | 79 | 38 |
| 2002 | 81 | 64 |
| 2003 | 46 | 52 |
| 2004 | 21 | 29 |
| 2005 | 28 | 18 |
| 2006 | 31 | 16 |
| 2007 | 47 | 24 |
| 2008 | 55 | 31 |
| 2009 | 31 | 30 |
| 2010 | 41 | 32 |
| 2011 | 19 | 26 |
| 2012 | 21 | 30 |
| 2013 | 29 | 12 |
| 2014 | 38 | 15 |
| Total | 740 | 534 |

*Source* WTO

In the light of India's status as the leading anti-dumping user among the WTO members in the last decade-and-half, this chapter seeks to examine India's injury and causation determination process and investigative methodologies. The larger objective is to examine the issues faced by one of the leading developing country users of trade remedy instruments. By looking at a sample of cases decided in the last two decades, this chapter examines whether India has been able to implement and domestically enforce the exacting WTO standards in injury and causation determination. As the WTO AD Agreement will have to carefully balance the concerns of members that are at varying levels of development, imposition of rigorous standards will have too little political appeal. At the same time, there is a need to ensure that such mechanisms are not used to derive undue protection in a global trading regime. In the above context, Sect. B of this chapter examines the rise in Indian antidumping actions; Sects. C and D provide a detailed analysis of the Indian antidumping practices on injury and causation. Section E provides a brief analysis of the injury and causation practices of the European Union, Australia, Brazil, China, Argentina, Mexico and South Africa and the United States. Section F summarises the conclusions and findings..

# B Rise of Antidumping in India: Legal Framework and Institutions

## 1 *India, Antidumping and the Uruguay Round*

As a founding Member of the GATT, India was indeed exposed to the complexities and the political economy considerations of using trade remedy measures. However, India did not introduce a formal legislation authorizing the use of trade remedies until several decades later. The Indian economy remained a relatively closed market for foreign products following its independence in 1947. During the post-independence period, domestic manufacturers continued to benefit from the licensing regime, high tariffs, and foreign exchange policies that impaired competition. India maintained quantitative restrictions on imports of nearly one-third of its tariff lines during the 1980s and 1990s citing balance of payment reasons. At the time of the 1991 economic reforms, the Indian import-weighted average tariff was 87 %; the simple average was 128 %, and some tariffs were in excess of 300 %. There were massive reductions in tariffs in the post-1991 reform period, but the import duties still remained very high. In view of the high protection that the Indian industry received, there was hardly any need for import relief laws in India. Furthermore, to quote Arvind Panagariya, there was a "benign neglect" of trade policy during this period.[7]

More than three decades after assuming various tariff obligations under the GATT, India finally incorporated legislative provisions in 1982 in the Customs Tariff Act, 1975. The legal framework for conduct of trade remedy investigations was established in 1982 through an amendment to the Customs Tariff Act of 1975. Sections 9A, 9AA, 9B and 9C were inserted in the Customs Tariff Act to govern various aspects of antidumping, countervailing duties and safeguard actions. Even after enactment of these legislative provisions, the law languished in the statute book for another decade. When India signed the Marrakesh Agreement establishing the WTO, India undertook further amendments to the Customs Tariff Act to incorporate the obligations under the Uruguay Round. In 1995, India also introduced the Customs Tariff (Identification, Assessment and Collection of Antidumping Duty on Dumped Articles and for Determination of Injury) Rules, 1995 for implementing the WTO Antidumping Agreement.

The rise of antidumping actions in India was rather unexpected considering India's slow embrace of this instrument in the context of the GATT. However, some studies indicate that antidumping remedies came into the center stage partly in response to the large tariff cuts undertaken in certain sectors of the economy. For example, Bown and Tovar find that the products that sought antidumping protection in the post reform period appeared to have received, on an average, larger tariff cuts during decade of the 1990s.[8]

---

[7] Arvind Panagariya, India: The Emerging Giant, 29 (2008).

[8] Chad P. Bown and P. Tovar, Trade Liberalization, Antidumping and Safeguards: Evidence from India's Tariff Reform, 96(1) Journal of Development Economics 115, 117(2011).

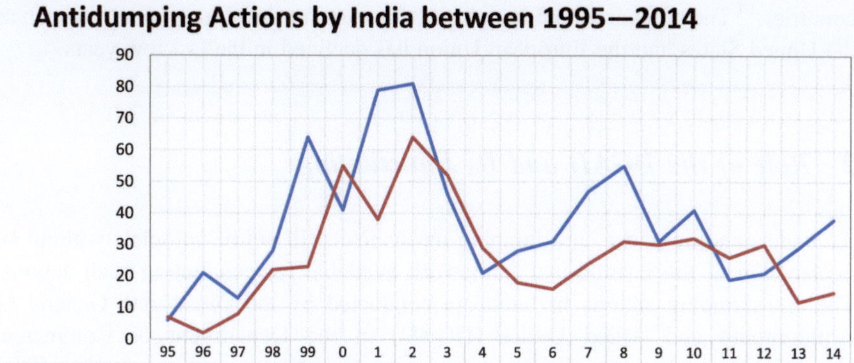


| | 95 | 96 | 97 | 98 | 99 | 0 | 1 | 2 | 3 | 4 | 5 | 6 | 7 | 8 | 9 | 10 | 11 | 12 | 13 | 14 |
|---|---|---|---|---|---|---|---|---|---|---|---|---|---|---|---|---|---|---|---|---|
| Anti-dumping Actions | 6 | 21 | 13 | 28 | 64 | 41 | 79 | 81 | 46 | 21 | 28 | 31 | 47 | 55 | 31 | 41 | 19 | 21 | 29 | 38 |
| Final Measures | 7 | 2 | 8 | 22 | 23 | 55 | 38 | 64 | 52 | 29 | 18 | 16 | 24 | 31 | 30 | 32 | 26 | 30 | 12 | 15 |



**Fig. 1** Trends in India's Antidumping Actions. *Source* WTO

Antidumping measures, despite attracting a protectionist tag in other developed countries did not suffer from any such public policy opposition in India. For example, the Supreme Court stated in *Reliance Industries v. Designated Authorities*[9] that antidumping was one of the mechanisms for advancing fair competition in India. As the Supreme Court of India noted, "[t]he industries which had been built up after independence with great difficulties must not be allowed to be destroyed by unfair competition".[10] The High Court of Madras also expressed the view that antidumping law being an economic legislation should be construed with the intention of developing the domestic industry.[11]

The sentiments echoed in the above appellate court decisions were apparently the leitmotif of the Indian antidumping enforcement. The antidumping actions were filed when the traditional forms of protection slowly waned. India initiated its first antidumping investigation in 1992 against the imports of Polyvinyl Chloride (PVC) in 1992.[12] The investigation was launched against imports from Brazil, Mexico, Korea and the United States. After a slow start, the number of actions peaked in the late 1990s/early 2000s [see Fig. 1]. A bulk of the actions has been concentrated in the chemicals and petrochemicals, pharmaceuticals, steel and the textiles sectors.[13] India's antidumping actions are increasingly against countries such as China, Republic of Korea (South Korea), Malaysia, Taiwan and other ASEAN

---

[9]2006 (10) SCC 368.

[10]*Id.*

[11]Nirma Limited v. Saint Gobain Glass India Limited, 2012 (281) ELT 321 (CESTAT, Madras).

[12]V. Lakshmi Kumaran, *The 10 Major Problems with the Antidumping Instrument in India*, 39 (1) Journal of World Trade 115 (2005).

[13]See Wu, *Antidumping in Asia's Emerging Giants,* supra note 4, at 32, 79.

countries.[14] The number of antidumping actions against developed countries such as the United States and the European Union has declined in the last few years.

## 2 *Role of the DGAD and Its Functioning*

An understanding of the anti-dumping mechanism will not be complete without an explanation of the institutional framework available for conducting such actions. The anti-dumping actions in India are conducted by the Directorate General of Antidumping and Allied Duties (DGAD) in the Department of Commerce. The DGAD is also vested with the powers of initiating and conducting CVD investigations. India's anti-dumping process has a single track determination of injury and dumping quite similar to the EU system. The DGAD, however, does not directly administer or implement the anti-dumping measures. The DGAD recommends anti-dumping measures including the rate at which the duties have to be imposed. Based on the recommendations of the DGAD, the measures are implemented by the Department of Revenue in the Ministry of Finance. The Department of Revenue has certain discretion in not giving effect to the recommendations of the DGAD.[15] In many ways, the functioning of the DGAD is modelled along the lines of the DG Trade in thc European Commission.[16]

The conventional and the widely accepted basis for initiation of anti-dumping investigation in India is through domestic industry applications. The DGAD initiates anti-dumping investigations upon written application by or on behalf of domestic industry. In certain cases, the DGAD initiates actions *suo motu* provided there is a justification to launch an investigation. The applications received from the domestic industry are scrutinized by the DGAD to ensure that they are adequately documented and provide sufficient and accurate information on dumping, injury and causal link. If the evidence is not adequate, the DGAD can issue a "deficiency letter".

For successful initiation of investigations, the domestic industry applicants must meet the domestic industry standing requirements. Rule 24(2)(i) of the Indian Antidumping Rules stipulates that the domestic industry complainants must account for at least 25 % of total domestic production of the like product or article. In addition, the domestic producers expressly supporting the petition must account for more than 50 % of the total production of the like article by those expressly

---

[14]Computations based on the WTO statistics. See World Trade Organization, *Anti-dumping Measures: Reporting Member vs. Exporting Country 01/01/1995–31/12/2010* [hereinafter WTO Statistics on AD Measures by Reporting Member v. Exporting Country] (last visited on November 1, 2014).

[15]For example, the Ministry of Finance took a decision not to implement the final measures as by the Department of Commerce.

[16]All antidumping complaints in the EU are investigated by a single entity, the Directorate General Trade ("DG Trade") in the European Commission. For more information about its handling of antidumping complaints, http://ec.europa.eu/trade/.

supporting and opposing the application. In line with the WTO Antidumping Agreement, dumping alone is not sufficient to claim relief. In addition to dumping, injury in the sense of material injury or material retardation in the setting up of the domestic industry will also have to be established.

For a petition to proceed, the DGAD must verify the accuracy and adequacy of the evidence provided with respect to dumping, injury, and a causal link. In addition, other injury causes have to be investigated so that they are not attributed to dumping. As dumping practices happen outside the country, collection of reliable and verifiable data regarding the three key elements of an anti-dumping investigation is not often easy. Perforce, the quality of evidence available to the DGAD at the time of initiation of the investigation with respect to these three elements can never match the quality of data that subsequently flows in. Nonetheless, there is an obligation on the domestic industry petitioners to provide all 'reasonably available' information at the time of the investigation. For example, while reviewing an anti-dumping investigation, the High Court of Rajasthan quoted a WTO panel in *Guatemala-Cements II* in support of the evidentiary thresholds.[17] The WTO panel in *Guatemala-Cement II* has set the widely quoted standard:

> An antidumping investigation is a process where certainty on the existence of all the elements necessary in order to adopt a measure is reached gradually as the investigations moves forward. However, the evidence must be such that an unbiased and objective investigating authority could determine that there was sufficient evidence of dumping… to justify an investigation.[18]

Before examining the legal framework and the conduct of investigations, it may be useful to examine the timelines involved in the conduct of an anti-dumping investigation in India. The initiation of anti-dumping investigations is made through public notices issued in the public gazettes. The DGAD informs the government of the exporting country, and issues a public notice with details of the initiation and the time-limits for interested parties to provide comments.

In an antidumping investigation, each exporter or producer can request for a separate margin of dumping. Under the Indian law, the Government is obliged to restrict the anti-dumping duty to the lower of the margin of dumping or the margin of injury, the details of which will be discussed later. Anti-dumping duties may remain in place for 5 years unless revoked earlier or extended by the DGAD.

A number of antidumping investigations do not reach final finding and are terminated. An investigation may be terminated by the DGAD, *inter alia*, on grounds of lack of injury or causal link. Cases with very little evidence of injury and causal link may not last their entire course and could be terminated, even based on the request of the domestic industry.

---

[17]Rajasthan Textiles Mills Association v. Designated Authority. 2002 (149) E.L.T. 45 (High Court of Rajasthan).

[18]Panel Report, *Guatemala – Definitive Anti-Dumping Measure on Grey Portland Cement from Mexico*, ¶ 8.35 WT/DS156/R (October 24, 2000).

In terms of Section 9C of India's Customs Tariff Act, 1975 as amended, appeals against the decisions of the DGAD (also referred to as "Designated Authority') regarding the existence, degree and effect of any dumping of an article, lies with the Customs, Excise and Service Tax Appellate Tribunal (CESTAT; known as CEGAT earlier) in the first instance. Only the final findings and reviews thereof, and the notification of the Department of Revenue imposing definitive duties can be appealed by an interested party before the CESTAT.[19] The CESTAT can examine all substantive and procedural issues including determination of domestic industry, standing, like article, normal value, export price, dumping margin, material injury, injury margin, causal link, etc. The CESTAT decision may be appealed to the Supreme Court under Article 136 of the Constitution of India.

## C Empirics of Injury and Causation Examination in India

The principles for determination of injury are provided under Annexure II of the Indian Antidumping Rules. The word "injury" defined in the operative part of Annexure II would include injury and threat of material injury to the domestic industry as well as material retardation of the establishment of such industry. Annexure II has listed most of the injury factors enumerated in Article 3.4 of the WTO Anti-Dumping Agreement. The factors include: natural[20] and potential declines in sales, profits, output, market share, productivity, return on investments or utilization of capacity; factors affecting domestic prices; the magnitude of the margin of dumping; actual and potential negative effects on cash flow, inventories, employment, wages, growth, and the ability to raise capital investments.

The injury is determined in accordance with Rule 11 of India's Antidumping Rules and the applicable principles are laid down in Annexure II of the Customs Tariff (Antidumping Duty) Rules 1995.

> The Designated Authority while determining the injury or threat of material injury to domestic industry or material retardation of the establishment of such an industry hereinafter referred to as "injury" and casual link between dumped imports and such injury, shall inter alia, take following principles under consideration:
>
> (i) A determination of injury shall involve an objective examination of both (a) the volume of the dumped imports and the effect of the dumped imports on prices in the domestic market for the like article and (b) the consequent impact of these imports on domestic producers of such products.
>
> (ii) While examining the volume of dumped imports, the said authority shall consider whether there has been a significant increase in the dumped imports, either in absolute terms or relative to production or consumption in India. With regard to the effect of the

[19] An interested party would include an importer or exporter or domestic industry or any interested person who had submitted representation to the Designated Authority in the course of investigation.

[20] The language used in the ADA is 'actual'. It is not entirely certain what the term 'natural' means.

dumped imports, on prices as referred to in Sub-rule (2) of Rule 18 the Designated Authority shall consider whether there has been a significant price undercutting by the dumped imports as compared with the price of like product in India, or whether the effect of such imports is otherwise to depress prices to a significant degree or prevent price increase which otherwise would have occurred, to a significant degree.[21]

Neither the Indian Antidumping legislation nor the WTO Anti-Dumping Agreement provides guidance on the period to be selected for injury examination. A recommendation of the WTO Committee on Anti-Dumping Practices provides that injury should be preferably be analyzed over a period of at least 3 years in order to detect the trends in volume, market shares and other economic factors.[22] The purpose is to examine the trends rather than the differences between the beginning and the end of the investigation period for a comprehensive injury examination.

## 1 *Examination of Volume and Price Effects*

According to the practice adopted by the DGAD, the injury is specifically analyzed in terms of the 'volume effect' and 'price effect' of the dumped imports. As examined in Chap. 3 and this chapter of this study, Article 3.2 of the Anti-Dumping Agreement (as also Article 15.2 of the Subsidies and Countervailing Measures Agreement) places an obligation on the investigating authorities to consider whether there is a significant increase in the volume of dumped imports either in absolute terms or relative to domestic production or consumption.

According to the practice followed in India, the DGAD focuses on the quantity of dumped imports and the effect it has on the market share of the domestic industry. The price effect, on the other hand, examines the domestic sales realization of the petitioning industry and the import prices. The price effect undertakes a temporal correlation between the trends in import prices and the trends in the indicators reflecting the conduct of the domestic industry. The volume and price effects have high probative value in establishing causal link in India.[23]

The DGAD conducts an enquiry regarding the effect of dumped imports on prices through the traditional price depression and price suppression analysis. First, the DGAD examines whether there has been a significant price undercutting by the dumped imports as compared with the price of the like domestic product in India.

[21]Customs Tariff (Identification, Assessment, and Collection of Antidumping Duty on Dumped Articles and for Determination of Injury) Rules, 1995, Gazette of India, section II(3)(i) (January 1, 1995) [hereinafter Indian Antidumping Rules].

[22]World Trade Organization, ADP Committee, *Recommendations for Data Collection for Antidumping Investigations*, ¶ 7.287 G/ADP/6 (May 16, 2000). A number of panels have referred to this recommendation, see Panel Report, *Argentina – Definitive Anti-Dumping Duties on Poultry from Brazil* (April 22, 2003).

[23]FAQ on Agreement on Antidumping, Centre for WTO Studies (CWS) Indian Institute of Foreign Trade (2011) *available at* http://wtocentre.iift.ac.in/FAQ/english/Anti-dumping.pdf.

Second, the DGAD examines whether the effects of such imports are otherwise to depress prices to a significant degree or to prevent price increases. Price depression is stated to take place under the Indian practice when the domestic industry's price levels are lower than the price levels during the previous period. Price suppression takes place when the increase in cost to make and sell the product is more than the increase in selling price of the domestic industry like product. Chapter 3 of this study examined the details of price undercutting and price underselling analysis in the context of WTO dispute settlement.

In order to conduct the price undercutting analysis, the DGAD computes the net sales realization. Net sales realization (NSR) is the selling price excluding taxes, duties, rebates, commission, etc. A price comparison for the product concerned is made between the landed value of imported product from subject countries and the NSR of the domestic industry. Landed value of imports is the assessable value of imports under the Customs Act and the applicable customs duties.[24] Further, a 1 percent handling charge is added to the landed value.

The DGAD also routinely uses the price underselling analysis in the injury and causation analysis. 'Underselling' is a term used in jurisdictions such as India and the E.U. to refer to the amount by which the dumped imports are at prices below the level necessary to eliminate injury. In India, the difference between fair selling price or the non-injurious price (NIP) and the landed value of imports is called the price underselling margin.[25] Price underselling can lead to price suppression. Price suppression takes place, when the increase in cost to make and sell is more than the increase in selling price of the domestic industry. In India, the NIP is determined on the basis of the weighted average cost of production of the domestic industry for the period of investigation (POI).[26]

The DGAD also takes into account the normated consumption norms and the raw material and utilities cost, actual expenses relating to overheads, capacity utilization, etc., to determine the cost of production. In addition, the DGAD makes provision for a certain amount for the return on capital employed (ROCE). The NIP is the price which the domestic industry would have charged under normal circumstances in the market during the period of investigation, or stated in other words, would have been the price at which the domestic industry would have been able to sell the product unaffected by the dumped imports. At the NIP level the domestic industry would be able to recover the cost of production, and a reasonable return on the capital employed after taking into account the consumption norms and practices of the domestic industry, the cost of raw materials, utilities and capacity utilization. NIP is often a useful benchmark for constructing the counterfactual price, i.e., a price which is not affected by dumped imports. NIP in certain other jurisdictions such as

[24]"Landed value" is the assessable value as determined under the Customs Act, 1962 (52 of 1962) and includes all duties of customs except duties levied under sections 3, 8B, 9 and 9A of the Customs Tariff Act.

[25]*See infra* Section C. 2 on Lesser Duty Rule for a detailed discussion.

[26]*See infra* Section C.2 on Lesser Duty Rule for more details.

Australia is referred to as the unsuppressed selling price, which as the name suggests, allows the domestic industry to operate as if dumping had not taken place.

The DGAD also cumulates the imports from more than one country if it is determined that (a) the margin of dumping established in relation to imports from each country is more than 2 % expressed as percentage of export price and the volume of the imports from each country is 3 % of the imports of like article, and (b) a cumulative assessment of the effect of imports is appropriate in light of the conditions of competition between the imported article and the like domestic article.[27]

## 2 *Lesser Duty Rule in India*

According to the WTO Anti-Dumping Agreement, once dumping and injury are established, an anti-dumping duty equal to the margin of dumping can be imposed. However, certain jurisdictions such as India, the European Union and Australia apply the lesser duty rule. According to the lesser duty rule, the antidumping duty is to be imposed in a lesser amount if such amount is sufficient to remove the injury to the domestic industry. Interestingly, the WTO Anti-Dumping Agreement has provided a choice between the two approaches.[28] The lesser duty rule is applied individually for each cooperating exporter.

The DGAD also calculates the NIP for the purpose of application of the lesser duty rule. The lesser duty rule operationalizes Article 9.1 of the Anti-Dumping Agreement. In practice, the lesser duty rule is based on the injury margin which is the difference between the ex-factory NIP and the landed value of the imported goods. In such a scenario, the calculation of the NIP serves the dual purpose of examining the price suppression or depression as well as the applicable antidumping duties.

The calculation of non-injurious price has a direct bearing in a number of anti-dumping investigations held in India. For example in the case of the anti-dumping proceedings on imports of purified terephthalic acid (PTA I) from Spain, Japan and Malaysia, no anti-dumping duty was recommended in respect of imports from Japan and Malaysia on the ground that the imports from these countries were above the non-injurious price. The Designated Authority at the same time had arrived at the margins of dumping for the manufacturers/exporters from Japan between 29 % and 34.26 %; for Malaysia at 68 %, and for Spain at 15 %. However, the Designated Authority held that there was no causal link between the imports from Japan and Malaysia. The Authority noted in the disclosure statement as follows:

[27]Antidumping Rules, Para III of Annexure II.

[28]WTO Antidumping Agreement, Art. 9.1. The text says that it is 'desirable that the duty be less than the margin of dumping, if such lesser duty would be adequate to remove the injury to the domestic industry.

> In the present proceedings the Authority does establish injury to the domestic industry on account of decline in the sales realization and profitability. However, its causal link with dumped imports is not established because the landed price of imports is found to be higher than the non-injurious price resulting in negative injury margin and the selling-price of the petitioner is found to be lower than the landed price. Since the landed prices of the imports are found to be higher than the sales realization there is no evidence of price undercutting or price depression resulting from the dumped imports.

Based on the finding, the Designated Authority imposed antidumping duties only against Spain.

The computation of the non-injurious price in India has been a highly contentious issue as the domestic industry would seek a higher non-injurious price and the exporters and importers would contest the basis for such a determination. For example, in the PTA-I case, one of the issues was whether the Designated Authority should use the actual price of raw material, utilities, etc., for the determination of the non-injurious price or whether such determination should be based on market price. For a backward integrated producer, the use of actual cost of transfer, i.e., the chain cost would be disadvantageous. The Appellant argued that it had drawn electricity from the power grid and had also utilized power from its captive power plants.

In PTA-I, the Designated Authority had worked out the cost of electricity taking into account the actual cost. In the Appeal, the CESTAT held that the Designated Authority was justified in using the actual cost of raw materials and utilities and observed that the actual cost is a more reliable basis for injury analysis. The Designated Authority also took the optimum capacity utilization (which is in excess of 100 %) in a block of 3 years for the apportionment of the fixed expenses per unit.

The decision of CESTAT in PTA-I, was appealed before the Supreme Court of India. The Supreme Court rejected the approach of the Designated Authority in using the optimal level of capacity utilization of the domestic industry. The Supreme Court noted, the "special advantages and disadvantages…domestic producers may have as a result of captive production should be ignored….".[29] This decision was considered to help the domestic industry in seeking a higher NIP and consequently a higher level of protection.

The use of 22 % return capital employed for calculating the NIP is not free from controversy. One of the widely held criticisms is that the 22 % is unusually high for certain industries and creates an artificial risk free return to capital. It is also felt that the ROCE would vary from industry to industry.[30] In 2011, the Government of India further amended the Custom Tariff (Identification, Assessment and Collection of Anti-dumping Duty on Dumped Articles and for Determination of Injury) Rules, 1995 to make a new set of rules of calculation of NIP. The new rules incorporated in Annexure III are entitled *Customs Tariff (Identification, Assessment and Collection of Anti-dumping Duty on Dumped Articles and for Determination of injury) Amendment Rules, 2011* (for short, *NIP Price Rules 2011)*. The amendment

[29]Reliance Industries v. Designated Authority, 2006 (10) SCC 368, ¶. 32.

[30]Indian Spinners Association v. Designated Authority, 2004(170) E.L.T 144 (Tri- Delhi).

has modified to some extent the law laid down by the Supreme Court of India in *Reliance Industries v. Designated Authority.*[31]

According to the NIP Rules 2011, the cost of production has to be calculated on the basis of:

- Cost of production based on the best utilization of raw materials by the constituents of domestic industry;
- The best utilization of utilities by the constituents of domestic industry, over the past three years period and the period of investigation;
- The best utilization of production capacities, over the past 3 years period and the period of investigation.

The NIP Rules 2011 also provide for the calculation of a reasonable return (pre-tax) on average capital employed for the product and includes allowances for recovery of interest, corporate tax and profit. According to Rule 4 (ix) the average capital employed is the sum of "net fixed assets and net working capital" which shall be taken on the basis of average of the same as on the beginning and at the end of the period of investigation.

### (a) Comparison Benchmarks for Price Effect Analysis

Price comparisons and the level of trade used in such comparisons play a crucial role in price effect and analysis and consequently causation analysis. In the antidumping investigation on *Poly Iso Butylene*, the DGAD imposed antidumping duties on all subject countries except the European Union (EU) although the imports from the EU were found to be dumped. The DGAD did not establish causal link in view of the fact that weighted average landed value of imports from the EU was higher that the NIP for the domestic industry.[32] The EU exporter contended before the CESTAT that significant quantities of imports had entered the market below the NIP which could have price effects. The question was whether the DGAD should adopt a weighted average price for all the imports or should it be on the basis of comparison between selective transactions. The Tribunal held:

> Para. 18. We are unable to accept the contention that weighted average is the only permissible or prudent method of analysis. We may first consider the position under the Rules. Separate Appendix lay down "Principles governing determination of normal value, export price and margin of dumping" (Appendix I) and "Principle for determination of injury (Appendix II). If the Rules allowed only the same principles to govern both, there would have been no requirement for separate Appendix. The first Appendix is about the 'determination' of certain prices and working out of margins (dumping and injury margins)... Appendix II deals with the determination of injury and causal link. These are assessments

[31]Reliance Industries v. Designated Authority, 2006 (10) SCC 368.

[32]The average landed value of imports from the EU was US $ 1000.94/MT whereas the NIP was determined to be higher than this amount. See Kothari Sugars and Chemicals Ltd. v. Designated Authority, 2005 (187) E.L.T 185 (CESTAT, Delhi).

> and, for that very reason, in the realm of opinion forming. Forming an opinion by its very nature cannot be reduced to a mechanical process of calculations, because it involves appreciation of data and forming of opinion based on such appreciation.[33]

The CESTAT rejected the contention of the DGAD and held that price effect analysis need not be conducted on a weighted average basis. This finding reiterates that the comparison methodologies that apply to dumping margin calculations need not apply to price effect analysis.

## D Survey of Injury and Causation in Indian Antidumping Cases

Chapters 2 and 3 of this study examined the political economy dynamics of trade remedies. Chapter 2 in particular examined how the public choice theory played its role in determining the injury and causation language of antidumping and other trade remedy legislations.

The objective of this chapter is to lay out the standards and approaches used by the Indian antidumping agency in establishing injury and causation. As Patrick Low noted, dumping and injury are always at the discretion of the domestic investigating authorities.[34] Especially, injury and causation findings provide a greater leeway to trade remedy investigating agency than any other substantive aspect of the investigation. Frequent findings of injury and causal link, have often lead to the criticism that such mechanisms are abused. For example, the Annual Economic Survey of India of 2012, published the Department of Economic Affairs echoed this view, "[t]hough India's anti-dumping policy has been directed to checking genuine cases of dumping, there is a need for some fine-tuning of its strategy to avoid unnecessary international criticism".[35]

The DGAD (including its predecessor) has initiated almost 700 antidumping cases, out of which nearly 535 have resulted in the imposition of final measures in the last two decades.[36] Given the volume and complexity of cases, it may not be possible to examine the injury and causation analysis in all the investigations. Furthermore, there is a possibility that some of the exporters might not have cooperated with the investigations. In the absence of adequate cooperation from the exporters, the investigating authority would not have been provided with alternative and rival arguments about the existence of other causes which may be causing injury to the domestic industry. In light of this difficulty, this study has identified 19 cases which span the last two

[33]Kothari Sugars and Chemicals Ltd. v. Designated Authority, 2005 (187) E.L.T 185 (CESTAT, Delhi).

[34]Patrick Low, The GATT and US Trade Policy 86 (1993).

[35]International Trade, *in* Annual Economic Survey- Government of India 271 (2012).

[36]Ministry of Commerce and Industry- India, Data on Anti-Dumping Investigations, http://commerce.nic.in/traderemedies/Data_Anti_dumping_investigations.pdf?id=25.

decades of antidumping activity (1994–2013). These cases also represent some of the key sectors that have traditionally petitioned for antidumping protection. These cases were categorized in two phases—Phase I and Phase II.

Phase I pertains to the 1994–2003 period, whereas Phase II pertains to the 2004–2013 period. The criterion for the selection of these cases was whether injury or causal link was one of the issues highlighted by at least one of the parties to the case. In order to identify the cases, the antidumping database prepared by Chad Brown was also consulted. In all the identified cases a finding of injury and causal link was a bone of contention and was contested by one of the parties, particularly by an affected exporter before the CEGAT/CESTAT or other appellate courts such as the High Courts and the Supreme Court of India.

Again, the years 2003–2004 mark an inflection point in the history of Indian anti-dumping enforcement. In December 2003, the European Communities (later the European Union) challenged India's imposition of antidumping duties on roughly 27 products.[37] Later, in January 2004, Bangladesh challenged India's imposition of anti-dumping duties on Lead acid batteries,[38] and in October 2004 Chinese Taipei (Taiwan) challenged certain antidumping measures.[39] These challenges were deftly handled by India and the WTO consultations did not culminate in the establishment of dispute settlement panels. However, the challenges resulted in tightening of procedural and substantive aspects of the proceedings. Therefore, the selection of these phases is not artificial, but could provide a vantage point to compare and contrast the methodologies used by the DGAD in the injury and causation determination.

## *1 Survey of Selected Indian Antidumping Cases*

The following section seeks to understand the practice of injury and causation examination in India by evaluating the analysis undertaken in the following antidumping investigations. The antidumping investigations examined in this chapter are the following (Table 2):

An evaluation of the injury and causation analysis of the above listed cases reveals certain important trends. In the initial years of implementation of trade remedy laws, India employed antidumping actions as a 'safety-valve' in the wake of lowered tariffs. The safety valve theory postulates that when the domestic industry is severely affected by increased foreign competition resulting from the lowered

---

[37]WTO, Dispute Settlement: India—Anti-Dumping Measures on Imports of Certain products from the European Communities, WT/DS304, *available* at https://www.wto.org/english/tratop_e/dispu_e/cases_e/ds304_e.htm (last visited May 26, 2015).

[38]Requesting for Consultations, *India- Antidumping Measures on Batteries from Bangladesh*, WT/DS 306 (February 2, 2004).

[39]WTO, Dispute Settlement: India – Anti-Dumping Measures on Certain Products from the Separate Customs Territory of Taiwan, Penghu, Kinmen and Matsu, WT/DS318 (Oct. 28, 2004).

**Table 2** List of Indian AD investigations in the qualitative analysis

**Phase I (1994- 2003) Cases**

- Hot Rolled Coils/Sheets/Plates/Strips from Russia, Kazakhstan and Ukraine (1998)
- Citric Acid from People Republic of China (1999)
- Purified Terephthalic Acid from Japan, Malaysia and Spain (2000)
- Optical Fibre from Korea R.P.( 1999 )
- Acrylic fiber from Turkey, Hungary and the European Union (2000))
- Bisphenol from European Union and Taiwan (2000)
- Hardened Forged Steel Rolls from Russia, Ukraine and Korea
- Lead Acid Batteries originating in or exported from Japan, Korea, China and Bangladesh (2001)
- Acyclic Alcohols from Republic of Korea, Malaysia, Taiwan and Thailand (2003)

**Phase II (2004-2013) Cases**

- Ball Bearing from China, Russia, Poland and Romania (2004)
- Coated paper from European Union and Malaysia (2004)
- PS Offset Aluminum Plate from China, Malaysia, Singapore and South Korea (2007)
- Acetone from EU, Chinese Taipei, Singapore, South Africa and USA (2008)
- Bias Tyres originating in or exported from China and Thailand (2007)
- Viscose Staple Fiber from China and Indonesia (2010)
- Circular Weaving Machine exported from China (2010)
- Digital Plate from China and Japan (2012)
- Melanin originating from EU, Iran, Indonesia and Japan (2012)
- Disodium carbonate (Soda ash) originating in Russia and Turkey (2013)

tariff, it will enforce antidumping laws that will temporarily raise tariffs, which could minimize or eliminate the tariff concession.[40] In the case of India, the autarkic policies adopted by the government for more than three decades after independence shielded the industry from any import competition. In 1991, when India was negotiating the Uruguay Round Agreements, the maximum tariff was 355 % and the simple average applied tariff rate was 125 %. In addition to the high tariffs, quantitative restrictions (QR) were placed on one-third of the tariff lines. The QRs remained perhaps the most visible form of protection for the Indian industry. These restrictions took various forms such as non-automatic licenses, imports through canalized agencies, special import licenses (SIL), and actual user criteria. The government imposed these restrictions on the grounds that India had unfavorable balance of payment (BoP) conditions.[41]

Some of the above mentioned quantitative restrictions were not fully phased out until April, 2001. Several studies conducted on Indian antidumping practices indicate

[40]According to this theory, antidumping increases a country's ex ante willingness to lower tariffs and enter trade negotiations.

[41]Rajesh Mehta, *Removal of QRs and Impact of India's Import*, 35(19) Economic & Political Weekly, 1667 (May 6, 2000).

that antidumping petitions enjoyed a very high "success rate" in India during 1994–2003.[42] This finding supports the criticism that virtually any industry that considered itself affected by foreign competition and presented a competently assembled petition had a good chance of claiming import relief during this time.[43] According to an analysis conducted by Aradhna Aggarwal of roughly 350 antidumping cases initiated during this period, the DGAD found justification for the imposition of antidumping duty in all except 12 cases.[44] The high success rate of antidumping actions during this period is attributed to the use of generally ambiguous provisions in the anti-dumping rules, which includes injury and causation.

Aggarwal found specifically three elements which resulted in the mushrooming of antidumping actions: the indiscriminate use of constructed normal value (CNV) methodology for calculating normal value; use of surrogate country methodology in the cases of non-market economies (NME) such as China, Ukraine and the former USSR countries, and; the asymmetrical dumping and injury margin comparisons. It is also noted that the benchmarks for determination of material injury and causation determination were extremely ambiguous, unguided and undefined. In addition, the DGAD *suo motu* initiated antidumping investigations. Such *suo motu* initiated cases augmented the cases which it had initiated on the basis of properly constituted applications. To provide a few illustrations, the DGAD initiated *suo motu* actions against imports of Bisphenol-A from the United States,[45] sports shoes and toys from China,[46] and dry batteries from China.[47] The DGAD was also perhaps one of the few anti-dumping agencies to have used the concept of "material retardation" to impose antidumping duties.[48]

---

[42]Prakash Narayanan, *Anti-dumping in India—Present State and Future Prospects*, 40(6) JOURNAL OF WORLD TRADE 1081, 1088–89 (2006).

[43]PATRIK LOW, TRADING FREE: THE GATT AND US TRADE POLICY 86 (1993).

[44]Aradhana Aggarwal, *Antidumping Law and Practice: An Indian Perspective* 3 (Indian Council for Research on International Economic Relations Working Paper No. 85, 2002).

[45]Imports of Bisphenol-A from the United States of America, No. 37/ADD/IW/95 (Ministry of Commerce, November 20, 1995) *available at* http://commerce.nic.in/adint_bisphenol_a_usa.htm (notice of initiation of antidumping).

[46]Imports of sport shoes (both branded and un-branded) originating in or exported from China, No. 56/1/2000-DGAD (Ministry of Commerce and Industry, November 20, 2000) (notice of initiation of antidumping).

[47]Imports of dry batteries originating in or exported from China, No. 53/1/2000- DGAD (Ministry of Commerce and Industry, November 11, 2000) (notice of initiation of antidumping).

[48]Imports of D (-) Para Hydroxy Phenyl Glycine Methyl potassium Dane Salt (PHPG Dane Salt originating in or exported from the China PR and Singapore ( Ministry of Commerce and Industry, June, 2003 (final findings); Imports of D (-) Para Hydroxy Phenyl Glycine Base (PHPG Base) originating in or exported from the European Union (Ministry of Commerce and Industry, March, 2003) (final findings); *Imports of D (-) Para Hydroxy Phenyl Glycine Methyl potassium Dane Salt (PHPG Dane Salt originating in or exported from China and Singapore*, No. 14/23/2002 (Ministry of Commerce, June 24, 2003) (final findings); Imports of fused magnesia from China PR-Final Findings (Ministry of Commerce and Industry, February, 1999) (final Findings).

**Table 3** Antidumping cases terminated on the request of the Domestic Industry

| S. No. | Case name | Initiation date | Reasons for termination |
|---|---|---|---|
| 1 | Vinyl Acetate from Singapore and Iran | 15 February 2002 | Withdrawn by domestic industry |
| 2 | Butter oil from New Zealand | 26 November 2002 | Withdrawn by domestic industry |
| 3 | Gypsum Plaster Board originating in or exported from Indonesia and Thailand. | 2 September 2003 | Withdrawn by domestic industry |
| 4 | Metallurgical Coke from Japan | 14 June 2004 | Withdrawn by domestic industry |
| 5 | Compressors from China and Malaysia | 13 July 2005 | Withdrawn by domestic industry |
| 6 | Vitamin B12 from China, Hong Kong and Japan | 29 October 2007 | Withdrawn by domestic industry in view of changed circumstances |
| 7 | Potassium Carbonate from US, Thailand and Russia | 23 January 2009 | Withdrawn by domestic industry |
| 8 | Penicillin-G originating in or exported from China | 22 May 2009 | Withdrawn by domestic industry |
| 9 | Power Steering Gear System originating in or exported from China | 5 June 2009 | Withdrawn by domestic industry |
| 10 | Hot Rolled Steel products from China, Indonesia, Iran, Japan, Kazakhstan, Malaysia, Philippines, Romania, Russia, South Africa, Saudi Arabia, Korea, Thailand and Turkey | 11 August 2009 | Withdrawn by domestic industry |
| 11 | Electrical Insulators originating in or exported from China | 9 April 2012 | Withdrawn by domestic industry |

*Source* DGAD

## 2 *Injury and Causation: Discussion of Phase I Cases*

During Phase I, a large number of antidumping actions were filed even if such actions were not well supported by evidence of material injury and causal link. For example, the antidumping investigation on *Butter Oil from New Zealand* was terminated in the absence of any concrete evidence on injury or causal link based on the domestic industry request itself.[49] A more detailed list of terminated cases is given in Tables 3 and 4.

It is not easy to find out whether the elements of injury and causation have been met merely by checking the data and the reasoning provided in any final antidumping order. However, one could examine the processes, methodologies and the reasoning provided by agencies to arrive at the finding of injury and causal link. A strong probative evidence of material injury to the domestic industry is the evidence of

[49]V.Lakshmi Kumaran, *The 10 Major Problems with the Antidumping Instrument in India*, 39 (1) Journal of World Trade 115, 177(2005).

**Table 4** Antidumping cases terminated for insufficient injury and causal link

| S. No. | Case name | Initiation date | Reasons for termination |
|---|---|---|---|
| 1 | Purified Terephthalic Acid | 22 April 1999 | Terminated against Japan, Malaysia and Taiwan |
| 2 | Carbon Black used in rubber applications originating in or exported from Australia, China, Iran, Malaysia, Russia and Thailand | 26 December 2008 | Terminated against Malaysia as the import price was above NIP |
| 3 | Polyester Staple Fiber (PSF) from Indonesia, Taiwan, Korea and Thailand | 25 June 2001 | Terminated against Indonesia and Thailand |
| 4 | SBR from Japan, Korea, Turkey, Chinese Taipei, US, Germany and France | 7 April 1998 | Terminated against Germany and France, since the import price from these countries were above the reasonable selling price of the domestic industry |
| 5 | Certain Phosphorus based chemical compounds originating in or exported from China & EU | 13 February 2009 | Terminated against European Union |

*Source* DGAD

adverse effects on the 15 injury factors provided under Article 3.4 of the Anti-dumping agreement. These 15 parameters have been incorporated in Appendix II of the Indian Antidumping Rules. Together with volume and price effects, it is possible to evaluate whether there is a reasonable correlation between dumping and material injury. While examining the Indian Antidumping cases included in Appendix I, this study has used the tick mark (✓) to indicate whether a particular injury factor was examined by the DGAD or not. If there is no indication of consideration of the concerned injury factor in the final finding, the terms 'Not Mentioned' or 'NM' are used to reflect this fact. As stated earlier, the purpose of this examination is to find out whether there is a qualitative methodology in the examination of injury and causation.

In the AD investigation on *Hot-Rolled Coils/Sheets/Plates/Strips* from Russia, Ukraine and Kazakhstan[50][Case# 14/1/97], the Designated Authority collected information on injury parameters of the domestic industry only for the previous year. Furthermore, of the 15 injury parameters examined, only 6 injury factors supported a finding of injury. Some of the key factors such as the productivity, cash flow, output, wages and employment remained unchanged in comparison with previous years. Although injury and causation were established in the final finding, such examination was not based on a trends analysis over a fairly long injury investigation period.

Acrylic fiber is one product which has been subject to multiple antidumping investigations in India. In *Acrylic yarn from Turkey, Hungary and the European Union*[51] [Case # 34/1/1998], the Designated Authority found increase in volume of the products from the subject countries and especially from Turkey. However, the

[50]Imports of Hot Rolled Coils, Sheets, plates and Strips from Russia, Khazakstan and Ukraine, No. 14/1/1997 (Ministry of Commerce and Industry, November 18, 1998) (Final Findings).

[51]Imports of Acrylic Fiber from Turkey, Hungary, and the European Union, No.34/1/1998 (Ministry of Commerce and Industry, March 24, 2000) (Final Finding).

Designated Authority did not examine injury trends over a long representative period. Among the trends examined, a finding of worsening of injury factors were found in respect of market share, price suppression, employment, profits and stocks. It is also noteworthy, that there is no reference to 5 out of the 15 parameters in the final finding. The Designated Authority had also calculated the non-injurious price and determined price suppression. However, the extent of decline in injury parameters was not clearly indicated in the final finding. A non-confidential index of the injury parameters was also not provided in the final finding. The final finding includes an assertion that the "[a]uthority has taken into account all indices regarding injury…. viz, the volume of dumped imports, their effect on prices in the domestic market, and its effect on the production, capacity utilization, sales, profits, market share of the domestic industry." While discussing causal link, the Authority made the following observation:

> In establishing that the material injury has been caused by the imports from the subject country, the Authority holds that the increase in market share of imports from Turkey resulted in decline in the market share of the petitioner. These imports undercut the prices of the domestic product forcing the domestic industry to seek at unremunerative prices. Resultantly, the domestic industry was, therefore, caused by dumped imports from the said country.[52]

In other words, findings on price depression and suppression were used to establish a finding of injury and causal link. The causal influence of other factors was not taken into account, at least in the final findings.

In the antidumping investigation on *Pure Terephthalic Acid from Japan, Spain, Malaysia and Taiwan*[53] [Case # 27/1/98] referred to as PTA-I earlier in this chapter, the Designated Authority found that most of the industry parameters had shown an improvement during the POI. The Designated Authority, however, noted that decreasing sales realization and increase in losses are sufficient to constitute material injury to the domestic industry. It is also pertinent that the Designated Authority did not provide any discussion of a number of injury parameters in the final finding. The Designated Authority had indicated that the other injury parameters were examined in the provisional findings; however, the tenets of 'objective examination' enshrined in Article 3.1 and 3.4 of the ADA may require an investigating authority to recapitulate all the injury factors in the final finding to provide a holistic picture of the condition of the domestic industry.[54]

In the antidumping investigation on *Lead Acid Batteries from Japan, China, Korea and Bangladesh*[55] [Case # 67/1/2000-DGAD], only 11 of the 15 injury parameters during the POI supported a claim of material injury. It is also pertinent

[52]Imports of Acrylic Fiber from Turkey, Hungary and the European Union, No. 34/1/1998- DGAD (Ministry of Commerce and Industry, March 24, 2000) (Final Findings).

[53]Imports of Pure Tephthalic Acid from Japan, Spain, Malaysia, and Taiwan, No.27/1/98 (Ministry of Commerce and Industry, April 20, 2000) (Final Findings).

[54]See Appellate Body Report, *Mexico – Definitive Anti–Dumping Measures on Beef and Rice, Complaint with Respect to Rice, ¶.180*, WT/DS295/AB/R (December 20, 2005).

[55]Imports of Lead Acid Batteries from Japan, China, Korea, and Bangladesh, 67/1/2000-DGAD (Ministry of Commerce and Industry) (Final Findings).

that the data was collected only for one previous year. Although one could say that the condition of the domestic industry had declined during the period of investigation, it was not clear whether the industry had performed relatively well in comparison with the previous years.

In the antidumping investigation on *Citric Acid from China*[56] [Case # 14/6/2011-DGAD], only 10 out of the 15 injury parameters supported a finding of injury. Factors such as capacity utilization and inventories showed significant improvement while profits came down. The final findings disclosed an analysis of only 5 or 6 of the listed 15 factors. Some of the remaining factors have been discussed in the preliminary findings. Furthermore, only a limited number of factors during the previous years were examined in detail and some of the key information such as trends on profitability were kept confidential. The Designated Authority arrived at a finding of material injury and causal link on the premise that not all economic parameters relating to domestic industry need to indicate injury.

In the antidumping investigation on *Polyester Staple Fibre from Korea R.P, Indonesia, Thailand, Taiwan*[57] [Case # 29/1/98] the Designated Authority found that the domestic industry had performed poorly in comparison with the previous years only in respect of domestic sales realization and profitability. In fact, the final finding indicated improvement in various other indicators although most of the injury parameters were not specifically listed in the final finding. Yet the Designated Authority had concluded that the domestic industry had suffered material injury.

The antidumping investigation on certain types of *Acyclic alcohols from Singapore, Romania, Malaysia and South Africa*[58] [Case # 63/1/2001] was initiated in the year 1999. The findings in this dispute were contested by the domestic industry, exporters and the importers before various judicial forums. The examination of the injury factors revealed that at least 5 out of the 15 factors had remained positive for the domestic industry. For example, capacity, capacity utilization, production, sales, market share, inventories, etc., had improved whereas the other factors such as employment and wages remained stable. However, the Designated Authority found that in view of the volume of dumped imports and the price effects, the domestic industry had suffered material injury. The Designated Authority placed emphasis on the profitability of the domestic industry. The Designated Authority acknowledged the improvement in several injury factors, but justified the finding the material injury on the ground that the improvement could be attributed to the imposition of antidumping duties on imports from other sources.[59]

---

[56] Import of Citric Acid from Peoples' Republic of China, No. 29/1/1997 (Ministry of Commerce and Industry, March 15, 1999) (Final Findings).

[57] Imports of Certain Polyester Staple Fibres (PSF) originating or exported from Korea, Thailand, Taiwan and Indonesia, No. 29/1/1998 (Ministry of Commerce and Industry, January 21, 2000) (Final Findings).

[58] Imports of Acyclic Alcohols originating in or exported from Singapore, Brazil, Romania, Malaysia and South Africa, No. 63/1/2001 (Ministry of Commerce and Industry, July 29, 20003) (Final Findings) [herein after *AD Investigation on Acyclic Alcohol*].

[59] *Id.*, ¶ 47.

*Bisphenol-A* is a chemical product that has been the subject matter of anti-dumping investigations for a long time. In the AD action on *Bisphenol A from European Union and Chinese Taipei*[60] [Case# 47/1/99-DGAD], the Designated Authority examined several injury parameters during the POI. In comparison with the previously examined cases during Phase I in this study, the *Bisphenol A* investigation provides relatively comprehensive data. The sales of the domestic industry improved during the POI and the previous 2 years; domestic output and market share also improved; capacity utilization exceeded 100 % during 1998–1999 and was 106 % in the POI; the closing stocks of domestic industry were the lowest during 12 months of the 18-month POI. In a growing market with high domestic demand, the domestic industry stepped up capacity and the licensed capacity was expected to increase during 1999–2000, which included six months of the POI. The argument of the domestic industry was that it suffered substantial losses during 1998–1999 and the POI. Despite the significant increase in imports from the subject countries, the Designated Authority noted that the landed value of *Bisphenol-A* from both the EU and Taiwan had been significantly higher than the selling price of the domestic industry. According to the DGAD, there was no price undercutting attributable to the imports. Although it appears that the Designated Authority had calculated the NIP for the domestic industry, it is not clear from the final finding whether there was any price suppression or not. According to the Designated Authority, as the landed value of Bisphenol-A from the European Union and Taiwan were above the net selling price of the domestic industry, the material injury established in the case of the domestic industry was not attributable to dumped imports. Bisphenol-A is one of the few cases where the Designated Authority arrived at a negative determination on injury and causal link.

An examination of the cases during Phase I indicates that the Designated Authority conducted the injury and causation analysis primarily based on the information provided during the Period of Investigation. The trends recorded during the entire injury investigation period were not given adequate consideration during this phase. All the 15 injury parameters were not included in the final findings, although some of such factors could have been discussed under the provisional finding. As the Appellate Body noted in *China—GOES*, an authority's consideration of price effects "must be reflected in the relevant documentation, so as to allow an interested party to verify whether the authority indeed considered such factors".[61] On the whole, the final findings were brief and a well-reasoned analysis was not very common at least during Phase I.

---

[60]Imports of Bisphenol-A originating in or exported from the European Union and Taiwan, 47/1/1999- DGAD (Ministry of Commerce and Industry, December 6, 2000) (Final Findings).

[61]Appellate Body Report, *China – Countervailing and Anti-Dumping Duties on Grain Oriented Flat-Rolled Electrical Steel from the United States*, ¶131, WT/DS414/AB/R (November 16, 2012) [hereinafter Appellate Body *China- GOES*].

## 3 *Injury and Causation: Discussion of Phase-II Cases*

For the purpose of this study, ten representative cases decided during the 2004–2013 period have been considered. These cases represent some of the key sectors subject to antidumping action in India.

In the anti-dumping investigation on *Coated paper boards of 80 GSM from European Union and Indonesia*[62] [Case #14/7/2003], the DGAD has provided a brief analysis of all statutory factors under the Antidumping Rules. As compared to the cases filed during Phase I, the final finding has provided an analysis of the 15 injury factors and certain factors such as loss of sales, and other threat of injury factors. The final finding disclosed a positive movement in sales, output, inventories as percentage of sale/production, productivity, wages, etc., while other factors such as capacity utilization, ability to raise capital, cash flow, growth, etc., did not show any adverse effect.

On the other hand, factors such as market share, profitability, return on investment and wages declined during the POI when compared to the previous year. This case is noteworthy in as much as the DGAD did not conclude that the domestic industry suffered material injury based on an assessment of factors such as domestic industry's reduced market share, profitability and return on investment which have been traditionally relied upon by the Authority. The margin of dumping from the subject countries was also rather significant. The volume effects of the dumped imports on the domestic industry injury parameters were also appreciable. The DGAD, however, paid particular attention to price effects. The DGAD noted an absence of price undercutting vis-à-vis imports from EU while price undercutting was marginally positive in respect of Indonesia. In other words, according to the DGAD, the prices of the dumped imports were higher than those of the domestic industry during the period of investigation. While the DGAD noted some reduction in the selling price of the domestic industry product, it could not find price underselling as the cost of production of the domestic product marginally declined.[63] Consequently, the DGAD held that the domestic industry did not suffer material injury during the period of investigation.

In the antidumping investigation on *Ball Bearing*[64] [Case #14/30/2002], the economic performance of the domestic industry was relatively unchanged when compared to the previous years. At least 6 injury parameters showed a decline, although several injury factors also showed an improvement. The DGAD in this case provided data for at least 3 years prior to the period of investigation. The DGAD also found that there was a significant increase in the volume of imports (especially from China) and a decline in market share, return on investment and

---

[62]Imports of Coated Paper Boards of 80 GSM from European Union and Indonesia, No. 14/7/2003 (Ministry of Commerce and Industry, December 15, 2004) (Final Findings).

[63]*Id*, ¶ 52.

[64]Imports of Ball Bearing from China, Russia, Poland and Romania, No. 14/30/2002-DGAD (Ministry of Commerce and Industry, March 19, 2004) (final findings).

employment for the domestic industry, but found improvements in regard to productivity, profits, inventories, output and capacity utilization. The DGAD, however, did not find evidence for material injury. This decision also highlights the reliance of the investigating authority on operating statistics. It is also seen from the reasoning that the absence of price underselling and price undercutting were some of the factors relied upon even for a negative finding on material injury.[65]

The antidumping investigation on *Acetone from European Union, Chinese Taipei, Singapore, South Africa and USA*[66] [Case #14/4/2006] discloses a qualitative improvement in the assessment of injury factors. There is a proper examination of all the 15 injury factors over a longer time horizon. The period of investigation in this case is July 2005 to June 2006. However, information on various macroeconomic and microeconomic factors is provided for the periods 2003–04, 2004–05, and 2005–06. Examination of data for three preceding years is helpful to understand how various injury factors have performed in comparison with the base year, although there is some improvement in the year immediately preceding the POI. In particular, financial parameters such as return on investment and ROCE showed significant improvement in the previous year and were healthy during the POI. A number of other factors such as employment, wages, sales, production, etc., improved during the POI. However, based on price depression and price suppression analysis the DGAD entered a finding on causation.

In the antidumping investigation on *Melamine from European Union, Iran, Indonesia and Japan*[67] [Case # 14/35/2010], the DGAD noticed negative movement in injury on a number of factors. The domestic industry was suffering losses during the POI. However, parameters such as capacity utilization, productivity, employment and wages remained relatively better during this period. Although the domestic sales during the POI had declined relative to the previous year, there was no marked trend indicating a decline during the injury investigation period. The Designated Authority concluded that the domestic industry has suffered material injury and that injury has been caused significantly by price and volume effects of dumped imports from the subject countries. Consistent with its earlier practice, the DGAD placed emphasis on price and volume effects for its conclusion for material injury and causation. The DGAD, based on its normal practice, placed emphasis on price undercutting and price suppression for reaching a finding on causal link.[68]

In the antidumping investigation on *Digital Plate from China and Japan*[69] [Case #14/7/2011], the DGAD's findings disclose that the injury parameters of the domestic industry were performing better when compared to the previous years. In

---

[65]*Id*, at 42 (i).

[66]Imports of Acetone from European Union, Chinese Taipei, Singapore, South Africa, and USA, No. 14/4/2006-DGAD (Ministry of Commerce and Industry, January 4, 2008) (Final Findings).

[67]Imports of Melamine from European Union, Iran, Indonesia and Japan, No. 14/35/2010-DGAD (Ministry of Commerce and Industry, June 1, 2012) (Final Findings).

[68]*Id*, ¶¶ 58-61.

[69]Imports of Digital Offset Printing Plates from China PR and Japan, No.14/7/2011-DGAD (Ministry of Commerce and Industry, October 3, 2012) (Final Findings).

fact, there was negative finding on 11 out of the 15 injury parameters. Even the market share of the domestic industry went up when the imports from the subject countries started increasing. In fact, the subject imports took the market share of other non-subject countries, while the domestic industry's market share remained unaffected. It is seen in this case that the DGAD based its finding of injury primarily on the basis of three financial parameters, namely, profitability, cash flow and return on investments. It is also seen that those factors which reflect the operating performance of the domestic industry tend to get greater weightage. However, a reasoned and adequate examination of how these parameters would outweigh the other positive factors was not discernible at least from the final finding. In respect of causation, the DGAD did not find any price undercutting margin with respect to Japan. The DGAD also did not establish any price underselling margin for Japan. In view of the negative price underselling and price undercutting margin, the DGAD terminated the action against Japan finding that there was no causation attributable to imports from Japan. Such finding was in line with the tradition of the DGAD to infer a break in causal link when the price undercutting and underselling margins are found to be negative.

In a recent antidumping investigation on *Di-sodium Carbonate originating from Russia and Turkey*[70] [Case #13/3/2011], the final finding of which was released in 2013, the DGAD examined the injury and causation factor in substantial detail. There was an existing antidumping order on the same product originating or exporting from Kenya, USA, etc. In this investigation, the DGAD provided an examination of all 15 injury factors. In order to establish the trends in injury factors, the data for the period of investigation and three preceding years were used. During the annualized POI, only 3 injury factors out of 15 showed a clear injury to the domestic industry; at least 8 injury factors out of 15 showed an improvement or marginal improvement, while 5 injury factors remained almost unchanged. The DGAD found injury and causal link primarily on the basis of price underselling, price suppression and price depression. The DGAD also noted that the cash profits, profitability and return on capital employed declined during the injury investigation period. The financial data indicated that the financial indicators had improved during the POI although they might have declined when compared to the base period. The correlation in the rise in imports from the subject countries and a decline in the profitability of the domestic industry was considered sufficient to establish injury and causation.

As a matter of policy, the DGAD is very likely to conclude that there is injury and causal link if there is underselling by the imports as was borne out by the investigation on *PTA-I* and *Soda Ash* investigations; conversely, like what happened in the investigation on *Digital plates* and *Ball Bearings*, the DGAD is likely to conclude that there is no causal connection if there is price overselling by the imports. To put it differently, if the DGAD finds that the landed value of imports

---

[70]Imports of Soda Ash originating in Russia and Turkey, No. 14/3/2011-DGAD (Ministry of Commerce and Industry) (Final Findings) [hereinafter *soda ash investigation*].

exceed the non-injurious price of the domestic industry, it will be reluctant to attribute the material injury to dumped imports. In addition to the price and volume effects, the DGAD pays particular attention to the question whether the domestic industry has lost market share at a time when the domestic demand for the product had risen. Furthermore, if the domestic sales quantity declines resulting in lesser capacity utilization during times of growing domestic demand like in the case of *Melamine*, it could be treated as a direct effect of dumped imports. Causation could be inferred in such cases.

In a number of investigations, the DGAD compares the injury factors in the POI with the base period, and not necessarily with the previous year. As an illustration, in the *Bias Tyres* [Case # 14/9/2005] as well as the *Circular Weaving Machine* [Case # 14/25/2008] investigations, the DGAD noted that certain injury factors have fared significantly worse when compared to the base period. Comparison with the base period may indicate a decline in injury parameters although the domestic industry would have performed significantly better during the POI when compared to the previous year. Specifically in the context of safeguard investigations, the WTO panels and the Appellate Body have held that such end point-to-end point comparisons are inappropriate in a trend analysis.[71]

An evaluation of the Indian antidumping practice in the selected cases does not indicate a uniform practice. As a WTO panel in *Thailand—H Beams*[72] noted, an investigating authority has to provide a thorough and persuasive explanation as to how positive movements in the evolution of certain injury factors were outweighed by certain other factors. However, when compared to Phase I, during the Phase II period, the DGAD has been enlisting most of the injury factors in its analysis. It may be noted that during Phase I, not more than 10 factors out of the 15, on an average, were enlisted at least in the final finding. Furthermore, the provisional and final findings in the Phase II period have provided more complete data on the evolution of various injury factors. At least in form, the injury analysis has improved. However, one should add that the DGAD still relies on qualitative analysis for injury determination.

It is also seen from the analysis of the limited cases that the assessment of material injury can be challenging. In most of the cases examined, some of the injury parameters had indicated positive trends, while a few others had showed negative trends. In certain cases, 10 or more injury factors had indicated a decline, while in certain others only 3 or 4 factors showed a decline. But the final findings invariably disclose that there was injury in all such cases. The focus of investigation seems to be limited to price suppression and depression. Significant emphasis is given on factors such as profits/profitability, ROCE and cash flow, which are always related. To certain extent, capacity utilization or inventories are also given

[71]Panel Report, Report, *Argentina – Safeguard Measures on Imports of Footwear*, ¶ 8.157, WT/DS121/AB/R (June 25, 1999).

[72]Appellate Body Report, *Thailand – Anti–Dumping Duties on Angles, Shapes and Sections of Iron or Non–Alloy Steel and H–Beams from Poland*, WT/DS122/AB/R, ¶ 128 (April 5, 2001).

some weightage. However, on the whole, an analysis that is rooted purely on price undercutting and price underselling margins will have its defects. Price undercutting need not be always on account of dumped imports, while price underselling is almost inevitable when the non-injurious price is decided on a hypothetical basis. The key issue is how material injury and causation could be established in such cases. In other words, what is the role of factors such as employment, wages, sales, etc., which are hardly addressed in detail in most cases?

An examination of the India's antidumping findings would indicate that there are persisting difficulties with the assessment of certain injury factors. Out of the 15 injury parameters, trends on at least 10 or so injury parameters are clear and unambiguous. However, certain parameters are elusive and unclear. Examples would include growth, ability to raise capital and factors affecting domestic prices. It is unclear whether growth should be viewed in respect of production, domestic sales or capacity utilization. Ability to raise capital can be interpreted in many ways. The DGAD examines the profitability of the domestic industry whereas the Antidumping Agreement refers to the term 'profits'.[73] These two terms have separate meanings. Although the dumping is a factor in the material injury examination, the role of injury margin is less clear. Especially since India calculates injury margin in all cases, injury margin may have a role in assessing injury. As it happened in the case of PTA-I and Digital plates investigations, a negative injury margin has resulted in a finding of lack of causation vis-à-vis that exporting country.

## *4 Non-attribution Analysis in Indian Antidumping Investigations*

As examined in Chap. 3, the non-attribution analysis is a key requirement in injury and causation analysis. The WTO panels and the Appellate Body have ruled against several trade remedy investigations in the absence of satisfactory non-attribution analysis. In terms of the existing WTO jurisprudence, investigating authorities are required to separate and distinguish the injury caused by factors other than dumping, subsidy or increased imports. Although the non-attribution obligation has been existing in the concerned WTO Agreements since 1995, this requirement attained significance only after the *US—Hot rolled Steel*[74] (Japan) ruling in 2001.

In the Indian antidumping investigations examined during Phase I, it is evident that the Designated Authority had hardly examined the existence of other factors causing injury to the domestic industry. Most of the cases examined during Phase I,

[73]While profit is an absolute number, profitability is a relative measure of the success or failure of a business. *See* https://edis.ifas.ufl.edu/fe939 (last visited on December 23, 2014).

[74]Appellate Body Report, *United States – Anti–Dumping Measures on Certain Hot–Rolled Steel Products from Japan*, ¶ 224, WT/DS184/AB/R (August 23, 2001).

did not even include a heading called "non-attribution" or "injury from other factors" or "other known factors". For example in the investigation on *Acrylic fibre* [Case # 4/1/98], there was enough evidence that the industry had suffered losses over the years since the raw material was not locally available and had to be imported. It was also known that Acrylic yarn was imported to India free of import duty under the Indo-Nepal Treaty, whereas Indian domestic industry had to pay import duty on the imported raw material.[75] Secondly, even when other causal factors were mentioned, it was in connection with the discussion on whether the domestic industry had suffered material injury or not and not in the context of causation. For example, the Designated Authority would have referred to contraction of demand, constraints of the domestic industry to increase capacity or productivity in the context of discussion of the listed 15 factors and not necessarily in the context of non-attribution.

During Phase I, the Designated Authority referred to only some of the listed known factors and not to most or all of them. Interestingly, even when the Authority referred to some of the listed known factors, the importance of such factors was summarily dismissed. For example, in the antidumping investigation on *Acyclic Alcohols* [Case # 63/1/2001], the Designated Authority summarily dismissed two of the listed known factors as follows: *"contraction in demand is not apparent and no technological development in the industry or any such factor which could have resulted in injury to the domestic industry has been noticed"*.[76] There was no further discussion on the causative significance of such factors.

In Phase II, one could observe a qualitative difference in the discussion of other known factors. For example, in *Coated Paper* Case [Case #14/7/2003], the Authority had discussed most of the listed known factors, except the volume and prices of the imports not sold at dumping prices. In the *Digital Plates* antidumping investigation [Case #14/7/2011-DGAD], the DGAD examined the various listed known factors. The discussion was very brief. The DGAD also noted in its final finding an observation from the Appellate Body report in *EC-Tube and Fittings*, which said: "*… previous panel and Appellate Body reports make it clear that while an investigating authority is required to consider the effects of other factors known to the investigating authority which may be causing injury to the domestic industry, there is no required basis for analysis in undertaking this analysis.*"[77]

In the *Digital plate* investigation, the DGAD examined other known factors such as the increase in raw material cost pursuant to imposition of safeguard duties on one of the inputs, namely, aluminium, additional investment by the domestic industry and the fact that the net sales realization (NSR) of the domestic industry was much higher than the

[75] VED PRAKASH, ANTIDUMPING, COUNTERVAILING DUTIES AND SAFEGUARD MEASURES IN MULTILATERAL TRADE REGIME 35 (2005).

[76] *AD Investigation on Acyclic Alcohol, supra* note 58, ¶ 52.

[77] Appellate Body, *European Communities – Anti-Dumping Duties on Malleable Cast Iron Tube or Pipe Fittings from Brazil*, ¶ 176, WT/DS219/ABR (July 22, 2003).

NIP. The DGAD found injury and causal link primarily on the basis that volume of imports from the subject countries had increased during the injury investigation period, and that the lower priced imports had caused price depression which had adversely affected the operating performance of the domestic industry. The DGAD relied on the decline in the profits and return on investments to establish its finding on injury and causal link. It is also evident from a perusal of the recent investigations including the *Digital plate* investigation that, unlike in the past, the DGAD has been examining all listed known factors and certain other known factors in performing the non-attribution analysis. However, each of these factors is introduced and summarily dismissed.

In the antidumping investigation on *Bias Retreaded Tyres from China and Thailand*[78] [Case #14/9/2005-DGAD], the interested parties had argued that the alleged injury to the domestic industry was on account of domestic competition, non-availability of raw material and rapid increase in its price, export of natural rubber by domestic producers and imposition of antidumping duties on the major raw material imported by the domestic industry. There was an oversupply in the market which might have caused alleged injury.[79] Admittedly this was a known factor whose injurious effect should have been properly examined and separated. This case illustrates the reluctance of the investigating agencies to go beyond the listed known factors in performing the non-attribution test.

In the anti-dumping investigation on *Soda ash* [Case #14/3/2011], the DGAD also performed a non-attribution analysis. Each of the listed known factors was briefly introduced. While examining the listed known factors, the DGAD notes that the injury to the domestic industry is on account of excess capacity, but concluded that listed known factors do not cause injury to the domestic industry. This was yet again a summary conclusion.

It appears that the non-attribution analysis is conducted in most of these cases on a *pro forma* basis without a detailed discussion or deliberation. It is often difficult to understand the injurious effects of some of the factors and whether they will have some impact on the causation already determined. It will be useful to have a detailed analysis of the complex facts and economic arguments in the consideration of "other factors". In this regard, it may be pertinent to refer to the observation of a WTO panel in *EC—DRAM*, although the observation was made in the context of the injury and causation under the SCM Agreement. The panel noted:

> It does not suffice for an investigating authority to merely to 'check the box'. An investigating authority must do more than simply list other known factors, and dismiss their role with bare qualitative assertions, such as 'the factor did not contribute in any significant way to the injury', or 'the factor did not break the causal link between subsidized imports and material injury.' In our view, an investigating authority must take a better effort to quantify the impact of other known factors, relative to subsidized imports, preferably using elementary constructs or models. At the very least, the non-attribution language of Article 15.5 requires an investigating authority a satisfactory explanation of the nature and extent of the

[78]Imports of Bias Tyres originating in or exported from China PR and Thailand, No. 14/9/2005-DGAD (Ministry of Commerce and Industry, June 29, 2007) (final findings).

[79]*Id., sub-¶ (e).*

> injurious effects of the other factors, as distinguished from the injurious effects of the subsidized imports.[80] (Italics original)

One may admit that as opposed to the Phase I period, during Phase II, there is at least a greater reference to most of the injury factors. Some data and figures are indeed mentioned in the final finding, although it will be a far cry from the rigorous standard outlined in WTO cases such as *US—Hot Rolled Steel.* There is a need to examine how the various causal factors interacted to analyse the impact and the proximity of such factors with the injury suffered. The sample cases selected during this time do not devote more than one or two sentences to discuss the role and impact of such factors. To quote Sapir and Trachtman, this type of an examination may not appear as an "assessment of the facts, but a guess at the facts".[81] It is also noted that, in addition to the seven listed other factors, the Indian antidumping cases do not routinely examine the role of other unlisted known factors which at the same time are causing injury to the domestic industry. The alternate causes were not examined probably on account of the failure of the parties to highlight such alternate causes at the appropriate time. However, a failure to take into account the other factors gives an impression that there were no other causal factors other than dumped imports. This is impliedly equating the dumped imports as the substantial cause of injury and assuming that no other causes could have caused injury to the domestic industry. Typically, industries alleging material injury could be suffering on account of factors such as increasing cost of capital, raw material, macroeconomic factors, global economic conditions, management decisions, *et al.* This list could be literally endless. But a summary rejection or disregard of the role of other factors is tantamount to treating correlation as causation, which is not what the WTO agreements require. In contrast, most of the WTO disputes that have been examined in Appendix I of this chapter had provided an examination of multiple known factors which could have caused injury. It is striking that the Indian Antidumping findings have limited their examination to only the listed factors, and that too even in the post-2003 period.

It is also evident from the examination of the investigations conducted in Phase II that the DGAD has not used regression analysis or statistical tools such as granger causality analysis for the purpose of isolating or quantifying the injuries to domestic industry. A review of the selected cases does not indicate the use of any such quantitative tools. However, on the positive side, during Phase II, the DGAD has started examining the trend over a 4 year period which includes the POI and three preceding years as well as a mandatory listing of other known causal factors mentioned in Articles 3.5 and 15.5 of the AD and SCM Agreements respectively.

---

[80]Panel Report, European Communities – Countervailing Measures on Dynamic Random Access Memory Chips from Korea, ¶ 7.405, WT/DS299/R (June 17, 2005).

[81]Andre Sapir and Joel P. Trachtman, Subsidization, Price Suppression, and Expertise: Causation and Precision in US- Upland Cotton, 21 (2011).

## 5 *Appellate Review of Injury and Causation in India*

Section 9C of the Customs Tariff Act, 1975 (as amended) provides an avenue for appealing a notification issued by the Ministry of Finance (MoF) implementing the findings of the DGAD. Accordingly, CESTAT is the statutory tribunal that could hear appeals on the DGAD's findings of dumping, injury and causal link. However, there is a view that if the MoF has terminated an action based on a finding of absence of dumping, injury and causal link, only a writ petition under Article 226 or 227 of the Constitution of India could lie to the High Court.

The constitutional courts such as the High Courts and the Supreme Court of India have given a significant amount of deference to the findings of the Designated Authority. Even appellate tribunals such as the CESTAT give considerable deference to findings of injury and causal link. For example, in *Urals Heavy Machine Building Plant v. Designated Authority*[82] which examined the AD proceedings on imports of induction hardened forged steel rolls, the CESTAT affirmed the findings of the DGAD.[83] In the underlying investigation, the DGAD had noted that a number of injury parameters such as sales, production, profits, inventories, and capacity of the domestic industry had improved. While the CESTAT acknowledged that these developments had taken place, it supported the finding of the DGAD that injury had occurred especially in view of the unremunerated prices. This case clearly demonstrates that evidence on price undercutting and price underselling have overwhelming influence in terms of establishing material injury and causal link.

Only in a limited number of cases have the appellate courts intervened in the matter of establishing causal link. In *Indian Refractory Makers Association v. Designated Authority,*[84] the CEGAT held that if dumped imports of an article do not or are not capable of causing injury to the domestic industry, imposition of antidumping duties is not warranted. In that case, it was found that dead burnt magnesite (DBM) of less than 4 % silica imported by the Indian domestic user was quite different from the DBM produced in India. Likewise, in the antidumping investigation concerning the importation of strontium carbonate, in granular form imported from China, CEGAT held that the importation of this product did not cause material injury to the domestic industry that was manufacturing Strontium Carbonate in the powder form.[85] The CEGAT, therefore, overturned the findings of the DGAD.

In *Agfa Gevaert A.G. v. Designated Authority,*[86] the CEGAT examined a plea by the exporters that the antidumping duty was imposed on the subject goods, namely,

---

[82]2005 (187) E LT 194 (CESTAT, Delhi).; *see* also, Automotive Tyre Manufacturer's Ass'n v. Designated Authority, 2013 (294) ELT 482 (CESTAT, New Delhi).

[83]Imports of Induction Hardened Forged Steel Rolls from Russia, Ukraine and Korea RP, No. 14/3/2002-DGAD (Ministry of Commerce and Industry, June 3, 2003) (final findings).

[84]2000 (119) ELT 319 (Tribunal).

[85]Videocon Narmada Glass v. Designated Authority, 2003 (151) ELT 80 (Tribunal Delhi).

[86]2001 (130) ELT 741 (Tribunal- Delhi).

black and white photographic paper without establishing causal link. There were only two industries out of which one industry was a new player while the other was an inefficient producer. The Designated Authority excluded the new player and assessed injury based on the data of the inefficient producer. However, the CESTAT found that the Designated Authority had used the data of the excluded producer for the calculation of the non-injurious price. The CESTAT held that causal link was not established because the only domestic producer had turned "sick" even before the imports had increased.

In the AD investigation on PSF, the petitioners challenged the finding of injury and causal link found by the DGAD on account of dumped imports from the subject countries. The High Court of Rajasthan observed, "[o]n independent consideration of the entire material and careful consideration of the contentions raised by the learned Counsel, …., the finding of fact recorded by the Designated Authority does not call for interference by us, in exercise of powers under Articles 226 and 227 of the Constitution of India".[87] Similarly in *Sasol-Solvents* case, the CESTAT ruled that it is not appropriate to impeach the finding of the DGAD without cogent evidence. According to CESTAT, when price undercutting and price underselling are properly calculated, there is no reason to interfere with the findings of the Designated Authority.[88]

## E Injury and Causation Determination: Practice of Other WTO Members

The experience of WTO members in conducting injury and causation was examined, to some extent, in Chap. 3 while examining the evolving WTO jurisprudence on injury and causation. Although it is desirable to examine the injury and causation methodologies in other key jurisdictions, it is not practically feasible given the scope of this study. Treating India as a prototype, this study examined the factors and methodologies that determine injury and causation in trade remedy investigations. Furthermore, an attempt is made to examine the injury and causation determination in anti-dumping proceedings in other jurisdictions based on secondary materials, especially journal articles and other internet resources to understand how various anti-dumping users are grappling with this important topic. Efforts were also made to understand the practice of other WTO members by searching on the websites of the concerned investigating authorities. The purpose is to examine whether these jurisdictions use practices which are more sophisticated than currently employed by India and to what extent such practices meet the causation standards espoused by the WTO panels and the Appellate Body.

---

[87]2002 (149) ELT 45.

[88]Sasol solvents v. Union of India, MANU/CUST/0057/2008 (CESTAT, Delhi).

## 1 Traditional Users

### (a) United States

The U.S. practices on establishing injury and causation in antidumping and CVD investigations have been extensively studied in Chaps. 2 and 3 of this study. The U.S. is one of the few jurisdictions that has used economic models to support its legal analysis in injury and causation determination.[89] In the U.S., the Commercial Policy Analysis System (COMPAS) model has been used widely by the USITC and participating parties in evaluating the impact of imports on local industries in AD/CVD proceedings.

The decision of the U.S. Court of Appeals for the Federal Circuit (USAFC) in *Bratsk Aluminum Smelter* v. *United States*[90] (hereinafter *Bratsk*) raises the question of the extent to which the USITC is required to examine the role and impact of imports not subject to investigation on the domestic industry. Although the subject imports might have undersold or depressed domestic prices and would have been eligible for import relief, according to the USAFC, the USITC was required to establish whether non-subject imports which were available in the domestic market would have replaced the subject imports.[91] This is widely known as the "replacement/benefit" test and was discussed for the first time in *Gerald Metals Inc v. United States*.[92] According to this test, the USITC must explain whether imports not subject to the antidumping petition would have replaced the imports from the subject countries without creating any beneficial effects on the domestic industry. There could be situations in which the subject imports might have undersold the domestic like product in significant quantities. However, the concern of the *Bratsk* court appears to be that fairly traded non-subject imports (a separate causal factor) were not given adequate examination by the USITC in the underlying investigation.[93] Admittedly, the *Bratsk* ruling is a separate domestic requirement in the U.S. and is not obviously influenced by the jurisprudence of any of the WTO disputes.

---

[89]A. Keck et al., *A 'Proababilistic Approach to Use of Econometric Modeling in Sunset Reviews*, 6 (3) World Trade Review 371 (2007).

[90]444 F. 3d 1369 (Fed. Cir. 2006).

[91]There is a view that the *Bratsk* ruling spoke on the potential effectiveness of an order. But subsequent decisions have clarified this position. *See* Mittal Steel Point Lisa Ltd. v. United States, Slip Op. 2007-1552 (Fed. Cir. Sep. 18, 2008) (holding that the USITC need to have "evidence in the record 'to show that the harm occurred 'by reason of' the LTFV imports,'" and requires that the USITC must not attribute injury from non-subject imports or other identified factors to subject imports).

[92]Gerald Metals Inc. v. United States 132 F. 3d716 ( U.S. Federal Circuit, 1997 (holding that the USITC has to explain why – despite the presence and significance of the non-subject imports – it concluded that the subject imports had caused material injury to the U.S. industry).

[93]E.P. Salonen, *The Bratsk Decision and Its Implications for Injury and Causation Analysis Under The Antidumping and Countervailing Duty Laws*, (2008) *available at* http://www.stewartlaw.com/Article/PublicationsByPracticeArea?PracAreaID=5 (last visited on May 26, 2015).

But in practice, this ruling could prevent the USITC from giving the benefit of antidumping protection, if non-dumped, non-subject, price-sensitive imports could have replaced the subject imports. In such a scenario, the dumped imports from the subject imports are not the real cause of injury, but something else. This may require an assessment of the competitive effects of other factors. Therefore, the *Bratsk* ruling entails disaggregation of the economic effects of causal factors other than dumped imports and may require sophisticated economic analysis.

Although the U.S. has been using the COMPAS model, according to Durling and McCullough, the USITC has developed only primitive tools in trade remedy cases.[94] It should be pointed out that although various panels and the Appellate Body have overturned the U.S. causation analysis, no WTO dispute settlement panel has per se questioned the use of any economic models.

### (b) European Union

Secondary literature on the EU antidumping practices reveals that the EU institutions enjoy a wide discretion in establishing injury and causation.[95] Generally, courts such as the European Court of Justice (ECJ) are reluctant in holding that the EU authorities are manifestly wrong in their assessment of injury.[96] The EU Antidumping and Anti-subsidy Regulations have adopted the language fairly similar to the WTO provisions. The only exception is the inclusion of an additional known factor in the non-attribution analysis which requires the Commission to examine "whether the industry is still in the process of recovering from the effects of past dumping or subsidisation".[97] Although this factor is assessed in the material injury determination, it appears that the purpose of this additional factor is to make sure that the weakened condition of the domestic industry in itself is not a reason for denying trade contingency relief.

The EU practice is to examine injury data for a period of three or four years preceding the period of investigation. The purpose is to examine the trends in volume, market share, and financial indicators such as profits, cash flow and ROCE.

According to the EU practice, microeconomic data will often play a more crucial role than macroeconomic indicators. European Courts have held that even if certain

---

[94]James P. Durling & Matthew P. McCullough, *Teaching Old Laws New Tricks: The Legal Obligation of Non-Attribution and the Need for Economic Rigor in Injury Analyses Under US Trade Law*, in HANDBOOK OF INTERNATIONAL TRADE (E. Kwan Choi & James Hartigan eds., 2004).

[95]Nakajima v. Council [1991] ECR I-2069, ¶ 86.

[96]P. Bentley & A. Silberston, ANTI-DUMPING AND COUNTERVAILING ACTION: LIMITS IMPOSED BY ECONOMIC AND LEGAL THEORY 39 (2007). For an exception *see*, Aluminium Silicon Mill Product Gmbh v. Council of the European Union (Court of First Instance (March 14, 2007) (holding that the Regulation was vitiated by a manifest error of judgement by wrongly attributing injury to imports from Russia whereas disregarding other factors such as the contraction in demand in the EU).

[97]Council Regulation No. 1225/ 2009 (Nov. 30, 2009), art 3(5).

criteria do not show injury, such findings will not discredit an affirmative finding.[98] Sale prices, profits and profitability could impact the industry's financial position and, therefore, occupy a central position in the material injury and causation analysis. Furthermore, the price undercutting and price underselling analysis are used to evaluate material injury as well as causation.

The EU has no single specific criterion for determining causation. In the anti-dumping investigation on Styrene-butadiene-styrene thermoplastic rubber originating in Korea, the Commission held that the dumped imports taken in isolation did not cause material injury.[99] The general practice seems to be that dumped imports 'if taken in isolation' could have injured the domestic industry, such a conclusion will not be affected by the existence of other factors.

The EU does not use quantitative methods for isolating and segregating the role of other factors on the domestic industry. The EU generally uses a mix of data reports, trends analysis and summary statistical tools, but use of complex regression models is not yet reported.[100] In 2005, a WTO panel condemned an EU countervailing duty measure for lack of sophistication in its causation analysis.[101] The EC-DRAM panel said that the EC's record is "devoid of even elementary quantitative analysis" of certain economic factors.[102] In respect of injury and causation, several studies have concluded that finding of 'no injury' are generally uncommon, although they may occur during expiry, interim and partial interim review proceedings.[103]

### (c) Canada

The Special Import Measures Act 1984 (SIMA) regulates the antidumping and subsidy countervailing duty imposition in Canada. The language on injury and causation under SIMA is substantially similar to the requirements under the Antidumping Agreement. An antidumping case under SIMA requires two separate sets of legal proceedings in order for a Canadian industry to obtain special tariff protection against dumped imports from another country. These legal proceedings comprise of the dumping investigation by the Canadian Border Service Agency and the injury investigation by the Canadian International Trade Tribunal (CITT).

It is for the CITT to find out whether material injury has occurred to the domestic industry and whether such injury is on account of dumped imports. CITT in practice focuses on certain financial and production related aspects which could give an

---

[98]*See* Miwon v. Council, ECR- II, 1841, ¶ 94 (Court of First Instance) (March 30, 2000); *see also* Sinochem v. Council ECR II- 85 (January 29, 1998).

[99]Council Regulation (EC) 1372/ 2005 (August 19, 2005).

[100]Thomas Prusa & Edwin Vermulst, *China countervailing and antidumping duties on Grain Oriented Flat-rolled Electrical Steel from the United States: exporting US AD/CVD methodologies through WTO dispute settlement,* 13 (2) World Trade Review 229, 260-269 (2014).

[101]Panel Report, *EC- DRAM*, ¶ 7.434.

[102]Panel Report, *EC- DRAM*, ¶¶ 7.413, 7. 420, 7.427.

[103]Edmond McGovern, EC Antidumping Law and Practice 41:4 (2013).

indication of injury. A number of considerations are taken into account by the CITT on a case-by-case basis. Typically, the CITT takes into account: (i) price erosion; (ii) lost sales and market sales; (iii) decline in production and under-utilization of capacity; (iv) reduced employment; (v) reduced investment; and (vi) declining gross or net profitability. It is not necessary to find that injury is exclusively due to dumping or subsidization, but rather that the latter are a cause of injury.

CITT has used quantitative economic estimates for assessing the effects of dumped and subsidized imports on the domestic industry. In some cases such estimates are prepared using the Commercial Policy Analysis System (COMPAS) partial equilibrium models. However, the use of such quantitative estimations has often been contested by interested parties in the investigations.[104]

### (d) Australia

Section 269TAE of the Australian Customs Act, 1901 (Act No. 6 of 1901 as amended) implements Article VI of the Agreement on Antidumping in Australia. Section 269 TAE does not provide a definition of what is meant by material injury. Such determinations are made by having regard to a range of factors mentioned under Article 3.4 of the AD Agreement. Australia specifically examines the price effects through price undercutting and price suppression analysis. As none of the antidumping measures imposed by Australia is subject matter of a WTO dispute, the WTO compatibility of Australia's injury and causation methodology is yet to be seriously tested.

Australia adopted a Ministerial Decision on Material Injury in 2012.[105] According to the Ministerial Decision, the Commissioner should, *inter alia*, use the following criteria in dumping or CVD investigation: (i) that the injury caused by dumping or subsidisation is material in degree; (ii) that material injury must be greater than that likely to occur in the normal ebb and flow of business, and (iii) that dumping and subsidisation need not be the sole cause of injury to the domestic industry. The Ministerial Decision reconfirms that factors such as profit forgone and a loss of market share (of the domestic industry) in an expanding market are relevant injury considerations.

The new principles adopted in the 2012 Ministerial Declaration are in a way a reiteration of the WTO AD/SCM Agreements as well as the well-settled jurisprudence in trade remedy law. However, Australia still depends on the qualitative assessment of injury and causation and is yet to introduce sophisticated economic tools.[106]

---

[104]Refined Sugar from the United States, Denmark, Germany, the Netherlands and the United Kingdom, Inquiry No. NQ-95-002 (Canadian International Trade Tribunal, November 6 and 21, 1995) (Findings and Reasons).

[105]Antidumping Commission, Australian Customs Dumping Notice No. 2012/24, New Ministerial Decision on Material Injury, *available at* http://www.adcommission.gov.au/notices/Documents/2012/XXACDN-StreamliningAustraliasAngti-DumpingSystem-MinisterialDirectiononMaterialInjury-FI_000.pdf.

[106]Weihuan Zhou, *Assessment of 'Material Injury' and* 'Causation', 9(10) GLOBAL TRADE AND CUSTOMS JOURNAL 282, 290 (2015).

## 2 *Injury and Causation Practices of 'New Users'*

There have been some studies on the antidumping practices of the new users of such instruments such as Argentina, Brazil, China and South Africa. The anti-dumping legislations of most of these countries are, by and large, based on the WTO AD Agreement.

### (a) Mexico

Mexico's anti-dumping as well as countervailing duty laws are similar in various aspects to the unfair trade laws of its North American Free Trade Agreement (NAFTA) partners.[107] Mexico has a single investigating authority to make both dumping and subsidy determination as well as material injury determinations.[108] This agency is known as the *Secretariat of the Economy* (*Secretarı´a de Economı´a*, or, for short, SECOFI). It is responsible for resolving investigations of unfair trade practices in international trade, as well as determining the compensatory tariffs resulting from said investigations. Within SECOFI, investigations are the responsibility of the *Unidad de Pra´cticas Comerciales* Internacionales (UPCI).[109] The UPCI is further divided into subdivisions for anti-dumping and countervailing, safeguards and international trade litigation.[110]

Under the Foreign Trade Law of Mexico, 'injury' is defined in Article 39 as including material injury, threat of injury or material retardation of the domestic industry. The concepts are the same as in the WTO AD/SCM Agreements, as indicated in SECOFI's regulations.[111]

The injury test is offered only to countries that provide an injury test on a reciprocal basis to Mexican exporters, presumably all other WTO members. Otherwise, compensatory duties can be imposed without the injury test. Mexico, in practice applies anti-dumping duties more frequently than countervailing duties.[112]

In the AD/CVD investigation, it must be established that dumped or subsidized imports are causing injury to the domestic industry, in accordance with the law.[113] Effects on the domestic industry caused by factors other than dumped imports are

---

[107] G.W. Bowman et al., *Antidumping and Countervailing Duty Law and Practice: The Mexican Experience*, Arizona Legal Studies Discussion Paper No. 10-10, 272 (2010).

[108] *Id.*

[109] *Id.*

[110] Id.

[111] *Id.* at 273.

[112] *Id.*

[113] *Id.* at 276.

required by the statute not to be attributed by the authority to such imports. In a proceeding initiated in the early 1990s, SECOFI determined that Canadian origin imports of hot-rolled steel sheet constituting only 6 % of total imports and 1.4 % of total consumption were sufficient to justify an injury finding.[114] This case implies that antidumping investigation can be launched even when dumped imports are not the predominant cause of injury.

Like many other WTO members, the Foreign Trade Law requires the Secretary to consider the volume of dumped imports, whether there has been a significant increase in absolute or relative terms, the effect on Mexican prices of the dumped or subsidized imports, and if the imports are sold at lower prices, whether they decrease Mexican prices or impede price increases that otherwise would have occurred.[115] In determining causation of injury to the Mexican industry, Foreign Trade Law places significant emphasis on factors such as actual or potential reduction of sales, production volume, market share, and capacity utilization; factors affecting local prices, including the magnitude of dumping margins, effects on investment and capital flows, employment and salaries, etc.[116] The coincidence in time analysis is used in several cases to establish a finding of causation.[117]

In the antidumping investigation on *Bovine Carcasses (2000),* the binational panel affirmed the right of the Secretary to make an affirmative injury finding although the determination had not found positive evidence of injury on the other injury factors. From an examination of the Mexican practice, it does not appear that the Foreign Trade Law recommends econometric models in the injury and causation determination. As is the case with many other WTO members, Mexico depends on the traditional trends analysis. In the anti-dumping investigation on Rice from the United States, the Ministry concluded that the investigated authorities had determined that dumped imports had caused injury, merely because dumping occurred at the same time as the domestic economic indicators had deteriorated.[118] This is a reconfirmation of the qualitative approach to injury and causation followed by Mexico in antidumping cases. While the parties to the antidumping practices have the option to submit statistical/econometric studies to the authorities, the use of such studies is not a pervasive practice.[119]

---

[114]Binational Panel, Hot Rolled Steel Sheet Originating in or Exported from Canada (Dumping) (June 16, 1997), MEX-96-1904-03, 33-36.

[115]*Id.*, at 277.

[116]*Id.*

[117]B. Leycegui and L. Torre, *The 10 Major Problems with the Antidumping Instrument in Mexico*, 39(1) Journal of World Trade 137, 141 (2005).

[118]K. Ito, Mexico, in Anti-dumping Laws and the Practices of the New Users 272 (Junji Nakagawa ed., 2007). *See also* Appellate Body Report, *Mexico—Definitive Anti Dumping Measures on Beef and Rice*, Complaint with Respect to Rice, WT/DS295/AB/R (December 20, 2005)

[119]I am grateful to Jorge Miranda for pointing out this fact.

### (b) Argentina

Unlike Brazil, India and Mexico, Argentina has adopted a binary system for the implementation of the dumping and the injury investigations. Dirección de Competencia Desleal ("DCD" or the Directorate of Unfair Trade) is the agency responsible for dumping determination, whereas Comisión Nacional de Comercio Exterior ("CNCE" or the National Foreign Trade Commission) is the agency responsible for injury determination. Although Argentina has adopted the WTO AD Agreement, its conduct of investigations has been challenged in several instances. For example, in *Argentina—Poultry* a WTO panel found that Argentina had violated its commitments by failing to provide an objective examination of material injury factors.[120] The panel found that the National Foreign Trade Commission did not assess (1) the magnitude of the margin of dumping, and (2) any actual or potential negative effects of the alleged dumping on cash flow, ability to raise capital or investment and, therefore, violated Article 3.4 of the Anti-Dumping Agreement. The injury and causation finding in a few other domestic antidumping proceedings have also been challenged before the WTO.[121]

A perusal of the WTO disputes outlined above indicates that CNCE is not using any quantitative models for evaluating and separating the role of various causal factors.

### (c) Brazil

In order to establish material injury, the Brazilian authorities take into account a totality of factors. DECOM, the anti-dumping agency in Brazil conducts the injury margin analysis. The injury margin is based on the price undercutting method which is the difference between the average price of the domestic industry like product with the average CIF landed price of the imports. In certain cases DECOM also disregards the domestic price on the assumption that the domestic prices are suppressed and constructs the price for the domestic like product, the cost calculation of which may be confidential.[122] Like in most jurisdictions, the injury and causation determination is based on volume and price effects.[123]

In regard to non-attribution analysis, the Brazilian authorities take into account the known factors enlisted in Article 3.5 of the Anti-Dumping Agreement. In addition to these factors, the Brazilian legislation requires the authorities to exclude

[120] Panel Report, *Argentina– Definitive Anti–Dumping Duties on Poultry from Brazil*, ¶ 7.327, WT/DS241/R (May 19, 2003).

[121] See Panel Report, *Argentina – Definitive Anti–Dumping Measures on Imports of Ceramic Floor Tiles from Italy*, WT/DS189/R (November 5, 2001). The European Communities did not challenge the injury findings of CNCE in this dispute.

[122] A. Caetano, *The 10 Major Problems with the Antidumping Instrument in Brazil*, 39(1) Journal of World Trade 87, 87-88 (2005).

[123] *Id.*

(i) the impact of the process of liberalization on domestic prices, (ii) captive consumption; and (iii) imports or resale of the imported product by the domestic industry.[124] There is no evidence that Brazil uses statistical or other quantitative models for assessing the extent and impact of various causal factors.[125]

### (d) China

As of 2015, China accounts for nearly 16 percent of global trade and has been a major target as well as a user of trade remedies. Specifically in regard to China's use of antidumping mechanism, it is seen that Ministry of Commerce (MOFCOM)[126] is relying heavily on volume and price effects in assessing injury and causation. However, the use of traditional techniques such as price undercutting and price selling analysis in establishing price effects is still not firmly established. For example, in a recent WTO dispute, namely *China–GOES*, the panel and the Appellate Body found that China sought to establish price depression and price suppression without conducting explicit price undercutting or price underselling analysis.[127] In the *China–GOES* dispute, the panel and the Appellate Body found lack of an objective examination in its price analysis. Likewise, another WTO panel *in China–X-Ray Equipment* ruled that China failed to ensure price comparability in its price effect analysis.[128] This dispute involved an antidumping investigation on non-medical x-ray scanning equipment. The Chinese dumping initiation covered scanning systems using more than 100 keV. However, the European exports (Smiths' scanners) were concentrated in low-energy scanning equipment whereas the Chinese sales (Nuctech's scanners) were of high-energy scanners.[129] This distinction was important in the injury analysis. In this investigation, MOFCOM made a determination of price undercutting and price suppression by comparing the weighted average unit price of all imported products with the annual weighted

[124]Marco Fonesca, Injury and Causation Determination in Brazil, Address at the International Conference on Trade Remedies organized by the Centre for WTO Studies, Indian Institute of Foreign Trade on April 9, 2015 in New Delhi (presentation on file with author).

[125]*Id.*

[126]Injury is assessed by Bureau of Industry Injury which is part of Ministry of Commerce.

[127]Appellate Body Report, *China—GOES*, at ¶.131.

[128]Panel Report, *China—Definitive Anti-Dumping Duties on X-Ray Security Inspection Equipment from the European Union*, ¶ 7.67, WT/DS425/R and Add.1 (April 24, 2013).

[129]It was stated that Nuctechs' scanners were used in cargo scanning such as railways and trucks whereas Smiths 'scanners were used for security scanning of airport luggage.

average unit prices of all domestic sales irrespective of the product types.[130] No model-to-model comparison was made. The Panel concluded that the MOFCOM's "price undercutting and price suppression analyses were not based on an objective examination."[131]

There is a criticism that there is insufficient disclosure of the basis of the determination of injury and causal link.[132] Article 8 of the *Antidumping Regulations of the People's Republic of China 2004*[133] lists the other known factors that need to be examined in the non-attribution analysis. However, Chinese implementing laws offer significant discretion in determining whether material injury had occurred and whether dumped imports had caused such injury. The legislation also does not contain detailed methodologies on how the impact of other known factors could be established. Secondary literature also confirms that the Ministry of Commerce does not use any quantitative tools in its injury and causation analysis. For example, while commenting on China's loss in *China—GOES*, Prusa and Vermulst suggest that China should look at "large body of statistical and econometric literature for guidance" for conducting its analysis in a rigorous way.[134] There is no evidence as of now that China has started using complex quantitative or statistical methods for determining injury and causation.

### (e) South Africa

In South Africa, the antidumping investigations are currently undertaken under the International Trade Administration Act, 71 of 2002 and the Antidumping Regulations (ADR). The Antidumping investigations are conducted by the Directorates (Trade Remedies I and II).

Article 13.2 of the ADR lists the factors that are to be considered for the assessment of material injury. Article 13.2 does not list the traditional factors such as import volumes, price undercutting, margin of dumping and factors affecting domestic prices in the material injury examinations. These factors are considered in the context of Article 16 of the ADR which specifically deals with the determination of causation. It is reported that the International Trade Administration Commission (ITAC) finds causation when there is a combination of increased

---

[130] *China–X-Ray Equipment,* ¶7.34.

[131] *Id.* ¶7.97.

[132] X. Wu, Anti-Dumping Law and Practice in China 417 (2009).

[133] PRC Trade Remedy Laws, Regulations and Rules, http://enforcement.trade.gov/trcs/downloads/documents/china/ (last visited on October 12, 2014).

[134] Thomas Prusa & Edwin Vermulst, *supra* note 100, at 261.

imports and price undercutting by dumped imports.[135] However, in a few investigations the ITAC has terminated the investigations citing lack of causal link[136] when the volume of dumped imports had been insignificant, or when the margin of dumping or the degree of price undercutting was low. The ITAC, however, is not reported to be employing quantitative or econometric tools for conducting causation analysis.

## F Conclusion

The adoption of the appropriate injury and causation standards in the domestic trade remedy proceedings has been one of the greatest challenges of trade remedy enforcement. This chapter in particular examined the injury and causation standards in antidumping proceedings in India, one of the leading users of antidumping mechanisms. In order to examine and understand the pattern and empirics of antidumping, this chapter examined 19 cases spread across the last two decades of antidumping enforcement in India. In addition, this chapter looked at the injury and causation standards prevailing in other key users of antidumping remedies to examine how these WTO Members have been conducting injury and causation and, in particular, the non-attribution requirement. The study also examined whether the WTO members are using plain qualitative techniques or whether they are using statistical tools such as granger causality regression or other econometric tools.

A review of the select cases in India indicates that injury and causation analysis was lax in the early phase, i.e., between 1994 and 2003. The final findings discussed only a few injury parameters. However, there is a qualitative improvement in the conduct of antidumping Investigation in India in the recent times. The DGAD provides a mandatory examination of all 15 injury parameters in the recent investigations. Adoption of tougher injury and causation standards could have crippled the domestic industry in India in the initial years in which the industry was facing global competition.

Causation determination is primarily based on an assessment of the volume and price effects. If there is price undercutting and price underselling by the subject imports accompanied by an increase in imports, causation is presumed. This trend continues even in the recent investigations. A proper assessment on the interaction

---

[135]Gustav Brink, Antidumping in South Africa (TRALAC Working Paper No. D12WP07, 2012), available at http://www.tralac.org/files/2012/07/D12WP072012-Brink-Anti-Dumping-in-SA-20120725final.pdf. See also G. Brink, The 10 Major Problems with the Antidumping Instrument in South Africa, 39(1) Journal of World Trade 147, 156 (2005).

[136]Polyethylene Terephthalate (originating in India, China, Indonesia, Korea, Chinese Taipei, Thailand) (Report 154); Stainless Steel Tubes and Pipes (originating in India, China and Malaysia (Report 160); Lysine (originating in United States) (Report 193); Toughened Glass (originating in China) (Report 184); Steel Wheel Rims (originating in Brazil, China, Chinese Taipei and Turkey) (Report 125).

between price effects and other industry parameters is still not observed in the injury and causation analysis across jurisdictions. As has been clarified by the Appellate Body in cases such as *Thailand—H Beams*, *Mexico—HFCS* a mere listing of data does not amount to evaluation. In that sense, an absence of a clear explanation of the interaction between various injury factors is a deficiency which India and other countries will have to address.

There are some interesting findings with respect to non-attribution analysis in India. During 1994–2003, the DGAD did not examine the role of other known factors as a mandatory requirement. Most of the final findings did not even mention the role of other listed known factors. However, in Phase II (2004–2013), the DGAD has provided a routine mention of the role of other factors. It is seen of late that the discussion on other known factors contains certain data and factual description of the role of other factors. Nonetheless, it does not appear that the findings contain the type of rigour expected in the various Appellate Body decisions on the need for "isolating and separating" the role of other factors. It is also noticed that most of the antidumping cases in India provide an examination of only the listed known factors and other additional factors which are known to the investigating authority during the proceedings are hardly addressed. There is very limited improvement in this regard even during the more recent phase, i.e. during 2004–2014.

While the injury and causation analysis in antidumping investigations in India has shown improvement in the last few years, it may still be falling short of the WTO requirement, especially in the matter of performing the non-attribution analysis. In this regard, an examination of the comparative practices in other WTO members was considered instructive. An analysis based on secondary literature indicates that most WTO members follow the approach currently implemented in India with a focus on volume and price effects. Price depression and suppression analysis remain central to antidumping investigations among all the major users. However, the use of constructed fair-selling or non-injurious prices increases the possibility of providing unwarranted protection to the domestic industry in certain cases.

One of the critical issues in causation is the use of quantitative tools. Except United States and Canada, no country examined in this chapter has been using quantitative tools on a consistent basis. Even in the United States, there is scepticism in the use of quantitative tools in trade remedy investigations and the use of such tools has been limited. In that context, the only acceptable tool for causation determination remains the volume and price analysis subsumed in the so-called trends analysis. In respect of non-attribution, most jurisdictions provide a descriptive assessment as opposed to a mathematical segregation. It is noticed that even the focus on the descriptive approach is a fairly recent trend. A review of causation methodologies of the major users of antidumping only goes to emphasise the practical difficulty in using quantitative methods, keeping aside the logical redundancy of such methods in the context of trade remedy investigations.

# Appendix

## Case 14/1/1997 # Anti-dumping Investigation Concerning Import of Hot Rolled Coils/Sheets/Plates/Strips from Russia, Kazakhstan and Ukraine

Petitioners: M/s Steel Authority of India Ltd. SAIL & M/s Essar Steel Ltd.
Period of Investigation: 1996–1997
Final Finding: November 18, 1998

**Material Injury—Consideration of 15 Injury Factors**

| | | 1995–96 Compared to previous year 1994–95 | | | 1996–97 (POI) Compared to previous year 1995–96 | | |
|---|---|---|---|---|---|---|---|
| S. No. | Factors | Worsened (−) | Improved (+) | Unchanged | Worsened (−) | Improved (+) | Unchanged |
| 1 | Sales | | | | ✓ | | |
| 2 | Profits | | ✓ | | ✓ | | |
| 3 | Output | | | NM | ✓ | | |
| 4 | Market share | | | | ✓ | | |
| 5 | Productivity | | ✓ | | ✓ | | |
| 6 | Return on Investments | | | | ✓ | | |
| 7 | Utilization of Capacity | | ✓ | | ✓ | | |
| 8 | Factors affecting domestic prices | | | NM | ✓ | | |
| 9 | Dumping Margin | | | – | | | |
| 10 | Cash flow | | | | ✓ | | |
| 11 | Inventories | | | NM | | ✓ | |
| 12 | Employment | | | NM | | | ✓ |
| 13 | Wages | | | NM | | | ✓ |
| 14 | Growth | | ✓ | | ✓ | | |
| 15 | Ability to raise capital or Investment | | | | ✓ | | |

*NM* means 'not mentioned'

| Non-attribution analysis | | |
|---|---|---|
| S. No. | Factors | Whether discussed or not |
| 1 | The volume and prices of the imports not sold at dumping prices | No |
| 2 | Contraction in demand or changes in the pattern of consumption | No |
| 4 | Trade-restrictive practices of and competition between foreign and domestic producers | No |
| 5 | Developments in technology | No |
| 6 | The export performance | No |
| 7 | Productivity of the domestic industry | None |

## Case 29/1/1997 # Anti-dumping Investigation Concerning Import of Citric Acid from People Republic of China

Petitioner: M/s. Citurgia Bio-chemicals Ltd
Period of Investigation (POI)—April 1996 to July 1997
Final Finding: March 15, 1999

**Material Injury—Consideration of 15 Injury Factors**

| | | 1995–96 Compared to previous year 1994–95 | | | 1996–97 (POI) Compared to previous year 1995–96 | | |
|---|---|---|---|---|---|---|---|
| S. No. | Factors | Worsened (−) | Improved (+) | Unchanged | Worsened (−) | Improved (+) | Unchanged |
| 1 | Sales | | | ✓ | ✓ | | |
| 2 | Profits | | | NM | ✓ | | |
| 3 | Output | | | ✓ | | | ✓ |
| 4 | Market share | | ✓ | | ✓ | | |
| 5 | Productivity | | | NM | ✓ | | |
| 6 | Return on Investments | | | NM | ✓ | | |
| 7 | Utilization of Capacity | | | ✓ | | ✓ | |
| 8 | Factors affecting domestic prices | | | NM | | | ✓ |
| 9 | Dumping Margin | | | | | | |
| 10 | Cash flow | | | NM | ✓ | | |
| 11 | Inventories | ✓ | | | | ✓ | |
| 12 | Employment | | | NM | | | NM |
| 13 | Wages | | | NM | | | NM |

(continued)

(continued)

| | | 1995–96 Compared to previous year 1994–95 | | | 1996–97 (POI) Compared to previous year 1995–96 | | |
|---|---|---|---|---|---|---|---|
| S. No. | Factors | Worsened (−) | Improved (+) | Unchanged | Worsened (−) | Improved (+) | Unchanged |
| 14 | Growth | | ✓ | | | | NM |
| 15 | Ability to raise capital or Investment | | | NM | | | NM |

*NM* means 'not mentioned'

| Non-attribution analysis | | |
|---|---|---|
| S. No. | Factors | Whether discussed or not |
| 1 | The volume and prices of the imports not sold at dumping prices | No |
| 2 | Contraction in demand or changes in the pattern of consumption | No |
| 4 | Trade-restrictive practices of and competition between foreign and domestic producers | No |
| 5 | Developments in technology | No |
| 6 | The export performance | No |
| 7 | Productivity of the domestic industry | No |
| 8 | Other known factors | None |

## Case 27/1/98 # Antidumping Investigation on Pure Terephthalic Acid from Japan, Malaysia, Spain and Taiwan

Petitioner: Reliance Industries Ltd.
Date of Final Finding: April 20, 2000

**Material Injury—Consideration of 15 Injury Factors**

| | | 1997–98 | | | April 1998-Dec. 1998 (POI) Compared to previous year | | |
|---|---|---|---|---|---|---|---|
| S. No. | Factors | Worsened (−) | Improved (+) | Unchanged/NM | Worsened (−) | Improved (+) | Unchanged/NM |
| 1 | Sales | | | NM | ✓ | | |
| 2 | Profits | | | NM | ✓ | | |
| 3 | Output | | | NM | | | NM |
| 4 | Market share | | | NM | | | NM |
| 5 | Productivity | | | NM | | | NM |
| 6 | Return on Investments | | | NM | | | NM |

(continued)

(continued)

| | | 1997–98 | | | April 1998-Dec. 1998 (POI) Compared to previous year | | |
|---|---|---|---|---|---|---|---|
| S. No. | Factors | Worsened (−) | Improved (+) | Unchanged/NM | Worsened (−) | Improved (+) | Unchanged/NM |
| 7 | Utilization of Capacity | | | NM | | | NM |
| 8 | Factors affecting domestic prices | | | NM | ✓ | | |
| 9 | Dumping Margin | | | | ✓ | | |
| 10 | Cash flow | | | NM | | | NM |
| 11 | Inventories | | | NM | | | NM |
| 12 | Employment | | | NM | | | NM |
| 13 | Wages | | | NM | | | NM |
| 14 | Growth | | | NM | | | NM |
| 15 | Ability to raise capital or Investment | | | NM | | | NM |

*NM* means 'not mentioned'

| Non-attribution analysis | | |
|---|---|---|
| S. No. | Factors | Whether discussed or not |
| 1 | The volume and prices of the imports not sold at dumping prices | No |
| 2 | Contraction in demand or changes in the pattern of consumption | No |
| 4 | Trade-restrictive practices of and competition between foreign and domestic producers | No |
| 5 | Developments in technology | No |
| 6 | The export performance | No |
| 7 | Productivity of the domestic industry | No |
| 8 | Other known factors | None |

## Case 34/1/1998 # Antidumping Investigation on Import of Acrylic Fiber from Turkey, Hungary and the European Union

Petitioner: M/s Indian Acrylics Ltd., Chandigarh, Pasupati Acylon Ltd., New Delhi and Consolidated Fibre and Chemicals Ltd., Calcutta
Period of Investigation: April 1998–December 1998
Date of Final Finding: March 24, 2000

**Material Injury—Consideration of 15 Injury Factors**

| | | During 1997–98 Compared to previous year | | | During (POI) 1998–1999 Compared to previous year | | |
|---|---|---|---|---|---|---|---|
| S. No. | Factors | Worsened (−) | Improved (+) | Unchanged | Worsened (−) | Improved (+) | Unchanged |
| 1 | Sales | | | NM | | ✓ | |
| 2 | Profits | ✓ | | | ✓ | | |
| 3 | Output | | ✓ | | ✓ | | |
| 4 | Market share | ✓ | | | ✓ | | |
| 5 | Productivity | | | | | | NM |
| 6 | Return on Investments | | ✓ | | ✓ | | |
| 7 | Utilization of Capacity | | | NM | | | NM |
| 8 | Factors affecting domestic prices | | | | ✓ | | |
| 9 | Dumping Margin | | | | ✓ | | |
| 10 | Cash flow | | | NM | | | NM |
| 11 | Inventories | ✓ | | | ✓ | | |
| 12 | Employment | | | NM | ✓ | | |
| 13 | Wages | | | NM | | | NM |
| 14 | Growth | | | NM | ✓ | | |
| 15 | Ability to raise capital or Investment | | | NM | ✓ | | |

*NM* means 'not mentioned'

| Non-attribution analysis | | |
|---|---|---|
| S. No. | Factors | Whether discussed or not |
| 1 | The volume and prices of the imports not sold at dumping prices | No |
| 2 | Contraction in demand or changes in the pattern of consumption | No |
| 4 | Trade-restrictive practices of and competition between foreign and domestic producers | No |
| 5 | Developments in technology | No |
| 6 | The export performance | No |
| 7 | Productivity of the domestic industry | No |
| 8 | Other known factors | None |

## Case 24/1/99 # Anti-dumping Investigations Concerning Import of Optical Fibre from Korea R.P

Petitioner: M/s. Sterlite Industries Ltd.
Period of Investigation (POI)—April 1998 to February 1999
Date of Provisional Finding: 5 November 1999

**Material Injury—Consideration of 15 Injury Factors**

| | | 1997–98 Compared to Previous year | | | 1998–99 (POI) Compared to previous year 1997–98 | | |
|---|---|---|---|---|---|---|---|
| S. No. | Factors | Worsened (−) | Improved (+) | Unchanged | Worsened (−) | Improved (+) | Unchanged |
| 1 | Sales | | ✓ | | | ✓ | |
| 2 | Profitability | ✓ | | | ✓ | | |
| 3 | Output | | | NM | | ✓ | |
| 4 | Market share | | ✓ | | ✓ | | |
| 5 | Productivity | | | NM | ✓ | | |
| 6 | Return on Investments | | | NM | | | NM |
| 7 | Utilization of Capacity | | ✓ | | ✓ | | |
| 8 | Factors affecting domestic prices | | | NM | ✓ | | |
| 9 | Dumping Margin | | | | ✓ | | |
| 10 | Cash flow | | | NM | | | NM |
| 11 | Inventories | | | NM | ✓ | | |
| 12 | Employment | | | NM | | | NM |
| 13 | Wages | | | NM | | | NM |
| 14 | Growth | | ✓ | | | | NM |
| 15 | Ability to raise capital or Investment | | | NM | | | NM |

*NM* means 'not mentioned'

| Non-attribution analysis | | |
|---|---|---|
| S. No. | Factors | Whether discussed or not |
| 1 | The volume and prices of the imports not sold at dumping prices | No |
| 2 | Contraction in demand or changes in the pattern of consumption | No |
| 4 | Trade-restrictive practices of and competition between foreign and domestic producers | No |
| 5 | Developments in technology | No |

(continued)

(continued)

| Non-attribution analysis | | |
|---|---|---|
| S. No. | Factors | Whether discussed or not |
| 6 | The export performance | No |
| 7 | Productivity of the domestic industry | No |
| 8 | Other unlisted known factors | None |

## Case 67/1/2000 # Anti-dumping Investigation Concerning Import of Lead Acid Batteries Originating in or Exported from Japan, Korea, China and Bangladesh

Petitioner: M/s Excide Industries Limited & M/s Amara Raja Batteries Ltd
Period of Investigation: January 2001–September 2001
Final Findings: 2001

**Material Injury—Consideration of 15 Injury Factors**

| | | 1998–99 | | | 2000 (POI) Compared to previous year 1998–99 | | |
|---|---|---|---|---|---|---|---|
| S. No. | Factors | Decline (−) | Improvement (+) | Unchanged | Decline (−) | Improvement (+) | Unchanged |
| 1 | Sales | | ✓ | | | ✓ | |
| 2 | Profits | | ✓ | | ✓ | | |
| 3 | Output | | | ✓ | | ✓ | |
| 4 | Market share | | | NM | ✓ | | |
| 5 | Productivity | | ✓ | | ✓ | | |
| 6 | Return on Investments | | | NM | ✓ | | |
| 7 | Utilization of Capacity | | | NM | ✓ | | |
| 8 | Factors affecting domestic prices | | | NM | ✓ | | |
| 9 | Dumping Margin | | | | ✓ | | |
| 10 | Cash flow | | | NM | | | NM |
| 11 | Inventories | | | NM | ✓ | | |

(continued)

(continued)

| | | 1998–99 | | | 2000 (POI) Compared to previous year 1998–99 | | |
|---|---|---|---|---|---|---|---|
| S. No. | Factors | Decline (−) | Improvement (+) | Unchanged | Decline (−) | Improvement (+) | Unchanged |
| 12 | Employment | | | NM | ✓ | | |
| 13 | Wages | | | NM | | | NM |
| 14 | Growth | | | NM | ✓ | | |
| 15 | Ability to raise capital or Investment | | | NM | ✓ | | |

*NM* means 'not mentioned'

| Non-attribution analysis | | |
|---|---|---|
| S. No. | Factors | Whether discussed or not |
| 1 | The volume and prices of the imports not sold at dumping prices | Yes |
| 2 | Contraction in demand or changes in the pattern of consumption | Yes |
| 3 | Trade-restrictive practices of and competition between foreign and domestic producers | No |
| 4 | Developments in technology | No |
| 5 | The export performance | No |
| 6 | Productivity of the domestic industry | No |
| | Other known factors | |
| 7 | Domestic companies introduced voluntary retirement scheme for its employees and reduced employment | |

## Case 47/1/99-DGAD # AD Investigation on Bisphenol-A Originating in or Exported from the European Union and Taiwan

Petitioner: M/s Kesar Petro Products
Period of Investigation: April 1998–September 1998
Date of Final Finding: December 6, 2000

**Material Injury—Consideration of 15 Injury Factors**

| | | 1997–1998 Compared to 1997–98 | | | 1998–1999 Compared to 1998–1999 | | | 1 April, 1998–30 Sep 1999 (POI) Compared to 1998–99 | | |
|---|---|---|---|---|---|---|---|---|---|---|
| S. No. | Factors | Worsened (−) | Improved | Unchanged | Worsened (−) | Improved | Unchanged | Worsened (−) | Improved | Unchanged |
| 1 | Sales | | ✓ | | | ✓ | | | ✓ | |
| 2 | Profits | ✓ | | | ✓ | | | ✓ | | |
| 3 | Output | | ✓ | | | ✓ | | | ✓ | |
| 4 | Market share | | | NM | | ✓ | | | ✓ | |
| 5 | Productivity | | | NM | | ✓ | | | ✓ | |
| 6 | Return on Investments | ✓ | | | ✓ | | | ✓ | | |
| 7 | Utilization of Capacity | | | NM | | ✓ | | | ✓ | |
| 8 | Domestic prices | | ✓ | | | ✓ | | | ✓ | |
| 9 | Dumping Margin | | | – | | | – | ✓ | | |
| 10 | Cash flow | | | NM | | | NM | | | NM |
| 11 | Inventories | | ✓ | | | ✓ | | | ✓ | |
| 12 | Employment | | | | | NM | | | | |
| 13 | Wages | | | | | NM | | | | NM |
| 14 | Growth | | | NM | | | NM | | ✓ | |
| 15 | Ability to raise capital or Investment | | | | | | | | | NM |

*NM* means ‘Not mentioned’

| Non-attribution analysis | | |
|---|---|---|
| S. No. | Factors | Whether discussed or not |
| 1 | The volume and prices of the imports not sold at dumping prices | No |
| 2 | Contraction in demand or changes in the pattern of consumption | No |
| 3 | Trade-restrictive practices of and competition between foreign and domestic producers | No |
| 4 | Developments in technology | No |
| 5 | The export performance | No |
| 6 | Productivity of the domestic industry | No |
| 7 | Other unlisted known factors | None |

**Case 64/1/2000 # AD Investigation on Hardened Forged Steel Rolls from Russia, Ukraine and Korea**

Petitioner: M/s Gontermann-Piper India Ltd.
Period of Investigation: April 2001–June 2002
Date of Final Finding: July 3, 2003

**Material Injury—Consideration of 15 Injury Factors**

| | | 1998–1999 Compared to 1997–1998 | | | Compared to 1999–2000 | | | 1 April, 2001–30 June 2002 (POI) Compared to 2000–2001 | | |
|---|---|---|---|---|---|---|---|---|---|---|
| S. No. | Factors | Worsened (−) | Improved (+) | Unchanged | Worsened (−) | Improved (+) | Unchanged | Worsened (−) | Improved (+) | Unchanged |
| 1 | Sales | | ✓ | | | ✓ | | | ✓ | |
| 2 | Profits | ✓ | | | ✓ | | | ✓ | | |
| 3 | Output | | ✓ | | | ✓ | | | ✓ | |
| 4 | Market share | | | NM | | ✓ | | ✓ | | |
| 5 | Productivity | | | NM | | ✓ | | ✓ | | |
| 6 | Return on Investments | ✓ | | | ✓ | | | ✓ | | |
| 7 | Utilization of Capacity | | | | | | NM | | ✓ | |
| 8 | Domestic prices | | ✓ | | | ✓ | | | ✓ | |
| 9 | Dumping Margin | | | | | | – | ✓ | | |
| 10 | Cash flow | | | NM | | | NM | ✓ | | |
| 11 | Inventories | | ✓ | | | ✓ | | | ✓ | |
| 12 | Employment | | | | | NM | | | | |
| 13 | Wages | | | | | | | | | |
| 14 | Growth | | | NM | | | NM | | | |
| 15 | Ability to raise capital or Investment | | | | | | | ✓ | | |

*NM* means 'Not mentioned'

| Non-attribution analysis | | |
|---|---|---|
| S. No. | Factors | Whether discussed or not |
| 1 | The volume and prices of the imports not sold at dumping prices | No |
| 2 | Contraction in demand or changes in the pattern of consumption | No |
| 3 | Trade-restrictive practices of and competition between foreign and domestic producers | No |
| 4 | Developments in technology | No |
| 5 | The export performance | No |
| 6 | Productivity of the domestic industry | No |
| 7 | Other unlisted known factors | None |

## Case 63/1/2001 #: Antidumping Investigation on Acyclic Alcohols Originating in or Exported from Singapore, Brazil, Romania, Malaysia and South Africa

Petitioner: M/s National Organic Chemicals Industries Ltd (NOCIL)
Period of Investigation: April 2000–June 2001
Date of Final Finding: July 29, 2003

**Material Injury—Consideration of 15 Injury Factors**

| | | 1999–2000 Compared to previous year 1998–1999 | | | 2000–2001(POI) Compared to previous year 1999–2000 | | |
|---|---|---|---|---|---|---|---|
| S. No. | Factors | Worsened (−) | Improved (+) | Unchanged (−) | Worsened (−) | Improved (+) | Unchanged |
| 1 | Sales | | ✓ | NM | | ✓ | |
| 2 | Profits | | | NM | ✓ | | |
| 3 | Output | | | NM | | ✓ | |
| 4 | Market share | | | ✓ | | ✓ | |
| 5 | Productivity | | | NM | | ✓ | |
| 6 | Return on Investments | | | NM | ✓ | | |
| 7 | Utilization of Capacity | | ✓ | | | ✓ | |
| 8 | Domestic prices | | | NM | ✓ | | |
| 9 | Dumping Margin | | | | ✓ | | |
| 10 | Cash flow | | ✓ | | ✓ | | |
| 11 | Inventories | ✓ | | | | ✓ | |

(continued)

(continued)

| | | 1999–2000 Compared to previous year 1998–1999 | | | 2000–2001(POI) Compared to previous year 1999–2000 | | |
|---|---|---|---|---|---|---|---|
| S. No. | Factors | Worsened (−) | Improved (+) | Unchanged (−) | Worsened (−) | Improved (+) | Unchanged |
| 12 | Employment | | | ✓ | | | ✓ |
| 13 | Wages | | ✓ | | | ✓ | |
| 14 | Growth | | | NM | | | NM |
| 15 | Ability to raise capital or Investment | | | NM | ✓ | | |

*NM* means 'Not mentioned'

| Non-attribution analysis | | |
|---|---|---|
| S. No. | Factors | Whether discussed or not |
| 1 | The volume and prices of the imports not sold at dumping prices | No |
| 2 | Contraction in demand or changes in the pattern of consumption | Yes |
| 4 | Trade-restrictive practices of and competition between foreign and domestic producers | No |
| 5 | Developments in technology | Yes |
| 6 | The export performance | No |
| 7 | Productivity of the domestic industry | No |
| 8 | Other unlisted known factors | None |

### Case 14/30/2002 #: Antidumping Investigation on Ball Bearing from China, Russia, Poland and Romania

Petitioner: Ball and Roller Bearing Manufacturers Association of India, New Delhi
Period of Investigation: January 2001–March 2002
Date of Final Finding: March 19, 2004

**Material Injury—Consideration of 15 injury factors**

| | | 1999–2000 Compared to previous year 1998–1999 | | | 2000–2001 Compared to previous year 1999–2000 | | | January 2001–March 2002 (POI) Compared to previous year 2000–2001 | | |
|---|---|---|---|---|---|---|---|---|---|---|
| S. No. | Factors | Worsened (−) | Improved (+) | Unchanged | Worsened (−) | Improved (+) | Unchanged | Worsened (−) | Improved (+) | Unchanged |
| 1 | Sales | ✓ | | | | ✓ | | | ✓ | |
| 2 | Profits | | | ✓ | | | NM | | ✓ | |
| 3 | Output | | | | | | NM | | ✓ | |
| 4 | Market share | | | NM | | | NM | ✓ | | |
| 5 | Productivity | | | NM | | | NM | | ✓ | |
| 6 | Return on Investments | | ✓ | | | ✓ | | ✓ | | |
| 7 | Utilization of Capacity | | ✓ | | | ✓ | | ✓ | | |
| 8 | Domestic prices | | | NM | | | NM | ✓ | | ✓ |
| 9 | Dumping Margin | | | | | | | ✓ | | |
| 10 | Cash flow | | ✓ | | | ✓ | ✓ | ✓ | | |
| 11 | Inventories | | ✓ | ✓ | ✓ | | | | ✓ | |
| 12 | Employment | ✓ | | | ✓ | | | ✓ | | |
| 13 | Wages | ✓ | | | | ✓ | | ✓ | | |
| 14 | Growth | ✓ | | | ✓ | | | ✓ | | |
| 15 | Ability to raise capital or Investment | | | NM | | NM | | | | NM |

*NM* means 'Not mentioned'

| Non-attribution analysis | | |
|---|---|---|
| S. No. | Factors | Whether discussed or not |
| 1 | The volume and prices of the imports not sold at dumping prices | No |
| 2 | Contraction in demand or changes in the pattern of consumption | No |
| 4 | Trade-restrictive practices of and competition between foreign and domestic producers | No |
| 5 | Developments in technology | No |
| 6 | The export performance | No |
| 7 | Productivity of the domestic industry | No |
| 8 | Other unlisted known factors | None |

### Case 14/7/2003 #: Antidumping Investigation on Coated Paper of 80 GSM Exported from European Union and Indonesia

Petitioner: BILT Graphics Papers
Period of Investigation: January 2002–December 2002
Date of Final Finding: December 15, 2004

**Material Injury—Consideration of 15 Injury Factors**

| | | Compared to previous year 1999–2000 | | | Compared to previous year 2000–2001 | | | 2002 (POI) Compared to previous year 2001–2002 | | |
|---|---|---|---|---|---|---|---|---|---|---|
| S. No. | Factors | Worsened (−) | Improved | Unchanged | Worsened (−) | Improved | Unchanged | Worsened (−) | Improved | Unchanged |
| 1 | Sales | | | NM | | ✓ | | | ✓ | |
| 2 | Profits | | | NM | | ✓ | | ✓ | | |
| 3 | Output | | ✓ | | | ✓ | | | ✓ | |
| 4 | Market share | ✓ | | | ✓ | | | ✓ | | |
| 5 | Productivity | | | NM | | ✓ | | | ✓ | |
| 6 | Return on Investments | | | | ✓ | | | ✓ | | |
| 7 | Utilization of Capacity | | | NM | ✓ | | | | | ✓ |
| 8 | Domestic prices | | | | ✓ | | ✓ | | | ✓ |
| 9 | Dumping Margin | | | | | | | ✓ | | |
| 10 | Cash flow | | | | | ✓ | ✓ | | | ✓ |
| 11 | Inventories | | ✓ | | | ✓ | | | ✓ | |
| 12 | Employment | | | NM | ✓ | | | ✓ | | |
| 13 | Wages | | | NM | | ✓ | | | ✓ | |
| 14 | Growth | | | NM | | | NM | | ✓ | |
| 15 | Ability to raise capital or Investment | | | NM | | | NM | | | NM |

*NM* means 'Not mentioned'

| Non-attribution analysis | | |
|---|---|---|
| S. No. | Factors | Whether discussed or not |
| 1 | The volume and prices of the imports not sold at dumping prices | No |
| 2 | Contraction in demand or changes in the pattern of consumption | Yes |
| 4 | Trade-restrictive practices of and competition between foreign and domestic producers | Yes |
| 5 | Developments in technology | Yes |
| 6 | The export performance | Yes |
| 7 | Productivity of the domestic industry | Yes |
| 8 | Other unlisted known factors | None |

## Case 14/9/2005 # Antidumping Investigation on Bias Tyres Originating in China PR and Thailand

Petitioner: Automotive Tyre Manufacturer Association (ATMA)
Date of Final Finding: June 29, 2007

**Material Injury—Consideration of 15 Injury Factors**

| | | Compared to previous year | | | Compared to previous year | | | 2002 (POI) Compared to previous year | | |
|---|---|---|---|---|---|---|---|---|---|---|
| S. No. | Factors | Worsened (−) | Improved (+) | Unchanged (−) | Worsened (−) | Improved (+) | Unchanged (−) | Worsened (−) | Improved (+) | Unchanged |
| 1 | Sales | | ✓ | | | ✓ | | | ✓ | |
| 2 | Profits | | ✓ | | ✓ | | | | ✓ | |
| 3 | Output | | ✓ | | | ✓ | | | ✓ | |
| 4 | Market share | | ✓ | | ✓ | | | ✓ | | |
| 5 | Productivity | | ✓ | | ✓ | | | | ✓ | |
| 6 | Return on Investments | ✓ | | | ✓ | | | | ✓ | |
| 7 | Utilization of Capacity | | ✓ | | | ✓ | | ✓ | | |
| 8 | Domestic prices | ✓ | | | ✓ | | | | ✓ | |
| 9 | Dumping Margin | | | | | | | ✓ | | |
| 10 | Cash flow | | ✓ | | ✓ | | | | ✓ | |
| 11 | Inventories | | ✓ | | ✓ | | | ✓ | | |
| 12 | Employment | | ✓ | | | ✓ | | | ✓ | |
| 13 | Wages | | ✓ | | | ✓ | | ✓ | | |
| 14 | Growth | | ✓ | | | ✓ | | | | |
| 15 | Ability to raise capital or Investment | | | −NM | | | NM | | | NM |

*NM* means 'Not mentioned'

| Non-attribution analysis | | |
|---|---|---|
| S. No. | Factors | Whether discussed or not |
| 1 | The volume and prices of the imports not sold at dumping prices | Yes |
| 2 | Contraction in demand or changes in the pattern of consumption | Yes |
| 4 | Trade-restrictive practices of and competition between foreign and domestic producers | No |
| 5 | Developments in technology | Yes |
| 6 | The export performance | Yes |
| 7 | Productivity of the domestic industry | Yes |
| 8 | Other unlisted known factors | None |

## Case 14/4/2006 # Antidumping Investigation on Acetone Originating in or Exported from EU, Chinese Taipei, Singapore, South Africa and USA

Petitioner: M/s Hindustan Organic Chemicals Ltd., Mumbai and M/s Schenectady Herdillia Ltd.
Date of Final Finding: January 4, 2008

**Material Injury—Consideration of 15 Injury Factors**

| | | 2003–04 Compared to previous year | | | 2004–05 Compared to previous year | | | 2005 (July)–2006 (June) (POI); Compared to previous year | | |
|---|---|---|---|---|---|---|---|---|---|---|
| S. No. | Factors | Worsened (−) | Improved | Unchanged | Worsened (−) | Improved | Unchanged | Worsened (−) | Improved | Unchanged |
| 1 | Sales | | ✓ | | ✓ | | | | | ✓ |
| 2 | Profits | ✓ | | | ✓ | | | ✓ | | |
| 3 | Output | | ✓ | | ✓ | | | | | ✓ |
| 4 | Market share | ✓ | | | | | ✓ | | | ✓ |
| 5 | Productivity | | ✓ | | | ✓ | | ✓ | | |
| 6 | Return on Investments | | ✓ | | ✓ | | | ✓ | | |
| 7 | Utilization of Capacity | ✓ | | | ✓ | | | | ✓ | |
| 8 | Domestic prices | | | NM | | | NM | ✓ | | |
| 9 | Dumping Margin | | | | | | | ✓ | | |
| 10 | Cash flow | | ✓ | | ✓ | | | ✓ | | |
| 11 | Inventories | ✓ | | | ✓ | | | ✓ | | |
| 12 | Employment | | | ✓ | | | ✓ | ✓ | | |
| 13 | Wages | | ✓ | | | ✓ | | | ✓ | |
| 14 | Growth | | ✓ | | ✓ | | | | ✓ | |
| 15 | Ability to raise capital/Invest | | ✓ | | ✓ | | | | | ✓ |

*NM* means 'Not mentioned'

| Non-attribution analysis | | |
|---|---|---|
| S. No. | Factors | Whether discussed or not |
| 1 | The volume and prices of the imports not sold at dumping prices | Yes |
| 2 | Contraction in demand or changes in the pattern of consumption | Yes |
| 4 | Trade-restrictive practices of and competition between foreign and domestic producers | Yes |
| 5 | Developments in technology | Yes |
| 6 | The export performance | Yes |
| 7 | Productivity of the domestic industry | Yes |
| 8 | Other unlisted known factors | None |

**Case 14/6/2006 # Anti-dumping Investigation on Imports of Pre-sensitized Positive Offset Aluminum Plates (PS Plates) from Bulgaria, China PR, Malaysia, Singapore and South Korea**

Petitioner: M/s Technova Imaging Systems (P) Ltd., and M/s. Stovec Industries Ltd.
Period of Investigation: April 2005–March 2006
Date of Final Finding: August 23, 2007

**Material Injury—Consideration of 15 Injury Factors**

| | | 2003–04 Compared to previous year 2002–03 | | | 2004–05 (POI) Compared to previous year 2003–04 | | | 2005–2006(POI) Compared to previous year 2004–05 | | |
|---|---|---|---|---|---|---|---|---|---|---|
| S. No. | Factors | Worsened (−) | Improved | Unchanged | Worsened (−) | Improved | Unchanged | Worsened (−) | Improved | Unchanged |
| 1 | Sales | | ✓ | | | ✓ | | | | ✓ |
| 2 | Profits | | ✓ | | ✓ | | | | ✓ | |
| 3 | Output | | ✓ | | | ✓ | | | ✓ | |
| 4 | Market share | | | ✓ | | ✓ | | | ✓ | |
| 5 | Productivity | | ✓ | | ✓ | | | ✓ | | |
| 6 | Return on Investments | | ✓ | | ✓ | | | ✓ | | |
| 7 | Utilization of Capacity | | ✓ | | ✓ | | | ✓ | | |
| 8 | Domestic prices | ✓ | | | ✓ | | ✓ | ✓ | | |
| 9 | Dumping Margin | | | | | | | ✓ | | |
| 10 | Cash flow | | ✓ | | ✓ | | | ✓ | | |
| 11 | Inventories | ✓ | | | ✓ | | | | ✓ | |
| 12 | Employment | | ✓ | | | ✓ | | | ✓ | |
| 13 | Wages | | | ✓ | | ✓ | | | ✓ | |
| 14 | Growth | ✓ | | | ✓ | | | ✓ | | |
| 15 | Ability to raise capital/Invest | | ✓ | | ✓ | | | ✓ | | |

*NC* means "not clear". *NM* means "not mentioned".

| Non-attribution analysis | | |
|---|---|---|
| S. No. | Factors | Whether discussed or not |
| 1 | Change in the pattern of consumption | Yes |
| 2 | Technological differences between product at issue and its substitutes | Yes |
| 3 | Trade restrictive practices and domestic competition | Yes |
| 4 | Contraction of demand | Yes |
| 5 | Export performance | Yes |
| 6 | Imports from third countries | Yes |
| 7 | Productivity of the domestic producers | Yes |
| 8 | Other unlisted known factors<br>a. Rising prices of aluminum | Yes |

**Case 14/6/2009 # Anti-dumping Investigation on Imports of Viscose Staple Fibre Excluding Bamboo Fibre Originating in or Exported from China PR and Indonesia**

Petitioners: Association of Man Made Fibre Industry of India (AMFII)
Period of Investigation: 2007–08
Date of Final Findings: May 17, 2010

**Material Injury—Consideration of 15 Injury Factors**

| | | 2006–07 Compared to previous year 2005–06 | | | 2007–08 (POI) Compared to previous year 2006–07 | | |
|---|---|---|---|---|---|---|---|
| S. No. | Factors | Worsened (−) | Improved | Unchanged | Worsened (−) | Improved | Unchanged |
| 1 | Sales | ✓ | | | | | ✓ |
| 2 | Profits | | ✓ | | | ✓ | |
| 3 | Output | | ✓ | | | ✓ | |
| 4 | Market share | ✓ | | | ✓ | | |
| 5 | Productivity | | ✓ | | | ✓ | |
| 6 | Return on Investments | | ✓ | | | ✓ | |
| 7 | Utilization of Capacity | | ✓ | | ✓ | | |
| 8 | Domestic prices | ✓ | | | ✓ | | |
| 9 | Dumping Margin | | – | | ✓ | | |
| 10 | Cash flow | | ✓ | | | ✓ | |
| 11 | Inventories | | ✓ | | ✓ | | |
| 12 | Employment | ✓ | | | ✓ | | |
| 13 | Wages | | ✓ | | | ✓ | |
| 14 | Growth | ✓ | | | ✓ | | |
| 15 | Ability to raise capital/Invest | | ✓ | | | ✓ | |

| Non-attribution analysis | | |
|---|---|---|
| S. No. | Factors | Whether discussed or not |
| 1 | Imports from third countries | Yes |
| 2 | Contraction in demand & Change in pattern of consumption | Yes |
| 3 | Conditions of competition | Yes |
| 4 | Development in technology | Yes |
| 5 | Export performance of the domestic industry | Yes |
| 6 | Other unlisted known factors<br>a. Global Downward Trend<br>b. Weakening of Indian Rupee<br>c. Rise in input costs | Yes |

## Case 14/25/2008 # Antidumping Investigation on Circular Weaving Machines Having Six or More Shuttles for Weaving PP/HDPE Fabrics Originating in or Exported from China PR

Petitioner: M/s Lohia Starlinger Ltd.
Period of Investigation: April 2008–December 2008
Date of Final Finding: November 16, 2010

**Material Injury—Consideration of 15 Injury Factors**

| | | 2006–07 Compared to previous year | | | 2007–08 Compared to previous year | | | Compared to previous year April 2008–Dec. 2008 | | |
|---|---|---|---|---|---|---|---|---|---|---|
| S. No. | Factors | Worsened (−) | Improved | Unchanged | Worsened (−) | Improved | Unchanged | Worsened (−) | Improved | Unchanged |
| 1 | Sales | | ✓ | | | ✓ | | | ✓ | |
| 2 | Profits | ✓ | | | | ✓ | | ✓ | | |
| 3 | Output | | ✓ | | | ✓ | | | ✓ | |
| 4 | Market share | ✓ | | | | ✓ | | ✓ | | |
| 5 | Productivity | | ✓ | | | ✓ | | | ✓ | |
| 6 | Return on Investments | ✓ | | | ✓ | | | ✓ | | |
| 7 | Utilization of Capacity | | ✓ | | ✓ | | | | ✓ | |
| 8 | Domestic prices | | | NM | | | NM | ✓ | | |
| 9 | Dumping Margin | | | | | | | ✓ | | |
| 10 | Cash flow | | ✓ | | ✓ | | | ✓ | | |
| 11 | Inventories | | | NM | | | NM | | | NM |
| 12 | Employment | | ✓ | | | ✓ | | | ✓ | |
| 13 | Wages | | ✓ | | | ✓ | | ✓ | | |
| 14 | Growth | | | | NM | | | NM | | NM |
| 15 | Ability to raise capital/Invest | ✓ | | | ✓ | | | ✓ | | |

*NM* means 'Not mentioned'

| Non-attribution analysis | | |
|---|---|---|
| S. No. | Factors | Whether discussed or not |
| 1 | The volume and prices of the imports not sold at dumping prices | Yes |
| 2 | Contraction in demand or changes in the pattern of consumption | Yes |
| 3 | Trade-restrictive practices of and competition between foreign and domestic producers | Yes |
| 4 | Developments in technology | Yes |
| 5 | The export performance | Yes |
| 6 | Productivity of the domestic industry | Yes |
| 7 | Other unlisted known factors | None |

## Case 14/7/2011 # Antidumping Investigation on Digital Offset Printing Plates Originating in or Exported from China PR and Japan

Petitioner: M/s Technova
Date of Final Finding: October 3, 2012

**Material Injury—Consideration of 15 Injury Factors**

| | | 2008–09 Compared to previous year 2007–08 | | | 2009–10 Compared to previous year 2008–09 | | | 2010–2011(POI) Compared to previous year 2009–10 | | |
|---|---|---|---|---|---|---|---|---|---|---|
| S. No. | Factors | Worsened (−) | Improved | Unchanged | Worsened (−) | Improved | Unchanged | Worsened (−) | Improved | Unchanged |
| 1 | Sales | | ✓ | | | ✓ | | | ✓ | |
| 2 | Profits | | ✓ | | ✓ | | | ✓ | | |
| 3 | Output | | ✓ | | | ✓ | | | ✓ | |
| 4 | Market share | | ✓ | | | ✓ | | | | ✓ |
| 5 | Productivity | | ✓ | | | ✓ | | | ✓ | |
| 6 | Return on Investments | | | | | | | ✓ | | |
| 7 | Utilization of Capacity | ✓ | | | | ✓ | | | ✓ | |
| 8 | Domestic prices | | | | | | | | ✓ | |
| 9 | Dumping Margin | | | | | | | | ✓ | |
| 10 | Cash flow | ✓ | | | | ✓ | | ✓ | | |
| 11 | Inventories | ✓ | | | ✓ | | | ✓ | | |
| 12 | Employment | | ✓ | | | ✓ | | | ✓ | ✓ |
| 13 | Wages | | ✓ | | | ✓ | | | ✓ | ✓ |
| 14 | Growth | | | NC | | | NC | | | NC |
| 15 | Ability to raise capital/Invest | | | | | | | | ✓ | |

*NC* means "not clear". The industry had volume growth, but suffered financial decline

| Non-attribution analysis | | |
|---|---|---|
| S. No. | Factors | Whether discussed or not |
| 1 | The volume and prices of the imports not sold at dumping prices | Yes |
| 2 | Contraction in demand or changes in the pattern of consumption | Yes |
| 3 | Trade-restrictive practices of and competition between foreign and domestic producers | Yes |
| 4 | Developments in technology | Yes |
| 5 | The export performance | Yes |
| 6 | Productivity of the domestic industry | Yes |
| 7 | Other unlisted known factors<br>a. safeguard duties on aluminum from China PR and the increase in raw material cost<br>b. NIP lower than NSR<br>c. Additional investment by domestic industry | Yes |

**Case 14/35/2010 # Antidumping Investigation on Melamine Originating in or Exported from European Union, Iran, Indonesia and Japan—Final Findings**

Petitioner: M/s. Gujarat State Fertilizers & Chemicals Ltd.
Period of Investigation: April 2009–June 2010
Date of Final Finding: June 1, 2012

**Material Injury—Consideration of 15 Injury Factors**

| | | 2007–08 Compared to previous year 2006–07 | | | 2008–09 Compared to previous year 2007–08 | | | April 2009–June 2010 (POI annualized) | | |
|---|---|---|---|---|---|---|---|---|---|---|
| S. No. | Factors | Worsened | Improved | Unchanged | Worsened | Improved | Unchanged | Worsened | Improved | Unchanged |
| 1 | Sales | | | | | | | | | |
| 2 | Profits | | ✓ | | ✓ | | | ✓ | | |
| 3 | Output | ✓ | | | ✓ | | | ✓ | | |
| 4 | Market share | ✓ | | | ✓ | | | ✓ | | |
| 5 | Productivity | ✓ | | | ✓ | | | | ✓ | |
| 6 | Return on Investments | | ✓ | | ✓ | | | ✓ | | |
| 7 | Utilization of Capacity | ✓ | | | ✓ | | | ✓ | | |
| 8 | Domestic prices | ✓ | | | | ✓ | | ✓ | | |
| 9 | Dumping Margin | | | – | | | – | ✓ | | |
| 10 | Cash flow | | ✓ | | ✓ | | | ✓ | | |
| 11 | Inventories | | ✓ | | | ✓ | | | ✓ | |
| 12 | Employment | | ✓ | | ✓ | | | ✓ | | |
| 13 | Wages | | ✓ | | | ✓ | | ✓ | | |
| 14 | Growth | ✓ | | | ✓ | | | ✓ | | |
| 15 | Ability to raise capital or Investment | | | NM | | | NM | ✓ | | |

*NM* means 'Not mentioned'

| Non-attribution analysis | | |
|---|---|---|
| S. No. | Factors | Whether discussed or not |
| 1 | The volume and prices of the imports not sold at dumping prices | Yes |
| 2 | Contraction in demand or changes in the pattern of consumption | Yes |
| 3 | Trade-restrictive practices of and competition between foreign and domestic producers | Yes |
| 4 | Developments in technology | Yes |
| 5 | The export performance | Yes |
| 6 | Productivity of the domestic industry | Yes |
| 7 | Other unlisted known factors | No |

### Case 14/3/2011 # Antidumping Investigation on Soda Ash Originating in Russia and Turkey

Petitioner: Alkali Manufacturer's Association of India
Date of Final Finding: February 9, 2013

**Material Injury—Consideration of 15 Injury Factors**

| | | 2009–10 Compared to previous year 2007–08 | | | 2010–11 Compared to previous year 2008–09 | | | 2011–2012(POI annualized) Compared to previous year 2009–10 | | |
|---|---|---|---|---|---|---|---|---|---|---|
| S. No. | Factors | Worsened | Improved | Unchanged | Worsened | Improved | Unchanged | Worsened | Improved | Unchanged |
| 1 | Sales | | ✓ | | | ✓ | | | ✓ | |
| 2 | Profits | ✓ | | | ✓ | | | | ✓ | ✓ |
| 3 | Output | | ✓ | | | ✓ | | | ✓ | |
| 4 | Market share | ✓ | | | | ✓ | | | | ✓ |
| 5 | Productivity | | ✓ | | | ✓ | | | ✓ | |
| 6 | Return on Investments | ✓ | | | ✓ | | | | ✓ | |
| 7 | Utilization of Capacity | | ✓ | | | | ✓ | | | ✓ |
| 8 | Domestic prices | | | | | | | ✓ | | |
| 9 | Dumping Margin | | | | | | | ✓ | | |
| 10 | Cash flow | ✓ | | | ✓ | | | | ✓ | |
| 11 | Inventories | | ✓ | | ✓ | | | | | ✓ |
| 12 | Employment | | ✓ | | ✓ | | | | | ✓ |
| 13 | Wages | | ✓ | | | ✓ | | | ✓ | |
| 14 | Growth | | | | | | | | ✓ | |
| 15 | Ability to raise capital or Investment | | | NM | | | NM | | ✓ | |

*NM* means 'Not Mentioned'

| Non-attribution analysis | | |
|---|---|---|
| S. No. | Factors | Whether discussed or not |
| 1 | The volume and prices of the imports not sold at dumping prices | Yes |
| 2 | Contraction in demand or changes in the pattern of consumption | Yes |
| 3 | Trade-restrictive practices of and competition between foreign and domestic producers | Yes |
| 4 | Developments in technology | Yes |
| 5 | The export performance | Yes |
| 6 | Productivity of the domestic industry | Yes |
| 7 | Other unlisted known factors | None |

# Chapter 5
# Injury and Causation in Safeguard Investigations: Experience of India and Other WTO Members

**Abstract** While the developed Members within the WTO have slowed down their recourse to safeguard measures, a number of developing countries such as India, Indonesia, Argentina and Turkey have become active users of such remedies. This chapter examines the practices and the tools developed by these emerging users in safeguards investigations. In particular this chapter seeks to examine whether the new users are conducting the injury and causation tests in conformity with the thresholds laid down by the WTO agreements and the jurisprudence developed by the panels and the Appellate Body.

## A Introduction

Safeguard investigations are relatively infrequent when compared to antidumping investigations and, therefore, attract limited publicity. Especially after the global safeguard investigations on steel by the Bush Administration in 2001, this mechanism has almost fallen into disuse among the traditional users.[1] The adverse rulings given by the WTO panels in some of safeguard investigations in the late 1990s and early 2000 too might have contributed to the falling popularity of safeguard instruments.[2] Nonetheless, following the 2008–09 economic crisis there was a worldwide upsurge in safeguard actions (see Fig. 1).

India has been a fairly active user of safeguards, although India's safeguard activity is significantly less when compared to its antidumping activity. India had initiated 36 safeguard actions during 1995–2014 which is by far the heaviest use of safeguard actions. Other leading users include Indonesia and Turkey, while there has been significant fall in the safeguard actions initiated by the traditional users such as the United States and European Union.

---

[1]The United States imposed special safeguard action passenger truck tyres from China under Section 421 of the U.S. Trade Act of 1974. The matter was later challenged by China at the WTO.
[2]Sheela Rai, Recognition and Regulation of Safeguard Measures Under GATT/WTO (2011).



J.J. Nedumpara, *Injury and Causation in Trade Remedy Law*,
DOI 10.1007/978-981-10-2197-8_5

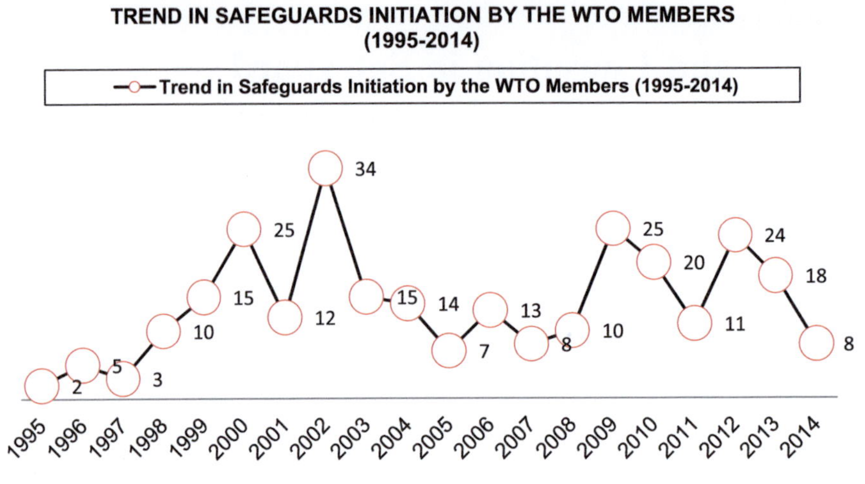


**Fig. 1** Trends in safeguards initiation by the WTO members. *Source* WTO

The legislative framework of safeguard investigations in India is provided by the Sections 8B and 8C of the Customs Tariff Act 1975. Section 8B deals with global safeguards while Section 8C relates to the transitional safeguard measures applied to imports from China. In addition, the Customs Tariff (Identification and Assessment of Safeguard Duty) Rules 1997, and the Customs Tariff (Transitional Products Specific Safeguard Duty) Rules 2002, describe the detailed procedures for the application of safeguard measures.

Unlike AD/CVDs, safeguard duties can be levied only for shorter periods of time which is necessary to prevent or remedy serious injury and to facilitate positive adjustment. Safeguard actions generally apply for short periods of time such as one or 2 years. There is an additional requirement that a safeguard measure in place for more than 1 year must be liberalized progressively at regular intervals. In rare circumstances, they may be applied for 4 years, but are scheduled to expire at the end of this period. However, the Central Government can extend the period of imposition upto a maximum of 10 years from first imposition of the duty if it is of the opinion that the domestic industry has taken measures to adjust to the injury or threat thereof and that the safeguard duty remains necessary. The safeguard measures are generally in the nature of customs tariffs, but the Foreign Trade (Development and Regulation) Amendment Act 2010 (No. 25 of 2010) also allows the use of quantitative restrictions as remedial measures.

In line with the previous chapter, this chapter seeks to examine India's conduct of injury and causation in safeguard investigations to find out the thrust, focus and the methodology of injury and causality analysis. A detailed analysis of the case studies is provided in the Appendix to this chapter. Like in the case of antidumping, the eight parameters provided in Article 4 of the Safeguards Agreement are analysed to find out how the DG Safeguards has performed the injury analysis in various investigations. Tick marks (√) have been used to indicate whether a particular injury factor was examined by the DG Safeguards or not. Furthermore, given the limited amount of safeguard activity, the focus of this study will be primarily on India, but will also consider the experience of some other WTO Members as well.

India has adopted almost the WTO treaty language in its safeguard legislation and rules and requires the domestic agency, namely, Director General of Safeguards (for short, "DG Safeguards") to establish that the subject goods are imported into India in such increased quantities and under such conditions as to cause or threaten to cause serious injury to the domestic industry. However, India's safeguard legislation or rules do not contain key provisions such as the requirement of "unforeseen development"[3]

It is also seen that several products which were subject to antidumping actions in India were also subject matter of safeguard investigations.[4] The objective may be to receive double remedies on nearly same or similar cause of injury, or perhaps to receive longer periods of protection especially after the elapse of one form of protection, or in some rare cases to receive import relief when the request for remedy under antidumping had failed or expired. The motivation for filing parallel or back-to-back investigations may have some bearing on injury and causation standards, but it is left out for the purposes of the present enquiry.

In order to conduct a qualitative research on injury and causation analysis in safeguard investigations, this study examined in depth twelve (12) safeguard investigations conducted over the last decade and a half. These cases represent nearly one-third of all safeguard investigations conducted by India. The purpose was to examine the injury parameters considered by the DG Safeguards in the causation analysis and whether the authority had conducted any non-attribution analysis as required under the WTO. The study also examined whether the DG Safeguards had applied any quantitative economic tools in this analysis.

---

[3]However, the DG Safeguards in India applies such requirements in practice. *See also*, Tarun Bhatti, Unforeseen development under safeguard investigations: International standard and Indian practices, http://www.lakshmisri.com/News-and-Publications/Publications/Articles/Tax/unforeseen-developments-under-safeguard-investigations# (last visited July 10, 205).

[4]The products that were subject to both antidumping and safeguards investigations include: Acetone, Bisphenol-A, Carbon Black, Caustic Soda, Certain Rubber Chemicals, Coated Paper and Paper Board, Electrical Insulators, Flexible Slabstock Polyol, Front Axle Beam and Steering Knuckle, Hot Rolled Flat Products of Stainless Steel, Hot Rolled Coils/Plates/Sheets and Strips, Phthalic Anhydride, Sodium Citrate, Sodium Nitrate, etc. Most of these actions were not parallel proceedings, but were filed by generally the same set of producers or associations. See DG Safeguards, http://dgsafeguards.gov.in (last visited October 5, 2014).

## B Assessment of Injury and Causation in India's Safeguard Investigations

The volume and rate of increase in imports is the centre of enquiry in safeguard investigations. Although the safeguard investigation refers to serious injury, which is a higher form of injury, the injury parameters required for establishing serious injury are fewer when compared to antidumping or countervailing duty investigations. While the Antidumping Agreement has listed fifteen (15) injury parameters, the Safeguards Agreement has listed only eight (8) parameters. There is no period of investigation per se in safeguard investigations, but there is a reference period for the examination of the data. The purpose of the reference period is to examine the volume of imports and the rate at which imports have entered the country.

In the investigation on *Flexible Slabstock Polyol*[5] [Case #1], the DG Safeguards paid particular attention to the volume of imports and the price effects caused to the domestic industry. The investigation also examined the data for 3 years. However, the finding of serious injury and causation was determined more on the basis of price undercutting especially on the fact that imports increased when the domestic demand also increased. The exporters alleged factors such as inefficiency of domestic producers, differences in quality and technical support available to the imported and domestic product, and the monopoly status of the domestic producers. The other factors were treated as significant, but there was no particular effort in segregating and separating the role of such factors. Accordingly, the safeguard duty was imposed in this case for a period of 18 months.

In the safeguard investigation on *Hard board (high density fiber board)*[6] [Case #2] the DG Safeguards used a 3 year reference period for examining injury. Serious injury was established on the ground that the imports had increased at a time when the domestic sales and price levels had declined. Although price effects are not given statutory significance, the DG safeguards attached specific importance to price undercutting. The authority also noted that there were other factors which might have caused injury to the domestic industry. For example, it was alleged that the domestic consumers had experienced short supply when buying the product from the domestic producers and had therefore shifted to imports. However, the final findings did not disclose how the injury on account of these factors was not attributed to increased imports.

---

[5]Imports of Flexible Slabstock Polyol from Singapore and Japan, No. SG/V/4/97, (DG Safeguards, Ministry of Finance, October 12, 1998) (final findings) [hereinafter *Flexible Slabstock Polyol*].

[6]Imports of Hard Board (High Density Fiber Board) from Thailand, South Africa, etc, (DG Safeguards, Ministry of Finance, November 12, 1998) (final findings).

While the trend analysis remains the focus of enquiry in a safeguard investigation, the reference period to be chosen for such comparison remains ambiguous. In the initial years of safeguard actions in India, the DG Safeguards used the trends analysis only for shorter periods which typically was a 3 year period. However, after 2001–02, it is seen that the DG Safeguards has started using a longer reference period for the injury analysis. For example, in the safeguard investigation on *Epichlorohydrin from Japan, United States, Belgium and Korea*[7] [Case #5] the investigating authority used a 5-year reference period. Furthermore, it is noticed that the investigating authority sought information on imports and domestic industry statistics on the most recent period. Even the information gathered post-initiation of the investigation is also considered in the final analysis.[8] It may be incidental that a series of safeguard investigations challenged in the WTO during the late 1990s and early 2000s pronounced that injury should be recent enough, sudden enough, sharp enough, significant enough, etc. It is apparent that the WTO rulings in some of the safeguard disputes had impacted the Indian safeguard practices during this time.

The rising share of imports in domestic consumption especially in the context of robust domestic demand is often given considerable weight in the injury and causation analysis. In the safeguard Investigation on *Bisphenol-A* [Case # 6] the Designated Authority noted that if imports occupy a higher market share and displace domestic production in a growing market, the injury so caused is "undoubtedly attributable to increased imports".[9] The correlation between the rise in imports and the declining market share was inferred as an evidence of a causal link between increased imports and serious injury. In this case, no additional analytical tool was used to establish causal link.

A linear growth in imports was not considered to be sufficient to constitute a 'sudden surge' in imports in certain circumstances. In the *safeguard investigation on Linear Alkyl Benzene (LAB)*[10] [Case # 10] the domestic industry alleged serious injury attributable to imports from Qatar, Iran and Saudi Arabia. The DG Safeguards found that the rate of increase of imports in the most recent period of the investigation, i.e. 2008–09 was 61.08 % as against 111.95 % during 2007–08, and 340.77 percent during 2006–07. The DG Safeguards also found that India was a net exporter of LAB and that the domestic industry lost market share primarily in view of the entry of another domestic producer and the loss in exports sales. In a rare finding, the

[7]Imports of Epichlorohydrin Japan, United States, Belgium and Korea, No. SG/INV/1/2002 (DG Safeguards, Ministry of Finance, June 25, 2002) (final findings).

[8]DG Safeguards referred to the WTO Panel and AB reports in *Argentina- Footwear* (EC) or its reliance on post-initiation data, See DG Safeguards, Final Findings, Safeguard Duty investigation against imports of Coated Paper and Paper Board into India (Nov. 13, 2009).

[9]Imports of Bisphenol - A from China, Germany, US, Singapore, Taiwan, Korea and Japan, No. SG/INV/1/2003, ¶.6(b) (DG Safeguards, Ministry of Finance, October 27, 2003) (final findings).

[10]Imports of Linear Alkyl Benzene from Iran, Saudi Arabia, Qatar and Switzerland, No. 2011/23/2008 (DG Safeguards, Ministry of Finance, November 18, 2009) (final findings).

DG Safeguards held that the export oriented design of the domestic industry and combination of domestic factors were more significant causes of injury to the domestic industry. The DG Safeguards did not find any causal link in this matter.

In addition to serious injury claims, applications based on threat of serious injury have also been filed before the DG Safeguards. In the *safeguard investigation on Phenol* [Case #3], the DG Safeguards found threat of serious injury mainly on the basis of increase in the share of imports in domestic consumption. A number of injury factors such as stocks and market share of the domestic industry showed improvement during reference period. This case indicates that the serious injury standard was met fairly easily on the basis of a coincidence in time analysis.

An examination of the select safeguard investigations indicates that the standards of serious injury and causation are not significantly higher in safeguard investigations when compared to antidumping proceedings, although serious injury is considered to be at a level higher than material injury. Serious injury in the Safeguards Agreement refers to the term "significant overall impairment" of the domestic industry. The exact meaning of this term is uncertain in the context of Indian safeguard investigations. For example, in *Coated paper and Paper Board*[11] [Case #12], the profitability and the market share of the domestic industry declined during the reference period. However, the DG Safeguards noted that a profit making domestic industry, which had high production, sales, capacity utilization and was undertaking capacity expansion during the entire period of consideration, could not be said to be in the position of significant overall impairment.

The key focus in the safeguard investigations is on the volume and rate of increase in imports and the market share ceded by the domestic industry to imports. For example, in the investigation on *Uncoated Paper and Copy paper*[12] [case # 11], the DG Safeguards held that if the increased imports are unable to take the market share of the domestic industry, it should be concluded that imports had no adverse effects on the domestic industry. The investigating authority, therefore, did not reach a finding of injury and causation. While profitability, return of capital employed (ROCE) and cash flow are given decisive importance in antidumping cases, such parameters are not often assessed on a consistent basis in India in safeguard investigations. It is striking to note that the DG Safeguards noted in the investigation on *Flexible Slabstock Polyol* [Case # 1] that ROCE is one of the reflections of the profit and losses made by the domestic industry and should be taken into account in the consideration of serious injury.[13] The recent safeguard investigations provide greater amount of data on profitability, ROCE and other factors in comparison with the earlier cases, but still an analysis of the financial parameters is not given the same weightage as is given in antidumping cases.

[11]Imports of Coated Paper and Paper Board from 22011/25/2009, (DG Safeguards, Ministry of Finance, April 24, 2009) (final findings).

[12]Imports of Uncoated Paper and Copy Paper from Indonesia, Thailand, Finland, China, Hong Kong, Japan, Singapore and the United States No. 22011/27/2009 (Ministry of Finance, November. 5, 2009) (final findings).

[13]Flexible Slabstock Polyol, ¶. 50.

The Safeguards Agreement requires the investigating authority to evaluate all other objective and quantifiable factors that are important to the situation of the domestic industry. The Indian safeguard investigations examined in this study indicate that not even the eight listed factors are examined in all cases. In a number of investigations the information pertaining to employment, productivity, etc. is missing. Domestic industry inventory (stocks) is also not examined in every case.

## C Non-attribution Analysis in India's Safeguard Investigations

Unlike the AD and SCM Agreements, the Safeguards Agreement does not provide a list of indicative factors that should be taken into account in the causation analysis. Nonetheless, a series of WTO panel and Appellate Body decisions have reiterated the importance of non-attribution analysis in safeguard investigations.[14] The Appellate Body noted in *US—Lamb* that the causal link between increased imports and serious injury can only be made after the effects of increased imports have been assessed, followed up by a separation of the effects by all different causal factors. In short, the non-attribution language casts an obligation on the investigating authority not to attribute the injury caused by other factors to increased imports.

The Indian safeguard investigations examined in this chapter clearly indicate that non-attribution in some form was conducted by the DG Safeguards even before this requirement became almost an unavoidable element of all trade remedy investigations. The other causal factors were not examined in any particular order or under any separate category of analysis in the final findings. An examination of the final findings also indicates that the other causal factors were often raised by the exporters in question and not necessarily discovered by the investigating authority on its own initiative. In the majority of cases examined, the DG Safeguards examined the role of product and quality differences and the export performance of the domestic industry. In certain other cases, factors such as the rise in raw material costs, utility costs or loss of productivity were examined. But the analysis, at best, is limited to only two or three other factors in that investigation. It will be instructive to examine the safeguard investigation on *Starch, Manioc (Cassava, Tapioco) based Sago and Modified Starches*[15] [Case # 7] which made a departure in analyzing the role of other factors. Unlike other safeguard investigations, the DG Safeguards had enumerated at least a dozen possible causal factors. Beyond listing these factors, however, there was no effort, either qualitative or quantitative, in separating the effects of these factors. It

---

[14]Appellate Body Report, *United States – Safeguard Measures on Imports of Fresh, Chilled or Frozen Lamb Meat from New Zealand and Australia*, WT/DS177/AB/R, WT/DS178/AB/R, ¶. 168 (May 16, 2001).

[15]Imports of Manioc (Cassava, Tapioca) based sugar modified starches, No. SG/INV/1/2004 (DG Safeguards, Ministry of Finance, February 16, 2005) (final findings).

appears that the various causal factors were raised by some of the interested parties not necessarily to disprove causation, but to argue why a higher import protection of safeguard duty is not called for. However, one could easily conclude that the requirement of separating the injurious effects of other factors, in the way the WTO panels and the Appellate Body had mandated, has remained almost an elusive concept in the context of Indian safeguard investigations.

## D Injury and Causation Determination: Experience of Other WTO Members

There has been a general slowdown in safeguard actions in the recent times. The traditional users are no longer invoking this mechanism. Among the developing countries India, Indonesia, Argentina and Turkey have been major users. The following section does not seek to provide an analysis of the injury and causation practices of all major users but only of a few representative jurisdictions.

### *1 Argentina*

Argentina is one of the active users of safeguard investigations and had conducted several such investigations in the wake of joining the WTO. The developments during the pre-Peso crisis period (1995–2001) and the intra-regional trade liberalization initiated with the signing of the MERCOSUR treaty led to a growth in imports in certain categories of goods and consequently to trade remedy measures.[16] Argentina initiated safeguard investigations on preserved peaches, footwear, toys, mopeds and motor cycles, to name a few products, during this period. Argentina's safeguard investigation on footwear was one of the first disputes to be challenged under the provisions of Article XIX of the GATT and the Agreement on Safeguards.[17] This case clarified the jurisprudence on several WTO issues and is frequently referred to in subsequent WTO cases. In this dispute the Appellate Body concluded that Argentina was not able to establish an increase in imports as well as injury and causation. The Appellate Body also concluded that the legality of safeguard measures depend upon the existence of "unforeseen developments", an expression which is mentioned only in Article XIX of the GATT.

Comisión Nacional de Comercio Exterior (CNCE) is the authority responsible for the analysis, investigation and regulation in the determination of injury to domestic production. Prior to the decision in *Argentina—Footwear*, the CNCE did

[16]The antidumping activity declined after the devaluation of peso which made the imports costlier.

[17]Appellate Body Report, *Argentina—Safeguard Measures on Imports of Footwear*, WT/DS121/AB/R(1999).

not separately establish the existence of unforeseen developments. As some of the disputes during the pre-Peso crisis period indicate, it was alleged that the competent authorities did not make any a priori finding nor demonstrate in their report the existence of unforeseen developments.[18] However, Argentina has apparently rectified this deficiency in its implementing legislation.

## 2 *Indonesia*

In recent times, Indonesia has been the most active user of safeguard instruments. The safeguard actions are initiated by the Komite Pengamanan Perdagangan Indonesia (KPPI or Committee on Trade Defense of Indonesia) under the legislation entitled "Safeguard of the Domestic Industry Against the Impact of Increased Imports". Indonesia generally takes into account the price and volume trends as the key indicators in the injury analysis. In order to conduct the volume trends, Indonesia generally takes into account 3 years as the injury investigation period.

While conducting the price trends analysis, comparisons are based on the average ex-works prices of the domestic producers with the landed price of imports. The landed price of imports is based on the CIF price along with the applicable customs duties and other ancillary costs.

Indonesia carries out the non-attribution analysis based on consideration of a standard set of factors. Checklist factors such as technology used by the domestic industry are often taken into account. This is apparently to make sure that the increase in imports is the major contributing factor to serious injury.[19] However the investigating authority does not generally consider factors other than the routinely considered causal events such as contraction in demand, export performance of the domestic industry, technology and domestic competition.

Indonesia's safeguard actions have been challenged by other WTO Members in recent times. For example, in a recent request for the establishment of panel by Chinese Taipei against Indonesia in respect of certain iron or steel products, the complainant has alleged that Indonesia had failed to provide a proper analysis of the unforeseen developments and a reasoned and adequate explanation of serious injury and causation.[20] In the meantime, Vietnam has raised concerns regarding the determination of unforeseen developments, serious injury and causal link in respect of flat-rolled products of iron or non-alloy steel.[21]

---

[18]*See* Panel Report, *Argentina—Peaches*, ¶. 7.35.

[19]Page 4 of the Notifications G/SG/N/10/IDN/2 G/SG/N/11/IDN/2 9 October 2009.

[20]World Trade Organization, Request for the Establishment of a Panel by the Separate Customs Territory of Taiwan, Penghu, Kinmen and Matsu, *Indonesia- Safeguard Action or Certain Iron or Steel Products,* WT/DS 490/2 (August 21, 2015).

[21]World Trade Organization, Committee of Safeguards, Minutes of the Regular Meeting, G/SG/M/46, March 24, 2015 [hereinafter Minutes of the Committee of Safeguards].

### 3 *Turkey*

Turkey is another jurisdiction that has frequently used safeguard measures in recent times. During 1995—2015 period, Turkey initiated 21 safeguard actions and was the third largest initiator among the WTO members.[22]

In Turkey, the authority to propose, apply and monitor safeguards measures is vested with the Ministry of Economy. The safeguard investigation is conducted by the Undersecretariat of Foreign Trade.[23]

Some concerns have been expressed by WTO Members regarding the safeguard practices of Turkey. One of the concerns was that Turkey had extended all its safeguard measures beyond their original term.[24] The objection was on the ground that the measures were not warranted because the share of imports had decreased and the production of the domestic industry had increased during the implementation of the measure.[25] India too had challenged the extension of safeguard measures on cotton yarn in 2012 and the matter was settled.[26] In regard to the investigation on printing, writing and copying paper, the European Union alleged that Turkey had imposed the measure without demonstrating 'recent, sudden or sharp increase in imports".[27] But none of these concerns has culminated in a completed WTO panel process.

## E Conclusion

Whilst the WTO treaty and dispute settlement jurisprudence on injury and causation in safeguard investigations present tough procedural and substantive standards, meeting such thresholds hitherto has not been that difficult in the context of Indian safeguard investigations. An overall coincidence of the upward trend in increased imports and the negative trend in injury factors over the reference period was considered sufficient enough for safeguards relief. In particular, a decline in the domestic industry's market share in periods of rising domestic demand was often considered as indicative of causation. Other causal factors were explored in the investigations, but the non-attribution analysis is often not conducted at depth or could be completely missing in some investigations. It is also not possible to find

---

[22]World Trade Organization, Trade Policy Review Body, Trade Policy Review: Report by the Secretariat: Turkey, WTO Doc. no. WT/TPR/S/331 (Feb. 9, 2016), at 69, ¶ 3.64.

[23]İthalatta Korunma Önlemlerine İlişkin Tebliğ (Tebliğ No: 2004/1).

[24]World Trade Organization, Committee of Safeguards, Minutes of the Regular Meeting, G/SG/M/46, (March 24, 2015).

[25]*Id.* ¶ 83.

[26]Request for Consultations by India, *Turkey — Safeguard measures on imports of cotton yarn (other than sewing thread),* WT/DS428/1 (Feb. 15, 2012).

[27]Minutes of the Committee of Safeguards, supra note 24, ¶ 85.

out any explicit methodology for separating the effects of other causal factors. It is also evident that the DG Safeguards does not use any quantitative tools in the causation determination. The available evidence demonstrates that the non-attribution in safeguards investigations is not significantly different from antidumping investigations conducted in India and is carried out purely on qualitative means. The analysis in this chapter has also demonstrated that the analytical tools employed by most of the recent users such as India, Indonesia, Argentina and Turkey look similar. Most of these jurisdictions have also experienced certain difficulty in assessing 'unforeseen development' as this requirement is not specifically incorporated in their domestic legal framework and are rather perfunctorily carried out.

## Appendix

### Case 1 # SG/IV/4/97: Safeguard Investigation Concerning Imports of Flexible Slabstock Polyol of Molecular Weight 3000–4000 Used in the Manufacture of Slabstock Foams and Polyurethane Foam Mattresses from Singapore and Japan

Petitioners: M/s Manali Petrochemicals Ltd. Chennai and M/s SPIC Organics Ltd., Chennai.
Date of Final Findings: September 17, 1998

**Consideration of Injury Parameters**

| | | 1995–96 | | | 1996–97 | | | 1997–98 | | |
|---|---|---|---|---|---|---|---|---|---|---|
| S. No. | Factors | W/D | I | U | W/D | I | U | W | I | U |
| 1 | Increased imports in absolute or relative terms | | ✓ | | | ✓ | | Imports Increased | | |
| 2 | Production | | ✓ | | | ✓ | | ✓ | | |
| 3 | Domestic sales | | ✓ | | | ✓ | | ✓ | | |
| 4 | Market share | ✓ | | | ✓ | | | ✓ | | |
| 5 | Stocks | | NM | | | NM | | ✓ | | |
| 6 | Capacity utilization | | NM | | | NM | | ✓ | | |
| 7 | Profits and losses | (stated to have declined over a period of time) | | | | | | | | |
| 8 | Employment | | NM | | | NM | | ✓ | | |
| 9 | Productivity | | NM | | | NM | | ✓ | | |

*NM* Not mentioned; *W/D* Worsened/Declined; *I* Improved/Increased; *U* Unchanged

| Non-attribution analysis | | |
|---|---|---|
| S. No. | Other unlisted factors | Whether discussed or not |
| 1 | Superior quality | Yes |
| 2 | Technical support | Yes |
| 3 | Inefficiency of domestic producers | Yes |
| 4 | Monopoly status of domestic producers | Yes |

## Case 2# SG-REP/4/98: Safeguard Investigation Concerning Imports of Hard Board (High Density Fibre Board) from Thailand, South Africa, Malaysia, Italy and Pakistan

Petitioners: All India Fibre Board Manufacturers Association.
Date of Final Findings: November 12, 1998.

**Consideration of Injury Parameters**

| | | 1995–96 | | | 1996–97 | | | 1997–98 | | |
|---|---|---|---|---|---|---|---|---|---|---|
| S. No. | Factors | W | I | U | W | I | U | W | I | U |
| 1 | Increased imports in absolute or relative terms | NM | | | Volume Increased | | | Volume Increased | | |
| 2 | Share of domestic market taken by increased imports | | NM | | | ✓ | | ✓ | | |
| 3 | Domestic sales | | NM | | | ✓ | | ✓ | | |
| 4 | Production | | NM | | | ✓ | | ✓ | | |
| 5 | Stocks | | NM | | | ✓ | | ✓ | | |
| 6 | Capacity utilization | | NM | | | ✓ | | ✓ | | |
| 7 | Profits and losses | | NM | | | NM | | | NM | |
| 8 | Employment | | NM | | | NM | | | NM | |
| 9 | Domestic consumption | | NM | | | NM | | | NM | |

*NM* Not mentioned; *W/D* Worsened/Declined; *I* Improved; *U* Unchanged

| Non-attribution analysis | | |
|---|---|---|
| S. No. | Other unlisted factors | Whether discussed or not |
| 1 | Import price of off-cut Hard board lower than that of standard size | Yes |
| 2 | Decline in domestic selling price | Yes |
| 3 | Quality | Yes |
| 4 | Differences in the end use of the imported and domestic products | Yes |
| 5 | Individual performance of the three domestic producers | Yes |

## Case 3 #SG/INV/2/98: Safeguard Investigation Concerning Imports of Phenol from Germany, Italy, US, Tokyo, Korea, Taiwan, South Africa and Switzerland

Petitioners: Hindustan Organic Chemicals Ltd. (HOC, Mumbai; Herdilia Chemicals Ltd. (HCL), Mumbai and Neyveli Lignite Corporation, Tamil Nadu.
Date of Final Findings: May 12, 1999

**Consideration of Injury Parameters**

| | | 1995–96 | | | 1996–97 | | | 1997–98 | | | 1998–99 | | |
|---|---|---|---|---|---|---|---|---|---|---|---|---|---|
| S. No. | Factors | W | I | U | W | I | U | W | I | U | W | I | U |
| 1 | increased Imports in absolute or relative terms | | ✓ | | ✓ | | | ✓ | | | Volume Increased | | |
| 2 | Production | | ✓ | | ✓ | | | | ✓ | | ✓ | | |
| 3 | Capacity utilization | | NM | | | NM | | | ✓ | | ✓ | | |
| 4 | Sales | | ✓ | | ✓ | | | | ✓ | | ✓ | | |
| 5 | Stocks | | NM | | | ✓ | | ✓ | | | | ✓ | |
| 6 | Employment | | | ✓ | | | ✓ | | | ✓ | | | ✓ |
| 7 | Profits and losses | | NM | | | NM | | | NM | | | NM | |
| 8 | Market share | ✓ | | | | ✓ | | ✓ | | | | ✓ | |

*NM* Not mentioned; *W/D* Worsened/Declined; *I* Improved; *U* Unchanged

| Non-attribution analysis | | |
|---|---|---|
| S. No. | Other unlisted factors | Whether discussed or not |
| 1 | Export performance of the domestic industry | Yes |
| 2 | Quality differences | Yes |
| 3 | Dumping of phenol in the Indian market | Yes |
| 4 | Captive consumption of phenol by the domestic industry | Yes |
| 5. | Monopoly/Duopoly by domestic producers | Yes |
| 6. | Global chemical industry recession | Yes |
| 7. | Shut down of operations for 15–40 days during 1998–99 | Yes |
| 8. | Productivity of the domestic industry | Yes |

## Case 4# SG/INV/2/2000: Safeguard Investigation Concerning Imports of Methylene Chloride from Taiwan and Hungary

Petitioners: Gujarat Alkalies and Chemicals Ltd. (GACL), Gujarat; Chemplast Sanmar Limited, Chennai and SRF Ltd., New Delhi.
Date of Final Findings: December 15, 2000

**Consideration of Injury Parameters**

| | | 1996–97 | | | 1997–98 | | | 1998–99 | | | 1999–2000 | | |
|---|---|---|---|---|---|---|---|---|---|---|---|---|---|
| S. No. | Factors | W/D | I | U | W/D | I | U | W | I | U | W | I | U |
| 1 | Increased imports in absolute or relative terms | Imports Increased | | | Imports Declined | | | Imports declined | | | Imports declined | | |
| 2 | Share of domestic market taken by increased imports | | NM | | | NM | | | NM | | | NM | |
| 3 | Domestic sales | ✓ | | | | ✓ | | | ✓ | | | ✓ | |
| 4 | Production | ✓ | | | | ✓ | | | ✓ | | | ✓ | |
| 5 | Productivity | | | ✓ | | | ✓ | | | ✓ | | | ✓ |
| 6 | Capacity utilization | ✓ | | | ✓ | | | | ✓ | | | ✓ | |
| 7 | Profits and losses | | NM | | | NM | | ✓ | | | ✓ | | |
| 8 | Employment | | | ✓ | | | ✓ | | | ✓ | | | ✓ |
| 9 | Domestic consumption | ✓ | | | | ✓ | | | ✓ | | | ✓ | |
| 10 | Stocks | ✓ | | | ✓ | | | | ✓ | | ✓ | | |

*NM* Not mentioned; *W/D* Worsened/Declined; *I* Improved; *U* Unchanged

| Non-attribution analysis | | |
|---|---|---|
| S. No. | Other factors | Whether discussed or not |
| 1 | Other unlisted known factors | No |

## Case 5# F. No. SG/INV/1/2002: Safeguard Investigation Concerning Imports Epichlorohydrin from Japan, US, Belgium and Korea

Petitioners: Tamil Nadu Petroproducts Limited (TPL) Chennai.
Date of Final Findings: June 25, 2002

**Consideration of injury parameters**

| | | 1997–98 | | | 1998–99 | | | 1999–2000 | | | 2000–01 | | | 2001–02 | | |
|---|---|---|---|---|---|---|---|---|---|---|---|---|---|---|---|---|
| S. No. | Factors | W | I | U | W | I | U | W | I | U | W | I | U | W | I | U |
| 1 | Increased imports in absolute or relative terms | Imports consistently increased | | | | | | | | | | | | | | |
| 2 | Share of domestic market taken by increased imports | ✓ | | | ✓ | | | ✓ | | | ✓ | | | | ✓ | |
| 3 | Domestic sales | ✓ | | | ✓ | | | | ✓ | | | ✓ | | | ✓ | |
| 4 | Production | ✓ | | | ✓ | | | | | ✓ | | ✓ | | ✓ | | |
| 5 | Productivity | ✓ | | | ✓ | | | | | ✓ | | ✓ | | | ✓ | |
| 6 | Capacity utilization | ✓ | | | ✓ | | | ✓ | | | | ✓ | | | | ✓ |
| 7 | Profits and losses | | ✓ | | | ✓ | | ✓ | | | | ✓ | | ✓ | | |
| 8 | Employment | ✓ | | | ✓ | | | ✓ | | | ✓ | | | ✓ | | |
| 9 | Stocks | ✓ | | | | ✓ | | | ✓ | | ✓ | | | | ✓ | |

*NM* Not mentioned; *W/D* Worsened/Declined; *I* Improved; *U* Unchanged

| Non-attribution analysis | | |
|---|---|---|
| S. No. | Other unlisted factors | Whether discussed or not |
| 1 | Export performance of the domestic industry | Yes |
| 2 | Quality difference | Yes |

## Case # 6: SG/INV/1/2003: Safeguard Investigation Concerning Imports of Bisphenol-A from China, Germany, US, Singapore, Taiwan, Korea and Japan

Petitioners: Kesar Petrochemicals Limited, Mumbai.
Final finding: October 27, 2003

**Consideration of Injury Parameters**

| | | 1998–99 | | | 1999–2000 | | | 2000–01 | | | 2001–02 | | | 2002–03 | | |
|---|---|---|---|---|---|---|---|---|---|---|---|---|---|---|---|---|
| S. No. | Factors | W/D | I | U | W/D | I | U | W | I | U | W/D | I | U | W | I | U |
| 1 | Increased imports—absolute or relative | | ✓ | | | ✓ | | ✓ | | | | ✓ | | | ✓ | |
| 2 | Share of domestic producers | ✓ | | | ✓ | | | | ✓ | | ✓ | | | ✓ | | |
| 3 | Domestic sales | | ✓ | | | ✓ | | | ✓ | | ✓ | | | ✓ | | |
| 4 | Production | | ✓ | | | ✓ | | ✓ | | | | ✓ | | ✓ | | |
| 5 | Productivity | | NM | | | NM | | | NM | | | NM | | | | NM |
| 6 | Capacity utilization | | | NM | | ✓ | | | NM | | ✓ | | | ✓ | | |
| 7 | Profits and losses | | NM | | | NM | | | NM | | | NM | | | | NM |
| 8 | Employment | | NM | | | NM | | | NM | | | NM | | | | NM |
| 9 | Domestic consumption | | ✓ | | | ✓ | | | ✓ | | | ✓ | | | ✓ | |

*NM* Not mentioned; *W/D* Worsened/Declined; *I* Improved; *U* Unchanged

| Non-attribution analysis | | |
|---|---|---|
| S. No. | Other unlisted factors | Whether discussed or not |
| 1 | Expansion of capacity by the domestic producers | Yes |
| 2 | Injury due to export performance | Yes |
| 3 | Demand- supply gap | Yes |
| 4 | Increase in raw material prices | Yes |
| 5 | Difference in quality and technical support | Yes |
| 6 | Inefficiency of domestic producers | Yes |

## Case # 7: Safeguard Investigation Concerning Imports of Starch; Manioc (Cassava, Tapioca) Based Sago and Modified Starches

Petitioners: A representation filed by the Farmers and Farmers Association of Tamil Nadu and Tamil Nadu Sago and Starch Manufacturers Welfare Association (TASSMA).
Date of final finding: February 16, 2005

**Consideration of Injury Parameters**

| | | 2002–2003 | | | 2003–2004 | | |
|---|---|---|---|---|---|---|---|
| S. No. | Factors | W/D | I | U | W/D | I | U |
| 1 | Increased imports in absolute or relative terms | ✓ | | | | ✓ | |
| 2 | Share of domestic market taken by increased imports | | ✓ | | ✓ | | |
| 3 | Domestic sales | ✓ | | | ✓ | | |
| 4 | Production | ✓ | | | | ✓ | |
| 5 | Productivity | | NM | | ✓ | | |
| 6 | Capacity utilization | ✓ | | | | ✓ | |
| 7 | Profits and losses | | ✓ | | ✓ | | |
| 8 | Employment | | | ✓ | ✓ | | |

*NM* Not mentioned; *W/D* Worsened/Declined; *I* Improved; *U* Unchanged

| Non-attribution analysis | | |
|---|---|---|
| S. No. | Factors | Whether discussed or not |
| 1 | Dumping of starch in the domestic market of India | Yes |
| 2 | Decline in export market share of the domestic industry | Yes |
| 3 | Captive consumption of starch must have been excluded from the investigation | Yes |
| 4 | Inefficiency of domestic producers | Yes |
| 5 | Self-inflicted injury by the domestic producers | Yes |
| 6 | Prices of raw materials | Yes |
| 7 | Ground water depletion | Yes |
| 8 | Increase in the cost of energy | Yes |
| 9 | Inability of small scale units to compete with large scale units | Yes |
| 10 | Withdrawal of preferential treatment in respect of Excise duty to small scale units vis-à-vis medium units | Yes |

## Case # 8: D-22011/07/2009: Safeguard Investigation Concerning Imports of Dimethoate Technical from China

Petitioners: M/s Shivalik Rasayan Limited
Date of Final Findings: May 14, 2009

**Consideration of Injury Parameters**

| | | 2006–2007 | | | 2007–2008 | | | 2008–2009 | | |
|---|---|---|---|---|---|---|---|---|---|---|
| S. No. | Factors | W | I | U | W | I | U | W | I | U |
| 1 | Increased imports in absolute or relative terms | ✓ | | | | ✓ | | | ✓ | |
| 2 | Share of domestic market taken by increased imports | ✓ | | | | ✓ | | | ✓ | |
| 3 | Domestic sales | | ✓ | | ✓ | | | ✓ | | |
| 4 | Production | | ✓ | | ✓ | | | ✓ | | |
| 5 | Productivity | | | ✓ | | | ✓ | | | ✓ |
| 6 | Capacity utilization | | ✓ | | ✓ | | | ✓ | | |
| 7 | Profits and losses | | ✓ | | | ✓ | | ✓ | | |
| 8 | Employment | | | ✓ | | | ✓ | ✓ | | |

*NM* Not mentioned; *W/D* Worsened/Declined; *I* Improved; *U* Unchanged

| Non-attribution analysis | | |
|---|---|---|
| S. No. | Factors | Whether discussed or not |
| 1 | Other unlisted factors | No |

## Case # 9: D-22011/32/2008-Safeguard Investigation Concerning Imports of Phthalic Anhydrite from Korea, Pakistan, Taiwan, Indonesia and Iran

Petitioners: M/s Thriumalai Chemicals Ltd.; M/s IG Petrochemicals Ltd.; M/s Mysore Petrochemicals Ltd.; M/s SI Group India Ltd.
Date of Final Findings: May 28, 2009

**Consideration of Injury Parameters**

| | | 2005–06 | | | 2006–2007 | | | 2007–2008 | | | 2008–2009 | | |
|---|---|---|---|---|---|---|---|---|---|---|---|---|---|
| S. No. | Factors | W | I | U | W | I | U | W | I | U | W | I | U |
| 1 | Increased imports in absolute or relative terms | | | NM | ✓ | | | | ✓ | | | ✓ | |
| 2 | Market share of the domestic producers | | | NM | | ✓ | | ✓ | | | ✓ | | |
| 3 | Domestic sales | | | NM | | ✓ | | | ✓ | | ✓ | | |
| 4 | Production | | | NM | | ✓ | | | ✓ | | ✓ | | |
| 5 | Productivity | | | NM | | | ✓ | | | ✓ | | | ✓ |
| 6 | Capacity utilization | | | NM | | ✓ | | | ✓ | | ✓ | | |
| 7 | Profits and losses | ✓ | | | | ✓ | | | ✓ | | ✓ | | |
| 8 | Employment | | | NM | | | ✓ | | | ✓ | ✓ | | |
| 9 | Stocks | | | NM | | ✓ | | | ✓ | | | ✓ | |

*NM* Not mentioned; *W* Worsened; *I*: Improved; *U* Unchanged

| Non-attribution analysis | | |
|---|---|---|
| S. No. | Factors | Whether discussed or not |
| 1 | Deterioration of export performance of the domestic industry | Yes |
| 2 | Losses suffered by the petrochemical industry due to the 2008 global recession | Yes |

**Case # 10 (F. No. D-22011/23/2008): Safeguard Investigation Concerning Imports of Linear Alkyl Benzene into India from Iran, Saudi Arabia, Qatar and Switzerland**

Petitioners: M/s. Reliance Industries Ltd., Mumbai; M/s Tamil Nadu Petroproducts Ltd., Chennai; M/s Nirma Ltd., Ahmedabad and M/s Indian Oil Corporation Ltd., New Delhi.

Date of Final Findings: November 18, 2009

**Consideration of Injury Parameters**

| | | 2006–2007 | | | 2007–2008 | | | 2008–2009 | | |
|---|---|---|---|---|---|---|---|---|---|---|
| S. No. | Factors | W | I | U | W | I | U | W | I | U |
| 1 | Increased imports in absolute or relative terms | | ✓ | | | ✓ | | | ✓ | |
| 2 | Share of domestic market | ✓ | | | ✓ | | | ✓ | | |
| 3 | Domestic sales | ✓ | | | ✓ | | | ✓ | | |
| 4 | Production | ✓ | | | | ✓ | | ✓ | | |
| 5 | Productivity | | ✓ | | | | ✓ | ✓ | | |
| 6 | Capacity utilization | ✓ | | | ✓ | | | ✓ | | |
| 7 | Profits and losses | ✓ | | | ✓ | | | | ✓ | |
| 8 | Employment | | | ✓ | | ✓ | | ✓ | | |
| 9 | Stocks | | | NM | | | NM | | | NM |

*M* Not mentioned; *W* Worsened; *I* Improved; *U* Unchanged

| Non-attribution analysis | | |
|---|---|---|
| S. No. | Other factors | Whether discussed or not |
| 1 | Improvement in domestic prices | Yes |
| 2 | Decline in domestic exports | Yes |
| 4 | Inter unit dynamics among producers in India | Yes |
| 5 | Overall position of the domestic industry | Yes |
| 6 | Export oriented design of the domestic producers | Yes |

### Case # 11: D-22011/27/2009: Safeguard Investigation Concerning Imports of Uncoated paper and copy Paper from Indonesia, Thailand, Finland, China, Hong Kong, Japan, Singapore and the US

Petitioners: ITC Limited—Paperboards and Specialty Papers Division; Ballarpur Industries Limited; JK Paper Limited; M/s The Andhra Paper Mills Ltd; M/s Tamil Nadu Newsprint and Papers Limited; Abhishek Industries Ltd.; Century Pulp and Paper; Emami Paper Mills Ltd.; Hindustan Paper Corporation Ltd.; Khanna Paper Mills Ltd.; The Mysore Paper Mills Ltd.; Orient Paper and Industries Ltd.; Pudumjee Pulp and Paper Mills Ltd.; Rama Newsprint and Papers Ltd.; Seshasayee paper and paper Board Ltd.; The Sirpur Paper Mills Ltd.; Star Paper Mills Ltd., The West Coast Paper Mills Ltd. and Yash Paper Mills Ltd.
Date of final findings: November 5, 2009

**Consideration of Injury Parameters**

| | | 2007–2008 | | | 2008–2009 | | |
|---|---|---|---|---|---|---|---|
| S. No. | Factors | Worsened | Improved | Unchanged | Worsened | Improved | Unchanged |
| 1 | Increased imports in absolute or relative terms | | ✓ | | | ✓ | |
| 2 | Share of domestic market taken by increased imports | | | ✓ | | | ✓ |
| 3 | Domestic sales | | ✓ | | ✓ | | |
| 4 | Production | | ✓ | | | ✓ | |
| 5 | Productivity | | NM | | | NM | |
| 6 | Capacity utilization | ✓ | | | | ✓ | |
| 7 | Profits and losses | | ✓ | | ✓ | | |
| 8 | Employment | | NM | | | NM | |

*NM* Not mentioned

| Non-attribution analysis | | |
|---|---|---|
| S. No. | Factors | Whether discussed or not |
| 1 | Other unlisted known factors | No |

## Case #12: D-22011/25/2009: Safeguard Investigation Concerning Imports of Coated Paper and Paper Board from China, Singapore, Japan, Hong Kong, Korea and Finland

Petitioners: ITC Limited—Paper Boards and Specialty Papers Dimension; Ballarpur Industries Limited and JK Paper Limited.
Date of Final Findings: November 13, 2009

**Consideration of Injury Parameters**

| | | 2007–2008 | | | 2008–2009 | | |
|---|---|---|---|---|---|---|---|
| S. No. | Factors | Worsened | Improved | Unchanged | Worsened | Improved | Unchanged |
| 1 | Increased imports in absolute or relative terms | | ✓ | | | ✓ | |
| 2 | Share of domestic market taken by increased imports | ✓ | | | ✓ | | |
| 3 | Domestic sales | | ✓ | | ✓ | | |
| 4 | Production | ✓ | | | ✓ | | |
| 5 | Productivity | | ND | | | ND | |
| 6 | Capacity utilization | | | ✓ | | ✓ | |
| 7 | Profits and losses | ✓ | | | ✓ | | |
| 8 | Employment | | ND | | | ND | |

*ND* No data for analysis; *W* Worsened; *I* Improved; *U* Unchanged

| Non-attribution analysis | | |
|---|---|---|
| S. No. | Factors | Whether discussed or not |
| 1 | Other unlisted known factors | No |

# Chapter 6
# Injury and Causation in Trade Remedies: Developments Under the Doha Round

**Abstract** This chapter examines the various proposals concerning the improvement to the treaty language on injury and causation under the Rules negotiations of the Doha Round. The proposals are made specifically in relation to the Antidumping as well as the Subsidies and Countervailing Measures Agreement. This chapter analyses the key proposals by the negotiating countries and whether there is any convergence of views among the WTO Members on any of the outstanding topics of injury and causation.

## A Introduction

The Doha Round of trade negotiations that were launched in November 2001 had an ambitious agenda. In the Doha Ministerial Declaration, WTO Members agreed to undertake "negotiations aimed at clarifying and improving disciplines under the Agreements on Implementation of Article VI of the GATT 1994 and on Subsidies and Countervailing Measures, while preserving the basic concepts, principles and effectiveness of these Agreements and their instruments and objectives, and taking into account the needs of developing and least-developed participants."[1] Reforming the trade remedy agreements was considered to be particularly important in the light of the increasing use of trade remedies in multiple jurisdictions. Negotiations on trade remedy instruments such as antidumping, subsidies and countervailing measures (including fisheries subsidies and RTAs, collectively known as Rules negotiations) turned out be one of the key areas of discussion under the Doha Round. Several proposals were made during 2002–2007, the initial and perhaps the most active phase of the Doha Round to reform or clarify the existing provisions of the Antidumping Agreement and the Subsidies and Countervailing Measures Agreement. Several proposals were initiated for clarifying the treaty provisions on injury and causality in these agreements as well. It is noteworthy that a similar exercise was not undertaken in the case of the Agreement on Safeguards.

---

[1]World Trade Organization, Ministerial Declaration of 14 November, 2001, WT/MIN (01)/DEC/1, 41 I.L.M. 746 (2002) (hereinafter *Doha Declaration*).



J.J. Nedumpara, *Injury and Causation in Trade Remedy Law*,
DOI 10.1007/978-981-10-2197-8_6

In December, 2005 at the WTO Ministerial Conference in Hong Kong, the Negotiating Group on Rules was directed "to intensify and accelerate the negotiating process" and also mandated the Chairman to prepare consolidated texts of the Anti-Dumping and Subsidies Agreements "that shall be the basis for the final stage of the negotiations." On the basis of the Ministerial Conference decision, the Chair of the Negotiating Group on Rules, Ambassador Guillermo Valles Galmés of Uruguay circulated to members on November 30, 2007 his first draft of consolidated texts on anti-dumping, subsidies and countervailing measures, including fisheries subsidies. The Chair's texts proposed a number of changes in the Anti-Dumping Agreement. The Chair of the Negotiating Group on Rules (NGR) subsequently issued a Chairman's text in 2011.

This chapter summarizes the various proposals submitted by the WTO members and analyses whether these proposals make substantial progress in elucidating the framework on injury and causation. By examining this issue, this chapter seeks to address the question whether there is consensus among the WTO members in using quantitative tools for establishing causation.

## B Rules Negotiations and Members' Proposals

By early 2002, various WTO panels and the Appellate Body (AB) had issued several landmark decisions in the field of injury and causation. The WTO panel and Appellate Body decisions, which I had examined exhaustively in Chap. 3, had already been issued and set the standard for the conduct of non-attribution analysis. The WTO panels and AB decisions in *EC—Bed Linen,*[2] and the panel's decision in *Thailand—H Beams*[3] had set important principles in the assessment of injury factors for determination of material injury and the assessment of other known factors which cause injury to the domestic industry at the same time as the dumped or subsidized imports. In the field of safeguard investigations, the WTO panels and the Appellate Body had clarified the scope of non-attribution analysis in cases such as the *Argentina—footwear,*[4] *US—Wheat Gluten,*[5] *US—Lamb,*[6] *US—Line*

[2]Appellate Body Report, *European Communities – Anti-Dumping Duties on Imports of Cotton-Type Bed Linens from India*, WT/DS141/AB/R/W (April 24, 2003).

[3]Appellate Body Report, *Thailand – Anti-Dumping Duties on Angles, Shapes and Sections of Iron or Non-Alloy Steel and H-Beams from Poland*, WT/DS122/AB/R (April 5, 2001).

[4]Appellate Body Report, *Argentina—Safeguard Measures on Imports of Footwear*, WT/DS121/AB/R (January 12, 2000).

[5]Appellate Body Report, *United States – Definitive Safeguard Measures on Imports of Wheat Gluten from the European Communities*, WT/DS166/AB/R (January 19, 2001).

[6]Appellate Body Report, *United States – Safeguard Measures on Imports of Fresh, Chilled or Frozen Lamb Meat from New Zealand and Australia*, WT/DS177/AB/R, WT/DS178/AB/R (May16, 2001).

*Pipe*[7] and *US—Tyres.*[8] These cases not only provided significant clarification in the conduct of the causation test, but also introduced standards which were generally non-existent or unheard of at the time of the conclusion of the Uruguay Round.

Immediately after the launch of the Doha Round, a group of countries including Brazil, Chile, Colombia, Costa Rica, Hong Kong, China, Israel, Japan, Korea, Mexico, Norway, Singapore, Switzerland, Thailand and Turkey submitted a series of proposals.[9] These set of countries known in the negotiating circles as the "Friends of Antidumping" (for short, "Friends Group" or "FAN") represent exporting countries that are often targeted in antidumping proceedings in major importing markets. The United States and European Union were also active in negotiations. The United States, in particular, was interested in improving the strength and effectiveness of the Antidumping Agreement.[10]

The following discussion focuses on some of the specific proposals in the field of causation under the Rules negotiations.

## C Relationship Between Material Injury and Causation

Under Article 3.1 of the ADA, an antidumping authority is to engage in an "objective examination" of "the volume of dumped imports", "the effect of dumped imports on prices in the domestic market for like products", and the consequent impact of dumped imports. Articles 3.2 and 3.4 of the ADA elaborate on these obligations, as does Article 3.7 of the ADA with respect to threat of injury determinations.

On November 22, 2002, the Friends Group made a proposal seeking to clarify the relationship between Articles 3.4 and other provisions of Article 3 to establish a more meaningful guidance for injury determination.[11] The Friends Group proposal noted that WTO dispute settlement panels and the Appellate Body have confirmed that the authorities must consider all elements as listed in Articles 3.1, 3.2 and 3.4 and all other known elements as listed in Article 3.5 in determining the existence of injury to domestic industry through the effects of dumping.

The Friends Group proposal referred to the WTO panel ruling in *Thailand—H Beams*[12] that the injury analysis must contain "a persuasive explanation as to how

[7]Appellate Body Report, *United States – Definitive Safeguard Measures on Imports of Circular Welded Carbon Quality Line Pipe from Korea*, WT/DS202/AB/R (March 8, 2002).

[8]Appellate Body Report, *United States – Measures Affecting Imports of Certain Passenger Vehicle and Light Truck Tyres from China*, WT/DS399/AB/R (October 5, 2011).

[9]*See* William Kerr and Laura Loppacher, *Anti-dumping in the Doha Negotiations: Fairy Tales at the World Trade Organization*, 38(2) JOURNAL OF WORLD TRADE 211, 216 (2004).

[10]*Id.* at 216.

[11]Negotiating Group on Rules, Paper by Friends of Antidumping, Antidumping: Illustrative Major Issues, TN/RL/W/6 (April 26, 2002).

[12]Panel Report, *Thailand – Anti-Dumping Duties on Angles, Shapes and Sections of Iron or Non-Alloy Steel and H-Beams from Poland*, WT/DS122/R ¶ 8.3(b) (April 5, 2001) as modified by the Appellate Body.

the evaluation of relevant factors led to the determination of injury." The proposal noted that the scope of review by panels and the Appellate Body on individual injury determinations were limited because Article 3 provides little guidance on how the authorities should analyze these factors in determining injury.

*FAN paper on interaction between Articles 3.1, 3.2, 3.4 and 3.5 of ADA.*

It is our view that Members should make substantial progress in clarifying a fair, reasonable and rigorous approach to the various injury factors as listed in Article 3.4, and to other factors set out in provisions of Articles 3.1 through 3.5. According to Article 3.1, injury determination involves, inter alia, an objective examination of both (a) the volume of the dumped imports and the effect of the dumped imports prices in the domestic market for the like product, and (b) the impact of those imports on domestic producers. These elements are further elaborated in Articles 3.2 and Article 3.4. Article 3.5 spells out the requirement for demonstration of a causal relationship leading to injury through the effects of dumping as set forth in Articles 3.2 and 3.4. Article 3.5 further provides guidance with respect to which factors other than the effects of dumped imports that shall be examined in determining such a causal relationship. It is therefore necessary to clarify the relationship between Article 3.4 and other provisions of Article 3 to establish more meaningful guidance for injury determination.

Friends Group made an additional submission seeking clarification of Article 3.4.[13] The proposal sought to elucidate the concept of 'material injury'. The FAN proposal included an amendment of footnote 9 of the ADA in order to clarify the definition of material injury:

*FAN Proposal: Article 3.4 of ADA*

The term 'material injury to a domestic industry' means the state of the domestic industry as demonstrated by an important and measurable deterioration in the operating performance of the domestic industry, based on an overall assessment of all relevant economic factors and indices having a bearing on the state of the domestic industry including those enumerated in Article 3.4.

The Friends Group proposal also noted that Article 3.4 of the current AD Agreement lists factors that must be considered when injury is determined, but does not provide adequate guidance to evaluate those factors. The United States too felt that the scope of the authority's obligation to examine "relevant factors and indices" other than the ones explicitly listed in Article 3.4 of the ADA and Article 15.4 of the ASCM is less clear. However, other members such as Australia had doubts about the additional need to clarify the examination of injury factors included in Article 3.4 of the ADA and its relationship with other provisions of Article 3 such as Article 3.1 and 3.2 and 3.5.

*Australia's questions on FAN proposals on Article 3.4 Injury parameters*

1. Do the proponents consider that this is an area where agreement could be reached on criteria used to evaluate injury factors?
2. Do the proponents consider that the ADA must specify all circumstances in relation to the factors outlined in Article 3.4? As Article 3.4 state in the last sentence, "this list is

[13]Negotiating Group on Rules, Paper from Friends of Antidumping, *Second Submission of Proposals on the Determination of Injury, Negotiating Group on Rules*, TN/RL/W/38 (March 23, 2005).

not exhaustive, nor can one or several of these factors necessarily give decisive guidance."

3. Could the proponents elaborate on what is meant by clarifying the relationship between Article 3.4 and other provisions of Article 3?

*Brazil's response to Australia's queries*

We have now had more than two decades of experience, with dozens of different countries and legal systems applying these factors to a wide variety of industries. Although we do not believe we can or should devise rigid mathematical formulas, we believe that the Members could make substantial progress in clarifying a fair, reasonable and rigorous approach to the various injury factors.

We do not consider that all circumstances must be specified in the ADA. However, the fact that we need not (indeed, could not) specify all circumstances is not a reason to avoid any and all efforts at clarification. There are many areas where clarification can and should be made, even if the list itself continues to be non-exhaustive.

On the other hand, certain other WTO Members such as Egypt observed that the various panel and Appellate Body reports have provided sufficient guidance on the obligations imposed on investigating authorities in injury determinations and that the case specific analysis of the injury factors should be left to the discretion of the investigating authorities.[14]

In regard to the relationship between Articles 3.1, 3.2, 3.4 and 3.5 of the ADA, the United States made a proposal in June 2003.[15] As is evident from the discussions in Chaps. 3 and 4 of this book, the volume of dumped imports is crucial in determining the volume effect in the injury and causation determination. The Appellate Body in the *EC—Bed Linen,*[16] observed that Articles 3.1 and 3.2 of the ADA "do not set out a specific methodology that investigating authorities are required to follow when calculating the volume of dumped imports". The Appellate Body also acknowledged that, in the light of ADA Article 6.10 (and under the circumstances described in the second sentence therein), these provisions must be interpreted in a way that does not require investigating authorities to investigate each producer or importer individually for the purposes of assigning a dumping margin. While the Appellate Body concluded that the EC's particular method of calculating the volume of "dumped imports" did not satisfy the requirements of Articles 3.1 and 3.2, it stated that there may be several possible ways of making such calculations that did satisfy these provisions. Members should consider whether the ADA should be clarified to specify methods that investigating authorities can readily implement in the injury investigation to calculate the volume of dumped imports for the purposes of Articles 3.1 and 3.2 especially when the investigating authorities may not be examining each individual producer or importer.

---

[14]Negotiating Group on Rules, Communication from Egypt, TN/RL/ W/56 (Feb. 10, 2003).

[15]Negotiating Group on Rules, Communication from the United States, TN/RL/W/130 (June 20, 2003).

[16]Appellate Body Report, *European Communities – Anti-Dumping Duties on Imports of Cotton-Type Bed Linens from India*, WT/DS141/AB/R/W (April 24, 2003).

## 1 Degree of Causal Relationship

According to the paper submitted by the Friends of Antidumping, the AD Agreement does not sufficiently describe the methodologies for establishing causal link between dumping and injury.[17] The FAN paper also noted that in practice authorities too often impose AD measures even when factors other than dumping are the substantial causes of the injury being experienced by the domestic industry. According to the Friends Group, in order to justify the imposition of AD measures, it is not sufficient that dumped imports merely have "contributed" to the material injury to some extent.[18] The FAN submission on causation noted as follows:

*FAN submission on causation*

"The obligations set forth in Article 3.5 should be rigorously observed. Moreover doesn't Article 3.5 merit further elaboration? In order to improve and clarify the Agreement, isn't it important to develop the procedures and criteria utilized to analyze the causal relationship, with a view to ensure that, even in the presence of other factors, a causal relationship will be found only when there is clear and substantial link between the dumped imports and the injury?"

In short, a key element of the paper was the need to introduce a substantial causal relationship between dumped imports and material injury to the domestic industry. In other words, if the cause of injury to the domestic industry is some other causal factor, then antidumping remedy should not be provided.

A similar proposal was made by China in 2003.[19] The proposal made by China imputed that the present framework of causation in the ADA/SCMA is inadequate. China stated that Article 3.5 should be clarified to ensure that a causal link could only be established when the dumped import is the "substantial reason" for the injury to the domestic industry. In the NGR, Australia specifically asked a question whether the use of the "substantial cause" standard would undermine the scope of the antidumping.[20] China however asserted that Article 3.5 of the ADA, as it stands, fails to provide a methodology of defining the causal relationship between dumping and injury. China also expressed the desire that WTO Members could distinguish the injury caused by dumped imports from the injury caused by other factors and that antidumping measures could be taken only when the dumped imports are the major cause of the injury.[21]

---

[17]WTO Negotiating Group on Rules, *Proposal of the People's Republic of China on the Negotiation on Antidumping,* TN/RL/W/66 (March 6, 2003).

[18]*Id.*

[19]*Id.*

[20]WTO Negotiating Group on Rules, Communication of Australia, Paper by Australia: Comments on Document TN/RL/W/6, TN/RL/W/22(October 15, 2002).

[21]WTO Negotiating Group on Rules, Submission from the People's Republic of China, Replies to the Questions and Comments of the WTO Members Concerning the Proposal of China, TN/RL/W/94 (May 5, 2003).

The Friends of Antidumping submitted a second proposal in 2005 in which they called for an amendment to Article 3.5 of the ADA.

*FAN proposal on the sufficiency of causal relationship*

"It must be demonstrated that the dumped imports in and of themselves are, through the effects of dumping, as set forth in paragraph 2 and 4, causing injury within the meaning of this agreement. (emphasis not original)"

## D Non-attribution Language

Article 3.5 of the ADA requires the establishment of a causal relationship between dumped imports and injury to the domestic industry. The investigating authorities are also required to examine any known factors other than the dumped imports which at the same time are injuring the domestic industry and the injuries caused by these other factors must not be attributed to dumped imports.

India also made a proposal on need for clarifying the "non-attribution" language in October 2002.[22] The 'non-attribution clause' i.e. requirement for segregating injury caused by factors other than dumped imports was particularly controversial in view of the Appellate Body decision in *US—Hot rolled steel.*[23] According to the Appellate Body, investigating authorities when conducting causation analysis should ensure that the injurious effects of the other known factors are not attributed to dumped imports. As the Appellate Body stated, this analysis requires the investigating authorities to appropriately assess the injurious effects of those other factors; such an assessment must involve separating and distinguishing the injurious effects of the other factors from the injurious effects of the dumped imports.

India acknowledged that separating and distinguishing the injurious effects from the different causal factors could be a difficult exercise. However, India stressed that for invoking anti-dumping measures, there is a need to specify an appropriate standard for establishing causality between dumped imports and material injury. While refraining from prescribing any standard, India proposed that there is a need to elaborate Article 3.5 so as to provide appropriate guidance to investigating authorities while separating and distinguishing the injurious effects of other factors from the injurious effects caused by the dumped imports.

Around the same time in October, 2002, Australia made a proposal, which opposed drastic changes to the injury and causation provisions. According to Australia, there was no lack of clarity in Article 3.5 of the ADA; Australia noted

---

[22]WTO Negotiating Group on Rules, *Second Submission of India: Antidumping Agreement*, TN/RL/W/26 (October 17, 2002).

[23]Appellate Body Report, *US- Hot rolled Steel,* ¶¶ 225-228.

that Article 3.5 only required adequate regard to other injury factors. Australia noted in its submission.[24]

*Australia's position on Article 3.5*

The question of causal link has been the subject of several recent WTO dispute settlement cases relating to anti-dumping and safeguards measures. The *Thailand Steel case* emphasized that although Article 3.5 requires that regard must be given by authorities to known factors other than dumped imports which are causing injury, this did not mean that there was an express requirement for an authority to examine these factors on their own initiative. However, they could choose to do so.

South Africa made a proposal in 2006 which reiterated the views expressed by Members such as the Friends of Antidumping, China and India.[25] South Africa acknowledged that it may not be possible to quantify exactly to what degree each factor is contributing to the injury affecting the domestic industry under investigation. However, according to South Africa, any inability at quantification of injury factors should not be a reason in granting import relief when other known factors contribute to a larger degree in the injury caused. In other words, according to South Africa, the injury caused by dumped imports must be at least as significant as the other known factors, individually or collectively. The extent of contribution should be borne out by the non-attribution, in South Africa's view.

As elaborately discussed in Chaps. 3 and 4 of this book, the most complex issue arising out of the implementation of the non-attribution analysis is the separation or isolation of the nature and extent of other known factors which may be causing injury to the domestic industry at the same time as the imports. While most of the WTO members agreed on the importance of this separation and segregation of effects, most of the proposals provided very little guidance on this issue. For example, Australia posed a couple of questions to China on the methodology for separation of the role of other known factors.

*Australia's questions to China*

Question: How does China envisage that these criteria of substantial reason can be made operational? Quantitative or qualitative assessment or should be even both examining causal link, and what should be done in practicable terms?

*China's answer to Australia's question*

Answer: As a common practice now, the causal relationship may be established if the investigating authorities determine that the dumped imports constitute one cause to the injury of the domestic industry in an antidumping investigation. Such loose provision leaves room for investigating authorities to discretionarily take measures to a great extent.

The purpose of the AD Agreement is to punish unfair trade practices, i.e. those measures which cause injury to the domestic industries of other Members through dumping. Article 3.5 of the AD Agreement provides that the investigating authorities shall also examine any

[24]WTO Negotiating Group on Rules, Communication of Australia, Paper by Australia: Comments on Document TN/RL/W/6, TN/RL/W/22 (October 15, 2002).

[25]Negotiating Group on Rules, Communication of South Africa (2006).

> known factors other than the dumped imports which at the same time are injuring the domestic industry, and the injuries caused by those other factors must not be attributed to the dumped imports. However, this Article fails to provide the methodology of defining the causal relationship between dumping and injury, which leads to the fact that, the investigating authorities in practice always neglect those other factors and take it for granted that the injuries are attributed to the dumping. China holds that in order to determine the causal relationship in a correct manner, the Agreement should provide that the investigating authorities shall separate and distinguish the injuries caused by other factors not attributed to the dumped imports from all the injuries, and should specify the method to separate and distinguish such injuries.
>
> As for the standard of assessment as well as the way of operation in practice, China is willing to discuss with other Members in a bid to establish an objective and operative standard.

In short, China did not specify any method for performing the non-attribution requirement. As Chaps. 3 and 4 of this book have examined, most users of antidumping have been using qualitative approaches for conducting non-attribution. It is revealing that most jurisdictions, including developed country Members such as the EU and Australia are not using quantitative tools in such examination. In several jurisdictions such as India, Brazil, Argentina, Turkey, Mexico and several other countries, the final antidumping proceedings have been at best qualitative and, in most cases, are based on a checklist approach. A particular known factor is raised only to be rejected as not being a cause. The possible causes of injury to the domestic industry could be several factors, but the findings, more often than not, do not discuss such factors. It is interesting to note that even a 2005 FAN proposal conceded the difficulty in separating and distinguishing the injurious effects of dumped imports from the injurious effect of other known factors.[26] It is pertinent to quote the FAN statement: "[i]t might be difficult, in most cases, to quantify precisely the degree to which dumped imports have contributed to the injury being experienced by the domestic industry relative to the effects of other factors".[27] The FAN Group proposal also suggests that such a separation of the injurious effects could be based on a qualitative information or less than perfect quantitative information or estimates based on such information. The FAN Group proposes that the purpose of any examination is to find out whether the dumped imports in and of themselves are causing material injury and as to what type of evidence was analyzed in reaching the conclusion.[28]

It is appropriate to mention in this regard that the United States had made two proposals in seeking to clarify the causation provision under Article 3.5 of the AD Agreement and Article 15.5 of the SCM Agreement. In the first paper, the United States proposed that any clarification should ensure "that any affirmative obligations

[26]WTO Negotiating Group on Rules, Paper from Friends of Antidumping, *Second Submission of Proposals on the Determination of Injury, Negotiating Group on Rules*, TN/RL/W/38 (March 23, 2005).

[27]*Id.* at 7.

[28]*Id.*

are clearly set forth in the Agreement and are workable for authorities to implement"[29] In the second paper, the United States also expressed the two key principles that any revision to the injury and causation provisions should embody (i) that an authority is not required to determine that dumped or subsidized imports are the sole cause of injury to the domestic industry.[30] This would confirm Members' current understandings and practice; and (ii) when authorities assess the effects of known factors other than dumped or subsidized imports, they should not be required to quantify the effects of these factors. The United States further noted that they were not aware of any reliable methodology.[31] Considering the fact that the United States was one of the very few jurisdictions that had used econometric models to quantify the extent of injury, this was an important statement. It is also pertinent to note that the US Court of Appeals for the Federal Circuit (USAFC) has insisted in *Bratsk Aluminum Smelter v. United States,*[32] that the U.S. International Trade Commission should provide quantitative explanation based on trade data in the injury determination.

In the subsequent paper, which was submitted in July 2005 and discussed at the September 2005 session of the Negotiating Group on Rules (NGR), the United States provided a further explanation of why clarification of the causation obligation established by Article 3.5 of the AD Agreement and Article 15.5 of the SCM Agreement would be useful. The United States also explained and suggested several specific ways in which the obligation should be clarified. In light of the above, the text proposed by the United States on causation included a modification of Art 3.5 of the ADA and the insertion of a new Article, namely Article 3.5.1. The United States also proposed a similar revision to the concerned provision under the SCM Agreement. It may be noted that the proposed deletions are struck through, while the proposed additions are underlined.

*Article 3.5 of the AD Agreement: U.S. Proposal*

"It must be demonstrated that the dumped imports are, through the effects of dumping, as set forth in paragraphs 2 and 4, causing injury within the meaning of this Agreement. The demonstration of a causal relationship between the dumped imports and the injury to the domestic industry shall be based on an examination of all relevant evidence before the authorities. The authorities shall also examine any known factors other than the dumped imports which at the same time are injuring the domestic industry. <u>As described in subparagraph 5.1, the authorities must not attribute</u> to the dumped imports ~~and~~ the injuries caused by these other factors ~~must not be attributed to the dumped imports~~. Factors which may be relevant in this respect include, inter alia, the volume and prices of imports not sold

[29]Communication from the United States, *Identification of Additional Issues Under the Anti-Dumping and Subsidies Agreements,* TN/RL/W/98 (May 6, 2003).

[30]Communication from the United States, *Causation (ADA Article 3.5; ASCM Article 15.5*), TN/RL/GEN/59 (July 13, 2005).

[31]*Id.* fn. 7.

[32]444 F.3d 1369 (Fed.Cir. 2006) (noting that the ITC will have to determine whether imposing the duties would benefit the domestic industry given the possibility of non-subject imports replacing the subject imports).

at dumping prices, contraction in demand or changes in the patterns of consumption, trade-restrictive practices of and competition between the foreign and domestic producers, developments in technology and the export performance and productivity of the domestic industry."

*Article 3.5.1 of the ADA: US Proposal*

"To make an affirmative determination that dumped imports are causing injury, the authorities must determine that the effects of the dumped imports are injurious notwithstanding the effects of the other known factors. The authorities need not isolate or quantify the effects of either the dumped imports or the other known factors, either individually or collectively. They also need not evaluate whether the effects of the dumped imports are more important than the effects of the other known factors, either individually or collectively"

On 30 November 2007, the Chair of the Negotiating Group on Rules issued a Draft Consolidated Chair Texts of the AD and SCM Agreements.[33] As the Chairman clarified, the draft texts on antidumping and subsidies/countervailing duties reflected a "bottom up" approach, identifying the most contentious issues contained in brackets with no legal text provided. The Chairman also noted that this was an interim step, pending the tabling of a revised text.

*Chairman's Text of the 2007 Working Document*

"Article 3.5: It must be demonstrated that the dumped imports are, through the effects of dumping, as set forth in paragraphs 2 and 4, causing injury within the meaning of this Agreement. The demonstration of a causal relationship between the dumped imports and the injury to the domestic industry shall be based on an examination of all relevant evidence before the authorities. The authorities shall also examine any known factors other than the dumped imports which at the same time are injuring the domestic industry, and the injuries ous effects of caused by these other factors must not be attributed to the dumped imports.[12] The examination required by this paragraph may be based on a qualitative analysis of evidence concerning, *inter alia*, the nature, extent, geographic concentration, and timing of such injurious effects. While the authorities should seek to separate and distinguish the injurious effects of such other factors from the injurious effects of dumped imports, they need not quantify the injurious effects attributable to dumped imports and to other factors, nor weigh the injurious effects of dumped imports against those of other factors. Factors which may be relevant in this respect include, inter alia, the volume and prices of imports not sold at dumping prices, contraction in demand or changes in the patterns of consumption, trade restrictive practices of and competition between the foreign and domestic producers, developments in technology and the export performance and productivity of the domestic industry.

[12] Factors which may be relevant in this respect include, *inter alia*, the volume and prices of imports not sold at dumping prices, contraction in demand or changes in the patterns of consumption, trade restrictive practices of and competition between the foreign and domestic producers, developments in technology and the export performance and productivity of the domestic industry.

[33] Negotiating Group on Rules, *Draft Consolidated Chair Texts of the AD and SCM Agreements*, TN/RL/W/213 (November 30, 2007).

The draft calls upon "the authorities [to] seek to separate and distinguish the injurious effects of such other factors from the injurious effects of dumped imports". One of the changes suggested in the 2007 Chairman's Text was that the non-attribution analysis may be based on qualitative assessment, rather than a quantitative assessment which was a significant development from the general tenor of discussions that prevailed in the early phase of the Doha Round. The delegations of Hong Kong, China, Japan, Korea R P, Norway, Switzerland, and the Separate Customs Territory of Taiwan, Penghu, Kinmen and Matsu submitted a paper which, inter alia, proposed certain amendments to the Chair's Text. The proposal in essence argues that "to the extent that a quantitative analysis is impracticable, the examination required by this paragraph may be based on a qualitative analysis of evidence".[34] This proposal indicates the differences among delegations in choosing an analytical tool in the causation analysis.

Subsequently, on May 8, 2008, the Chairman of the Negotiating Group on Rules issued a working document regarding negotiations on rules.[35] The document, which included a cover note and three Appendices relating to anti-dumping, horizontal subsidies and fisheries subsidies, sought to capture the full spectrum of issues and the reactions of delegations to the Chair's 2007 draft. The Chairman issued another Text on Rules on December 19, 2008. The 2008 Chairman's text included the following observation on causation.

*Chairman's Text on causation in 2008*

[CAUSATION OF INJURY: Delegations maintain a wide range of views on such questions as whether it should be mandatory to separate and distinguish the effects of dumped imports and other factors, the extent to which authorities should be required to conduct a quantitative (as opposed to qualitative) analysis of non-attribution, and the extent to which authorities should be required to weigh the injurious effects of dumped imports against the effects of other factors.][36]

On April 21, 2011, the Chairman of the Negotiating Group on Rules issued a new legal text on Antidumping.[37] The objective of preparing the Chairman's text is to "capture" the current situation in the Rules negotiations. The Chairman's Text indicates that the language on causation is still bracketed, which indicates that there is no agreement or convergence of views on this important issue.

---

[34]Negotiating Group on Rules, Hong Kong, China; Japan; Korea, Rep. of; Norway; Switzerland; and the Separate Customs Territory of Taiwan, Penghu, Kinmen and Matsu, TN/RL/W/233 (March 12, 2008).

[35]Negotiating Group on Rules, *Working Document from the Chairman*, TN/RL/W/232(May 28, 2008).

[36]Negotiating Group on Rules, *New Draft Consolidated Chair Texts for AD and SCM Agreements*, TN/RL/W/236 (December 19, 2008).

[37]Negotiating Group on Rules, *Communication from the Chairman, Agreement on the Implementation of Article VI of the General Agreement on Tariffs and Trade*, TN/RL/W/254 (April 11, 2011).

*Chairman's Text on Causation in 2011*

[CAUSATION OF INJURY: Delegations continue to hold widely diverging views on issues relating to causation of injury. Recent discussions have focused on two issues: whether it should be mandatory to separate and distinguish the effects of dumped imports and other factors, and the extent to which authorities should be required to conduct a quantitative (as opposed to qualitative) analysis of non-attribution. Although there seems to be a shared view that authorities should carefully consider the effects of factors other than dumped imports, and ensure they are not attributed to dumped imports, there are substantial gaps regarding the degree of precision that can or should be required.]

The Chairman's text on Article 3.5 of the Antidumping Agreement reflect the lack of consensus and understanding in identifying an acceptable standard on injury and causality (causation) in antidumping proceedings.

# E Negotiations on Subsidies and Countervailing Measures

Although there have been fewer proposals on subsidies than on anti-dumping, a wide range of proposals have nevertheless been submitted regarding prohibited subsidies, actionable subsidies and export credits. In the SCMA negotiations, the Friends Group or other developing countries were not as active as they were in reformulating the language of injury and causation in antidumping proceedings. The United States made, perhaps the only substantive proposal in the negotiations on Agreement on Subsidies and Countervailing Measures.

*U.S. Proposal on Causation in SCMA*

"15.5 It must be demonstrated that the subsidized imports are, through the effects [footnote] of subsidies, causing injury within the meaning of this Agreement. The demonstration of a causal relationship between the subsidized imports and the injury to the domestic industry shall be based on an examination of all relevant evidence before the authorities. The authorities shall also examine any known factors other than the subsidized imports which at the same time are injuring the domestic industry; As described in subparagraph 5.1, the authorities must not attribute to the subsidized imports ~~and~~ the injuries caused by these other factors ~~must not be attributed to the subsidized imports~~. Factors which may be relevant in this respect include, inter alia, the volume and prices of non-subsidized imports of the product in question, contraction in demand or changes in the patterns of consumption, trade restrictive practices of and competition between the foreign and domestic producers, developments in technology and the export performance and productivity of the domestic industry.

15.5.1 To make an affirmative determination that subsidized imports are causing injury, the authorities must determine that the effects of the subsidized imports are injurious notwithstanding the effects of the other known factors. The authorities need not isolate or quantify the effects of either the subsidized imports or the other known factors, either individually or collectively. They also need not evaluate whether the effects of the subsidized imports are more important than the effects of the other known factors, either individually or collectively."

Notwithstanding the few submissions that were made in clarifying and elaborating the injury and causation provisions, the 2008 Chairman's Text did not include any suggested changes to Article 15 of the SCMA. It is also noteworthy that the Chairman of the Negotiating Group on Rules did not release any text in 2011.

## F Conclusion

As the Chairman's text indicates, consensus on a widely acceptable language on injury and causal link in the context of Rules Negotiations has turned out to be almost elusive and extremely difficult in the WTO. Although most WTO members are in favour of rigorous assessment of injury and causation assessment, there is very little unanimity in the methodologies to be used. A bone of contention is whether the WTO members should necessarily segregate and isolate the injurious effects of other known factors as opposed to the injurious effects of dumped or subsidized imports. While a number of new users such as China, India and the FAN Group have suggested the importance of non-attribution analysis, they are yet to suggest concrete methodologies or analytical tools for carrying out the "segregation or separation" of effects of other factors. The new users are yet to endorse the use of econometric or statistical tools, whereas traditional users such as the United States that have developed sophisticated economic models are not in support of recommending such models. These contrasting positions call into question whether non-attribution in its strict sense is ever possible in trade remedies. Although the Rules negotiations have produced some serious discussion on causation, the debate on the use of quantitative as opposed to qualitative assessment is still inconclusive. In other words, the discussion on injury and causation in trade remedy instruments reflects the deeply divisive role of trade contingent protection among various WTO members. It also reaffirms the hypothesis of this study that trade remedies are inherently political instruments and that achieving scientific precision in injury and causation should neither be the goal nor the short term objective of trade remedy investigations.

# Chapter 7
# General Principles of Law on Causation: Application in the Field of Trade Remedy Investigations

**Abstract** This chapter explores the possibility of formulating the causation standard in trade law based upon the general theories of causation in law. In particular, this chapter also explores the suitability of the "necessary element of a sufficient set" (NESS) test which incorporates a weak necessity and strong sufficiency element. The chapter also compares the efficacy of the NESS test vis-à-vis the "but-for" test in the context of trade remedy investigations.

## A Introduction

As the previous chapters of this book have indicated, identifying the language of causation is perhaps the most difficult and politically contentious part of trade remedy investigations. Industries that wanted import relief have always lobbied for flexible causation standards while sectors that were targeted in antidumping wanted rigorous causation standards to render its use rare and infrequent. The negotiations on injury and causation under the WTO Rules Negotiations typify the controversial character of this debate.[1] As some of the submissions under the WTO Rules negotiations indicate, a number of delegations including China and the FAN Group would like to include a strong causation language in trade remedies. Some of these submissions, in particular, point to the "substantial cause" language. At the same time, Members such as Australia consider that the current language is appropriate and does not require drastic changes.[2]

While the WTO treaty language of causation is fairly broad and open-ended, a number of dispute settlement panels have examined the dictionary meaning of the term "cause".[3] While the dictionaries can provide tautological definitions, there has been very little effort to understand some of the dominant philosophical theories on

[1]For a discussion on the negotiating proposals, see Chap. 6 of this study, supra section titled "Degree of Causal Relationship".
[2]*Id.*
[3]Panel Report, *United States – Definitive Safeguard Measures on Imports of Wheat Gluten from the European Communities*, WT/DS166/R (January 19, 2001).



J.J. Nedumpara, *Injury and Causation in Trade Remedy Law*,
DOI 10.1007/978-981-10-2197-8_7

causation. The purpose of this chapter is to examine some of the commonly referred to theories of causation in law, and restate how the causation analysis in WTO trade remedies can be rendered logically coherent and fit well with the established notions of causation. Furthermore, instead of assuming the causal significance of factors, as is generally done in trade remedy investigations, it is necessary to make an intuitively plausible legal framework for causal determination which is consistent with the dominant theories of causation.

## B The Concept of Causation: From Hume to Hart and Honoré

This study examined the dictionary meaning of the term "cause" in Chap. 3. However, in order to fully explicate the meaning of this term, it is essential to revisit the philosophical debates on causation. In a way, the modern genealogy of causation starts with David Hume, the renowned Scottish Philosopher. Hume was of the opinion that generalizations or causal laws constituted the idea of causation in its entirety.[4] Causation for Hume had a certain universal application. Hume also believed that there was a truth that every event had to have a cause.[5]

Hume's concept of causation was revised by John Stuart Mill.[6] Mill did not reject the principle that there are certain general causes for events. On the other hand, Mill argues that there are broad generalizations that are at play regarding causation and that there are multiple conditions that are integrally related to the occurrence of an event. Stated differently, Mill argues that in certain scenarios there could be specific anomalies that could be the cause of an event.[7]

Legal Philosopher H.L.A. Hart and his colleague Tony Honoré revisited this topic in the late 1950s. They were of the opinion that causation could only be understood with reference to specific acts. For Hart and Honoré, the answer to the question '*what caused the event?*' could not be answered by an empirical generalization of cause and effect, but they argued that the question could be answered by analyzing the circumstances of a specific case.[8] Hart and Honoré observe that these

---

[4]David Hume, A Treatise of Human Nature 14-15(A Selby-Biggee and P. Nidditch eds., 2nd edn., 1978).

[5]*Id.*

[6]John s. Mill, A System of Logic Ratiocinative and Inductive (8th edition, London, 1886).

[7]Jane Stapleton, *Unpacking Causation, in* Relating to Responsibility: Essays for Tony Honore on his Eightieth Birthday 145, 145-46 (Peter Cane & John Gardner eds, Hart Publishing, 2001). Hart and Honore use the analogy of a railway accident to clarify Mil's point. If the speed of a train, the nature of the track, a bent rail and other externalities are all required for a particular accident to happen, all the factors being equally relevant and important to cause the accident, Mill is of the opinion that the bent rail, being the most recent act is the cause. Though Mill notes the arbitrary nature of this, he seems to think that the answer lies in principles of common sense.

[8]Hart and Honoré, Causation in Law 35-36 (2nd ed. 1985).

generalizations are based on common sense and logic and need not refer to any particular scientific theory. In their view, causal knowledge can be based on reasoning by analogy from empirical observations or can be acquired through education or even from imagination.

According to Hart and Honoré, a 'cause' of an event is a distinct idea from mere 'conditions' that enable an event to happen. A cause is to be treated at a higher level than a mere condition. This classification that Hart and Honoré have created responds to Mill's assertion that every condition in a causal chain is as important as any other condition; thus picking a cause is an arbitrary exercise which invariably ends in the most recent condition being picked.[9] Hart and Honoré explained this difference through a facile illustration. A fire can never happen without Oxygen. Oxygen is essential to the starting of a fire, but it is not an anomaly; it is a mere condition[10] and not a cause. But, the throwing of a matchstick can be the cause of fire as it is an anomaly that does not constantly happen. Hart and Honoré have succinctly elaborated the difference using another set of illustration.

> The cause of a great famine in India may be identified by the Indian peasant as the drought, but the World Food Authority may identify the Indian government's failure to build up reserves as the cause and the drought as mere condition. A woman married to a man who suffers from ulcerated condition of the stomach might identify eating parsnips as the cause of indigestion: a doctor might identify the ulcerated condition of his stomach as the cause and the meal as a mere condition.[11]

According to Hart and Honoré, a contributing factor is a "cause" rather than a "mere condition" if it satisfies two requirements. The first requirement is that it must be (a) a voluntary human intervention that was intended to produce the consequence —for example, deliberately shooting someone, or (b) an abnormal action, event, or condition in the particular context—for example, a freak storm or driving carelessly, and (2) it must be the last intervention or independent abnormal occurrence.[12]

In a legal proceeding, not every contributing condition or reason for an outcome can be treated as a "cause". In principle, all contributing conditions are causes, but only one or two such conditions are treated as cause(s) based on a notion that such a condition or factor could be the most significant or relevant in the context of the causal enquiry. For example, if a train collides with a bus crossing an unmanned level crossing, the presence of the unmanned level crossing itself could be considered as the relevant cause although the bus driver might have missed the train's whistle or driven the vehicle at an excessive speed so as to disregard the incoming train. Maintaining an unmanned level crossing itself would be regarded as the abnormal condition, or more appropriately, the causally relevant factor for the accident. Likewise, in the case of trade remedy law, the petitioning domestic industry might be suffering business loss and injury on account of a plethora of factors, but the causally

---

[9] *Id.*

[10] See the discussions in Chapter I entitled Philosophical Preliminaries, at 9–25.

[11] Hart and Honoré, Causation in Law, at 35–36.

[12] *Id.*

relevant factor in the underlying investigation is whether the industry has suffered injury on account of fair or unfair imports. In both the examples given above, a particular act or condition is treated as a statutory cause and is assumed to have certain causal significance. In other words, all trade remedy investigations assume that the subject imports are a cause or a potential cause of injury, and the purpose of the causation enquiry is either to reaffirm or reject this assumption.

## C Addressing a Plurality of Causes in a Trade Remedy Setting

The 'but-for' concept of causation acquired a fair amount of attention in trade remedy law and practice and was discussed briefly in Chap. 3.[13] Under the but-for test, X is a causally relevant factor for the occurrence of Y when Y would not have occurred but for the occurrence of X. In a vast majority of cases, the but-for test works quite well as a test of causation. But in situations involving complex facts matrix, it results in a finding of no causation, even though it is clear that the act in question contributed to the injury. In a way, the but-for test makes the necessary condition almost the exclusive criterion for causal contribution. The but-for test also reflects a deeply rooted belief that a condition cannot be a cause of some event unless it is, in some sense, necessary for the occurrence of the event. As is demonstrated in Chap. 3 of this book, the but-for test is singularly inapplicable in cases of over-determination. The cases of over-determined causation include the following at a minimum: cases in which a factor other than the specified act would have been sufficient to produce the injury, but its effects either (1) were preempted by the more immediately operative effects of the specified act, or (2) combined with or duplicated those of the specified act to jointly produce the injury.

In the context of trade remedies, dumping or subsidization of export sales is not a single act performed at a particular moment in time similar to activities like pulling a gun trigger, feeding a spoonful of poison, dealing a physical blow, or lighting a fire. It is a recurrent and sustained activity, conducted over a period of several weeks and months, if not years, the cumulative effects of which might have caused an injury to the domestic industry. Domestic and export transactions examined in the case of trade remedies deal with hundreds and thousands of shipments involving multitude of sellers, exporters, importers and other intermediaries. The industry itself would have passed through several phases of business cycles during this time. In such a situation requiring that fair or unfair imports themselves should have caused injury is essentially an implausible requirement. In essence, any causation in the context of trade remedies should be an inclusive test, with the possibility of accommodating multiple causes as causally relevant factors.

[13]Dukgeun Ahn & William J. Moon, *Alternative Approach to Causation Analysis in Trade Remedy Investigations: 'Cost of Production' Test*, 44(5) Journal of World Trade 1023-1052 (2010).

According to Mackie, a proponent of the but-for test, attempts to define causation in terms of the most obvious conceptual tools—necessary conditions, sufficient conditions, or necessary and sufficient conditions—have all failed to provide a comprehensive and satisfactory framework.[14] Accordingly, Mackie developed the Insufficient but Necessary part of an Unnecessary but Sufficient set (INUS test)—a test which treats a condition as cause if it is an insufficient but non-redundant part of a condition which is itself unnecessary. For example, the damage to a shipping vessel from a fire that occurred due to oil spillage in a wharf where certain welding and repair work too was carried out, cannot be attributed to the fire sparks in a normal setting. The fire sparks are insufficient to cause the damage by themselves, but the damage would not have caused without the fire sparks. The fire sparks could constitute an INUS cause. However, the INUS test requires strong necessity and can be characterized as a modified version of but-for test, which this study has rejected as inappropriate in a trade remedy setting. However, scholarly writings point out that some of the recent frameworks provide intelligible and plausible framework for explaining causal judgments when plurality of causes are involved. The following paragraphs will examine the relevance of the NESS test suggested by Hart and Honoré.

## D A Causation Framework for Trade Remedies: Necessity Test

Hart and Honoré recognize that there may be a plurality of causes in a particular instance. Hart and Honoré noted in their landmark book entitled *Causation in Law* that the "necessary element of a sufficient set" (NESS) test of causal contribution follows directly from the dominant "regularity" account of the meaning of causation initially developed by David Hume and elaborated by John Stuart Mill. According to Hume, singular causal judgments are not based on direct perception of causal qualities.[15] Causal judgments are based on the belief that certain succession of events instantiates one or more causal laws.[16] The essence of causation under this philosophic account is that a particular condition was a cause of (condition contributing to) a specific consequence if and only if it was a necessary element of set of antecedent actual conditions that was sufficient for the occurrence of the consequence.[17] However, in order to avoid including causally irrelevant conditions in

[14]John Mackie, *Causes and Conditions*, 4 (2) American Philosophical Quarterly, 245, 245-255 (1965) (arguing that the INUS test, i.e. Insufficient but Necessary part of an Unnecessary but Sufficient set, could explicate the causal relationship)

[15]David Hume, A Treatise of Human Nature 14-15 (A Selby-Biggee ed., rev'd P. Nidditch 1978).

[16]Richard Wright, *Causation, Responsibility, Risk, Probability, Naked Statistics, and Proof: Pruning the Bramble Bush by Clarifying the Concepts*, 73 Iowa Law Review 1001, 1788-91 (1988) (hereinafter *Bramble Bush*).

[17]*Id.*

this sufficient set, the antecedent conditions must be limited to those that are necessary for the sufficiency of the set.[18]

The NESS is also in harmony with the dominant philosophic literature on causation. The literature continues to be characterized by arguments based on necessary conditions, sufficient conditions, or necessary and sufficient conditions. The following formulations are based on the various degrees of necessity or sufficiency and both.

- Stringent & strong necessity test: Dumping (D) be necessary for the occurrence of Injury (I), whenever (I) occurs.
- Less stringent & strong necessity test: Dumping (D) have been necessary for the occurrence of Injury (I) on that particular occasion.
- Least stringent, weak necessity test: Dumping (D) have been a necessary element of some set of actual conditions that was sufficient for the occurrence of Injury (I).
- Stringent sufficiency test: Dumping (D) be sufficient by itself for the occurrence of the Injury (I).
- Less stringent, strong sufficiency test: Dumping (D) be a necessary element of some set of existing conditions that was sufficient for the occurrence of Injury (I).
- Least stringent, weak sufficiency test: Dumping (D) be a part of some of the existing conditions that was sufficient for the occurrence of Injury (I).

Legal philosophers have described the NESS test as a test of weak necessity or strong sufficiency. The sufficiency can be stated as follows: when 'D' happens, 'I' also happens. A causal inference of 'I' is drawn whenever 'D' takes place. It may be possible to point out here that dumping (or, subsidy or increased imports as the case may be) itself is an arbitrary causal choice. As Tony Honoré points out in his book *Responsibility and Cause*, it is the breach of responsibility that determines an otherwise arbitrary choice as a relevant causal choice.[19] Dumping, being part of a set causing a certain harm is picked as the cause because dumping results in the breach of a legal obligation as and when it causes an injury to the industry. In other words, the dumping is a statutory cause as provided under the trade remedy statute and cannot be treated as an arbitrary causal choice in NESS set.

In the above scenarios, the strict necessity and strict sufficiency tests are too strict and rigid. Both the strict necessity and strict sufficient test could be considered appropriate to test the counterfactual enquiry. As stated earlier, the stringent and strong necessity test can be practically implemented through the but-for test without much difficulty. However, as this study examined in Chap. 3, the but-for test is not an inclusive test and does not admit the possibility of any other factor causing injury to the domestic industry. Likewise, few, if any, conditions are sufficient by

---

[18]*Id.* See also Wright, *Causation in Tort Law*, 73 CALIFORNIA LAW REVIEW 1735, 1788-91 (1985).
[19]*See* generally, TONY HONORÉ, RESPONSIBILITY AND FAULT 14-32 (1999).

themselves for the occurrence of any result.[20] Accordingly, this study pointed out the infirmities of the but-for test as a causative tool in a trade remedy scenario.

The element of strong sufficiency in the NESS test does not appear inconsistent with the limited WTO jurisprudence. In some of the safeguard investigations, the WTO panels have suggested a language that increased imports shall "in and of themselves", or "per se" cause injury to the domestic industry.[21] Although the rigour of this language has been whittled down by the WTO Appellate Body,[22] the element of strong sufficiency still appears to be guiding such investigations. The FAN Group also made a proposal suggesting a similar language in the context of Article 3.5 of the Antidumping Agreement.[23] While the but-for test cannot clearly accommodate a 'weak necessity and strong sufficiency' standard, it needs to be still examined whether the requirement of non-attribution could fit well within the contours of the NESS test.

It is important to revisit Hart and Honoré's initial formulation of the NESS to answer this query. Hart and Honoré do not require that each of the causal factors has been actively operating, but they seem to require that each has been sufficient by itself for the occurrence of the injury. For example, in the burnt house example, Hart and Honoré assume that each fire would have been sufficient by itself for the destruction of the plaintiff's house. The NESS test then confirms causal contribution by each fire. Each fire was necessary for the sufficiency of a set of actual antecedent conditions that did not include the other fire. The requirement that each factor has been sufficient by itself (when combined with the background conditions) is too restrictive and is not part of the basic concept of causation that is reflected in the NESS test.

The next enquiry is whether each of the statutory causes such as dumping, subsidized imports or increased imports should be independently sufficient to constitute the injury. Hart and Honoré apparently require that a duplicative cause be independently sufficient—in the NESS sense of sufficiency—for the cause. A condition can be a cause under the NESS test, even if it was neither necessary nor independently sufficient. The question is whether a particular set of conditions identified in a set is sufficient to produce a particular result.

The independent sufficiency is not always followed by courts. Richard Wright has demonstrated this aspect eloquently. In an illustration that he has provided, five units of pollution was necessary and sufficient for a particular environmental harm and seven defendants released one unit of pollution.[24] Each unit of pollution in itself was neither necessary nor independently sufficient for the environmental

---

[20]T. Beauchamp & A. Rosenberg, Hume and the Problem of Causation 23, 88-91 (1981).

[21]Panel Report, *United States – Definitive Safeguard Measures on Imports of Wheat Gluten from the European Communities*, ¶ 8.140 WT/DS166/R (January 19, 2001), as modified by Appellate Body Report WT/DS166/AB/R;

[22]Appellate Body, *US—Wheat Gluten*, ¶ 66.

[23]For a discussion on the negotiating proposals, see Chap. 6 of this study, supra section titled "Degree of Causal Relationship".

[24]Richard Wright, *Bramble Bush*, supra note 16, at 1035.

harm, but each unit of pollution was a NESS cause. To restate this scenario in the context of the NESS test, each unit of pollution was necessary for the sufficiency of an actual set that included four other units of pollution, and the sufficiency of each set was not affected by the presence of two other duplicate causes of causation. The hallmark of the NESS test is that there should be a set of causal factors that is adequate in itself to cause an injury.

In two duplicative causation cases involving merged fires and noisy motor vehicles, the courts did not require the plaintiff to prove the independent sufficiency of each contributing factor, but rather required the plaintiff to prove only that each factor contributed to the injury. The following example will explain this aspect better: If any two or three fires were sufficient for the injury, but none by itself was sufficient, each was a cause of the injury since each was necessary for the sufficiency of a set of antecedent conditions that included only one of the other fires. The same causal connection exists even if there were only two fires, one of which was independently sufficient and the other of which was not. The first was clearly a cause, since it was independently sufficient. But the second fire was also a cause. It was necessary for the sufficiency of a set of actual antecedent conditions which included another fire (the first) that was at least large enough to be sufficient for the injury if it merged with a fire the size of the second fire.

As Richard Wright argues, in certain conditions the NESS test for a causally relevant factor is superior to the alternative but-for test.[25] A reference may be made to an example used by Richard Wright (with minor modifications) to illustrate the utility of NESS in the non-attribution analysis in trade remedies. Assume a situation where fire X and fire Y, both having nearly the same intensity and proportions broke out in a congested housing locality. Fire X reached a bit early, while fire Y reached after the house had already been destroyed. There was only one actually sufficient set—a set that contains fire X but not fire Y. There is also a probable set that includes fire Y. However, the earlier arrival of fire X preempted the sufficient set that included fire Y, making it causally neither necessary nor sufficient. In this scenario fire Y was neither a but-for cause nor a NESS cause, but only a preempted condition. Even fire X is also not a but-for cause, because Fire Y could have done the same damage had it not been preempted by fire X. However, understanding the factors that could possibly establish multiple set of conditions is essential to understanding the concept of causation.

It is necessary to revisit the non-attribution analysis in the WTO trade remedies in the light of the above understanding. The non-attribution language requires that the injury to the domestic industry or producers on account of other factors shall not be attributed to imports. The non-attribution analysis requires the parties and the investigating authorities to identify the 'causes' which affect the domestic industry. Assume a scenario where the anticompetitive practices in the domestic industry are a known cause of injury. The investigating authority conducts a counterfactual analysis and determines that in the absence of anticompetitive practices within the

[25]Richard Wight, *Bramble Bush*, *supra* note 16.

domestic industry, the alleged injury would not have happened. Assuming that dumped imports also played a contributing role, should the investigating agency terminate the investigation on the ground that there is no causal link? Such a conclusion does not appear from a reading of the text of antidumping or other trade remedy agreements such as SCM Agreement or Safeguards Agreement. The injury and causation standards in all the three agreements admit the possibility of plurality of causes and no causal factor can be treated as rival candidates. One could therefore argue that the non-attribution language does not require a but-for analysis in considering the degree of contribution of other factors. However, the investigating agency can consider whether the role of dumped/subsidized imports have been preempted by any other known factor. Only if the evidence of this preemption is so overwhelming and clear, is there is a need for an investigating authority to terminate the trade remedy action for want of causal link.

This study would argue that the NESS test would be more appropriate even when there is a plurality of causes. Mackie, a preeminent philosopher of causation, also suggests that when multiples causes can be pointed out for the eventual outcome and when none of the causes in itself is sufficient to bring out the concerned result, an aggregate but-for test can be used. In one of Mackie's examples, a man dies when two bullets, each of which by itself would have been immediately fatal, enter the victim's heart simultaneously. A detailed causal enquiry could not determine whether as to which among the two bullets was necessary to cause the death. Mackie suggests that death would not have caused without the volley, which includes the aggregate effect of the two bullets. Mackie offers the aggregate but-for test as the best possible formulation when we cannot precisely know which item in the cluster caused the result.

Richard Wright has provided a comprehensive response to Mackie's aggregated but—for test and in arguing why the NESS test would have none of these philosophic or pragmatic objections. According to Wright, problems associated with examples given by Mackie can be correctly addressed by the NESS test. While reverting to illustration dealing with the hypothetical discussing the death caused by the volley of bullets, the NESS test could treat each bullet as necessary for the sufficiency of a set of actual antecedent conditions which do not include the second bullet. Furthermore, the sufficiency of each set is not affected by the simultaneous existence of the alternative set. If one causal factor gets triggered and the result (victim's death) occurs before the arrival of the second, the NESS test would treat the first causal factor as the cause of the outcome and the second one as the preempted condition. In this scenario, the first factor would be necessary for the sufficiency of a set of antecedent conditions that does not include the second factor. In this scenario, the second factor was not necessary for the sufficiency of any set of actual antecedent conditions. Based on this characterization, there is no conceivable weaker necessity test than the NESS test.

The non-attribution test suggested in the WTO dispute settlement jurisprudence need not find it difficult to embrace the NESS test. The WTO language only insists that the injury attributable to dumped/subsidized or increased imports should not be "polluted" by the injurious effects of the remaining factors.[26] The causal effects can be polluted only if a cluster of causes is aggregated so as to constitute a "single cause". It can happen in a causal enquiry comprising the aggregate but-for scenario. The aggregated but-for test could include both causally relevant factors, causally irrelevant factors and pre-empted conditions and examines whether injury could have taken place in the absence of the aggregated factors. Such an analysis does not seek to distinguish actual causes from the irrelevant causes or preempted conditions. The Appellate Body came down strongly against such aggregation of such causes in *US—Hot rolled Steel* when it ruled that "… if the injurious effects of dumped imports and other known factors remain lumped together and indistinguishable, there was simply no means of knowing whether injury ascribed to dumped imports was, in reality, caused by other factors."[27]

## E Conclusion

The foregoing discussions indicate that in trade remedy law there is a need to formulate a causation standard which is not based on the strong necessity linked but-for test. The NESS test admits the possibility of accommodating more than one cause in a set of causally relevant factors which could be sufficient to cause the alleged injury to the domestic industry. The NESS test will also be appropriate in eliminating the role of causally irrelevant factors which may cloud the aggregate but-for situation or in performing the non-attribution. This study has also demonstrated that the NESS test is intuitively superior to the popular but-for test which is seen to be inadequate while dealing with plurality of causes that may be identified as injuring the domestic industry in the context of trade remedy law.

[26]Panel Report, *United States – Safeguard Measures on Imports of Fresh, Chilled or Frozen Lamb Meat from New Zealand and Australia*, ¶ 224 WT/DS177/AB/R (March 16, 2001).

[27]Appellate Body Report, *United States – Anti-Dumping Measures on Certain Hot-Rolled Steel Products from Japan*, ¶ ¶. 224, 228 WT/DS184/AB/R (Aug. 23, 2001).

# Chapter 8
# Findings and Conclusions

**Abstract** This book explored the evolution of injury and causation standards in trade remedy investigations covering a time span of almost a century. While there is no exact science on the choice of the appropriate standard for injury and causation in trade remedies, the historical evolution and negotiating history emphasise the policy dependent character of such remedies. While quantitative tools may be desirable in estimating injury and causation, this study makes a finding that in addition to the trends analysis, a well-reasoned descriptive analysis of the effects and role of other causal factors could satisfy the applicable injury and causation standards uder the existing WTO rules. In addition, the book highlights the utility of the "necessary element of a sufficient set" (NESS) test which incorporates a weak necessity and strong sufficiency element in making the injury and causation standards more robust and reliable.

The average tariff protection among most members of the WTO has come down significantly in the post-WTO phase. When tariff protection has declined, trade remedy measures have served as some form of proxy protection. Importantly, most trade remedy measures are implemented as tariff measures and serve to protect the domestic industry for reasonably long periods of time.

One of the assumptions addressed in this study is that injury and causality in trade remedy investigations is a highly policy dependent standard. The chapter on the historical evolution of trade remedies, especially antidumping, indicates how antidumping evolved from antitrust which provided protection to competition from predatory pricing practices. In a way, antidumping had its roots in international price discrimination but tied this principle to a verifiable requirement of injury to domestic industry which was affected by import competition. This study also traced how inextricably the concepts of antidumping and antitrust were originally connected at least in the context of the United States—one of the first countries to implement these laws in a major scale. The study also examined how the injury and causality standards in the United States influenced the respective provisions in multilateral trade treaties such as GATT 1947, the Kennedy and Tokyo Antidumping Codes. The policy dependent nature of the causation standards were



J.J. Nedumpara, *Injury and Causation in Trade Remedy Law*,
DOI 10.1007/978-981-10-2197-8_8

clearly demonstrated while tracing the negotiating history of the Kennedy Code which introduced the concept of "principal cause" in antidumping investigations and later removed this requirement owing to domestic compulsions. The developments in the Tokyo and Uruguay Rounds only reaffirmed the policy significance of injury and causation provisions, as the active users of antidumping pushed for flexible and easy-to-meet standards whereas the targets of antidumping bargained for tougher and stringent injury and causation standards. This trend continued even in the negotiations on Rules under the ongoing Doha Round trade negotiations where a number of Members, especially the Friends of Antidumping (FAN) Group proposed a series of proposals on the injury and causation standards in antidumping and countervailing duty provisions.

While the history of antidumping and other trade remedy agreements indicated a relaxation of causation standards, the WTO panels and the Appellate Body attempted to render the injury and causality standards more scientific and precise. The decision of the Appellate Body in *US—Hot-rolled Steel*[1] is a clear example of this trend. A review of the WTO panel and Appellate Body decisions indicates that the degree and role of dumped/subsidized or increased imports in effecting the alleged injury to the domestic industry has been significantly altered through dispute settlement decisions. While tools such as coincidence-in-time or trends analysis have remained the traditional tools, the creation of an artificial construct called the "non-attribution" requirement has posed significant interpretative ambiguity and operational difficulty. As the analysis in Appendix of Chap. 3 demonstrates, there is no certainty on the types of causes whose presence have to be identified and separated. Some of the listed causes may not be relevant for a particular industry while a number of known causes may not be brought to the notice of the investigating agencies at the time of the investigation. There could be other hidden causes, whose effects or roles the investigating authority or other interested parties may not be aware of. In certain other cases, some of the perceived causes need not be causes, but mere conditions for another cause to operate or an event to take place. In the above context—as the review of WTO jurisprudence indicated–the non-attribution test is not serving the purpose of isolating and distinguishing the role of causal factors other than dumping, subsidy or increased imports and making sure that the remedy is given only when the cause is well established.

As this study demonstrates in Chaps. 3 and 4, a proper non-attribution, i.e., separating and distinguishing the role of other factors can be properly undertaken only through a quantitative or econometric approach. Given this difficulty, some of the WTO panels have been more pragmatic. The *Mexico–Olive Oil* panel approved even a qualitative approach; the *EC–DRAM* panel suggested that some data analysis would suffice. However, some other panels are still emphasizing the need for "disentangling" (i.e., separating and distinguishing) the role of other causal factors. The panel in *China–GOES* is one such example. While there are indications that the

[1]Appellate Body Report, *United States – Anti-Dumping Measures on Certain Hot-Rolled Steel Products from Japan*, WT/DS184/AB/R ( August 23, 2001).

non-attribution test is here to stay in trade remedies, the Appellate Body has not revisited this issue in recent times and clarified its approach. Ideally, the Appellate Body should restate and clarify its position in future disputes.

Having analyzed the jurisprudence on injury, causality and the non-attribution test, this study enquired in Chaps. 4 and 5 regarding the methodologies followed by key users of trade remedies. This study also examined how some of the frequent users are establishing injury and what tools they are using for conducting the non-attribution test. The study also examined India as a prototype given its role as the leading user of antidumping and safeguards measures. The examination of the antidumping practices in India and other key users clearly indicates that the non-attribution analysis is carried out in a perfunctory manner. It was also found that most investigating agencies generally provide only an examination of the listed known factors and the other additional factors were seldom taken into consideration in the ultimate analysis. The analysis indicates that the non-attribution analyses are not made with any explicit method but are generally done on a *pro forma* basis. Again, the use of a checklist approach for performing non-attribution analysis was also noticed while examining the safeguard cases involving India. This was amply clear from the analysis in Chap. 5. In other words, a study of injury and causation practices of India and other WTO members do not indicate that the rigorous standards of segregating and separating the role of other factors, in terms of the strict requirements imposed by the WTO Appellate Body are scrupulously followed.

A review of the WTO disputes examining the injury and causality determination of domestic authorities in Chaps. 2 and 3 and a separate analysis of the country practices in Chaps. 4 and 5 reveal that the most commonly used tool for injury and causality is the coincidence-in-time or the trends analysis. The practices in India and other jurisdictions demonstrated the probative force of the price undercutting and price underselling analysis. This view was also fortified by the recent Appellate Body ruling in a series of cases involving China. Illustrative cases include the *China-GOES,*[2] *China—X-ray*[3] and *China—Broiler products.*[4] These cases emphasize the inestimable role of price effects analysis both in establishing injury and causal link.

In the light of the limitations in finding a generally acceptable methodology for conducting injury and causation, the trends analysis is becoming perhaps the most reliable tool in establishing injury and causality. This is demonstrated from a review of the WTO jurisprudence and the country practices undertaken in Chaps. 3, 4 and 5 of this study. In addition to the trends analysis, a well-reasoned descriptive analysis on the effect and role of other causal factors can satisfy the requirements of

---

[2]Appellate Body Report, *China – Countervailing and Anti-Dumping Duties on Grain Oriented Flat-Rolled Electrical Steel from the United States*, ¶ 131 WT/DS414/AB/R (November 16, 2012).

[3]Panel Report, *China – Definitive Anti-Dumping Duties on X-Ray Security Inspection Equipment from the European Union*, ¶ 7.67 WT/DS425/R and Add.1 (April 24, 2013).

[4]Panel Report, *China – Anti-Dumping and Countervailing Duty Measures on Broiler Products from the United States,* WT/DS427/R and Add. 1 (September 25, 2013).

most of the trade remedy agreements. The decisions of the WTO panel in *Mexico-Olive Oil* and *EC-DRAM* indicate this possibility.[5] While the WTO members are divided on the issue of use of sophisticated statistical or quantitative tools, this study argues that quantitative tools could, in certain cases, augment qualitative tools. It is not a matter of preference, but a matter of reinforcement or reaffirmation of injury and causation findings, subject to the financial and manpower resources an investigating authority may have.

This study has also identified a few areas where improvement could be made in the conduct of the non-attribution test. This is in regard to raising other known or knowable causes of injury. The analysis of WTO cases examined in Chap. 3 indicated that in addition to the listed causes there are several other factors which may be contributing to injury. Some of the commonly cited factors include the rise in input costs, currency fluctuation, and changing consumer habits. It is suggested that these factors could be included in the illustrative list of 'known factors'. In addition, there is a need to recast the burden of proof requirements to elicit the parties who are in possession of certain facts or information to share it with the authority during the investigation to make sure that such known causes are also taken into account. Such causes can be identified by including separate interested party questionnaires and inviting industry experts to testify before the investigating authorities.

Based on a review of WTO cases and country practices, this study recommends that there is a need to strengthen the injury and causality determination in most jurisdictions. It was also found that in most jurisdictions, in the absence of a clear non-attribution analysis, the causation is determined on an assessment of the volume and price effects which falls within the realm of the trends analysis. In other words, if price undercutting and price underselling are observed, causation is presumed. While the trends analysis remains a useful and probabilistic tool for determining causation, this study has identified certain deficiencies in its implementation in various jurisdictions and has recommended certain ways of improving this examination. It is observed that a proper assessment of the interaction between price effects and industry parameters is missing in most investigations. An overall assessment of even the domestic industry injury parameters is also non-existent. Part of the reason for this inadequate assessment is that at least four or five indicators of material injury determination are themselves vague or undefined under AD and SCM Agreements. Factors such as growth, ability to raise capital or investment and factors affecting domestic production are a few illustrations. This study recommends that a rigorous analysis of the price effects and the movement in domestic industry injury parameters can strengthen the trends or correlation analysis and could result in improved qualitative approaches to causation determination. In addition to this, investigating authorities could also give certain emphasis on the margin of dumping or subsidy in making affirmative findings, although most

[5]Panel Report, *Mexico – Definitive Countervailing Measures on Olive Oil from the European Communities*, WT/DS341/R (October 21, 2008).

jurisdictions do not provide weightage to the dumping or subsidy margin in the causality determination.

This study also examined the reform proposals submitted in the Rules Negotiations of the ongoing Doha Round of trade negotiations. Several proposals submitted in the Doha Round have suggested the need for a tougher injury and causality test. But as is established in Chap. 6 of this book, most WTO members are currently using soft injury and causality standards based on a qualitative assessment of injury and causal link. Given this reality, a number of proposals in the Doha Round are suggesting the reintroduction of injury and causality provisions like "substantial cause", "genuine and substantial means of cause and effect", dumping and subsidy "in and of themselves", etc. Those terms have been specifically rejected by the GATT Contracting Parties in the past during the Kennedy, Tokyo and Uruguay Rounds of trade negotiations and are unlikely to gather support among key users of trade remedy instruments. Furthermore, most WTO members, even the traditional users, have not developed adequate tools for weighing and grading the role of causal factors. In fact, based on an analysis of WTO cases and country practices, this research argues against the incorporation of various degrees or tiers of causal relationships such as "substantial cause", "principal cause", "major cause", "genuine and substantial means of cause and effect", "a cause on its own", etc. As the negotiating history indicates, such terms were clearly rejected in various iterations of trade negotiations, and there is no need to resuscitate them through either judicial reasoning or future negotiations.

Finally, this book addressed the question whether or not it is possible to reframe the causation determination in trade remedy investigations in accordance with extant Common law tests. In Chaps. 3 and 7, this study argued why a strong-necessity based 'but-for' test is inappropriate in the case of causation determination in trade remedies especially in view of the plurality of causes of injury. In the alternative, the "Necessary Element of a Sufficient Set" (NESS) analysis which incorporates a weak necessity and strong sufficiency test was suggested. The NESS test admits the possibility of accommodating more than one cause in a set of causally relevant factors which could be sufficient to cause the alleged injury to the domestic industry. The NESS test will also be appropriate in eliminating the role of causally irrelevant factors which may cloud the aggregate but-for situation or in performing the non-attribution.

Overall, on the basis of an understanding of the negotiating history, existing dispute settlement jurisprudence in the WTO, and the trade remedy practices of individual Member countries, this study concludes that injury and causation determination has always been a policy dependent concept in trade remedy investigations. The overwhelming evidence of negotiating history and country practices indicate that trade remedy measures were designed as adjustment or response tools to relieve an industry from the pains of trade liberalization and import competition. While it might be possible to quantify the exact role of imports in the injury caused to the industry considering the developments in econometrics and mathematics, it may not be advisable to provide or deny import relief based on scientific or mathematical tests alone. Such an approach will defeat the very purpose of trade remedies. Any negotiation (especially the Doha Round negotiations or any subsequent initiative) on reforming injury and causation in trade remedies should steer clear of this danger. On the other hand, it may be possible to discipline the process requirements of satisfying injury and causation. For example, explaining the exact meaning of the 15 parameters of injury in antidumping (or 8 injury parameters in the case of safeguards) or detailing the procedural and burden of proof requirements especially in identifying the other 'known factors' in the non-attribution analysis could introduce rigour and a systemic method in the injury and causality determination. Furthermore, framing the injury and the causality analysis in terms of the NESS test could bring a much needed conceptual clarity to this debate.

# Bibliography

## Books

I.V. Bael and J. Bellis, Anti-Dumping and other Trade Protection Laws of the European Community (5th edn., 2011).
K. Bagwell, and R.W. Staiger, The Economics of the World Trading System (2002).
T.L. Beauchamp and Rosenberg, Hume and the Problem of Causation (1981).
A. Benitah, The Law of Subsidies Under the GATT/WTO System (2001).
P. Bentley QC and A. Silberston, Anti-Dumping and Countervailing Action – Limits Imposed by Economic and Legal Theory (2007).
J. Beseler, and A. Williams, Anti-Dumping and Anti-Subsidy Law: The European Communities (1986).
J. Bhagwati, Protectionism (8th edn., 1989).
J. Barcelo III, *Subsidies, Countervailing Duties and Anti-dumping After the Tokyo Round*, 13(2) Cornell International Law Journal 257 (1980).
R. Bhala, Modern GATT Law: A Treatise on the General Agreement on Tariffs and Trade (2005).
J.S. Bhandhari and A.O. Sykes, Economic Dimensions in International Law: Comparative and Empirical Perspectives (1997).
P.V. Bossche, and W. Zdouc, The Law and Policy of the World Trade Organization: Text, Cases and Materials (3rd edn., 2013).
P. Cane, *et al*, Relating to Responsibility: Essays in Honour of Tony Honore on his 80th Birthday (2001).
E.K. Choi and J.C. Hartigan, Handbook of International Trade: The Economic and Legal Analysis of Trade Policy and Institutions (Volume II ed., 2004).
T. Cottier, and M. Oesch, International Trade Regulation: Law and Policy in the WTO, the European Union and Switzerland: Cases, Materials and Comments (2005).
J. Croome, Reshaping the World Trading System: A history of the Uruguay Round (1999).
J. Czako, *et al*, A Handbook on Anti-Dumping Investigations (2003).
K.W. Dam, The GATT: Law and International Economic Organization (1970).
J.M. Finger, Anti-Dumping: How it Works and Who Gets Hurt (1993).


J.J. Nedumpara, *Injury and Causation in Trade Remedy Law*,
DOI 10.1007/978-981-10-2197-8

G. GANDOLFO, INTERNATIONAL ECONOMICS I: THE PURE THEORY OF INTERNATIONAL TRADE (2nd edn., 1994).

H.L.A. HART, and T. HONORE, CAUSATION IN THE LAW, (2nd edn., 2002).

B.M. HOEKMAN and M.M. KOSTECKI, THE POLITICAL ECONOMY OF THE WORLD TRADING SYSTEM (3rd edn., 2013).

H. HORN and P.C. MAVROIDIS, THE WTO CASE LAW OF 2001 (2011).

H. HORN, and P.C. MAVROIDIS, THE AMERICAN LAW INSTITUTE REPORTERS' STUDIES ON WTO CASE LAW: LEGAL AND ECONOMIC ANALYSIS (2010).

J. JACKSON and E.A. VERMULST, THE ANTIDUMPING LAW AND PRACTICE: A COMPARATIVE STUDY (1990).

J.H. JACKSON, THE WORLD TRADING SYSTEM: LAW AND POLICY OF INTERNATIONAL ECONOMIC RELATIONS (2nd ed., 1997).

A.O. KRUEGER, THE WTO AS AN INTERNATIONAL ORGANIZATION (January 5, 2001).

C. LIM, and M. LIANG, ECONOMIC DIPLOMACY: ESSAYS AND REFLECTIONS BY SINGAPORE'S NEGOTIATORS (2011).

M. MATSUSHITA, *et al*, THE WORLD TRADE ORGANIZATION: LAW, PRACTICE AND POLICY (2nd edn., 2006).

P.C. MAVROIDIS *et al*, THE LAW OF THE WORK TRADE ORGANIZATION (WTO): DOCUMENTS, CASE & ANALYSIS (1st edn., 2010).

P.C. MAVROIDIS, *et al*, THE LAW AND ECONOMICS OF CONTINGENT PROTECTION IN THE WTO (2010).

E. MCGOVERN, EUROPEAN COMMUNITY ANTI-DUMPING AND TRADE DEFENCE LAW AND PRACTICE (2008).

J. NAKAGAWA, ANTI-DUMPING LAWS AND PRACTICES OF THE NEW USERS (2007).

A. NARLIKAR *et al*, THE OXFORD HANDBOOK ON WORLD TRADE ORGANIZATION (2012).

NORTON and BUSH, ANTIDUMPING INVESTIGATIONS IN CHINA: DEVELOPMENT AND PROBLEMS (2005).

NORTON, A TREATISE OF HUMAN NATURE (2000).

A. PANAGARIYA, INDIA: THE EMERGING GIANT (2011).

F. PIEROLA, THE CHALLENGE OF SAFEGUARDS IN THE WTO (2014).

V. PRAKASH, ANTIDUMPING, COUNTERVAILING DUTIES AND SAFEGUARD MEASURES IN MULTILATERAL TRADE REGIME (2005).

S. RAI, RECOGNITION AND REGULATION OF SAFEGUARD MEASURES UNDER GATT/WTO (2011).

K.D. RAJU, WORLD TRADE ORGANIZATION AGREEMENT ON ANTI-DUMPING: A GATT/WTO AND INDIAN LEGAL JURISPRUDENCE (2008).

D. RODRIK, ECONOMICS RULES (2015).

D. RODRIK, ONE ECONOMICS, MANY RECIPES: GLOBALIZATION, INSTITUTIONS, AND ECONOMIC GROWTH (2008).

A. SAPIR and J.P. TRACHTMAN, SUBSIDIZATION, PRICE SUPPRESSION, AND EXPERTISE: CAUSATION AND PRECISION IN US- UPLAND COTTON, (2011).

T. STEWART *et al*, THE GATT URUGUAY ROUND: A NEGOTIATING HISTORY 1986-1992 (1999).

A.O. SYKES, THE WTO AGREEMENT ON SAFEGUARDS: A COMMENTARY (2006).

M.J. TREBILCOCK, and R. HOWSE, THE REGULATION OF INTERNATIONAL TRADE (2005).

M.J. TREBILCOCK, UNDERSTANDING TRADE LAW (2011).
D. VAUS, RESEARCH DESIGN IN SOCIAL RESEARCH 10 (2001).
J. VINER, DUMPING: A PROBLEM IN INTERNATIONAL TRADE (1923).
J. WELLINGTON, and M. SZCERBINSKI, RESEARCH METHODS FOR SOCIAL SCIENCES (2008).
X. WU, ANTI-DUMPING LAW AND PRACTICE IN CHINA (2009).

**Dictionaries**

BLACK LAW DICTIONARY (6TH EDS, 1990).
WEBSTER'S THIRD NEW INTERNATIONAL DICTIONARY (1981).

**Scholarly Articles**

D. AHN, and W.J. MOON, *Alternative Approach to Causation Analysis in Trade Remedy Investigations: 'Cost of Production' Test*, 44(5) JOURNAL OF WORLD TRADE 1023 (2010).
R.P. ALFORD, *Why a private right of action against dumping would violate GATT?* 66 NEW YORK UNIVERSITY LAW REVIEW 696 (1991).
ANGELIONOS and VERMULST, *Injury in Anti-Dumping Proceedings – The Need to Look Beyond the Uruguay Round Results*, 28(5) JOURNAL OF WORLD TRADE 61 (1994).
BARCELO III, *A History of GATT Unfair Trade Law*, 14(3) THE WORLD ECONOMY 311 (1991).
BARCELO III, *Antidumping Laws As Barriers to Trade: The United States and the International Antidumping Code*, 57(4) CORNELL LAW REVIEW 491 (1972).
R. BHALA, *Rethinking Antidumping Law,* 29(1) GEORGE WASHINGTON JOURNAL OF INTERNATIONAL LAW AND ECONOMICS 11 (1995).
R.D. BOLTUCK, *An Economic Analysis of Dumping*, 21(5) JOURNAL OF WORLD TRADE LAW 45 (1987).
BOWMAN *et al*, *Antidumping and Countervailing Duty Law and Practice: The Mexican Experience*, ARIZONA LEGAL STUDIES DISCUSSION PAPER NO. 10-10, 272 (June 2010).
C.P. BOWN, and MEAGHER, N.M., *Mexico- Olive Oil: Remedy Without a Cause*, 9(1) WORLD TRADE REVIEW 85 (2010).
C.P. BOWN, and TOVAR, P., *Trade Liberalization, Antidumping and Safeguards: Evidence from India's Tariff Reform*, 96(1) JOURNAL OF DEVELOPMENT ECONOMICS 115 (2011).
C.P. BOWN, *Trade Remedies and WTO Dispute Settlement: Why are so few challenged?* 34(2) JOURNAL OF LEGAL STUDIES, 515 (2004).
C.P. BOWN, *Why are Safeguards Under the WTO so Unpopular*, 1(3) WORLD TRADE REVIEW 47 (2002).
G. BRINK, *The 10 Major Problems with the Antidumping Instruments in South Africa*, 39(1) JOURNAL OF WORLD TRADE 147 (2005).
G. BRONZ, *The Tariff Commission as a Regulatory Agency*, 61(3) COLUMBIA LAW REVIEW 463 (1961).
A. CAETANO, *The 10 Major Problems with the Antidumping Instrument in Brazil*, 39 (1) JOURNAL OF WORLD TRADE 87 (2005).

D.J. Carloni, *An Analysis of Material Injury under the 1979 Trade Agreements Act*, 4 Loyola of Los Angeles International and Comparative Law Review 87 (1981).

S. Cho, *Anticompetitive Trade Remedies: How Antidumping Measures Obstruct Market Competition*, 87(2) North Carolina Law Review 357 (2009).

Conrad, *Dumping and Anti-Dumping Measures from a Competition and Allocation Perspective*, 36(3) Journal of World Trade 563 (2002).

A. Das, and Sharafudeen, M., *Sunset Reviews: Important Provisions Made Irrelevant?,* 5(1) Jindal Global Law Review 79 (2014).

DeGrandis, *Proving Causation in Anti-dumping Cases*, 20(2) The International Lawyer 563 (1986).

J.J. Fetzer, *Inference for Economic Modeling in Antidumping, Countervailing duty and Safeguard Investigations*, 8(4) World Trade Review 545 (2009).

J.M. Finger, *The Origins and Evolution of Antidumping Regulation*, World Bank Working Papers Series 783 (1991).

R.D Fumerton, *Causation and the Law: Preemption Lawful Sufficiency and Causal Sufficiency* 64(4) Law and Contemporary Problems 83 (2001).

Grossman and A.O. Sykes, *United States–Definitive Safeguard Measures on Imports of Certain Steel Product*, 6(1) World Trade Law Review 89 (2007).

Grossman, *Imports as a Cause of Injury: The Case of the US Steel Industry*, 20(3) Journal of International Economics 201 (1986).

K. Grybowski, *et al*, *Towards Integrated Management of International Trade-The U.S. Trade Act of 1974*, 26 International and Comparative Law Review 283 (1979).

Andrew T.Guzman, *Determining the Appropriate Standard of Review in WTO Disputes*, 42 (1) Cornell international law journal 45 (2009).

Hansen and Prusa, *Economics and Politics: An Empirical Analysis of ITC Decision Making*, 5(2) Review of International Economics 230 (1997).

G. Horlick and E.C. Shea, *The World Trade Organization Anti-Dumping Agreement*, 29(1) Journal of World Trade 5 (1995).

G. Horlick, *History of the One/Three Formula for Antidumping*, 8(1) Global Trade and Custom Journal 25 (2013).

D.A. Irwin, *Causing Problems: The WTO Review of Causation and Injury in Section 201 Cases*, 2(3) World Trade Review 297 (2003).

D.A. Irwin, *The Rise of U.S. Antidumping Activity in Historical Perspective,* 28(5) The World Economy 651 (2005).

A. Keck, *A Probabilistic Approach to Use of Econometric Modeling in Sunset Reviews*, 6(3) World Trade Review 371 (2007).

K. Kelly, *An analysis of Causality in Escape Clause Cases*, 37(2) Journal of Industrial Economics 187 (1998).

Kerr and Loppacher, *Anti-dumping in the Doha Negotiations: Fairy Tales at the World Trade Organization*, 38(2) Journal of World Trade 211 (2004).

L. Kumaran, *The 10 Major Problems with the Antidumping Instrument in India*, 39 (1) Journal World Trade 115 (2005).

Ledet, *Causation of Injury in Safeguard Cases: Why the US Can't Win*, 34(3) Georgetown Journal of International Law and Policy 713 (2003).

LEYCEGUI and LUZ DE LA TORRE, *The 10 Major Problems with the Antidumping Instrument in Mexico*, 39(1) JOURNAL OF WORLD TRADE 137 (2005).
J. MACKIE, *Causes and Conditions*, 4(2) AMERICAN PHILOSOPHICAL QUARTERLY 245 (1965).
R. MEHTA, *Removal of QRs and Impact of India's Import*, 35(19) ECONOMIC AND POLITICAL WEEKLY 1667 (May 2000).
J. MIRANDA, *Causal Link and non-attribution as interpreted in WTO Trade Remedy Disputes*, 44(4) JOURNAL OF WORLD TRADE 730 (2010)
P. NARAYAN, *Injury Investigation in "Material Retardation" Antidumping Cases*, 25(1) NORTHWESTERN JOURNAL OF INTERNATIONAL LAW AND BUSINESS 37 (2004).
P. NARAYANAN, *Anti-dumping in India- Present State and Future Prospects*, 40(6) JOURNAL OF WORLD TRADE 1081 (2006).
J. J. NEDUMPARA, Causation in Trade Remedy Law: Problems with the Test, 10 (11&12) GLOBAL TRADE AND CUSTOMS JOURNAL 402 (2015).
I. NEUFELD, *Anti-Dumping and Countervailing Procedures – Use or Abuse? Implications for Developing Countries*, POLICY ISSUES IN INTERNATIONAL TRADE AND COMMODITIES STUDY SERIES NO. 9, UNCTAD (2001).
N.D. PALMETER, *Countervailing Subsidized Imports: The International Trade Commission Goes Astray,* 2(1-2) UCLA PACIFIC BASIC LAW JOURNAL 21 (1983).
N.D. PALMETER, *Dumping Margins and Material Injury: The USITC is Free to Choose*, 21(4) JOURNAL OF WORLD TRADE, 173 (1987).
PANGRATIS & VERMULST, *Injury in Anti-Dumping Proceedings: The Need to Look Beyond the Uruguay Round Results*, 28(5) JOURNAL OF WORLD TRADE 61 (1994).
R.S. PINDYCK, and J.J. ROTEMBERG, *Are Imports to Blame? Attribution of Injury under the 1974 Trade Act*, 30 JOURNAL OF LAW AND ECONOMICS 101 (1987).
PINTOS and MURPHY, *Congress Dumps the International Antidumping Code*, 18 CATHOLIC UNIVERSITY LAW REVIEW 180 (1969).
T.J. PRUSA and D.C. SHARP, *Simultaneous Equations in Antidumping Investigations*, 14(1) JOURNAL OF FORENSIC ECONOMICS 63 (2001).
T. PRUSA & E.VERMULST, *China countervailing and antidumping duties on Grain Oriented Flat-rolled Electrical Steel from the United States: exporting US AD/CVD methodologies through WTO dispute settlement,* 13(2) WORLD TRADE REVIEW 229 (2014).
J. D. RUE, *Returning to the Roots of the Bramble Bush: The 'But for' Regains Primacy in Causation Analysis in the American Law Institute's Proposed Restatement (Third) of Torts,* 71 (6) FORDHAM LAW REVIEW 1744 (1985).
E.P. SALONEN, *The Bratsk Decision and its Implications for Injury and Causation Analysis Under the Anti-Dumping and Countervailing Duty Laws*, STEWARD & STEWARD PUBLICATION (2008).
W. SHENG, *Reforming Trade Remedies*, 34 MICHIGAN JOURNAL OF INTERNATIONAL LAW 151 (2012).
T.P. STEWART, *et al*, *Trends in the Last Decade of Trade Remedy Decisions: Problems and Opportunities for the WTO Dispute Settlement System*, 24(1) ARIZONA JOURNAL OF INTERNATIONAL AND COMPARATIVE LAW 251 (2007).

A.O. SYKES, *A Safeguard Mess: A Critique of WTO Jurisprudence*, 2(3) WORLD TRADE REVIEW 261 (2003).

A.O. SYKES, *Countervailing Duty Law: An Economic Perspective*, 89(2) COLUMBIA LAW REVIEW 199 (1989).

A.O. SYKES, *The Economics of Injury in Antidumping and Countervailing Duty Cases*, 16, INTERNATIONAL REVIEW OF LAW AND ECONOMICS 5 (1996).

A.O. SYKES, *The Persistent Puzzles of Safeguards: Lessons from the Steel Dispute*, 7(3) JOURNAL OF INTERNATIONAL ECONOMIC LAW ANTI-DUMPING LAW AND PRACTICE IN CHINA 523 (2004).

M.J. TREBILCOCK and T.M. BODDEZ, *The Case for Liberalizing North American Trade Remedy Laws*, 4(1) MINNESOTA JOURNAL OF GLOBAL TRADE 6 (1995).

E. VERMULST, *Adopting and Implementing Antidumping Laws: Some Suggestions for Developing Countries*, 31(2) JOURNAL OF WORLD TRADE 5 (2002).

R. WRIGHT, *Causation in Tort Law*, 73 CALIFORNIA LAW REVIEW 1735 (1985).

R. WRIGHT, *Causation, Responsibility, Risk, Probability, Naked Statistics, and Proof: Pruning the Bramble Bush by Clarifying the Concepts*, 73 IOWA LAW REVIEW 1001 (1988).

M. WU, *Antidumping in Asia's Emerging Giants*, 53(1) HARVARD INTERNATIONAL LAW JOURNAL 101 (2012).

M.O. MOORE and M. WU, *Antidumping and Strategic Industrial Policy: Tot-for-Tat Trade Remedies and the China—X-Ray Equipment Dispute* (Robert Schuman Centre for Advanced Studies Global Governance Programme- 150, 2014).

M. ZANARDI, *Anti-dumping: What are the Numbers to Discuss at Doha?* 27(3) THE WORLD ECONOMY 403 (March 2003).

**Working Papers**

A. AGGARWAL, *Antidumping Law and Practice: An Indian Perspective* (WORKING PAPER NO. 85, INDIAN COUNCIL FOR RESEARCH ON INTERNATIONAL ECONOMIC RELATIONS 2002).

G.W. BOWMAN *et al*, *Antidumping and Countervailing Duty Law and Practice: The Mexican Experience* Arizona Legal Studies Discussion Paper No. 10-10, 272 (2010).

C.P. BOWN, *Global antidumping database version 1.0* (Policy Research Working Paper Series 3737, The World Bank 2005).

G. BRINK, *Antidumping in South Africa* (Working Paper No. D12WP07, Trade Law Center 2012).

M. FINGER, *The Origins and Evolution of Antidumping Regulation*, 26 (World Bank Working Papers, 783, October 1991).

D.A. IRWIN, S. LAIRD, J. NOGUES, *Trade Policy and Debt Crisis* 18 (World Bank Working Paper Series No. 99, Sept. 1988).

D.A. IRWIN, *Causing Problems: The WTO Review of Causation and Injury Attribution in US Section 201 Cases*, (Working paper No. 9815, National Bureau of Economic Research 2003).

K.H. KELLY and M.E. MOKRE, *One Lump or Two: Unitary Versus Bifurcated Measures of Injury at the USITC* (Federal Trade Commission Working Paper No. 282) 2006.

**Internet Sources**

Australian Customs Dumping Notice, *New Ministerial Direction on Material Injury,* No.2012/24, (1 June 2012) *available at* http://www.adcommission.gov.au/adsystem/referencematerial/Documents/ACDN2012-24.pdf (last visited May 26, 2015).

Centre for WTO Studies (CWS) Indian Institute of Foreign Trade (IIFT), *FAQ on Agreement on Antidumping* (2011) *available at* http://wtocentre.iift.ac.in/FAQ/english/Anti-dumping.pdf (last visited May 26, 2015).

C.P. Bown, *Global Antidumping Database*, The World Bank (2014), http://econ.worldbank.org/ttbd/gad/ (last visited May 26, 2015).

*International Trade, in Annual Economic Survey- Government of India* (2012) *available at* http://indiabudget.nic.in/survey.asp (last visited May 25, 2015).

Ministry of Commerce and Industry of India, *Data on Anti-Dumping Investigations*, http://commerce.nic.in/traderemedies/Data_Anti_dumping_investigations.pdf?id=25 (last visited on September 30, 2014).

U.S. Committee on Finance - US Senate, *The Antidumping Act 1921 and the International Dumping Code* (July 5, 1968) *available at* http://www.finance.senate.gov/library/prints/ (last visited May 26, 2015).

World Trade Organization, *Anti-Dumping Initiations: By Exporting Country 01/01/1995 –31/12/2013*, http://www.wto.org/english/tratop_e/adp_e/AD_InitiationsByExpCty.pdf (last visited 11 Oct. 2014).

World Trade Organization, *Anti-Dumping Initiations: By Reporting Member 01/01/1995 – 31/12/2013*, http://www.wto.org/english/tratop_e/adp_e/AD_InitiationsByRepMem.pdf (last visited Oct. 11, 2014).

World Trade Organization, *Dispute settlement Gateway*, http://www.wto.org/english/tratop_e/dispu_e/dispu_e.htm (last visited October 12, 2014).

World Trade Organization, *Safeguard Initiations: by reporting Member*, *available at* https://www.wto.org/english/tratop_e/safeg_e/safeg_e.htm (last visited May 26, 2015).

World Trade Organization, *WTO Trade Remedies Gateway*, *available at* http://www.wto.org/english/tratop_e/adp_e/adp_e.htm (last visited December 31, 2013).

World Trade Organization, *Statistics on Antidumping*, *available at* http://www.wto.org/english/tratop_e/adp_e/adp_e.htm (last visited May 26, 2015).

# Index




J.J. Nedumpara, *Injury and Causation in Trade Remedy Law*,
DOI 10.1007/978-981-10-2197-8

MIX
Papier aus verantwortungsvollen Quellen
Paper from responsible sources
FSC® C105338
FSC
www.fsc.org

If you have any concerns about our products,
you can contact us on
**ProductSafety@springernature.com**

In case Publisher is established outside the EU,
the EU authorized representative is:
**Springer Nature Customer Service Center GmbH**
**Europaplatz 3, 69115 Heidelberg, Germany**

Printed by Libri Plureos GmbH
in Hamburg, Germany

SAMMLUNG GÖSCHEN BAND 782/782a

# FINANZWISSENSCHAFT

von

DR. HEINZ KOLMS
o. Professor an der Universität Kiel

## IV
## ÖFFENTLICHER KREDIT
## ÖFFENTLICHER HAUSHALT
## FINANZAUSGLEICH

WALTER DE GRUYTER & CO.
vormals G. J. Göschen'sche Verlagshandlung · J. Guttentag, Verlagsbuchhandlung · Georg Reimer · Karl J. Trübner · Veit & Comp.
BERLIN 1964

Die Gesamtdarstellung umfaßt folgende Bände:

Band I: Grundlegung. Öffentliche Ausgaben (Band 148)

Band II: Erwerbseinkünfte. Gebühren und Beiträge. Allgemeine Steuerlehre (Band 391)

Band III: Besondere Steuerlehre (Band 776)

Band IV: Öffentlicher Kredit. Öffentlicher Haushalt. Finanzausgleich (Band 782)

 — Archiv-Nr. 7521643 — Satz und Druck: Paul Funk, Berlin 30. — Printed in Germany.

## Inhaltsverzeichnis

Seite

# Kapitel VIII. Öffentlicher Kredit

## § 1. Definition des öffentlichen Kredits

Wird im Rahmen der Einnahmelehre vom öffentlichen Kredit gesprochen, so meint man den sogenannten Passiv-Kredit, d. h. den Kredit, den die öffentliche Hand aufnimmt, im Gegensatz zum Aktiv-Kredit, bei dem die öffentliche Hand als Kreditgeber auftritt.

Die Aufnahme von Krediten durch die öffentliche Hand wird in traditioneller Sicht als *außerordentliche*, *vorläufige* (provisorische) und *marktwirtschaftliche Einnahme* bezeichnet. Diese Begriffsmerkmale bedürfen einer näheren Interpretation.

Zur *Außerordentlichkeit* des öffentlichen Kredits ist zu sagen, daß er „bis um die Wende vom 18. zum 19. Jahrhundert nicht als reguläres Mittel zur Deckung des außerordentlichen Bedarfs, sondern als (ein) ... im Rahmen einer gesunden Finanzwirtschaft im Grunde ungehöriges Deckungsmittel" (Landmann) betrachtet wurde. Diese Auffassung wurzelt in der Praxis der Fürsten, notfalls Schulden — häufig gegen Verpfändung von Vermögensgegenständen — aufzunehmen, wenn die normalen Einnahmen verwirtschaftet waren.

Eine zumeist skeptische Beurteilung erfuhr die Staatsverschuldung durch die englischen Klassiker. D. Ricardo fürchtete, die öffentliche Kreditaufnahme würde einerseits Ersparnisse binden und privaten Investitionsvorhaben entziehen und andererseits unproduktiven Staatsverbrauch fördern. Dadurch werde der „Reichtumszuwachs" der Nation gemindert. C. Dietzel wies dagegen auf eine mögliche entgegengesetzte Wirkung der öffentlichen Kreditnahme hin. Sie könne „disponible Kapitalien" einer produktiveren als der privaten Verwendung zuführen. Auch andere Vertreter der traditionellen deutschen Finanzwissenschaft stan-

---

Bei der Sammlung und Durcharbeitung des umfangreichen Materials zu diesem Band IV haben mir die Herren Dr. H. Bydekarken, Dipl.-Ing. E. A. Conrad und Dipl.-Ing. N. Thissen zur Seite gestanden. Ihnen sei dafür auch an dieser Stelle gedankt.

den der Staatsschuld optimistisch gegenüber. C. A. v. Struensee schlug vor, den „inneren Wohlstand des Landes" durch inländische und auch durch ausländische Kredite für rentable öffentliche Investitionen zu heben. A. Wagner legte eine ähnliche Anschauung seinen Deckungsgrundsätzen für den öffentlichen Haushalt zugrunde. Staatliche Kreditaufnahme sei zulässig, wenn sie zur Deckung rentablen außerordentlichen Aufwandes, d. h. zur Finanzierung einer „Zinskosten deckenden Kapitalanlage", verwendet werde. Aus dieser Einstellung heraus sind auch die noch heute gültigen gesetzlichen Regelungen der staatlichen Kreditaufnahme formuliert worden. Das Merkmal „außerordentliche" Einnahmen ist heute nur mehr in diesem haushaltsrechtlichen Sinne zu verstehen. Eine Sonderstellung nimmt in dieser Hinsicht allerdings der Kassenkredit ein (vgl. unten § 2, 6a). Innerhalb der neueren auf Keynes aufbauenden Lehre der „monetary-fiscal policy" tritt das Kriterium der Außerordentlichkeit in den Hintergrund, weil vom traditionellen Postulat des jährlich auszugleichenden Haushalts abgerückt wird. Der öffentliche Kredit wird als ein Instrument der Beschäftigungspolitik gewertet.

Das Begriffsmerkmal *„vorläufige"* Einnahme weist darauf hin, daß der Kredit eines Tages zurückgezahlt werden muß, bei „echter" Tilgung durch die entsprechende Verwendung ordentlicher (definitiver) Einnahmen, vor allem aus Steuern. Ist jedoch die Staatsschuld als dauernde Institution etabliert, so ist auch eine Rückzahlung eines bestimmten Kredits durch eine gleichzeitige Neuverschuldung denkbar, ja typisch. Weiterhin mag eine wirtschaftsbelebende Wirkung kreditfinanzierter Staatsausgaben die Steuereinnahmen auf längere Sicht derart anheben, daß nicht nur die Kreditrückzahlung möglich ist, sondern darüber hinaus der öffentlichen Hand eine Nettoeinnahme bleibt. In diesem Falle wäre — letztlich doch als Folge einer Kreditaufnahme — sogar eine endgültige Einnahme entstanden.

Das Begriffsmerkmal *„marktwirtschaftlich"* weist darauf hin, daß bei der Aufnahme von Krediten eine spezielle, ökonomisch äquivalente Gegenleistung vorhanden ist. Sie besteht in der Rückzahlung der Kreditsumme und der Verzinsung bzw. in der wertäquivalenten Zahlung einer Rente. Dieses Merkmal wird eingeschränkt, wenn — etwa durch übermäßige Anspannung des öffentlichen Kredits — Geldwertverschlechterungen eintreten und Verzinsung und Tilgung in entwertetem Geld erfolgen, der Staat also realiter einen Teil des Kredits einbehält. Dadurch würde auch das Merkmal „Vorläufigkeit" eingeschränkt! Andererseits kann dann nicht von „marktwirtschaftlicher" Einnahme gesprochen werden, wenn die Privaten dem Staat nicht freiwillig aufgrund marktwirtschaftlicher Erwägungen, sondern durch hoheitlichen Zwang bedingt, Kredite geben (vgl. unten § 2, 7).

Das Merkmal *„Einnahme"* ist zwar allgemeingültig, doch ist zu fragen, ob es immer das primäre Ziel der Kreditaufnahme darstellen muß. Nach neueren finanzpolitischen Vorstellungen können durchaus allgemein wirtschaftspolitische Zielsetzungen vor das Ziel der Mittelbeschaffung gestellt werden. Ein extremer Vorschlag in Richtung auf ausschließliche Orientierung der Kreditaufnahme an der beschäftigungspolitischen Zielsetzung ist z. B. von der „Functional Finance" (A. P. Lerner) unterbreitet worden.

Der öffentliche Kredit ist damit unter Berücksichtigung der gegebenen Einschränkungen von den übrigen finanziellen öffentlichen Einnahmen, die sämtlich den Charakter endgültiger, also nicht „provisorischer" Einnahmen aufweisen, unterschieden. Seine Kennzeichnung als „marktwirtschaftliche" Einnahme unterscheidet ihn ferner von den Zwangseinnahmen (Steuern, Gebühren, Beiträgen). Von den Steuern ist er insbesondere noch dadurch abgegrenzt, daß diesen keine speziellen und keine ökonomisch äquivalenten Gegenleistungen gegenüberstehen.

## § 2. Formen und Technik des öffentlichen Kredits

Der Kredit der öffentlichen Hand kann nach verschiedenen Gesichtspunkten gegliedert werden. Diese Unterscheidungen sollen im folgenden kurz dargestellt und begründet werden, sofern sie für die Erklärung der Kredittechnik, für die Kenntnis des institutionellen Rahmens oder für die Theorie des öffentlichen Kredits von wesentlicher Bedeutung sind.

Da die einzelnen Gliederungen an *unterschiedliche* Eigenschaften des öffentlichen Kredits anknüpfen, schließen sie sich nicht gegenseitig aus. Vielmehr ergibt sich eine abgerundete Beschreibung eines gegebenen praktischen Falles erst durch Einordnung unter *alle* aufgeführten Gliederungsgesichtspunkte.

### 1. Gliederung nach den Schuldarten

Kredite können nach Schuldarten unterschieden werden, die sich im Laufe der Entwicklung des Kreditwesens herausgebildet haben und die durch typische rechtliche Regelungen und technische Formen gekennzeichnet sind.

Grundzüge der Kredittechnik werden bei der Behandlung der einzelnen Schuldarten dargestellt. Dabei werden insbesondere die Methoden der Unterbringung, der Verzinsung, der Tilgung und der Änderung der Bedingungen während der Laufzeit eines öffentlichen Kredits behandelt.

#### a) *Anleihen*

Bei den Anleihen werden die Ansprüche des Gläubigers aus einer langfristigen Kapitalüberlassung durch ein Wertpapier (Obligation, Teilschuldverschreibung), das im allgemeinen auf den Inhaber lautet oder durch eine Schuldbucheintragung dokumentiert. Die Forderungen werden an der Börse zu einem Marktkurs gehandelt.

α) Die *Unterbringung* (Emission) erfolgt heute allgemein auf freiwilliger Basis[1]) bei Kapitalsammelstellen und bei dem Publikum (private Haushalte und Unternehmungen). In technischer Hinsicht ist zu unterscheiden zwischen der heute seltenen Selbstemission, bei der der öffentliche Kreditnehmer den Verkauf der Papiere selbst durchführt,

---

1) Den hier nicht behandelten Gegensatz bildet die Zwangsanleihe. Vgl. dazu unten 7b.

und der Fremdemission[1]), bei der eine Bank oder ein Bankenkonsortium zwischengeschaltet wird. Die Emission wird durch ein *Zeichnungsangebot* (Prospekt), in dem Ausstattung und Zeichnungsbedingungen der Anleihe genannt werden, öffentlich angekündigt.

Die Schuldart der Anleihe wird gewählt, wenn ein großer Betrag von einer Vielzahl von Kreditgebern aufgenommen werden soll. Zu diesem Zweck wird der Betrag aufgespalten *(Stückelung)*. Häufig werden Stücke mit unterschiedlichen Nennbeträgen gebildet, um den Wünschen unterschiedlicher Anlegergruppen entgegenzukommen. Durch das Angebot kleiner Stücke (so z. B. im Werte von DM 100,—) soll privaten Kleinanlegern die Möglichkeit zur Zeichnung gegeben und damit eine breite Streuung angestrebt werden.

Der *Form* nach werden öffentliche Anleihen allgemein als Briefschuld oder als Buchschuld begründet. Bei der *Briefschuld* besitzt der Gläubiger einen in einem Wertpapier verbrieften — an das Papier als Sache gebundenen — Anspruch. Sie weist den Vorteil der leichten Übertragbarkeit aber den Nachteil der Gefährdung des Anspruches (durch Verlust des Papiers) auf. Bei der *Buchschuld* wird der Anspruch des Gläubigers durch namentliche Eintragung auf einem besonderen Konto eines Schuldbuches (z. B. des von der Bundesschuldenverwaltung geführten Bundesschuldbuches) dokumentiert. Schuldbucheintragungen sind verlustsicher aber verkehrsunbequem.

In der Bundesrepublik Deutschland werden bei Anleihen des Bundes und seiner Sondervermögen den Zeichnern heute in der Regel neben den genannten Formen auch die *Einlegung in ein Sammeldepot* bei einer Wertpapiersammelbank zur Wahl gestellt. In Höhe des gesamten auf sie entfallenden Sammelbetrages stellt der Emissionär dieser Bank Wertpapiere (oder ent-

[1]) Dabei können die Banken in verschieden starkem Maße mitwirken. Die stärkste Form der Fremdemission liegt vor, wenn die Banken eine Anleihe unter eigenem Namen auflegen und den Erlös öffentlichen Kreditnehmern als Darlehen zur Verfügung stellen (vor allem bei kommunalen Sammelanleihen). Gradweise schwächere Funktionen erfüllen die Banken bei der festen Übernahme (Negotiation), bei der Kommission und bei der Geschäftsbesorgung.

sprechende Schuldbuchforderungen) in Form weniger Globalstücke zur Verfügung, die im Portefeuille der Bank verbleiben und als einheitlicher Sammelbestand gelten. Die Zeichner besitzen daran gemäß ihres Anteils Miteigentum, über das sie auf dem Buchungswege (Wertpapiergiroverkehr) verfügen können. Durch diese Technik, deren Entwicklung auf den Zweiten Weltkrieg zurückgeht, gestalten sich Emission und Verfügungen wesentlich einfacher.

β) die *Verzinsung* erfolgt, bei in der Regel halbjährlicher Zahlung, zu einem festen, auf einhundert Einheiten des Nennbetrages bezogenen Jahressatz (Nominalzinssatz). Ist die Anleihe anders als bei der *Pariemission* — hier sind Ausgabe- und Einlösungskurs (Nennbetrag) einander gleich — zu einem niedrigeren Kurs als dem Einlösungskurs begeben worden, man spricht dann von *Unterpariemission,* so sind bei der Ermittlung der *Effektivverzinsung* in bekannter Weise neben der festen Nominalverzinsung und dem Einlösungskurs auch der Ausgabekurs und die Laufzeit zu berücksichtigen. Das gilt auch von der selteneren *Überpariemission,* bei der die Begebung zu einem höheren als dem Einlösungskurs erfolgt.

γ) Nach den *Rückzahlungsbedingungen* ist zwischen Tilgungsanleihen und Rentenanleihen zu unterscheiden.

Bei den *Tilgungsanleihen mit fristgebundener Tilgung* übernimmt der öffentliche Schuldner die Verpflichtung, eine Tilgung mindestens in dem in den Anleihebedingungen genannten Umfange durchzuführen. Dabei kann eine Gesamtrückzahlung zu einem bestimmten Termin oder eine Teilrückzahlung durch Auslosung einzelner Stücke oder von Serien zu bestimmten Terminen[1]) vorgesehen werden. Über diese Verpflichtung hinaus behält der Staat sich häufig das Recht vor, die *Tilgung* durch zusätzliche Auslosungen zu *verstärken* oder die gesamte *Anleihe vorzeitig* zu *kündigen.* Eine solche Regelung mag aus Gründen

---

1) Eine Sonderform stellt die Zeitrente (Annuität) dar, bei der der Gläubiger während einer endlichen Laufzeit Anspruch auf eine gleichbleibende Zahlung hat, die sich aus Verzinsung und Tilgung zusammensetzt. Wird die Annuität gezahlt, solange der Gläubiger lebt, so liegt die heute im öffentlichen Kredit seltene Form der Leibrente vor.

der Konjunkturpolitik bedeutungsvoll sein oder getroffen werden, um dem Staat Gelegenheit zu bieten, sich bei günstiger Kassenlage entschulden zu können. Ist zu diesem Zeitpunkt der landesübliche Zinsfuß im Verhältnis zum Nominalzinssatz der Anleihe niedrig, so werden die Stücke zu einem höheren Kurs als dem Nennwert gehandelt. Die Rückzahlung zum Nennwert bedeutet dann einen Verlust für die Gläubiger[1]).

Bei den *Rentenanleihen* hat der Gläubiger keinen Anspruch auf Tilgung, sondern nur auf laufende Rentenzahlungen. Es sind von seiten des Staates kündbare und beiderseitig unkündbare (ewige) Rentenanleihen zu unterscheiden.

Die öffentliche Hand kann versuchen, die Unterbringung ihrer Anleihen dadurch zu *fördern*, daß sie diese mit besonders attraktiven Bedingungen ausstattet oder besondere Vergünstigungen gewährt.

Bei den *Lotterie- und Prämienanleihen* soll durch eine Gewinnchance, die neben oder anstelle der Tilgung bzw. Verzinsung besteht, ein besonderer Anreiz ausgeübt werden. Bei der (heute seltenen) Lotterieanleihe wird der Anspruch auf Tilgung gegen einen höheren Gewinn ausgespielt; bei der Prämienanleihe bleibt der Rückzahlungsanspruch unangetastet, der Anspruch auf Zinszahlung wird ganz oder teilweise gegen eine höhere Prämie ausgelost. Zwischenformen sind denkbar.

Einige besondere Anreize kann nur der Staat gewähren. Dazu zählen die Einräumung von *Steuervergünstigungen* und die *Steuerbefreiung*, die dem Gläubiger oft bedeutende materielle Vorteile bringen können.

δ) Wegen der langen Laufzeit einer Anleihe kommt den Möglichkeiten der *nachträglichen Änderung der Anleihebedingungen* Bedeutung zu.

Bei der *Konversion* handelt es sich um eine Veränderung des Zinsfußes[2]). Im Falle der freiwilligen Konversion kündigt der Staat aufgrund eines vorbehaltenen Kündigungs-

---

1) Abgesehen davon hat der Staat — und das gilt auch für die im nächsten Absatz genannten Rentenanleihen — die Möglichkeit, sich durch den Kauf von Kredittiteln am Markte seiner Schuld aus den Anleihen zu entledigen. Nur kann er dabei die Schuldtitel allein zum geltenden Marktkurs erwerben, der im übrigen bei bedeutenden Rückkäufen anziehen mag.

2) In seltenen Fällen der Kapitalschuld.

rechts die Anleihe vorzeitig und bietet eine neue niedriger verzinsliche an. Die Gläubiger können sich ihre Forderung zum Nennwert auszahlen lassen. Bei der Zwangskonversion erklärt der Staat, ohne eine Rückzahlung anzubieten, daß er in Zukunft eine geringere Verzinsung vornehmen werde. Die Staatsgläubiger erleiden Vermögensverluste insofern, als die Kurse der Schuldtitel infolge der Zinssenkung ebenfalls sinken.

Auch der Fall einer Zinserhöhung, einer sogenannten *Arrosierung*, zumeist um den Kurs der Papiere zu stützen und u. U. damit ein günstigeres Klima für Neuemissionen zu schaffen, ist geschichtlich zu belegen.

Eine *Unifizierung* liegt vor, wenn mehrere Anleihen mit verschiedenen Bedingungen zusammengefaßt und dafür einheitliche neue Titel geschaffen werden.

An dieser Stelle sei auch die *Fundierung* erwähnt. Darunter versteht man die Umwandlung einer bestehenden Schuld hinsichtlich der Schuldart in der Weise, daß kurzfristige Schuldarten durch langfristige, z. B. durch Anleihen, ersetzt werden.

Unifizierung und Fundierung werden gelegentlich auch gemeinsam als *Konsolidierung* bezeichnet.

Stellt schon die Konversion eine Beeinträchtigung der Interessen der Gläubiger dar, so werden diese im besonderen Maße geschädigt, wenn der Staat seine bei der Kreditaufnahme eingegangenen Verpflichtungen überhaupt nicht mehr erfüllen kann (*Staatsbankrott*). Eine solche Situation ist allerdings in entwickelten Ländern heute nicht mehr denkbar. Eine nur vorübergehende Einstellung der Zins- und Tilgungszahlungen wird als *Zwangsmoratorium* bezeichnet.

In diesem Zusammenhang ist auch die *Entwertung* der Gläubigeransprüche durch Geldwertverschlechterungen zu nennen. Durch übermäßige Kreditbeanspruchungen kann der Staat eine Inflation auslösen und auf diesem Wege den realen Wert seiner Schuld dezimieren, im Grenzfall sich völlig davon befreien.

Sind die Kreditgeber aufgrund gegebener Erfahrungen mißtrauisch bezüglich der Beständigkeit des Geldwertes, so hat der Staat die Möglichkeit, *wertbeständige Anleihen* aufzulegen, die entweder auf Sachwerte lauten oder mit einer Wertsicherungsklausel verbunden sind.

Etwa mangelndem Vertrauen potentieller Kreditgeber in die künftige Zahlungsfähigkeit des Kreditnehmers kann dieser durch besondere Sicherungen entgegenzuwirken suchen, wie durch die Zweckbindung bestimmter Einnahmequellen zum Schuldendienst (z. B. bei Tilgungsfonds), durch eine Verpfändung von Vermögensteilen oder sogar durch die Einräumung einer Finanzkontrolle.

### b) Schuldscheindarlehen

Hier wird dem Gläubiger vom Schuldner über die Kreditgewährung in der Form eines Darlehens ein auf den Namen lautender Schuldschein ausgestellt. Diese Urkunde stellt grundsätzlich kein Wertpapier dar[1]), sondern hat nur Bedeutung als Beweispapier; die Ansprüche des Gläubigers gründen sich also allein auf den Darlehensvertrag. Die Unterbringung erfolgt allgemein bei Kapitalsammelstellen und Banken, also nicht bei einem breitgestreuten Publikum. Jedoch können durch Stückelung des gesamten Darlehens in Abschnitte auch mehrere Kreditgeber herangezogen werden. Der Schuldner verpflichtet sich zur regelmäßigen festen Verzinsung. Die Rückzahlung erfolgt, häufig auch in Teilbeträgen, nach einem festgelegten Tilgungsplan. Schuldscheindarlehen sind nicht börsenfähig und somit keinen Kursschwankungen ausgesetzt.

### c) Verzinsliche Schatzanweisungen

Die Kreditaufnahme gegen Ausgabe von verzinslichen Schatzanweisungen weist rechtlich und technisch starke Ähnlichkeiten mit der Emission von Anleihen auf. Es werden regelmäßig mit einem festen Satz zu verzinsende, in der Regel auf den Inhaber lautende Wertpapiere begeben, die zu einem Marktkurs an der Börse gehandelt werden.

[1]) Eine Ausnahme wird nach herrschender Meinung durch die Ausstellung einer Urkunde seitens der Bundesschuldenverwaltung geschaffen. Derartigen Urkunden wird rechtsbegründende Wirkung zugesprochen. Vgl. Dieben, HdF², III, 40.

Im Gegensatz zur langfristigen Anleihe handelt es sich jedoch um mittelfristige Titel. Ihre Tilgung erfolgt an einem im voraus festgesetzten Termin, gelegentlich kommen auch auslosbare Schatzanweisungen vor.

Eine Sonderform der verzinslichen Schatzanweisungen bilden die *Kassenobligationen.* Sie werden en bloc oder in großen Teilbeträgen in der Regel fest bei Banken und anderen Großanlegern (insbesondere Kapitalsammelstellen) untergebracht. Dagegen werden die sogenannten *Baby-Bonds* mit der besonderen Absicht begeben, private Kleinsparer zu gewinnen. Ihre Stücke lauten deshalb auf sehr kleine Beträge. Vgl. dazu die Prämienschatzanweisungen der Bundesrepublik von 1951. In den Vereinigten Staaten kommen neben anderen auch auf den Namen lautende unverzinsliche, d. h. auf Diskontbasis begebene, Baby-Bonds vor.

### *d) Unverzinsliche Schatzanweisungen*

Unverzinsliche Schatzanweisungen sind Wertpapiere mit kurzen Laufzeiten, heute allgemein 6--24 Monate, die im Wege der Diskontierung untergebracht werden[1]).

Bei der Diskontierung wird vom Kreditgeber bei der Übernahme nicht der volle Nennbetrag des Papiers im Kaufpreis vergütet, sondern ein Abschlag (Diskont) vorgenommen. Am Fälligkeitstermin löst der Staat das Papier zum Nennwert ein. Der Zins wird also bei den sogenannten unverzinslichen Schatzanweisungen vom Gläubiger in der Form einer Differenz zwischen Übernahme- und Rückzahlungsbetrag des Papiers von vornherein einbehalten und nicht wie bei den festverzinslichen Papieren später vom Schuldner ausgezahlt. Materiell gesehen findet in beiden Fällen eine Verzinsung statt, der Unterschied liegt nur in der Technik. Die unverzinslichen Schatzanweisungen werden üblicherweise auf große Beträge ausgestellt und vom Geldmarkt aufgenommen und gehandelt. Die Deutsche Bundesbank darf solche Papiere nicht diskontieren, sondern nur lombardieren oder damit Offenmarktgeschäfte betreiben, wobei diese zu Marktsätzen, die sich nach Angebot

---

[1]) Für unverzinsliche Schatzanweisungen (auch „U-Schätze" genannt) und für Schatzwechsel findet man auch die Sammelbezeichnung Schatzscheine.

und Nachfrage richten, abgewickelt werden. Das gilt übrigens auch für das Offenmarktgeschäft mit Schatzwechseln.

### e) *Schatzwechsel*

Hier handelt es sich um Wertpapiere, auf die die Vorschriften des Wechselrechts Anwendung finden. Regelmäßig sind es eigene (Sola-)Wechsel, denen als reinen Finanzwechseln kein Kausalgeschäft zugrunde liegt. Sie werden wie die unverzinslichen Schatzanweisungen diskontiert. Die Laufzeit beträgt allgemein drei Monate. Die Unterbringung erfolgt auf dem Geldmarkt. Die Deutsche Bundesbank kann Schatzwechsel diskontieren, jedoch sind dabei die Vorschriften über den Kreditplafond zu beachten, in den auch die im Offenmarktgeschäft angekauften Schatzwechsel einbezogen werden (vgl. unten 3, 4a).

### f) *Buchkredite*

Auch die Buchkredite werden in den Kreditplafond der Deutschen Bundesbank einbezogen. Ihre Kreditsumme überwiegt im übrigen derzeit bei dem kurzfristigen öffentlichen Kredit die der Schatzwechsel. Bei den Buchkrediten wird kein Wertpapier ausgestellt und allgemein keine Schuldbuchforderung begründet, es wird also keine Dokumentation des Anspruchs mit rechtsbegründender Wirkung vorgenommen, vielmehr erscheint der Kredit nur in den Handelsbüchern. An dieser Stelle ist auch der Kontokorrentkredit zu erwähnen, der namentlich im kurzfristigen kommunalen Kreditgeschäft von Bedeutung ist.

### g) *Besondere Schuldarten*

Während der NS-Zeit ist eine Reihe von *Sonderformen* staatlicher Kreditnahme entwickelt worden, so 1933 zur Finanzierung der Arbeitsbeschaffung die sogenannten *Arbeitsbeschaffungswechsel* und seit 1935 zur Finanzierung der Aufrüstung die sogenannten *Mefowechsel.* Auf diesem Wege sollte eine vermehrte Begebung von Schatzwechseln vermieden werden, deren Übernahme durch die Reichsbank gesetzlich begrenzt war. Von einer Lockerung dieser Vorschrift befürchtete man das Wachwerden unliebsamer Erinnerungen an die große Inflation der Zwanziger

Jahre. Arbeitsbeschaffungs- sowie Mefowechsel wurden von den mit Staatsaufträgen bedachten Firmen ausgestellt und von besonderen Instituten, wie der Gesellschaft für öffentliche Arbeit (Öffa) und der 1933 geschaffenen Metallurgischen Forschungsgesellschaft (Mefo) akzeptiert. Dadurch, sowie durch andere Manipulationen rein formeller Art, welche die an sich mittel- bis langfristigen Kredite äußerlich als kurzfristige erscheinen ließen, wurde die Diskontierung durch die Reichsbank institutionell ermöglicht. Damit wurden die Papiere für die Banken interessant. Bei den Mefowechseln wurde übrigens aus Geheimhaltungsgründen noch die Golddiskontbank eingeschaltet, welche gegen Mefowechsel eigene (Sola-)Wechsel ausgab, die von den Banken aufgenommen wurden. Andere Sonderformen der NS-Zeit waren die *Lieferschatzanweisungen* von 1938, die *Steuergutscheine* von 1939[1]) und die *Wehrmachtsverpflichtungsscheine*. In all diesen Fällen wurden Staatspapiere zur Bezahlung von Staatsaufträgen unter Anwendung staatlichen Zwanges abgegeben.

Weiterhin wurden während des Zweiten Weltkriegs bei den Unternehmungen infolge Lagerabbaus und mangelnder Reinvestitionsmöglichkeit auflaufende liquide Mittel mit Hilfe steuerlicher Anreize in der Form der sogenannten *Warenbeschaffungsguthaben* und der *Betriebsanlageguthaben* dem Staate kreditähnlich zur Verfügung gebracht.

Aus systematischen Gründen ist an dieser Stelle auch das *Staatspapiergeld* zu nennen, das in der geschichtlichen Entwicklung vielfach eine Rolle gespielt hat. Staatspapiergeld wird vom Staat ausgegeben und in der Regel mit Zwangskurs ausgestattet, d. h. zum gesetzlichen Zahlungsmittel gemacht und für uneinlöslich erklärt. Es ist streng zu trennen von den Banknoten, die von einer Bank ausgegeben werden (heute Monopol der Bundesbank) und eine Forderung gegenüber der Bank dokumentieren.

### 2. Gliederung nach der Laufzeit

Eine in der Schuldenstatistik häufig verwendete Gliederung ist die in schwebende und fundierte Schulden. Dabei

---

[1]) Steuergutscheine sind Wertpapiere, die zu einem späteren Zeitpunkt von den Finanzkassen anstelle fälliger Steuerzahlungen angenommen werden. Die Steuergutscheine von 1939 sind nicht zu verwechseln mit den Steuergutscheinen der Ära Papen von 1932, die eine verdeckte Steuersenkung bezweckten. Die Steuergutscheine von 1939 dagegen waren ein Instrument staatlicher Ausgabenfinanzierung, d. h wurden den Staatslieferanten an Zahlungs Statt aufgezwungen.

wird heute[1]) in der Regel an der planmäßigen Laufzeit des Kredits angeknüpft.

*a) Schwebende Schulden*

Darunter versteht man mit der Absicht der baldigen Rückzahlung, bis spätestens nach zwei Jahren, aufgenommene Schulden. Durch Prolongation können schwebende Schulden allerdings effektiv auch längere Laufzeiten erreichen.

*b) Fundierte Schulden*

Das sind für längere Zeit, allgemein über zwei Jahre, aufgenommene Schulden. Hierzu zählen alle Kredite, die in mittelfristigen (2 bis 10 Jahre), langfristigen (mehr als 10 Jahre) und ewigen Schuldarten begeben worden sind.

3. Gliederung nach dem Kreditnehmer

Schuldner eines öffentlichen Kredits können Finanzwirtschaften verschiedener Ebene sein. In der Bundesrepublik Deutschland sind das der Bund, die Länder (einschl. der Stadtstaaten), die Gemeinden (einschl. der Gemeindeverbände), Sondervermögen des Bundes sowie sonstige öffentlich-rechtliche Körperschaften.

Die Kreditnehmer unterscheiden sich durch ihre Stellung auf dem Kreditmarkt, insbesondere in bezug auf die Kreditgewährung durch die Bundesbank. Damit hängt eine unterschiedliche Inanspruchnahme der verschiedenen Schuldarten zusammen. Aus den spezifischen Aufgaben der Kreditnehmer ergeben sich unterschiedliche Zwecke der Kreditaufnahme.

*a) Der Bund*

Über die Struktur der Verschuldung des Bundes gibt die Tabelle V Auskunft. An dieser Stelle ist es wichtig, darauf hinzuweisen, daß dem Bund außer anderen Kreditquellen auch die Bundesbank im Rahmen der gesetzlichen Begrenzungen zur Verfügung steht. Der Regelung gerade dieser

[1]) Die Unterscheidung stammt aus der mittelalterlichen Kreditwirtschaft. Als „fundierte Schuld" wurde ursprünglich ein durch Pfänder gesicherter Kredit verstanden.

Beziehungen zwischen Staat und Zentralbank kommt im Zusammenhang mit der Geldmengen-Problematik (s. u. § 3) besondere Bedeutung zu.

Es hat Zeiten gegeben, in denen der Staat praktisch unbegrenzt von der Zentralbank Kredit erhalten konnte. So das Deutsche Reich in der Zeit in und nach dem Ersten Weltkriege und im Zweiten Weltkrieg. Wegen der darauf folgenden Inflationsentwicklung sind, so nach 1923 und 1948, die gesetzlichen Regelungen mit der Absicht verschärft worden, dem Staat den Zugang zur Zentralbank zu erschweren. So durfte nach dem Reichsbankgesetz von 1924 in Verbindung mit der Banknovelle von 1926 die Reichsbank nur Reichsschatzwechsel bis zum Betrage von 400 Mill. RM übernehmen. Heute ist die Kreditaufnahme des Bundes bei der Deutschen Bundesbank begrenzt. Es besteht nach § 20 des Bundesbankgesetzes (BBG) ein Kreditplafond in Höhe von 3 Mrd. DM für Kassenkredite. In diesen Plafond werden auch die von der Bundesbank im Offenmarktgeschäft übernommenen Schatzwechsel einbezogen.

Hinsichtlich des Zwecks der Kreditaufnahme ist hervorzuheben, daß bei der Zentralregierung auch bestimmte wirtschaftspolitisch gewünschte Wirkungen, insbesondere auf Geldmenge und Beschäftigung gerichtete, bedeutungsvoll sein können, die Kreditaufnahme also auch aus anderen als aus rein einnahmepolitischen Gründen erfolgen kann.

### *b) Länder und Stadtstaaten*

Aufgrund des föderativen Aufbaus der Bundesrepublik nimmt der Kredit der Länder eine ähnliche Stellung ein wie der des Bundes.

Die Länder können sich der gleichen Schuldformen bedienen, insbesondere auch Schatzwechsel und Schatzanweisungen begeben. Sie verfügen ebenfalls über einen gesetzlich festgelegten Plafond für Kassenkredite bei der Bundesbank (BBG, § 20). Er beträgt je Einwohner 20 DM, in Berlin, Hamburg und Bremen 40 DM.

Hinsichtlich des Zweckes der Kreditaufnahme ist zu bemerken, daß in der Regel einnahmepolitische Zwecke im Vordergrund stehen. Es kann aber nicht ausgeschlossen werden, ja es ist zu wünschen, daß die Länder eine wirtschaftspolitisch ausgerichtete Kreditpolitik des Bundes unterstützen.

*c) Gemeinden und Gemeindeverbände*

Den Gemeinden ist die Möglichkeit einer Verschuldung bei der Bundesbank verschlossen. Die bedeutendsten und charakteristischen Kreditquellen der Gemeinden sind die Sparkassen, Girozentralen, Landesbanken u. ä. Anstalten, mit denen die Gemeinden z. T. ohnehin institutionell und personell eng verbunden sind. Die häufigsten Schuldarten stellen für lang- und mittelfristige Kredite das Schuldscheindarlehen und für Kassenkredite der Kontokorrentkredit dar. Die Kreditaufnahme, die praktisch ausschließlich einnahmepolitischen Zwecken dient, wird durch die Gemeindeordnungen geregelt und ist an die Genehmigung (Globalgenehmigung, Einzelgenehmigungen) der staatlichen Aufsichtsbehörde gebunden. Dabei wird u. a. zur Voraussetzung gemacht, daß es sich um einen dringenden außerordentlichen Bedarf handelt, der sich aus der Erfüllung einer satzungsgemäßen Aufgabe ergibt und der nur durch Aufnahme eines Darlehens gedeckt werden kann. Kassenkredite dürfen nur im Rahmen einer allgemeinen Ermächtigung (Kreditplafond) der staatlichen Aufsichtsbehörde aufgenommen werden.

*d) Sondervermögen des Bundes*

Bundesbahn, Bundespost, Lastenausgleichsfonds weisen als Sondervermögen des Bundes z. Z. eine relativ bedeutende Verschuldung auf. Ihnen steht ebenfalls ein limitierter Kassenkredit der Bundesbank zur Verfügung. Die Kreditaufnahme dient insbesondere einnahmepolitischen Zwecken innerhalb der spezifischen Aufgabenbereiche der Sondervermögen. Es ist aber darauf hinzuweisen, daß starke wirtschaftlich relevante Wirkungen infolge der vorliegenden Größenordnungen zu erwarten sind und nicht außer acht gelassen werden sollten.

### *e) Sonstige öffentlich-rechtliche Körperschaften*

Neben den Gebietskörperschaften und den Sondervermögen des Bundes treten eine Anzahl anderer öffentlichrechtlicher Körperschaften als Kreditnehmer auf. Dabei handelt es sich um Stiftungen, Zweckverbände und ähnliche Körperschaften auf der Ebene der Länder und der Gemeinden. Die Verschuldung der letzteren wird zusammen mit der der gemeindlichen Gebietskörperschaften auch als „Kommunalkredit" bezeichnet. Die Kreditnahme auf kommunaler Ebene erfolgt regelmäßig nur unter einnahmepolitischen Gesichtspunkten. Im übrigen sind hier weitgehende Ähnlichkeiten zur privaten Kreditaufnahme anzunehmen.

## 4. Gliederung nach dem Kreditgeber

Die Kreditgeber weisen Unterschiede auf bezüglich ihrer Möglichkeit zur Kreditschöpfung und der Grenzen, in denen Kredite gewährt werden können, sowie im Hinblick auf ihre Kreditnehmer.

### *a) Zentralbank*

Die Fähigkeit der Zentralbank zur Ausweitung des Kredits durch Ausgabe von Banknoten und Einräumung von Buchgeldguthaben ist institutionell gesehen eine Frage der Währungsgesetzgebung.

Nach Abbau früherer „Bremsen", wie Golddeckungs- und Einlösungsvorschriften, ist die Fähigkeit der Zentralbanken zur Geld- und Kreditschöpfung gegenwärtig größer als im Zeitalter der Goldwährungen. Allerdings unterliegen die Zentralbanken auch heute in dieser Hinsicht gewissen institutionellen Beschränkungen.

So darf die Deutsche Bundesbank — wie schon erwähnt — nur bestimmten öffentlichen Kreditnehmern und nur in gesetzlich limitierter Höhe Kredite einräumen.

Im Bundesbankgesetz wird der Deutschen Bundesbank die Aufgabe zugesprochen, die Währungsstabilität zu sichern. Diese Aufgabenstellung wirkt sich als indirekte Einschränkung der Geldschöpfungsmöglichkeit der Bundesbank ebenso aus wie die institutionellen Festlegungen hinsichtlich des Zahlungsverkehrs mit dem Ausland. Nach dem Bundesbankgesetz hat die Deutsche Bundesbank — unter Sicherung der Währungsstabilität — die allgemeine Wirtschaftspolitik der Bundesregierung zu unterstützen. Diese ihrerseits hat sich durch den Beitritt zum Internationalen Währungsfonds verpflichtet, den Wechselkurs innerhalb gewisser Bandbreiten stabil zu halten und nur unter besonderen Ausnahmebedingungen (fundamentales Ungleichgewicht) größere Wechselkursänderungen vorzunehmen. Dazu kommen noch vertragliche Bindungen aus dem Europäischen Währungsabkommen (Konvertibilität). Auch aus diesen Verpflichtungen ist der Deutschen Bundesbank keine unbeschränkte Geldschöpfung möglich, da sie sich in gewissem Umfange in fremden Währungen liquide halten muß.

### *b) Geschäftsbanken*

Den Geschäftsbanken ist die Kreditgewährung an alle Kreditsuchenden, darunter gegebenenfalls also auch die öffentliche Hand, nach Maßgabe bankwirtschaftlicher Grundsätze (Rentabilität, Liquidität, Sicherheit) möglich. Die Fähigkeit zur Kreditschöpfung in der Form der Einräumung von Buchgeldguthaben ist der einzelnen Bank im Rahmen ihrer Überschußreserven gegeben; die Geldschöpfungsmöglichkeit des gesamten Geschäftsbankensystems kann ein Vielfaches der Überschußreserven betragen (Giralgeldschöpfungsmultiplikator); sie wird einerseits durch die Bargeldabflüsse ins Publikum und andererseits durch Mindestreservevorschriften der Zentralbank begrenzt. Durch Offenmarktpolitik kann ferner der Kreditspielraum der Geschäftsbanken beeinflußt werden.

### *c) Sparkassen und andere Kapitalsammelstellen*

Bei den Kreditgeschäften der *Sparkassen* im traditionellen Sinne handelte es sich um eine Weitergabe eingelegter Sparguthaben. Heute ist die Abgrenzung Sparkasse—Geschäftsbank weitgehend verwischt. In bezug auf den öffentlichen Kredit werden bei den Sparkassen vor allem Körperschaften auf kommunaler Ebene berücksichtigt.

Die *Girozentralen* haben als Zentralinstitute der Sparkassen ebenfalls Aufgaben auf dem Gebiete des kommunalen Kreditwesens, insbesondere durch die Ausgabe kommunaler Sammelanleihen, übernommen.

Bei den *Versicherungen* (u. ä. Kapitalsammelstellen) ist eine Kreditgewährung grundsätzlich an alle Kreditsuchenden (zumeist langfristig und in großen Beträgen) üblich, um liquide Mittel rentabel anzulegen.

### *d) Publikum*

Für die Unterbringung öffentlicher Kredittitel beim privaten Publikum kommen vor allem Anleihen und verzinsliche Schatzanweisungen, auch in spezieller Form (Baby-Bonds), infrage. Vor und während des Zweiten Weltkrieges sind in Deutschland für die Kreditierung durch Unternehmungen Sonderformen entwickelt worden wie die oben bereits erwähnten Lieferschatzanweisungen, Betriebsanlage- und Warenbeschaffungs-Guthaben. Die privaten Haushalte wurden auf indirekte Weise zum Staatskredit herangezogen, indem die Sparkassen (und andere Kapitalsammelstellen) über das bisherige Maß hinaus Staatstitel übernahmen (sogenannte „geräuschlose Kriegsfinanzierung").

### *e) Gebietskörperschaften*

Von Bedeutung sind ferner Kredite, die öffentliche Gebietskörperschaften untereinander gewähren. Dabei handelt es sich insbesondere um solche Kredite, die von übergeordneten Gebietskörperschaften an nachgeordnete im Rahmen von Förderungsmaßnahmen gegeben werden. In diesem Zusammenhang sind auch Kredite zu nennen, die durch die Sondervermögen des Bundes, ERP-Sondervermögen und Lastenausgleichsfonds an öffentliche Finanzwirtschaften gegeben werden.

## 5. Gliederung nach der örtlichen Herkunft der Mittel

Bei der Unterbringung eines öffentlichen Kredits ist ferner nach dem Sitz des Kreditgebers zwischen *Inlands-* und *Auslandskredit* zu unterscheiden.

Eine ähnliche Unterscheidung wie die in Inlands- und Auslandsschulden ist die in *innere* und *äußere* Verschuldung. Diese Begriffsbildung hat den Vorteil, daß sie auch auf den Ebenen der Gemeinden, der Länder und sogar supranationaler Organisationen anwendbar ist, wenn zum Ausdruck gebracht werden soll, ob die Verschuldung innerhalb oder außerhalb des Gebiets der kreditaufnehmenden Finanzwirtschaft untergebracht worden ist.

Bei der Entscheidung über die alternative Aufnahme von Inlands- oder von Auslandsschulden ist nicht nur die Unterbringungsmöglichkeit — das ist, wie wir später sehen werden, eine auch von institutionellen Gegebenheiten abhängige Frage —, sondern auch die Wirkung auf die Güterversorgung bedeutungsvoll:

### *a) Inlandsschulden*

In einer *vollbeschäftigten* Volkswirtschaft ist die gesamte inländische Güterversorgung einer Zeitperiode eine gegebene Größe. Durch inländische Kreditaufnahme finanzierte zusätzliche Nachfrage der öffentlichen Hand bedingt daher zu gleicher Zeit und in gleicher Höhe einen Verzicht auf Güterversorgung an anderer Stelle innerhalb der Volkswirtschaft.

Es ist allerdings zu bedenken, daß in einer *nicht vollbeschäftigten* Volkswirtschaft auch eine inländische Kreditaufnahme durch ihre Ankurbelungswirkung die gesamte Güterversorgung erhöhen kann.

### *b) Auslandsschulden*

Die Unterbringung öffentlicher Kredite im Ausland mag entweder infolge institutioneller Begrenzung im Inland oder aus güterwirtschaftlichen Gründen von Bedeutung sein.

Handelt es sich um einen Sachkredit, so werden dem Schuldner unmittelbar zusätzliche Güter und Dienste zur Verfügung gestellt. Wird der Kredit in Form von Devisen gewährt, so kann angenommen werden, daß entweder durch Käufe im Gläubigerland oder — bei Verwendung der Mittel im Inland — über die Wirkung von Außenwirtschaftsmechanismen letztlich dem Schuldnerland zusätzliche Güter und Dienste aus dem Ausland zufließen.

Der Erschließung zusätzlicher Güterquellen, die besonders bei inländischer Vollbeschäftigung oder bei Kapitalmangel in Aufbausituationen wichtig sein kann, steht andererseits ein Rückfluß von Gütern und Diensten im Zusammenhang mit der späteren Tilgung der Kredite gegenüber. Ferner ist während der Laufzeit des Kredits wegen der Zinszahlungen mit einem laufenden Abfluß inländischen Realeinkommens an das Ausland zu rechnen. Zwischenzeitlich kann jedoch in den bezeichneten Grenzen der verfügbare Bestand an Gütern und Diensten im Inland vergrößert werden. Dadurch wird es möglich, eine reale Belastung, die einer Volkswirtschaft durch gegenwärtige öffentliche Investitionen entsteht, auf die Laufzeit des Kredits — eventuell also über mehrere Generationen — zu verschieben. Dieser Gesichtspunkt ist besonders bei Entwicklungskrediten von Bedeutung.

### 6. Gliederung nach der haushaltsrechtlichen Stellung

Ein öffentlicher Kredit kann als *Haushalts*einnahme in den Haushaltsplan eingestellt werden (Haushaltskredit, Finanzierungskredit), er kann andererseits aufgenommen werden, um einen vorübergehenden Mangel an *Kassen*mitteln zu überbrücken (Kassenkredit, Betriebsmittelkredit).

Diese unterschiedlichen Funktionen des öffentlichen Kredits bedingen unterschiedliche rechtliche Regelungen. Darin einbegriffen unterscheiden sich Kassenkredit und Haushaltskredit normalerweise durch ihre Fristigkeit und, damit zusammenhängend, durch die zu wählenden Schuldarten. In einigen Fällen hat sich ferner die Inanspruchnahme bestimmter Kreditgeber als typisch erwiesen.

Die getroffene Gliederung spielt unter *traditioneller* Betrachtungsweise eine wesentliche Rolle für die Frage nach der Zulässigkeit und Begrenzung der Kreditaufnahme. Kassenkredite dürfen nach dieser Auffassung kurzfristig und in begrenztem Umfange aufgenommen werden, sie sind nach Eingang der ordentlichen Einnahmen zurückzuzahlen. Die Aufnahme von Haushaltskrediten wird mit Skepsis betrachtet; nach dem eng gefaßten Postulat des ausgeglichenen Staatshaushaltes sollen die Ausgaben die ordentlichen Einnahmen nicht übersteigen (vgl. dazu unten, IX, § 2, 8). Einer Sonderbeurteilung unterliegen allerdings Haushaltskredite, die für die Erstellung von Anlagen (Staatsinvestitionen) werbenden Charakters verwendet werden sollen, d. h. für die aus den Erträgen der Anlage die laufende Verzinsung und Tilgung möglich ist oder möglich erscheint.

Wie die folgenden Ausführungen zeigen, lehnen sich die geltenden gesetzlichen Regelungen dieser traditionellen Auffassung stark an.

Die Theorie der Fiskalpolitik erkennt dieser historisch begründeten Entscheidung keine derart wesentliche Bedeutung mehr zu, sondern beurteilt die Zulässigkeit öffentlicher Kreditaufnahme vorwiegend von der gesamtwirtschaftlichen, insbesondere der konjunkturellen Situation aus. Von diesem Standpunkt her mögen die bestehenden rechtlichen Regelungen sich allerdings als hinderlich für den wirtschaftspolitischen Mitteleinsatz erweisen.

### *a) Kassenkredit*

Ein vorübergehender Mangel an Betriebsmitteln (Liquiditätsmangel) der Hauptkasse einer öffentlichen Finanzwirtschaft kann auftreten, obwohl nach einem für das Rechnungsjahr ausgeglichenen Haushaltsplan gewirtschaftet wird. Das kann sein, wenn geplante Ausgaben im Verlauf der Planperiode zu tätigen sind, bevor die geplanten Einnahmen in entsprechendem Umfange eingegangen sind und der Kasse tatsächlich zur Verfügung stehen. Zur Überbrückung derartiger zeitlicher Verschiebungen dient der Kassenkredit[1]).

Wenn die geplanten Einnahmen allerdings auch am Ende der Periode nicht eingegangen sind, muß der Kassenkredit u. U. entstandene Kassenlücken bis in das neue Rechnungsjahr hinein ausgleichen. Daraus hat die Praxis die Übung entwickelt, Kassenkredite auch für den kassenmäßigen Ausgleich eines Haushalts-

---

[1]) Eine Alternativlösung zur Aufnahme von Kassenkrediten ist die Anhäufung eines genügend großen Betriebsmittelfonds, aus dem alle die Einnahmen vorübergehend übersteigenden Ausgaben bestritten werden können, und der beim späteren Eingang der Einnahmen wieder aufgefüllt werden muß.

defizits in Anspruch zu nehmen und ihn damit nachträglich in ein echtes Finanzierungsinstrument umzuwandeln.

Die Exekutivorgane in Bund, Ländern und Gemeinden dürfen Kassenkredite nicht in beliebiger Höhe aufnehmen. Vielmehr wird ein Höchstbetrag (Kreditermächtigung)[1]) von der Legislative der Gebietskörperschaft im Haushaltsgesetz (bei Gemeinden in der Haushaltssatzung) des betreffenden Rechnungsjahres festgesetzt.

Aus der Überbrückungsfunktion des Kassenkredits ergibt sich seine Kurzfristigkeit: Die Laufzeit ist gesetzlich begrenzt. Übliche Schuldarten sind Kontokorrentkredite, Schatzanweisungen, Schatzwechsel und kurzfristige Schuldscheindarlehen. Kassenkredite des Bundes, der Länder und der Sondervermögen des Bundes werden vor allem bei der Bundesbank aufgenommen (gesetzlich begrenzte Kreditplafonds)[1]), jedoch sind auch andere Kreditgeber denkbar und kommen vor, so z. B. die Körperschaften der Sozialversicherung und der Lastenausgleichsfonds als Kreditgeber des Bundes. Die Gemeinden, denen die Bundesbank verschlossen ist, wenden sich regelmäßig an ihre kommunalen Kreditorganisationen.

### *b) Haushaltskredit*

Durch einen Haushaltskredit als Einnahme im haushaltsrechtlichen Sinne soll eine Unterdeckung der Einnahmen gegenüber den geplanten Ausgaben, die ohne Kreditaufnahme zu erwarten wäre, vermieden werden.

Allgemeine rechtliche Regelungen für die Aufnahme von Haushaltskrediten finden sich für den Bund im Grundgesetz, für die Länder in den Verfassungen der Länder und für die Gemeinden in den Gemeindeordnungen der Länder.

So schreibt Satz 1 des Artikels 115 GG vor: „Im Wege des Kredites dürfen Geldmittel nur bei außerordentlichem Bedarf und in der Regel nur für Ausgaben zu werbenden Zwecken und

---

[1]) Die Kreditplafonds der Bundesbank sind also von den Kreditermächtigungen in den Haushaltsgesetzen durchaus zu unterscheiden. Die ersten binden die Bundesbank als speziellen Kreditgeber, die zweiten die öffentliche Finanzwirtschaft als Kreditnehmer.

nur auf Grund eines Bundesgesetzes beschafft werden"[1]). Die Verfassungen der Länder und die Gemeindeordnungen folgen den Grundsätzen dieser Vorschrift in mehr oder weniger strengem Maße; in jedem Falle ist jedoch die Aufnahme von Haushaltskrediten nur zur Finanzierung außerordentlichen Bedarfs zulässig; es wird also untersagt, Kreditmittel als Einnahme in den ordentlichen Haushalt einzustellen.

Wie beim Kassenkredit wird auch beim Haushaltskredit der Exekutive der Gebietskörperschaften die zulässige Gesamthöhe der Kreditaufnahme (Kreditermächtigung) durch die Legislative vorgeschrieben. Das geschieht in der Regel im jährlichen Haushaltsgesetz, bei den Gemeinden in der Haushaltssatzung; hier ist noch eine Genehmigung durch die kommunale Kreditaufsicht erforderlich.

Der Kredit erscheint als Einnahmeposten im Haushaltsplan. Die Finanzierung außerordentlichen Bedarfs durch Haushaltskredite bedeutet in der Regel eine Festlegung der Mittel für längere Zeit. Der Kredit muß darum langfristig zur Verfügung stehen, dem entsprechen als Schuldarten die Anleihe und das langfristig gegebene Schuldscheindarlehen. Ist ausnahmsweise nur eine mittelfristige Bindung erforderlich, so kommt als Schuldart vor allem die verzinsliche Schatzanweisung in Betracht.

Kreditgeber können Banken, Publikum, Sparkassen und andere Kapitalsammelstellen sein.

### 7. Gliederung nach der Ausübung staatlichen Zwanges

Der Leser mag über diesen Gliederungsgesichtspunkt mit Recht insofern erstaunt sein, als oben (§ 1) der öffentliche Kredit als marktwirtschaftliche Einnahme bezeichnet wurde. Diese — heute im allgemeinen wohl mehr oder weniger berechtigte — Bezeichnung setzt allerdings voraus, daß die öffentliche Hand sich wie ein privater Kreditnehmer verhält. Jedoch kann der Staat die ihm eigenen Möglichkeiten derart einsetzen, daß er eine von den privaten Kredit-

---

[1]) Die oben behandelte Möglichkeit der Aufnahme von Kassenkredit ist bei dieser Vorschrift stillschweigend als Ausnahme zugelassen.

nehmern sich unterscheidende Position erhält. Unter diesem Gesichtspunkt ist zu gliedern in freiwilligen und erzwungenen Kredit.

*a) Freiwilliger Kredit*

Dabei vermeidet es die öffentliche Hand, sich durch rechtliche Regelungen auf dem Kapitalmarkt eine Sonderstellung im Vergleich zu privaten Keditnachfragern zu verschaffen.

*b) Erzwungener Kredit*

Der Staat verfügt aber auch über Möglichkeiten, die Übertragung von Kaufkraft an die öffentliche Hand durch rechtlichen oder ökonomischen Zwang zu erreichen, zumindest zu unterstützen:

Durch differenzierende rechtliche Regelungen kann der Staat der öffentlichen Hand eine Sonderstellung gegenüber den Privaten als Nachfrager auf dem Kreditmarkt verschaffen, z. B. durch steuerlich günstigere Behandlung öffentlicher Anleihen oder durch ein Verbot wie auch anderweitige Beschränkung privater Emissionen.

Der Staat kann auf bestimmte private Wirtschaftssubjekte auch unmittelbar einen rechtlichen Zwang zur Kreditgewährung an die öffentliche Hand ausüben, z. B. durch die Auflegung einer Zwangsanleihe.

Daneben kann sich der Staat — unter bestimmten institutionellen Voraussetzungen — durch geldwirtschaftliche Maßnahmen, wie durch die Ausgabe von Staatspapiergeld oder durch eine verstärkte Anspannung des Notenbankkredits, zusätzliche Kaufkraft verschaffen. Wird dadurch der Geldwert vermindert, so entspricht dem Einkommen der Privaten — sofern ihr Nominaleinkommen gleichgeblieben oder nicht in entsprechendem Maße mitgewachsen ist — eine geringere Menge an Gütern und Diensten. Die auf Geldeinheiten lautenden Vermögensteile der Privaten haben real ebenfalls an Wert verloren. Auf diese Weise kann der Staat sich übrigens auch teilweise oder sogar annähernd völlig von seinen auf Nominalwerte lautenden Schulden befreien. Aufgrund solcher Fakten, die z. B. in der großen Inflation der Zwanziger Jahre eine wesentliche

Rolle gespielt haben, kann der Staat seinen Anteil am Sozialprodukt vergrößern, ohne von den oben geschilderten rechtlichen Maßnahmen Gebrauch zu machen, aber auch, ohne daß Private freiwillig auf die Ausübung ihrer Kaufkraft verzichtet und dem Staat Kredit eingeräumt hätten.

## § 3. Öffentlicher Kredit und monetäre Nachfrage

Im folgenden soll der Einfluß behandelt werden, den der öffentliche Kredit auf die umlaufende Geldmenge und die monetäre Nachfrage in der Gesamtwirtschaft ausübt. Damit wird die fiskalpolitische Fragestellung wiederum aufgegriffen.

### 1. Schöpfungskredit und Übertragungskredit

In der Theorie des öffentlichen Kredits findet man zu dieser Frage Aussagen, die hier ganz vereinfacht dargestellt werden sollen. Danach besteht ein wesentlicher Unterschied im Hinblick auf die Veränderung der Geldmenge darin, bei wem die staatlichen Kredittitel untergebracht werden. Eine Unterbringung bei der Zentralbank und bei den Geschäftsbanken würde eine Expansion der Geldmenge mit sich bringen, sei es in der Form von Bargeld oder von Giralgeld der Zentralbank, sei es in der Form von Kreditbankengiralgeld; die Bankbilanzen verlängern sich. Diese Art der Kreditierung wird auch als *„Schöpfungskredit"* bezeichnet. Anders wäre es, wenn die staatlichen Kredittitel beim Publikum unmittelbar oder mittelbar bei Kapitalsammelstellen untergebracht würden. Hier würde die Geldmenge nicht vermehrt werden, es handelte sich also lediglich um *„Übertragungskredit"*. — Umgekehrt würde eine echte, d. h. nicht etwa durch neue Kreditaufnahme finanzierte, Tilgung von im Bankensystem untergebrachten Schuldtiteln die umlaufende Geldmenge kontrahieren lassen, während eine solche Tilgung von im Publikum untergebrachten Titeln die umlaufende Geldmenge unberührt ließe.

Aus all dem ist auch der Schluß gezogen worden, daß selbst bei gleichbleibendem Schuldenstand der öffentlichen Hand eine Manipulation der Geldmenge dadurch möglich wäre, daß auslaufende Schulden der einen Unterbringungskategorie durch solche einer anderen Kategorie ersetzt werden. Würde die öffentliche Hand Schuldtitel, die bisher im Bankensystem untergebracht waren, mit Hilfe von Geldmitteln tilgen, die sie sich durch Unterbringung von Schuldtiteln im Publikum beschafft, wäre die Folge eine Kontraktion der Geldmenge, vice versa eine Expansion, wenn man nämlich bisher im Publikum untergebrachte Schulden mit Hilfe einer Aufnahme von Schulden tilgt, die jetzt im Bankensystem untergebracht werden. Aus diesen Wirkungen auf die Geldmenge wird vielfach auf gleichgerichtete Nachfragewirkungen geschlossen.

2. Wirkungen auf die gesamte Nachfrage

Inwiefern bestehen wirklich diese unterschiedlichen Wirkungen der Unterbringung öffentlicher Kredittitel, insbesondere, inwiefern hat ihre Unterbringung beim Publikum tatsächlich eine *neutrale* Wirkung auf die gesamte Nachfrage nach Gütern und Diensten?

Vorwegnehmend ist zu betonen, daß auch bei dem sogenannten Übertragungskredit der beschriebenen Art eine expandierende Wirkung auf die gesamte monetäre Nachfrage dann auftritt, wenn durch den Akt der Kreditgewährung vorher stillgelegt gewesene Gelder (Barhorte und Deposithorte im Sinne H. Gestrichs) in den Kreislauf dadurch zurückfließen, daß der Staat diese Mittel wieder ausgibt. In der Sprache der älteren Geldtheorie: Die Umlaufgeschwindigkeit des Geldes wird erhöht. Man kann in solchem Fall von einer *Aktivierung* von Geldmitteln sprechen („müßiges“ Geld wird zu „aktivem“ Geld).

Abgesehen davon würde der Ausdruck „Übertragung“ im Sinne einer neutralen Wirkung auf die gesamte Nachfrage bedeuten müssen, daß die Privaten deswegen, weil von ihnen Staatstitel gezeichnet werden, um soviel weniger nachfragen, wie der Staat nunmehr mit Hilfe der überlassenen Geldmittel mehr nachfragt[1]). Das ist fraglich aus mehreren Gründen:

Eine Zeichnung von Staatstiteln bedingt keineswegs, daß die Zeichner weniger *konsumieren*[2]). Sie mögen vielmehr lediglich, anstatt ihre Ersparnisse bei Sparinstituten, bei Banken oder in privaten Wertpapieren anzulegen, eine alternative Wahl derart treffen, daß sie nunmehr staatliche Kredittitel kaufen. Es müßte sich aber um eine zusätzliche Ersparnis, d. h. um eine wirkliche Einschränkung der konsumtiven Nachfrage der Privaten handeln, wenn der Name „Übertragungskredit“ im Sinne eines geldmengen- und nachfrageneutralen Kredits gerechtfertigt sein soll.

Zum anderen ist zu fragen, ob etwa aus der Zeichnung von Staatstiteln durch das Publikum eine Einschränkung der privaten *Investitions*nachfrage zwingend folgt. Auch das ist zu verneinen. Wenn nämlich die Unternehmer zur Finanzierung ihrer Investitionen anstelle von Krediten aus dem Publikum Bankkredite erhalten, muß ihre Nachfrage nicht notwendig eingeschränkt werden. Allgemein läßt sich zunächst sagen, daß wo immer der Staatskredit auch untergebracht wird, eine gleichzeitig erfolgende Kontraktion des Kredits an private Unternehmer die privaten Investitionen ceteris paribus einschränken wird. Daraus kann sich eine geldmengen- und nachfrageneutrale Gesamtwir-

---

[1]) Übrigens käme es dann auch noch darauf an, welche Güter der Staat im Verhältnis zu den Privaten nachfragen würde. Wären es ausländische Güter oder Grundstücke, während die Privaten inländische Produkte gekauft hätten, so würde die monetäre Nachfrage nach dem inländischen Sozialprodukt ceteris paribus geringer werden. Würde andererseits der Staat Inlandsprodukte kaufen, während die Privaten Auslandsprodukte nachgefragt hätten, so würde selbst bei privater Konsumeinschränkung die Inlandsnachfrage wachsen.

[2]) Die unter der Voraussetzung der Konsumfreiheit, d. h. der freien Entscheidungsmöglichkeit der Einkommensbezieher zur Verwendung ihres Einkommens zur Konsumtion oder zur Ersparnis sowohl theoretisch als auch empirisch sich ergebende Konsumfunktion weist den Konsum und damit die Höhe der Gesamtersparnis ceteris paribus als ziemlich fest bestimmt durch die Höhe des verfügbaren Einkommens aus. Eine Zeichnung von Staatstiteln wird daher ohne besondere Nebenbedingungen (etwa Rationierung in Notzeiten) nur die Anlage in privaten Schuldtiteln zurückdrängen, nicht aber die privaten Konsumausgaben.

kung ergeben. Die Frage ist nun, unter welchen Bedingungen diese gleichzeitige Kontraktion der Kredite an Private zu folgern ist.

Im Falle der Unterbringung von staatlichen Kredittiteln bei der *Zentralbank* könnte diese von ihren Möglichkeiten Gebrauch machen, den Kreditspielraum der privaten Geschäftsbanken einzuengen, etwa, indem sie die gesetzlichen Mindestreserveanforderungen heraufsetzt und/oder die Rediskontkontingente herabsetzt. Bei mangelnden Überschußreserven und voller Inanspruchnahme der begrenzten Refinanzierungsmöglichkeiten müßten die Geschäftsbanken ihr Kreditvolumen einschränken; im äußersten Fall müßten sie vielleicht sogar bestehende Kreditzusagen zurücknehmen, was die Einschränkung der privaten Investitionen bewirken würde. Es muß aber betont werden, daß hier ein besonderes Eingreifen der Zentralbank erforderlich ist, um den geschilderten Effekt zu erreichen. Unternimmt sie nichts, z. B. wenn Konjunkturlage und Außenhandelssituation es gestatten, so wird in der Tat der Fall des geldmengen- und nachfrageexpandierenden „Schöpfungskredites" verwirklicht.

Wird dagegen der Staatskredit bei den *Geschäftsbanken* untergebracht, so kann auch ohne besondere politische Maßnahmen der Zentralbank eine Kreditrestriktion gegenüber privaten Kreditnehmern Platz greifen. Dann nämlich, wenn die Geschäftsbanken keine Überschußreserven haben und auch sonst für sie keine Refinanzierungsmöglichkeiten bei der Zentralbank bestehen und demzufolge bei bestehenden Pflichtreservesätzen und gegebenem Einlagenbestand dem Staat nur in dem Maße Kredit gewähren können, wie sie den Kredit gegenüber privaten Unternehmern einschränken.

Aber auch die Kreditnachfrageseite ist zu berücksichtigen. Da der Staat nicht in dem Maße Rentabilitätsüberlegungen anzustellen braucht wie private Kreditnehmer, kann er bei begrenztem Kreditangebot durch attraktive Konditionen, insbesondere hohen Zins dafür sorgen, daß seine Kreditnachfrage zum Zuge kommt, während die Investitionsneigung der Unternehmer und damit auch ihre Kreditnachfrage wegen erhöhter Zinsbelastung und verschärfter Kreditbedingungen zurückgeht.

Außer durch diese marktwirtschaftlichen Mittel kann der Staat in besonderen Situationen durch Zwangsmaßnahmen private Kreditnahme zugunsten staatlicher zurückdrängen.

Wenn im Gegensatz zur bisherigen Voraussetzung die Geschäftsbanken Überschußreserven haben und mit deren Hilfe eine Kreditexpansion vollzogen wird, wird eine Unterbringung staatlicher Schuldtitel bei den Geschäftsbanken ebenso wie bei der Zentralbank einen „Schöpfungskredit" bewirken.

Zeichnet das *Publikum* die staatlichen Kredittitel, so wird es ebenfalls nur dann zu einer Einschränkung der Kredite für private Investitionen kommen müssen, wenn die Geschäftsbanken keine Überschußreserven und/oder Refinanzierungsmöglichkeiten haben[1]). Denn zwischen der Zeichnung durch das Publikum und der Situation der Geschäftsbanken bestehen bestimmte Zusammenhänge:

Sofern es bei der Zeichnung der staatlichen Schuldtitel nicht zu einer Aktivierung von Bar- und Deposithorten kommt, ist der Erwerb der staatlichen Schuldtitel erstens durch dementsprechende Auflösung *bestehender* privater Sparguthaben möglich. Wenn nun die staatlichen Sichtguthaben bei den Geschäftsbanken steigen, ohne daß die Sichtguthaben des Publikums zurückgehen, wären höhere Mindestreserven erforderlich. Sind aber keine Überschußreserven oder Refinanzierungsmöglichkeiten bei der Zentralbank vorhanden, so sind die Geschäftsbanken gezwungen, die Kreditzusagen für private Unternehmer einzuschränken, um auf diese Weise die Gesamtsumme an Sichtverpflichtungen konstant zu halten und damit die sonst erforderliche Erhöhung der Mindestreserven zu umgehen.

Werden dagegen als zweite Möglichkeit Anleihen aus *laufender* privater Ersparnis gezeichnet, die im übrigen als gleichbleibend angenommen wird, so gehen nicht nur die Zugänge auf private Sparkonten zurück, sondern auch die Möglichkeiten für private Unternehmer, langfristige Papiere auf dem Kapitalmarkt unterzubringen, werden eingeschränkt.

Es braucht nicht betont zu werden, daß für diese Aus-

[1]) Selbstverständlich gilt auch dabei die Voraussetzung, daß die Zentralbank keine liquidisierende Politik (auch nicht durch Offenmarktpolitik) betreibt.

führungen durchweg die Voraussetzung gelten soll, daß die privaten Haushalte nicht zusätzlich sparen, d. h. ihre bisherige Konsumnachfrage nicht einschränken. Nur dann können nämlich die Liquiditätseinschränkungen auftreten, die unter den beschriebenen Bedingungen einen bremsenden Einfluß auf die private Investition ausüben werden. Zusammenfassend lassen sich diese Bedingungen dahingehend charakterisieren, daß eine *automatische,* d. h. ohne besondere politische Maßnahmen der Zentralbank eintretende Einschränkung der privaten Investitionen als Folge öffentlicher Schuldaufnahme nur dann zu erwarten ist, wenn die Unterbringung der Schuldtitel beim Publikum oder bei den Geschäftsbanken nicht nur keine Aktivierung von „müßigem Geld" mit sich bringt, sondern auch den Geschäftsbanken Überschußreserven und Refinanzierungsmöglichkeiten bei der Zentralbank fehlen.

Weiterhin ist noch auf folgenden wichtigen Tatbestand hinzuweisen, der den oben in diesem Abschnitt behandelten Fall der Unterbringung von Staatsschuldtiteln bei den Geschäftsbanken ergänzend beleuchtet: Werden öffentliche Kredittitel bei der Zentralbank untergebracht, ohne daß gleichzeitig Maßnahmen der Zentralbank mit dem Ziel einer Reduktion des privaten Kreditvolumens erfolgen, so erhöhen die zusätzlichen Staatsausgaben bei unveränderten Ausgaben der Privaten die Liquidität der gesamten Wirtschaft. Damit wächst aber auch die Liquidität der Geschäftsbanken (Überschußreserven). Es wächst dann auch die Kreditfähigkeit der Geschäftsbanken und damit wiederdie Chance, daß nicht nur der Staat weitere Kredittitel im Bankensystem unterbringen kann, sondern auch, daß Private neben dem Staat auf der Grundlage des Kredits ihre Investitionsnachfrage erhöhen können, zumindest aber, sie nicht einschränken müssen.

Aus dem Vorhergehenden zeigt sich die große Bedeutung, die die Möglichkeit der Unterbringung von Staatstiteln bei der Zentralbank (vgl. dazu § 2, 3 und § 5 dieses Kapitels) und die Politik der Zentralbank zur Beeinflussung der Kreditpolitik der Geschäftsbanken haben.

## § 4. Grenzen der Staatsverschuldung

Im Zusammenhang mit dem Ansteigen der Staatsverschuldung, insbesondere in Kriegszeiten, deren Entwicklung noch in § 5 an einigen Beispielen zu zeigen ist, sind immer wieder Fragen nach der maximal möglichen Höhe, den „Grenzen der Staatsverschuldung" gestellt worden. Dabei handelt es sich im wesentlichen um drei Fragestellungen, einmal um die nach der möglichen Begrenztheit der nominellen Kreditaufnahme, zweitens um die Frage nach den Grenzen der „realen" güterwirtschaftlichen Wirksamkeit aufgenommener Staatskredite und schließlich um einen Fragenkomplex wirtschaftspolitischer Natur: Ist eine hohe Staatsverschuldung mit gewissen wirtschafts- und sozialpolitischen Zielsetzungen kompatibel?

### 1. Begrenztheit der nominellen Kreditaufnahme

#### *a) Institutionelle „Grenzen"*

Durch institutionelle Regelungen kann öffentlichen Haushaltswirtschaften die unbeschränkte Kreditaufnahme verwehrt sein. Hinzuweisen ist in diesem Zusammenhang einmal auf mögliche Deckungs- und Einlösungsvorschriften bei der Zentralbank und Mindestreservevorschriften bei den Kreditbanken, die diesen Instituten die unbegrenzte Aufnahme staatlicher Schuldtitel unmöglich machen können. Andererseits kann der Umfang staatlicher Kreditaufnahme auch direkt durch gesetzlich vorgegebene Kreditplafonds begrenzt sein, vgl. dazu § 2, 3 und 4. Obwohl diese Regelungen in einer verfassungsrechtlich fixierten Situation der staatlichen Kreditaufnahme und damit dem finanzpolitischen Handeln kurzfristig unüberschreitbare Barrieren setzen mögen, bleibt festzustellen, daß diese institutionellen „Grenzen" niemals notwendige und absolute Gültigkeit beanspruchende ökonomische Grenzen für die Staatsverschuldung darstellen. Das läßt sich besonders deutlich aus dem mehr oder minder verdeckten Aufheben solcher institutionellen Begrenzungen in Kriegszeiten augenfällig machen.

Es ist also zu fragen, ob *ökonomische* Grenzen für die staatliche nominelle Kreditaufnahme bestehen, über die die Staatsverschuldung — ganz abgesehen von irgendwelchen institutionellen „Grenzen" — auf jeden Fall nicht hinausgehen könnte.

### *b) Grenzen für die Schuldaufnahme aus dem Kreislauf?*

Bei sehr einfacher Betrachtungsweise könnte die Idee aufkommen, daß sowohl für die privaten Kreditsuchenden als auch für die öffentlichen Haushaltswirtschaften nur ein durch private Sparbeträge gespeister begrenzter Kreditfonds zur Verfügung steht, nach dessen Erschöpfung „nichts mehr zu holen" ist.

Eine solche Vorstellung täuscht nicht nur im Hinblick auf die grundsätzliche Möglichkeit einer über die privaten Sparentscheidungen hinausgehenden Geldschöpfung (ein Thema der allgemeinen Geld- und Kredittheorie), sondern darüber hinaus auch im Hinblick auf die spezifischen Möglichkeiten des Staates, sich Zugang zu dementsprechenden Kreditquellen zu verschaffen.

Die makroökonomische Kreislaufanalyse vermag durchaus zu zeigen, daß die Auffassung, nach der die privaten Ersparnisse u. U. nicht ausreichen mögen, um den Staat mehr ausgeben zu lassen als er aus ordentlichen Einnahmen einnimmt, fehlgeht. Von M. Kalecki ist der Satz formuliert worden, daß ein Staatsdefizit sich selber finanziere, das soll heißen, daß Staatsdefizit und private Investition immer durch eine private Ersparnis in gleicher Höhe aufgewogen werden.

Das mag vereinfacht wie folgt dargestellt werden:

Gemäß einer bekannten Bilanzgleichung der Volkswirtschaftlichen Gesamtrechnung ist das Nettosozialprodukt zu Marktpreisen $E_m$ gleich der gesamten monetären Nachfrage, die sich aus der privaten Konsumnachfrage C, der privaten Netto-investitionsnachfrage I und der staatlichen Nachfrage nach Gütern und Diensten $A_{st}$ zusammensetzt[1]):

$$(1) \qquad E_m = C + I + A_{st}$$

Andererseits ist das Nettosozialprodukt zu Marktpreisen nach der Verwendungsseite aufgeteilt gleich der Summe aus privater Konsumtion C, privater Ersparnis S und den Steuern T[1]):

$$(2) \qquad E_m = C + S + T$$

Wenn die Staatsausgaben mit den Steuern übereinstimmen:

$$(3a) \qquad A_{st} = T$$

so ist durch Gleichsetzung von (1) und (2) und Kürzung der jeweils identischen Glieder leicht zu sehen, daß

$$(4a) \qquad S = I$$

gelten muß.

Unterscheiden wir dagegen den anderen Fall, daß die Staatsausgaben höher als die Steuereinnahmen gewesen sind, so hat sich ein Defizit Kr (Stromgröße) ergeben, und es gilt die folgende Beziehung:

$$(3b) \qquad A_{st} = T + Kr$$

Setzen wir nun (3b) in (1) ein, so ergibt sich nach Gleichsetzung mit (2) und Kürzung der jeweils identischen Glieder:

$$(4b) \qquad S = I + Kr$$

Man kann also in der Tat sagen, daß auch bei einem Defizit die private ex post-Ersparnis (im Sinne des nicht konsumierten Einkommens) gemäß (4b) immer gerade so hoch ist, daß sie nicht nur die privaten Nettoinvestitionen, sondern auch das staatliche Defizit deckt.

Diese Aussage, als solche unbestreitbar hinzunehmen, schildert aber nur eine ex post-Identität. Sie ist insofern trivial, als sie nur die Selbstverständlichkeit feststellt, daß, wenn der Staat mehr an den privaten Sektor ausgegeben hat (durch $A_{st}$) als er von ihm erhalten hat (durch T), der private Sektor notwendig — in Höhe der gleichen Differenz Kr — mehr an Einkommen bekommen haben muß

---

[1]) Wir vernachlässigen in der folgenden Betrachtung aus Übersichtsgründen die staatlichen Erwerbseinkünfte, den Außenbeitrag und die Transferausgaben der öffentlichen Hand. (Vgl. dazu Volkswirtschaftliche Gesamtrechnung, IX, § 4, 2).

als er ausgegeben hat, d. h. in Höhe von Kr über seine Invistion I hinaus gespart hat.

Es könnte zwar sein, daß die privaten Haushalte diese über die private Investition hinausgehende Ersparnis auch ex ante, d. h. von vornherein, geplant haben, indem sie in dieser Höhe auf Konsum verzichten, um mit den so gesparten Mitteln das staatliche Defizit über den Kauf von Anleihepapieren zu finanzieren[1]); keineswegs gilt das aber allgemein.

Es mag vielmehr so sein, daß die Mittel, die der Staat aufnimmt, um die über seine Einnahmen hinausgehenden Ausgaben zu tätigen, von der Zentralbank oder den Kreditbanken geschöpft sind, während die private Konsum- und Investitionsnachfrage keine Einschränkungen erfährt, d. h. also auch keine höhere Ersparnis geplant wird. Da nun die staatliche Nachfrage steigt, kommt es zu einer allgemeinen Einkommenssteigerung, die — wie am Modell erkennbar — eine ex post-Erhöhung der privaten Ersparnis bedeutet, die nun aber — im Unterschied zu dem eben behandelten Fall — über ihre ex ante geplante Höhe hinausgeht. Erfolgt daraufhin als Reaktion der Privaten auf diese Einkommenssteigerung eine erhöhte Konsum- und Investitionsnachfrage, so ergeben sich im weiteren Verlauf erneute Einkommens- und Nachfragesteigerungen, d. h. es folgt ein kumulativer Expansionsprozeß[2]).

Weiter ist zu sagen, daß solche durch die Einschleusung zusätzlicher Kaufkraft entstehenden Nachfrageexpansionen

---

1) In diesem Fall halten sich staatliche Ausgabensteigerung und private Nachfrageeinschränkung durch verringerte Konsumneigung, d. h. erhöhte Sparneigung, die Waage, so daß das Gleichgewichtseinkommen erhalten bleibt. Gleichgewicht kann auch erhalten bleiben, wenn Konsum und Ersparnis unverändert bleiben, dafür aber die private Investition eingeschränkt wird, vgl. dazu oben § 3.

2) Ob dieser Prozeß zu einem neuen Gleichgewichtseinkommen konvergiert, hängt vornehmlich von den Investitionsreaktionen und vom weiteren Verhalten des Staates ab. Bei konstanter (autonomer) Investition und unverändert auf dem „neuen" Ausgabenniveau verharrender Staatsnachfrage stellt dieser Expansionsvorgang nichts anderes dar als den bekannten Multiplikatorprozeß, der das Einkommen gegen den neuen Gleichgewichtswert konvergieren läßt, bei dem die ex ante-Ersparnis mit der gestiegenen ex post-Ersparnis wieder übereinstimmt.

dann zu einer inflatorischen Entwicklung führen, wenn die reale Produktion nicht entsprechend der gestiegenen Nachfrage ausgeweitet werden kann, z. B. bei Vollbeschäftigung und/oder ausgelasteten Kapazitäten. Beiläufig sei bemerkt, daß sich in einem solchen Fall die Einkommenssteigerungen wegen der Preiserhöhungen vorwiegend als Gewinnsteigerungen niederschlagen; diese ex post eingetretenen ungeplanten Ersparniserhöhungen bei den Unternehmerhaushalten werden auch als „windfall-profits" bezeichnet. Praktische Bedeutung hat dieser Zusammenhang insbesondere für die Erklärung von Kriegsgewinnen. Aus dem zuletzt Gesagten lassen sich gewisse wirtschaftspolitische Schlußfolgerungen für die anzustrebende Höhe der staatlichen Kreditaufnahme ziehen, auf die wir unten noch zu sprechen kommen werden. Wie auch immer aber diese Schlußfolgerungen lauten mögen, es bleibt festzustellen, daß die geplante Ersparnis der Privaten im Sinne des ex ante vorgenommenen Konsumverzichtes keine unüberschreitbare Grenze für die nominelle Kreditaufnahme des Staates bildet.

### *c) Grenzen für die Schuldsumme aus der Vermögensbilanz?*

Wenn soweit aus der Kreislaufanalyse keine Grenzen für die laufende Kreditaufnahme (als Stromgröße) ersichtlich sind, bleibt doch zu fragen, ob der Höhe der Staatsschuldsumme (als Bestandsgröße, die sich aus der Kumulation aller Schuldaufnahmen abzüglich aller Tilgungen ermittelt) Grenzen gesetzt sind. Soweit es sich dabei um eine innere Schuldaufnahme handelt und soweit eine Geldverfassung ohne „bremsende" Deckungsregeln und auch ohne das Fehlen sonstiger institutionellen „Grenzen" vorausgesetzt werden können, ist auch hier keine Begrenzung für die Staatsschuld erkennbar. Wie Otto Donner (Weltwirtschaftliches Archiv, 1942) festgestellt hat, kann sich dann weder ein Ungleichgewicht in der Vermögensbilanz noch die Gefahr einer Insolvenz des Staates ergeben:

„Sehr vereinfachend, aber doch den Kern der Sache treffend, kann man sagen, daß die innere Staatsschuld eine Schuld an sich selbst ist. In seiner Eigenschaft als Besitzer von Staatspapieren wird das Volk Gläubiger des Staates, also seiner selbst, und ebenso bringt es in seiner Eigenschaft als Steuerzahler die für die Bedienung seiner Kapitalansprüche gegen den Staat erforderlichen Mittel selbst auf. Die Zunahme der Staatsverschuldung kann deshalb niemals ein bilanzielles Ungleichgewicht herbeiführen. Was bei den Privaten an Forderungen gegen den Staat zuwächst, erhöht gleichzeitig die Aufbringungsverpflichtung der Privaten um genau den gleichen Betrag. Weder wird das Volk im ganzen durch Geldkapitalbildung in der Form des Erwerbs von Staatstiteln reicher, noch durch Zunahme der Staatsschuld, die ja nur die andere Seite desselben Vorganges ist, ärmer .... Es wird lediglich von einer Tasche in die andere gezahlt."

### 2. Die Begrenzung der realen Wirksamkeit des Staatskredits

Die bisher festgestellte Möglichkeit eines „unbegrenzten" staatlichen Kredits bezieht sich aber nur auf die nominelle Kreditaufnahme; es ist jetzt zu fragen, inwieweit monetäre Kreditaufnahmen auch real gesehen als zusätzliche Verfügung über Güter und Dienste wirksam gemacht werden können.

Solange noch nicht Vollbeschäftigung und/oder Kapazitätsauslastung besteht, wird eine zusätzliche kreditfinanzierte Nachfrage des Staates ohne große Schwierigkeiten eine zusätzliche Güterproduktion hervorrufen, so daß dem zusätzlichen Kredit auch eine zusätzliche staatliche Verfügung über Güter und Dienste entspricht. Problematischer ist dagegen die Situation bei Vollbeschäftigung und/oder Kapazitätsauslastung.

#### *a) Auswirkungen zusätzlichen Staatskredites in einer vollbeschäftigten Verkehrswirtschaft*

Zunächst sei eine Verkehrswirtschaft vorausgesetzt, wobei es in diesem Zusammenhang insbesondere darauf ankommt, daß weder Produktionsvorschriften, Preis- und Lohnstop-Verordnungen noch Rationierungen existieren; ferner sei Vollbeschäftigung gegeben. Wie schon unter 1b) beschrieben, führt eine zusätzliche kreditfinanzierte Nachfrage des Staates dann zu einer nominellen Einkommens-

und Preisniveau-Steigerung, wenn nicht die Privaten ex ante durch Minderung ihrer Konsumnachfrage eine Erhöhung ihrer Ersparnisse bewirken oder aber eine Einschränkung der privaten Investitionsnachfrage erfolgt. Da — wie in § 3 erläutert wurde — eine Kreditaufnahme des Staates nicht notwendig zu einer Einschränkung der privaten Nachfrage führen muß, mag es unter den genannten Bedingungen sehr wohl zu einer solchen Preisniveau- und nominellen Einkommenssteigerung kommen. Aus Gründen einer vereinfachten Darstellung sei als „Periode" eine „mittlere"[1]) Reaktionszeit (time-lag) bezeichnet, die zwischen der Entstehung privaten Einkommens und dem marktmäßigen Wirksamwerden der von ihm bestimmten Konsum- und Investitionsnachfrage verstreicht.

Gehen wir davon aus, daß vor der zusätzlichen Kreditaufnahme des Staates zu Nachfragezwecken nicht nur Vollbeschäftigung bei ausgelasteter Kapazität gegeben sei, sondern auch Nachfragegleichgewicht, d. h., daß das auf den Markt kommende gesamte Angebot an Gütern und Diensten, zu Preisen der Vorperiode bewertet, der gesamten Wertsumme der Nachfrage (private Konsum- und Investitionsnachfrage und staatliche Nachfrage) entspricht. In dieser ersten Periode würde daher das Preisniveau konstant auf dem Wert der Vorperiode beharren können. Jetzt werde in der folgenden zweiten Periode eine zusätzliche staatliche Nachfrage geltend gemacht, ohne daß die private Nachfrage zurückgeht, mit anderen Worten: die zusätzliche staatliche Nachfrage würde durch neu in den Kreislauf fließende Mittel finanziert. Dann überwiegt die Nachfrage das Angebot zu Preisen der Vorperiode, und es kommt zu einer Steigerung der Preise und der Nominaleinkommen der Privaten. Da jedoch die Erhöhung der privaten effektiven Nachfrage aufgrund dieser höheren Nominaleinkommen voraussetzungsgemäß erst in der nächsten dritten Peri-

---

[1]) Eine Berücksichtigung des Tatbestandes, daß in der Realität unterschiedliche Reaktionszeiten vorliegen, insbesondere was den time-lag bei Konsumtion einerseits und Investition andererseits anbelangt, würde nur die Darstellung erschweren, ohne den im Text beschriebenen Prozeß grundsätzlich aufzuheben.

ode erfolgen kann, gelingt es dem Staat, in dieser zweiten Periode durch seine Kreditaufnahme eine höhere reale Verfügung über Güter und Dienste auf Kosten der Privaten durchzusetzen, denn die Nachfrage der letzteren ist noch am kleineren Einkommen der Vorperiode orientiert, während der Staat im Gegensatz dazu bereits jetzt größere Mengen an Gütern und Diensten bei steigenden Preisen kauft. Würde nun die nominelle staatliche Nachfrage in der nächsten, dritten, Periode die gleiche Größe behalten wie in der zweiten, so würde die reale Verfügung des Staates über Güter und Dienste in der dritten Periode zurückgehen, weil jetzt die Privaten mit dem höheren Einkommen aus der Vorperiode nachfragen und so einiges von dem verlorenen Terrain an realer Güterversorgung zurückgewinnen. Bei dem vorausgesetzten unelastischen Angebot an Gütern und Diensten käme es zu einer weiteren Preissteigerung, wodurch wegen der zunächst vorausgesetzten konstanten nominellen Nachfrage des Staates dieser einen Kaufkraftverlust erfahren würde. Nur dann, wenn der Staat eine weitere kreditfinanzierte Steigerung seiner nominellen Nachfrage in der dritten Periode vornehmen würde, könnte es ihm gelingen, die reale Wirksamkeit des in der Vorperiode aufgenommenen Kredites aufrechtzuerhalten, d. h. sich die gegenüber dem Ausgangspunkt höhere Güterversorgung weiterhin zu sichern.

Unter diesen Umständen würden Preis- und Nominaleinkommenssteigerung in der dritten Periode größer sein als ohne Erhöhung der Kredite mit der Folge, daß auch die private Nachfrage der nächsten Periode verstärkt steigt, woraus sich für den Staat erneut die Notwendigkeit zur nominellen Kreditausweitung ergeben würde, wenn er den Umfang seiner Güterversorgung aufrechterhalten (geschweige, wenn er sie ausdehnen) will. Wieder würde es zu erheblichen Preis- und Nominaleinkommenssteigerungen kommen usf. Dieser Inflationsprozeß, dessen Stärke wesentlich von der Größe des durch Kredite zu finanzierenden zusätzlichen Staatsbedarfes, von der Konsum- und Investitionsneigung der Privaten und von ihrer Reaktionsgeschwindigkeit abhängen würde[1]), zeigt auf, daß der realen Wirksamkeit der Schöpfungskreditfinanzierung, wenn sie nicht dauernd und schließlich erheblich gesteigert wird, in einer vollbeschäftigten Verkehrswirtschaft enge Grenzen gesetzt sind.

Nur bei begrenzter Schöpfungskreditfinanzierung zusätzlicher Staatsausgaben dürfte sich der Inflationsprozeß in beherrschbaren Maßen halten. Andernfalls würde die fortschreitende Zerrüttung der Währung eine ungestörte Aufrechterhaltung der staatlichen Güterversorgung letztlich in Frage stellen.

In einem verkehrswirtschaftlichen System wäre also die Finanzierung zusätzlichen Staatsbedarfs von erheblicher Größenordnung, wie in Kriegen, überwiegend durch Steuern vorzuziehen — trotz der dadurch eintretenden negativen Leistungsanreize.

### *b) Die Bedeutung der staatlichen Kreditaufnahme in einer gelenkten Wirtschaft*

Geht der Staat allerdings zu direkter Steuerung der Produktion über, bedient er sich Preis- und Lohnstop-Verordnungen sowie der Rationierung der Konsumgüter, so können — wie Otto Donner in dem oben bereits erwähnten Aufsatz gezeigt hat — die Grenzen für eine real wirksam bleibende staatliche Kreditnahme erheblich hinausgeschoben werden. Theoretisch kann der private Bedarf an Gütern und Diensten auf das Existenzminimum festgesetzt und durch Produktionsbefehle einerseits und Rationierung andererseits auch durchgesetzt werden. Der private Konsum hätte dann gleichbleibend die nominelle Höhe des zu den gestoppten Preisen bewerteten rationierten Existenzbedarfes. Die private Investition würde auf den absolut notwendigen Ersatz — ebenfalls zu vorgeschriebenen Preisen bewertet — beschränkt sein. Alles, was vom realen Sozialprodukt nicht für die eben genannten privaten Zwecke abgezweigt wird, steht dem Staat zur Verfügung.

---

1) Bei längerdauernden Inflationsprozessen kommt es zumeist zu einer Steigerung dieser Reaktionsgeschwindigkeit.

Bewertet man diesen maximalen realen Staatsbedarf ebenfalls zu den konstant gehaltenen Preisen, so hätte man den maximalen Finanzbedarf ermittelt, der notwendig und hinreichend ist, um diesen realen Staatsbedarf zu erwerben. Dieser Finanzbedarf wird zumTeil durch Steuern gedeckt. Nur soweit das nicht der Fall ist, ist eine Kreditaufnahme sinnvoll, denn eine höhere Kreditaufnahme als durch die Differenz zwischen maximalem Finanzbedarf und Steueraufkommen angegeben wird, würde dem Staat nicht mehr an Gütern und Diensten geben können, als er durch seine Mengenregulierungen ohnehin für sich reserviert hat.

Die genannte Differenz kann — insbesondere bei geringer Steuerbelastung — recht hoch werden, d. h. die „Grenze", innerhalb derer der Staatskredit real wirksam bleibt, kann unter diesen Umständen recht weit gesteckt sein. Die Unterbringungsart spielt hier nur insofern eine Rolle, als in dem Maße, wie der Staatskredit durch Geld- und Kreditschöpfung und nicht durch private freiwillige Anleihezeichnung oder durch gesetzliches Zwangssparen finanziert wird, eine Aufstauung an Liquidität beim Publikum entsteht, die eine spätere Aufhebung der Rationierung sehr problematisch machen kann.

Insbesondere bei der Finanzierung des Zweiten Weltkrieges ist man den hier geschilderten Weg — wenigstens in Ansätzen — gegangen. Für die Kriegsfinanzierung scheint diese Aufhebung der verkehrswirtschaftlichen Ordnung — vor allem wegen höherer Leistungsanreize infolge einer „milden" Besteuerung — in der Tat ein geringeres Übel zu sein als eine extrem hohe Besteuerung bei freier Verkehrswirtschaft.

### 3. Die Auswirkungen einer hohen Staatsverschuldung unter wirtschafts- und sozialpolitischen Aspekten

Besondere politische Umstände mögen ergeben, daß der Staat sein absoluten Vorrang beanspruchendes Ziel einer maximalen Güterinanspruchnahme bei mäßiger Steuerbelastung zu erreichen versucht, so daß zur Erreichung dieses

Zieles die Ausnutzung einer möglichst hohen real wirksamen Kreditaufnahme erforderlich wird. Daraus können sich unerwünschte Nebenwirkungen ergeben, die in Widerspruch zu anderen, wirtschafts- und sozialpolitisch begründeten Zielsetzungen stehen.

*a) Konjunktur- und wachstumspolitische Nebenfolgen*

α) Zunächst seien die konjunktur- und wachstumspolitischen Nebenfolgen der *Schuldaufnahme* und *Mittelverwendung* betrachtet. Hinsichtlich der konjunkturpolitischen Nebenfolgen sind die bei hoher staatlicher Kreditaufnahme zu befürchtenden Inflationsprozesse von besonderer Bedeutung.

In einer gelenkten Wirtschaft ist in dieser Hinsicht weniger zu befürchten als in einer Verkehrswirtschaft; allerdings kann — wie schon erwähnt wurde — eine spätere Aufhebung von Rationierungs- und Preisvorschriften nachträglich noch zu inflationären Entwicklungen führen, wenn während der Kreditaufnahme eine völlige Abschöpfung der überschüssigen Kaufkraft der Privaten durch Steuern und/oder Unterbringung der staatlichen Schuldtitel beim Publikum nicht möglich gewesen ist. In diesem Fall würde das Inflationsproblem nur aufgeschoben, nicht aber aufgehoben.

In einer *vollbeschäftigten* Verkehrswirtschaft könnten die Inflationsfolgen nur dann vermieden werden, wenn der staatlichen Nachfrageausweitung in vollem Umfange eine private Nachfrageeinschränkung entsprechen würde. Inwieweit das durch staatliche Kreditaufnahme geschehen kann, ist allerdings fraglich. Es käme zunächst vor allem darauf an, daß die Unterbringung von Staatsschuldtiteln derart erfolgt, daß damit nach Möglichkeit ex ante eine erhöhte Sparneigung, d. h. zusätzliche Konsumeinschränkung der Privaten hervorgerufen wird.

Beim Publikum untergebrachten Anleihen ist in dieser Hinsicht schon vom Ansatzpunkt her eine größere Chance einzuräumen als einer Schuldaufnahme bei der Zentralbank oder den Kreditbanken. Allerdings sind die oben

(§ 3) gemachten Bemerkungen zu berücksichtigen, nach denen der Unterbringung der Staatsschuldtitel beim Publikum unter gewissen Umständen[1]) zwar ein gleichgewichtsfördernder Einfluß durch eine Hemmung der privaten Investitionen zuzusprechen ist, daß jedoch diese Unterbringungsart als solche nicht notwendig zu einer Einschränkung des Konsums führen muß, vielmehr bei gleichgebliebener Sparneigung nur die Wahl einer anderen Anlageart bedeuten mag. Wenn aber bei einer Erhöhung der Staatsausgaben erhöhte Steuern ebenso wenig erwünscht sein sollten wie die Einschränkung der privaten Investitionen, andererseits die konjunkturelle Situation eine generelle Steigerung der Nachfrage verbietet, muß die Unterbringung der Kredittitel beim Publikum durch solche finanz- und kreditpolitische Maßnahmen ergänzt werden, die die erforderlichen Anreize für ein *erhöhtes* Sparen durch Konsumeinschränkung schaffen. Ebenso wie für die Unterbringung beim Publikum seit jeher in erster Linie langfristige Papiere in Frage kommen, ist aus institutionellen Gründen und zur Erzielung einer gewissen langfristigen Stabilität die Förderung langfristiger Sparformen vorzuziehen. An erster Stelle sind diejenigen finanzpolitischen Maßnahmen zu nennen, die den Einkommensteuerzensiten nach Maßgabe der aus laufenden Einkommen langfristig angelegten Mittel eine Steuervermeidungsmöglichkeit, z. B. durch Gewährung der Abzugsfähigkeit solcher Ersparnisse als „Sonderausgaben", einräumen, was zweifellos einen Anreiz zu erhöhtem Sparen darstellt. In der gleichen Richtung mögen sich vielleicht neben einer Werbung für langfristiges Sparen auch kredittechnische Maßnahmen bemerkbar machen, die die Ausgestaltung und Mannigfaltigkeit der angebotenen Kredittitel hinsichtlich der Zinssätze, der Ausgabekurse, der Verfallzeiten und der Stückelung betreffen.

Die Auswirkung dieser finanz- und kreditpolitischen Maßnahmen im Sinne eines Anreizes zu erhöhtem Sparen ist aber als verhältnismäßig begrenzt anzusehen, so daß

---

1) Keine Überschußreserven oder Refinanzierungsmöglichkeiten der Geschäftsbanken und keine expandierende Geldpolitik der Zentralbank.

insofern sich in gewissen Grenzen haltende zusätzliche Staatsausgaben und dementsprechende Kreditaufnahmen zu empfehlen wären. Gehen die Staatsausgaben und die zu ihrer Finanzierung notwendigen Kreditaufnahmen über diese Grenze hinaus, wären inflationäre Folgen nur in dem Maße vermeidbar, wie es zu einer Einschränkung der privaten Investitionsnachfrage kommen würde. Wie in § 3 dargestellt, kann — auch bei unveränderter privater Sparneigung — eine vermehrte Zeichnung staatlicher Schuldtitel durch das Publikum zu einer Einschränkung der privaten Investitionen dann führen, wenn — wegen mangelnden Kreditspielraumes der Geschäftsbanken und bei restriktiver Geld- und Kreditpolitik der Zentralbank — die privaten Investoren für ihre Projekte umso weniger Kredit erhalten können, je mehr das unveränderte Sparvolumen vom öffentlichen Kreditnehmer in Anspruch genommen wird. Soweit die genannten Voraussetzungen wirksam sind, könnten also Inflationswirkungen durch Investitionseinschränkungen vermieden werden.

Allerdings treten dann in *wachstumspolitischer* Sicht unangenehme Nebenwirkungen ein; das insofern, als durch das Unterlassen von Nettoinvestitionen notwendigerweise das Wachstum der volkswirtschaftlichen Realkapitalausrüstung und damit auch das Wachstum der Produktionskapazitäten zurückgehen würde. Diese in längerfristiger Hinsicht bedenklichen Nebenfolgen könnten das Gewicht der Argumentation wiederum zugunsten der Steuerfinanzierung zusätzlicher Staatsausgaben verschieben:

Geht man davon aus, daß Vollbeschäftigung gegeben ist und zur Vermeidung inflationärer Prozesse die gesamte Nachfrage und damit das Nettosozialprodukt zu Marktpreisen konstant bleiben soll, oder genauer gesagt von Periode zu Periode nur geringfügig nach Maßgabe des unter Vollbeschäftigungsbedingungen möglichen realen Wachstums steigen soll, so muß einer über das reale Wachstum hinausgehenden Staatsnachfragesteigerung $\Delta A_{st}$ eine verringerte private Nachfrage ($\Delta I + \Delta C$) entsprechen, d. h. es muß gelten: $\Delta I + \Delta C = -\Delta A_{st}$ oder

$$(1) \qquad \Delta I = -\Delta A_{st} - \Delta C.$$

Wenn angenommen werden kann, daß die marginale Konsumquote b durch die staatlichen Maßnahmen zur Mittelbeschaffung nicht wesentlich beeinflußt wird, kann die Änderung des Konsums $\Delta C$ genügend genau mit dem b-fachen der Änderung des privaten verfügbaren Einkommens angesetzt werden.

Eine Finanzierung von $\Delta A_{st}$ durch zusätzliche *Steuern* $\Delta T$, d. h. $\Delta T = \Delta A_{st}$, vermindert unter diesen Voraussetzungen das private verfügbare Einkommen um $\Delta T$ und demzufolge die private Konsumtion um $b \cdot \Delta T$, d. h. es ist $\Delta C = -b \cdot \Delta T = -b \cdot \Delta A_{st}$. Die zur Vermeidung eines Nachfrageüberschusses erforderliche Verringerung der Investition ist unter diesen Umständen nach (1):

$$(2) \qquad \Delta I = -(1-b) \cdot \Delta A_{st}$$

Wird dagegen $\Delta A_{st}$ durch *Kredite* finanziert (dabei darf es sich zur Vermeidung von Inflationsprozessen nicht um Schöpfungskredite handeln; vielmehr müssen diese Kredite aus der gegebenen ex ante-Ersparnis auf Kosten der Kreditierung privater Investitionsvorhaben gespeist werden), so kommt es anders als bei der Steuerfinanzierung zu keiner Senkung des privaten verfügbaren Einkommens. Unter der oben gemachten Voraussetzung folgt dann aber auch keine Senkung der Konsumnachfrage, d. h. $\Delta C = 0$. Die zur Erhaltung der Bedingung (1) erforderliche Senkung der privaten Investitionsnachfrage beträgt dann:

$$(3) \qquad \Delta I = -\Delta A_{st}$$

Durch Vergleich der rechten Seiten der Gleichungen (2) und (3) ist ersichtlich, daß die Investitionseinschränkung bei Kreditfinanzierung um $b \cdot \Delta A_{st}$ größer sein muß als bei Steuerfinanzierung. Übrigens hat schon Ricardo aus ähnlichen Überlegungen eine Kriegsfinanzierung aus Steuern befürwortet.

Bei all dem ist zu betonen, daß die Schlußfolgerung in vollem Umfange nur dann gilt, wenn annahmegemäß die Kreditnahme des Staates die private Konsumnachfrage unverändert läßt (vgl. oben § 3).

Bedenkt man aber die bei extrem hoher Besteuerung eintretenden negativen Leistungsanreize, so bleibt eine wenigstens teilweise Finanzierung hoher Staatsausgaben durch Kredite zu empfehlen. In Kriegszeiten mag der Übergang zu einem wenigstens teilweise gelenkten System (vgl. 2 b) die praktisch vertretbarste Lösung sein, um Inflationswirkungen und den Rückgang des Kapazitätswachstums wenigstens für gewisse Zeit in Grenzen halten zu können. Abschließend sei nochmals darauf hingewiesen, daß die gemachten Ausführungen sich nur auf die Situation eines — wegen hoher Staatsnachfrage zu vermutenden — Nachfrageüberschusses bei Vollbeschäftigung beziehen. Ist dagegen ein Nachfragedefizit zu befürchten, verliert die staatliche Schuldaufnahme, auch und insbesondere bei der Zentralbank, nicht nur ihren Charakter als mögliche Ursache von unerwünschten konjunkturellen Nebenwirkungen, sondern wird geradezu zu einer wirtschaftspolitischen Notwendigkeit, um durch eine Ausweitung staatlicher Nachfrage das gesamtwirtschaftliche Nachfrage-Angebotsgleichgewicht zu erhalten oder bei Unterbeschäftigung durch steigende Gesamtnachfrage zu steigender Beschäftigung zu führen.

β) Nunmehr sind die konjunkturellen und wachstumspolitischen Wirkungen der *Schuldbedienung* durch Verzinsung und Tilgung zu behandeln.

Soweit es sich dabei um Schulden beim privaten Publikum handelt, würde eine Finanzierung des Schuldendienstes durch Steuern den Privaten ebenso viel Mittel entziehen, wie ihnen andererseits durch die Leistungen des Schuldendienstes zufließen würden. Wenn sich auch aus diesem Grund die Auswirkung auf die effektive Gesamtnachfrage in Grenzen halten wird, so mögen doch insofern Nachfragewirkungen auftreten, als verschiedene Einkommensgruppen durch Steuern und Zinsen in verschiedenem Maße begünstigt oder benachteiligt werden, so daß sich einmal wegen unterschiedlich hoher Konsumneigung der verschiedenen Einkommensgruppen Effekte auf die Höhe der konsumtiven Nachfrage ergeben, zweitens je nach Bevorzugung oder Benachteiligung der Gewinneinkommen die Investitionen mehr oder weniger beeinflußt werden und schließlich durch solche Verteilungswirkungen auch die Struktur der Nachfrage nach den verschiedenen Gütern und Diensten sich ändern wird. Weil durch eine Steuerfinanzierung des Schuldendienstes den Privaten soviel an

Mitteln entzogen wird, wie ihnen andererseits zufließt, ist der konjunkturelle Effekt auf die Gesamtnachfrage verhältnismäßig unbeachtlich. Wirkungen ergeben sich vornehmlich im Hinblick auf die Nachfrage-Angebotssituation auf den Einzelmärkten. Die dabei aber nicht auszuschließenden Wirkungen auf die Investitionen erfordern dagegen wegen ihrer wachstumspolitischen Bedeutung durchaus Beachtung.

All solche Wirkungen würden zwar auch auftreten, wenn der öffentliche Schuldendienst an private Gläubiger durch Kreditaufnahme beim Bankensystem finanziert wird. Dazu kann aber dann ein Ansteigen der gesamten Nachfrage treten, wenn das Bankensystem nicht gleichzeitig die Kredite an private Unternehmer entsprechend kürzt. Genau die gegenteilige, d. h. eine kontrahierende Wirkung würde übrigens ein Schuldendienst zeigen, der Schulden bei der Zentralbank mit Hilfe von Steuereinnahmen bedient.

Von entscheidender Bedeutung kann das Problem der konjunktur- und wachstumspolitischen Auswirkungen des Schuldendienstes in Nachkriegszeiten werden. Die während des Krieges durch bei Banken und Privaten aufgenommene Kredite finanzierten Kriegsgüter sind zerstört oder für private Zwecke unbrauchbar, so daß sie der privaten Verwendung endgültig entzogen sind. Die Kriegsersparnisse der Privaten sind entweder wegen unzureichender Besteuerung und hoher Geldschöpfung in einem verkehrswirtschaftlichen System vornehmlich durch Kriegsgewinne entstanden oder in einem gelenkten System auf unzureichende Abschöpfung „überflüssiger" (s. h. privat nicht verwendbarer) Einkommensteile zurückzuführen. Würden diese Kriegsersparnisse oder ihre Zinserträge nach dem Kriege als zusätzliche Nachfrage am Markt geltend gemacht werden, so müßte es notwendigerweise zu inflationären Prozessen kommen. Ein staatlicher Schuldendienst ohne gleichzeitige zusätzliche Besteuerung ist daher unter diesen Umständen zu verurteilen. Bei der zusätzlich erforderlichen Besteuerung ist aber daran zu denken, daß nicht nur die Besitzer von Staatsschuldtiteln (durch Einlösung ihrer Schuldtitel oder durch Zinsen) die Mittel für zusätzliche Nachfrage in Händen haben, sondern auch alle anderen Einkommensempfänger, die im Kriege nur einen Teil ihres Einkommens konsumieren konnten. Wenn man also den Gedanken einer vorzüglichen Belastung der im Kriege entstandenen Vermögen hegt, müßte man *sämtliche* in der Kriegszeit entstandenen Ersparnisse zu erheblich verstärkter Besteuerung heranziehen, was wahrscheinlich am zweckmäßigsten und gerechtesten durch eine Besteuerung des im Kriege stattgefundenen Vermögenszuwachses durch geeignete Zuwachssteuern (vgl. Bd. III, Kap. VII, § 5) zu erreichen wäre. Eine vorzügliche Belastung der im Kriege entstandenen Vermögen rechtfertigt sich erstens insofern, als die entsprechenden Einkommen zu einem erheblichen Teil nicht auf besondere ökonomische Leistungen der Einkommensbezieher, sondern nur auf den Verzicht des Staates auf rigorose Besteuerung bei hoher Schöpfungskreditfinanzierung zurückzuführen sind und zweitens daraus, daß eine Besteuerung der laufenden Einkommen aus laufenden produktiven Diensten in der Nachkriegszeit gerade den Leistungsanreiz der Zensiten in der Wiederaufbauperiode schwächen würde.

### *b) Verteilungspolitische Nebenfolgen*

In der oben (1c) zitierten Aussage O. Donners, daß lediglich von „einer Tasche in die andere gezahlt" würde, wird das Problem der verteilungspolitischen Nebenfolgen der Staatsverschuldung umgangen.

α) Zunächst sind die Wirkungen der *Ausgabe* der vom Staat aufgenommenen Kreditmittel auf die Einkommens- und Vermögensverteilung zu nennen, durch die verschiedene Einkommensgruppen und Einkommensschichten in durchaus unterschiedlicher Weise profitieren können.

Während bei den Steuereinnnahmen schon der Akt zusätzlicher Mittelbeschaffung durch Erhöhung der Tarife bestehender oder durch Einführung neuer Steuern die Verteilung der privaten Nettoeinkommen verändern kann, ist bei dem Akt der Kreditaufnahme als solchem — ganz gleich, ob der Kredit bei Banken oder beim Publikum untergebracht wird — kein derartiger Einfluß zu verzeichnen, da die bestehende Verteilung der Nettoeinkommen unverändert bleibt. Dagegen führt die Ausgabe der Kreditmittel in aller Regel zu Verteilungsänderungen.

$\alpha_1$) Zunächst sei angenommen, daß mit der Kredithingabe, u. U. gestützt durch besondere politische Maßnahmen, eine *Einschränkung* der *privaten Nachfrage* in gleicher Höhe erreicht worden ist. Unter diesen Umständen wird es zwar nicht zu einer generellen Nachfrageerhöhung kommen; jedoch ist zu betonen, daß die zusätzliche staatliche Nachfrage nicht auf allen einzelnen Märkten für Güter und Dienstleistungen um genauso viel höher sein kann, wie jeweils der Rückgang der privaten Nachfrage ausmacht; es wird also auf einzelnen Märkten zu Nachfrageüberschüssen, Preis- und Einkommenssteigerungen kommen, auf anderen dagegen zu Nachfragerückgängen, Preis- und Einkommensminderungen.

In Kriegszeiten z. B. lassen sich regelmäßig Gewinnsteigerungen derjenigen Unternehmer feststellen, die Rüstungsgüter zu produzieren in der Lage sind. Ebenso wie sich Einkommensverschiebungen zwischen den einzelnen Unternehmern ergeben, können sich natürlich auch Einkommensverschiebungen zwischen verschiedenen Berufsgruppen von Arbeitnehmern zeigen. Darüber hinaus sind durchaus auch Einkommensverschiebungen zwischen Unternehmern und Arbeitnehmern denkbar. Schränken die Privaten z. B. ihre Nachfrage auf Gütermärkten ein und fragt andererseits der Staat vermehrt nach unselbständigen Arbeitskräften nach, so könnten die Unternehmergewinne zurückgehen und dafür die Löhne und Gehälter ansteigen. Wie immer lassen sich auch hier leichter Aussagen über die funktionelle als über die personelle Einkommensverteilung machen. Immerhin können mit einiger Vorsicht aus den funktionellen Ergebnissen auch Vermutungen über die Veränderung der personellen Einkommensverteilung gewonnen werden. Da z. B. Unternehmereinkommen im allgemeinen höher sind als die anderer Berufsgruppen, dürfte eine relative Steigerung der Unternehmereinkommen mit einiger Wahrscheinlichkeit eine ungleichmäßigere personelle Einkommensverteilung mit sich bringen.

$\alpha_2$) Die soeben geschilderten Wirkungen auf die Einkommensverteilung sind insofern unvermeidbar, als sie notwendig mit jeder zusätzlichen Staatsnachfrage verbunden sind, die sich ja nach den von privaten Bedürfnissen grundsätzlich unterschiedlichen Gemeinbedürfnissen richtet. Derartige Wirkungen treten daher auch dann auf, wenn die staatliche Kreditaufnahme und Mittelausgabe *nicht* bei gleichzeitiger *privater Nachfrageeinschränkung* erfolgt, wenn also Schöpfungskreditfinanzierung und allgemeiner Nachfrageüberschuß zu verzeichnen sind. Im Unterschied zu der zuvor ($\alpha_1$) angenommenen Situation werden nun aber die nominellen Einkommenssteigerungen, die einzelne Einkommensgruppen infolge zusätzlicher Staatsnachfrage erfahren, nicht durch Einkommenseinschränkungen anderer kompensiert. Die oben genannten Einkommensverschiebungen bleiben aber auch hier als Verschiebungen der Einkommensrelationen festzustellen. Z. B. ist der Fall, daß durch zusätzliche Staatsnachfrage auf Dienstleistungsmärkten den Arbeitnehmern, oder einzelnen Berufsgruppen von ihnen, eine relative Einkommensverbesserung gegenüber den Unternehmern gelingt, theoretisch durchaus denkbar. Historisch gesehen ist allerdings vor allem der gegensätzliche Fall von nennenswerter Bedeutung gewesen: In Kriegszeiten, insbesondere im Ersten Weltkrieg, kam es über die schöpfungskreditfinanzierte Ausdehnung der Staatsnachfrage nach Gütern, bei verhältnismäßig unveränderter privater Nachfrage, zu einer recht erheblichen Steigerung der Gewinneinkommen, der die Steigerung der Lohneinkommen nicht entsprach.

$\beta$) Auch der *Schuldendienst* wird Auswirkungen auf die Einkommensverteilung zeigen; die erforderliche Bedienung der Staatsschuld mag einen Rückgriff auf Steuereinnahmen notwendig machen. Dann darf aber auch die Frage nach unterschiedlichen Einkommensbelastungen nicht mehr vernachlässigt werden, weil man die lediglich durch Aggregation künstlich geschaffene Identität der Zinszahlungen empfangenden und Steuerzahlungen leistenden Einkommensgruppen aufheben muß. Damit wird der Tatbestand der Betrachtung zugänglich gemacht, daß diese Einkommensgruppen in praxi kaum identisch sein dürften.

Jede Anlage in zinsbringenden Titeln, ganz gleich welcher Art, wirkt sich ceteris paribus für den Anleger als zukünftiges Mehreinkommen aus. Soweit die staatliche Schuldaufnahme bei Privaten erfolgt ist, ist also mit Einkommenserhöhungen dieser privaten Kapitalgeber zu rechnen. Haben diese die staatlichen Schuldtitel anstelle sonst erworbener privater Schuldtitel gewählt, bleibt das durch die Zinseinkünfte zukünftig erzielte Mehreinkommen unverändert; kommt es dagegen in Höhe der emittierten Staatsschuldtitel zu einer zusätzlichen Ersparnis, erzielen die Kapitalgeber einen verstärkten Einkommenszuwachs[1]).

Es liegt nun zwar nahe, daraus eo ipso auf eine Verschiebung der Einkommensrelationen zugunsten der Kapitalgeber zu schließen; wie sich aber zeigen läßt, ist diese Schlußfolgerung nicht ohne weiteres zwingend. Zunächst ist daran zu denken, daß auch die übrigen Einkommensbezieher durch Entwicklungsprozesse von Angebot und Nachfrage auf den Faktorenmärkten einen entsprechenden relativen Einkommenszuwachs haben könnten wie die Kapitalgeber durch ihre Zinseinkünfte. Eine solche Entwicklung wird ohne inflationäre Spannungen nur dann möglich sein, wenn auch das reale Sozialprodukt jeweils in gleichem Maße mitwächst.

Es ist durchaus denkbar, daß durch Kreditaufnahmen des Staates für *Investitionen,* die zur Ausdehnung der produktiven Kapazität der Volkswirtschaft beitragen (neben Ausgaben für werbende Zwecke auch solche zur Verbesserung der Infrastruktur, für Erziehung usw.), das Wachstum des realen Sozialproduktes selbst dann nicht ge-

---

[1]) Die Zinseinkommen — auch der Gläubiger von Privaten — können sich darüberhinaus dadurch erhöhen, daß staatliche Kreditnachfrage eine Steigerung des Zinsniveaus bewirkt.

hindert wird, wenn wegen der staatlichen Investitionsaktivität ein Teil der privaten Investitionen, zwecks Vermeidung inflationärer Spannungen, unterlassen werden muß. Es ist jedenfalls nicht von vornherein auszuschließen, daß dabei die Zuwachsrate des realen Sozialprodukts und damit aller Einkommen die gleiche Höhe erreicht wie die Zuwachsrate der Einkommen der Kapitalgeber, so daß eine unveränderte Einkommensverteilung zumindest im Bereiche des Möglichen liegt. — Durch dieses Wachstum des Sozialproduktes würde übrigens, auch bei unverändertem Steuersystem, das Steueraufkommen wachsen, so daß haushaltsmäßig die Finanzierung der Staatsschuldzinsen überwiegend durch Steuern denkbar wäre.

Andererseits werden hohe Kreditaufnahmen des Staates für rein *konsumtive* Zwecke das reale Wachstum hindern, so daß mit wachsendem Konsumanteil der Staatsausgaben das zuvor geschilderte Ergebnis immer unwahrscheinlicher werden würde. Wollte man dennoch eine gleichbleibende Einkommensverteilung erreichen, könnte man vielleicht daran denken, die Bedingung konstanten Preisniveaus aufzugeben und fragen, ob nicht ein entsprechend hohes Wachstum der nominellen Einkommen der Nicht-Kapitalgeber die Einkommensverteilung unverändert lassen würde. Wegen der durch solche inflationäre Entwicklung in aller Regel auftretenden Verschiebungen zugunsten der Unternehmereinkommen ist die Frage aber zu verneinen. Dagegen könnte man durch Änderung des Steuersystems vielleicht gleichbleibende Relationen der verfügbaren Einkommen herstellen. Theoretisch müßte den Kreditgebern gerade soviel durch zusätzliche Besteuerung genommen werden, daß dann die Rate ihres Nettoeinkommenswachstums der geringeren allgemeinen Wachstumsrate der übrigen nominellen Nettoeinkommen entspräche. — Dabei könnte man durch Erhöhung der Steuereinnahmen sowohl inflationäre Spannungen vermeiden als auch die steuerliche Finanzierung der Zinszahlungen erreichen.

Allerdings läßt sich eine Besteuerung nur der Kapitalgeber deshalb nicht rechtfertigen, weil dadurch Bezieher kleinerer Einkommen, die Zinseinkünfte erhalten, über Gebühr benachteiligt werden. Gerechter erscheint eine zusätzliche progressive Besteuerung der höheren Einkommensschichten, bei denen man wegen der höheren Sparneigung ohnehin den erheblicheren Teil der zusätzlichen Zinseinkommen suchen mag.

Es ist in diesem Zusammenhang darauf hinzuweisen, daß eine verstärkte Besteuerung zwar auch diejenigen Einkommensbezieher trifft, die in früheren Perioden Kapital gegeben haben, aber nicht nur diese. Es kann dazu kommen, daß noch vermögensarme aufstrebende Unternehmer, die gegenwärtig durch besondere Leistungen versuchen, Differentialeinkommen zu erhalten, durch die zusätzliche progressive Besteuerung in ihrer gegenwärtigen wirtschaftlichen Entwicklung stärker behindert werden als „ältere" Unternehmer, die zwar auch zusätzliche Steuern zu entrichten haben, diese Belastung aber gegebenenfalls durch ihre Zinseinkommen kompensieren oder überkompensieren. Schließt man sich dem theoretischen Bild des frühen Schumpeter[1]) an, nach dem die wirtschaftliche Entwicklung gerade durch vermögenslose junge „Pionier"-Unternehmer vorwärtsgetrieben wurde, so würde man sagen können, daß unter den geschilderten Umständen eine hohe Staatsschuldzinslast den wirtschaftlichen Fortschritt hemmt[2]). Mag dieses Bild historisch gesehen gegenüber der Wirklichkeit verblassen[3]); ist man dem der wirtschaftshistorischen Entwicklung gegenüber reformistischen Idealbild der „Sozialen Marktwirtschaft" zugetan, so würde sich aus wirtschaftspolitischen Gründen ein weiteres Argument gegen eine hohe Staatsschuld ergeben, soweit nämlich dadurch Startchancen junger Unternehmer vermindert werden können.

Abschließend sei noch darauf hingewiesen, daß die wirtschafts- und gesellschaftspolitische Entscheidung über die anzustrebende Einkommensverteilung notwendig werturteilsbestimmt ist. Man kann einen besonderen Einkom-

---

1) Theorie der wirtschaftlichen Entwicklung, 1911.

2) Nicht nur ihre dem Aufbau des Eigenkapitals dienenden Gewinne würden ohne Gegengabe (Zinszahlungen) gekürzt werden, auch die „Incentives" würden wesentlich geschmälert werden.

3) Vgl. dazu den späten Schumpeter in: Capitalism, Socialism, and Democracy, 1942.

mensvorteil für die Zinsempfänger für gerechtfertigt halten, etwa mit der Begründung, daß die ursprüngliche Kapitalhingabe einen Verzicht auf unmittelbaren konsumtiven Nutzen aus laufendem Leistungseinkommen bedeutet, der in der Zukunft eine Gegenentschädigung rechtfertige. Auch den Staatsschuldgläubigern könnte man daher einen relativen Vorteil bei der Entwicklung der Einkommensverteilung lassen. Dagegen muß man für die *Kriegsschulden*[1]) allerdings den Tatbestand geltend machen, daß schon bei der Entstehung der Einkommen und bei der Bildung der Ersparnisse von einem freiwilligen Opfer aus Leistungseinkommen vielfach kaum die Rede sein kann, so daß eine wenigstens teilweise nachträgliche Wegsteuerung dieser Einkommensvorteile nicht unbedingt als „ungerecht" klassifiziert werden sollte (vgl. dazu auch die Schlußbemerkung zu 3aβ).

### *c) Die Belastung des Staatshaushaltes*

Eine hohe Staatsschuld mag, da ihre Bedienung einen großen Teil der laufenden Staatsausgaben von vornherein bindet, eine merkliche Unfreiheit der *Budgetgestaltung* zur Folge haben. Das betrifft einmal die konkurrierenden Ausgaben für soziale und andere Zwecke, zum anderen, daß die Elastizität des Haushalts insgesamt geringer wird, was sich vor allem hinsichtlich fiskalpolitischer Zielsetzungen hinderlich auswirken mag.

Man könnte zwar darauf hinweisen, daß bei größeren Zinsverpflichtungen die übrigen Ausgaben nicht unbedingt darunter zu leiden hätten, wenn man ausgleichend für höhere Steuereinnahmen sorgen würde. Insbesondere

---

[1]) Es ist in diesem Zusammenhang darauf hinzuweisen, daß in der Volkswirtschaftlichen Gesamtrechnung — nach weitgehender internationaler Übereinkunft — Staatsschuldzinsen auf rein konsumtiv aufgenommene Kredite (überwiegend Kriegsschulden) statistisch als T r a n s f e r z a h l u n g e n aufgefaßt werden, d. h. also als Zahlungen o h n e p r o d u k t i v e G e g e n l e i s t u n g, die das jeweilige Sozialprodukt nicht erhöhen wie z. B. in der Volkswirtschaftlichen Gesamtrechnung der Bundesrepublik Deutschland (vgl. Kap. IX, § 4, 2). Dagegen werden die Zinsen auf Kredite für Staats i n v e s t i t i o n e n vielfach als Transformationszahlungen, d. h. als Bestandteil des laufenden Sozialproduktes angesehen.

würde das private steuerbelastungsfähige Einkommen durch die Staatsschuldzinsen ja auch in positivem Sinn beeinflußt. Dagegen ist allerdings zu sagen, daß erstens eine höhere Steuerbelastung ganz sicher auf politische Widerstände und Steuerwiderstände stößt und daß zweitens die Notwendigkeit, einen größeren Teil des Sozialproduktes durch die Staatskassen zu leiten, unvermeidbar zu steigenden Verwaltungskosten führt und damit den Staatsapparat ineffizienter macht.

### *d) Die relativierte Bedeutung stetig steigender Staatsschulden im langfristigen Wachstum*

Im Vorangegangenen sind einige der wichtigsten Argumente gegen eine „unbegrenzte" Staatsverschuldung dargestellt worden. Sie treffen vor allem ihr ruckartiges Wachsen, wie es bei der Kriegsfinanzierung in Erscheinung tritt. Setzt man dagegen kontinuierlich wachsende Staatsschulden voraus, die vom Staate für produktive Zwecke der Wirtschaftsförderung aufgenommen werden, worunter auch die für beschäftigungspolitische Zwecke aufgenommenen inbegriffen sein sollen, so verlieren jene Gegenargumente allerdings an Gewicht. Denn durch solche Kredite wird, bei erfolgreicher Verwendung, die Basis der Finanzkraft des Staates, das Sozialprodukt, verstärkt, aus dem letzten Endes die Bedienung der Staatsschuld erfolgt.

Zu solchen Schlüssen, die die Besorgnis über die wachsende Zinslast in Grenzen zu halten vermögen, kommt man, wenn man Berechnungen folgt, die von E. Domar u. a. vorgenommen wurden. Es kann gezeigt werden, daß eine jährliche Nettoschuldaufnahme (Haushaltsdefizit), die einen konstanten Bruchteil des Sozialproduktes ausmacht, bei einem wachsenden Sozialprodukt und d. h. dann auch bei absolut wachsender jährlicher Nettoschuldaufnahme, nicht etwa zu einer im Verhältnis zum Sozialprodukt über alle Grenzen wachsenden Staatsschuldsumme führt, sondern, daß das Verhältnis zwischen Schuldsumme und Sozialprodukt einem bestimmten Endwert zustrebt

Sei D die Summe der jeweiligen Staatsschuld, E das Sozialprodukt, k das Verhältnis der laufenden Nettoschuldaufnahme zum Sozialprodukt (relative Nettoschuldaufnahme) und r die Wachstumsrate des Sozialproduktes, so strebt das Verhältnis $\frac{D}{E}$ im Zeitablauf dem Werte $\frac{k}{r}$ zu. Bei einem Zinssatz von i % nähert sich die Zinsbelastung des Sozialproduktes (relative Zinsbelastung) dem Werte

$$\frac{k}{r} \cdot i\,\%.$$

Würde z. B. die Nettoschuldaufnahme 1 % des Sozialproduktes betragen, die Wachstumsrate 4 %, so würde das Verhältnis zwischen Staatsschuld und Sozialprodukt dem Werte $^1/_4$ zustreben. Bei einem Zinssatz von 3 % würde in Endwerten eine Belastung von $^3/_4$ % des Sozialproduktes durch Zinszahlungen die Folge sein. Man sieht daraus, daß bei wachsendem Sozialprodukt trotz absolut wachsender Gesamtverschuldung die Belastung sich makroökonomisch in manipulierbaren Grenzen halten kann.

Wenn in Endwerten die relative Zinsbelastung $\frac{k}{r} \cdot i$ kleiner ist als die relative Nettoschuldaufnahme k, würde die jeweilige Nettoschuldaufnahme nicht nur ausreichen, die fälligen Zinsen zu finanzieren, sondern ein Rest könnte für die Finanzierung anderer Staatsaufgaben eingesetzt werden. Diese Bedingung ist immer dann erfüllt, wenn der Zins i kleiner ist als die Wachstumsrate des Sozialproduktes r. Ist dagegen i größer als r, reicht eine — sich in konstantem Verhältnis zum Sozialprodukt haltende — Nettoschuldaufnahme nicht für die jeweils fällig werdenden Zinsverpflichtungen aus. Ein Rest der Zinsen müßte aus dem übrigen Haushalt finanziert werden.

Die grundsätzliche Problematik der Staatsschuld und der Staatsschuldzinsen, wie sie in den vorangegangenen Abschnitten aufgezeigt wurde, bleibt dabei unberührt; jedoch ist die Verteilungsproblematik, insbesondere, wenn die für die Verzinsung zu erhebenden Steuern zumindest nicht regressiv wirken, in dem Maße als weniger negativ anzunehmen, wie eine breite Streuung der Schuldtitel erreicht werden kann. Das aber ist im Falle einer mäßig wachsenden Schuld eher möglich als dann, wenn die Schuld abrupt steigt, wie es sich im Falle der Kriegsfinanzierung in aller Regel gezeigt hat.

## § 5. Statistiken zur Staatsverschuldung

An Hand einiger Tabellen soll eine Übersicht über interessante Perioden der Entwicklung der Staatsverschuldung in den USA und Deutschland sowie über den Stand der öffentlichen Schuld in der Bundesrepublik gegeben werden.

### 1. Langfristige Entwicklungen der Staatsverschuldung

#### *a) Entwicklung in den Vereinigten Staaten von Amerika*

Die Entwicklung der Bundesschuld der Vereinigten Staaten (Tabelle I) läßt sich seit der Entstehung der ersten Schuld durch die Übernahme der Schulden der Staaten (Funding Act, 1790) bis in die heutige Zeit verfolgen, ohne daß währungsvernichtende Inflationen Friktionen hervorriefen.

Die markantesten Veränderungen der Schuldsumme sind die durch Kriege bedingten sprunghaften Steigerungen (nach 1810, 1860, 1897, 1916, 1940).

In Friedenszeiten bestand früher stets die Tendenz, die Schuld allmählich abzutragen (nach 1820, 1869, 1899, 1920). Seit 1929 wurde diese Praxis durchbrochen, zunächst, um die Etats-Defizite auszugleichen, die infolge der Weltwirtschaftskrise entstanden waren, nach 1933 im Zuge des neuen Wirtschaftsprogramms zur Steigerung der Beschäftigung (New Deal) und der bald darauf einsetzenden Aufrüstung. Nach dem Zweiten Weltkrieg erlaubte die angespannte Haushaltslage es nicht, die Schuldsumme wesentlich zu verringern. Seit 1929 besteht daher eine mehr oder weniger starke Anstiegstendenz der Schuldsumme.

Die Relation der Bundesschuld zum Volkseinkommen ist jeweils in den Nachkriegsjahren (nach 1869, 1899, 1920, 1946) zurückgegangen, wobei sich Schuldenstand und Volkseinkommen gegenläufig bewegten, bis auf die Zeit nach dem Zweiten Weltkrieg, in der die Schuldsumme sich relativ geringfügig erhöhte.

Besondere Beachtung verdient die Zeit der Weltwirtschaftskrise: Sowohl steigende Schuld als auch stark sinkendes Volkseinkommen bewirkten eine erhebliche Steigerung der genannten Relation. Bemerkenswert ist ferner, daß nach dem Zweiten Weltkrieg die Bundesschuld der USA größer war als das Volkseinkommen eines Jahres und daß 1961 das Verhältnis von Bundesschuld zum Volkseinkommen mehr als doppelt so groß war wie nach Beendigung des Ersten Weltkrieges. — Die Relation in der letzten Spalte der Tabelle I zeigt an, welcher Teil des Volkseinkommens auf Zinszahlungen für die Bundesschuld entfällt.

### *b) Entwicklung in Deutschland*

Tabelle II zeigt die Entwicklung der Reichs- bzw. der Bundesschuld in Deutschland.

Die deutsche Staatsschuld wurde zweimal vom Staate abgewälzt: einmal nach dem Ersten Weltkriege infolge der großen Inflation und der Währungsumstellung 1923/24, zum anderen nach dem Zweiten Weltkriege mit der Währungsreform 1948. Beide Male wurden die Anleihegläubiger nur in sehr beschränktem Umfange entschädigt (Anleiheablösungsgesetz vom 16. 7. 1925 und Allgemeines Kriegsfolgengesetz vom 5. 11. 1957). Nach den beiden Währungsumstellungen weist die Entwicklung des Schuldenstandes darum scharfe Einschnitte auf.

Das ruckartige Ansteigen der Schuld als Folge der Kriege zeigt sich auch in Deutschland nach 1913 und 1938. Jedoch hat sich hier, im Gegensatz zur früheren Entwicklung in den USA, auch die Verschuldung ständig erhöht. Vor dem Ersten Weltkrieg lag die Ursache dafür vor allem

Tabelle I

Entwicklung der Bundesschuld

| Jahr | Bundesschuld[1]) Mrd. $ | Bundesschuldzinsen[3]) Mrd. $ | Volkseinkommen[4]) Mrd. $ | Bundesschuld in % des Volkseinkommens |
|---|---|---|---|---|
| 1791 | 0,075 | 0,002 | · | · |
| 1810 | 0,048 | 0,003 | · | · |
| 1820 | 0,090 | 0,005 | · | · |
| 1860 | 0,065 | 0,003 | · | · |
| 1869 | 2,545[2]) | 0,131 | 6,2 | 41 |
| 1897 | 1,227 | 0,038 | 14,6 | 8 |
| 1899 | 1,437 | 0,040 | 14,6 | 10 |
| 1916 | 1,225 | 0,023 | 34,8 | 4 |
| 1920 | 24,299 | 1,020 | 79,1 | 31 |
| 1929 | 16,931 | 0,678 | 87,8 | 19 |
| 1933 | 22,539 | 0,689 | 40,2 | 56 |
| 1940 | 42,968 | 1,041 | 81,6 | 53 |
| 1946 | 269,422 | 4,722 | 180,9 | 149 |
| 1957 | 270,527 | 7,244 | 364,0 | 74 |
| 1961 | 288,971 | 8,957 | 427,8 | 68 |

Quelle: Historical Statistics of the United States, Colonial Times to 1957. A Statistical Abstract Supplement, Washington D. C. 1960; Statistical Abstract of the United States, 1962.

1) Stand am Jahresende.

der Vereinigten Staaten

| Zinsen in % des Volkseinkommens | Historisches Ereignis |
|---|---|
| . | Funding Act (1790): Bund übernimmt die Schulden der Staaten |
| . | |
| . | Englisch-amerikanischer Krieg (1812—1814) |
| . | |
| 2,1 | Sezessionskrieg (1861—1865) |
| 0,3 | |
| 0,3 | Krieg USA gegen Spanien um Kuba (1898) |
| 0,1 | Erster Weltkrieg (Teilnahme der USA: |
| 1,3 | 1917—1918) |
| 0,8 | Weltwirtschaftskrise (1929—1933) |
| 1,7 | New Deal, Aufrüstung |
| 1,3 | Zweiter Weltkrieg (Teilnahme der USA |
| 2,6 | 1941—1945) und anschl. Umstellung auf |
| . | Friedensproduktion |
| 2,0 | Periode wirtschaftlichen Wachstums nach dem Zweiten Weltkrieg |
| 2,1 | . |

2) Für 1866: 2,756 Mrd. $

3) Bis 1820 Kalenderjahre, später Rechnungsjahre, endend am 30. Juni.

4) Für 1869: „Net National Product", Durchschnitt 1869—1873; später: „National Income"; für 1897, 1899: Durchschnitt 1897—1901 („Net National Product" dieser Periode zum Vergleich: 15,8); für 1916: Durchschnitt 1912—1916; später Kalenderjahre.

Tabelle II

## Entwicklung der Reichs- bzw. der Bundesschuld in Deutschland[1])

(Milliarden M, RM, DM)

| Ausgewählte Jahre | Schuld des Reiches/Bundes[2]) | | | | | Staatsschuldzinsen[5]) | Volkseinkommen[6]) | Gesamtschuld in % des Volkseinkommens | Zinsen in % des Volkseinkommens |
|---|---|---|---|---|---|---|---|---|---|
| | gesamt | Ausland (soweit erfaßt) | Inland | | | | | | |
| | | | Altschulden[3]) | Neuverschuldung[4]) | | | | | |
| | | | | fundiert | schwebend | | | | |
| 1872 | 0,04 | . | 0,04 | 0,00 | 0,00 | 0,001 | . | . | . |
| 1881 | 0,31 | . | 0,00 | 0,27 | 0,04 | 0,011 | . | . | . |
| 1891 | 1,3 | . | 0,00 | 1,3 | — | 0,056 | 24,8 | 5 | 0,2 |
| 1900 | 2,3 | . | 0,00 | 2,3 | — | 0,079 | 30,9 | 7 | 0,3 |
| 1910 | 4,9 | . | — | 4,9 | — | 0,168 | 44,0 | 11 | 0,4 |
| 1913 | 4,8 | . | — | 4,8 | — | 0,179 | 50,1 | 10 | 0,4 |
| 1915 | 16,7 | . | — | 9,5 | 7,2 | 1,265 | . | . | . |
| 1918 | 104,9 | . | — | 71,9 | 33,0 | 5,808 | . | . | . |
| 1920 | 184,5 | . | — | 93,0 | 91,5 | 10,953 | . | . | . |
| 1923 | 6.660,7 | . | — | 59,6 | 6.601,1 | . | . | . | . |
| 1925 | 2,8 | 0,9 | 1,4 | 0,0 | 0,4 | 0,009 | 60,0 | 5 | 0,0 |
| 1929 | 8,2 | 0,9 | 5,2 | 1,2 | 0,9 | 0,150 | 75,9 | 11 | 0,2 |
| 1933 | 11,7 | 3,0 | 4,4 | 2,7 | 1,5 | 0,2 | 46,5 | 25 | 0,4 |
| 1938 | 19,1 | 1,3 | 3,5 | 12,0 | 2,3 | 1,3 | 82,1 | 23 | 1,6 |
| 1942 | 137,7 | 1,2 | 2,7 | 66,9 | 66,9 | 5,9 | . | . | . |
| 1945 | 379,8 | 1,3 | 2,1 | 135,4 | 241,0 | . | . | . | . |
| 1950 | 6,1 | . | 5.5 | 0,0 | 0,6 | 0,151 | 74,5 | 8 | 0,2 |
| 1955 | 20,1 | 9,4 | 7,9 | 2,3[7]) | 0,5 | 0,368 | 137,5 | 15 | 0,3 |
| 1961 | 30,8 | 5,7 | 12,0 | 12,5[7]) | 0,6 | 0,682 | 240,8[8]) | 13 | 0,3 |

**Quellen:**

Statistisches Handbuch für das Deutsche Reich, Berlin 1907, erster Teil;

Statistisches Jahrbuch für das Deutsche Reich (1881—1942);

Statistisches Handbuch von Deutschland, München 1949;

Statistisches Jahrbuch für die Bundesrepublik Deutschland (1952—1961);

Reichshaushaltsrechnung (1925—1929);

Bundeshaushaltsrechnung (1950—1960);

Grünig, F.: Die Anfänge der „Volkswirtschaftlichen Gesamtrechnung" in Deutschland, a.a.O.

Auskünfte der Bundesschuldenverwaltung, Bad Homburg v. d. Höhe.

---

1) Alle Größen sind auf den jeweiligen Gebietsstand bezogen. Währungseinheiten: bis 1923 Mark, 1925—1948 Reichsmark, dann Deutsche Mark.

2) Schuldenstand jeweils am 31. März, für 1961: 31. Dezember. Nicht berücksichtigt: Reichskassenscheine und Darlehnskassenscheine (vgl. Tab. III), Mefo-Wechsel und sonstige Reichsschulden (vgl. Tab. IV), sonstige Schulden des Bundes (vgl. Tab. V, Fußnote 1).

3) bis 1900: Schulden des Norddeutschen Bundes; 1925—1945: vor dem 1. 4. 1924 entstandene Schulden, einschl. Festwert- und Valutaschulden; ab 1950: vor dem 21. 6. 1948 entstandene Schulden.

4) Schulden, die nicht zu den Altschulden gezählt werden (vgl. Fußnote 3).

5) Für 1872 und 1961 Kalenderjahr, sonst Rechnungsjahr, das am 1. 4. des genannten Jahres beginnt; Nettoausweis nach den Haushaltsrechnungen, für 1918 nach dem Haushaltsplan.

6) In jeweiligen Preisen. Bis 1938 nach der Definition des Statistischen Reichsamtes, nach 1950 Nettosozialprodukt zu Faktorkosten.

7) Darin enthalten: Kredite bei der Bundesbank für Beteiligungen an internationalen Einrichtungen sowie Forderungen der Bundesbank wegen Änderung der Wechselkurse und Forderungserwerb aus Nachkriegswirtschaftshilfen.

8) Vorläufiges Ergebnis.

in der Schwäche der Reichsfinanzen (geringe Reichsbesteuerung bei zunehmenden Ausgabenverpflichtungen, insbesondere für die Ausrüstung von Heer und Marine). Nach der schuldvernichtenden Währungsumstellung 1923/24 begann die Verschuldung des Reiches wieder schnell anzuwachsen, zunächst zum Teil als Folge der Reparationsverpflichtungen, später infolge der Weltwirtschaftskrise und der damit verbundenen schlechten Finanzlage des Reiches (hohe notstandsbedingte Ausgabenverpflichtungen bei gleichzeitigem Rückgang der Steuereinnahmen). Nach 1933 bedingten Arbeitsbeschaffungspolitik und später die Aufrüstung eine weitere Zunahme der Verschuldung bis zum Übergang zur Kriegsfinanzierung. Auch nach dem Zweiten Weltkrieg hat die Bundesrepublik ihren Finanzbedarf zu einem allerdings geringen Teil durch Kredite gedeckt.

*Auslandsschulden* des Deutschen Reiches werden bis 1923 nicht ausgewiesen. 1924 wurde zur Abdeckung von Reparationsverpflichtungen und zur Stabilisierung der jungen RM-Währung die Dawes-Anleihe gezeichnet, der andere Auslandsanleihen folgten (u. a. Young-Anleihe, Kreuger-Anleihe). Im Londoner Schuldenabkommen 1953 wurden die Auslandsschulden Deutschlands neu geregelt (Anteil danach 1961 3,3 Mrd. DM).

Zu den *Altschulden* wurden für die Zeit nach der Reichsgründung die Schulden des vormaligen Norddeutschen Bundes gerechnet, die schnell abgetragen wurden. Nach 1923 wurden unter dieser Bezeichnung Schulden zusammengefaßt, die vor der Währungsumstellung entstanden waren und in irgendeiner Form noch anerkannt werden mußten („Ablösungsschulden"). Nach 1948 handelt es sich ebenfalls um Ablösungsschulden sowie um Ausgleichsforderungen und Deckungsforderungen, die infolge der Währungsreform entstanden sind.

Unter *Neuverschuldung* wird der Stand, nicht etwa der jährliche Zugang, der Verschuldung verstanden, soweit es sich nicht um Altschulden handelt.

Die *schwebenden Schulden* waren in Friedenszeiten stets verhältnismäßig gering. Dafür sorgten strenge Bestimmungen der Währungsgesetzgebung. Die Lockerungen dieser gesetzlichen Bremse in Kriegszeiten ermöglichten starke Expansionen der schwebenden Schulden, die inflationierend wirkten (vgl. auch Tab. III und IV).

## 2. Kriegsfinanzierung in Deutschland

### a) Erster Weltkrieg

Die in den Kriegsjahren steil ansteigenden Reichsausgaben wurden mangels einer dementsprechenden Steuerpolitik, vor allem in der Ära Helfferich (bis 1916), weitgehend durch Kredite[1]) finanziert (Tabelle III). Es erfolgte eine laufende Kreditaufnahme in Form schwebender Verschuldung vor allem bei der Reichsbank; durch die dabei eintretende Geldschöpfung flossen den Privaten liquide Mittel zu. Da aber in den ersten Kriegsjahren wegen der noch großen Opferwilligkeit die Bereitschaft der Privaten groß war, ihre Liquiditätsreserven für die Zeichnung von Anleihen zu verwenden, war eine Fundierung der laufenden schwebenden Schuldaufnahme in erheblichem Umfang möglich, so daß die Statistik einen verhältnismäßig großen Zuwachs an fundierten Schulden zeigt.

Ab 1917 mit den erhöhten Kriegsanstrengungen des „Hindenburg-Programms" ist jedoch ein relativ stärkerer Zuwachs der schwebenden Verschuldung auch in der Statistik bemerkbar. Das zeigt, daß Anleihen immer weniger und wegen der fortschreitenden Inflation ab 1920 überhaupt nicht mehr — wer langfristige Kredite gab, verlor sein Geld — untergebracht werden konnten.

Die große, bis 1923 dauernde Inflation ist als Folge der Kriegsfinanzierung zu deuten. Die umlaufende Geldmenge wurde — bei verminderter Erzeugung privater Güter und Dienste — stark vergrößert. Die Geldmengenvermehrung entstand auf folgende Weise: die Änderung in der Reichsbankgesetzgebung von 1914 gestattete die Aufnahme unverzinslicher Schatzanweisungen in die Restdeckung des Banknotenumlaufes (zuvor nur Handelswechsel bestimmter Qualität). In die Primär- oder Dritteldeckung (zuvor Gold) konnten nunmehr auch Darlehnskassenscheine[2]) auf-

[1]) Den Deckungsgrundsätzen wurde formal dadurch genügt, daß die Kriegsausgaben in den außerordentlichen Haushalt eingestellt wurden. Vgl. Bd. I, III, § 1, 6.

[2]) Diese wurden von der Darlehnskasse gegen Lombardierung von Wertpapieren (auch von Staatspapieren!) ausgegeben und galten als Zahlungsmittel (Umlauf Jahresdurchschnitt 1920: 13,1 Mrd. M).

**Tabelle III**

**Reichsverschuldung und Geldumlauf im 1. Weltkrieg und in der großen Inflation**
(Milliarden Mark)

| Jahr (Stand am 31. 3.) | Reichsschuld | | | | | Umlauf an Stückgeld[1]) (Jahresdurchschnitt) | |
|---|---|---|---|---|---|---|---|
| | gesamt | fundiert | | schwebend | | | |
| | | Anleihen[2]) | verzinsl. Schatzanweisungen | gesamt | davon bei der Reichsbank in % | Münzen | Papiergeld (insbesondere Reichsbanknoten und Darlehnskassenscheine)[4]) |
| 1913 | 4,8 | 4,6 | 0,2 | . ( . ) | . | 3,7 | 2,4 |
| 1914 | 4,9 | 4,7 | 0,2 | . ( . ) | . | 3,4 | 3,6 |
| 1915 | 16,7 | 8,3 | 1,2 | 7,2 (43) | 83 | 2,1 | 6,8 |
| 1916 | 39,5 | 28,3 | 1,9 | 9,3 (24) | 86 | 1,2 | 9,2 |
| 1917 | 68,9 | 45,6 | 4,7 | 18,6 (27) | 70 | 0,5 | 14,4 |
| 1918 | 104,9 | 64,1 | 7,8 | 33,0 (31) | 47 | 0,1 | 22,7 |
| 1919 | 156,1 | 81,0 | 11,4 | 63,7 (41) | 47 | 0,1 | 40,9 |
| 1920 | 184,5 | 82,4 | 10,7 | 91,5 (50) | 47 | 0,2 | 67,7 |
| 1921 | 248,5 | 73,0 | 9,2 | 166,3 (67) | 39 | 0,4 | 90,4 |
| 1922 | 337,6 | 58,6 | 7,0 | 271,9 (81) | 54 | . | 351,7 |
| 31. 3. 23 | 6.660,7 | 53,0 | 6,6 | 6.601,1 (99) | 69 | . | 5.542,9 |
| 30. 9. 23 | 46.716.676 | 54,0 | 6,5 | 46.716.616,4 (100) | 97 | . | 28.244.405,8 |
| 15. 11. 23 | 191.580.465.500 [5]) | | . | 191.580.465.422,1 (100) | 99 | . | 92.900.000.000 [5]) |

Quellen: Statistisches Jahrbuch für das Deutsche Reich 1923; Deutschlands Wirtschaft, Währung und Finanzen, Berlin 1924.

1) Gesetzliche Zahlungsmittel; außerdem 1922 und 1923 insgesamt ca. 314 Trillionen M. Papiermarknotgeld und ca. 425 Mio. Goldmark wertbeständiges Notgeld ausgegeben, zwischenzeitlich aber teilweise wieder zurückgenommen. Buchgeld statistisch nicht erfaßt.

2) Reichsanleihen; ab 1920 einschließlich Prämienanleihen.

3) Diskontierte unverzinsliche Schatzanweisungen, bei der Reichsbank oder im freien Verkehr. In Klammern der Anteil der schwebenden Verschuldung an der gesamten Reichsschuld in %.

4) Ferner einschl. in immer geringer werdendem Anteil Privatbanknoten und Reichskassenscheine.

5) Geschätzt.

genommen werden. Von diesen Möglichkeiten wurde in steigendem Umfang Gebrauch gemacht. Insbesondere als nach 1920 fundierte Schulden nicht mehr unterzubringen waren, der Staatsbedarf bei hohen Ausgabenverpflichtungen hoch blieb, während infolge der Inflation der Realwert der Steuererträge laufend sank, hat sich das Reich in verstärktem Maße kurzfristig bei der Reichsbank verschulden müssen, wodurch der Geldumlauf alsbald eine außerordentliche Höhe erreichte.

Eine zusätzliche Beschleunigung der Inflation wurde in den Nachkriegsjahren dadurch hervorgerufen, daß infolge des Vertrauensschwundes in die Wertbeständigkeit des Geldes die Privaten die Umlaufgeschwindigkeit des Geldes durch möglichst schnelles Umwandeln von Geld in Güter (Sachwerthunger) erhöhten und erwartete künftige Preissteigerungen in gegenwärtigen erhöhten Preisforderungen und Preishinnahmen antizipierten. Interessant ist dabei, daß wegen der galoppierend steigenden Preise und damit zusammenhängend der wachsenden für Umsatzzwecke benötigten Geldmittel Banknoten sogar zeitweilig knapp wurden, so daß eine durchaus beachtliche Ausgabe von Notgeld, z. T. auch durch Private, erfolgte. Der Inflation wurde endlich seit Mitte November 1923 in einem sowohl für die Theorie der Finanz- als auch der Geldpolitik lehrreichen dramatischen Akkord finanz- und geldpolitischer Maßnahmen Einhalt geboten: Ausgleich des Staatshaushalts durch rigorose Ausgabenkürzungen auf der einen, Steueranspannungen auf der anderen Seite; Einführung einer knapp gehaltenen Hilfswährung, der Rentenmark; Stabilisierung des Währungsgeldes (4,2 Billionen Mark = 1 U.S.-Dollar). Wesentlich war, daß das Geld knapp gehalten, vor allem aber das „Loch“ im Staatshaushalt — durch das bisher zusätzliches Geld in den Wirtschaftskreislauf eingeflossen war — geschlossen wurde.

Die reale Staatsverschuldung ist durch die staatsfinanziell verursachte große Inflation in Verbindung mit der Rechtsprechung durch das höchste Gericht (Mark = Mark), praktisch fast völlig vom Staate abgewälzt worden. Der reale Wert der Staatsanleihen war am Ende der Inflation auf 0,002 Milliarden der Rechnungseinheit Goldmark zusammengeschrumpft.

### *b) Zweiter Weltkrieg*

Tabelle IV zeigt die Entwicklung der Reichsverschuldung im Zusammenhang mit dem Zweiten Weltkrieg.

Zur Finanzierung der einsetzenden militärischen Aufrüstung wurden in Deutschland ab 1935 die sogenannten „Mefo-Wechsel" geschaffen. Sie konnten von der Reichsbank diskontiert werden und auf diese Weise eine Vergrößerung der umlaufenden Geldmenge bewirken. Durch das Reichsbankgesetz vom 15. 6. 1939 wurde dann auch der Ankauf von kurzfristigen Schatzanweisungen und Reichswechseln in praktisch unbegrenzter Höhe durch die Reichsbank zugelassen. Dadurch erhielt das Reich die Möglichkeit der unbegrenzten Geldschöpfung für Zwecke der Staatsfinanzierung. Schwebende Verschuldung, Notenumlauf und Buchgeldbestand haben sich in der Folgezeit bis Kriegsende stark vergrößert. Die Anleiheunterbringung wurde wesentlich anders gehandhabt als im Ersten Weltkrieg. Die NS-Machthaber zeigten — trotz aller Rücksichtslosigkeit in bezug auf die Persönlichkeitsrechte — eine beachtliche Vorsicht gegenüber den wirtschaftlichen Reaktionen der Beherrschten. Da nach der Entwertung der Staatspapiere im und nach dem Ersten Weltkrieg eine Emission von Kriegsanleihen beim Publikum ungünstige psychologische Wirkungen erwarten ließ, wurden Anleihen zum großen Teil als sogenannte „Liquiditätsanleihen" bei Kapitalsammelstellen "geräuschlos", d. h. ohne Propagandaaufwand untergebracht. Über diesen indirekten Weg dienten auch die — insbesondere bei Sparkassen eingelegten — Mittel der Privaten der Kriegsfinanzierung. Ferner entstand während des Krieges eine allerdings relativ unbedeutende Verschuldung des Reiches in den Sonderformen der „Warenbeschaffungs- und Betriebsanlageguthaben" (vgl. dazu oben § 2, 1g).

Tabelle IV

Reichsverschuldung und Notenumlauf vor und während des Zweiten Weltkrieges
(Milliarden Reichsmark)

| Jahr (Stand am 31. 3.) | Neuverschuldung[1]) im Inland | | | | | sonstige Reichsschuld[3]) | Umlauf Mefo-wechsel | Noten-Umlauf |
|---|---|---|---|---|---|---|---|---|
| | gesamt | fundiert | schwebend | | | | | |
| | | | gesamt[2]) | davon unverzinsl. Schatzanw. | davon Reichswechsel | | | |
| 1934 | 5,5 | 3,6 | 1,9 (35) | 1,5 | 0,4 | 2,6 | — | 3,7 |
| 1936 | 8,9 | 6,0 | 2,9 (33) | 2,4 | 0,4 | 1,4 | 4,9 | 4,3 |
| 1938 | 14,3 | 12,0 | 2,3 (16) | 1,9 | 0,4 | 0,6 | 12,0 | 5,6 |
| 1939 | 26,1 | 19,6 | 6,5 (25) | 6,1 | 0,4 | 0,2 | 11,9 | 8,3 |
| 1940 | 43,5 | 25,5 | 18,0 (41) | 11,3 | 6,5 | 4,2 | 11,4 | 12,2 |
| 1941 | 81,9 | 43,7 | 38,2 (47) | 21,3 | 14,9 | 3,7 | 10,8 | 14,2 |
| 1942 | 133,8 | 66,9 | 66,9 (50) | 35,1 | 26,0 | 4,4 | 10,1 | 22,1 |
| 1943 | 191,9 | 88,4 | 103,5 (54) | 57,5 | 37,3 | 2,1 | 9,5 | 24,4 |
| 1944 | 269,8 | 115,6 | 154,2 (57) | 88,9 | 61,2 | 1,9 | 8,8 | 33,7 |
| 1945[4]) | 376,4 | 135,4 | 241,0 (64) | 102,7 | 116,0 | 2,0 | 8,1 | 60,0 |
| 21. 4. 45 | 384,2 | 137,7 | 246,6 (64) | 104,3 | 131,3 | 2,0 | 8,1 | 73,0[5]) |

Quellen: Statistisches Handbuch von Deutschland, Berlin 1949; Wolf, E.: Geld- und Finanzprobleme der deutschen Nachkriegszeit, a.a.O.; Dieben, W.: Die innere Reichsschuld seit 1933, in: Finanzarchiv, Neue Folge, Bd. 11, Jg. 1949.

1) Nach dem 1. 4. 1924 entstandene Schulden.

2) In Klammern der Anteil der schwebenden Verschuldung an der gesamten Neuverschuldung im Inland in %.

3) Anleiheablösungsschuld ohne Auslosungsrechte, Steuergutscheine, Betriebsanlageguthaben und Warenbeschaffungsguthaben, Wehrmachtsverpflichtungsscheine.

4) Alle Angaben für 1945 „ungefähr" bzw. „geschätzt".

5) Ungefähre Größe bei Kriegsende.

Die bedeutende Vermehrung des Notenumlaufs und des Buchgeldbestandes als Folge der erheblichen Geldschöpfung bei gleichzeitig stark vermindertem Angebot an zivilen Gütern und Diensten hätte bei freiem Spiel der Kräfte zu einer starken Geldentwertung und u. U. wie nach dem Ersten Weltkrieg, weiterhin zu einer galoppierenden Inflation führen müssen. Durch staatliche Zwangsmaßnahmen, wie Preis- und Lohnstop, sowie durch Rationierungen wichtiger Güter, die im Gegensatz zu den Praktiken des Ersten Weltkrieges außerordentlich rigoros durch Strafgesetze gesichert waren, wurden diese Erscheinungen weitgehend vermieden, d. h. die Inflation wurde „zurückgestaut". Der dadurch als Nebenfolge auftretende „Nachfrageüberhang" bei staatlich fixierten Preisen förderte allerdings die Tendenz zur Bildung „schwarzer Märkte". Vor der Aufgabe der Zwangsmaßnahmen war — sollte ein akutes Eintreten der durch diese Maßnahmen nur zurückgestauten Inflation vermieden werden — eine Reduzierung der Geldmenge entsprechend der Menge der vorhandenen Güter und Dienste notwendig. Das geschah durch die Währungsreform 1948, die die durch übermäßige Anspannung des Staatskredits verursachte Abwertung der in Geld oder Geldforderungen bestehenden Vermögensteile der Privaten sichtbar vollzog.

## 3. Schuldenstand der öffentlichen Gebietskörperschaften in der Bundesrepublik

Die Verschuldung des *Bundes* (vgl. Tabelle V) besteht noch zu einem bedeutenden Teil aus „Altschulden aus Kreditmarktmitteln". Dabei handelt es sich im wesentlichen um Ausgleichsforderungen, insbesondere der Deutschen Bundesbank, die im Zusammenhang mit der Währungsreform 1948 entstanden sind und zu einem geringen Teil u. a. um Ablösungsschulden gegenüber Gläubigern von auf RM lautenden Forderungen. Von den „Neuschulden aus Kreditmarktmitteln und sonstigen Forderungen" entfällt der größte Posten auf die „Kredite der Deutschen Bundesbank einschließlich Forderungen", der sich wie folgt aufteilt: 2,2 Mrd. DM Kredite für Einzahlungen an internationale Einrichtungen, 1,2 Mrd. DM Forderungen der Bundesbank wegen Änderung der Wechselkurse, 2,5 Mrd. DM Forderungserwerb aus Nachkriegswirtschaftshilfen. Kassenkredite, die im Laufe des Haushaltsjahres mehrmals in unterschiedlicher Höhe beansprucht wurden, sind jedoch in diesem Posten nicht enthalten. Der Bestand an Buchkrediten bei der Deutschen Bundesbank belief sich am Stichtag auf 0,7 Mrd. DM. Unter den Gebietskörperschaften hat der Bund mit 2,6 Mrd. DM die größten Verpflichtungen aus der Aufnahme von Anleihen (darunter 1,2 Mrd. DM 5 %-Anleihe für Entwicklungshilfe). Schatzwechsel wurden im Jahre 1962 wie auch schon im Vorjahr von keiner der dazu berechtigten Gebietskörperschaften (Bund und Länder) ausgegeben. An den „Neuschulden aus öffentlichen Sondermitteln" — hier spielen insbesondere die Träger der Sozialversicherung eine bedeutende Rolle — und an den Auslandsschulden (davon beim Bund 3,3 Mrd. DM gemäß Londoner Schuldenabkommen) ist der Bund am stärksten beteiligt. Er weist jedoch keine Schulden bei anderen Gebietskörperschaften und beim Lastenausgleichsfonds auf.

Auch bei den *Ländern* spielen die „Altschulden aus Kreditmarktmitteln" eine bedeutende Rolle. Unter den Neuschulden treten die Anleihen und die Schulden bei Banken und Sparkassen hervor. Charakteristisch für die Struktur der Verschuldung der Länder ist seit einigen Jahren der hohe Anteil der Schulden bei Gebietskörperschaften und beim Lastenausgleichsfonds. Darin sind große Beträge an Darlehen des Bundes zur Förderung des Wohnungsbaues enthalten. Die Länder wiesen am Stichtag keinen Bestand an Kassenkrediten auf; sie haben jedoch im Laufe des Jahres 1962 vorübergehend einen geringen Bundesbankkredit in Anspruch genommen.

Bei der Verschuldung der *kommunalen* Gebietskörperschaften fällt der hohe Anteil der Schulden bei Banken

Tabelle V

Stand der öffentlichen Schulden in
(Milliarden

| Art der Schulden |
|---|
| Altschulden aus Kreditmarktmitteln ..................... |
| Neuschulden aus Kreditmarktmitteln und sonstige Forderungen |
| Anleihen ................................ |
| Verzinsliche Schatzanweisungen ..................... |
| Kassenobligationen ............................ |
| unverzinsliche Schatzanweisungen .................. |
| Schatzwechsel ............................... |
| Kredite der Deutschen Bundesbank einschl. Forderungen .. |
| Schulden bei Banken und Sparkassen ................ |
| Schulden bei Versicherungen und Bausparkassen ........ |
| übrige Schulden ............................ |
| Neuschulden aus öffentlichen Sondermitteln ............... |
| Kredite der Bundesanstalt f. Arbeitsverm. u. Arbeitslosenversicherung ........................ |
| Kredite von sonstigen Trägern der Sozialversicherungen .. |
| ERP-(ECA-)Kredite ......................... |
| übrige Schulden ............................ |
| Auslandsschulden .............................. |
| Schulden bei Gebietskörperschaften u. bei Lastenausgleichsfonds |
| Gesamtverschuldung |
| Kassenkredite .............................. |

Quelle: Statistisches Jahrbuch für die Bundesrepublik Deutschland 1963, S. 433 (zusammengefaßt).

1) Einschließlich Berlin (West).

2) Ohne die durch die Bundesvermögensrechnung nachgewiesenen „Anderen Schulden" des Bundes.

der Bundesrepublik[1]) am 31. 12. 1962
DM)

| Bund[2]) | Länder (einschl. Stadtstaaten) | Gemeinden (einschl. Gemeindeverbände | insgesamt[3]) |
|---|---|---|---|
| 12,1 | 9,1 | 0,0 | 21,3 |
| 10,0 | 3,7 | 14,0 | 27,7 |
| 2,6 | 1,7 | 0,4 | 4,7 |
| 0,4 | 0,0 | — | 0,5 |
| 0,4 | 0,0 | — | 0,4 |
| 0,5 | 0,0 | — | 0,5 |
| — | — | — | — |
| 5,9 | — | — | 5,9 |
| 0,1 | 1,5 | 11,0 | 12,6 |
| — | 0,4 | 2,3 | 2,7 |
| — | 0,1 | 0,2 | 0,4 |
| 3,2 | 1,2 | 1,4 | 5,8 |
| 0,4 | 0,4 | 0,1 | 0,9 |
| 2,8 | 0,3 | 0,7 | 3,8 |
| — | 0,5 | 0,5 | 1,0 |
| — | 0,0 | 0,1 | 0,1 |
| 4,5 | 0,2 | 0,1 | 4,8 |
| — | 17,5 | 2,5 | 20,0 |
| 29,8 | 31,7 | 18,0 | . [4]) |
| 0,7 | — | 0,0 | 0,8 |

[3]) Außerdem: Innere Verschuldung: 1,0 Mrd. DM (nur für Gemeinden [Gv.] nachgewiesen); Schulden des Lastenausgleichsfonds 4,3 Mrd. DM und Schulden der Bundesbahn und Bundespost 17,6 Mrd. DM (einschließlich deren Schulden bei Gebietskörperschaften).

[4]) Wegen Doppelzählung nicht summiert.

und Sparkassen auf. Die Sparkassen und Girozentralen können als die typischen Gläubiger des Kommunalkredits bezeichnet werden. Eine gewisse Rolle spielen daneben noch die Versicherungen, Bausparkassen und die Träger der Sozialversicherungen. An dem Bestand von Kassenkrediten sind die Gemeinden mit 0,04 Mrd. DM beteiligt. Die „innere Verschuldung"[1]) der Gemeinden wird mit 1,0 Mrd. DM (vgl. Fußnote 3 zur Tabelle V) angegeben.

Die Verschuldung der öffentlichen Gebietskörperschaften insgesamt beträgt ohne den Posten „Schulden bei öffentlichen Gebietskörperschaften und beim Lastenausgleichsfonds" 59,5 Mrd. DM (31. 12. 61: 58,5 Mrd. DM). Der letztgenannte Posten weist einen Betrag von 20,0 (19,0) Mrd. DM auf und darf, um Doppelzählung zu vermeiden, bei der Ermittlung der Gesamtverschuldung nicht addiert werden.

# Kapitel IX. Öffentlicher Haushalt

## § 1. Objekt der Lehre vom öffentlichen Haushalt; Funktionen des öffentlichen Haushalts

### 1. Objekt der Lehre vom öffentlichen Haushalt

Sowohl das Haushaltswesen — als Inbegriff aller institutionellen Regelungen, die für die formale Gestaltung des Haushaltsplanes, für seine Aufstellung, seinen Vollzug, Rechnungslegung und Kontrolle Anwendung finden sollen — als auch die Bestimmung von Struktur und Höhe des öffentlichen Haushalts (Budget, Etat) sind Mittel zur Erreichung bestimmter Zielsetzungen. Die Lehre vom öffentlichen Haushalt sollte daher als Erläuterung und Begründung der Zusammenhänge gesehen werden, die zwischen Haushaltswesen und Haushalt als Mittel und den

[1]) Dieser Begriff wird hier in einem engeren Sinn gebraucht als bei der oben genannten geographisch orientierten Gliederung (vgl. § 2, 5) und bedeutet, daß eigene Mittel der Gemeinden, die für einen anderen Zweck angesammelt oder treuhänderisch gebunden waren (i. d. R. Rücklagen), herangezogen worden sind

damit möglicherweise zu erreichenden Zielsetzungen bestehen oder bestehen können. Haushalt und Haushaltswesen erhalten somit instrumentale Funktionen, die zweckmäßigerweise nach dem Charakter der verschiedenen Zielsetzungen zu gliedern sind. Die Erkenntnis über solche Funktionen des öffentlichen Haushaltswesens und des öffentlichen Haushalts ist in der Vergangenheit auf das engste verknüpft gewesen mit der historisch-politischen Entwicklung finanzpolitischer Systeme und ihrer Widerspiegelung in der finanzwissenschaftlichen Theorie. So ist es schwer möglich, die Funktionen des Haushalts und des Haushaltswesens als ein für allemal in gleicher Weise geltend zu beschreiben, zumal auch zu jeder Zeit zwischen Idee und Praxis Unterschiede zu verzeichnen sind.

## 2. Funktionen von Haushaltswesen und Haushalt

### *a) Die Ordnungsfunktion des öffentlichen Haushaltswesens*

Die Ordnungsfunktion wird vom Haushaltswesen dann erfüllt, wenn es so organisiert ist, daß das Zwischenziel einer ordentlichen, d. h. *übersichtlichen* und *rationalen* Handhabung der Staatsfinanzen erreicht werden kann. Dieses Zwischenziel ist seinerseits wieder Mittel im Sinne einer möglichst rationalen und ökonomischen Erreichung weiterer Zielsetzungen, die weltanschaulich, politisch und wirtschaftspolitisch ganz verschieden geprägt sein mögen.

Diese Funktion des Haushaltswesens ist vornehmlich haushaltstechnisch zu umreißen: Wie sollen *rechenmäßig* Einnahmen und Ausgaben erfaßt werden und in welcher *Form* soll die Zusammenfassung zu übersichtlichen Rechenwerken erfolgen? Auf diese Frage gibt z. B. ein großer Teil der im Laufe der Zeit entwickelten Haushaltsmaximen oder Budgetprinzipien (vgl. § 2) spezifizierte Anwort.

Heute ist dazu die Frage getreten, wie diese Rechenwerke zur Klärung der Zusammenhänge genutzt werden können, wie sie zwischen staatsfinanziellem Handeln und der gesamten Volkswirtschaft bestehen (Volkswirtschaftliche Gesamtrechnungen, Nationalbudgets, vgl. § 4).

### *b) Die machtpolitische Funktion des öffentlichen Haushaltswesens*

Wie auch immer das Haushaltswesen im einzelnen ausgestaltet sein mag, stets sichern seine institutionellen Vorschriften explizite oder implizite politischen Entscheidungsträgern Machteinflüsse. Das Haushaltswesen hat somit die Funktion, d. h. es dient dem Zwischenziel, den Einfluß politischer Institutionen auf die Staatsfinanzen zu regeln und zu erhalten. Die Problematik dieser Funktion des Haushaltswesens kreist um die Frage: Wer plant, wer kontrolliert, mit anderen Worten, wer hat Einfluß und wie weit geht dieser? Von vornherein ist zu betonen, daß das, was wir heute in der freien Welt als Lehre vom öffentlichen Haushalt verstehen, auf das engste verbunden ist mit dem Werden der Staatsgebilde, die im parlamentarischen Rechtsstaat ihren ideellen und weitgehend praktizierten Ausdruck gefunden haben.

Das betrifft vorzüglich diejenigen Haushaltsmaximen, die insbesondere mit staatspolitisch liberalen Ideen verbunden sind, die sich gegen die Staatsallmacht richten; historisch gesehen, zunächst gegen die Allmacht der Fürsten, im weiteren Verlauf gegen die auch im Rahmen parlamentarisch-demokratischer Systeme immer wieder aufkommende Macht der Exekutive überhaupt.

Aber auch der tatsächlich sich vollziehende Budgetkreislauf (vgl. § 3), der das Leben des Haushalts von seiner ex ante-Planung über Durchführung, ex post-Haushaltsrechnung, Kontrollen bis zur Entlastung umfaßt, ist zutiefst von der staatspolitischen und mit ihr verbundenen finanz- und wirtschaftspolitischen Ordnung geprägt.

### *c) Allgemeine staats- und wirtschaftspolitische Funktionen des öffentlichen Haushaltes*

Während die beiden bisher genannten Funktionen des Haushaltswesens die institutionellen Voraussetzungen für geordnetes finanzpolitisches Handeln gewährleisten sollen, betreffen die nun zur Sprache kommenden Funktionen als

Funktionen des quantitativ bestimmten Haushaltes das politische Handeln selbst, soweit es seinen ökonomischen Niederschlag in den Staatsfinanzen findet. In Bd. I, Kapitel II wurde bereits eine Fülle von staats- und wirtschaftspolitischen Zielsetzungen genannt, die der Staat mit finanzpolitischen Mitteln erreichen kann. Diese finanzpolitischen Mittel sind die verschiedenen Arten von Ausgaben und Einnahmen; daraus folgt, daß der öffentliche Haushalt als Zusammenfassung aller Ausgaben und Einnahmen selbst als Instrument zur Erreichung all der genannten Zielsetzungen aufgefaßt werden kann, d. h. daß auch der öffentliche Haushalt als quantitative Festlegung der verschiedenen Einnahmen und Ausgaben staats- und wirtschaftspolitische Funktionen hat. Im Unterschied zu der Rolle der einzelnen Ausgaben und Einnahmen als Mittel zu Zielen tritt aber beim Staatshaushalt in viel größerem Umfang das Problem der Rangordnung, der Kompatibilität und der Nebenfolgen bei mehreren Zielsetzungen auf, weil hier die Zahl der verschiedenen in Frage kommenden Zielsetzungen unendlich viel größer ist als im Falle einer einzelnen Ausgabe oder Einnahme. Der Staatshaushalt kann in gewissem Sinn als quantitative Widerspiegelung der Rangordnung der verschiedenen Zielsetzungen angesehen werden, die vom politischen Entscheidungsträger gewählt worden ist. Das betrifft nicht nur die Ausgabenseite, vielmehr auch die Einnahmen, bei denen neben sonstigen Zielsetzungen insbesondere auch belastungspolitische Vorstellungen ihren Ausdruck finden können. Hinsichtlich der mangelnden Kompatibilität oder unerwünschter Nebenfolgen mag der Hinweis auf den möglichen Widerspruch zwischen einer nach kultur-, sozial- oder außenpolitischen Gründen erforderlichen Ausgabenerhöhung einerseits und konjunkturellen Gesichtspunkten andererseits genügen. Wenn in dieser Situation die Erhöhung ordentlicher Einnahmen aus politischen Gründen inopportun und eine Kreditfinanzierung wegen etwa drohender Inflationsgefahr nicht angebracht erscheinen, kann eine gleichzeitige Realisierung aller Ziele nicht erfolgen. So kommt dem politischen Entscheidungsträger immer wieder von neuem die Aufgabe zu, für eine Koordination der verschiedenen Elemente des Staatshaushaltes Sorge zu tragen; das gilt nicht nur für die Abstimmung der verschiedenen Ausgaben oder Einnahmen untereinander, sondern ebenso für die Gegenüberstellung von Ausgaben und Einnahmen. In neuerer Zeit hat diese Gegenüberstellung eine besondere Bedeutung dadurch erfahren, daß Differenzen dieser Größen, d. h. Haushaltsdefizite oder -überschüsse geradezu als bewußtes Instrument der Fiskalpolitik gewertet werden.

### 3. Geschichtliches

Das Werden des gebietskörperschaftlichen (Flächen-) Staates mit seiner starken Betonung der ordnenden Macht des *Fürsten* war mit Kämpfen der ständischen, insbesondere der adeligen Gewalten verbunden, die sich nicht nur ihres politischen Einflusses beraubt sahen, sondern auch wirtschaftlich-sozialer Privilegien. Der Fürst wurde zum alleinigen Träger der Willensbildung. In seiner Hand lagen Planung und Kontrolle, wenn sie auch aus rein technischen Gründen in Maßen an ausführende Organe delegiert wurden.

Während und nach dem Kampf um die machtpolitischen Einflußmöglichkeiten wurden in den absoluten Fürstenstaaten der Neuzeit — mit Vorläufern in dem Haushaltswesen der Städte — unter dem Druck der Notwendigkeit zur Beherrschung der sich aus Machtkämpfen nach innen und außen ergebenden finanziellen Schwierigkeiten, Etatsysteme entwickelt, die eine fortschreitende Rationalisierung der Staatsfinanzen zum Ziele hatten. Bemerkenswert ist, daß damals bei der Planung neben dem Hauptziel, der Mittelbeschaffung und ihrer Verwaltung, auch wirtschaftspolitische, Struktur und Wachstum der Wirtschaft beeinflussende Momente eine hervorragende Rolle spielten (Merkantilismus, Kameralismus).

Die folgende Periode des staatspolitischen *Liberalismus* ließ den letzten Gesichtspunkt stark in den Hintergrund treten, während der Drang nach Durchleuchtung des staatsfinanziellen Tuns wuchs, wodurch die Entwicklung des Haushaltswesens im Sinne der Ordnungsfunktion an sich gefördert wurde. Ziel der politischen Kämpfe war aber eine Zurückdrängung der Staatsallmacht. Keineswegs war mit diesen Zielen — idealtypisch gesehen — die Neigung verbunden, dem Staate Instrumente zu verschaffen, welche ihm eine aktive wirtschaftspolitisch orientierte Finanzpolitik erleichtern würden, wie es auf längere Sicht in der Tat der Fall war. Noch heute findet man gelegentlich eine aus altliberaler Sicht geborene Abwehr gegen Aufzeichnungen, von denen man glaubt, daß sie dem Staat zuviel Einsicht, damit Wissensmacht und dadurch möglicherweise die Fähigkeit zu „herrschen" geben. „Herrschaft des Staates" im wirtschaftlichen Raum aber provoziere die Möglichkeit von Fehlentwicklungen, in Abkehr vom ökonomischen Optimum.

Im Gegensatz dazu wird in der Gegenwart eine andere, aus geschichtlicher Erfahrung gewonnene und durch erweiterte theoretische Einsicht geläuterte Auffassung vertreten. Je mehr die öffentlichen Haushalte infolge ihrer wachsenden absoluten und relativen zahlenmäßigen Größe von nicht zu übersehender Bedeutung für das gesamte Wirtschafts- und Sozialgeschehen geworden sind, und dieses offenbar zumindest derzeitig irreversible Geschehen (vgl. Bd. I, Kap. III, Entwicklung der Staatsausgaben) bewußt wird, umsomehr ist zu fordern, den Staatshaushalt neben den einflußpolitischen Aspekten des Haushaltswesens verstärkt in seiner wirtschaftspolitischen Funktion zu erfassen. Daraus ergeben sich spezifische Reformbestrebungen über die Form der staatsfinanziellen Rechenwerke, vor allem hinsichtlich ihrer Einordnung in die volkswirtschaftlichen Rechenwerke (Volkswirtschaftliche Gesamtrechnungen, Nationalbudgets).

Bei all dem bleibt dennoch ein *Problem* bestehen. Gewiß schließt eine Nutzung der Staatsfinanzen als bewußt eingesetztes Instrument der Wirtschaftspolitik eine Einflußnahme der Legislative nicht aus. Sie wird sogar erleichtert, wenn die Rechenwerke im Sinne des eben Genannten erstellt werden. Aber wenn der Staatshaushalt als wirtschaftspolitisches Instrument genutzt werden soll, so muß man ihn auch elastisch genug handhaben können, um bei wechselnden Wirtschaftslagen seine Positionen schnell genug zu variieren. Hier ist die Hauptfrage, wie die Notwendigkeit schneller Reaktion in bezug auf wechselnde Wirtschaftslagen vereinbar ist mit dem Legalprinzip vorheriger Planung durch die gesetzgebenden Gewalten. Ist es möglich, im Sinne der dargestellten Auffassung sachliche Notwendigkeiten in Einklang zu bringen mit den einflußpolitischen Erfordernissen? Die legale Prinzipien erfüllende Haushaltsplanung erfordert Zeit, während die Sachproblematik eine schnelle Entscheidung verlangen mag. Sonach mögen sich hier durchaus immer wieder Widersprüche zwischen den wirtschaftspolitischen Funktionen des Staatshaushalts und den machtpolitisch bestimmten Funktionen des Haushaltswesens ergeben.

Diese Problematik ist daher bei der Behandlung der folgenden §§ dieses Kapitels immer im Auge zu behalten. So sind bei den Budgetprinzipien (§ 2) nicht nur die machtpolitischen Einflußfragen, sondern auch ihre Beziehung zum Ordnungsproblem des Haushaltswesens und zu den wirtschaftspolitischen Funktionen des Haushalts zu beachten, desgleichen bei der Behandlung des Budgetkreislaufs (§ 3). Bei der Darstellung der Zusammenhänge zwischen Staatshaushalt und Wirtschaftskreislauf (§§ 4 f.) sind andererseits die machtpolitischen Belange nicht völlig zu vernachlässigen, wenn sie auch leicht in den Hintergrund treten mögen.

## § 2. Budgetprinzipien

Im Verlauf der finanzpolitischen Entwicklung sind eine Reihe von Haushaltsmaximen oder Budgetprinzipien entwickelt worden, die bei der Aufstellung und Durchführung des Haushaltsplans zu beachten sind. Es ist nochmals zu betonen, daß diese Grundsätze im engen Zusammenhang stehen mit den Kämpfen der Parlamente gegen die Allmacht oder um die Kontrolle der Fürsten in der konstitutionellen Monarchie, weiterhin aber auch um die Kontrolle der Exekutive in der parlamentarischen Demokratie.

M. a. W., die Budgetprinzipien haben soweit Bedeutung in machtpolitischer Hinsicht. Das soll und darf aber nicht heißen, daß sie nicht auch Bedeutung für die Ordnungsfunktion des Haushaltswesens haben. Das, indem sie durch Festlegung von Regeln zugleich zur Klarheit, Rechenhaftigkeit usw. beitragen (vgl. z. B. das Bruttoprinzip). Z. T. binden sie nicht nur die Exekutive, sondern auch die Legislative (vgl. z. B. Prinzip des materiellen Haushaltsausgleichs).

Die Budgetprinzipien sind in der Literatur in vielfältiger Gliederung und Beziehung zu finden; folgende Aufstellung erhebt deshalb keinen Anspruch auf Vollständigkeit.

### 1. Prinzip der Öffentlichkeit

Dieses Prinzip wendet sich gegen die Finanzpraxis sowohl des Ancien Régime mit seinen Geheimbudgets als auch gegen ähnliche Tendenzen in totalitären Regimen der Neuzeit. Im Gegensatz dazu sollen sich alle Stadien des Haushaltskreislaufs (Aufstellung, Bewilligung, Durchführung, Kontrolle und Entlastung) dergestalt im Lichte der Öffentlichkeit abspielen, daß jeder Staatsbürger sich grundsätzlich ein treffendes Bild von ihnen verschaffen kann (Neumark). Die Erfüllung dieses Grundsatzes ist weiterhin Voraussetzung für eine Integration der öffentlichen Meinung in den Prozeß der politischen Willensbildung (Schmölders). Es kommt für ein erfülltes demokratisches Staatsleben darauf an, daß die Bürger nicht lediglich die Ergebnisse des Regierungshandelns zu spüren bekommen, sondern daß der ganze Prozeß staatsfinanziellen Tuns einschließlich der Arbeit der Volksvertreter dem staatspolitischen Interesse der Bürger erfaßbar gemacht wird. Das könnte insbesondere der Sparsamkeit der Staatsführung dienlich sein. Über die Erfüllung des formalen Prinzips ist darüber hinaus zweifellos Voraussetzung die verfassungsrechtlich und praktisch vorhandene Sicherung, daß kritische Äußerungen ohne Nachteil für den, der sie tut, getan werden dürfen. Aber das ist nicht alles. Es muß auch ein tatsächliches Interesse der Bürger vorhanden sein oder geweckt werden, welches über die vielfach allein vorhandene Neigung hinausgeht, lediglich über gegebene steuerliche Belastungen ungehalten zu sein, nicht aber der Ursache dieser Belastung nachzuspüren.

*Ausnahmen* vom Prinzip der Öffentlichkeit bilden sog. Geheimvermerke. Das sind z. B. in den Haushaltsplänen der Bundesrepublik Haushaltsvermerke, die bestimmen, daß die Kontrolle der betreffenden Mittel nur vom Präsidenten des Bundesrechnungshofes vorgenommen werden darf. Solche Geheimvermerke mögen ein legitimes Interesse der Staatsführung erfüllen, wie z. B. im Falle von Mitteln für Geheimdienste. Im Falle des sogenannten Reptilienfonds des Bundeskanzlers (Kap. 0403, Titel 300) ist immer wieder Kritik laut geworden, daß hier der Öffentlichkeit zu wenig Einblick in sie interessierende Belange gewährt wird.

### 2. Prinzip der Klarheit

Öffentlichkeit in dem Sinne, wie soeben ausgeführt, setzt auch voraus, daß es dem interssierten Staatsbürger möglich ist, sich in den Budgetverfahren, insbesondere aber in den staatsfinanziellen Zahlenwerken zurechtzufinden. Darum schließt sich zur Erfüllung des Prinzips der Öffentlichkeit mit Notwendigkeit die Forderung nach Klarheit an. Danach sollen der Haushaltsplan und die nach dessen Vollzug vorzulegende Haushaltsrechnung in einer Form abgefaßt werden, daß sich der interessierte Staatsbürger in den veröffentlichten Zahlen nicht nur prinzipiell, sondern auch praktisch zurechtfinden kann. Hier liegt in besonderem Maße ein Desideratum vor.

### 3. Prinzip der Genauigkeit

Während vorgenannter Grundsatz ein formales Prinzip in dem Sinne ist, daß das, was einmal Inhalt des Zahlenwerkes ist, klar und deutlich zum Ausdruck kommen soll, hat das Prinzip der Genauigkeit bereits stärker inhaltliche Bezüge. Denn es fordert, daß die veranschlagten Zahlen des Haushaltsplans bestimmten Kriterien genügen. Sie sollen „genau" sein einmal in dem Sinne, daß nicht etwa nur ein die wirkliche Situation verschönender, lediglich „papiermäßiger" Ausgleich des Haushalts erfolgt. Zum anderen sollen aber auch nicht geheime Reserven, durch eine Überschätzung der Ausgabenvoranschläge oder eine Unterschätzung der Einnahmenvoranschläge, gebildet werden. Auch in diesem Falle würde die Rationalität der Haushaltsführung leiden.

Abgesehen von der Schwierigkeit, geschätzte Voranschlagszahlen mit den sich aus der tatsächlichen Entwicklung ergebenden Zahlen in Einklang zu bringen — das hat insbesondere Bedeutung bei den Steuererträgen — kann die Bildung solcher geheimen Reserven auch finanztaktischen Belangen dienen. Einmal als Argument im Kampfe um zukünftige größere Zuteilungen im Rahmen des Finanzausgleichs. Vgl. dazu die jüngste Diskussion um die vom Bund geforderte Erhöhung der Beteiligungsquoten an der Einkommen- und Körperschaftsteuer in der Bundesrepublik Deutschland, in der die Länder in ihrer Gegenargumentation immer wieder darauf hingewiesen haben, daß der Bund seine erwarteten Steuereinnahmen unterschätze. — Zum anderen aber erscheint die Bildung geheimer Reserven oft im Zusammenhang mit der Planaufstellung innerhalb eines Ressorts. Wegen des in der Praxis oft gerechtfertigten Verdachts solcher Reservebildungen werden die Haushaltsansätze der ihre Wünsche anmeldenden unteren Stellen (vgl. Aufstellung des Planentwurfs § 3, 1) in der Regel durch die jeweils höheren Stellen gekürzt. Wenn diese Kürzungen, wie oft der Einfachheit halber, proportional für die Ansätze aller Haushaltsstellenträger erfolgen, so mag jedes für eine Haushaltsposition verantwortliche Gremium seine Ausgabenvoranschläge höher ansetzen, um im Verhältnis zu „den anderen" nicht zu schlecht wegzukommen. Wer dagegen von vornherein die tatsächlich benötigten Sätze nennt, mag dann benachteiligt werden. Dadurch aber treten Verzerrungen in der Haushaltsstruktur ein, die nicht der Rationalität der Haushaltsführung dienen. Im übrigen wird dem Parlament die Bewilligung des wirklichen Bedarfs der Haushaltsstellenträger erschwert.

### 4. Prinzip der Vollständigkeit

Nach diesem Grundsatz soll der Haushaltsplan derart aufgestellt werden, daß er die voneinander gesonderten

Voranschläge sämtlicher Einnahmen und Ausgaben enthält. Nächst der Forderung, daß alle Einnahmen und Ausgaben im Haushaltsplan verzeichnet werden sollen, d. h. nicht etwa bestimmte Einnahmen und Ausgaben aus dem Haushaltsplan herausgenommen werden, fordert das Prinzip der Vollständigkeit speziell, daß nicht nur die Salden aus diesen Einnahmen und Ausgaben (Nettoprinzip), sondern gemäß dem Bruttoprinzip alle Einnahmen und alle Ausgaben in voller Höhe unsaldiert verzeichnet, d. h. der gesetzgebenden Körperschaft und der Öffentlichkeit klargelegt werden. Sinn des Grundsatzes ist es, eine umfassende Planung zu ermöglichen und der Volksvertretung einen Gesamtüberblick über die geplante Staatstätigkeit zu verschaffen.

Allerdings sind *Ausnahmen* vom Prinzip der Vollständigkeit zu verzeichnen. Nur einige seien genannt. So wird z. B. bei solchen öffentlichen Unternehmungen, die der Sachlage entsprechend mehr kaufmännisch betonte Führung verlangen, das Nettoprinzip angewandt. Hier könnte ja, wenn schnelles Reagieren auf veränderte Marktlagen erforderlich ist, die vollständige Planung aller Einzelheiten, wie sie das Bruttoprinzip erfordert, wirtschaftliches Verhalten hemmen. Über die Problematik in einflußpolitischer Sicht vgl. aber Bd. II, Kapitel IV, § 3. Dann können bei zweckgebundenen Sondervermögen Ausnahmen vom Vollständigkeitsprinzip auftreten. Auch die sogenannten Rückeinnahmen, die z. B. durch den Planvermerk „Einnahmen fließen den Mitteln zu" möglich sind, stellen eine Ausnahme vom Prinzip der Vollständigkeit dar. Dagegen sind allerdings Bedenken angemeldet worden, weil durch die eigenmächtige Verfügung über Rückeinnahmen von der Verwaltung Ausgaben getätigt werden, auf die das Parlament keinen Einfluß hat.

### 5. Prinzip der Einheit

Nach dieser Haushaltsmaxime sind alle veranschlagten Einnahmen und Ausgaben einer Gebietskörperschaft innerhalb eines *einzigen Haushaltsplans* aufzuführen. Damit soll die Übersichtlichkeit der Haushaltgebarung, auch zwecks politischer Kontrolle, erreicht werden. Somit ergeben sich auch Verbindungslinien zum Prinzip der Klarheit.

Das Prinzip der Budgeteinheit sichert allerdings noch nicht die Budgetvollständigkeit. Diese ist erst zu erreichen, wenn der Einheitsgrundsatz durch den Grundsatz der *fiskalischen Kasseneinheit* ergänzt wird. Danach sollen alle Einnahmen in einen allgemeinen Fonds zur Finanzierung aller Ausgaben zusammengefaßt werden. Diese Forderung, auch Grundsatz der *Non-Affektation* (Nicht-Zweckbindung) genannt, ist dagegen gerichtet, Einnahmen für besondere Zwecke abzuzweigen, d. h. für Spezialkassen, Zweckkassen, zu reservieren. Zwar waren Spezialfonds zu Beginn einer rationalen Finanzwirtschaft gegenüber bisheriger fürstlicher Mißwirtschaft gewiß ein fortschrittliches Instrument, um überhaupt Mittel für wichtige Aufgaben zu sichern. Im weiteren Verlauf der Durchrationalisierung dagegen erwiesen sie sich als hinderlich, indem sie einer aus freiem Entschluß der politischen Gewalten entspringenden Verteilung der Mittel für alle gewollten Zwecke im Wege standen. Sie wurden daher im allgemeinen abgebaut. Jedoch gibt es noch heute Ausnahmen von dem Prinzip der fiskalischen Kasseneinheit, so z. B. bei den sogenannten Sondervermögen, bei denen eine spezielle und direkte Verbindung zwischen Einnahmen und Ausgaben besteht.

Aus dem Prinzip der Budgeteinheit mag man die Forderung nach der Aufstellung eines *Einheitsbudgets* ableiten. Ein Einheitsbudget ist dadurch charakterisiert, daß alle Einnahmen und Ausgaben in einer einzigen Zusammenstellung erscheinen.

Einheitsbudgets sind nicht in allen Ländern üblich. Vielmehr werden vielfach, ohne daß dadurch der Grundsatz der Budgeteinheit[1]) zerstört wird, „*doppelte*" Budgets aufgestellt. Die Einheitlichkeit ist dadurch gewahrt, daß die Planaufstellung in einem einheitlichen Vorgang erfolgt, unabhängig davon, daß der Gesamtplan aus zwei Aufstellungen besteht, die aber untrennbar miteinander verbunden sind.

---

[1]) Dabei ist ja allein wichtig, daß die gesetzgebenden Körperschaften den ordnenden und einflußmäßigen Überblick behalten.

So gibt es in einigen Ländern, wie z. B. auch in der Bundesrepublik Deutschland neben dem *„ordentlichen"* einen *„außerordentlichen"* Haushalt. In den außerordentlichen Haushaltsplan werden die durch außerordentliche Einnahmen, in der Regel durch Kredite zu finanzierenden Ausgaben eingestellt. Nach Neumark sind es vor allem zwei Motive gewesen, die Anlaß zu solcher Budgetordnung waren. Einmal der Wunsch, ein als unerwünscht angesehenes Defizit des Gesamthaushalts dadurch zu verschleiern, daß man den außergewöhnlichen „einmaligen" Charakter bestimmter Ausgaben zum Anlaß nimmt, sie von „normalen" zu unterscheiden, um so ihre kreditmäßige Deckung rechtfertigen zu können. Zum anderen aber die Vorstellung, daß gewisse „produktive" bzw. rentable Ausgaben eine Anleihefinanzierung zulassen oder erfordern. Schmölders hat jüngst die Aufstellung von außerordentlichen Haushaltsplänen aus finanzpsychologischen Gründen verteidigt: Es würde durch die Bezeichnung „außerordentlich" den Abgeordneten ein Zeichen gesetzt, daß Kreditfinanzierung nicht die Regel, sondern eine Ausnahme sei. Die Frage, wann und wann nicht Defizitfinanzierung angebracht ist, läßt sich aber so einfach nicht lösen, sondern erfordert tieferreichende Erwägungen.

Dann kann ein doppeltes Budget in der Art aufgestellt werden, daß eine Trennung zwischen einem laufenden Betriebsbudget und einem Kapitalbudget erfolgt. Die Transaktionen, die den Vermögensstatus des Staates berühren, Investitionen auf der Ausgaben-, Anleihen auf der Einnahmenseite, werden im *Kapitalbudget,* alle anderen (Steuern u. a. laufende Einnahmen sowie Verbrauchsausgaben) werden im *Betriebsbudget* verzeichnet. Durch Einstellung bestimmter Ausgaben für den Kapitalfonds (z. B. der Zinsen für Staatsschulden, Abschreibungen für Investitionen) einerseits und Einnahmen aus dem Kapitalfonds (z. B. der Gewinne aus öffentlichen Betrieben) andererseits in die laufende Betriebsrechnung, wird auch eine Durchleuchtung gewisser staatswirtschaftlicher Kosten versucht. Das Defizit im laufenden Haushalt und nur dieses, da die für Investitionen aufgenommenen Anleihen als defizit-unwesentlich gelten, wird, so z. B. in Schweden, einem Budgetausgleichfonds belastet, entsprechende Überschüsse ihm gutgeschrieben.

Hinsichtlich der Frage, welche Arten von Investitionen im Kapitalbudget verbucht werden, unterscheidet man mehrere Methoden. Bei der *Methode der ertragbringenden Vermögensgegenstände* werden nur die werbenden Anlagen im Kapitalbudget verbucht und anleihefinanziert, ohne daß ein „Defizit" im laufenden Haushalt erscheint. Nichtwerbende Anlagen werden im laufenden Budget verbucht. Die Zuordnung zu den beiden Gruppen ist oft nicht hinreichend exakt durchzuführen. In Schweden z. B. setzt man bei bestimmten Gebäuden den nichtwerbenden Teil der Investition schematisch fest, so bei Dienstgebäuden 25 %, bei Schulen 50 % (und bei Militäranlagen 100 %). Bei der *Reinvermögensmethode* dagegen werden die Ausgaben für alle Investitionen im Kapitalbudget verbucht, gleich, ob sie Ertrag bringen oder nicht.

Eine Sonderfrage ist, wie die Staatshaushaltsrechenwerke für die *Volkswirtschaftliche Gesamtrechnung* aufbereitet werden können[1]). Hier ist ein konsolidiertes Budget, und zwar ein alle Regierungsebenen umfassendes, deswegen Voraussetzung, weil Transaktionen zwischen einzelnen Gebietskörperschaften für die Zwecke der Einkommensanalyse irrelevant sind. Weiterhin muß dabei eine andere Gliederung der Ausgaben, nach den Kriterien, wie sie die Volkswirtschaftliche Gesamtrechnung (VGR) erfordert, gewählt werden (vgl. Bd. I, Kap. III, § 1,3). Im übrigen wird darauf hingewiesen, daß für die Einkommensanalyse bei den Einnahmen nicht der tatsächliche Kasseneingang (Kassenbudget), sondern die Entstehung der Zahlungsverpflichtung gebucht werden muß (wie auch in der Praxis vieler VGR die Regel), um den Zeitpunkt der Buchung mehr mit dem Zeitpunkt der Wirkung auf den privaten Sektor in Einklang zu bringen. Jedoch ist das auch bestritten worden unter Hinweis darauf, daß der tatsächliche Zahlungsvorgang, da er die Liquidität der Privaten berührt, von wesentlicher Bedeutung für deren wirtschaftliche Entscheidungen ist.

## 6. Prinzip der Spezialität

Durch das Prinzip der Spezialität erfolgt eine Bindung der Exekutive an den Haushaltsplan dadurch, daß die bewilligten Ausgaben nur für die vorgesehenen Zwecke (sachliche oder qualitative Spezialität), nur in der vorgesehenen Höhe (größenmäßige oder quantitative Spezialität) und nur innerhalb des vorgesehenen Zeitraums (zeitliche Spezialität) getätigt werden dürfen.

[1]) Ihre Aufstellung von vornherein allein für diesen Zweck dürfte vor allem daran scheitern, daß dann, wie es Ziel vor allem des nach dem Ministerialprinzip gegliederten Budgets ist, die politische Verantwortlichkeit nicht mehr klar ersichtlich würde.

*a) Sachliche Spezialität*

Durch eine weitgehende Aufgliederung des Haushaltsplans in Einzelpläne, Kapitel, Titel usw. soll, nächst Festlegung der politischen Verantwortlichkeit, eine Bindung der Exekutive hinsichtlich der sachlichen Verwendung der bewilligten Mittel erreicht werden. Die Legislative engt den Spielraum der Exekutive dadurch ein, daß allgemein die *Appropriationsklausel* gilt, wonach keine andere Verwendung als die im Haushaltsplan vorgesehene erlaubt ist. Nicht für den bestimmten Zweck verwendete Mittel verfallen.

Soll dagegen *ausnahmsweise* eine Verwendung von Mitteln auch für andere als die bewilligten Zwecke erlaubt sein, so muß der Haushaltsplan eine sogenannte *Deckungsklausel* enthalten, die genau anzugeben hat, für welche anderen Titel oder seine Untertitel eine „Deckungsfähigkeit" gelten soll. Bei einseitiger Deckungsfähigkeit ist nur erlaubt, die bei einer Haushaltsposition ersparten Mittel zur Deckung von Mehrbedarf an einer anderen Stelle zu verwenden. Bei gegenseitiger Deckungsfähigkeit dagegen können in den Haushaltsplan eingestellte Mittel in beiden Richtungen, von der einen auf die andere Position und umgekehrt, verschoben werden.

*b) Größenmäßige Spezialität*

Danach sollen Ausgaben nur in der Höhe erfolgen, wie Mittel im Haushaltsplan veranschlagt wurden. Diese aus dem Begriff der Planung notwendigerweise sich ergebende Forderung mag jedoch in praxi auf Schwierigkeiten stoßen. Deshalb besteht in den meisten Ländern die Möglichkeit, durch Nachtragspläne oder durch besondere, haushaltsrechtlich genau festgelegte Verfahren Haushaltsüberschreitungen zu vermeiden bzw. zuzulassen. Es ist aber zu beachten, daß für Nachtragshaushalte dieselben rechtlichen Regeln gelten wie für die Bewilligung des Haushalts selbst, m. a. W. die Exekutive dadurch in ihrer Bindung an das Parlament befangen bleibt. Ist aus besonderen Gründen ein schnelles Handeln der Regierung erforderlich, so können besondere Regelungen in Kraft treten. Vgl. z. B. das sogenannte Notbewilligungsrecht des Finanzministers nach Art. 112 des Grundgesetzes für die Bundesrepublik Deutschland (GG), wonach Haushaltsüberschreitungen und außerplanmäßige Ausgaben möglich sind, aber der Zustimmung des Bundesministers der Finanzen bedürfen. Diese darf nur im Falle eines unvorhergesehenen und unabweisbaren Bedürfnisses erteilt werden.

### *c) Zeitliche Spezialität*

Der Grundsatz der zeitlichen Spezialität engt den Entscheidungsspielraum der Exekutive dadurch ein, daß die in den Haushaltsplan eingestellten Mittel nur für den Zeitraum der Haushaltsperiode, also einen festen Zeitraum, bewilligt werden. Mittel, die am Ende einer Periode nicht verbraucht sind, verfallen und müssen, falls eine spätere Verwendung beabsichtigt ist, nochmals bewilligt werden.

Neben dem vor allem einflußpolitisch zu verstehenden Sinn dieses Grundsatzes ist es dessen „ordnender" Nebensinn, die Sparsamkeit der Ausgabengestaltung zu fördern. Es ist jedoch eine andere Frage, ob dieses Ziel damit allemal erreicht wird oder ob nicht vielmehr gerade dadurch eine gewisse subalterne Verschwendung gefördert wird, indem die ausgabeberechtigten Stellen die bewilligten Mittel „rechtzeitig" auch dann verbrauchen, wenn es sachlich gesehen gar nicht nottut, um nicht den „Verdacht" zu erregen, daß die Haushaltssätze zu hoch waren und deshalb in Zukunft gekürzt werden könnten.

Sollen *ausnahmsweise* bestimmte Mittel auch in einer späteren Haushaltsperiode ausgegeben werden dürfen, so muß eine sogenannte *Übertragungsklausel* in den Haushaltsplan eingestellt werden. Es ist dabei darauf hinzuweisen, daß eine solche Klausel nach dem in der Bundesrepublik geltenden Haushaltsrecht dann nicht notwendig ist, wenn es sich bei den bewilligten Mitteln um einmalige und außerordentliche handelt, die von Gesetzes wegen als übertragbar gelten.

In gewisser Weise ist mit dem Begriff der zeitlichen Spezialität verbunden das in vielen Darstellungen erwähnte Prinzip der

*Jährlichkeit.* Beide beinhalten eine „zeitliche Begrenzung", die beim Prinzip der Jährlichkeit die Aufstellung, dagegen beim Prinzip der zeitlichen Spezialität die Durchführung des Haushaltsplanes betrifft. Teilweise ist das Prinzip der Jährlichkeit, zumindest als Periodisierung schon im Begriff des Budgets enthalten. Die Tatsache, daß diese Periode ein Jahr ist und der Haushaltsplan nur für ein Jahr gelten soll, engt die Entscheidungsfreiheit der Regierung bewußt ein. Es handelt sich damit um einen einflußpolitischen Grundsatz, während aus sachlichen Gründen vielleicht eine langfristige Planung in bestimmten Fällen besser wäre. Immerhin ist dabei zu bedenken, daß eine jährliche Veranschlagung nicht die Bewilligung von Ausgaben für einen längeren Zeitraum ausschließt (vgl. Art. 110, 2 Satz 3 zweiter Halbsatz GG). Im übrigen gilt gemäß Art. 110, 2 Satz 4 GG das sogenannte Bepackungsverbot, nach dem in das Haushaltsgesetz keine Bestimmungen aufgenommen werden dürfen, die über das Rechnungsjahr hinausgehen oder sich nicht auf die Einnahmen und Ausgaben des Bundes oder seiner Verwaltung beziehen.

Die unter den Begriff Spezialität fallenden Grundsätze tragen vorzüglich einflußpolitischen Charakter. Dabei ergibt sich folgendes Problem: Soll der Haushalt als Instrument einer antizyklischen Politik dienen, so muß die Regierung die Möglichkeit haben, gegebenenfalls auf wechselnde Wirtschaftslagen zu reagieren. Unter diesem Gesichtspunkt mag es sich als notwendig erweisen, daß die Exekutive durch bewußte finanzielle Maßnahmen eingreift, die u. U. den durch die genannten Grundsätze der größenmäßigen und zeitlichen Spezialität gesteckten Rahmen durchbrechen. Nach G. Colm sollten Haushaltspläne „serve as a guide and tool for gouvernment operations and not as a straitjacket". In den Überlegungen der Wissenschaftlichen Beiräte beim Bundeswirtschaftsministerium und beim Bundesfinanzministerium[1]) nimmt vor allem eine Verstärkung der Möglichkeit, Ausgaben zeitlich zu verschieben, Raum ein. Auch die Möglichkeit, Eventualbudgets aufzustellen, wurde in die Erwägungen einbezogen.

---

[1]) Instrumente der Konjunkturpolitik und ihre rechtliche Institutionalisierung, Gutachten vom 3. 6. und 8. 7. 1956.

## 7. Prinzip der Vorherigkeit

Nach diesem Grundsatz ist der Haushaltsplan vor Beginn der Haushaltsperiode festzustellen, d. h. vorzulegen und zu beschließen, für die er gelten soll. Das hat einmal ordnende Bedeutung, da die Verwaltung ohne vorherige Kenntnis der Planansätze nicht klug disponieren kann, zum anderen einflußpolitische, um ein bindungsloses Vakuum zu vermeiden. Diese aus dem Wesen des Haushalts als einer ex ante-Planung sich ergebende Forderung hat andererseits die mißliche Folge, daß dadurch eine reagible Finanzpolitik im Hinblick auf etwa schnell wechselnde Wirtschaftslagen erschwert wird. So wichtig die oben genannten Gründe, insbesondere der einflußpolitische, sind, so wird andererseits dadurch die im vorigen Punkte 6 zu b und c bezeichnete Problematik institutionell verfestigt. Denkbare Abhilfen sind unter ähnlichen Gesichtspunkten zu betrachten wie die dort angeführten.

## 8. Prinzip des Haushaltsgleichgewichts

Nach diesem Grundsatz sollen die Ausgaben von vornherein durch Einnahmen gedeckt sein. Er kann formell oder materiell aufgefaßt werden.

Als *formeller* Grundsatz sagt er aus, daß alle in den Haushalt eingestellten Ausgaben auch durch planmäßige Einnahmen gedeckt sein sollen. Soweit bindet das Prinzip bereits den Gesetzgeber, für alle geplanten Ausgaben auch an Einnnahmen zu denken, d. h. nicht Ausgabenbeschlüsse zu fassen, ohne sich über die damit verbundenen Belastungen klar zu sein. Es ist daher von grundlegender Bedeutung, sagt aber noch nichts über die Art der Deckungsmittel aus, läßt also auch Kredite grundsätzlich zu.

Wird dagegen das Prinzip des Haushaltsgleichgewichts so aufgefaßt, daß alle Ausgaben durch „ordentliche" Einnahmen gedeckt sein müssen, daß also eine Defizitfinanzierung durch Kredite ausgeschlossen ist, so handelt es sich um eine ökonomisch *materielle* Vorschrift. Würde das materielle Prinzip gelten, so wäre damit die Möglichkeit einer ausgleichenden Fiskalpolitik wesentlich eingeschränkt. Die Frage, ob ein Ausgleich des Haushalts auch durch einen Kredit erfolgen darf, betrifft die sogenannten Deckungsgrundsätze und wurde bereits im Kapitel VIII, Öffentlicher Kredit gestreift. Weiterhin wurde sie auch im Zusammenhang mit dem Prinzip der Budgeteinheit angeschnitten, als dort die Aufstellung eines außerordentlichen Haushalts neben dem ordentlichen Haushalt und eines Kapitalhaushalts neben dem laufenden Haushalt erwähnt wurde. Der außerordentliche Haushalt bedeutet ja geradezu eine institutionalisierte Möglichkeit für Kreditaufnahmen, da diese in aller Regel als außerordentliche Einnahmen verstanden werden. Die Möglichkeit, den öffentlichen Kredit bewußt als Instrument der Beschäftigungspolitik zu nutzen, wird in der Bundesrepublik durch die Vorschrift des Artikels 115 GG in dem Sinne eingeengt, daß Kredite nur bei außerordentlichem Bedarf und in der Regel nur für Ausgaben zu werbenden Zwecken aufgenommen werden dürfen.

Hier muß aber eines ganz deutlich gemacht werden. Die eben gemachte Anknüpfung an die deutsche Praxis des außerordentlichen Haushalts darf auf keinen Fall zu der Meinung Anlaß geben, daß eine Defizitfinanzierung nur bei doppelten Haushalten möglich ist; vielmehr ist das auch denkbar bei Einheitsbudgets. Nur bietet sich uns die Anknüpfung an das bekannte Beispiel insbesondere an. — Die Trennung des Haushalts in ein laufendes oder Betriebsbudget und ein Kapitalbudget, wie z. B. in Schweden, bietet in zweifacher Hinsicht finanztechnische Vereinfachungen für eine antizyklische Politik: Einmal dadurch, daß mehr oder weniger hohe Investitionsausgaben über das Kapitalkonto kreditmäßig finanziert werden können, wodurch bereits eine die gesamte Nachfrage steuernde Möglichkeit eröffnet ist. Zum anderen dadurch, daß auch bei den laufenden Ausgaben, die über das Betriebsbudget laufen, je nachdem eine Defizit- oder Überschußfinanzierung möglich ist — etwa auftretende Salden können völlig legal mit einem Budgetausgleichsfonds verrechnet werden. Aber auch hier ist zu beachten, was schon Hansen[1]) betont hat, daß die Frage, ob bestimmte Ausgaben durch Steuern oder Kredite finanziert werden sollen, sich nicht durch diese Form der Budgetierung automatisch lösen läßt. Vielmehr sind alle Entscheidungen über Richtung und Ausmaß der Fiskalpolitik auf der Grundlage wirtschaftspolitischer Überlegungen zu treffen.

## § 3. Der Kreislauf des Budgets

Der Budgetkreislauf, der die Lebensphasen eines für eine bestimmte Periode, meist ein Jahr, geltenden Haushalts von seiner Aufstellung bis zur Kontrolle und Entlastung der Regierung umfaßt, ist das Ergebnis historischer Entwicklung. Deshalb findet man in den einzelnen Ländern durchaus Unterschiede. Abgesehen davon zeigt sich in den freien Ländern etwa folgende idealtypische Struktur. Der Budgetkreislauf umfaßt folgende Phasen, die zum Teil streng zeitlich aufeinander folgen, zum Teil aber auch nebeneinander laufen. Zeitlich folgen aufeinander: *Aufstellung* des Haushaltsplanes mit seinen Teilphasen Entwurf, Beratung und Feststellung, der *Vollzug* und die *Entlastung*. Die *Entlastung* hat zur Voraussetzung die *Kontrolle*. Diese ist jedoch zeitlich nicht eindeutig zu bestimmen. Sie ist vor allem nachherige, aber auch mitlaufende, ja sogar auch vorherige Kontrolle. Insgesamt gesehen dauert der Kreislauf des für ein Haushaltsjahr geltenden Haushalts in der Regel mindestens drei Jahre. Daß bei diesem Tatbestand sich zeitliche Überlappungen ergeben, d. h. daß während des Vollzugs eines Haushaltsplanes die Vorarbeiten für den der nächsten Periode normalerweise bereits begonnen haben, während andererseits die Abwicklung des Planes der vorherigen Periode noch läuft, ist am Rande zu vermerken.

---

[1]) Fiscal Policy and Business Cycles, S. 202.

## 1. Aufstellung des Haushaltsplanes

Bei der Aufstellung des Haushaltsplanes wird in der Regel vom zeitlich vorhergehenden ausgegangen, dem Zusatzgrößen (in der Regel positive, seltener negative) angefügt werden. Das ist vor allem schon praktisch-technisch begründet. Dadurch ergibt sich ein traditionelles Element der Haushaltsplanung. Bedeutende Änderungen sind nur nach umstürzenden politischen Ereignissen zu erwarten.

### *a) Entwurf des Haushaltsplanes*

Die Feststellung des Entwurfs des Haushaltsplanes erfolgt durch die Exekutive. Bei der Erarbeitung der Planung geht man in der Regel von unten nach oben vor. Die unteren Verwaltungseinheiten geben ihre Wünsche und Vorschläge bekannt, die jeweils auf der nächsthöheren Verwaltungsstufe auf ihre Realisierbarkeit im Rahmen der hin und her erwogenen finanziellen Gesamtplanung und auf ihre Berechtigung im Verhältnis zu den Wünschen anderer nebengeordneter Stellen hin abgestimmt werden.

Aufgrund der von den Fachressorts für ihren Geschäftsbereich erarbeiteten und eingereichten Unterlagen nimmt dann der Finanzminister die rechnerische Aufstellung des Planentwurfs vor[1]). Dieser wird nach Beratung durch das Kabinett dem Parlament vorgelegt. Auf die dadurch gegebene gewisse, zumindest budgettechnisch begründete, Vormachtstellung der Exekutive gegenüber der Legislative sei von vornherein hingewiesen. Vgl. dazu aber sofort auch die Frage der sogenannten Legislativinitiative.

### *b) Beratung des Planentwurfs*

Der Planentwurf wird dann von der Legislative, der gesetzgebenden Gewalt, beraten. Die Beratung erfolgt in der Regel in mehreren „Lesungen", denen ins einzelne gehende

[1]) Die im Text genannten Bezeichnungen decken die in Bund und Ländern üblichen. In den Städten, die gleichzeitig den Charakter eines Landes haben, und in den anderen Gemeinden treten an ihre Stelle analoge Bezeichnungen, z. B. Finanzsenator oder Stadtkämmerer anstatt Finanzminister.

Beratungen durch Haushaltsausschüsse zwischengeschaltet sind. Die Technik der Beratung als Voraussetzung zur Feststellung des Haushaltsplans variiert im übrigen je nach gegebener Aufteilung der Legislativgewalt, d. h. ist abhängig davon, ob es sich um ein Einkammer- oder um ein Zweikammersystem handelt und im letzten Falle, welche Rolle die einzelnen Kammern spielen. In der Bundesrepublik Deutschland ist neben dem Bundestag als der gewählten Volksvertretung der Bundesrat, durch den die Länder bei der Gesetzgebung und Verwaltung des Bundes mitwirken, in den Budgetprozeß eingeschaltet. Ihm geht der Regierungsentwurf zunächst im „ersten Durchgang" zu, bevor der Bundestag tätig wird.

Nunmehr ist ein bereits angekündigtes Wort zur „Legislativinitiative" am Platze: Dem Wesen der parlamentarischen Demokratie entsprechend kann das Parlament Änderungen am Haushaltsplanentwurf vornehmen. Das betrifft in aller Regel vor allem Abstriche in den Planzahlen. Für Änderungen, die Ausgabenvermehrungen mit sich bringen, gelten vielfach besondere Bestimmungen. So bedürfen z. B. in der Bundesrepublik Deutschland Beschlüsse des Bundestages und des Bundesrates, welche die von der Bundesregierung vorgeschlagenen Ausgaben des Budgetentwurfs erhöhen oder neue Ausgaben in sich schließen oder für die Zukunft mit sich bringen, nach Artikel 113 GG der Zustimmung der Bundesregierung. Im übrigen wird nach § 96, 3 der Geschäftsordnung des Bundestages ein Antrag, der eine Finanzvorlage darstellt, nur dann beraten, wenn er mit einem Ausgleichsantrage zu ihrer Deckung verbunden ist.

Für Ergänzungsvorlagen, die von der Regierung während der Beratung des ursprünglichen Planentwurfs eingebracht werden, gelten die gleichen Bestimmungen wie für einen normalen Entwurf.

### *c) Feststellung des Haushaltsplanes*

Die nächste Teilphase im Budgetkreislauf ist die Feststellung des Haushaltsplans durch die Legislative. Diese erfolgt durch das Haushaltsgesetz, bei den Gemeinden durch die Haushaltssatzung.

Einige Worte zu dem Fall, daß der von der Regierung vorgelegte Haushaltsplanentwurf nicht oder nicht rechtzeitig vom Parlament verabschiedet wird. Im preußischen Verfassungskonflikt, der über die vom König geplante Heeresform ausbrach und seit 1862 dazu führte, daß Ausgaben ohne Bewilligung durch das Parlament getätigt wurden, ist von Bismarck die sogenannte „Lückentheorie" vertreten worden: Wenn kein Budget zustande käme, wäre eine tabula rasa gegeben. Die Verfassung böte keinen Ausweg. Die Regierung aber müsse handeln. In der Weimarer Republik haben mehrfach Nothaushaltsgesetze eine Rolle gespielt, durch die der Regierung für einen bestimmten Zeitabschnitt die Vollmacht erteilt wurde, ohne ein im einzelnen bewilligtes Budget die Finanzgeschäfte des Reiches zu führen. Rechtsgrundlage war der Artikel 48 der Reichsverfassung (Eingriffsrecht des Reichspräsidenten), zu dem das in dessen Absatz 2 vorgesehene Ausführungsgesetz übrigens nie erlassen wurde. Der Artikel 48 hat dann bei der Aushöhlung des Sinnes der Verfassung und den Geschehnissen von 1933 eine bedeutende Rolle gespielt. — In der NS-Zeit hat die vorliegende Frage infolge der weiteren Aushöhlung der Verfassung kaum noch eine Rolle gespielt. Das Budget verlor seine politische Funktion, Bindung der Regierung an die Beschlüsse der Legislative, praktisch völlig, es bestand nunmehr nur noch als internes Verwaltungsgerüst weiter. Die politische Funktion des Budgets wurde durch das Grundgesetz für die Bundesrepublik von 1949 wieder hergestellt. Aber auch hier hat sich ein Nothaushaltsrecht niedergeschlagen. So hat die Regierung nach Artikel 111 GG die Möglichkeit, Ausgaben auch vor Genehmigung des Budgets zu tätigen, wenn dieses nicht rechtzeitig zustande kommt. Auch darf die Bundesregierung die zur Aufrechterhaltung der Wirtschaftsführung erforderlichen Mittel bis zur Höhe eines Viertels der Endsumme des abgelaufenen Haushaltsplanes im Wege des Kredits flüssig machen. Vgl. auch das vielgestaltige Nothaushaltsrecht in den Ländern.

Werden nach der gesetzlichen Feststellung Änderungen des Haushaltsplanes notwendig, so können diese durch einen Nachtragshaushalt bewirkt werden. Der Entwurf des Nachtragshaushaltsplanes ist wie der eines normalen Haushaltplanes zu behandeln, d. h. er ist der parlamentarischen Beratung und Beschlußfassung zu unterwerfen.

## 2. Vollzug des Haushaltsplanes

### *a) Bindung der Exekutive*

Die zweite Hauptphase im Budgetkreislauf ist der Vollzug des Haushaltsplans. Die Exekutive ist gehalten, den Willen der Legislative zu erfüllen. Bei den *Ausgabe*ansätzen ist die Exekutive an Zweck, Höhe und Zeit jedoch nur da im strengeren Sinne gebunden, wo durch außerbudgetäre Gesetze (Versorgungsgesetze, Besoldungsgesetze, Angestellten- und Arbeitertarife usw.) oder durch vertragliche Bindungen gegenüber Dritten rechtlich begründete Ausgabeverpflichtungen bestehen[1]). Zu den übrigen Ausgaben, d. h. in dem durch Sondergesetze oder anderweitige Bindungen nicht geregelten freien Raum ist die Exekutive lediglich ermächtigt, sie trägt die Verantwortung für ihr Tun oder auch Unterlassen. Im übrigen müssen die Ausgaben sachlich und ökonomisch gerechtfertigt sein. Bei den *Einnahme*voranschlägen besteht zwar eine Bindung für die Erhebung nach Maßgabe der die Erhebung von Steuern und anderen Abgaben begründenden außerbudgetären Gesetze. Jedoch hat die Exekutive Abweichungen von den Ansätzen im Haushaltsplan nicht zu verantworten, da diese als Voranschläge auf Schätzungen beruhen und ihre tatsächliche Entwicklung auch von Faktoren abhängt, deren numerische Bedeutung z. Z. der Planaufstellung nicht immer voll vorausgesehen werden konnte. Denn die Einnahmeerträge hängen, wie wir wissen, nicht nur von den Steuersätzen und allen übrigen in den Steuergesetzen enhaltenen Bestim-

---

[1]) Das Haushaltsgesetz selbst, soweit es den Haushaltsplan betrifft, begründet nach deutschem Haushaltsrecht weder Ansprüche Dritter noch hebt sie diese auf. Das gleiche gilt für Verbindlichkeiten Dritter (§ 24 der Reichshaushaltsordnung [RHO]). Es ist soweit nur ein Gesetz im sogenannten formellen Sinne. Die Bindung der Exekutive an den Inhalt des Haushaltsplans ist nur eine öffentlich-rechtliche. Das Verhältnis zwischen Individuum und Regierung wird durch den Haushaltsplan nicht berührt und regelt sich ausschließlich nach den dafür maßgeblichen Gesetzen.

mungen, sondern im Rahmen dieser institutionellen Daten von der Entwicklung der Wirtschaftslage ab (Konjunkturempfindlichkeit der Steuererträge).

Die tatsächliche Entwicklung der Einnahmen und der Ausgaben weicht deshalb oft von den budgetierten Größen ab. Auch für diesen Fall gelten besondere Regelungen. In der Bundesrepublik Deutschland bedürfen nach Artikel 112 GG (vgl. auch § 33 RHO) Haushaltsüberschreitungen und außerplanmäßige Ausgaben der Zustimmung des Finanzministers. Sie darf nur im Falle eines unvorhergesehenen und unabweisbaren Bedürfnisses erteilt werden. Nach § 83 RHO ist aufgrund der Haushaltsrechnung eine nachträgliche Genehmigung der über- und außerplanmäßigen Ausgaben durch die gesetzgebenden Körperschaften erforderlich. Im Falle größerer Beträge wird der Finanzminister in der Regel die Bewilligung bereits durch einen Nachtragshaushalt zu erreichen suchen.

### *b) Öffentliches Kassen- und Rechnungswesen*

Zum technisch-rationalen Vollzug des Haushaltsplans ist ein durchgebildetes Kassen- und Rechnungswesen erforderlich. Im folgenden wird das öffentliche Kassen- und Rechnungswesen im Bereich der Bundesrepublik Deutschland in seinen Grundzügen beschrieben.

#### *α)* Kassenwesen

Die Durchführung des Haushaltsplanes vollzieht sich in den Bereichen der Verwaltungen und der Kassen. Erstere verwalten die Haushaltsmittel, haben aber selbst kein Geld. Letztere dagegen haben das Geld, dürfen aber ohne Anweisung von Verwaltungsstellen nicht darüber verfügen. Durch eine scharfe Trennung von Anordnung und Ausführung, d. h. von Verwaltung und Kasse, gesichert durch eine Überwachung beider durch Finanzkontrollbehörden, soll eine den gesetzlichen Normen entsprechende Verwendung der öffentlichen Mittel erreicht werden. Die Kassen haben die Aufgabe, Gelder einzuziehen und auszuzahlen, darüber buchzuführen und so Unterlagen für die Rechnungslegung zu erstellen.

$\alpha_1$) Hinsichtlich des *Kassenaufbaus* unterscheidet man bei den Kassen des *Bundes* drei Ebenen: Zentralkasse, Oberkassen und

Amtskassen. Die Zentralkasse des Bundes ist die Bundeshauptkasse, bei der alle Einnahmen und Ausgaben des Haushalts zusammenfließen. Die Ober- und Amtskassen sind nach Verwaltungszweigen und Gebieten gegliedert. Die Einrichtung von Oberkassen soll den Abrechnungsverkehr zwischen den Amtskassen und der Zentrale erleichtern.

Die Kassenorganisation der *Länder* ist ähnlich wie die des Bundes. Auf der *kommunalen* Ebene ist für jede Gemeinde eine Gemeindekasse gesetzlich vorgeschrieben, in deren Büchern alle Einnahmen und Ausgaben der Gemeinde geführt werden müssen. Für bestimmte Einrichtungen der Gemeinde, wie z. B. für Krankenhäuser, ist die Errichtung von Nebenkassen möglich, die jedoch Teile der Gemeindekasse sind und mit ihr in Abrechnungsverkehr stehen.

Daneben können von den Gemeinden Sonderkassen errichtet werden für Institutionen, die eine besondere Rechnung außerhalb der allgemeinen Jahresrechnung erfordern. Sonderkassen sind möglich für Eigenbetriebe, rechtlich selbständige Stiftungen und rechtlich unselbständige Stiftungen, sofern ein besonderer Haushaltsplan für sie aufgestellt wird.

$\alpha_2$) Im *Zahlungsverkehr* mit den Kassen können Zahlungen in bar oder unbar wie durch Überweisung, Postscheck usw. erfolgen. Einzahlungen dürfen nur von den für diese Zahlung zuständigen Kassen angenommen werden. Auszahlungen dürfen lediglich auf schriftliche Anordnung oder aufgrund von Gesetzesvorschriften an den genau bezeichneten Empfänger erfolgen, der sich bei Barauszahlungen über seine Person auszuweisen hat.

Einzahlungen für den Bund dürfen nur für Bundeszwecke verwendet werden. Entsprechendes gilt für die Länder und Gemeinden. Der Kassenbestand, der aus Barmitteln und Guthaben bei den Geldinstituten besteht, unterliegt hinsichtlich Höhe und Anlegung bestimmten Sicherheitsvorschriften. Beträge, die den zulässigen Kassenbestand der Amts- und Oberkassen übersteigen, sind an die Zentralkasse abzuführen. Bleiben die Einnahmen hinter den Ausgaben zurück, so ist eine sogenannte „Verstärkung" der Betriebsmittel der Zentralkasse oder des Kassenbestandes der nachgeordneten Kassen erforderlich. Im Bund oder betreffenden Land werden die erforderlichen Beträge einer Betriebsmittelrücklage entnommen oder im Wege des Kredits (Kassenkredit) beschafft. Die Amts- oder Oberkassen beziehen im wesentlichen die Kassenverstärkungen von der Zentralkasse. Bei den Gemeinden wird ähnlich verfahren: Mittel zur Kassenbestandsverstärkungen werden aus Rücklagen oder Krediten beschafft.

$\alpha_3$) Die *Buchführung* der Kassen erfolgt in Form der kameralistischen oder Verwaltungsbuchführung und erstreckt sich auf die Aufzeichnung von Einnahmen und Ausgaben und den Vermögens- und Schuldennachweis. Die Buchführung wird in zeitlicher und sachlicher Ordnung des Haushaltsplans vollzogen und endet in der Rechnungslegung.

$\alpha_4$) Wichtig für eine ordnungsmäßige Führung der Kassengeschäfte ist eine wirksame *Kassenaufsicht.* Sie obliegt grundsätzlich dem Vorsteher der Behörde, der auch eine Weisungsbefugnis hat. Weil bei größeren Behörden der Vorsteher kaum der Aufsicht in genügendem Maße nachkommen kann, wird durch Gesetz oder Verwaltungsvorschrift bestimmt, daß ein Kassenaufsichtsbeamter zu bestellen ist, der sich von der ordnungsmäßigen Erledigung der Kassengeschäfte zu überzeugen hat. Im Gegensatz zum Behördenvorsteher hat er dem Leiter oder einem Beamten der Kasse gegenüber keine Weisungsbefugnis.

In den Gemeinden unterliegt die Aufsicht der Kasse dem Bürgermeister (Gemeindedirektor). Auch hier ist die Übertragung der Aufsicht auf einen Beigeordneten oder einen Kassenaufsichtsbeamten möglich.

$\alpha_5$) Die Ordnungsmäßigkeit der Kassenführung soll durch ordentliche (meist monatliche) und außerordentliche (mindest einmal jährliche) *Kassenprüfungen* gewährleistet sein. Bei den Gemeinden unterscheidet man regelmäßige, unvermutete und überörtliche Kassenprüfungen, die durch Beauftragte der staatlichen Aufsichtsbehörde oder der in verschiedenen Ländern üblichen Gemeinde-(Kommunal-)Prüfungsämter vorgenommen werden.

### *β*) Rechnungslegung

Grundsätzlich ist über die Verwaltung überantworteter Mittel Rechenschaft abzulegen. Dieser Grundsatz gilt wie im privaten Rechtsleben so ganz besonders für die öffentliche Verwaltung.

Die Rechnungslegung im öffentlichen Bereich, auch Rechenschaftslegung genannt, umfaßt insbesondere die geordnete Aufstellung der Haushaltseinnahmen und -ausgaben und ihre Belegung sowie den Nachweis, daß diese Transaktionen gemäß den Weisungen des Haushaltsplanes und unter Beachtung sonstiger gegebener Grenzen und Vorschriften erfolgten. Man unterscheidet drei Arten von Rechnungen: Kassen-, Haushalts- und Vermögensrechnung.

Die *Kassenrechnung* hat den Nachweis zu liefern, daß die Haushaltseinnahmen und -ausgaben nach den entsprechenden Gesetzen und Vorschriften erhoben oder geleistet wurden und ordnungsgemäß belegt sind. Darauf baut die *Haushaltsrechnung* auf; hier werden die Einnahmen und Ausgaben jeder Haushaltsstelle nach dem Haushaltsplan geordnet dargestellt. Mit der Haushaltsrechnung geben die Exekutivorgane Rechenschaft über die Ausführung des Haushaltsplanes. Die *Vermögensrechnung* enthält den Bestand des Vermögens oder der Schulden am Anfang und Ende des Rechnungsjahres und die Veränderungen.

β1) Bei *Bund* und *Ländern* unterscheidet man hinsichtlich der *Kassenrechnungen* nach den Stufen der Rechnungslegung Einzel- und Gesamtrechnungslegung. Bei der Einzelrechnungslegung steht die einzelne Haushaltseinnahme oder -ausgabe und ihr Beleg im Mittelpunkt. Weil die Bewirtschaftung einer Ausgabebewilligung aber oft durch mehrere Behörden und Kassen erfolgt, läßt sich aufgrund der Einzelrechnungslegung die Einhaltung des Haushaltsplans nicht überprüfen. Dazu muß eine entsprechende Gruppierung und Summierung der Einzelrechnungen erfolgen. Für die Gesamtrechnungslegung werden von den zuständigen Oberkassen oder Rechnungsstellen sogenannte Oberrechnungen aufgestellt, die die Einnahme- und Ausgabesumme je Titel und Kapitel ausweisen. Für jeden Einzelplan werden sodann sogenannte Zentralrechnungen erstellt, deren Summierung die sogenannte Hauptrechnung ergibt; sie zeigen das Gesamtergebnis der Einnahmen und Ausgaben des ordentlichen und außerordentlichen Haushalts.

Die Ergebnisse der Kassenrechnungen des Bundes und der Länder werden zu *Haushaltsrechnungen* zusammengestellt. Die Summen der Einnahmen und Ausgaben von Titeln, Kapiteln und Einzelplänen werden dem Aufbau des Haushaltsplans entsprechend den jeweiligen Haushaltsansätzen und etwaigen verbliebenen Haushaltsresten des Vorjahres gegenübergestellt. Die nachgeordneten Behörden liefern dem zuständigen Fachminister die Beiträge zur Haushaltrechnung. Besonders geeignet hierfür sind Abschriften der Zentralrechnungen der Kassen, die ergänzt und erläutert dem Finanzminister weitergegeben werden. Dieser legt für die Bundes- oder Landesregierung — für die meisten Länder wird entsprechend diesen Ausführungen verfahren — der gesetzgebenden Körperschaft über die Haushaltsführung Rechnung.

Dem Bund ist durch Art. 114 GG die Aufstellung einer *Ver-*

*mögensrechnung* vorgeschrieben, in der Bundestag und Bundesrat eine Übersicht über das Vermögen und die Schulden des Bundes vorgelegt wird. In den Ländern werden nur selten Vermögensrechnungen erstellt. Die Länderverfassungen enthalten keine Vorschriften über einen Vermögensnachweis. Die Aufstellung der Vermögensrechnung des Bundes erfolgt ähnlich wie bei der Kassenrechnung. Ausgehend von der Einzelrechnungslegung in Form einer Vermögensrechnungsnachweisung über den Anfangsbestand zu Beginn, der Zu- und Abgänge während und den Endbestand am Schluß des Rechnungsjahres erfolgt die Gesamtrechnungslegung über Ober-, Zentral- und Hauptrechnung.

$\beta_2$) Die Rechnungslegung der *Gemeinden* umfaßt ebenfalls eine Kassen-, Haushalts- und Vermögensrechnung. Mit der *Kassenrechnung* wird vom Kassenverwalter gegenüber dem Bürgermeister oder Gemeindedirektor nachgewiesen, daß die Einnahmen und Ausgaben entsprechend der Verwaltungsordnung erhoben bzw. geleistet wurden, und weiter dargelegt, wie sich diese Istbeträge zum Soll des entsprechenden Haushaltsplans verhalten. Auf der Kassenrechnung baut die *Haushaltsrechnung* auf. Dem Aufbau des Haushaltsplans entsprechend werden die Einnahmen und Ausgaben der einzelnen Haushaltsstellen zusammengefaßt. Einzelheiten sind in den jeweiligen Gemeindeordnungen festgelegt. Mit der Haushaltsrechnung legt der Bürgermeister oder Gemeindedirektor gegenüber der Gemeindevertretung und der Aufsichtsbehörde Rechenschaft ab; die Haushaltsrechnung ist somit Grundlage für die Entlastung der Verwaltung und für die Rechnungsprüfung.

Den Gemeinden und Gemeindeverbänden ist ebenso wie dem Bund eine *Vermögensrechnung* vorgeschrieben, die Anfangs- und Endbestand sowie Veränderungen während des Rechnungsjahres auszuweisen hat.

## 3. Kontrolle der Haushaltsführung

Bei der Kontrolle der Haushaltsführung treten verschiedene Kontrollinstanzen auf, die im folgenden der Gliederung dienen. Zeitlich gesehen ist dabei zu unterscheiden zwischen vorheriger, mitlaufender und nachheriger Kontrolle.

### *a) Administrative Kontrolle*

Eine erste administrative Kontrolle erfolgt durch die Verwaltung (Selbstprüfung der Administrative) selbst. Die

Prüfung wird durch eigene Abteilungen in den Behörden auf den einzelnen Verwaltungsstufen vollzogen. Sie kann vorher, mitschreitend oder nachher erfolgen. In der Bundesrepublik besteht bei jeder obersten Bundesbehörde, bei nachgeordneten Dienststellen je nach Anordnung, eine Vorprüfungsstelle. In den Ländern (mit Ausnahme von Bayern) lehnen sich die Vorprüfungsordnungen eng an die des Bundes an. In den Gemeinden ist das Moment der „Aufsicht von oben" stärker ausgeprägt.

### *b) Rechnungskontrolle*

Den Vorprüfungen durch die Administrative selbst folgen Prüfungen durch eine Rechnungsprüfungsbehörde, die sich weitgehend als ein externes Organ mit selbständiger Stellung in allen Ländern herausgebildet hat. In der Bundesrepublik z. B. ist das für den Bund der Bundesrechnungshof, der auf den Ergebnissen der Vorprüfung die „Rechnungsprüfung" aufbaut. Der Bundesrechnungshof ist wie die Gerichte an Weisungen nicht gebunden; seine Mitglieder besitzen volle richterliche Unabhängigkeit.

Eine Erweiterung des Tätigkeitsbereiches des Bundesrechnungshofes ist insofern gegeben, als sich seine Tätigkeit nicht mehr auf die Rechnungsprüfung beschränkt, sondern seine Prüfer schon zu Beratungen im Voranschlagsstadium des Haushaltsplanes herangezogen werden.

In den Ländern bestehen Landesrechnungshöfe, die in einigen Ländern zugleich oberstes Prüfungsorgan für die Gemeinden des Landes sind.

### *c) Politische (parlamentarische) Kontrolle*

Die politische Kontrolle erfolgt durch die Legislative. Übliche Organe der politischen Haushaltskontrolle durch das Parlament sind der Haushaltsausschuß (Finanzkommission) und die Rechnungsprüfungskommission, die bisweilen eine Unterkommission des Haushaltsausschusses ist. In totalitären Staaten behalten sie vielfach ihre traditionellen Bezeichnungen bei, verändern aber, da das Parlament bestenfalls akklamatorische Bedeutung hat, mit diesem ihre Funktion.

In der Bundesrepublik dienen als Unterlagen für die parlamentarische Prüfung der Bundeshaushaltsrechnung durch den Rechnungsprüfungsausschuß des Bundestages: Die Bundeshaushaltsrechnung selbst, dazu die Bemerkungen des Bundesrechnungshofes mit dem Bericht über die Prüfung der Unternehmen mit eigener Rechtspersönlichkeit und die Denkschrift des Präsidenten des Bundesrechnungshofs. In den Ländern tritt an die Stelle der Berichte des Bundesrechnungshofs der Prüfungsbericht des Landesrechnungshofs.

Es ist von Heinig und Vialon bemerkt worden, daß die Kontrolltätigkeit der Parlamente nicht mehr ausschließlich auf die nachherige Kontrolle beschränkt geblieben ist, sondern, obgleich dazu die gesetzliche Grundlage fehle und diese Praxis an sich nicht mit dem Prinzip der Gewaltenteilung übereinstimme, z. T. schon in den Budgetvollzug eingeschaltet ist. Um „Schwierigkeiten bei der späteren Prüfung der Haushaltsüberschreitungen und bei der Entlastung" zu entgehen, würden heute von der Exekutive Parlamentsmitgliedern Informationen über den Haushaltsablauf gegeben. So käme eine mitlaufende, z. T. sogar eine vorherige Kontrolle zustande. „Am plastischsten ist vielleicht die Feststellung, daß die ausführliche Beratung des Voranschlags für das künftige Rechnungsjahr die wirksamste Kontrolle der laufenden Haushalts- und Finanzgebarung einer Behörde ist. Hier kann sich der zuständige Parlamentsausschuß aus dem laufenden Rechnungsjahr alles vorlegen lassen, Übersichten, vergangene und künftige Zahlungen, Empfänger, Schuldner oder was sonst von Bedeutung ist."

Soweit das zutrifft, würde dadurch die sonst so oft bemerkte Vorherrschaft der Exekutive, z. B. bei der Planaufstellung, durchaus gedämpft werden. Es bleibt dennoch die Frage, wieweit dabei nicht trotz allem infolge des größeren Sachverstandes der Verwaltung diese den größeren Einfluß behält.

### 4. Entlastung

Die Kontrolle wird abgeschlossen durch die Entlastung. Diese erfolgt durch das Plenum des Parlaments. Mit der Entlastung der Regierung durch das Parlament ist der Kreislauf eines Jahreshaushaltsplanes abgeschlossen.

Wird die Entlastung verweigert, so bleibt die staatsrechtliche Verantwortung der Regierung für die zurückliegende Zeit in der Schwebe. Einer Verweigerung der Entlastung können verschiedene Motive zugrunde liegen: Das Parlament verweigert, obgleich die Haushaltsführung als solche in Ordnung war, die Entlastung aus sogenannten politischen Gründen. In einem solchen Fall steht der Regierung in der Bundesrepublik für die damit gegebene Verfassungsstreitigkeit der Klageweg vor dem Bundesverfassungsgericht offen. Anders liegen die Dinge, wenn erhebliche Verstöße gegen die Grundsätze einer ordentlichen Haushaltsführung aufgetreten sind. Dann kann das Parlament verschieden verfahren. Es kann unter dem Vorbehalt der Durchführung entsprechender Maßnahmen die Entlastung aussprechen. Es kann aber auch die Entlastung aussetzen und die Regierung veranlassen, die erforderlichen Maßnahmen zunächst zu treffen, ehe es die Entlastung ausspricht. Im Falle sehr erheblicher Verstöße mag das Parlament der Gesamtregierung oder einzelnen ihrer Minister das Mißtrauen aussprechen. Voraussetzung ist, daß die Verfassung dieses zuläßt. In der Bundesrepublik ist es nicht möglich, wie zur Zeit der Weimarer Republik durch Mehrheitsbeschluß dem Kanzler und auch einzelnen Ministern das Vertrauen zu entziehen, sodaß sie zurücktreten müssen. Denn es gilt das sogenannte konstruktive Mißtrauensvotum, wonach der Bundestag dem Bundeskanzler das Mißtrauen nur dadurch aussprechen kann, daß er mit der Mehrheit seiner Mitglieder einen Nachfolger wählt und den Bundespräsidenten ersucht, den Bundeskanzler zu entlassen.

Es bleibt zu bemerken, daß im Falle einer Gesetzesverletzung die schuldigen Beamten oder Angestellten privatrechtlich oder disziplinär zur Rechenschaft zu ziehen sind.

## § 4. Staatshaushalt und Wirtschaftskreislauf

### 1. Vorbemerkungen

Finanzwirtschaftliches Handeln des Staates und wirtschaftliches Handeln der Privaten, von Betrieben und

Haushalten, sind in ihren Auswirkungen nicht isoliert zu sehen; sie stehen vielmehr in einem gegenseitigen Zusammenhang. Einmal: Staatliches finanzwirtschaftliches Handeln wirkt auf die von den privaten Sektoren ausgehenden Wirtschaftsgrößen ein. Zum anderen: Das wirtschaftliche Handeln der Privaten hat Einfluß auf eine Reihe von Größen, die sich dann in den Staatsrechnungen ex post niederschlagen.

Das und weiteres wurde im einzelnen in den vorhergehenden Kapiteln bereits behandelt. Im Vordergrund standen dabei durchaus Detailgesichtspunkte; nur gleichsam am Rande sind Ausführungen im Hinblick auf eine Zusammenschau aller simultan wirkenden Elemente des Staatshaushaltes und der Interdependenz zu den übrigen volkswirtschaftlichen Größen erfolgt. Immerhin wurde im ersten Band dieser Finanzwissenschaft — wo im Kapitel II auch die beschäftigungspolitische Zielsetzung der modernen Fiskalpolitik und ihre Problematik in ihren Grundzügen dargestellt wurde — bereits manches über die Zusammenhänge zwischen den Elementen des Staatshaushalts, Einnahmen und Ausgaben, und dem Wirtschaftskreislauf gesagt.

Grundsätzlich bieten sich zwei Ansatzpunkte dar: Die klassische, insbesondere die neoklassische Preis- und Verteilungstheorie und die von Quesnay ausgehende Kreislaufanalyse. Diese von Keynes und seinen Nachfolgern als Einkommensanalyse weiterentwickelte Methode spielt heute eine hervorragende Rolle, insbesondere auch deswegen, weil sie durch die ihr eigentümliche makroökonomische Methode leichter quantitativ zugänglich ist. Das heißt nicht, daß die Preistheorie keine Rolle für die kreislaufmäßige Betrachtung der Einkommensanalyse spielt. Zunächst ist darauf hinzuweisen, daß die Größen, mit denen die Einkommensanalyse arbeitet, Summen sind aus Produkten, deren Faktoren Preise und Mengen sind. Soweit ist der Hintergrund aller Ergebnisse, die in die makroökonomischen Kreislaufschemata eingehen, das Geschehen auf den einzelnen Märkten. Während hier Angebot und Nachfrage nach einzelnen Gütern im Vordergrund stehen, so in der Kreislaufanalyse deren Gesamtgrößen. Bei der Behandlung von Kreislaufproblemen durch die Einkommensanalyse geht man im allgemeinen so vor, daß die Marktformenstruktur als gegeben betrachtet wird. Dadurch und durch den Verzicht auf ein allzu tiefes Eindringen in das Geschehen auf den Einzelmärkten wird mehr Wert auf die Klärung der Entwicklung des Preisniveaus gelegt als auf die des Preisgefüges. Immerhin ist zu vermerken, daß durch eine weitere Aufgliederung der Kreislaufschemata in Richtung auf intersektorale Untersuchungen hier durchaus weitergeforscht werden kann. Jedoch können im Rahmen dieses Lehrbuches nur die einfachsten Ansätze der Einkommensanalyse gezeigt werden.

## 2. Der Staatshaushalt in der volkswirtschaftlichen Gesamtrechnung

Volkswirtschaftliche Gesamtrechnungen (VGR) sind als Weiterentwicklungen der Statistik des Volkseinkommens Darstellungen von Fakten. Sie zeigen nicht, warum etwas geschehen ist, sondern lassen nur die Ergebnisse des Geschehens sichtbar werden[1]). Bahnbrechend für die Entwicklung der VGR in Deutschland sind die Arbeiten des Deutschen Instituts für Wirtschaftsforschung gewesen. Seinen Forschungen kommt eine entscheidende Bedeutung insbesondere für die kurzfristige konjunkturpolitische Diagnose zu, da vorläufige Zahlen schon nach einem Vierteljahr verfügbar sind. Seit einigen Jahren wird auch vom Statistischen Bundesamt eine VGR veröffentlicht, die hier in einer für unsere Zwecke stark verkürzten und vereinfachten Form wiedergegeben wird (vgl. Tabelle VI).

Es wurde die Aufteilung und detaillierte Unterteilung der einzelnen Konten vereinfacht und gestrafft, um dem Leser einen einprägsamen Überblick zu geben. Insbesondere kommt die Entstehung des Sozialproduktes zu kurz; für eine Darstellung der Rolle der Staatsfinanzen im Wirtschaftskreislauf sind die

---

1) Bei Vorhandensein einer genügenden Zahl solcher Rechnungen (statistisch: Zeitreihen) können über ökonometrische Modelle Schlüsse auf zukünftiges Geschehen versucht werden.

Tabelle VI. Vereinfachtes Kontenschema der Volkswirt-

| Buchg. | (1) Produzierende Einheiten[3]) — Ausgaben — | Gegenbuchg. | Mrd. DM |
|---|---|---|---|
| 101 | Verteilte Einkommen aus Produktion und Dienstleistungen[4]) ................ | 251, 351 | 204,57 |
| 102 | Unverteilte Gewinne der Untern. m. eig. Rechtspers.[4]) ...................... | 353, 551 | 14,80 |
| 103 | Indirekte Steuern abzügl. Subventionen[4]) | 352, 451 | 38,93 |
| 104 | Abschreibungen ...................... | 553 | 24,10 |
| | Bruttosozialprodukt zu Marktpreisen .... | | 282,40 |

| Buchg. | (2) Private Haushalte — Ausgaben — | Gegenbuchg. | Mrd. DM |
|---|---|---|---|
| 201 | Laufende Übertragungen an übrige Welt | 452 | 0,68 |
| 202 | Direkte Steuern (18,93), Soz.vers.beitr (27,73) u. sonst. lfd. Übertrag.[6]) ........ | 353 | 46,81 |
| 203 | Private Konsumtion .................... | 151 | 160,52 |
| 204 | Ersparnis der privaten Haushalte ...... | 552 | 27,53 |
| | Gesamteinkommen der privaten Haushalte | | 235,54 |

| Buchg. | (3) Öffentliche Haushalte[8]) — Ausgaben — | Gegenbuchg. | Mrd. DM |
|---|---|---|---|
| 301 | Lfde. Übertragungen an übrige Welt[9]) .. | 452 | 5,26 |
| 302 | Transfer-Ausg. an priv. Haushalte[7]) .... | 252 | 34,98 |
| 303 | (Eigen-)Verbrauch des Staates .......... | 152 | 38,43 |
| 304 | Ersparnis der öffentl. Haushalte ........ | 552 | 22,12 |
| | Summe .............................. | | 100,79 |

| Buchg. | (4) Übrige Welt — Ausgaben — | Gegenbuchg. | Mrd DM |
|---|---|---|---|
| 401 | Außenbeitrag[5]) .......................... | 154 | 7,75 |
| 402 | Lfde. Übertragungen an Staat[11]) ........ | 354 | 2,26 |
| 403 | Lfde. Übertragungen an priv Haushalte | 253 | 0,07 |
| | Summe ............................... | | 10,08 |

| Buchg | (5) Kapitalveränderung — Ausgaben — | Gegenbuchg. | Mrd DM |
|---|---|---|---|
| 501 | Bruttoinvest. i. Unternehmungssekt.[13]) (Netto: 43,27) ........................... | 153 | 66,31 |
| 502 | Bruttoinvest. i. öffentl. Sektor[8]) (Netto: 8,33) ............................. | 153 | 9,39 |
| 503 | Zuwachs d Forderungssaldos gegen die übrige Welt[12]) .......................... | 453 | 4,08 |
| | Summe ............................... | | 79,78 |

schaftlichen Gesamtrechnung[1]) der Bundesrepublik[2]) 1960

| Buchg. | (1) Produzierende Einheiten[3]) — Einnahmen — | Gegenbuchg. | Mrd. DM |
|---|---|---|---|
| 151 | Private Konsumtion .................. | 203 | 160,52 |
| 152 | Staatliche Konsumtion ................. | 303 | 38,43 |
| 153 | Bruttoinvestition (dav. Lagerinvest.: 8,00) | 501, 502 | 75,70 |
| 154 | Außenbeitrag[5]) ......................... | 401 | 7,75 |
| | Bruttosozialprodukt zu Marktpreisen .... | | 282,40 |

| Buchg | (2) Private Haushalte — Einnahmen — | Gegenbuchg. | Mrd. DM |
|---|---|---|---|
| 251 | Vert. priv. Eink. aus Produktion und Dienstl. (davon aus unselbständiger Arbeit: 133,61) .......................... | 101 | 200,49 |
| 252 | Transferzahlungen vom Staat[7]) .......... | 302 | 34,98 |
| 253 | Lfde. Übertragungen v. d. übrigen Welt | 403 | 0,07 |
| | Gesamteinkommen der privaten Haushalte | | 235,54 |

| Buchg. | (3) Öffentliche Haushalte[8]) — Einnahmen — | Gegenbuchg. | Mrd. DM |
|---|---|---|---|
| 351 | Nettoeinkünfte aus wirtschaftl. Tätigk.[10]) | 101 | 4,08 |
| 352 | Indirekte Steuern abzügl. Subv. (1, 38) .. | 103 | 38,87 |
| 353 | Direkte Steuern (26, 81), Soz.vers.beitr. (27, 73) u. sonstige lfde. Übertragungen .. | 102, 202 | 55,58 |
| 354 | Lfde Übertragungen v. d. übrig. Welt[11]) | 402 | 2,26 |
| | Summe ............................ .... | | 100,79 |

| Buchg | (4) Übrige Welt — Einnahmen — | Gegenbuchg. | Mrd DM |
|---|---|---|---|
| 451 | Indirekte Steuern (Umlagen der Montanunion) .................................. | 103 | 0,06 |
| 452 | Lfde Übertragungen von privaten Haushalten und Staat .......................... | 201, 301 | 5,94 |
| 453 | Zuwachs des Schuldensaldos gegenüber d. Inland[12]) ............................ | 503 | 4,08 |
| | Summe .................................. | | 10,08 |

| Buchg | (5) Kapitalveränderung — Einnahmen — | Gegenbuchg. | Mrd. DM |
|---|---|---|---|
| 551 | Verfügb.[14]) Nettogew. d. Untern.[13]) m. eig. Rechtspers. ........................ | 102 | 6,03 |
| 552 | Ersparnis der privaten und öffentlichen Haushalte ............................ | 204, 304 | 49,65 |
| 553 | Abschreibungen (davon im öffentlichen Sektor: 1,06) ..................... ...... | 104 | 24,10 |
| | Summe .................................. | | 79,78 |

Bemerkungen zu Tabelle VI:

[1]) Quelle: Stat. Jb. d. BRD 1963, S. 524 ff. — [2]) Ohne Westberlin. — [3]) Private und öffentliche Unternehmungen (inkl. Wohnungswesen, Bundesbahn und -post), Dienstleistungen (auch Unselbständiger bei der öffentlichen Hand). — [4]) Die Summe der ersten zwei Buchungen (101 und 102) ist das Nettosozialprodukt zu Faktorenkosten (219,37 Mrd. DM), die der ersten drei (101, 102 und 103) das Nettosozialprodukt zu Marktpreisen (258,30 Mrd. DM). — [5]) Ausfuhrüberschuß (8,17 Mrd. DM) abzüglich Differenz zwischen Erwerbseinkommen (auch Zinszahlungen des Staates an übrige Welt: 0,14 Mrd. DM) von Ausländern im Inland und Inländern in der übrigen Welt (0,42 Mrd. DM). — [6]) Erstattungsbeträge im Rahmen öffentlicher Fürsorge u. ä. — [7]) Von den Haushalten empfangene Leistungen der Sozialversicherungen, Pensionen, Renten usw — [8]) Gebietskörperschaften, Lastenausgleich, Sozialversicherungen. — [9]) Davon an Berlin: 3,15 Mrd. DM — [10]) Insgesamt im öffentlichen Sektor produzierte Wertsumme an Gütern und Diensten abzüglich der notwendigen Vorleistungen, Arbeitskosten, Abschreibungen und indirekten Steuern, zuzüglich der an den Staat ausgeschütteten Gewinne, abzüglich gezahlter Staatsschuldzinsen (1,63 Mrd. DM) — [11]) Davon aus Berlin (Bundessteuern etc.) 2,23 Mrd. DM — [12]) Abgesehen von stattgefundenen Vermögensübertragungen, die in diesem Schema nicht berücksichtigt worden sind. — [13]) Einschließlich öffentlicher Unternehmungen. — [14]) Nach Abführung direkter Steuern und sonstiger laufender Übertragungen an den Staat.

---

Aspekte der *Verteilung* und *Verwendung* des Sozialprodukts bedeutsamer, die einigermaßen ausführlich berücksichtigt werden.

Wenn man von der Wertsumme aller in der Periode erzeugten Güter und Dienstleistungen die Vorleistungen an Rohstoffen und Zwischenprodukten abzieht, die zur Erzeugung dieser Güter und Dienste erforderlich waren, erhält man das Bruttosozialprodukt zu Marktpreisen als die Summe der Güter und Dienste, die für Konsumtions- und Investitionszwecke zur Verfügung stehen. Bringt man von dieser Summe die Abschreibungen in Abzug, die dem Verschleiß des genutzten Realkapitals entsprechen sollen, so erhält man das Nettosozialprodukt zu Marktpreisen, welches die Wertsumme darstellt, die die Volkswirtschaft entweder konsumiert, als Nettoinvestition für die Aufstokkung des Realkapitals oder als Außenbeitrag für einen Forderungszuwachs gegenüber dem Ausland verwendet hat, vgl. Konto (1). Von dieser Wertsumme muß man die indirekten Steuern (minus Subventionen) abziehen, um das Nettosozialprodukt zu Faktorenkosten (Volkseinkommen) zu erhalten, welche alle Einkommensteile umfaßt, die den Faktoren zuzurechnen sind. Der Hauptteil davon ist an die

Faktoren verteilt worden: einmal an die privaten Haushalte als Einkommen aus Produktion von Gütern und Diensten, zum anderen an den Staat als Einkünfte aus seiner und der öffentlichen Unternehmen wirtschaftlichen Tätigkeit.

Nicht das ganze Volkseinkommen wird aber in dieser Weise verteilt. Auszunehmen sind nämlich die unverteilten Bruttogewinne der privaten und öffentlichen Unternehmen mit eigener Rechtspersönlichkeit (z. B. Kapitalgesellschaften), die bei diesen unmittelbar für Investitionszwecke Verwendung finden, vgl. Konto (5), soweit sie nicht als direkte Steuern (vor allem Körperschaftsteuern) an den Staat entrichtet werden müssen, vgl. Konto (3).

Zu den verteilten Einkommen, welche die privaten Haushalte aus Produktion und Diensten erhalten haben, kommen noch die „abgeleiteten Einkommen" aus laufenden Transferzahlungen, entweder vom Staat (als Pensionen, Sozialversicherungsleistungen usw.) oder von der übrigen Welt hinzu, zu der in diesem Schema allerdings auch nicht-ausländische Gebiete gehören. Um vom sich so ergebenden privaten Gesamteinkommen zum verfügbaren Einkommen der Haushalte zu gelangen, werden zunächst die Zahlungen an die öffentliche Hand, wie direkte Steuern, Sozialversicherungsbeiträge und sonstige lfd. Übertragungen[1]) abgezogen, sodann als „abgeleitete Einkommenszahlungen" die laufenden Übertragungen an die übrige Welt.

Das verfügbare private Einkommen kann entweder konsumiert oder gespart werden. Die private Ersparnis stellt eine der Gegenbuchungen auf der Finanzierungsseite des Kapitalveränderungskontos dar.

Unter den *Einkommensströmen*, die dem *Staat* aus dem Kreislauf zufließen oder zuzurechnen sind, sind zunächst die Nettoeinkünfte des öffentlichen Sektors aus wirtschaftlicher Tätigkeit zu nennen. Sie sind hier ermittelt als Überschuß der Wertsumme der vom Staatssektor an Private und an den Staat selbst umgesetzten Güter und Dienste

---

[1]) Z. B. Erstattungsbeträge im Rahmen öffentlicher Fürsorge u. ä.

über die dabei anfallenden Kosten, zuzüglich der an den Staat ausgeschütteten Gewinne, abzüglich der von ihm gezahlten Zinsen. Weiter erhält der Staat Steuern und Sozialversicherungsbeiträge und sonstige laufende Einkommensübertragungen von Unternehmungen und privaten Haushalten. Dazu kommen noch die laufenden Übertragungen von der übrigen Welt.

Unter den *Ausgaben* des Staates erscheinen die Subventionen nicht, da sie (vgl. Bd. I) als negative indirekte Steuern verstanden und bei den Einnahmen aus indirekten Steuern abgezogen werden können.

Der *Eigenverbrauch* des Staates (Staatskonsum) ist der Teil der dem Staat aus Eigenproduktion und aus Käufen von Privaten zugeflossenen Güter und Dienste, der von ihm selbst als laufender Verbrauch in Anspruch genommen wird. Er enthält nicht die selbst erstellten Anlageinvestitionen, die in der staatlichen Bruttoinvestition (Konto 5) enthalten sind.

Die *Staatsschuldzinsen* werden in der Rechnung des Statistischen Bundesamtes nicht als Transformationszahlungen angesehen und sind somit auch weder integrierender Bestandteil des Staatskonsums noch des Bruttosozialproduktes. Wegen statistischer Schwierigkeiten sind die Staatsschuldzinszahlungen an private *Haushalte* nicht gesondert angegeben, sondern werden zusammen mit den Zinszahlungen an Unternehmen geschlossen als staatlicher Transfer an den Unternehmenssektor aufgeführt. (Wegen der hier gebotenen Vereinfachungen kann dieser Transfer in Tabelle VI nicht dargestellt werden). In der vorliegenden VGR sind die an private Haushalte verteilten Einkommen aus Produktion von Gütern und Diensten um die Zinszahlungen an private Haushalte höher, obwohl diese Einkommen an sich nur Transformationszahlungen umfassen sollten. Sie müßten daher um die Zinszahlungen an private Haushalte niedriger und entsprechend müßten die Transferzahlungen des Staates an private Haushalte und die Nettoeinkünfte des öffentlichen Sektors um den gleichen Betrag höher sein. Die Zinszahlungen des Staates an die übrige Welt sind bei der Berechnung des Außenbeitrages mit berücksichtigt worden.

Auf der Finanzierungsseite des *Kapitalveränderungskontos* sind die verfügbaren Nettogewinne der Unternehmen mit eigener Rechtspersönlichkeit, die staatliche und private Ersparnis und die Abschreibungsbeträge zusammen größer als auf der Ausgabenseite die gesamte Bruttoinvestition im Inland. Das bedeutet, daß ein inländischer Ersparnisüberschuß sich in einem Forderungszuwachs gegenüber der übrigen Welt in Höhe des angegebenen Saldos niedergeschlagen hat.

Die in den Konten (3) und (5) erscheinende Ersparnis des Staates ist nur zum Teil für eigene Investitionen verwendet worden, zum anderen haben die öffentlichen Haushalte damit Forderungen gegenüber anderen Wirtschaftseinheiten erworben. Soweit dieser Forderungserwerb zu einer Thesaurierung der Geldmittel im Bankensystem geführt hat, ist dadurch eine Dämpfung der gesamten Nachfrage erfolgt. In dem Maße aber, wie die öffentlichen Haushalte direkt oder indirekt Aktivkredite an Unternehmungen und private Haushalte gegeben haben, die damit zusätzliche Nachfrage, insbesondere für Investitionszwecke, entfalten konnten, wird dieser Teil des Finanzierungsüberschusses nicht zu einer Dämpfung der gesamten Nachfrage geführt haben. Aktivkredite haben gerade in den letzten Jahren in der Bundesrepublik Deutschland eine bedeutende Rolle gespielt; insbesondere der Bund hat in beträchtlicher Höhe Kredite für Investitionszwecke, vor allem im Wohnungsbau, gegeben. Zur Durchleuchtung dieser Zusammenhänge wird z. B. vom Deutschen Institut für Wirtschaftsforschung in Berlin im Rahmen seiner Volkswirtschaftlichen Gesamtrechnung neben der Einkommenskreislaufanalyse eine spezifizierte kreislaufmäßige Darstellung der Geldvermögensbildung gegeben.

## 3. Nationalbudgets und Entscheidungsmodellanalysen

### *a) Begriffe und Voraussetzungen*

*α) Nationalbudgets.* Während die Volkswirtschaftlichen Gesamtrechnungen im Sinne der Nationalen Buchführung das Ergebnis des Spiels der wirtschaftlichen Kräfte — einschließlich der vom Staat ausgehenden Entscheidungen — einer vergangenen Periode beschreiben, d. h. ex post-Größen „konstatieren", zielen die Nationalbudgetrechnungen in die Zukunft. Das Rechenwerk enthält[1]) Zahlen, wie sie sich als Ergebnis des Zusammenwirkens der wirtschaftlichen Kräfte in einer zukünftigen Periode, auch hier unter Einschluß der vom Staat ausgehenden Entscheidungen, am Ende dieser zukünftigen Periode zeigen mögen oder doch zeigen sollten. Es handelt sich um *antizipierte* ex post-Rechnungen im Gegensatz zu den realisierten der Volkswirtschaftlichen Gesamtrechnung. Sinn solcher Rechnungen ist es u. a., die möglichen Auswirkungen der finanziellen Tätigkeit der öffentlichen Haushalte auf den Wirtschaftskreislauf aufzuzeigen. Dabei ist es notwendig, die Reaktionen der Privaten auf das staatsfinanzielle Tun in die Überlegungen mit einzubeziehen, was am besten anhand eines „Modells" erfolgt.

β) *Modelle.* Modelle sind Gleichungssysteme, deren Unbekannte die zu erklärenden wirtschaftlichen Größen darstellen und die aus ebenso vielen Gleichungen bestehen müssen, wie Unbekannte vorhanden sind. Diese Unbekannten bezeichnet man auch als *endogene* Variablen, d. h Variablen, die aus dem Systemzusammenhang errechnet werden müssen, in der Realität: sich aus dem Spiel der ökonomischen Kräfte ergeben, im Gegensatz zu den *exogenen* Variablen des Systems, von denen angenommen wird, daß sie nur Ursache, aber nicht Wirkung im Wirtschaftsablauf sind und die daher für die reine wirtschaftstheoretische Analyse als gegebene Voraussetzung bekannt sind. Zu letzteren gehören insbesondere die Variablen des Systems, die allein der staatlichen Entscheidung unterliegen, wie Ausgaben, Steuersätze usw., die man auch als „Instrumentvariablen" bezeichnet.

Ein solches Modell enthält stets mindestens zwei Typen von Gleichungen:

---

1) Bei möglicherweise der Nationalen Buchführung gleichender aber auch in gekürzter, im übrigen in einzelnen Ländern unterschiedlicher formaler Darstellung.

(1) *Identitäts- oder Bilanzgleichungen,* die aufgrund definitorischer Setzungen als stets erfüllte Identitäten „selbstverständlich" sind; so ist z. B. das Nettosozialprodukt zu Marktpreisen $E_m$ notwendig gleich der Summe der privaten Konsumtion C und der Nettoinvestition (einschl. Lagerbestandsveränderungen) I, der staatlichen Nachfrage nach Gütern und Diensten $A_{st}$ und dem Außenbeitrag A.

(2) *Funktionen,* wie z. B. Konsum-, Investitions-, Produktions-, Steuerertragsfunktionen usw. Solche Funktionen sind im Gegensatz zu den Identitäten nicht a priori bestimmt, sondern müssen konzipiert werden. Wenn ein Modell aufgrund theoretischer Überlegungen aufgestellt worden ist, wobei die Koeffizienten der Funktionen zunächst nur in unbestimmter Form vorliegen, kann mit Hilfe statistisch-ökonometrischer Forschungsmethoden versucht werden, sowohl diese unbestimmten Koeffizienten zu ermitteln als auch überhaupt die statistische Verläßlichkeit der vom Theoretiker versuchten Funktionen zu prüfen.

(3) Gewisse Modelle enthalten neben diesen Beziehungen auch noch *Gleichgewichtsbedingungen,* z. B. des Gleichgewichts zwischen Angebot und Nachfrage auf einen speziellen Markt oder des Gleichgewichts zwischen (ex ante) geplanter Investition und (ex ante) beabsichtigter Ersparnis. Die Einfügung einer Gleichgewichtsbedingung in ein Modell kann grundsätzlich zweierlei bedeuten: Entweder man setzt voraus, daß die Reaktionen der Wirtschaftssubjekte auf Ungleichgewichtssituationen so schnell und so gut dosiert erfolgen, daß die Existenz des betreffenden Gleichgewichts in der Realität zumindest annähernd gesichert erscheint oder aber man gibt das Gleichgewicht als ein durch geeigneten Einsatz der im Modell enthaltenen staatlichen Instrumentvariablen zu erreichendes Ziel vor: Die Gleichgewichtsbedingung ist dann eine Zielfunktion, wie sie in Entscheidungsmodellen auftreten kann.

γ) *Entscheidungsmodellanalysen.* Ist das zugrundeliegende Modell entwickelt, so kann eine Entscheidungsmodellanalyse einsetzen. Darunter werden bestimmte *wirtschaftspolitische* Analysen mit Hilfe von Modellen verstanden. Dabei ist der Aspekt ein anderer als in den rein wirtschaftstheoretischen Modellanalysen, wie sie z. B. in einfacher

Form in Band I und Band II dargestellt wurden. Hier waren die Handlungen des Staates und damit auch die exogenen Größen der staatlichen Instrumentvariablen als bekannt vorgegeben und es wurde nach ihrer Auswirkung auf die anderen, endogenen Größen wie Konsum, induzierte Investition, Volkseinkommen gefragt, d. h. letztere wurden aus dem Gleichungssystem des Modells errechnet. Bei den Entscheidungsmodellanalysen dagegen werden aus diesen endogenen Variablen diejenigen ausgewählt, die bestimmten staatlichen Zielsetzungen entsprechen, und als Zielvariable größenmäßig fixiert vorgegeben. Auch können Zielfunktionen vorgegeben werden, in denen die Zielvariablen nicht größenmäßig fixiert sind, seien es Gleichgewichtsbedingungen, seien es Maximierungsregeln oder Optimierungsregeln für Entscheidungen bei mehreren, nicht voll miteinander vereinbaren Zielen. Die Fragestellung richtet sich nun auf die Instrumentvariablen, die aufgrund des Gleichungssystems des Modells erforderlich sind, um die Ziele zu verwirklichen. M. a. W., die Ziele erscheinen hier als gegebene Größen oder Funktionszusammenhänge, während die Instrumentvariablen die zu errechnenden Unbekannten des Systems sind[1]).

Der besondere Wert der Entscheidungsmodellanalysen liegt darin, daß mit ihrer Hilfe die Entscheidungen für gedachte Ziele hinsichtlich ihrer Nebenfolgen und ihrer Kompatibilität überprüft werden. Oft genug wird sich dabei herausstellen, daß gewisse Ziele nicht kompatibel, d. h. nicht gleichzeitig ereichbar sind, was eine Erörterung des Ranges und der Gewichtung, die man den einzelnen Zielgrößen zumessen will, erforderlich macht.

δ) *Nationalbudgetanalysen.* Als Nationalbudgetanalysen sollen vereinfachte Spezialfälle von Entscheidungsmodellanalysen bezeichnet werden, in denen die vorkommenden Variablen Einkommensgrößen und andere Wertsummengrößen einer VGR sind. In Nationalbudgetanaly-

---

1) Eine Instrumentvariable kann zuweilen auch identisch mit einer Zielgröße sein, z. B. können bestimmte Staatsausgaben, d. h. also auch exogene Größen, in vorgegebener Höhe schon Ziel an sich sein.

sen tauchen also unmittelbar keine Mengen und keine Preise als Modellvariablen auf. Diese vereinfachte Struktur der Nationalbudgetanalysen ist ein Vorteil, wenn es nur um die grundsätzliche Darstellung der wirtschaftspolitischen Modellanalysen geht, weshalb auch gerade hierfür Beispiele ausgewählt wurden; sie wird aber, was die Verläßlichkeit der gefundenen Erkenntnisse anbelangt, in der Regel hinter den umfangreicheren allgemeineren Entscheidungsmodellanalysen, wie sie insbesondere von Ragnar Frisch und Jan Tinbergen entwickelt wurden, zurückstehen. Inwieweit die aus der Modellanalyse gefolgerten Änderungen der VGR-Wertsummengrößen wirklich Mengen- und Beschäftigungsänderungen sind und inwieweit diese nur Preisänderungen bedeuten, muß dann außerhalb des Nationalbudgetmodells durch eine weitere Analyse geklärt werden. Will man z. B. konstantes Preisniveau, so darf die Wertsumme des Bruttosozialprodukts nicht stärker ansteigen, als die zu erwartende reale Ausstoßsteigerung.

### *b) Beispiele für Nationalbudgetanalysen*

*α*) Zunächst sei auf ein *Modell der Bundesregierung* aus dem Jahre 1952 hingewiesen. Im Zusammenhang mit den Bestrebungen, die Bundesrepublik stärker zu den gemeinsamen Verteidigungslasten heranzuziehen, fand Anfang 1952 eine Diskussion über die der Bundesrepbulik als tragbar zuzumutende Verteidigungslast statt. Gegenüber dem weitergehenden Gutachten der „Drei Weisen" Plowden, Harriman und Monnet überreichte die Bundesregierung den NATO-Sachverständigen am 1. 2. 1952 ein Gegengutachten[1]), das auf einer Nationalbudgetanalyse beruhte und zu anderen Schlußfolgerungen kam (geringere Staatsausgaben für Verteidigungszwecke möglich als von den „Drei Weisen" vorgesehen). Das Gutachten interessiert heute in materieller Hinsicht kaum noch, dennoch ist es in formell theoretischer Hinsicht grundsätzlich interessant. Es sei hier nicht wörtlich wiedergegeben, jedoch in einfacher Modell-

---

[1]) Die Neue Zeitung vom 3. 2. 1952.

weise dargestellt. Das Grundmodell enthält folgende Variablen:

BSP = Bruttosozialprodukt zu Marktpreisen
A = Außenbeitrag[1])
I = Bruttoinvestition
C = private Konsumtion
$A_{st}$ = Staatsausgaben (staatl. Bruttoinvestition + staatlicher Konsum incl. Verteidigungsbeitrag)

Es gilt die Bilanzgleichung

$$(1)\ BSP = I + C + A_{st} + A$$

BSP soll nach dem Wunsch der Regierung seine maximale Größe erlangen. Von einer Schätzung der möglichen realen Entwicklung des BSP zu Faktorenkosten im jeweils nächsten Jahr ausgehend, wie es durch eine möglichst weitgehende Förderung des wirtschaftlichen Wachstums, bei annähernd konstanten Preisen, erreicht werden könnte, wird — unter Einschätzung der indirekten Steuern (abzüglich Subventionen) — das BSP errechnet. Damit ist eine Größe der Gleichung als realisierbar erscheinende Zielgröße BSP vorherbestimmt. Die zweite Größe, die Bruttoinvestition, kann ebenfalls als anzustrebende Zielvariable I gesetzt werden. Man kann sich dabei von der Überlegung leiten lassen, daß für das weitere Wachstum des BSP in den nächsten Jahren eine bestimmte Realkapitalerhöhung (Investition) erforderlich ist. Für diese erforderliche Investition wurde ein konstanter Anteil vom Bruttogesamtbetrag der im Inland verfügbaren Güter und Dienste, d. h. von (BSP — A[2]), angenommen. (Problematisch ist diese Setzung deshalb, weil die Investitionsreaktionen der Unternehmer von dieser „erforderlichen" Größe abweichen können).

Es besteht nur noch ein *Freiheitsgrad*, d. h. nur noch eine Variable kann frei bestimmt werden. Würde nun als dritte

---

1) Der Außenbeitrag entspricht im wesentlichen Exporten abzüglich Importen. Da seinerzeit noch Importüberschuß vorlag, war A eine negative Größe.

2) A wurde geschätzt: $\bar{A}$

Größe noch die Summe der Staatsausgaben für Güter und Dienste $A_{st}$ festgelegt werden, so wäre damit auch die mögliche Größe der Konsumausgaben bestimmt. Es ist die Frage, wieweit dieses möglich ist, ohne den Charakter der Wirtschaftsordnung als Marktwirtschaft mit freier Konsumwahl zu verlassen. Deshalb setzen an dieser Stelle Überlegungen ein, wie sich bei Freiheit der Einkommensverwendung die Konsumausgaben entwickeln werden, wenn das BSP wächst. Diese Überlegungen können in die Form einer weiteren Gleichung, in die uns schon bekannte Konsumfunktion gebracht werden. Zunächst ist das verfügbare Einkommen $E_v$ zu bestimmen. Es gilt:

$$(2) \quad E_v = BSP - T + Tr - G_z - Ab$$

wobei T = Steuern (abzüglich Subventionen)
Tr = Transferzahlungen
$G_z$ = zurückgehaltene Gewinne und
Ab = Abschreibungen
sind.

Wäre es möglich, das verfügbare Einkommen in eine eindeutige Relation zu BSP zu bringen, d. h. in einer Funktion auszudrücken, in der die verschiedenen Zu- und Abschlagsgrößen, wie Steuern, Transferzahlungen usw. nicht mehr explicite auftauchen, so könnte die Konsumtion als Funktion von BSP ausgedrückt werden.

Steuern, Transferzahlungen, zurückgehaltene Gewinne und Abschreibungen können, was ökonometrisch belegbar ist, für kurze Zeiträume ohne große Fehler in linearer Funktion von BSP ausgedrückt werden. Denkt man sich dieses ausgeführt, so stellt die rechte Seite von Gleichung (2) eine Kombination von linearen Abhängigkeiten von BSP dar, d. h. also insgesamt auch wieder eine lineare Funktion von BSP, so daß damit $E_v$ eine lineare Funktion von BSP ist. Setzt man die so gewonnene Funktion in die bekannte Konsumfunktion[1]) $C = a + b \cdot E_v$ ein, so erhält man, wenn auch mit anderen Koeffizienten, nämlich a' und b', den Konsum als ökonometrisch recht gut verifizierbare Funktion von BSP:

$$(3) \quad C = a' + b' \cdot BSP$$

1) Vgl. dazu Bd. I, Kap. III, § 2, 3.

Da BSP als Zielgröße $\overline{BSP}$ vorgegeben wurde, ist infolge der Funktion (3) der Konsum nicht mehr frei, sondern nimmt den Wert $\overline{C} = a' + b' \cdot \overline{BSP}$ an. Da nunmehr die drei Variablen $BSP = \overline{BSP}$, $I = \overline{I}$, $C = \overline{C}$ bestimmt sind, ferner der Außenbeitrag A durch den Schätzwert $\overline{A}$ gegeben ist, ist die mögliche Höhe der fünften Variablen $A_{st}$ ebenfalls bestimmt. Sie kann aus der Gleichung (4) errechnet werden, die durch Umformung der Gleichung (1) gewonnen wird:

$$(4)\quad \overline{A}_{st} = \overline{BSP} - \overline{I} - \overline{C} - \overline{A}$$

Würden die Staatsausgaben $A_{st}$ als ins Auge gefaßte Zielvariable größer gewählt werden als nach (4) zu errechnen, so würde die gesamte Nachfrage $(I + C + A + A_{st})$ das mögliche Angebot zu ursprünglich gegebenen Preisen $(\overline{BSP})$ übertreffen und es würde eine „Inflationslücke" entstehen, die zu einer Preissteigerung führen müßte, solange bis das Angebot sich auf den Wert der Nachfrage verteuert hätte[1]).

$A_{st}$ war von den „Drei Weisen" höher angesetzt worden als nach Gleichung (4) des Modells zu errechnen. Finanzpolitisch könnte auch bei größerem $A_{st}$ ein Ausweg gefunden werden. Wenn nämlich die Steuern erhöht werden, fließt den Haushalten ein geringerer Anteil des wachsenden BSP zu. Da nach dem Willen der Bundesregierung damals von einem weiteren Anziehen der Steuerschraube Abstand genommen werden sollte, blieb, da auch Inflationsvermeidung und Erhaltung der Konsum- und Sparfreiheit gleichfalls politisches Ziel waren, nur die Begrenzung der Größe $A_{st}$.

$\beta$) Es liegen auch Versuche vor, über die kurzfristige Analyse hinausgehend Nationalbudgets für eine Reihe von Jahren im voraus aufzustellen. So hat Nicholaus *Kaldor* im Jahre 1944 ein Modell für die britische Wirtschaft in

---

[1]) Wir sehen hier einmal von der in diesem Fall u. U. eintretenden Desinvestition durch Lagerabbau ab, bei der die Angebot-Nachfrage-Gleichheit auch ohne Preiserhöhung möglich ist, weil die eingetretene Nachfrageerhöhung aus Vorräten gespeist wird. Dieser Fall hätte seinerzeit — zum Modellzeitpunkt — praktisch kaum Bedeutung gehabt.

der Nachkriegszeit, d. h. für das Jahr 1948, entwickelt. Kaldors Modelle zeigen an einem praktischen Versuch die Möglichkeit, mit Hilfe verschiedener staatsfinanzieller Mittel ein gegebenes Ziel zu erreichen. Gleichzeitig geben sie ein Bild von den möglichen Nebenfolgen im Hinblick auf das Staatsdefizit bei diesen verschiedenen Wegen.

γ) Dann sind, neben anderen, die Versuche der *National Planning Association* in Washington bemerkenswert, im Jahre 1945 Nationalbudgets für das Jahr 1950 aufzustellen, deren erstaunlich gute Annäherung an die wirkliche Entwicklung festgestellt werden konnte. Die Arbeiten der National Planning Association sind später (1952) durch Gerhard *Colm* für das Jahr 1960 weitergeführt worden. Colm geht von den in der amerikanischen Wirtschaft liegenden Produktionsmöglichkeiten aus und entwickelt anhand verschiedener Modelle alternative Möglichkeiten insbesondere einer finanzpolitische Instrumente nutzenden Wirtschaftspolitik, um eine expandierende Wirtschaftsentwicklung bei Vollbeschäftigung zu stützen. Indem er dann die materielle Konsistenz der bei unterschiedlichem politischen Mitteleinsatz zu erzielenden Gesamtgrößen überprüft, d. h. fragt, ob die jeweils gewählte Politik mit der zu erwartenden Verhaltensweise der Privaten, insbesondere der Konsumenten, im Gesamtrahmen der erstrebten Ziele verträglich ist, kommt er unter Verwerfung aller anderen zu einem „adjusted model", das er als Diskussionsbeitrag gewertet wissen möchte. Die weitere Überprüfung der Ergebnisse dieser Arbeit mit der wirklichen Entwicklung hat eine recht gute Übereinstimmung erwiesen. Colms Arbeit verdient besonderes Interesse gerade im Zusammenhang mit den Problemen einer gleichmäßigen langfristigen Wirtschaftsentwicklung.

### 4. Das Haavelmosche Theorem

Das von Trygve Haavelmo 1945 entwickelte Theorem besagt, daß auch ein Staatshaushalt, der ohne zusätzliche Kreditaufnahme expandiert — zusätzliche Staatsausgaben werden voll durch zusätzliche Steuern finanziert — zu einer Vergrößerung des Sozialprodukts und Volkseinkommens führe. Diese Aussage ist das Ergebnis folgender Analyse: Es seien $E_m$ das Nettosozialprodukt zu Marktpreisen, C der private Konsum, I die private Nettoinvestition und $A_{st}$ die Ausgaben des Staates für Güter und Dienste. Vernachlässigt man den Außenbeitrag, so ergibt sich folgende Identität:

(1) $E_m = C + I + A_{st}$

Werden vom Nettosozialprodukt zu Marktpreisen die Steuern T abgezogen, so ergibt sich das verfügbare Einkommen[1]) $E_v = E_m - T$. Die private Konsumtion hänge, entsprechend der bekannten Konsumfunktion folgendermaßen von dem verfügbaren Einkommen ab:

(2) $C = a + b \cdot E_v = a + b \cdot (E_m - T)$.

Setzt man (2) in (1) ein und löst nach $E_m$ auf, so erhält man

$$(3)\ E_m = \frac{a}{1-b} + \frac{1}{1-b} \cdot I + \frac{1}{1-b} \cdot A_{st} - \frac{b}{1-b} \cdot T$$

Unter der Voraussetzung, daß I konstant ist (d. h. $\Delta I = 0$), ergibt sich der Zuwachs des Nettosozialprodukts zu Marktpreisen $\Delta E_m$ als Funktion der Änderungen der Staatsausgaben $\Delta A_{st}$ und der Änderung der Steuern $\Delta T$:

$$(4)\ \Delta E_m = \frac{1}{1-b} \cdot \Delta A_{st} - \frac{b}{1-b} \cdot \Delta T$$

Diese Gleichung stellt das Ergebnis der Wirkung des Staatsausgabenmultiplikators $\frac{1}{1-b}$ und des negativen Steuermultiplikators $-\frac{b}{1-b}$ dar (vgl. Bd. II, Kap. VI, § 10,1).

---

1) Genau genommen müßten noch Nettoeinkünfte aus wirtschaftlicher Staatstätigkeit, die Sozialbeiträge und die unverteilten Gewinne abgezogen und die Transferzahlungen hinzugerechnet werden, was hier der Einfachheit halber unterbleibt.

Bei ausgeglichenem Staatshaushalt ist $\Delta A_{st} = \Delta T$; unter dieser Bedingung ergibt sich:

$$(5)\quad \Delta E_m = \left( \frac{1}{1-b} - \frac{b}{1-b} \right) \Delta A_{st} = \Delta A_{st} = \Delta T$$

Das bedeutet, daß der „Gesamt-Multiplikator“ im Haavelmo-Fall gleich 1 ist. Das Nettosozialprodukt zu Marktpreisen steigt bei voll durch Steuern finanzierter Staatsausgabenerhöhung um eben den Betrag der Staatsausgabenerhöhung.

Man kann zeigen, wie es z. B. Erich Schneider getan hat, daß dieses Ergebnis modifiziert werden muß, wenn man unterschiedliche marginale Konsumquoten b für die verschiedenen Einkommensgruppen zugrunde legt. Der Multiplikator wird größer (kleiner) als 1 sein, wenn vornehmlich Gruppen mit höheren (niedrigeren) Einkommen von der Steuererhöhung betroffen werden, oder wenn die Ausgabe der empfangenen Steuern durch den Staat vornehmlich das Einkommen der unteren (höheren) Einkommensklassen erhöht. Diese Schlußfolgerungen ergeben sich aus der Annahme einer niedrigen (hohen) marginalen Konsumquote b für die höheren (unteren) Einkommensklassen. Diese Fragestellung sei hier nicht weiter ausgeführt; man kann dieses Ergebnis leicht ableiten, wenn man sich der obigen Analyse bedient und nur verschiedene Einkommensgruppen mit verschiedenen marginalen Konsumquoten, mit verschiedenen Steuerzahlungen und verschiedenem Anteil an den zusätzlichen Staatsausgaben in die Gleichungen einführt.

Die Haavelmosche Analyse ist eine komparativ-statische, d. h. es wird ein möglicher Gleichgewichtszustand vor Expansion des Staatshaushalts mit einem zweiten nach Expansion des Staatshaushalts verglichen. Der Erhöhung der von den Privaten zu zahlenden direkten und indirekten Steuern entspricht die Erhöhung des Nettosozialprodukts zu Marktpreisen um den gleichen Betrag, so daß ihr privates Nettoeinkommen und in Funktion davon ihr Konsum unverändert erhalten bleibt.

Die Erhöhung des Nettosozialprodukts zu Marktpreisen kann dabei durchaus eine reale Produktionsvergrößerung bedeuten, wenn vorher Unterbeschäftigung vorlag und Überkapazitäten vorhanden waren. In diesem Fall beibt das gesamte nach Abzug der Steuern verbleibende Nettorealeinkommen der Privaten gleich, wobei allerdings das Einkommen der zusätzlich Beschäftigten und das Einkommen aus zusätzlich in Anspruch genommenen bisher brach liegenden Kapazitäten auf Kosten der bisher beschäftigten Faktoren geht; deren Einkommen wurden ja durch zusätzliche Steuern gekürzt. Die Produktionssteigerung kommt dem Staate zugute. Wenn jedoch vorher Vollbeschäftigung und Kapazitätsauslastung bestand, ergeben sich bei unveränderter Gesamtproduktion und marktwirtschaftlicher Wirtschaftsordnung notwendigerweise Preis- und Lohnsteigerungen.

Diese Preis- und Lohnsteigerungen erhöhen zwar das nominelle Bruttoeinkommen der Gesamtheit der Privaten. Da aber wegen der gleichzeitig erhöhten Steuern ihr nominelles Nettoeinkommen konstant bleibt (jedenfalls im einfachen Haavelmoschen Modell), ergibt sich somit wegen der Preissteigerungen eine Einschränkung des Realeinkommens der Gesamtheit der privaten Einkommensbezieher zugunsten einer verbesserten Güterversorgung des Staates. Es ist dabei aber durchaus denkbar, daß einzelne Gruppen von Einkommensbeziehern — jedenfalls kurzfristig — in unterschiedlichem Maße von der Realeinkommenssenkung betroffen werden.

Bei all dem kann jedoch die Frage nicht unterdrückt werden, ob die grundlegende Voraussetzung des Haavelmoschen Modells, daß die privaten Investitionen unbeeinflußt bleiben, d. h. daß $\Delta I = 0$ ist, wirklich schlechthin Gültigkeit beanspruchen kann. Wenn angenommen werden darf, daß die privaten Investitionen sowohl von der Finanzierungsmöglichkeit aus erzielten Nettogewinnen als auch von den zukünftig erwarteten Nettogewinnen bestimmt werden, so mag es wegen der Steuererhöhung, insbesondere bei Gewinnsteuern, zu einer Senkung der gegenwärtigen Investitionen kommen. In der komparativ-statischen Analyse müßte man dann also mit einem negativen

$\Delta$ I rechnen, d. h. die eintretende Einkommensänderung würde gemäß (3) um $\frac{1}{1-b} \cdot \Delta$ I kleiner sein als oben unter (5) festgestellt wurde, was u. U. den beschriebenen Haavelmo-Effekt gänzlich aufheben mag.

Man beachte, daß bei einer marginalen Konsumquote von z. B. 0,8 sich ein Investitionsmultiplikator $\frac{1}{1-b} = 5$ ergibt, d. h. es genügt eine Einschränkung der privaten Investitionen um nur $^1/_5$ der zusätzlichen Staatsausgaben oder Steuern, um den Haavelmo-Effekt zunichte zu machen. — Der Leser sei in diesem Zusammenhang auf die große Ähnlichkeit der Theoreme von Haavelmo und Föhl (vgl. Bd. II, Kap. VI, § 9, 4d$\gamma_2$) hingewiesen, jedenfalls, was die modelltheoretischen Annahmen anbelangt. Bei beiden unterliegt die gesamte private Nachfrage trotz Steuern keiner Einschränkung, so daß die zusätzliche steuerfinanzierte Staatsnachfrage zu einer allgemeinen *Brutto*einkommensexpansion führt, die bei Föhl speziell als Bruttogewinnsteigerung und damit Gewinnsteuerüberwälzung erscheint.

Es bleibt abschließend zu betonen, daß selbst dann, wenn die Voraussetzung hinsichtlich der Konstanz der Investitionen zuträfe, der Staat durch Erzielung eines geeignet hohen Überschusses, d. h. $\Delta T > \Delta A_{st}$, in der Lage ist, auch bei Ausdehnung der Staatsnachfrage ($\Delta A_{st} > 0$) die Gesamtnachfrage konstant zu halten oder sogar kontrahieren zu lassen. Auch gilt unter der gleichen Voraussetzung und bei gegebener Konsumfunktion nach wie vor die Aussage, daß eine zusätzliche kreditfinanzierte Staatsnachfrage eine viel größere Multiplikatorwirkung zeigen wird als eine steuerfinanzierte Ausgabensteigerung. Oder anders ausgedrückt: Um eine bestimmte Erhöhung der Gesamtnachfrage zu erreichen, müssen im ersten Falle die Staatsausgaben in geringerem Maße ansteigen als im zweiten. Grundsätzlich bliebe also auch unter den Haavelmoschen Annahmen das Instrumentarium konjunktureller Fiskalpolitik erhalten.

## 5. Staatshaushalt und Fiskalpolitik[1])

### a) Langfristige Fiskalpolitik

Es erscheint zweckmäßig, die Frage nach den Bedingungen für langfristiges Vollbeschäftigungsgleichgewicht vor dem mehr kurz- und mittelfristigen Problem der Konjunkturpolitik zu erörtern. Damit hängt die Frage nach der *langfristigen* Fiskalpolitik im Falle andauernder Stagnation zusammen, zu der andeutungsweise schon einiges in Band I (vgl. Kap. II, § 8, 3c) gesagt wurde.

Als reales Vollbeschäftigungssozialprodukt V sei das zu Marktpreisen einer Basisperiode bewertete Nettosozialprodukt zu Marktpreisen bezeichnet, das in der jeweiligen Periode bei Beschäftigung des gesamten Arbeitspotentials produziert werden könnte.

V, als das bei Vollbeschäftigung denkbare, allerdings nicht immer realisierte, Sozialprodukt, steigt durch den technischen Fortschritt und das Wachstum des Arbeitspotentials, das weitgehend vom Bevölkerungswachstum bestimmt ist. Damit dieses denkbare Wachstum auch wirklich erreicht wird, ist eine gewisse private reale Investition $\bar{I}$ als *erforderliche* Investition notwendig, um die Kapazitäten entsprechend dem Arbeitspotentialwachstum auszuweiten und entsprechend dem technischen Fortschritt qualitativ umzugestalten. Von der erforderlichen Investition $\bar{I}$ ist die aufgrund ihrer Investitionsneigung von den Unternehmern *tatsächlich* vorgenommene Investition I zu unterscheiden.

Es sei zunächst angenommen, daß $I = \bar{I}$ sei; dann würde für die gesamte effektive Nachfrage N gelten[2]):

$$(1) \quad N = C + \bar{I} + A_{st}$$

Für die Konsumfunktion kann man unter langfristigen Aspekten annähernd den Ansatz einer proportionalen Funktion des privaten nach Abzug der Steuern T verfüg-

---

1) Formulierungen dieses Abschnittes von H. Bydekarken.

2) Der Außenbeitrag kann hier vernachlässigt werden.

baren[1]) Einkommens machen, so daß bei Vollbeschäftigung sich folgender Konsum ergeben würde:

$$(2) \quad C = b \cdot (V - T)$$

Damit wird vorläufig angenommen, daß V als das Angebot von Gütern und Diensten bei Vollbeschäftigung auch auf eine entsprechend hohe Nachfrage N trifft, so daß das Vollbeschäftigungseinkommen als Gleichgewichtsgröße realisiert wird. Allerdings ist diese Annahme sogleich noch zu überprüfen.

Nun ist die Definitionsgleichung für das Staatsdefizit Kr zu berücksichtigen:

$$Kr = A_{st} - T \text{ oder:}$$

$$(3) \quad T = A_{st} - Kr$$

Setzt man nun (3) und (2) in (1) ein, so erhält man:

$$(4) \quad N = b \cdot V + \bar{I} + (1 - b)\, A_{st} + b \cdot Kr$$

Um Gleichgewicht zu realisieren, müßte $N = V$ gelten. Wäre $N > V$, würde sich ein preissteigernder Nachfrageüberschuß, wäre dagegen $N < V$, würde sich ein Nachfragedefizit ergeben. Es würde dann das Angebot nicht abgesetzt werden können, d. h. es würde zu Preis- und Einkommensverlusten und zu Beschäftigungsrückgang kommen; und da nach (2) für die Konsumnachfrage Vollbeschäftigungseinkommen vorausgesetzt wurde, würde in diesem Fall der Konsum die nach (2) angegebene Höhe gar nicht erreichen können, so daß die Nachfragelücke noch größer werden würde. Ein langfristiges Gleichgewichtswachstum aller Größen wäre unter diesen Umständen ausgeschlossen.

Setzt man die Nachfragelücke[2]) $D = V - N$ ins Verhältnis zu V, so erhält man die relative Nachfragelücke:

$$(5) \quad \frac{D}{V} = (1 - b) - \frac{\bar{I}}{V} - (1 - b) \cdot \frac{A_{st}}{V} - b \cdot \frac{Kr}{V}$$

[1]) Hinsichtlich der Vernachlässigung der Transferzahlungen und anderer Größen, die das verfügbare private Einkommen beeinflussen, sollen hier schon die im vorigen Abschnitt vorgenommenen Vereinfachungen gelten.

[2]) Positive D verkörpern eine Nachfrage l ü c k e, negative D einen Nachfrage ü b e r s c h u ß.

Die Fragestellung geht nun dahin, über die Größenordnung der relativen Nachfragelücke Aussagen zu machen. Die sogenannte Stagnationsthese, an die sich eine bestimmte Konzeption der langfristigen Fiskalpolitik anschließt, beantwortet die Frage dahingehend, daß es in der Tat zu solch einer Nachfragelücke kommen kann, wenn die staatliche Aktivität unzureichend ist.

Anhand von (5) kann diese Ausage ein wenig präzisiert werden. Das erste Glied (1—b) von (5) ist stets positiv, da b immer kleiner als 1 ist. Die Nachfragelücke wird also nur dann verschwinden, wenn die folgenden drei abzuziehenden Glieder so groß wie (1—b) werden. $\bar{I}/V$ ist — wie schon gesagt wurde — in seiner Größenordnung vom Bevölkerungswachstum und vom technischen Fortschritt abhängig. Es mag zwar sein, daß für gewisse Zeiträume (großes Bevölkerungswachstum und „industrielle Revolutionen") diese Einflüsse so stark sind, daß $\bar{I}/V$ schon so groß ist, daß selbst bei kleinen Größen für $A_{st}/V$ und $Kr/V$ die Nachfragelücke verschwindet. Andererseits hat A. Hansen mit Recht darauf hingewiesen, daß das keineswegs schlechthin Gültigkeit beanspruchen könne, weil $\bar{I}/V$ nicht immer so groß wäre[1]), um (1—b) annähernd zu kompensieren. Dann müssen $A_{st}/V$ und $Kr/V$ als politische Parameter so groß gewählt werden, daß gemäß (5) gerade $D/V = O$ wird, da nur dann Nachfragegleichgewicht und gleichgewichtiges Wachstum möglich ist.

Unter diesen Umständen würden die „klassischen" Forderungen erstens nach *minimalem* öffentlichem Haushalt, d. h. $A_{st}$ soll nur so groß sein, daß es zur Erfüllung der unbedingt erforderlichen Grundfunktionen des Staates im Sinne von Smith (vgl. Bd. I, Kap. II § 2, 1) ausreicht, und zweitens nach *ausgeglichenem* Haushalt, d. h. $Kr = 0$, als politische Maxime mehr als fragwürdig sein, da *diese* Wahl der politischen Parameter die Nachfragelücke nicht beseitigen würde.

Es wäre z. B. vorstellbar, daß $b = 0{,}85$ und $\bar{I}/V = 0{,}075$ wäre. Wenn man für $A_{st}$ nur die minimalen Staatsausgaben im Sinne Smiths wählen würde, könnte z. B. $A_{st}/V$ nur 15 % be-

[1]) Man beachte, daß es hier nur um das verhältnismäßig kleine Wachstum bei Vollbeschäftigung geht. Fur einen Konjunkturaufschwung nach einer Depression können und werden die Investitionsmöglichkeiten viel größer sein.

tragen, so daß ohne Kreditaufnahme des Staates sich dann gemäß (5) eine relative Nachfragelücke von 5,25 % ergeben würde. Bei Aufrechterhaltung der Forderung nach ausgeglichenem Haushalt müßte man $A_{st}/V$ bis auf 50 % steigern, um die Nachfragelücke zu vermeiden. Würde man diese Relation der Staatsausgaben zum Sozialprodukt für zu hoch halten und anstatt dessen $A_{st}/V$ z. B. in Höhe von 40 % ansetzen, so müßte man eine relative Kreditaufnahme von $Kr/V = 1{,}76\,\%$ zulassen, um die Nachfragelücke zu vermeiden.

Bei der Bestimmung der politischen Parameter[1]) $A_{st}/V$ und $Kr/V$ zur Vermeidung einer Nachfragelücke besteht ein Freiheitsgrad, d. h. eine dieser beiden Größen kann frei gewählt werden, die andere ergibt sich dann aus der Bedingung $D/V = 0$. Dabei sind zwei interessante Feststellungen zu machen: Erstens ist zu sagen, daß eine Vergrößerung von $A_{st}/V$ um einen bestimmten Prozentsatz viel weniger effizient im Hinblick auf die Verkleinerung der Nachfragelücke ist als die Vergrößerung von $Kr/V$ um den gleichen Prozentsatz. Zweitens läßt sich die Aussage machen, daß wenn einmal $A_{st}/V$ und $Kr/V$ so gewählt worden sind, daß $D/V$ verschwindet, eine politische Entscheidung hinsichtlich einer weiteren Erhöhung der Staatsausgaben nach (5) notwendig zu einer Verkleinerung von Kr führen muß, wenn $D/V = 0$ bleiben soll, d. h. nach (3) müssen die Steuern T stärker ausgedehnt werden als die Staatsausgaben.

Nun muß allerdings darauf hingewiesen werden, daß bei der Berechnung der Nachfragelücke immer vorausgesetzt wurde, daß die aufgrund der Investitionsneigung oder der Investitionsfunktion erfolgende Investition I tatsächlich so groß sei, wie die für Beibehaltung des optimalen Wachstums erforderliche Investition $\bar{I}$. Wenn aber die staalichen Parameter variiert werden, ist daran zu denken, daß eine rein steuerfinanzierte Staatsausgabensteigerung nicht nur die Konsumnachfrage trifft — sondern höchstwahrscheinlich auch über die Minderung der Nettogewinne zu einer verringerten Investition I führen wird. Damit wäre die

---

[1]) Politische Parameter im eigentlichen Sinn sind die absoluten Größen und Ast und Kr Da die im Nenner stehende Bezugsgroße V wächst, beinhaltet eine Fixierung von Ast/V und Kr/V auch eine ständige proportionale Vergrößerung von Ast und Kr.

bisher angenommene Voraussetzung $I = \bar{I}$ in Frage gestellt. Man müßte daher unter Umständen durch andere Maßnahmen dafür sorgen, daß die tatsächliche private Investition die Höhe der erforderlichen Investition $\bar{I}$ erreicht.

Grundsätzlich bieten sich zwei Möglichkeiten an. Erstens könnten die Bruttogewinne der Unternehmer angehoben werden, so daß dadurch die steuerlichen Einbußen soweit kompensiert würden, daß eine negative Auswirkung auf die Investition unterbleibt. Wenn man von einer Lohnsenkung absieht, wäre dafür eine Preisniveausteigerung erforderlich. Will man diese vermeiden, muß man die zweite Möglichkeit ins Auge fassen, durch gesetzliche Steuerbegünstigungen für Investitionen die Investitionsneigung der Unternehmer in erforderlicher Höhe zu erhalten.

Neben der bisher geschilderten Möglichkeit, auftretende Nachfragelücken durch Veränderung der Globalgrößen $A_{st}$ und T zu schließen, ist noch zu erwähnen, daß — bei unveränderten Globalgrößen — eine steuerliche Redistributionspolitik, wie sie in Bd. I und Bd. II erläutert wurde, die volkswirtschaftliche marginale Konsumquote b und damit die private Konsumnachfrage erhöhen kann. Wie dort bereits ausgeführt, ist dabei immer das Problem der möglichen negativen Rückwirkung einer schärferen Belastung der höheren (insbesondere der Gewinn-) Einkommen auf die Investition zu beachten, worauf auch in den vorangegangenen Ausführungen erneut hingewiesen wurde.

Abschließend bleibt festzustellen, daß die Konzeption langfristiger Fiskalpolitik, nämlich durch bewußte Gestaltung von Staatsausgaben und Steuern und damit auch der staatlichen Kreditnahme zu einem Wachstumsgleichgewicht bei Vollbeschäftigung beizutragen, als wirtschaftspolitische Forderung voll zu unterstützen ist. Dabei ist zu beachten, daß wenn der aus liberalen Gedanken kommende Wunsch nach einer Begrenzung der Höhe der öffentlichen Ausgaben geäußert wird, einmal daran zu denken ist, daß dann — zur Erfüllung der Bedingung $D/V = O$ — unter Umständen eine Kreditfinanzierung öffentlicher Ausgaben erforderlich wird. Zum anderen darf aber auch niemals die außerordentliche Bedeutung gewisser Staatsausgaben (Infrastruktur, Erziehungswesen, Gesundheit usw.) als Wachstumsvoraussetzung selbst übersehen werden, so daß von dieser Seite gegen eine allzu kleinliche Behandlung öffentlicher Ausgaben ernste Bedenken geltend zu machen sind.

### *b) Antizyklische Fiskalpolitik*

Während das Schwergewicht der Betrachtung bei der Konzeption langfristiger Fiskalpolitik auf den Stabilitätsbedingungen für langfristiges Vollbeschäftigungswachstum liegt, zielt die Idee der *antizyklischen* Fiskalpolitik auf die Bekämpfung kurzfristiger Ungleichgewichte im Konjunkturablauf mit finanzpolitischen Mitteln. Beide Konzeptionen haben aber die gleichen Zielsetzungen, nämlich erstens Vollbeschäftigung und zweitens Preisstabilität zu erreichen.

Die bekannte Grundformulierung im Konzept der *gesteuerten* antizyklischen Fiskalpolitik (vgl. Bd. I, II, § 8, 3b$\beta$) lautet: Bewußte und rechtzeitige Senkung der Staatsausgaben und Erhöhung der Steuereinnahmen kurz vor und in der Hochkonjunktur, Erhöhung der Staatsausgaben und Senkung der Steuereinnahmen im Abschwung und in der Depression. Das führt zu einem Überschuß der Steuereinnahmen über die Ausgaben des Staates im ersten, zu einem entsprechenden Defizit im zweiten Falle. Dabei — wie auch in den folgenden Ausführungen — wird vorausgesetzt, daß im Falle des Überschusses die Geldmittel thesauriert werden, z. B. durch Einzahlung bei der Zentralbank, und nicht etwa auf dem Wege über Aktivkredite an Unternehmungen und Haushalte deren Nachfrage erhöhen. Vgl. dazu die abschließenden Bemerkungen zu § 4,2. Entsprechendes gilt, vice versa, für den Fall des Defizits.

Das Konzept der gesteuerten antizyklischen Fiskalpolitik schließt alerdings einen Konflikt zwischen den verschiedenen Zielsetzungen der Fiskalpolitik nicht aus: Dämpfungsmaßnahmen in der Hochkonjunktur sollen die Preise, können aber auch die Beschäftigung senken; Förderungsmaßnahmen in einer Depression sollen die Beschäftigung, können aber auch die Preise ansteigen lassen. Für eine einigermaßen befriedigende Beantwortung der Fragestellung nach den Möglichkeiten, diesen Konflikt zu vermeiden, ebenso wie nach dem „Wann“ und dem „Wieviel“ des Staatseingriffes, wäre eine ausführliche konjunkturtheoretische Betrachtung notwendig, für die hier nicht der Raum ist. Es mögen daher einige Andeutungen genügen.

Im Konjunkturabschwung, in der Depression und wahrscheinlich in einer ersten Phase des Aufschwunges wird sowohl mit unbeschäftigten Arbeitskräften als auch mit nicht ausgelasteten Kapazitäten zu rechnen sein. Einer Expansionspolitik des Staates durch vermehrte Staatsausgaben und verminderte Steuern eine Ausdehnung der Gesamtnachfrage zu erreichen, steht dann grundsätzlich nichts im Wege. Denn der erhöhten Nachfrage kann unter diesen Umständen rasch eine Steigerung der realen Produktion folgen, so daß es zunächst nicht zu nennenswerten Preissteigerungen kommen wird (abgesehen von Fällen, in denen vorangegangene depressive Preissenkungen unter die Durchschnittskosten erst wieder wettgemacht werden müssen, bevor an Produktionsausdehnung gedacht werden kann). In solchen Situationen wird also die Steigerung der effektiven Nachfrage zu Beschäftigungssteigerungen bei annähernd konstantem oder nur wenig erhöhtem Preisniveau führen können.

In einer späteren Phase des Aufschwungs, in der durchaus noch unbeschäftigte Arbeitskräfte vorhanden sind, wird es zu einer Auslastung der Produktionskapazitäten kommen. Das liegt nicht zuletzt daran, daß während der Depression regelmäßig Ersatzinvestitionen unterlassen werden, wodurch Realkapitalbestand und Produktionskapazität verkleinert worden sind.

Würde nun — etwa um die Unterbeschäftigung noch schneller zu beseitigen als es ohnehin schon im Zuge des Aufschwungs geschieht — eine staatliche Expansionspolitik verfolgt, müßte es in verstärktem Maße zu Preissteigerungen kommen, da die wachsende Nachfrage wegen der ausgelasteten Kapazitäten ohnehin auf ein nicht schnell genug wachsendes Angebot stößt. Zwar werden im Zuge der während des Aufschwunges eingetretenen Nachfragesteigerungen und Verbesserungen der Rentabilitätssituation der Unternehmungen wieder steigende Nettoinvestitionen durchgeführt; jedoch vor dem Kapazitätseffekt jeder Investition und der dadurch eintretenden Angebotssteigerung liegt ihr Effekt auf Nachfrage, Einkommen und erneuter Konsumnachfrage, so daß es auch ohne besondere staatliche Expansionspolitik zu einem Vorwegeilen der Nachfrage und damit zu Nachfrageüberschüssen und Preissteigerungen kommen wird.

Sinnvoller erscheint in dieser Konjunkturphase (also schon vor Erreichen der Vollbeschäftigung) eine Politik, die dafür sorgt, daß Nachfrageüberschüsse soweit wie möglich vermieden werden; dabei soll das Wachstum der Nachfrage entsprechend dem Wachstum der Ausstoßmengen nicht ausgeschlossen werden, aber — ideal-typisch gesehen — zu jedem Zeitpunkt nur um soviel mehr Nachfrage geltend gemacht werden, wie produziertes reales Angebot vermehrt auf die Märkte strömt. Durch zusätzliche Steuern, insbesondere Einkommensteuern, müßte das Wachstum der Konsumnachfrage und durch Ausgabeneinschränkung das Wachstum der Staatsnachfrage gedrosselt werden[1]). Wichtig wäre allerdings, die bei solcher Politik möglicherweise eintretenden negativen Wirkungen auf Netto-Gewinne und Investitionen zu beachten, die dann unvermeidbar sind, wenn nicht durch besondere finanzpolitische Maßnahmen die Investition so gefördert wird, daß die an sich zu erwartenden Investitionshemmungen dadurch kompensiert oder sogar überkompensiert werden. Zu denken wäre vor allem an Einkommensteuerbefreiungen für Investitionsvorhaben (zweckmäßigerweise schon im Planungszeitpunkt, um die Finanzierung zu erleichtern, z. B. durch entsprechende Kürzungen der Steuervorauszahlungen), die ja gerade wegen der gleichzeitig bestehenden hohen Einkommensbesteuerung und des damit gegebenen großen Anreizes zur Steuervermeidung zweifellos ihre Wirkung nicht verfehlen dürften. Auch an befristete Umsatzsteuersenkungen wäre zu denken, die — bei gegebener effektiver Nachfrage und gegebenem Preisniveau — zu Gewinnsteigerungen bei

---

[1]) Die Möglichkeit, bisher unbeschäftigte Arbeitskräfte durch öffentliche Arbeiten zu beschäftigen, bleibt aber insofern erhalten, als man durch Einkommensteuern die gesamte private Konsumnachfrage auch dann drosseln kann, wenn das private Bruttoeinkommen (infolge der Mehrbeschäftigung) steigt.

den Unternehmern und dadurch zu erhöhter Investition führen.

Möglicherweise würde es im Zuge all dieser Maßnahmen schon in dieser Konjunkturphase zu einem staatlichen Budgetüberschuß kommen. Aber wegen der Steuerbefreiungen zur Investitionsförderung mag das erst in der folgenden Konjunkturphase der Fall sein, wenn nämlich die Investitionsförderung aufgehoben werden muß. Die Notwendigkeit dazu ergibt sich aus dem Tatbestand, daß unmittelbar vor Erreichen der Vollbeschäftigung und bei Vollbeschäftigung die reinen *Erweiterungsinvestitionen,* die während des Aufschwunges eine entscheidende Bedeutung für die erforderlichen Kapazitätserweiterungen hatten, auf ein niedrigeres, durch das Wachstum des Arbeitspotentials bestimmtes Maß zurückgehen müssen. Zwar sind in dieser Siutation die *Rationalisierungsinvestitionen* von größerer Bedeutung als vorher; zweifellos wird aber das ökonomisch sinnvolle Ausmaß der Nettoinvestition viel kleiner als während des Aufschwunges sein.

Es ist zu bemerken, daß dieser Rückgang von privater Investition bei Vollbeschäftigung nach einer Aufschwungperiode mit starker Investitionstätigkeit auch bei einem völlig ungesteuerten Konjunkturverlauf spätestens dann eintreten wird, wenn sich bei den Unternehmungen Überkapazitäten gebildet haben; denn das bisherige Realkapitalwachstum kann — abgesehen von Fällen äußerst intensiven technischen Fortschritts — nicht als ökonomisch sinnvoll aufrecht erhalten werden.

Aus diesem Grunde ist es angebracht, kurz vor dem Erreichen der Vollbeschäftigung die Investitionsförderung einzustellen. Der eintretende Rückgang der privaten Investitionsnachfrage einerseits und die infolge der vorangegangenen Kapazitätserweiterungen allmählich eintretenden Angebotserhöhungen andererseits lassen nunmehr einer größeren Konsumnachfrage und größeren Staatsnachfrage auch dann mehr Raum, wenn eine inflationäre Entwicklung nach wie vor ausgeschlossen bleiben soll. Da aber die im Aufschwungsprozeß ebenfalls eingetretene Bruttoeinkommenssteigerung der Privaten schon bei unveränderten Steuersätzen eine erhebliche Konsumnachfragesteigerung bewirken, sollten die Einkommensteuersätze nur allmählich gesenkt und die Staatsausgaben nur allmählich erhöht werden. Die dadurch sich immerhin ergebende defizitäre Auswirkung auf den Staatshaushalt wird zunächst noch überkompensiert durch Zurücknahme der Steuerbefreiungen für Investitionszwecke und gegebenenfalls durch die Erhöhung der Umsatzsteuer (zwecks Senkung gegenwärtiger Gewinne und damit zukünftiger Investitionen) einerseits und die mit einem lag in die Staatskassen einströmenden, noch hohen Gewinnsteuereinnahmen (höhere Gewinne und höhere Steuersätze in der Vorperiode) andererseits, so daß in dieser Phase unmittelbar vor der Vollbeschäftigung mit einem Haushaltsüberschuß zu rechnen ist.

Einige Zeit nach Erreichen der Vollbeschäftigung wird der Kapazitätseffekt aller während des Aufschwungsprozesses vorgenommenen Investitionen voll zum Tragen gekommen sein; da die für das laufende Vollbeschäftigungswachstum jetzt noch erforderliche Investition $\bar{I}$ verhältnismäßig klein ist (vgl. a), bleibt ein größerer Raum für C und $A_{st}$. Beide müssen diesen Raum auch in Anspruch nehmen, da nur so von nun an das Nachfragegleichgewicht bei Vollbeschäftigung zu gewährleisten ist.

Es ist in diesem Zusammenhang bemerkenswert, daß in neueren Konjunkturtheorien der Konjunkturzusammenbruch allgemein aus dem unvermeidbaren Rückgang der Investitionsnachfrage erklärt wird, dem bei mangelnder Steuerung keine ausreichende Erhöhung der Konsumnachfrage oder der Staatsnachfrage entgegenwirkt.

Wenn in dieser Situation durch staatliche Steuerungsmaßnahmen der entstehende Raum für C und $A_{st}$ auch in Anspruch genommen wird, so bedeutet das nichts anderes, als daß die politischen Parameter Staatsausgaben und Steuern (oder Kredite) gemäß den Ausführungen zu a) so dimensioniert werden, daß D/V verschwindet und sich somit von nun an ein gleichgewichtiges Vollbeschäftigungswachstum ergibt. Wie in a) ausgeführt, kann das langfristige Gleichgewicht so beschaffen sein, daß eine laufende staatliche Kreditnahme sinnvoll und notwendig ist.

Einer staatlichen Politik, die — im Gegensatz zum bisher Geschilderten — erst bei Vollbeschäftigung mit ihren Maßnahmen einsetzen würde, wäre eine Inflationsbekämpfung nur in beschränktem Maße möglich, da es dann — wie angedeutet — schon während des Aufschwunges zu Preissteigerungen kommen mag. Besonders müßte man dann aber darauf achten, daß die inflationsbekämpfenden Maßnahmen der Nachfragedrosselung, die zunächst auch nach Erreichen der Vollbeschäftigung ihren preisstabilisierenden Sinn behalten, weil die Auftriebstendenzen aus dem Aufschwung noch weiter fortwirken, sofort in dem Augenblick aufgehoben werden, wenn es zum beschriebenen Rückgang der Investitionsnachfrage kommt. Würde eine staatliche Überschußpolitik (hohe Steuern, niedrige Ausgaben) dann nämlich beibehalten werden, würde der Rückgang der Investitionsnachfrage noch weniger als im ungesteuerten Konjunkturzyklus durch Erhöhung der privaten Konsumnachfrage oder der staatlichen Nachfrage aufgefangen werden können, so daß es zu einer Nachfragelücke mit negativen Auswirkungen auf die Beschäftigung kommen würde.

Insbesondere in dem zuletzt beschriebenen Zusammenhang ist die Konzeption *automatischer* antizyklischer Politik der „built-in flexibility" kritisch zu betrachten. Wegen des time-lags der Steuereinnahmen hinter dem Einkommen können Überschüsse selbst dann noch auftreten, wenn der Rückgang der Nachfrage bereits eingesetzt hat. Abgesehen davon ist es erstens sehr fraglich, ob automatische Stabilisatoren einen zyklischen Verlauf überhaupt stabilisieren, und zweitens bleibt völlig offen, auf welchem Beschäftigungsniveau eine Stabilisierung, gesetzt sie sei erreichbar, Platz greifen würde.

In jüngster Zeit ist die Konzeption automatischer Stabilisierung durch die sogenannte „formula-flexibility" (vgl. insbesondere Phillips, Keiser) erweitert worden. In Anlehnung an die Regeltechnik sollen festgestellte Abweichungen zwischen der tatsächlich realisierten und der politisch erwünschten Größe einer ökonomischen Variablen in eine Formel eingesetzt werden, aufgrund derer dann die Größe des politischen Instrumentparameters (z. B. Staatsausgaben) „automatisch" errechnet[1]) wird, die daraufhin in der folgenden Periode zur Beseitigung der unerwünschten Differenz zwischen Zielgröße und realisierter Größe eingesetzt wird. Das große Problem dabei ist freilich, die geeignete Formel zu finden, und so interessant die gemachten Untersuchungen auch sind, es zeigt sich nach den vorliegenden Ergebnissen, daß das genannte Regelverfahren nicht immer zum Ziele führt.

# Kapitel X. Finanzausgleich

## § 1. Gliederung der Finanzwirtschaften und ihrer Beziehungen

### 1. Gliederung der Finanzwirtschaften

Im vorigen Kapitel wurde ganz grundsätzlich von der Gestaltung und vom Vollzug des Haushaltsplanes gesprochen. Nunmehr ist eine Erweiterung vorzunehmen. Es gibt innerhalb eines Staatswesens nicht nur einen Haushaltsplan, sondern viele, und sie hängen miteinander zusammen. Die Finanzwirtschaft eines Staates besteht in aller Regel aus vielen Einzelfinanzwirtschaften. Diese sind vertikal und horizontal zu gliedern. Man spricht von einer *vertikalen* Gliederung zwischen vor- und nachgeordneten Gebietskörperschaften. Dabei kann je nach dem Staatsaufbau Zweistufigkeit (Staat, Gemeinden) oder Dreistufigkeit (Gesamtstaat, Gliedstaaten, Gemeinden) gegeben sein, ja es sind auch noch mehr Stufen denkbar. In der Bundesrepublik Deutschland, einem Bundesstaat, besteht eine Dreistufigkeit: Bund, Länder, Gemeinden (und Gemeindeverbände). Die *horizontale* Gliederung bezieht sich auf das Nebeneinander der dem Gesamtstaat nachgeordneten Körperschaften gleicher Ebene, in einem Bundesstaat der Gliedstaaten einerseits, der Gemeinden andererseits, in einem zweistufigen System der Gemeinden, nebeneinander.

---

[1]) Bei dieser Konzeption werden durchaus — im Gegensatz zur „einfachen" built-in flexibility — bewußte Variationen der politischen Parameter erforderlich; ihre quantitative Festlegung soll allerdings dem Automatismus der Formel überlassen bleiben.

Es ist zu bemerken, daß neben den Finanzwirtschaften im nationalen Rahmen heute auch Finanzwirtschaften bestehen, die auf überstaatlicher Ebene basieren. Nationale Finanzwirtschaften sind mit diesen sowohl im Hinblick auf Aufgaben als auch im Hinblick auf die Mittelverteilung verbunden.

## 2. Finanzwirtschaftliche Beziehungen

Die überstaatlichen Finanzbeziehungen ausgeklammert bestehen zwischen den genannten Finanzwirtschaften mehrere Beziehungsreihen. Wie sind diese geordnet und welche Folgen ergeben sich dadurch?

### *a) Ordnung der finanzwirtschaftlichen Beziehungen*

Die Ordnung der finanzwirtschaftlichen Beziehungen umfaßt einmal ($\alpha$) die Verteilung der öffentlichen Aufgaben und der sich daraus ergebenden Ausgaben („Passiver“ Finanzausgleich), dann ($\beta$) die Verteilung der Mittel (aktiver“ Finanzausgleich), in vertikaler sowohl als auch in horizontaler Sicht. An dritter Stelle ($\gamma$) ist ein Blick auf die beide der genannten Materien betreffenden Revisionsklauseln zu richten.

$\alpha$) *Verteilung der Aufgaben.* Nach Moll gebührt der logische Primat bei der Ordnung des Finanzausgleichs in einem Staate nicht der Verteilung der Einnahmequellen zwischen den verschiedenen öffentlichen Körperschaften, sondern der Abgrenzung ihrer Aufgaben. Wieweit das in der politischen Realität zutrifft, ist eine Tatfrage. Gestützt wird die Aussage von Moll aus dem politischen Bereich dann, wenn, wie z. B. jüngst von den Ländern der Bundesrepublik Deutschland im Steuerverteilungsstreit, das Interesse vor allem auf die Aufgabenverteilung gerichtet wird. Als die Länder aufgefordert wurden, einer anderen Verteilung der Mittel zugunsten des Bundes zuzustimmen, erfolgte ihre vorläufige Ablehnung vor allem wegen der Befürchtung, daß der Bund dann auch Aufgaben an sich ziehen würde, die sie im Sinne föderativen Staatsaufbaus als ihnen zustehend annehmen (vgl. die von Popitz sogenannte Anziehungskraft des größeren Etats). Die Länder waren eher geneigt, einer anderen Verteilung der Aufgaben als einer anderen Verteilung der Einnahmen zuzustimmen.

$\alpha_1$) Das führt sofort zum Problem der *vertikalen* Aufgabenverteilung. Hier steht politisch die Frage der Zentralisierung oder der Dezentralisierung staatlicher Aufgabenkompetenzen im Vordergrund.

Nach dem Prinzip der Subsidiarität sollten Aufgaben, die von unteren Instanzen erledigt werden können, diesen auch zugewiesen werden. Der Befolgung dieses Prinzips, das auch dem Gedanken einer Verbreiterung demokratischer Selbstverwaltung zielmäßig zugeordnet werden kann, sind allerdings auch rationale Grenzen gesetzt. So mögen z. B. sozialpolitische Aufgaben auf erste Sicht zwar besser bei den unteren Instanzen aufgehoben sein, weil diese eine bessere Kenntnis der Lage der zu betreuenden Bürger haben. Jedoch: Gerade an Mitteln arme Gebietskörperschaften müssen hier relativ mehr öffentliche Mittel bereitstellen als reiche, die sich zudem notfalls mehr auf die private Übernahme von sozialen Aufgaben verlassen können. Mit anderen Worten: Aus der Überlassung gerade solcher Aufgaben an untere Instanzen mag — bei gegebener Verteilung eigener Einnahmequellen — die Notwendigkeit mittelseitigen Finanzausgleichs gerade wachsen. Zum anderen ist folgendes zu bedenken: Öffentliche Ausgaben wirken auf die Beschäftigung ein. Die gerade bei unteren Instanzen begrenzten Zugriffsmöglichkeiten zu außerordentlichen Finanzmitteln — die Gemeinden z. B. haben nur einen begrenzten Zugang zum Kredit, dessen Gewährung oft von dem Vorhandensein sonstiger ordentlicher Mittel abhängig gemacht wird — haben zur Folge, daß hier öfter eine gesamtwirtschaftlich unerwünschte Parallelpolitik eingeschlagen wird.

Der Selbständigkeitsgrad der öffentlichen Finanzwirtschaften unterer Ebene in bezug auf ihre Aufgaben- und damit ihre Ausgabengestaltung ist auch bestimmt durch die Verteilung der Aufgaben in Selbstverwaltungsaufgaben und Auftragsangelegenheiten. *Selbstverwaltungsaufgaben* werden die „eigenen" Angelegenheiten der Gemeinden genannt, deren Erfüllung ihnen nach dem Grundsatz der Allseitigkeit des Wirkungskreises eigenverantwortlich durch eigene Organe unter der grundsätzlich auf die Kontrolle der Rechtmäßigkeit beschränkten Aufsicht des Staates zusteht. Diese Betätigung freier Gemeinden erfährt jedoch eine Einschränkung durch Pflichtaufgaben, genehmigungspflichtige Aufgaben und Auftragsangelegenheiten. Als *Auftragsangelegenheiten* bezeichnet man die den kommunalen Gebietskörperschaften übertragenen staatlichen Verwaltungsaufgaben, die unter Dienstaufsicht des Staates durchzuführen sind. Es wird in diesem Zusammenhang darüber geklagt, daß durch eine wachsende Zahl von Pflichtaufgaben, genehmigungspflichtigen Aufgaben und Auftragsangelegenheiten die freiwillig übernommenen Selbstverwaltungsaufgaben an Zahl und Finanzvolumen zurücktreten.

$\alpha_2$) Auch im Hinblick auf die *horizontale* Aufgabenverteilung ist die vertikale Verteilung der Aufgaben von Bedeutung. Es mögen dadurch bedingt untere Instanzen Aufgaben zu erfüllen haben, die ihnen — gegenüber auf der gleichen Ebene liegenden anderen — unterschiedliche Kosten aufbürden, d. h. Lasten, die bei den einen, nicht aber bei den anderen Aufgabenverpflichtungen zur Folge haben, zumindest aber bedeutsame Unterschiede mit sich bringen. Gerade auch dadurch können sich besondere Mittelverteilungsprobleme ergeben; vgl. dazu unten $\beta_2$.

$\beta$) *Verteilung der Mittel.* Die Frage der Aufgabenverteilung in bestimmter Weise geregelt, ergibt sich mit Notwendigkeit die Frage der Mittelbereitstellung.

$\beta_1$) In *vertikaler* Sicht lassen sich idealtypisch folgende Systeme unterscheiden, die in der Wirklichkeit allerdings selten in reiner Form auftreten, vielmehr auch Elemente anderer Systeme enthalten:

(1) *Trennsystem.* Hier obliegen dem Zentralstaat wie den Gliedstaaten je selbständige sich nicht überschneidende Aufgaben. Jede Körperschaft beschafft sich die für die Erfüllung ihrer Aufgaben erforderlichen Mittel selbst. Bei *freiem* Trennsystem oder Konkurrenzsystem steht jeder Regierungsebene die Auswahl und die Höhe (Tarife) der

erhobenen Abgaben frei, bei *gebundenem* Trennsystem allein deren Höhe.

(2) *Verbundsystem.* Hier hat (haben) nur die Gebietskörperschaft(en) einer Stufe des Finanzsystems eigene Finanzeinnahmen, während die Gebietskörperschaft(en) der anderen Stufen ihre Einnahmen in der Form von Zuweisungen erhält (erhalten). Es kann sich dabei um ein *Beitrags-* oder Umlagesystem (Zahlungen von „unten" nach „oben") oder um ein *Überweisungs*system (Zahlungen von „oben" nach „unten") handeln.

(3) *Mischsystem.* Hier beschaffen sich die einzelnen Gebietskörperschaften die erforderlichen Finanzmittel z. T. selbst, z. T. aber erhalten sie diese von den Gebietskörperschaften höherer oder unterer Ebenen durch Überweisungen oder Beiträge.

Bei den Überweisungen oder Beiträgen gemäß (2) und (3) ist noch zu unterscheiden, ob diese mehr oder weniger *automatisch* erfolgen oder einer *diskretionären* Steuerung zugänglich sind. Grenzbeispiele sind Überweisungen oder Beiträge auf der Grundlage des Steuerverbundes[1]) mit langfristig festen Beteiligungsqouten auf der einen Seite; hier ist die Zahlung automatisches Ergebnis einer Formel. Das andere Grenzbeispiel ist die Festlegung von Überweisungen oder Beiträgen auf der Grundlage des „Bedarfs" der empfangenden Ebene, wenn die „gebende" Instanz den „Bedarf" nach in ihrem Ermessen liegenden Kriterien festsetzt. Dazwischen liegen eine Reihe von Übergängen, z. B. Beteiligungen bei variablen Steuerquoten, die einen immer erneuten Kampf um die Höhe der Quoten mit sich bringen[2]). Über Revisionsklauseln vgl. unter γ) dieses Abschnittes.

---

[1]) Gebietskörperschaften mehrerer Ebenen teilen sich den Ertrag einer Steuer.

[2]) Bei dem hier nicht erwähnten Zuschlagsystem erfolgen keine Überweisungen. Vielmehr erhält eine finanzwirtschaftliche Ebene das Recht, oder wird dazu verpflichtet zu Steuern, die von einer anderen finanzwirtschaftlichen Ebene erhoben werden, Zuschläge zu erheben. Vgl. z. B. bei der früheren preußischen Einkommensteuer das Zuschlagsrecht der Gemeinden.

$\beta_2$) *Horizontale* Gesichtspunkte der Mittelverteilung. Während in vertikaler Sicht des mittelseitigen Finanzausgleichs die Frage der Zentralisierung und Dezentralisierung auf „vor-" und „nach"geordnete Gebietskörperschaften im Vordergrund steht (vgl. noch b, $\alpha$), so in horizontaler Sicht die *Unterschiedlichkeit* der Finanzkraft und damit auch der finanzpolitischen Gestaltungsmöglichkeit der Gebietskörperschaften jeweils *gleicher* Ebene.

Bei dem Begriff der Finanzkraft ist mit Notwendigkeit ein Rückblick auf die Aufgabenproblematik am Platze. Der Begriff Finanzkraft hat gewiß zwei Aspekte: Einmal die Frage der Aufgaben und zum anderen die zu ihrer Erfüllung benötigten Finanzmittel. Wie wir bereits wissen, können Aufgaben zentral festgelegt werden (Auftragsangelegenheiten) oder dem mehr oder weniger freien Ermessen der jeweiligen Gebietskörperschaften unterliegen (autonome oder Selbstverwaltungsangelegenheiten), zumindest, was ihre Höhe angeht. Mangelnde Finanzkraft hat deshalb mehrere Ursachen: (1) Ein Gemeinwesen mag deswegen arm erscheinen, weil es infolge der Sozialstruktur seiner Bevölkerung zu höheren Aufgaben im Sinne autonomer Aufgaben gezwungen ist. D. h. ein Gemeinwesen mit einer armen Bevölkerung mag sich in stärkerem Maße vor die Notwendigkeit gestellt sehen, Aufgaben „staatlicherseits" zu übernehmen als es notwendigerweise einem Gemeinwesen mit wohlhabenden Gliedern oder Gruppen von Gliedern gegeben ist. Hier ist eher die Delegierung gewisser Aufgaben an einzelne oder Gruppen von einzelnen möglich, es kann mehr auf privater Ebene getan werden. (2) Dann aber kommt es darauf an, welche Art von Aufgaben den verschiedenen Ebenen zugewiesen werden. Ungleiche Lasten mögen sich bei zentraler Festlegung von Aufgaben dann ergeben, wenn die Tatbestände, die zur Ausgabe führen, in ungleicher Weise bei den nachgeordneten Gebietskörperschaften zutreffen. Beispiele: Ausbau und Erhaltung von Hafenanlagen, Deichbauten, Unterstützungszahlungen. (3) Man fühlt sich arm oder ist arm, weil man bei selbst gestellten oder zugewiesenen Aufgaben diese deshalb nicht erfüllen kann, weil die zur Verfügung stehenden Mittel nicht ausreichen. Erst an diesem Punkte kommt die Frage der Einnahmeungleichheit als Ursache mangelnder Finanzkraft in die Debatte.

Die *reine* Form des einnahmemäßigen horizontalen Finanzausgleichs ist der *echte zwischengebietskörperschaft-*

*liche* Ausgleich, der ohne diskretionäres Eingreifen zentraler Instanzen nach einmal festgelegten Regeln vor sich geht. Beispielhaft sei auf den heutigen Länderfinanzausgleich in der Bundesrepublik verwiesen. Horizontale Ausgleichswirkungen können aber auch erstrebt werden oder können sich ergeben bei der Zwischenform des so zu nennenden vertikal-horizontalen Ausgleichs (vgl. dazu $\beta_3$).

$\beta_3$) Zwischen *vertikaler* und *horizontaler* Mittelverteilung bestehen gewisse *Zusammenhänge*.

Bereits die *vertikale* Verteilung der Einnahmen präjudiziert unter Umständen auch eine gewisse horizontale Verteilung der Mittel. So, wenn z. B. einkommens- oder vermögensabhängige Steuern den unteren Gebietskörperschaften zugewiesen werden. Arme Gemeinwesen sind dann schlechter gestellt als reiche. An diesem Tatbestand hängen dann noch andere Probleme wie die Standortfrage (vgl. b$\beta$) und die Frage einer zentralen Beschäftigungspolitik mit Hilfe finanzpolitischer Instrumente (vgl. b$\gamma$).

Dann kann aber auch bei vertikalen Zahlungen z. B. in der Form von Überweisungen eine horizontale Ausgleichswirkung sich ergeben oder sogar erstrebt werden. Wir sprechen dann von einem *vertikal-horizontalen* Mittelausgleich. Dabei schaltet die Oberinstanz sich ein, ihr zunächst zufließende Mittel werden an die Unterinstanzen verteilt, gewiß nach Regeln, aber im Einzelfalle so, daß dabei auf individuelle Merkmale der Finanzkraft der Unterinstanz Rücksicht genommen wird. Finanzarme erhalten mehr als finanzstarke. Es handelt sich hierbei also um einen vertikalen Ausgleich mit einer gleichzeitig horizontalen Ausgleichswirkung. Beispielhaft sei dazu auf den heutigen Gemeindefinanzausgleich in der Bundesrepublik (§ 3, 3) verwiesen.

Im Falle des Verbundsystems in der Form des Beitragssystems (Zahlungen von unten nach oben) ist ein gewisser vertikal-horizontaler Ausgleich dann gegeben, wenn arme Gemeinwesen weniger zahlen als reiche.

$\gamma$) *Revisionsklauseln* bilden ein Zwischenglied im Rahmen des vertikalen Finanzausgleichs. Wie die Ausgaben für die Erfüllung der einmal den jeweiligen Ebenen zugeordneten Aufgaben eine entsprechende Mittelverteilung erfordern, so hat der Gesetzgeber häufig auch Bestimmungen für den Fall erlassen, daß sich in Zukunft Einnahmen und Ausgaben unterschiedlich entwickeln. Die Vorschriften über die Beseitigung eines derartigen Ungleichgewichts werden in sogenannten *allgemeinen* Revisionsklauseln abgefaßt.

Daneben gibt es auch sogenannte *spezielle* Revisionsklauseln, auch *Sicherungsklauseln* genannt. Sie sollen die Finanzwirtschaften der nachgeordneten Ebene davor schützen, daß ihnen durch die übergeordnete Ebene neue Aufgaben zugewiesen werden, ohne daß gleichzeitig für die Bereitstellung der für diese Aufgaben notwendigen Mittel gesorgt wird. Analoges kann für den Fall gelten, daß der Oberverband dem Unterverband Einnahmen entzieht, ohne ihn aber von Aufgaben zu entlasten.

An den Revisions- und Sicherungsklauseln wird wiederum deutlich, daß der Finanzausgleich immer unter dem doppelten Aspekt der Aufgabenverteilung einerseits und der Mittelverteilung andererseits gesehen werden muß.

### *b) Politische und ökonomische Probleme, die sich aus der Ordnung der finanzwirtschaftlichen Beziehungen ergeben.*

Mit der Ordnung der finanzwirtschaftlichen Beziehungen in dieser oder jener Weise hängen eine Reihe staats- und wirtschaftspolitischer Fragen zusammen:

*α) Dezentralisation und Zentralisation.* Dem einer politisch betonten Wirtschaftslehre zugewandten Leser drängt sich die Frage auf, wie den verschiedenen Ordnungen der Mittelverteilung eine dieser Fragestellung entsprechende Deutung gegeben werden kann. Folgende Spannungsreihe — ähnlich wie von Albers vorgeformt — bietet sich an, die von einer extrem föderativen, dezentralisierten, bis zu einer konsequent unitarischen, zentralisierten Mittelverteilungsordnung geht:

(1) Verbundsystem in der Form des Beitragssystems

(2) freies Trennsystem
(3) gebundenes Trennsystem
(4) Mischsystem in der Form des Beitragssystems
(5) Mischsystem in der Form des Überweisungssystems
(6) Verbundsystem in der Form des Überweisungssystems.

D. h. im Falle (1) ist der Einfluß der unteren, im Falle (6) der der Zentralebene am größten, bei schrittweisen Übergängen in den anderen Ordnungen.

Dabei ist aber weiterhin zu beachten, daß bei den Überweisungen das Maß der Zentralisierung größer ist, je weniger sie automatisiert sind, vielmehr diskretionärem Zugriff der Zentralebene unterliegen. Bei Beiträgen ist das gerade umgekehrt. Unterliegen diese Zahlungen Automatismen, so ist der dezentrale Einfluß geringer als im anderen Falle.

Wenn somit die vertikale Mittelverteilung vor allem als ein einflußpolitisches Problem erscheint: Welche Ebene hat vorzüglich Macht und Möglichkeit, Aufgaben zu setzen und zu erfüllen, so ist nicht zu übersehen, daß mit dieser Verteilung nicht nur die vertikale Ordnung, sondern auch Verteilungsfragen auf horizontaler Ebene berührt werden. Diese mögen auf die vertikale Ordnung zurückwirken. Die Einkommensungleichheit zwischen gleichgeordneten Finanzwirtschaften wird möglicherweise verstärkt, wenn ihnen allein und vorzüglich Einnahmequellen zur Verfügung stehen, deren Erträge von der Wirtschaftskraft ihrer Bürger in besonderem Maße abhängen, wie z. B. bei einkommens- und ertragsabhängigen Steuern. Das kann den Wunsch nach einer anderen Verteilung der Einnahmequellen mit gleichmäßigeren Einnahmeergebnissen zur Folge haben. Dabei muß die vertikale politische Ordnung an sich nicht verändert werden: Der Grad der Zentralisierung muß nicht wachsen. Das ist aber ganz anders, wenn einnahmearme Finanzwirtschaften nach Finanzzuweisungen rufen, und zwar dem individuellen Mangel entsprechend nach individuell höheren. Denn hier handelt es sich um eine in bezug auf die Eigenständigkeit resignierende Forderung, die ein Beugen unter den Willen der höheren Instanz nach sich zieht, in ganz besonderem Maße deswegen, weil es sich — wie es dem Wesen des Problems entspricht — um Überweisungen handeln muß, bei deren Zuteilung diskretionäre Züge Platz finden. So mag eine bestimmte vertikale Verteilung der Einnahmequellen dann, wenn eine Lösung durch eine qualitativ andere Verteilung versperrt ist, den Hang zur Zentralisierung gerade durch Wünsche unterer Ebenen zwangsläufig stärken.

*β) Standortproblem.* Andererseits wird durch die Verteilung von einkommens- oder ertragsabhängigen Einnahmequellen an Finanzwirtschaften auf der unteren Ebene unter Umständen eine Veränderung der Standorte gewerblicher Betriebe dann begünstigt, wenn die Höhe der Steuersätze im Sinne einer Dezentralisierung in das Belieben dieser Finanzwirtschaften gestellt wird. Es können auf der einen Seite Attraktionswirkungen zur Errichtung neuer oder zum Ausbau bestehender Betriebe von solchem Gemeinwesen ausgehen, die z. B. deswegen, weil sie bereits in größerem Umfange steuerkräftige gewerbliche Betriebe beherbergen, finanzstark sind und deshalb die Steuersätze niedrig halten oder auch großzügig Stundungen oder Nachlässe gewähren können (Steueroasen). Dazu kommt, alternativ oder auch kumulativ die Möglichkeit, durch verstärkte gewerblichen Belangen dienende Ausgaben für Verkehrsanlagen, Geländebereitstellung, aber auch für kulturelle Zwecke auf Gewerbebetriebe attraktiv zu wirken. Andererseits mögen Abstoßwirkungen von solchen Gemeinwesen ausgehen, die wegen ihrer geringen Finanzkraft die Sätze der ihnen zur Ausbeute überlassenen Steuern anspannen müssen und/oder nur in geringem Umfange gewerbliche Betriebe attrahierende Ausgaben machen können. Es ergibt sich also ein Teufelskreis, denn eine solche Finanzpolitik verstärkt das Finanzgefälle noch mehr. Daraus mag man schließen, daß aus gesamtwirtschaftlichen Gründen, eben weil bei stark dezentralisierter Finanzordnung leicht „Verzerrungen“ in der Standortstruktur hervorgerufen, zumindest aber begünstigt würden, eine stärker zentralisierte Finanzordnung eine bessere Lösung bietet. Dazu ist aber wiederholt auf jene Lehrmeinungen zu verweisen, die die besondere Bedeutung der politischen Betätigung in den Gemeinwesen der unteren Ebene hervorheben. Und echte verantwortliche Betätigung erfordert nicht nur die Disposition über Ausgaben, sondern auch die Sorge für Einnahmen aus eigenen Quellen. Bei der alleinigen Verantwortung für die Ausgaben, die von denen „da oben" zu finanzieren sind, schleicht sich eher eine Form der echte Verantwortung abwehrenden Subalternität ein als wenn auch für Einnahmen geradegestanden werden muß, die dann unter Umständen die Zensiten im eigenen Gemeinwesen stärker belasten.

γ) *Beschäftigungspolitische Problematik.* Dazu kommt ein gesamtwirtschaftlich relevantes Problem: Die Durchschlagskraft konjunkturpolitischer Maßnahmen, die vom Gesamtstaat eingeleitet werden, wird gemindert, wenn untere Gebietskörperschaften wie die Gemeinden eine antizyklisch ausgerichtete Finanzpolitik nicht mitmachen, vielmehr Parallelpolitik betreiben. Dazu können sie aber, z. B. im Falle einer aus zentraler Sicht erwünschten und auch zentral eingeleiteten Politik der Ausgabenverstärkung geradezu gezwungen sein, wenn ihnen vorzüglich oder sogar allein solche Steuerquellen zur Verfügung stehen, deren Erträge stark konjunkturempfindlich sind. Denn in einer depressiven Periode fehlen ihnen dann die für eine Erhöhung der Ausgaben nötigen Finanzmittel. Dazu kommt, daß ihnen andere Einnahmequellen, z. B. aus Krediten, nur in ganz begrenztem Maße zur Verfügung stehen. Sie haben keinen Zugang zur Zentralbank. Bei anderen Kreditquellen aber ist es oft so, daß die Kreditfähigkeit von dem Vorhandensein anderer Einnahmen abhängig gemacht wird. So ist dann eine Einschränkung der Ausgaben die notwendige Folge. Auch hier drängt sich die Frage einer Änderung der finanzwirtschaftlichen Ordnung auf. Man muß sich aber bewußt sein, daß das in diesem Falle eine stärkere Zentralisierung zur Folge hat, wenn der Ausweg über diskretionäre Überweisungen gesucht wird. Auch die Gewährung von Krediten von oben nach unten geht letzten Endes in diese Richtung.

## § 2. Entwicklung des Finanzausgleichs in Deutschland

### 1. Bismarck-Reich

Von Interesse ist hier allein der vertikale Finanzausgleich zwischen dem Reich und den Bundesstaaten mit stark föderativen Interessen. Dem Reich waren das Wehrwesen, die auswärtige Vertretung und einzelne Zweige der inneren Verwaltung übertragen, während die Hauptaufgaben der inneren Verwaltung, insbesondere die Kultur- und Wohlfahrtspolitik, aber auch große Teile der Wirtschaftspolitik sowie der Rechtspflege, von gewissen oberen Instanzen abgesehen, den Bundesstaaten verblieben. An Finanzmitteln wurden dem Reich zunächst die aus den Zöllen, den gemeinschaftlichen Verbrauchsteuern und den aus dem Post- und Telegraphenwesen fließenden Einnahmen zugebilligt. Insoweit durch diese die Ausgaben nicht gedeckt wurden, sollten sie, „solange Reichssteuern nicht eingeführt sind“[1]), durch Matrikularbeiträge der einzelnen Bundesstaaten nach Maßgabe ihrer Bevölkerung aufgebracht werden. Es lag soweit ein Mischsystem in der Form des Beitragssystems vor. Um das Reich nicht „Kostgänger“ der Bundesstaaten bleiben zu lassen, versuchte der Reichskanzler Bismarck mit Hilfe der Zolltarifreform 1879 dem Reich durch erhöhte Zolleinnahmen zusätzliche eigene Mittel zu beschaffen, die ihn zudem von dem lästigen Bewilligungsrecht des Parlamentes befreit hätten. Dem trat jedoch die vom Parlament beschlossene „Franckensteinsche Klausel“ entgegen, wonach das Reich von den Einnahmen aus den Zöllen und der Tabaksteuer, später auch der „Reichsstempelabgaben“ und der Branntweinsteuer nur 130 Millionen ohne weiteres für sich behalten durfte, während der

---

[1]) Clausula Miquel. Sollte dem Reich auch Erhebung direkter Steuern ermöglichen. Dennoch bildete sich das politische Dogma heraus, daß die direkten Steuern allein den Einzelstaaten zustünden.

Rest den Bundesstaaten zu überweisen war. Dadurch blieb für das Reich der Zwang beibehalten, notfalls das Bewilligungsrecht des Parlaments für Matrikularbeiträge in Anspruch zu nehmen. Infolge der Überweisungen traten Elemente eines Mischsystems in der Fom des Überweisungssystems in den Finanzausgleich ein. Zeitweilig sind die Überweisungen sogar höher gewesen als die Matrikularbeiträge. 1896 und 1906 wurden sie abgebaut, 1918 beseitigt.

Durch die Finanzreformen der Jahre 1906 ff. wurden dem Reich, nachdem bisher auch noch nachher vorzüglich eine Reihe zusätzlicher indirekter Steuern eingeführt oder bestehende ertragreicher ausgestaltet wurden, auch die Erschließung einiger direkter Steuern ermöglicht, so 1906 die bisher den Ländern zustehende Erbschaftsteuer, 1913 der Wehrbeitrag — eine einmalige Vermögensteuer — sowie die „Besitzsteuer". Soweit die Einzelstaaten, wie bei der Erbschaftsteuer, an den Erträgen beteiligt wurden, wurde das Überweisungssystem durch einen quotalen Steuerverbund bereichert.

## 2. Weimarer Republik

Die junge Republik hatte finanziell einen schweren Start wegen der außerordentlich hohen Kriegsfolgelasten. Bereits dadurch ist das Streben nach wachsender Zentralisierung der Einnahmekompetenzen zu verstehen, wie überhaupt die Zeit durch einen Zug zur Zentralisierung gekennzeichnet war, auch in der Steuerverwaltung. Im Hinblick auf die Zentralisierung der Einnahmekompetenzen ist vor allem auf die „Verreichlichung" der jetzt steuerertragsmäßig bedeutend ausgebauten Personalsteuern, der Einkommensteuer, der Körperschaftsteuer und der zeitweilig als besondere Steuer konzipierten Kapitalertragsteuer hinzuweisen. Dies hatte beachtliche Folgen für den vertikalen Finanzausgleich zwischen Reich und Ländern insofern, als letztere für die ihnen entzogenen Steuerquellen durch Beteiligungen „entschädigt" werden mußten. Die Länder erhielten von den Erträgen der Einkommensteuer und der Körperschaftsteuer 2/3 vorab, darüber hinaus gewährleistete das Reich eine Überweisung aus der Einkommensteuer in der Mindesthöhe des Aufkommens an Landes- und Gemeindeeinkommensteuern im Steuerjahr 1919 zuzüglich einer Steigerung von 25 %. Diese Sätze wurden später mehrfach geändert. Das gilt auch für Überweisungen, die die Länder aus der Umsatzsteuer erhielten. Weitere Überweisungen erfolgten aus der Grunderwerbsteuer, Kraftfahrzeugsteuer u. a. Reichssteuern, die im Interesse der Länder und Gemeinden erhoben wurden und bei denen nur eine Erhebungsquote dem Reich verblieb. Das zentrale Element im vertikalen Reichsländerfinanzausgleich wurde, zumal die Matrikularbeiträge in Fortfall gekommen waren, nach dieser Regelung im Sinne eines Mischsystems (die Länder hatten auch eigene Einkommenquellen) in der Form des Überweisungssystems verstärkt — wenn auch bei weitem nicht in dem Maße wie später in der NS-Periode, als die automatisch geregelten Beteiligungen durch diskretionäre Zuweisungen abgelöst wurden.

Hinsichtlich des Länder-Gemeindefinanzausgleichs wurden die Länder zwar durch Reichsrecht verpflichtet, für einen Lastenausgleich unter den Gemeinden, insbesondere auf dem Gebiete der Armen-, Schul- und Polizeilasten zu sorgen, aber der nach Landesrecht vollzogene gemeindliche Finanzausgleich war nach wie vor von Land zu Land ziemlich verschieden.

### 3. NS-Staat

Hier gelangten Zentralisierungstendenzen eindeutig zum Durchbruch. Staatspolitisch wurden, vorbereitet durch das Vorläufige Gesetz zur Gleichschaltung der Länder mit dem Reich vom 31. 3. 1933, die Länder durch das Gesetz über den Neuaufbau des Reiches vom 30. 1. 1934 ausgeschaltet. (Artikel 1: Die Volksvertretungen der Länder werden aufgehoben. Artikel 2, 1: Die Hoheitsrechte der Länder gehen auf das Reich über. Artikel 2, 2: Die Länderregierungen unterstehen der Reichsregierung). Finanzpolitisch relevant waren folgende Stationen: Die Realsteuerreform von 1936 brachte den Übergang der Ertragshoheit der jetzt reichsgesetzlich geregelten Realsteuern auf die Gemeinden, die Grundsätze über den Finanz- und Lastenausgleich vom 10. 12. 1937 eine reichsgesetzliche Regelung der Gemeindeanteile an den Reichssteuerüberweisungen. Weiterhin kam es in den Jahren 1935 bis 1940 durch mehrere Gesetze zur Änderung des Finanzausgleichs zu erheblichen Kürzungen der Länderanteile an den Überweisungssteuern (Einkommen-, Körperschaft- und Umsatzsteuer). Dies hatte zur Folge, daß die Länder ihre finanziellen Verpflichtungen nicht mehr voll erfüllen konnten; vom 1. April 1941 an mußte das Reich die Länder mit Finanzzuweisungen unterstützen. Erst mit der Verordnung über die einstweilige Regelung des Finanz- und Lastenausgleichs vom 30. Oktober 1944 wurde das Nebeneinander von Überweisungen und Zuweisungen rückwirkend beseitigt. Nach dieser Verordnung gewährte das Reich ab 1941 den Ländern Finanzzuweisungen „nach Maßgabe ihres Bedarfs". Diese ersetzten die bisherigen Reichssteuerüberweisungen und einige der den Ländern verbliebenen Landessteuern. Für die Rechnungsjahre 1941 bis 1943 verblieb es bei den vom Reich bereits gezahlten Zuweisungen. Die Gemeinden erhielten ab 1944 Schlüsselzuweisungen unmittelbar vom Reich. Die Mittelverteilung erfolgte also nunmehr für den Reich-Länderfinanzausgleich so gut wie ganz nach dem Verbundsystem in der Form eines zudem diskretionären Überweisungssystems, welches das größte Maß an Zentralisation enthält. Aus dem Finanzausgleich mit den Gemeinden waren die Länder als selbständig entschließende Instanzen ausgeschlossen; dieser war alleinige Reichssache, und zwar im Sinne eines Mischsystems in der Form des Überweisungssystems geregelt; die Gemeinden hatten eigene Einnahmen, vor allem aus den reichsrechtlich geregelten Grund- und Gewerbesteuern, dazu erhielten sie Schlüsselzuweisungen des Reiches.

Die Zerschlagung des Deutschen Reichs nach dem verlorenen Kriege von 1939—1945 brachte eine ganz neue Situation, eine völlige Umkehrung der finanzpolitischen

Beziehungen: Die unteren Instanzen erhielten zunächst die Ausgaben-Einnahmekompetenzen, und nur langsam erfolgte wiederum ein Hineinwachsen in eine gesamtstaatliche Finanzordnung. Im Zusammenhang mit den weltpolitisch bedeutsamen Ost-West-Gegensätzen wurde Deutschland gespalten und das Folgende (§ 3) gilt nur für den freiheitlichen Teil Deutschlands, die Bundesrepublik, nach dem Willen der Väter der Verfassung die Keimzelle für ein neues ganzes Deutschland.

## § 3. Der Finanzausgleich in der Bundesrepublik Deutschland

### 1. Vertikaler Finanzausgleich Bund—Länder

#### *a) Aufgabenverteilung*

Nach 1945 hatten zunächst die unteren Gebietskörperschaften, dann die z. T. nach anderen als historischen Gegebenheiten zusammengefaßten Länder außer ihren eigentlichen Verwaltungsaufgaben weitere übernehmen müssen, die bisher der Reichskompetenz unterlagen.

Einen vertikalen Finanzausgleich gab es bis zum Erlaß des Grundgesetzes nicht. Jedes Land hatte für sich die in seinem Gebiete und für seine Bevölkerung anfallenden Lasten aller Art zu tragen und alle staatlichen Aufgaben zu erfüllen.

Die Gründung der Bundesrepublik Deutschland 1949 brachte die Aufgabe einer bundesgesetzlichen Regelung. Die eigene Reaktion auf Erfahrungen mit einem radikal zentralstaatlichen Reich sowie der Einfluß der Alliierten brachten stark föderative Züge in das finanzpolitische System hinein.

Nach Artikel 106, 4 des Grundgesetzes (GG) tragen Bund und Länder gesondert die Ausgaben, die sich aus der Wahrnehmung ihrer Aufgaben ergeben. Gemäß den Artikeln 30 und 83 GG ist die Ausübung der staatlichen Befugnisse und die Erfüllung der staatlichen Aufgaben Sache der *Länder*, soweit das Grundgesetz keine andere Regelung trifft oder zuläßt, und: Die Länder führen die Bundesgesetze als eigene Angelegenheit aus, soweit das Grundgesetz nichts anderes bestimmt oder zuläßt. Die wesentlichen Aufgaben des *Bundes* erstrecken sich auf die Pflege der Beziehungen zu auswärtigen Staaten, das Wehrwesen, die Kriegsfolgelasten sowie auf Teile der Sozialleistungen, des Polizei-, Nachrichten- und Verkehrswesens, der Finanzverwaltung und der Maßnahmen zur Förderung der Wirtschaft.

Neben dem Grundgesetz sind dabei insbesondere die in Ausführung der Bestimmungen des Artikels 120, 2 GG erlassenen fünf Gesetze zur Überleitung von Lasten und Deckungsmitteln auf den Bund vom 28. 11. 1950, 21. 8. 51, 4. 1. 52, 27. 4. 55 und 30. 6. 59 zu beachten, die gleichzeitig die Realisierung des Übergangs bestimmter Steuereinnahmen auf den Bund brachten.

Es ist dabei zu erwähnen, daß das 3. Überleitungsgesetz die Stellung des Landes Berlin (West) im Finanzsystem des Bundes regelt. Solange Berlin aus weltpolitischen Gründen am Finanzausgleich unter den Ländern (horizontaler Finanzausgleich) nicht teilnimmt, erhält es zur Deckung eines auf andere Weise nicht auszugleichenden Haushaltsfehlbedarfes einen Bundeszuschuß. Im übrigen trägt der Bund auch in Berlin im wesentlichen die Lasten aus Aufgaben, wie er sie in den anderen Bundesländern im Sinne der vertikalen Aufgabenverteilung übernommen hat, erhält dafür andererseits die Erträge der Bundessteuern und den im GG geregelten Anteil aus der Einkommen- und Körperschaftsteuer. Deren Sätze sind allerdings in Berlin infolge von Steuererleichterungen zur Förderung der Berliner Wirtschaft, die auch die Umsatzsteuer umfassen, niedriger als im Bundesgebiet.

Trotz des zunächst kleinen Katalogs von Bundesaufgaben haben sich die Ausgaben des Bundes im Verhältnis zu denen der Länder relativ erhöht, ja sie liegen höher als die des Reiches in der Zeit vor dem Ersten Weltkriege und in der Zeit der Weimarer Republik. Während die Reichsausgaben 1913 32 % der gesamten Ausgaben von Reich, Ländern und Gemeinden ausmachten, betrugen in den letzten Jahren die entsprechenden Ausgaben des Bundes über 40 %. Vgl. dazu Tabelle VII.

Folge ist, bei gegebener Einnahmenverteilung, eine Finanzklemme des Bundes, bei durchaus weniger angespannter Finanzlage der Gesamtheit der Länder. Das hat zu Änderungswünschen hinsichtlich der Verteilung von Lasten und/oder Einnahmen geführt.

Zu beachten ist dabei bereits hier die in bezug auf die Verteilung der Einnahmen aus der Einkommen- und Körperschaftsteuer im Artikel 106, 4 neue Fassung des Grundgesetzes[1]) eingebaute Revisionsklausel, die die enge Verbindung zwischen Aufgaben- und Einnahmeproblematik aufzeigt.

### *b) Mittelverteilung*

Vor Gründung der Bundesrepublik kamen den Ländern und Gemeinden zunächst die Erträge aller Steuern zu, seit der Bildung des Vereinigten Wirtschaftsgebiets unter Ausnahme der Zölle und der Kaffeesteuer, seit 1949 auch der Teesteuer. Das Grundgesetz brachte dann folgende Regelung: Während in Art. 105 die Gesetzgebungshoheit bei den Finanzmonopolen und den Steuern einschließlich der Zölle geregelt wurde, so in Artikel 106 die Aufteilung der Einnahmen, d. h. die Ertragshoheit. Danach stehen dem Bund zu: Der Ertrag der Finanzmonopole und das Aufkommen aus den folgenden Steuern: Zölle, Verbrauchsteuern, soweit sie nicht nach Absatz 2 den Ländern zustehen, Umsatzsteuer, Beförderungsteuer, die einmaligen Vermögensabgaben und die zur Durchführung des Lastenausgleichs erhobene Ausgleichsabgabe, die Abgabe „Notopfer Berlin“ und die Ergänzungsabgabe zur Einkommen- und Körperschaftsteuer. Das Aufkommen folgender Steuern dagegen steht den Ländern zu: Vermögensteuer, Erbschaftsteuer, Kraftfahrzeugsteuer, Verkehrsteuern, soweit sie nicht nach Absatz 1 dem Bund zustehen, Biersteuer, Abgaben von Spielbanken, Steuern mit örtlich bedingtem Wirkungskreis. Vom Aufkommen der Einkommensteuer und der Körper-

[1]) Die Artikel 106, 107 GG wurden durch das „Gesetz zur Änderung und Ergänzung der Finanzverfassung (Finanzverfassungsgesetz)“ vom 23. 12. 1955 und das Änderungsgesetz vom 24. 12. 1956 geändert und ergänzt.

Tabelle VII: Die Entwicklung der Ausgaben[1]) der öffentlichen Haushalte in der Bundesrepublik Deutschland 1959—1963

| Verwaltungsebene | Rechnungsjahr | | Rumpf-Rechnungsjahr[2]) | | Kalenderjahre | | | | | |
|---|---|---|---|---|---|---|---|---|---|---|
| | 1959 | | 1960 | | 1961 | | 1962 | | 1963 | |
| | Mrd. DM | % | Mrd. DM | % | Mrd. DM | % | Mrd. DM | % | Mrd. DM | % |
| Bund[3]) | 37,60 | 42,0 | 30,31 | 40,6 | 44,46 | 40,7 | 49,5 | 40,4 | 54,0 | 41,3 |
| Lastenausgleichfonds | 4,71 | 5,3 | 3,26 | 4,4 | 4,13 | 3,8 | 4,7 | 3,8 | 3,9 | 3,0 |
| Länder (einschließlich Stadtstaaten[4]) | 28,98 | 32,3 | 24,95 | 33,4 | 37,04 | 33,9 | 41,8[5]) | 34,1 | 44,3 | 33,8 |
| Gemeinden (GV)[4]) | 18,33 | 20,5 | 16,07 | 21,5 | 23,57 | 21,6 | 26,5 | 21,6 | 28,7 | 21,9 |
| Gesamt | 89,62 | 100,0 | 74,59 | 100,0 | 109,20 | 100,0 | 122,5 | 100,0 | 130,9 | 100,0 |

Quelle: Finanzbericht 1964, hrsg. vom Bundesministerium der Finanzen, S. 34.

1) Gesamtausgaben ohne Zuführung an Rücklagen (nach Abgrenzung der Finanzstatistik). Abweichungen in den Summen durch Runden der Zahlen.

2) 9 Monate, wegen Umstellung von Rechnungsjahr auf Kalenderjahr

3) Ohne durchlaufende Mittel.

4) Die Differenzen im Verrechnungsjahr sind nicht berücksichtigt.

5) Ohne den einmaligen Länderbeitrag 1962 zum Ausgleich des Bundeshaushaltes.

schaftsteuer erhalten der Bund 39 v. H. und die Länder 61 v. H.[1]). Die Absätze 4 und 5 des Artikels 106 GG sehen Änderungsmöglichkeiten der Ertragsverteilung vor.

So enthält Absatz 4 des Artikels 106 GG eine sogenannte *allgemeine Revisionsklausel*, die eine Änderung des Beteiligungsverhältnisses an der Einkommen- und Körperschaftsteuer unter den beiden folgenden Bedingungen vorsieht: 1. Es müssen sich die Verhältnisse zwischen Einnahmen und Ausgaben des Bundes einerseits und der Länder andererseits unterschiedlich entwickeln. Zur Anwendung der Revisionsklausel genügt also nicht nur die Verschlechterung der Finanzlage eines Partners. Vielmehr muß der saldenmäßigen Verschlechterung des Verhältnisses zwischen Einnahmen und Ausgaben des einen Partners eine saldenmäßige Verbesserung bei dem anderen Partner gegenüberstehen. 2. Es muß in der Haushaltswirtschaft des Bundes oder der Länder ein so erheblicher Fehlbedarf entstehen, daß eine entsprechende Berichtigung geboten ist. Ergänzend ist zu bemerken, daß es sich im Falle einer gebotenen Verbesserung zugunsten der Länder um die Haushaltswirtschaft der Länder schlechthin und nicht um die eines oder einiger Länder handeln muß. Derartige Ungleichgewichte zwischen „reichen" und „armen" Ländern sind im Rahmen des horizontalen Länderfinanzausgleichs zu beseitigen. Die Anwendung der allgemeinen Revisionsklausel erfolgt durch ein Bundesgesetz, das der Zustimmung des Bundesrates bedarf.

Daneben enthält der Absatz 5 des Art. 106 GG noch eine sogenannte *spezielle Revisionsklausel*, auch *Sicherungsklausel* genannt. Diese Sicherungsklausel sieht eine Änderung des Beteiligungsverhältnisses zugunsten der Länder für den Fall vor, daß diesen durch den Bund zusätzliche Aufgaben auferlegt oder Einnahmen entzogen werden. Dadurch wird der Bund verpflichtet, bei einer Übertragung neuer Aufgaben auf die Länder für eine entsprechende Bereitstellung der Mittel zu sorgen, was bei einer

---

[1]) Diese Regelung gilt für 1964 bis 1966, während für 1963 ein Verhältnis von 38 v. H Bundesanteil, 62 v. H Länderanteil galt. Vom 1. 4. 1958 bis 1962 betrug der Bundesanteil 35 v. H., der Länderanteil 65 v. H., bis zum 31. 3. 1958 33 1/3 bzw. 66 2/3. Bis zum Erlaß des Finanzverfassungsgesetzes vom 23. 12. 1955 galt eine andere Regelung. Die Einkommen- und die Körperschaftsteuern waren den Ländern zugewiesen. Jedoch konnte der Bund einen Teil ihrer Erträge in Anspruch nehmen, eine jährlich neu auszuhandelnde Angelegenheit. M. a. W., insgesamt und nachträglich gesehen zeigte sich bisher praktisch eine Regelung variabler Verteilungsquoten im Sinne der Systematik des allgemeinen Teils dieses Kapitels (§ 1, 2 $B_1$). Die „Automatik" galt jeweils nur für eine begrenzte Zeit.

vorübergehenden Belastung auch durch Finanzzuweisungen geschehen kann.

Die oben im Katalog der dem Bund zustehenden Steuern erscheinende Abgabe Notopfer Berlin ist mit Ausnahme einer Erhebung bei den Körperschaften aufgehoben worden. Sie wurde seit 1958 nicht mehr gesondert erhoben, sondern ist in die Körperschaftsteuer eingebaut worden. Damit hat sich im Rahmen des Steuerverbundes bei der Einkommen- und Körperschaftsteuer der Gesamtanteil der Länder erhöht.

Von der Möglichkeit, eine Ergänzungsabgabe zur Einkommen- und Körperschaftsteuer zu erheben, hat der Bund bisher aus politischen Gründen keinen Gebrauch gemacht.

Die einnahmemäßigen Beziehungen zwischen Bund und Ländern sind im Sinne der obigen Systematik (§ 1, 2 a β) zu kennzeichnen als ein *Mischsystem* in der Form des *Beitragssystems*, da es die Länder sind, welche bestimmte Anteile der von ihnen zunächst vereinnahmten Einkommen- und Körperschaftsteuern „automatisch" an den Bund abführen. Die der Automatik zugrundeliegenden Verteilungssätze sind allerdings, wie oben betont (vgl. vorhergehende Fußnote), des öfteren geändert worden.

## 2. Horizontaler Finanzausgleich zwischen den Ländern

### *a) Aufgabenverteilung*

Zunächst, d. h. solange nach dem Kriege die Länder unter anderem auch die zahlenmäßig bedeutsamen Lasten zu tragen hatten, die sich aus dem Erbe dieses Krieges ergaben, und die bei den einzelnen Ländern sehr ungleichmäßig anfielen, war damit in stärkstem Maße eine ungleichmäßige Verteilung der Lasten gegeben, der andererseits keine dementsprechende Verteilung der Einnahmen gegenüberstand. Es ergab sich daraus bei einigen Ländern, insbesondere den Flüchtlingsaufnahmeländern, eine typische relative Finanzschwäche gegenüber anderen weniger benachteiligten Ländern.

### *b) Mittelverteilung*

Dieses Problem lösende Finanzausgleichsbestimmungen fehlten. Die Länder haben sich jedoch bereits im Jahre 1948 der Notwendigkeit nicht verschließen können, eine notdürftige Abhilfe durch horizontale Vereinbarungen zu schaffen und dem durch Flüchtlingslasten insbesondere betroffenen Land Schleswig-Holstein eine Finanzhilfe von 87 Millionen DM zu gewähren. Für das Rechnungsjahr 1949 wurde vom Wirtschaftsrat das „Gesetz zur vorläufigen Regelung der Kriegsfolgelasten" vom 6. 8. 1949 erlassen, das einen Ausgleichsbetrag von 500 Millionen DM an die benachteiligten Länder (Bayern, Niedersachsen, Schleswig-Holstein) vorsah, der durch andere Länder (Nordrhein-Westfalen, Hessen, Baden-Württemberg, Hamburg und Bremen) aufzubringen war. Dem folgte ein vom inzwischen konstituierten Bundestag mit Zustimmung des Bundesrates beschlossenes Gesetz vom 21. 3. 1950 zur Regelung der Kriegsfolgelasten im 2. Rechnungshalbjahr 1949.

Danach wurde der Finanzausgleich zwischen den Ländern durch Gesetze geregelt, die die Materie von Jahr zu Jahr ordneten. Erst das Gesetz über den Finanzausgleich unter den Ländern (Länderfinanzausgleichsgesetz) vom 27. 4. 1955 war als Dauerlösung gedacht, wurde dann durch das Länderfinanzausgleichsgesetz 1958 ersetzt, das durch die Neufassung vom 23. 6. 1961 als Länderfinanzausgleichsgesetz 1961 den Finanzausgleich unter den Ländern regelt.

Nach diesem Gesetz werden zur Durchführung des Finanzausgleichs unter den Ländern aus Beiträgen der ausgleichspflichtigen Länder (Ausgleichsbeiträge) Zuschüsse an die ausgleichsberechtigten Länder (Ausgleichszuweisungen) geleistet. *Ausgleichspflichtig* sind Länder, deren Steuerkraftmeßzahl ihre Ausgleichsmeßzahl übersteigt. *Ausgleichsberechtigt* dagegen sind Länder, deren Steuerkraftmeßzahl 95 v. H. ihrer Ausgleichsmeßzahl nicht erreicht.

Die *Steuerkraftmeßzahl* soll die Steuerkraft eines bestimmten Landes anzeigen. Sie ergibt sich aus der Summe der Steuereinnahmen des Landes (also vor allem aus dem Länderanteil der Einkommen- und Körperschaftsteuer) und der Realsteuereinnahmen seiner Gemeinden, abzüglich gewisser Beträge zur Abgeltung von Sonderbelastungen (Hafenlasten der Länder Bremen, Hamburg, Niedersachsen) und der übermäßigen Belastungen von Schleswig-Holstein. Als Realsteuereinnahmen gelten für alle Länder einheitlich „herabgesetzte" Steuerkraftzahlen der Grundsteuern und der Gewerbesteuern vom Ertrag und vom Kapital. Bei der Ermittlung der Steuerkraftzahlen der Gemeinden eines Landes werden, um besondere Anstrengungen einzelner Gemeinden nicht zu „bestrafen", die einnahmemäßigen Auswirkungen unterschiedlicher Hebesätze eliminiert, vielmehr werden für die einzelnen Steuern einheitliche v. H.-Sätze in Rechnung gestellt.

Die *Ausgleichsmeßzahl* dagegen soll die auf ein bestimmtes Land bezogene und durch Bedarfselemente modifizierte bundesdurchschnittliche Finanzkraft (cum grano salis: „Steuerkraftsollzahl") kennzeichnen. Sie ist die Summe der beiden Meßzahlen, die zum Ausgleich der Steuereinnahmen der Länder und der Realsteuereinnahmen gesondert festgestellt werden. Diese Meßzahlen ergeben sich aus den auszugleichenden Steuereinnahmen je Einwohner im Bundesdurchschnitt, vervielfacht mit der Einwohnerzahl des Landes. Dabei werden die Elemente des Bedarfs insofern berücksichtigt, als bei den Realsteuereinnahmen der Gemeinden eine höhere Gewichtung mit wachsender Einwohnerzahl erfolgt (Hamburg und Bremen zuzüglich 10 %). Bei den Landessteuern werden im allgemeinen 100 % angesetzt, bei Bremen 125 % und Hamburg 135 %.

Die *Ausgleichszuweisungen* (an die „armen" Länder) werden von den Beträgen errechnet, um die die Steuerkraftmeßzahl hinter 95 % der Ausgleichsmeßzahl zurückbleibt. Ab 1. 1. 1959 wird als Ausgleichszuweisung der volle Betrag festgesetzt, der an 85 % der Ausgleichsmeßzahl fehlt, und 60 % des Betrages, der von 85 bis 95 %

der Ausgleichsmeßzahl fehlt[1]). Die *Ausgleichsbeiträge* (der „reichen“ Länder) werden mit einem einheitlichen Hundertsatz von dem Betrag errechnet, um den die Steuerkraftmeßzahl die Ausgleichsmeßzahl übersteigt. Dabei wird die Steuerkraft zwischen 100 und 110 v. H. der Ausgleichsmeßzahl nur mit drei Vierteln, über 110 v. H. hinaus jedoch voll angesetzt[2]) (Sonderregelung für die Hansestädte). Der einheitliche Hundertsatz, mit dem die Ausgleichsbeiträge berechnet werden, wird so festgelegt, daß die Summen von Ausgleichszuweisungen und -beiträgen gleich sind[3]).

Der Sinn dieser Errechnungen von Ausgleichsbeiträgen und Zuweisungen ist offenbar nicht eine volle Nivellie-

---

1) Man kann das formelmäßig darstellen: Bezeichnen wir die Steuerkraftmeßzahl mit S, die Ausgleichsmeßzahl mit A und die Ausgleichszuweisung mit Z, dann

gilt für $S < 0{,}85$ A:

$$Z = (0{,}85\ A - S) + 0{,}6\ (0{,}95 - 0{,}85)\ A$$

$$Z = 0{,}91\ A - S$$

und für $0{,}85\ A < S < 0{,}95\ A$

$$Z = 0{,}6\ (0{,}95\ A - S)$$

2) Mit Hilfe einer formelmäßigen Darstellung: Bezeichnet man den einheitlichen Hundertsatz, der zur Übereinstimmung der Ausgleichszuweisungs- und Ausgleichsbeitragssumme führen soll, mit h, den Ausgleichsbeitrag mit B, ferner, wie bereits oben, die Steuerkraftmeßzahl mit S und die Ausgleichsmeßzahl mit A, dann gilt

für $S > 1{,}1$ A

$$B = h\ [(S - 1{,}1\ A) + 0{,}75\ (1{,}1 - 1{,}0)\ A]$$

$$B = h\ [S - 1{,}025\ A]$$

und für $A < S < 1{,}1$ A

$$B = h\ [0{,}75\ (S - A)]$$

3) Kennzeichnet man die Zuweisungen der empfangenden Länder mit dem Index i, die Meßzahlen und Beiträge derjenigen Länder, deren Steuerkraftmeßzahl über 110 % der Ausgleichsmeßzahl liegt, mit dem Index j und die Meßzahlen und Beiträge der übrigen beitragsverpflichteten Länder mit dem Index k, so soll — wie oben beschrieben — gelten:

$$\sum_i Z_i = \sum_j B_j + \sum_k B_k$$

Entsprechend der vorhergehenden Anmerkung gilt dafür auch:

$$\sum_i Z_i = h \left\{ \sum_j (S_j - 1{,}025\ A_j) + \sum_k 0{,}75\ (S_k - A_k) \right\}$$

Also ergibt sich: $h = \dfrac{\sum_i Z_i}{\sum_j (S_j - 1{,}025\ A_j) + \sum_k 0{,}75\ (S_k - A_k)}$

Danach können dann die einzelnen $B_j$ $B_k$ wie ausgeführt ermittelt werden.

rung, sondern es soll nur eine Annäherung erreicht werden, damit Anreize bestehen bleiben.

Während des Ausgleichsjahres wird der Finanzausgleich aufgrund vorläufiger Bemessungsgrundlagen vollzogen. Der Zahlungsverkehr erfolgt dabei so, daß die Ablieferung des Bundesanteils an der von den Ländern eingezogenen Einkommen- und Körperschaftsteuer bei den ablieferungspflichtigen Ländern um die vorläufigen Ausgleichsbeiträge erhöht, bei den ausgleichsberechtigten Ländern dagegen um die vorläufigen Ausgleichszuweisungen in entsprechendem Maße gesenkt wird. Einige Länder erhalten Vorauszahlungen auf den durch den Bundesanteil nicht gedeckten Teil ihrer vorläufigen Ausgleichszuweisungen. — Später, nach Abschluß der Rechnung erfolgt dann eine endgültige Abrechnung. Rechnungstechnisch ist also der vertikale Bund-Länderausgleich mit dem horizontalen Länderfinanzausgleich verknüpft.

Die Beiträge und Zuweisungen im Länderfinanzausgleich 1958 bis 1. Halbjahr 1963 sind aus der Tabelle VIII zu ersehen.

## 3. Gemeindefinanzausgleich

Eine Übersicht über den Gemeindefinanzausgleich wird dadurch erschwert, daß die Materie in den einzelnen Ländern durchaus unterschiedlich geordnet ist. Deshalb kann in den folgenden Ausführungen nur auf die Grundzüge eingegangen werden, wobei die allen idealtypischen Darstellungen immanente Gefahr bleibt, daß in Einzelheiten die mehr abstrakte Darstellung mit den in concreto vorzufindenden Ordnungen nicht völlig übereinstimmt.

### *a) Aufgaben der Gemeinden*

Die Aufgaben der Gemeinden lassen sich in Selbstverwaltungsangelegenheiten und Auftragsangelegenheiten gliedern.

*Selbstverwaltungsangelegenheiten* sind die eigenen Angelegenheiten der Gemeinden, die von ihnen unter eigener Verantwortung durchgeführt werden und lediglich der

Tabelle VIII

Beiträge und Zuweisungen im Länderfinanzausgleich 1958 — I. Halbjahr 1963[1])

| | Abrechnung Mill. DM | | | | | |
|---|---|---|---|---|---|---|
| | 1958[2]) | 1959[2]) | 1960[3]) | 1961[4]) | 1962[4]) | 1. Halbjahr 1963 |
| *Beiträge der ausgleichspflichtigen Länder:* | | | | | | |
| Nordrhein-Westf. | 486,6 | 500,0 | 517,9 | 752,5 | 722,9 | 311,5 |
| Baden-Württbg. | 119,7 | 149,6 | 107,8 | 191,1 | 275,7 | 121,1 |
| Hessen | 72,2 | 56,0 | 67,8 | 155,3 | 191,8 | 133,4 |
| Hamburg | 265,2 | 318,5 | 221,1 | 332,9 | 376,9 | 214,7 |
| Bremen | 11,0 | 1,4 | — | — | — | — |
| zusammen | 954,7 | 1025,5 | 914,6 | 1431,8 | 1567,3 | 780,7 |
| *Zuweisungen an die ausgleichsberechtigten Länder:* | | | | | | |
| Bayern | 220,3 | 233,1 | 185,0 | 219,3 | 228,9 | 66,3 |
| Niedersachsen | 266,8 | 258,0 | 259,6 | 446,6 | 491,3 | 255,8 |
| Rheinl.-Pfalz | 224,6 | 279,9 | 256,7 | 332,8 | 347,7 | 190,1 |
| Schlesw.-Holst. | 243,0 | 254,5 | 213,3 | 305,2 | 355,0 | 186,0 |
| Saarland | — | — | — | 127,9 | 144,4 | 77,8 |
| Bremen | — | — | — | — | — | 4,7 |
| zusammen | 954,7 | 1025,5 | 914,6 | 1431,8 | 1567,3 | 780,7 |

1) Quelle: Finanzbericht 1963, herausgegeben vom Bundesministerium der Finanzen, Bonn, S. 189; ebenda. 1964, S. 283.
2) Rechnungsjahre.
3) 9 Monate, wegen Umstellung von Rechnungsjahr auf Kalenderjahr.
4) Kalenderjahre.

Aufsicht des Staates über ihre Rechtmäßigkeit unterliegen. Die Selbstverwaltungsangelegenheiten erstrecken sich auf Selbstverwaltungsaufgaben, die *freiwillig* übernommen (Theater-, Musik-, Heimatpflege u. a.) oder *gesetzlich* zugewiesen (Wasserversorgung, Straßenwesen u. a.) werden. *Auftragsangelegenheiten* sind die Aufgaben, die den kommunalen Gebietskörperschaften gesetzlich übertragen werden und die sie nach mehr oder weniger detaillierten Weisungen des Oberverbandes durchzuführen haben. Beispiele für diese Aufgaben, gelegentlich auch Pflichtaufgaben genannt, sind die Durchführung von Wahlen, die Besorgung des Standesamts-, Bauaufsichtswesens u. ä.

Um die Gemeinden (Gemeindeverbände) vor der Übertragung neuer Aufgaben und damit neuer Lasten seitens des Oberverbandes zu schützen, ohne daß für eine entsprechende Mittelbereitstellung gesorgt wird, tragen auch hier die meisten Gesetze eine *Revisionsklausel* in sich. Die Mehrzahl der Länder sieht für die Übertragung neuer Aufgaben eine spezielle Revisionsklausel (Sicherungsklausel) vor. Einzelheiten können hier nicht dargelegt werden, da die Länder die Voraussetzungen und Folgen einer solchen Revision teilweise unterschiedlich abgefaßt haben.

### *b) Mittelverteilung*

*α) Allgemeines.* Die Finanzmittel der Gemeinden (kommunale Finanzmasse) setzen sich aus eigenen Mitteln und den vom Staat zugewiesenen Mitteln zusammen.

$\alpha_1$) Die *eigenen* Mittel der Gemeinden sind die Summe der Erwerbseinkünfte, der Gebühren und Beiträge und der kommunalen Steuern (Realsteuern und eine Reihe kleinerer Steuern mit örtlich bedingtem Wirkungskreis).

$\alpha_2$) Bei den vom Staat *zugewiesenen* Mitteln ist zu unterscheiden zwischen denen aus dem allgemeinen und aus dem Sonderlastenausgleich. Der *Sonderlastenausgleich* bezieht sich insbesondere auf die Aufgaben, bei denen die Länder (z. T. auch der Bund, z. B. bei den Verwaltungsaufgaben für die Lastenausgleichsämter) Teile der den Gemeinden aufgetragenen *gemeinsamen* Aufgaben (Schulen, Polizei, Fürsorge usw.) lastenmäßig übernehmen. Er bringt nach Popitz eine Lasten*beteiligung* des Staates.

Der *allgemeine Lastenausgleich* erfolgt dagegen unabhängig von einzelnen Aufgaben der Gemeinden. Er soll nach Popitz eine Lasten*verteilung* durch Finanzzuweisungen bringen, zur Ergänzung der unzureichenden eigenen Finanzmittel.

Die den Gemeinden im Rahmen des allgemeinen und des Sonderlastenausgleichs zufließenden Mittel werden als „Ausgleichsmasse" bezeichnet.

$\alpha_3$) Schließlich ist auch noch auf einen Finanzstrom in umgekehrter Richtung hinzuweisen, der eine *Kürzung* der Finanzmittel bedeutet. Durch Umlagen und Beiträge an höhere Instanzen im Sonderlastenausgleich werden die zur eigenen Verwendung bereitstehenden Finanzmittel der Gemeinden verringert.

In Anpassung an die allgemeine Systematik dieses Kapitels soll im folgenden unterschieden werden zwischen vertikaler (*β*), vertikal-horizontaler (γ) und rein horizontaler Mittelverteilung (δ).

*β*) *Vertikale Mittelverteilung.* Dieses betrifft die eigenen Mittel. Die Verteilung der Steuererträge zwischen Ländern und Gemeinden ist in Artikel 106, 6 Satz 1 des Grundgesetzes neue Fassung geregelt. Danach steht das Aufkommen der Realsteuern den Gemeinden zu. Mit dieser „Realsteuergarantie" macht der Bund von seinem Gesetzgebungsrecht über die Realsteuern Gebrauch und sichert den Gemeinden (nicht auch den Gemeindeverbänden) das Aufkommen aus den Grundsteuern und der Gewerbesteuer.

Nach Maßgabe der Landesgesetzgebung können den Gemeinden auch andere Landessteuern zur Verfügung gestellt werden. In allen Ländern ist dies der Fall bei den Steuern mit örtlich bedingtem Wirkungskreis wie Vergnügungsteuer, Getränkesteuer, Schankerlaubnissteuer, Hundesteuer u. a., deren Erhebung teils fakultativ, teils obligatorisch ist. Es wäre denkbar, den Gemeinden auch andere Landessteuern wie die Kraftfahrzeugsteuer zur Ausbeute zu überweisen.

Daneben gibt es noch ein sogenanntes Steuererfindungsrecht der Gemeinden, das sie befugt, neben den ihnen gesetzlich überlassenen neue Steuern einzuführen und zu erheben. Dieser Befugnis kommt allerdings nur eine geringe Bedeutung zu, weil nach den bundesgesetzlichen oder landesrechtlichen Bestimmungen alle größeren Steuern schon in der Hand des Bundes oder der Länder sind. Das Steuererfindungsrecht kann sich daher nur auf Steuern erstrecken, die zahlenmäßig und ertragsmäßig nicht ins Gewicht fallen.

γ) *Vertikal-horizontale* Mittelverteilung. Im Artikel 106, 6 Satz 3 des Grundgesetzes wird bestimmt, daß von dem Länderanteil an der Einkommen- und der Körperschaftsteuer den Gemeinden und Gemeindeverbänden insgesamt ein von der Landesgesetzgebung zu bestimmender Vomhundertsatz zufließen soll. Im übrigen soll die Landesgesetzgebung bestimmen, ob und inwieweit das Aufkommen der Landessteuern den Gemeinden (Gemeindeverbänden) zufließt. Die Länder sind in der Ausführung dieser grundsätzlichen Regelung durch das Grundgesetz unterschiedlich verfahren.

Soweit ist nur die allgemeine Regelung über die in die Ausgleichsmasse fließenden Mittel betroffen. Von besonderem Interesse ist nunmehr die Aufteilung dieser Mittel auf die einzelnen Gemeinden selbst. Zwar erfolgen diese Zahlungen in vertikaler Richtung, von den Ländern an die kommunalen Einheiten, aber es ist zu bemerken, daß bei der Verteilung an die einzelnen Gemeinden in starkem Maße die finanzielle Individualstruktur der Gemeinden, d. h. ihre unterschiedliche Steuerkraft und Bedarfsstruktur, über das „Ob" und „Wieviel" solcher Zuweisungen entscheidet, d. h. aber, daß durch diese Finanztransaktionen in indirekter Weise ein Ausgleich unter den Gemeinden erfolgt. Man kann daher insoweit von einem vertikal-horizontalen Ausgleich sprechen.

Auch hier ist zu betonen, daß dabei in den einzelnen Ländern durchaus unterschiedlich verfahren wird. Dennoch zeigen sich gewisse Gemeinsamkeiten. Zu den *allgemeinen* Finanzzuweisungen, die den allgemeinen Lastenausgleich betreffen, gehören Schlüsselzuweisungen, Bedarfszuweisungen, Ausgleichszuweisungen, die Grundsteuerausfallentschädigung für zerstörten Grundbesitz usw.

Wichtig sind vor allem die *Schlüsselzuweisungen*, die den weitaus größten Teil dieser Mittel ausmachen. Hierbei wird im Prinzip wie folgt verfahren: Es werden für die einzelnen Gemeinden Bedarfsmeßzahlen und Steuerkraftmeßzahlen ermittelt. Durch die *Bedarfsmeßzahl* soll die durchschnittliche Ausgabenbelastung einer Gemeinde durch eine Punktzahl ausgedrückt werden. Zunächst wird ein Hauptansatz gebildet; er geht von der Einwohnerzahl der Gemeinde aus, wobei jedoch, entsprechend erfahrungsgemäß höheren Pro-Kopf-Ausgaben in größeren Gemeinden, diese Zahlen in größeren Gemeinden stärker gewichtet werden. Durch Ergänzungsansätze werden die Bevölkerungsstruktur der Gemeinde (Arbeitnehmer-, bzw. Kinderanteil) sowie weitere Besonderheiten (Zuwachs bzw. Rückgang der Bevölkerung, Zonennähe, besondere Kriegszerstörungen usw.) berücksichtigt. Die Summe aus Hauptansatz und Ergänzungsansätzen ergibt den Gesamtansatz, auch veredelte Einwohnerzahl genannt. Dieser wird mit einem einheitlichen Grundbetrag multipliziert, der für jedes Jahr so festgelegt wird, daß die Geldsumme, die für Schlüsselzuweisungen zur Verfügung steht, aufgebraucht wird. Bei der Berechnung der *Steuerkraftmeßzahl* werden nur die Realsteuern (ohne Lohnsummensteuer) zugrunde gelegt. Da es gilt, die durchschnittliche Steuerkraft zu ermitteln, werden dabei nicht die tatsächlichen Hebesätze der einzelnen Gemeinden, sondern ein für alle Gemeinden gleicher fingierter Hebesatz (Nivellierungssatz) angewandt. Die Summe der so für die einzelnen Steuerarten errechneten Steuerkraftzahlen ergibt die Steuerkraftmeßzahl jeder Gemeinde. Nur bei der Grundsteuer B sind die Nivellierungssätze in den meisten Ländern nach der Summe der Meßbeträge progressiv gestaffelt. Die Schlüsselzuweisungen werden dann durch *Gegenüberstellung* der Bedarfsmeßzahl und der Steuerkraftmeßzahl für jede Gemeinde ermittelt. Ist die Steuerkraftmeßzahl größer, erhält die Gemeinde nichts, ist sie kleiner als die Bedarfsmeßzahl, so steht der Gemeinde in den meisten Ländern die Hälfte des Unterschiedes als Schlüsselzuweisung zu.

Die meisten Länder verbessern die Ergebnisse der Schlüsselberechnung zugunsten besonders schwacher Gemeinden durch *Sonderschlüsselzuweisungen*, sogenannte *Sockelgarantien*, durch die entweder die Steuerkraft auf eine bestimmte Höhe aufgefüllt wird oder die Summe aus Steuerkraftmeßzahl und Schlüsselzuweisung einen bestimmten Prozentsatz der Bedarfsmeßzahl erreicht.

Alle Länder gewähren den Gemeinden und Gemeindeverbänden *Bedarfszuweisungen* aus einem Ausgleichsstock; sie sollen außergewöhnlichen Lagen und Belastungen, sowie besonderen Aufgaben und Notlagen Rechnung tragen. Ferner werden Bedarfszuweisungen dazu bestimmt, Härten auszugleichen, die bei der Durchführung der Finanzausgleichsgesetze entstehen; in einigen Ländern wird als besonderer Zweck erwähnt, den Haushalt der Gemeinden und Landkreise auszugleichen, die dazu trotz sparsamer Haushaltsführung und Ausschöpfung aller verfügbaren Einnahmequellen nicht imstande sind.

Beim *Sonderlastenausgleich* ist die leitende Idee die Lasten*beteiligung* an Aufgaben durch Staatszuschüsse, auch zweckgebundene Finanzzuweisungen oder Zweckzuweisungen genannt. Bei diesen Aufgaben handelt es sich um Gemeinschaftsaufgaben, die von Ländern und Gemeinden gemeinsam zu tragen sind, und um Auftragsangelegenheiten. Soweit die Aufgabenanteile bei den einzelnen Gemeinden unterschiedliche Höhe erreichen und die besonderen Zuwendungen des Oberverbandes diesen interkommunal bedeutsamen Unterschied in der Belastung ausgleichen, darf man den Sonderlastenausgleich wohl mit der vertikal-horizontalen Systematik in Beziehung bringen.

Es soll ergänzend noch darauf hingewiesen werden, daß den Zuschüssen teilweise auch ein Strom in umgekehrter Richtung als Beiträge der Gemeinden an die Länder gegenübersteht. Dies ist dann der Fall, wenn bei Gemeinschaftsaufgaben das Land Kostenträger ist und hierzu von den Gemeinden Beiträge verlangt.

Die Bemessung der Staatszuschüsse kann nach mancherlei Maßstäben erfolgen. Die Möglichkeiten reichen von Anreizen zu einem erwünschten Verhalten über gezielte Hilfsmaßnahmen in Katastrophenfällen bis zu gesetzlich festgelegten Beteiligungen bei Auftragsangelegenheiten.

Soweit die Zuschüsse als Anreiz dienen und die Länder Eigenbeteiligungen der Gemeinden an den Ausgaben für bestimmte Objekte (wie Theater, Museen) verlangen, ist eine horizontale Ausgleichswirkung mitunter in Frage gestellt. Das ist dann der Fall, wenn die Eigenbeteiligungen so hoch sind, daß ohnehin nur finanzstarke Gemeinden sie tragen können, finanzschwache dagegen nicht. Das kann dazu führen, daß die bestehenden finanziellen Unterschiede nicht ausgeglichen, sondern sogar noch verschärft werden.

Die gesetzlichen Regelungen sind z. T. in den Finanzausgleichsgesetzen, z. T. aber auch in einer großen Zahl von Spezialgesetzen niedergelegt.

δ) *Horizontale Mittelverteilung* Eine rein horizontale Mittelverteilung ist im Rahmen des interkommunalen Finanzausgleichs im Zusammenhang mit der ertragsmäßigen Regelung der Gewerbesteuer in bestimmten Fällen vorgesehen:

Eine „Zerlegung“ des einheitlichen Steuermeßbetrages für die Gewerbeertrag- und Gewerbekapitalsteuer sieht das Gewerbesteuergesetz vor, wenn sich eine Betriebstätte über mehrere Gemeinden erstreckt oder ein Unternehmen in mehreren Gemeinden Betriebstätten unterhält. Dadurch soll den beteiligten Gemeinden ein entsprechender Anteil am Gewerbesteuermeßbetrag gesichert werden. Bei der Gewerbesteuer nach der Lohnsumme (Lohnsummensteuer) ist eine Zerlegung nur erforderlich, wenn sich eine Betriebstätte über mehrere Gemeinden erstreckt, da die Lohnsummensteuer — anders als die Gewerbeertrag- und Gewerbekapitalsteuer — für jede Betriebstätte gesondert berechnet wird.

Ein „Gewerbesteuerausgleich" zwischen Wohngemeinde und Betriebsgemeinde findet dann statt, wenn Arbeitnehmer in der einen Gemeinde wohnen oder ihren gewöhnlichen Aufenthaltsort haben (Wohngemeinde), aber in einer anderen Gemeinde (Betriebsgemeinde) beschäftigt sind. Da der Betriebsgemeinde der Gewerbesteuerertrag zunächst ganz zufließt, hat die Wohngemeinde als Ausgleich für die Lasten der Arbeitnehmerbevölkerung einen Anspruch an die Betriebsgemeinde auf einen Ausgleichszuschuß. Voraussetzungen und Höhe dieses Zuschusses sind nach den einzelnen Landesgesetzen geregelt. Sind Wohn- und Betriebsgemeinde durch eine Landesgrenze getrennt, so wird ein „überregionaler Gewerbesteuerausgleich" notwendig. Entsprechende Ländervereinbarungen bestehen z.B. zwischen Hamburg und Niedersachsen, Schleswig-Holstein und Hamburg sowie Bremen und Niedersachsen.

Weitere Finanzausgleichsprobleme auf der kommunalen Ebene entstehen durch die Inanspruchnahme von Einrichtungen der Gemeinden (Schulen, Krankenhäuser, Theater usw.) durch Bürger einer anderen Gemeinde. Das mag geregelt werden entweder durch eine Kostenbeteiligung oder durch einen Zusammenschluß zur Errichtung oder zur Benutzung solcher Einrichtungen.

ε) *Gemeindeverbände.* Zum interkommunalen Finanzausgleich gehören auch die Beiträge und Umlagen, die die Gemeinden an die Gemeindeverbände abzuführen haben. Daneben erhalten die Landkreise Finanzzuweisungen von den Ländern, bei deren Berechnung in ähnlicher Weise verfahren wird wie bei den Finanzzuweisungen an die Gemeinden. Es sei erwähnt, daß die Kreise nur über sehr geringe eigene Steuereinnahmen verfügen, nämlich in der Regel über Jagd- und Fischereisteuer, Schankerlaubnissteuer sowie über den gemeindlichen Zuschlag zur Grunderwerbsteuer.

## Literaturhinweise

### Für Kap. VIII


Zu § 1:

Gerloff, W., Die öffentliche Finanzwirtschaft, 2. Aufl., Bd. 2, Frankfurt a. M. 1950

Landmann, J., „Geschichte des öffentlichen Kredits", in: Handbuch der Finanzwissenschaft, 2 Aufl., 3. Bd., Teil X, Tübingen 1958

Nöll v. d. Nahmer, R., „Kredit, öffentlicher; (II) Theorie", in: Handwörterbuch der Sozialwissenschaften, 6. Bd., Tübingen-Göttingen 1959

Nöll v. d. Nahmer, R., Lehrbuch der Finanzwissenschaft, Bd. 1, Köln u. Opladen 1964

Preiswerk, S., Geschichtlicher Überblick über die Theorien der Staatsverschuldung, Basel 1942

Schwarz, O., „Die öffentlichen Kredite", in: Handbuch der Politik, 2. Bd., I. Teil, Berlin u. Leipzig 1914

Das Staatsschuldenproblem, 16. Bd. der ausgewählten Lesestücke zum Studium der politischen Ökonomie, hrsg. von K. Diehl und P. Mombert, Karlsruhe 1923

Terhalle, F., Die Finanzwirtschaft des Staates und der Gemeinden, Berlin 1948

Weichmann, H., „Kassenkredit, öffentlicher", in: Handwörterbuch der Sozialwissenschaften, 5. Bd., Tübingen-Göttingen 1956

Willeke, F.-U., „Kredit, öffentlicher; (I) Geschichte", in: Handwörterbuch der Sozialwissenschaften, 6. Bd., Tübingen-Göttingen 1959

Zu § 2:

Barocka, E., Kommunalkredit und kommunale Finanzwirtschaft, Frankfurt a. M. 1958

Dieben, W und Ebert, K., „Die Technik des öffentlichen Kredits", in: Handbuch der Finanzwissenschaft, 2. Aufl., 3. Bd., Teil X, Tübingen 1958

Ebert, K., „Die Erscheinungsformen der öffentlichen Schulden unter besonderer Berücksichtigung des Rechts der Bundesrepublik Deutschland", in: Österreichisches Bank-Archiv, Bd. IV, 7. Jahrg., Wien 1959

Giere, G., „Kommunales Schuldenwesen", in: Handbuch der kommunalen Wissenschaft und Praxis, hrsg. von H. Peters, 3. Bd., Berlin-Göttingen-Heidelberg 1959

Jèze, G., „Die Technik des öffentlichen Kredits", in: Handbuch der Finanzwissenschaft, 1. Aufl., 2. Bd., Tübingen 1927

Musgrave, R. A., „Theorie der öffentlichen Schuld", in: Handbuch der Finanzwissenschaft, 2 Aufl., 3. Bd., Teil X, Tübingen 1958

Nicolas, M., Finanzmathematik, Berlin 1959

Obst, G. und Hintner, O., Geld-, Bank- und Börsenwesen, 35. Aufl., Stuttgart 1963

Stucken, R., Deutsche Geld- und Kreditpolitik 1914 bis 1963, 3. Aufl., Tübingen 1964

Timm, H., „Anleihen, öffentliche", in: Handwörterbuch der Sozialwissenschaften, 1. Bd., Tübingen-Göttingen 1956

Vialon, F. K., Öffentliche Finanzwirtschaft, Berlin u. Frankfurt a.M. 1956
Vialon, F. K., Haushaltsrecht — Haushaltspraxis, Berlin u. Frankfurt a. M. 1959

## Zu §§ 3 und 4:

Albers, W., „Staatsverschuldung und Geld- und Kreditpolitik", in: Finanzarchiv, N.F., Bd. 21, Tübingen 1961/62
Andel, N., Probleme der Staatsschuldentilgung (Finanzwissenschaftliche Forschungsarbeiten, N.F Heft 30), Berlin 1964
Benning, B., „Aufbringung der Kriegskosten, Kapitalfreisetzung und Geldüberfluß", in: Weltwirtschaftliches Archiv, Bd. 56, Jena 1942
Benning, B., „Expansion und Kontraktion der Geldmenge", in: Weltwirtschaftliches Archiv, Bd. 58, Jena 1943
Bowen, W. G., Davis, G. D., Kopf, D. H., „The Public Debt: A Burden on Future Generations?" in: American Economic Review, Vol. L, 1960
Buchanan, J. M., Public Principles of Public Debt, Homewood (Ill.) 1958
Burkheiser, K., Grenzen des Staatskredits, Berlin 1937
Dieben, W., „Die innere Reichsschuld seit 1933", in: Finanzarchiv, N.F., Bd. 11, Tübingen 1949
Domar, E. D., „The 'Burden of the Debt' and the National Income", in: American Economic Review, Vol. XXXIV, 1944, abgedruckt in: Readings in Fiscal Policy, London 1955
Donner, O., „Die Grenzen de: Staatsverschuldung", in: Weltwirtschaftliches Archiv, Bd. 56, Jena 1942
Due, J. F., Government Finance, 3. Aufl., Homewood (Ill.) 1963
Föhl, C., Geldschöpfung und Wirtschaftskreislauf, 2. Aufl., Berlin 1955
Föhl, C., „Steuern und Staatskredit", in: Finanzarchiv, N.F., Bd. 11, Tübingen 1948
Gestrich, H., Kredit und Sparen, 3. Aufl., Düsseldorf u. München 1957
Hahn, A., Volkswirtschaftliche Theorie des Bankkredits, 3. Aufl., Tübingen 1930
Haller, H., Finanzpolitik, 2. Aufl., Tübingen-Zürich 1961
Haller, H., „Zur Problematik der Kreditfinanzierung öffentlicher Ausgaben", in: Finanzarchiv, N.F., Bd. 19, Tübingen 1958/59
Haller, H., „Staatsbudgetsalden und Konjunktur", in: Konjunkturpolitik, Heft 7, Berlin 1961
Hansen, A. H., Monetary Theory and Fiscal Policy, New York 1949
Hansmeyer, K. H., „La dette publique comme moyen de reporter des charges sur les générations futures", in: Revue de Science Financière, Anneé 55, Paris 1963
Hart, A. G. und Kenen, P. B., Money, Debt and Economic Activity, 3. Aufl., Englewood Cliffs (N.J.) 1961
Jöhr, W. A., „Das Problem der Schuldentilgung", in: Finanzarchiv, N.F., Bd. 11, Tübingen 1948
Lehmann, G.-D., Entwicklung und Probleme der Staatsverschuldung in der Bundesrepublik Deutschland Zürich 1962
Lerner, A. P., „Functional Finance and Federal Debt", in: Social Research, Vol. X, 1943, abgedruckt in: Readings in Fiscal Policy, London 1955
Lütge, F., „Die deutsche Kriegsfinanzierung im ersten und zweiten Weltkrieg", in: Beiträge zur Finanzwissenschaft und zur Geldtheorie, Festschrift für R. Stucken, hrsg. von F. Voigt, Göttingen 1953

Mishan, E. J., „Is the National Debt a Burden?", in: The Banker, Vol. CXIII, London 1963

Modigliani, F., „Long-Run Implications of Alternative Fiscal Policies and the Burden of the National Debt", in: The Economic Journal, Vol. LXXI, 1961

Monatsberichte der Bank Deutscher Länder, bzw. der Deutschen Bundesbank, Frankfurt a. M. (lfd.)

Musgrave, R. A., „Theorie der öffentlichen Schuld", in: Handbuch der Finanzwissenschaft, 2. Aufl., 3. Bd., Teil X, Tübingen 1958

Musgrave, R. A., The Theory of Public Finance, New York-Toronto-London 1959

„Die öffentlichen Einlagen im Bankensystem", in: Monatsberichte der Deutschen Bundesbank, Frankfurt a.M., Mai 1962

Pigou, A. C., The Political Economy of War, Chapter IV, London 1921

Preiser, E., Bildung und Verteilung des Volkseinkommens; (Gesammelte Aufsätze zur Wirtschaftsordnung und Wirtschaftspolitik), Göttingen 1957, siehe insbesondere.
„Sparen und Investieren", aus: Jahrb. f. Natök. u. Stat., Bd. 159, 1944;
„Multiplikatorprozeß und dynamischer Unternehmergewinn", aus: Jahrb. f. Natök u. Stat., Bd. 167, 1955;
„Wesen und Methoden der Wirtschaftslenkung", aus: Finanzarchiv, N.F., Bd. 8, 1941;
„Der Begriff des Preisniveaus und das Problem der Kaufkraftstabilisierung", aus: Jahrb. f. Natök. u. Stat., Bd. 158, 1943
„Die Sanierung des Geldwesens und der Finanzen in Deutschland", 1946

Preiswerk, S., Geschichtlicher Ueberblick über die Theorien der Staatsverschuldung, Basel 1942

Readings in Fiscal Policy, hrsg. von der American Economic Association, ausgewählt von A. Smithies und J. K. Butters, Homewood (Ill.)-London 1955

Readings in Monetary Theory, hrsg. von der American Economic Association, ausgewählt von F. A. Lutz und L. W. Mints, Homewood (Ill.)-London 1952

Ricardo, D., „Funding System", in: Supplement to the Fourth, Fifth and Sixth Editions of the Encyclopaedia Britannica, 1820, abgedruckt in: The Works and Correspondence of David Ricardo, hrsg. von P. Straffa, Vol. IV, Cambridge 1951

Schneider, E., Einführung in die Wirtschaftstheorie, III. Teil, 7. Aufl., Tübingen 1962

Shoup, C. S., „Debt Financing and Future Generations", in: The Economic Journal, Vol. LXXII, 1962 (mit ausführlichen Literaturhinweisen zu diesem Problem)

Stucken, R., Deutsche Geld- und Kreditpolitik 1914 bis 1963, 3. Aufl., Tübingen 1964

Stucken, R., Geld und Kredit, 2. Aufl., Tübingen 1957

Timm, H., „Gedanken zur Staatsverschuldung", in: Finanzarchiv, N.F., Bd. 9, Tübingen 1941/43

Wolf, E., „Geld- und Finanzprobleme der deutschen Nachkriegswirtschaft", in: Die deutsche Wirtschaft zwei Jahre nach dem Zusammenbruch, hrsg. vom Deutschen Institut für Wirtschaftsforschung, Berlin 1947

## Zu § 5:

Allgemeine Vorbemerkungen zum Bundeshaushaltsplan für das Rechnungsjahr . (1954—60), in: Bundeshaushaltsplan für das Rechnungsjahr ... (1954—60) hrsg. vom Bundesministerium dei Finanzen, Bonn 1954—60

„Anleihe- und Schuldenpolitik der öffentlichen Hand in der Bundesrepublik" (Schriftenreihe des Instituts „Finanzen und Steuern", Heft 28), Bonn 1953

„Die Anleiheverschuldung der öffentlichen Hand im Rahmen der gesamten öffentlichen Neuverschuldung", in: Monatsberichte der Deutschen Bundesbank, Frankfurt a. M., November 1963

Benning, B., „Aufbringung der Kriegskosten, Kapitalfreisetzung und Geldüberfluß", in: Weltwirtschaftliches Archiv, Bd. 56, Jena 1942

„Bundeshaushaltsrechnung für das Rechnungsjahr ... (1949 ff.), hrsg. vom Bundesministerium der Finanzen, Bonn 1949 ff.

Dieben, W., „Die innere Reichsschuld seit 1933", in: Finanzarchiv, N.F., Bd. 11, Tübingen 1949

Finanzbericht ... (1961 ff.); (Die volkswirtschaftlichen Grundlagen und die wichtigsten finanzwirtschaftlichen Probleme des Haushaltsplans der Bundesrepublik Deutschland), hrsg. vom Bundesministerium der Finanzen, Bonn 1961 ff.

Grünig, F., „Die Anfänge der ‚Volkswirtschaftlichen Gesamtrechnung' in Deutschland", in: Beiträge zur empirischen Konjunkturforschung, hrsg. vom Deutschen Institut für Wirtschaftsforschung, Berlin 1951

Historical Statistics of the United States, Colonial Times to 1957, A Statistical Abstract Supplement, Washington (D.C.) 1960

Monatsberichte der Bank deutscher Länder, bzw. der Deutschen Bundesbank, Frankfurt a. M. (lfd.)

Nevin, E., The Problem of the National Debt, Cardiff 1954

Public Debt 1914—1946, hrsg. v. d. United Nations, Department of Economic Affairs, Lake Success-New York 1948

Reichshaushaltsrechnung ..., hrsg. vom Reichsminister der Finanzen, Berlin 1925 ff.

Statistical Abstract of the United States, hrsg. vom U.S. Department of Commerce, Washington (D.C.) 1962

Statistisches Handbuch für das Deutsche Reich, hrsg. vom Kaiserlichen Statistischen Amt, Berlin 1907

Statistisches Handbuch von Deutschland 1928 bis 1944, hrsg. vom Länderrat des Amerikanischen Besatzungsgebiets, München 1949

Statistisches Jahrbuch für das Deutsche Reich, hrsg. vom Kaiserlichen Statistischen Amt, bzw. vom Statistischen Reichsamt, Berlin 1880—1942

Statistisches Jahrbuch für die Bundesrepublik Deutschland, hrsg. vom Statistischen Bundesamt, Wiesbaden 1952 ff.

Wolf, E., „Geld- und Finanzprobleme der deutschen Nachkriegswirtschaft", in: Die deutsche Wirtschaft zwei Jahre nach dem Zusammenbruch, hrsg. vom Deutschen Institut für Wirtschaftsforschung, Berlin 1947

## Für Kap. IX

### Zu § 1:

Allgemeine Vorbemerkungen zum Bundeshaushaltsplan für das Rechnungsjahr ... ((1954—60), in: Bundeshaushaltsplan für das Rechnungsjahr ... (1954—60), hrsg. vom Bundesministerium der Finanzen, Bonn 1954—60

Der Bundeshaushalt (Schriftenreihe des Instituts „Finanzen und Steuern", Heft 15, Bd. 1 ff., Bonn 1952 ff.

Colm, G., „Haushaltplanung, Staatsbudget, Finanzplan und Nationalbudget", in: Handbuch der Finanzwissenschaft, 2. Aufl., 1. Bd., Teil IV, Tübingen 1952

Colm, G., „Wirtschaftsverfassung, Finanzwirtschaft und Finanzwissenschaft", in: Finanzarchiv, N.F., Bd 19, Tübingen 1959

Finanzbericht ... (1961 ff); (Die volkswirtschaftlichen Grundlagen und die wichtigsten finanzwirtschaftlichen Probleme des Haushaltsplans der Bundesrepublik Deutschland), hrsg. vom Bundesministerium der Finanzen, Bonn 1961 ff.

Heinig, K., Das Budget, 3 Bde., Tübingen 1949—1951

Jèze, G., Allgemeine Theorie des Budgets, deutsche Ausgabe von F. Neumark, Tübingen 1927

Mann, F. K., Finanztheorie und Finanzsoziologie, Göttingen 1959

Mayer, Th., „Geschichte der Finanzwirtschaft vom Mittelalter bis zum Ende des 18. Jahrhunderts", in: Handbuch der Finanzwissenschaft, 2. Aufl., 1. Bd., Teil II, Tübingen 1952

Musgrave, R. A., The Theory of Public Finance, New York-Toronto-London 1959

Neumark, F., „Theorie und Praxis der Budgetgestaltung", in: Handbuch der Finanzwissenschaft, 2. Aufl., 1. Bd., Teil IV, Tübingen 1952

Senf, P., „Budget; (I) Haushaltplan", in: Handwörterbuch der Sozialwissenschaften, 2. Bd., Tübingen-Göttingen 1959

Terhalle, F., „Geschichte der deutschen öffentlichen Finanzwirtschaft vom Beginn des 19. Jahrhunderts bis zum Schlusse des zweiten Weltkrieges", in: Handbuch der Finanzwissenschaft, 2. Aufl., 1. Bd., Teil II, Tübingen 1952

### Zu § 2:

Budgetary Structure and Classification of Government Accounts, United Nations, Department of Economic Affairs, New York 1951

Colm, G., „Wirtschaftsverfassung, Finanzwirtschaft und Finanzwissenschaft", in: Finanzarchiv, N.F., Bd. 19, Tübingen 1959

Gegenwartsprobleme des öffentlichen Haushalts (Schriftenreihe der Hochschule Speyer, Bd. 12), Berlin 1962

Hansen, A. H., Fiscal Policy and Business Cycles, New York 1941

Heinig, K., Das Budget, Bd. I—II, Tübingen 1949—1950

Hicks, J. R., The Problem of Budgetary Reform, Oxford 1948

Hicks, J. R. and Hicks, U. K., „The Reform of Budgetary Accounts", in: Bulletin of the Oxford University Institute of Economics and Statistics, Vol. 2, Oxford 1963

Jessen, J., Deutsche Finanzwirtschaft, Hamburg 1938

Jèze, G., Allgemeine Theorie des Budgets, deutsche Ausgabe von F. Neumark, Tübingen 1927

Laufenburger, H., „L'Elargissement du Concept du Budget", in: Finanzarchiv, N.F., Bd. 12, Tübingen 1950
Lindahl, E., Studies in the Theory of Money and Capital, London 1939
Musgrave, R. A., „Theorie der öffentlichen Schuld", in: Handbuch der Finanzwissenschaft, 2. Aufl., 3 Bd., Teil X, Tübingen 1958
Myrdal, G., „Fiscal Policy in the Business Cycle", in: American Economic Review, Vol. XXIX, 1939
Neumark, F., „Theorie und Praxis der Budgetgestaltung", in: Handbuch der Finanzwissenschaft, 2. Aufl., 1 Bd., Teil IV, Tübingen 1952
Probleme des öffentlichen Budgets, Beiträge von P. Senf, W. Dreißig, R. Stucken, W Ehrlicher, G. Schmölders und H. C. Recktenwald, hrsg. von H. Jecht (Schriften des Vereins für Socialpolitik, N.F., Bd. 31), Berlin 1964
Recktenwald, H. C., „Kapital- und Investitionshaushalt", in: Probleme des öffentlichen Budgets, hrsg von H Jecht (Schriften des Vereins für Socialpolitik, N F., Bd. 31), Berlin 1964
Schmölders, G., „Der Grundsatz der Budgetpublizität", in: Finanzarchiv, N.F., Bd. 18, Tübingen 1957/58
Schmölders, G., „Politische und institutionelle Probleme der Budgetgliederung", in: Probleme des öffentlichen Budgets, hrsg. von H Jecht (Schriften des Vereins für Socialpolitik, N.F., Bd. 31), Berlin 1964
Senf, P., „Budget; (I) Haushaltplan", in: Handwörterbuch der Sozialwissenschaften, 2. Bd., Tübingen-Göttingen 1959
Senf, P., „Probleme der Gliederung des öffentlichen Haushalts (nach funktionalen und ökonomischen Gesichtspunkten)", in: Gegenwartsprobleme des öffentlichen Haushalts (Schriftenreihe der Hochschule Speyer, Bd 12), Berlin 1962
Smith, H D., „Das Budget als Mittel der legislativen Kontrolle und der Verwaltungsführung", in: Finanzarchiv, N.F., Bd. 12, Tübingen 1950
The Swedish Budget 1963/64, hrsg. vom Schwedischen Finanzministerium, Stockholm 1963
Vialon, F K., Haushaltsrecht — Haushaltspraxis (Kommentar zur Haushaltsordnung [RHO] und zu den Finanzbestimmungen des Bonner Grundgesetzes), Berlin und Frankfurt a. M. 1959
Wagner, A., Finanzwissenschaft, 3. Aufl., Teil 1, Leipzig 1883

## Zu § 3:

Heinig, K., Das Budget, Bd. I—II, Tübingen 1949/51
Heinig, K. und Vialon, F K., „Budget; (III) Budgetkontrolle", in: Handwörterbuch der Sozialwissenschaften, 2. Bd., Tübingen-Göttingen 1959
Helmert, O., Haushalts-, Kassen- und Rechnungswesen, Berlin 1961
Senf, P., „Budget; (I) Haushaltplan", in: Handwörterbuch der Sozialwissenschaften, 2. Bd., Tübingen-Göttingen 1959
Vialon, F K., Haushaltsrecht — Haushaltspraxis (Kommentar zur Haushaltsordnung [RHO] und zu den Finanzbestimmungen des Bonner Grundgesetzes), Berlin und Frankfurt a. M. 1959
Vialon, F. K., Öffentliche Finanzwirtschaft, Berlin u. Frankfurt a. M. 1956
Weichmann, H., „Budget; (II) Budgetrechnung", in: Handwörterbuch der Sozialwissenschaften, 2. Bd., Tübingen-Göttingen 1959

## Zu § 4:

## Außer der Literatur zu Bd. I, Kap. II, § 8 und zu Bd. II, Kap. VI, § 10 noch folgende:


Allen, R. G. D., Mathematical Economics, 2. Aufl., London-New York 1959

Allgemeine Vorbemerkungen zum Bundeshaushaltsplan für das Rechnungsjahr ... ((1954—60), in: Bundeshaushaltsplan für das Rechnungsjahr ... (1954—60), hrsg. vom Bundesministerium der Finanzen, Bonn 1954—60

Bartels, H., „Probleme der volkswirtschaftlichen Gesamtrechnung", in: Wirtschaft und Statistik, N.F., Heft 6, Stuttgart 1951

Bombach, G., „Staatshaushalt und volkswirtschaftliche Gesamtrechnung", in: Finanzarchiv, N.F., Bd. 17, Tübingen 1957

Colm, G., „Fiscal Policy and the Federal Budget", in: Income Stabilization for a Developing Democracy, hrsg. von M. F. Millikan, New Haven 1953

Colm, G., „Haushaltplanung, Staatsbudget, Finanzplan und Nationalbudget", in: Handbuch der Finanzwissenschaft, 2. Aufl., Bd. 1, Teil IV, Tübingen 1952

Colm, G., „Der Staatshaushalt und der Haushalt der Gesamtwirtwirtschaft", in: Finanzarchiv, N.F., Bd. 11, Tübingen 1949

Colm, G. und Young, M., The American Economy in 1960, hrsg. von der National Planning Association, Washington (D.C.) 1952

Domar, E. D., „Capital Expansion, Rate of Growth, and Employment", in: Econometrica, Vol. 14, 1946, abgedruckt in: Domar, E. D., Essays in the Theory of Economic Growth, New York 1957

Edey, H. C. und Peacock, A. T., National Income and Social Accounting, London 1954

Finanzbericht ... (1961 ff.): (Die volkswirtschaftlichen Grundlagen und die wichtigsten finanzwirtschaftlichen Probleme des Haushaltsplans der Bundesrepublik Deutschland), hrsg. vom Bundesministerium der Finanzen, Bonn 1961 ff.

Föhl, C., „Möglichkeiten einer künftigen Fiskalpolitik", in: Weltwirtschaftliches Archiv, Bd. 79, Hamburg 1957

Frisch, R., „Economic Planning and the Role of Econometrics", in: Statsøkonomisk Tidsskrift, Bd. 78, Olso 1964

Frisch, R. Price — Wage — Tax — Subsidy Policies as Instruments in Maintaining Optimal Employment (E/CN. 1/Sub. 2/13, 18. April 1949, United Nations, Economic and Social Council)

Galbraith, J. K., The Affluent Society, London 1958. Dt.: Gesellschaft im Überfluß, übersetzt von R. Mühlfenzl, München-Zürich 1959

Goodwin, R. M., „The Non-Linear Accelerator and the Persistence of Business Cycles", in Econometrica, Vol. 19, 1951

Haavelmo, T., „Multiplier Effects of a Balanced Budget", in: Econometrica, Vol. 13, 1945, abgedruckt in: Readings in Fiscal Policy, London 1955

Hall, Ch. A., Fiscal Policy for Stable Growth, New York 1960

Hansen, A. H., „The Stagnation Thesis", in: Fiscal Policy and Business Cycles, New York 1941, abgedruckt in: Readings in Fiscal Policy, London 1955

Hansen, A., „Three Methods of Expansion through Fiscal Policy", in: American Economic Review, Vol. XXXV, 1945

Harrod, R. F., Towards a Dynamic Economics, London 1948

Harrod, R. F., The Trade Cycle, Oxford 1936

Hicks, J. R., A Contribution to the Theory of the Trade Cycle, Oxford 1950

Kaldor, N., „The Quantitative Aspects of the Full Employment Problem in Britain", in: Beveridge, W. H., Full Employment in a Free Society, Appendix C, 3. Aufl., London 1945

Kalecki, M., „A Macrodynamic Theory of Business Cycles", in: Econometrica, Vol. 3, 1935

Kalecki, M., Theory of Economic Dynamics, London 1954

Keiser, N. F., „The Development of the Concept of ‚Automatic Stabilizers'", in: The Journal of Finance, Vol. XI, 1956

Kolms, H., Marktwirtschaft und Wirtschaftspolitik, Frankfurt a. M. 1958

Kolms, H., „Volkswirtschaftliche Gesamtrechnungen, Nationalbudgets und ökonometrische Gesamtmodelle", in: Weltwirtschaftliches Archiv, Bd. 71, Hamburg 1953

Krelle, W., Volkswirtschaftliche Gesamtrechnung, Berlin 1959

Laufenburger, H., „L'Elargissement du Concept du Budget", in: Finanzarchiv, N.F., Bd. 12, Tübingen 1950

Lerner, A. P., The Economics of Control, New York 1946

Musgrave, R. A., The Theory of Public Finance, New York-Toronto-London 1959

National Budgets for Full Employment, in: Planning Pamphlets No. 43—44, hrsg. von der National Planning Association, Washington (D.C.) 1945

The National Budget of Norway, hrsg. vom Königlich Norwegischen Finanzministerium, Oslo (lfd.)

Paulsen, A., Allgemeine Volkswirtschaftslehre, Bd. IV, 2. Aufl., Berlin 1962

Philip, K., „Finanzpolitik und wirtschaftliche Aktivität", in: Weltwirtschaftliches Archiv, Bd. 57, Jena 1943

Phillips, A. W., „Stabilisation Policy and the Time-Forms of Lagged Responses", in: The Economic Journal, Vol LXVII, 1957

Phillips, A. W., „Stabilisation Policy in a Closed Economy", in: The Economic Journal, Vol. LXIV, 1954

Preiser, E., Bildung und Verteilung des Volkseinkommens (Gesammelte Aufsätze zur Wirtschaftsordnung und Wirtschaftspolitik), Göttingen 1957

Readings in Fiscal Policy, hrsg. von der American Economic Association, ausgewählt von A. Smithies und J. K. Butters, Homewood (Ill.)-London 1955

Richter, R., und Selten, R., „Dynamische Theorie der Built- in Flexibility", in: Zeitschrift für die gesamte Staatswissenschaft, Bd. 119, Tübingen 1963

Ruggles R., An Introduction to National Income and Income Analysis, New York-Toronto-London 1949. Dt.: Volkseinkommen und volkswirtschaftliche Gesamtrechnung, übers. von R. Mortenthaler, Wien-Stuttgart 1952

Ruggles, R., National Income Accounting and its Relation to Economic Policy, Paris 1949

Samuelson, P. A., „Interactions between the Multipler Analysis and the Principle of Acceleration", in: The Review of Economics and Statistics, Vol. XXI, 1939, abgedruckt in: Readings in Business Cycle Theory, Philadelphia-Toronto 1944

Schmölders, G., Finanzpolitik, Berlin 1955

Schneider, E., Einführung in die Wirtschaftstheorie, I. Teil, 10. Aufl., Tübingen 1963

Schneider, E., „Zur Frage der Wirkung finanzpolitischer Maßnahmen auf die wirtschaftliche Aktivität" in: Finanzarchiv, N.F., Bd 10, Tübingen 1945

Senf, P., „Wesen, Aufgaben und Probleme des Nationalbudgets" in: Zeitschrift für die gesamte Staatswissenschaft, Bd. 107, Heft 2, Tübingen 1951

Smithies, A., „Federal Budgeting and Fiscal Policy", in: A Survey of Contemporary Economics, hrsg. von H. S. Ellis, Philadelphia 1948

A Standardized System of National Accounts, hrsg. von der OEEC, Paris 1958

Statistisches Jahrbuch für die Bundesrepublik Deutschland, Abschnitt „Volkswirtschaftliche Gesamtrechnung" hrsg. vom Statistischen Bundesamt, Wiesbaden 1952 ff.

Stone, R., und Croft-Murray, G., Social Accounting and Economic Models, London 1959

Taylor, Ph. E., The Economics of Public Finance, 3. Aufl. New York 1961

Theil, H., „Econometric Models and Welfare Maximisation", in: Weltwirtschaftliches Archiv, Bd. 72, Hamburg 1954

Timm, H., „Bemerkungen zum multiplikativen Effekt eines wachsenden ausgeglichenen Budgets", in: Finanzarchiv, N.F., Bd. 18, Tübingen 1957/58

Tinbergen, J., „Government Budget and Central Economic Plan", in: Public Finance, Vol. IV, 1949

Tinbergen, J., Einführung in die Ökonometrie, Wien-Stuttgart 1952

Tinbergen, J. und Stuvel, G., „Das Nationalbudget" in Handbuch der Finanzwissenschaft, 2. Aufl., Bd. 1, Teil IV, Tübingen 1952

Tinbergen, J., On the Theory of Economic Policy, Amsterdam 1952

Vierteljahreshefte zur Wirtschaftsforschung, hrsg. vom Deutschen Institut für Wirtschaftsforschung (Institut für Konjunkturforschung), Berlin 1949 ff.

Vogt, W., „Einige Unklarheiten in der Diskussion über die Multiplikatorwirkung eines ausgeglichenen Budgets", in: Weltwirtschaftliches Archiv, Bd. 85, Hamburg 1960/II

## Für Kap. X

### Zu § 1:

Albers, W., Finanzausgleich; (III) Deutschland", in: Handwörterbuch der Sozialwissenschaften, Bd. 3, Tübingen-Göttingen 1961

Allgemeine Vorbemerkungen zum Bundeshaushaltsplan für das Rechnungsjahr ... (1954-60), in: Bundeshaushaltsplan für das Rechnungsjahr ... (1954—60), hrsg. vom Bundesministerium der Finanzen, Bonn 1954—60

Bickel, W., „Der Finanzausgleich", in: Handbuch der Finanzwissenschaft, 2. Aufl., Bd. 2, Teil IX, Tübingen 1956

Due, J. F., Government Finance, 3. Aufl., Homewood (Ill.) 1963

Finanzbericht ... (1961 ff.), hrsg. vom Bundesministerium der Finanzen, Bonn 1961 ff.

Götz, P., Grundprobleme des Finanzausgleichs in der Bundesrepublik, Frankfurt 1957

Hacker, H., „Finanzausgleich" in: Handbuch der kommunalen Wissenschaft und Praxis, hrsg. von H. Peters, Bd. 3, Berlin-Göttingen-Heidelberg 1959

Haller H., Finanzpolitik, 2. Aufl., Tübingen 1961
Hensel, A., Der Finanzausgleich im Bundesstaat in seiner staatsrechtlichen Bedeutung, Berlin 1922
Keller, Th., „Finanzausgleich; (I) Allgemeines", in: Handwörterbuch der Sozialwissenschaften, Bd. 3, Tübingen-Göttingen 1961
Keller, Th., „Finanzausgleich; (II) Außerdeutsche Länder", in: Handwörterbuch der Sozialwissenschaften, Bd. 3, Tübingen-Göttingen 1961
Moll, B., Probleme der Finanzwissenschaft, Leipzig 1924
Nöll v. d. Nahmer, R., Lehrbuch der Finanzwissenschaft, 2 Bde., Köln und Opladen 1964
Philip, K., Intergovernmental Fiscal Relations, Kopenhagen 1954
Popitz, J., Der künftige Finanzausgleich zwischen Reich, Ländern und Gemeinden (Gutachten), Berlin 1932
Schmölders, G., „Zentralismus und Föderalismus in der amerikanischen Finanzverfassung", in: Europa-Archiv, Folge 13, Frankfurt a. M. 1949
Statistisches Jahrbuch für die Bundesrepublik Deutschland, Abschnitt „Öffentliche Finanzen", hrsg. vom Statistischen Bundesamt, Wiesbaden 1952 ff.
Stucken, R., „Der Finanzausgleich in der Bundesrepublik", in: Finanzarchiv, N.F., Bd. 14, Tübingen 1953/54
Terhalle, F., „Das Finanz- und Steuersystem der Bundesrepublik Deutschland", in: Handbuch der Finanzwissenschaft, 2. Aufl., Bd. 3, Teil XI, Tübingen 1958
Timm, H., „Finanzpolitische Autonomie untergeordneter Gebietskörperschaften (Gemeinden) und Standortverteilung", in: Kommunale Finanzen und Finanzausgleich, hrsg. von H. Timm und H. Jecht, Berlin 1964
Vialon, F. K., Haushaltsrecht — Haushaltspraxis (Kommentar zur Haushaltsordnung [RHO] und zu den Finanzbestimmungen des Bonner Grundgesetzes), Berlin und Frankfurt a.M. 1959
Vialon, F. K., Öffentliche Finanzwirtschaft, Berlin und Frankfurt a.M. 1956

## Zu §§ 2 und 3:

Albers, W., „Das Popitzsche Gesetz der Anziehungskraft des übergeordneten Haushalts", in: Strukturwandlungen einer wachsenden Wirtschaft, hrsg. von F. Neumark, Schriften des Vereins für Socialpolitik, N.F., Bd. 30/II, Berlin 1964
Allgemeine Vorbemerkungen zum Bundeshaushaltsplan für das Rechnungsjahr... (1954-60), in: Bundeshaushaltsplan für das Rechnungsjahr... (1954—60), hrsg. vom Bundesministerium der Finanzen, Bonn 1954—60.
Becker, E., „Der Finanzausgleich, der Verwaltungsverbund und die Selbstverwaltungsgarantie", (Schriftenreihe der Hochschule Speyer, Bd. 8), Stuttgart 1960
Begemann, E., Die Finanzreformversuche im Deutschen Reiche von 1867 bis zur Gegenwart, Göttingen 1912
„Finanzausgleich", in: Finanzen und Steuern, Fachserie L, Reihe 1, IV, hrsg. vom Statistischen Bundesamt Wiesbaden 1960 ff.
„Finanzausgleich", in: Finanzen und Steuern, Fachserie I, Steuern", Heft 17), Bonn 1952
Finanzbericht... (1961 ff.) (Die volkswirtschaftlichen Grundlagen und die wichtigsten finanzwirtschaftlichen Probleme des Haushaltsplans der Bundesrepublik Deutschland), hrsg. vom Bundesministerium der Finanzen, Bonn 1961 ff.

Zur gegenwärtigen Problematik der Gemeindefinanzen, Gutachten des Wissenschaftlichen Beirats beim Bundesministerium der Finanzen, Köln 1959

Gerloff, W., Die Finanz- und Zollpolitik des Deutschen Reiches, Jena 1913

Gerloff, W., Die Finanzgewalt im Bundesstaat, Frankfurt a.M. 1948

Zum Gewerbesteuerausgleich zwischen Betriebsgemeinden und Wohngemeinden (Grüne Briefe, Nr. 54, hrsg. vom Institut „Finanzen und Steuern"), Bonn 1963

Görg, H., „Geschichtliche Entwicklung und gegenwärtige Problematik des kommunalen Finanzsystems" (Schriftenreihe der Hochschule Speyer, Bd. 8), Stuttgart 1960

Görg, H., „Probleme der Bundesfinanzverfassung, in: Staats- und verwaltungswissenschaftliche Beiträge, hrsg. von der Hochschule für Verwaltungswissenschaften Speyer, Speyer 1957

Haller, H., „Probleme einer konjunkturpolitisch orientierten Finanzpolitik unter besonderer Berücksichtigung des Finanzausgleichs" in: Zeitschrift für die gesamte Staatswissenschaft", Bd. 116, Tübingen 1960

Hettlage, K. M., „Die Neuordnung der deutschen Finanzverfassung", in: Finanzarchiv, N.F., Bd. 14, Tübingen 1953

Hornschu, H.-E., „Die Entwicklung des Finanzausgleichs im Deutschen Reich und in Preußen von 1919 bis 1944", in: Kieler Studien, 3, Kiel 1950

Popitz, J., „Der Finanzausgleich", in: Handbuch der Finanzwissenschaft, 1. Aufl., Bd. 2, Tübingen 1927

Popitz, J., „Das Finanzausgleichsproblem in der deutschen Finanzwissenschaft der Vorkriegszeit", in: Finanzarchiv, N.F., Bd. 1, Tübingen 1933

Strickrodt, G., „Die Finanzverfassung des Bundes als politisches Problem" (Schriftenreihe der Hochschule Speyer, Bd. 6), Tübigen 1951

Terhalle, F., Die Finanzwirtschaft des Staates und der Gemeinden, Berlin 1948

Teschemacher, H., Reichsfinanzreform und innere Reichspolitik 1906—1913, Berlin 1915

Vialon, F. K., Haushaltsrecht — Haushaltspraxis (Kommentar zur Haushaltsordnung [RHO] und zu den Finanzbestimmungen des Bonner Grundgesetzes), Berlin und Frankfurt a.M. 1959

Vialon, F. K., Öffentliche Finanzwirtschaft, Berlin und Frankfurt a.M. 1956

Wagner, A., Finanzwissenschaft, 3. Aufl., Teil 1, Leipzig 1883

## Zeitschriften

The American Economic Review, Menasha (Wisc.)

Econometrica, Menasha (Wisc.) u. a.

The Economic Journal, London

Finanzarchiv, N.F., Tübingen

Openbare Finanzien / Public Finance / Finances Publiques (N. Samson N.V.) Alphen a.d.Rijn

The Quarterly Journal of Economics, Cambridge (Mass.)

Steuer und Wirtschaft, München-Berlin-Göttingen-Heidelberg

Weltwirtschaftliches Archiv, Hamburg

Zeitschrift für die gesamte Staatswissenschaft, Tübingen

## Handbücher, Sammelwerke und Schriftenreihen

Beiträge zur Finanzwissenschaft, Festgabe für Georg Schanz, (2 Bde.) Tübingen 1928

Hauptprobleme der Finanzwissenschaft, in: Die Wirtschaftstheorie der Gegenwart, Bd. IV, hrsg. von H. Mayer, Wien 1928

Handbuch der Finanzwissenschaft, 1. Aufl., hrsg. von W. Gerloff und F. Meisel (3 Bde.), Tübingen 1926—1929

Handbuch der Finanzwissenschaft, 2. Aufl., hrsg. von W. Gerloff und F. Neumark (3 Bde.), Tübingen 1952—1958

Handwörterbuch der Sozialwissenschaften, Stuttgart-Tübingen-Göttingen 1956 ff.

Handwörterbuch der Staatswissenschaften, 4. Aufl., hrsg. von L. Elster, A. Weber und F. Wieser, Jena 1923—1929

Readings in Fiscal Policy, hrsg. von der American Economic Association, London 1955

Readings in Monetary Theory, hrsg. von der American Economic Association, London 1952

Schriftenreihe des Instituts „Finanzen und Steuern", hrsg. vom Institut „Finanzen und Steuern", Bonn

Schriftenreihe des Vereins für Socialpolitik, Berlin

Viewpoints on Public Finance, hrsg. v. H. M. Groves, New York 1947

Wörterbuch der Volkswirtschaft, 4. Aufl., hrsg. v. L. Elster, Jena 1931—1933

(Zusammengestellt von K. Schneider)

# Namensregister

# Sachregister

NOTIZEN

Kolibri 360 GmbH
Ferdinand-Jühlke-Straße 7
99095 Erfurt, Deutschland
produktsicherheit@kolibri360.de